Communications
in Computer and Information Science   218

Song Lin   Xiong Huang (Eds.)

Advances in Computer Science, Environment, Ecoinformatics, and Education

International Conference, CSEE 2011
Wuhan, China, August 21-22, 2011
Proceedings, Part V

 Springer

Volume Editors

Song Lin
International Science & Education Researcher Association
Wuhan Branch, No.1, Jiangxia Road, Wuhan, China
E-mail: 1652952307@qq.com

Xiong Huang
International Science & Education Researcher Association
Wuhan Branch, No.1, Jiangxia Road, Wuhan, China
E-mail: 499780828@qq.com

ISSN 1865-0929   e-ISSN 1865-0937
ISBN 978-3-642-23356-2   e-ISBN 978-3-642-23357-9
DOI 10.1007/978-3-642-23357-9
Springer Heidelberg Dordrecht London New York

Library of Congress Control Number: Applied for

CR Subject Classification (1998): I.2, C.2, H.4, H.3, D.2, H.5

Typesetting: Camera-ready by author, data conversion by Scientific Publishing Services, Chennai, India

Printed on acid-free paper

Springer is part of Springer Science+Business Media (www.springer.com)

Preface

The International Science & Education Researcher Association (ISER) puts its focus on the study and exchange of academic achievements of international teaching and research staff. It also promotes educational reform in the world. In addition, it serves as an academic discussion and communication platform, which is beneficial for education and scientific research, aiming to stimulate the interest of all researchers.

The CSEE-TMEI conference is an integrated event concentrating on the field of computer science, environment, ecoinformatics, and education. The goal of the conference is to provide researchers working in this field with a forum to share new ideas, innovations, and solutions. CSEE 2011-TMEI 2011 was held during August 21–22, in Wuhan, China, and was co-sponsored by the International Science & Education Researcher Association, Beijing Gireida Education Co. Ltd, and Wuhan University of Science and Technology, China. Renowned keynote speakers were invited to deliver talks, giving all participants a chance to discuss their work with the speakers face to face.

In these proceeding, you can learn more about the field of computer science, environment, ecoinformatics, and education from the contributions of several researchers from around the world. The main role of the proceeding is to be used as means of exchange of information for those working in this area.

The Organizing Committee made a great effort to meet the high standards of Springer's *Communications in Computer and Information Science* (CCIS) series. Firstly, poor-quality papers were rejected after being reviewed by anonymous referees. Secondly, meetings were held periodically for reviewers to exchange opinions and suggestions. Finally, the organizing team held several preliminary sessions before the conference. Through the efforts of numerous people and departments, the conference was very successful.

During the organization, we received help from different people, departments, and institutions. Here, we would like to extend our sincere thanks to the publishers of CCIS, Springer, for their kind and enthusiastic help and support of our conference. Secondly, the authors should also be thanked for their submissions. Thirdly, the hard work of the Program Committee, the Program Chairs, and the reviewers is greatly appreciated.

In conclusion, it was the team effort of all these people that made our conference such a success. We welcome any suggestions that may help improve the conference and look forward to seeing all of you at CSEE 2012-TMEI 2012.

June 2011   Song Lin

Organization

Honorary Chairs

Chen Bin   Beijing Normal University, China
Hu Chen   Peking University, China
Chunhua Tan   Beijing Normal University, China
Helen Zhang   University of Munich, Germany

Program Committee Chairs

Xiong Huang   International Science & Education Researcher
                  Association, China
Li Ding   International Science & Education Researcher
                  Association, China
Zhihua Xu   International Science & Education Researcher
                  Association, China

Organizing Chairs

ZongMing Tu   Beijing Gireida Education Co. Ltd, China
Jijun Wang   Beijing Spon Technology Research Institution,
                  China
Quan Xiang   Beijing Prophet Science and Education
                  Research Center, China

Publication Chairs

Song Lin   International Science & Education Researcher
                  Association, China
Xiong Huang   International Science & Education Researcher
                  Association, China

International Program Committee

Sally Wang   Beijing Normal University, China
Li Li   Dongguan University of Technology, China
Bing Xiao   Anhui University, China
Z.L. Wang   Wuhan University, China
Moon Seho   Hoseo University, Korea
Kongel Arearak   Suranaree University of Technology, Thailand
Zhihua Xu   International Science & Education Researcher
                  Association, China

Co-sponsored by

International Science & Education Researcher Association, China
VIP Information Conference Center, China

Reviewers

Chunlin Xie	Wuhan University of Science and Technology, China
Lin Qi	Hubei University of Technology, China
Xiong Huang	International Science & Education Researcher Association, China
Gang Shen	International Science & Education Researcher Association, China
Xiangrong Jiang	Wuhan University of Technology, China
Li Hu	Linguistic and Linguidtic Education Association, China
Moon Hyan	Sungkyunkwan University, Korea
Guang Wen	South China University of Technology, China
Jack H. Li	George Mason University, USA
Marry. Y. Feng	University of Technology Sydney, Australia
Feng Quan	Zhongnan University of Finance and Economics, China
Peng Ding	Hubei University, China
Song Lin	International Science & Education Researcher Association, China
XiaoLie Nan	International Science & Education Researcher Association, China
Zhi Yu	International Science & Education Researcher Association, China
Xue Jin	International Science & Education Researcher Association, China
Zhihua Xu	International Science & Education Researcher Association, China
Wu Yang	International Science & Education Researcher Association, China
Qin Xiao	International Science & Education Researcher Association, China
Weifeng Guo	International Science & Education Researcher Association, China
Li Hu	Wuhan University of Science and Technology, China,
Zhong Yan	Wuhan University of Science and Technology, China
Haiquan Huang	Hubei University of Technology, China
Xiao Bing	Wuhan University, China
Brown Wu	Sun Yat-Sen University, China

Table of Contents – Part V

The Research on Real-Time Bus Strategy in Distributed Simulation Based on STK

Deyu Zhang and Wenbo Zhang[*]

Communication and Network Institute, Shenyang Ligong University, Shenyang, China
zhang_de_yu@163.com, zhangwenbo@yeah.net

Abstract. As a new distributed interactive simulation architecture, HLA in visual distributed simulation is limited in real-time. To solve this problem, this paper proposes a distributed simulation based on real-time bus strategy. It uses the real-time bus to command the basis simulation time of the system which ensure time synchronization among the federal members, and then achieve the entire distributed system time synchronization. Through testing and application, it shows that the real-time bus strategy is reliable and stable.

Keywords: Distributed Simulation, Satellite ToolKit (STK), Real-Time Bus Strategy.

1 Introduction

As one of the hotspots researches of simulation, distributed interactive simulation system structure HLA (High Level Architecture) is designed by bottom operation support environmental RTI (Run Time Infrastructure) to provide a general infrastructure and extensible services, in order to separate the simulation application and the bottom supporting environment. Time synchronization is the key of distributed simulation technology, although HLA specification has its own time scheduling criterion; in high real-time demand simulations HLA also have the following questions:

(1) The RTI of HLA not only doesn't provide how to handling the news by real-time schedule, but also doesn't provide an end-to-end prediction and a real-time functional mechanism;

(2) HLA only support two transfer modes: Transmission as soon as possible and reliable, the two methods cannot satisfy the requirements of relay messages under the real-time distributed interactive simulation.

As a new development direction of the simulation technology, visual simulation technology injects new vitality into the modern distributed simulation, which makes it become one of the main research contents of distributed interactive simulation technology. STK is a visual analysis software that made by the AGI company of American. Using its powerful analysis and lifelike 2D, 3D visual dynamic scenes and accurate graphic forms of various analysis resultsto determine the optimal solutions [1].

---

[*] Corresponding author.

S. Lin and X. Huang (Eds.): CSEE 2011, Part V, CCIS 218, pp. 1–5, 2011.

In order to resolve the worse real-time problems of HLA as above and also introduce the visual technology into the distributed simulation applications, this paper proposes the thinking of using real-time control bus strategy. Through design the link agent of STK and RTI, realize control the whole system time synchronization in distributed environment.

2   The Propose of Simulation Framework by Real-Time Bus Strategy Based on Link Agent

As the important connection module of STK, STK/Connect provides a quick way to connect with STK in C/S mode. STK/Connect includes a series of commands function that initialize Connect module, open the connection to STK, send STK/Connect instructions, and receive the data that STK returns and stop the connection with STK after the interactive be finished.

As mentioned, HLA has problems in real-time distributed simulation.when a federal member request time iterative, may not get the RTI response immediately, then it cannot meet the system in real-time [2]. In order to resolve worse real-time problem of HLA, this paper put forward build the link agent of STK and HLA, which based on STK/Connect module. Put STK and operation support environmental RTI of HLA together; propose the real-time bus strategy in distributed simulation based on link agent. Realize that use HLA mechanism in the whole simulation framework, but in high real-time demands simulation parts use the real-time bus strategy. By link agent realize the functions such as synchronous coordination between federal members and real-time control bus parts, information exchange and so on. Make the whole simulation system becomes a collaborative simulation environment. The simulation framework of real-time control bus is showed as figure 1.

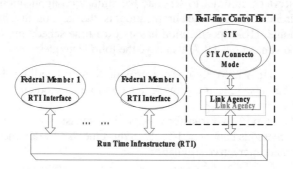

Fig. 1. The simulation framework of real-time control bus

In the real-time control bus of distributed simulation based on link agent, different federal members can run on different computer in LAN, the network communication among federal members and time management are realized by RTI, meanwhile the federal members may establish a connection with STK rely on link agent that real-time driving and obtain the display action and relate data information in STK interface.

The system design real-time control bus parts through link agency establish a connection with RTI, responsible collaborative interoperate, receive data, conversion and distribute in RTI and STK real-time simulation part. On the one hand, it bound with STK, maintain benchmark the simulation time of system.It can control the advance speed of the simulation system by RTI. The time synchronization strategy is: with STK demo clock as reference clock, through STK/Connect module, use link agency bind visual simulation federal members and STK time synchronization, thus establish the time base of simulation world; through RTI to ensure time synchronization among the federal members, and then make the distributed system are time synchronization. Specific operational process of simulation as shown in figure 2:

3 Effective Real-Time Controls for STK in Real-Time Strategy

How to realize efficient real-time control between application and STK in distributed simulation environment is the key factor for the real-time strategy to be implemented successful [3]. Therefore, in order to complete the real-time bus strategy of distributed simulation, it is necessary to improve the time control algorithm of STK simulation.

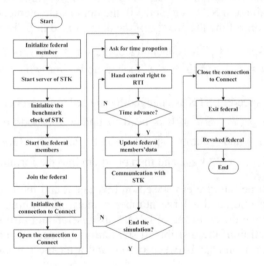

Fig. 2. Operational process of simulation

3.1 STK Real-Time Control Method

STK provides two kind of real-time control method: "Time Step" pattern and "Real Time/X Real Time" pattern [4].

"Time Step" pattern is a way that drives STK by set time step. In this driving mode, if the external connect command doesn't promote time step, STK's internal clock and scene wouldn't make any advance and refresh, this will make the objects of the scene jump from one position to another, so the actions in the scene doesn't smooth.

"Real Time/X Real Time" pattern is the way that doesn't interrupt each object in their respective time propulsion after each STK interaction renewal. In the process of update scene, it can extrapolate the object data on each time point by multiple speeds or pose extrapolate method, optimization the object's state in the scene. Use "Real Time/X Real Time" pattern can reduce the sending quantity of external control instruction, and ensure the fluency of pictures show; therefore this paper chooses this way to realize the real-time control on STK [5].

3.2 Obtaining the Improved Algorithm of STK Simulation Time

This paper put forward a more efficient real-time algorithm for STK under the "Real Time / X Real Time" mode, in the promoting time principles of the internal STK: the program of federal member on the server demo and the main program of STK are designed on the same computer (for sharing the CPU time of the same host). Under the "Real Time / X Real Time" mode, the promoting time principle of internal STK is [1]: it is assumed that the demo time of STK is t1 when the machine time is T1, the demo time of STK is t2 when the machine time is T2, and the demo speed V remains the same size when time is between T1 and T2.Thus:

$$t_2 = t_1 + V * (T_2 - T_1) \tag{1}$$

It is assumed that the initial simulation time is T0 (machine time), the demo time and demo speed gained of STK is t0 and V0; the demo state element program in server is responsible for controlling the change of the demo speed in STK:

(1) If the demo speed of STK is unchanged, the simulation time t of STK can gained by the formula $1: t = t_i + V_i * (T - T_i)$ .T1 is a node time which is the closest to the machine time T;

(2) If the demo speed of STK is changed by the federal member in server when the machine time is $T_{i+1} (T_{i+1} \le T$). It is need to update the node data, and regain the demo time ti+1 and demo speed Vi+1 at the time Ti+1, causing $T_i = T_{i+1}$, $t_i = t_{i+1}$, $V_i = V_{i+1}$, and then put them into the formula (1).

Using the real-time bus strategy based on link agent and the real-time access STK time algorithm, on one hand a large number of network commands transmission is reduced, also improve the real-time of HLA transmission and also improve the ability of real-time interaction of the distributed simulation systems. Figure 3 is the network delay effects comparison char between before and after the introduction of real-time control bus.

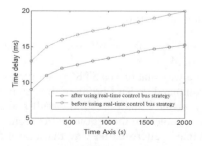

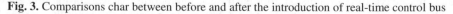

Fig. 3. Comparisons char between before and after the introduction of real-time control bus

From the test results, although the simulation time delay increases with the simulation time going, there is a more improvement in the time delay of the simulation system based on real-time control bus than not. It is proved that it can improve the real-time ability of the distributed simulation systems based on real-time control bus.

4 Summary

Although HLA is widely used in distributed simulation, its defects in real-time make its application is restricted. To solve this problem, this paper puts forward the real-time control bus strategy method, and through designs the link agency between STK and RTI to realize it.

References

1. Ying, Y., Qi, W.: STK in Computer Simulation of Application. National Defence Industrial Press (2005)
2. Xu, D.-y., Jiang, X.-y., Zhang, Y.-h.: Real-Time Extension To HLA. The Computer Simulation 23(1), 124–127 (2006)
3. Rui, L., Zeng, D.-x.: Applying STK to System Simulation Based on Network. Aerospace Control 6(23), 64–68 (2005)
4. Ma, Z.-q., Du, C.-l.: Research on Real-time RTI Based Distributed Interactive Simulation. Science Technology and Engineering 7(8), 1810–1812 (2007)
5. He, X.-h., Zhao, Z.-l., Liu, X.-q.: Test to real time performance of real-time simulation method based on HLA. Computer Engineering and Design 30(22), 5140–5143 (2009)

Research on Medieval English Literature Teaching Based on Data Analysis

XiuLi Zhang

School of Foreign Languages, Anhui University of Science and Technology,
Huainan, Anhui, China
xllczhang@gmail.com

Abstract. To teach undergraduate students the medieval English literature for many teachers is a great challenge. Teachers perhaps need to revise many of their traditional approaches to a literature which has seemed to many students difficult to comprehend. Better preparation of texts and broader use of recordings are needed to deal with this problem in the classroom practices.

Keywords: medieval English literature, undergraduate, video and audio-materials.

1 Introduction

At undergraduate levels most of Chinese scholars probably spend more time teaching and supervising their students than doing research, and teaching medieval English language and literature for undergraduate students is somewhat limited to the introductory courses more than anything else. For instance, during their third- and fourth-year students at the school of foreign languages receive their first exposure to Old and Middle English language and literature in a course on the history of the English language, or the quick survey of the history of English literature, the latter being more restricted to the works like Beowulf and Chaucer due to the teachers' unwillingness of teaching the medieval English itself, and the students' disinclination for the grammatically hard reading materials and to some extent old fashion stories. Even for Beowulf and Chaucer's works, usually The Caterbery Tales, some teachers just mentioned the story line without specific explanation of the texts. The English is so far away from the Chinese students, even that of the English major, that student find it boring to read it and try very hard to find unsurprising meanings from the difficulty words and poetic lines. Therefore, some teachers choose to skip the reading of those texts. Students are required only to memorize the names of the author and their works in the examinations. In addition, the audio and video materials are hard to find on the internet, and the education institutions do not provide any of that kind. For example, there is no recording of the text, and teachers have no access to these kinds of materials. Therefore, listening to the texts is impossible, at least in my university currently. Someone would say that the teachers can record by themselves. That is also beyond the normal circumstance. Average teachers who teach English language and literature are not so professional enough to make it and they are reluctant to do so. They themselves even feel boring of teaching medieval literature, compare with the other period English literature. They are not keen on researching on this period; in fact, most of them show

S. Lin and X. Huang (Eds.): CSEE 2011, Part V, CCIS 218, pp. 6–10, 2011.

little enthusiasm toward academic research. Thus the most lightly and easy to be taught become their favorite. And there is another important factor that influences the teaching preference. The most recent education reformation states that teachers' performance are mostly decided by the students who have the right to give marks to their teachers and ask the teachers to behave like this or that. Thus, most teachers prefer to change themselves to satisfy the needs of the students, at least in inexplicit way. The medieval period is probably the most unattractive to the students, and is doomed to be skipped.

2 Pedagogical Challenges and Solutions

Teaching medieval English literature effectively to Chinese college students presents unique pedagogical challenges. It requires an understanding of what such students are like and an adaptation of teaching methods and materials to deal with their unique characteristics.

Better preparation of the texts is the first step to teach well of the medieval English literature. Compare with the other stages of the English literature, the ME literature has the following characteristics. First, the Medieval literature is a broad subject, encompassing essentially all written works available in Europe and beyond during the Middle Ages (encompassing the one thousand years from the fall of the Western Roman Empire ca. AD 500 to the beginning of the Florentine Renaissance in the late 15th century).It is a complex and rich field of study, from the utterly sacred to the exuberantly profane, touching all points in-between. Because of the wide range of time and place it is difficult to speak in general terms without oversimplification, and thus the literature is best characterized by its place of origin and/or language, as well as its genre. Second, ME literature texts have different versions that it is hard to choose the most suitable for the students. Then, the language it uses is hard to explain and students will find it much difficult to understand. And most of the literary texts are of religious subjects, which is unattractive to the Chinese students. Unlike the literary works in other periods, the ones in ME period are less concern with the common subjects. Thus, teachers have to be well prepared for the class and the following tips perhaps would help.

First, the history shall be illustrated clearly to the students. Without knowing the history of this period and the ones before and after this period, there will be hard for the students who know almost nothing of the early English history to fully appreciate the literature of this period. Contextual information from history, art and architecture, had greatly enhanced undergraduate study of the texts. It was agreed that teaching the texts through manuscript culture was one particularly effective technique and the increasing availability of electronic and online manuscript resources was welcomed in this regard. Gail Ashton (2010) suggested that an electronic package of contextual resources (images, sound clips, MS images, text excerpts, plot summaries) would prove very helpful as learning and teaching resource.

Second, the most understandable version of the texts shall be used for a better understanding for the students. The ME literature is just a beginning or a small part of the history of English literature, that if the texts are to frustrated to read, students will feel exhausting to continue this course. In the 'Teaching Medieval Romance' day conference organized by the collaboration of Jonathan Gibson at the English Subject

Centre and Raluca Radulescu, who hosted the event at the Centre for Medieval Studies, University of Wales, Bangor, in May, delegates discussed how issues of textual variation loomed large in study of the medieval romances. Students might often encounter romances in parallel text editions; individual editions vary greatly in the amount of guidance provided in terms of glossaries, textual notes etc. There was evaluation and comparison of editions commonly used in teaching the romances. Alison Wiggins presented a number of issues involved in producing a student-friendly edition. Ros Allen introduced the topic of in-house editions of romances which university lecturers produce for their students, in the absence of enough available copies of several texts. It was widely agreed that teachers from various universities could cooperate in exchanging ideas in order to improve student access to medieval romance texts.

Then, translation is needed to better understand the contents and thoughts of the ME literary work. Many teachers who teach the English major students English literature prefer to use English in the whole teaching process. Translation has been used by foreign language learners to facilitate language learning for centuries, but translation has played various roles under different language teaching methods. While some foreign language educators may consider translation as a critical means to ensure students' comprehension and an important writing exercise, other teachers may totally ban or discourage the use of the native language and translation in the classroom. While for the medieval English literature, a more difficult part, I believe that translation is a better resolution. It will help the students to grasp the main ideas of the mostly poetic diction. Although the use of translation in learning a foreign language is much maligned by language teachers, translation is widely used in learners' foreign language learning process. It appears that learners often use translation as a learning strategy to comprehend and remember. As Malmkjær stated, 'the issue of the use of translation in language teaching is one on which most language teachers have a view' [3](1998: 1), but fairly often, teachers' views are not strongly in favor of it. Particularly from the turn of the twentieth century onwards, Posen Liao argues that[5], many theoretical works and practical methods in language teaching have assumed that a second language (L2) should be taught without reference to the learners' first language (L1). It has become a popular belief among teachers that the translation of L1 gets in the way with the acquisition of L2. While many foreign language educators may have ignored the role of translation in language teaching, from the learners' perspective, translation is still widely used. For instance, Naiman et al. (1978) aimed to identify strategies used by Good Language Learners (GLLs), and found that one of the strategies often used by GLLs was to 'refer back to their native language(s) judiciously (translate into L1) and make effective cross-lingual comparisons at different stages of language learning'[4].

The next approach to the teaching of the ME literature is the employ of the video and audio-materials. This has been proved to be an effective way, especially for the ME literature teaching. Students tend to be more active when they watch a video. And on the internet there are many such materials. However, 90%of the students don't have a computer. For the ones who have, the speed of their net is very slow, because all of them have to use the net provided by the university and it works not well. Also, more than 90% of the students rely on the teachers as the source of knowledge, having scare awareness of e-learning by themselves. Therefore, teachers should provide the students more materials from the internet, something new and different from the textbooks.

These materials are fresh for them, and will provide them another perspective to acquire the required knowledge, thus are better received in the classroom. In this semester, spring of the 2011, I have two classes of the same level, the English major students in their second year. They are separated into two classes, and I have taught the same lecture twice, which provides me the opportunity of comparing the different teaching methodologies. A questionnaire is carried out to evaluate the effect of these opposite teaching methods, the one group taught with the assistant of the video and audio-materials and the other without.

For example, when teaching the history of the medieval English, or the origin of England, only interpretation of the book texts is not enough. Students find it too confusing to understand the happening in an unknown land of an unknown people. The foreignness of the big names stands as blocks to their full comprehension of the events. While if the names and images and sounds are combined together, students show their willingness and interest on the one hand, and receive more deep impression of this period on the other hand, which is clearly a better approach. Without the assistance of the video and audio-materials, both the teacher and the student would feel boring in the classroom. And in many teacher training programs, video recordings in micro-teaching practice are well-established. They have, however, been little used in the teaching practices. Most of the universities and colleges are reluctant to adopt it. There are some reasons for it. First, as classrooms are more and more student-centered, teachers have to confine his or her teaching to traditional teaching methodologies. If not, some students and their parents would "have a talk" with the school director or the dean, the boss or the senior of the teachers, and the results would be not good for the teachers and as well the department just because of this kind of complaints. Thus, most teachers are reluctant to use new methods of teaching for the old one, the one that are familiar to students and parents, is more "safe". There is one event that one student accused his teacher of showing movie in the classroom to the master of the university, and the result was an unofficial rule that teachers should use as few as possible movie things in the English teaching classroom. Second, such video and audio-materials that are suitable to teaching in the college classroom are hard to access to. Owning to finance shortage, managers and teachers tend to use the ways that they can handle with.

In fact, video is highly motivating for the learner. According to Chris Kennedy, video can expose him to 'live' instances of communication rather than the usual simulations which teachers or text-book writers have to resort to. It can show him the situations he will have to operate in, can present examples of successful and unsuccessful interaction, and more important can show why misunderstandings might occur and how to avoid breakdowns in communication. The learner's terminal behavior can be brought into the classroom rather than exist as an abstract ideal outside it [7]. The problem is that the video and audio-materials are not discriminated before they go into the students' minds, which is more harmful. Some materials from the internet are mingling of good and evil. Teachers should choose the most suitable materials for the students. Therefore, in order to help students better understand and comprehend the truth of English literature, teachers shall go with the world, and act as an employable leader.

3 Summary

At undergraduate levels most of Chinese teachers tend to overpass the medieval period when teaching the history or anthology of English literature, for the teaching practices present many challenges to teachers. However, better preparation of texts and broader use of recordings can help deal with this problem.

References

1. Danker, F.E.: Teaching Medieval English Literature: Texts, Recordings, and Techniques. College English 32(3), 340–357 (1970), http://www.jstor.org/stable/374482
2. Ashton, G.: Medieval English Romance in Context. Continuum International Publishing Group Ltd (2010)
3. Malmkjær, K. (ed.): Translation & Language Teaching: Language Teaching & Translation. St. Jerome Publishing, UK (1998)
4. Naiman, N., Frohlich, M., Stern, H.H., Todesco, A.: The Good Language Learner (Toronto: Ontario Institute for Studies in Education), p. 14. Ontario Institute for Studies in Education, Toronto (1978)
5. Liao, P.: EFL Learners' Beliefs about and Strategy Use of Translation in English Learning. RELC Journal 37, 191 (2006)
6. Radulescu, R., Dalrymple, R.: Teaching Medieval Romance, http://www.english.heacademy.ac.uk/explore/publications/newsletters/newsissue11/radulescu.htm
7. Kennedy, C.: Video in ESP. RELC Journal 10(1), 60 (1979)

On Training the Practical and Creative Ability of Professional Engineering Management Students Based on Web Resources

Yanhong Qin and Ying Yang

School of Management, Chongqing Jiaotong University,Chongqing, China
qinyanhong24@163.com, yy15802322926@163.com

Abstract. With the development of building industry in China, it requires a lot of engineering management professionals, so the colleges and universities should focus on developing and training the practical and innovative ability of engineering management students, and strengthening the practice of teaching and research actively in order to make students adapt to market requirements and industry development demands on practical and innovation capacities. Besides, they should make contributions to train applicable professionals for society.

Keywords: Engineering management, Practical teaching, Innovation.

1 Introduction

Since the "enrollment expansion", Chinese higher education has achieved leaps and bounds development, higher education has entered a stage of popular education. In this context, when facing up to the engineering management professional which has a character of practice, how to improve the level and quality of professional education of engineering management, it is a urgent problem must be resolved to improve the rate of employment and competitiveness in the market for engineering management students.

At present, the mainly problems of our school's engineering management professional teaching are as follows: teaching contents are relatively falling behind the practice, thus, what students have learned cannot be put into practice; on the other hand, professional teachings are not well combined with social and enterprises' practical needs, what's more, the students cannot quickly adapt to their posts after graduating. To solve these problems, this paper studies how to develop the abilities of professional practice and innovation for engineering management students, and strive to enhance the ability of students to combine theory and practice as unit so that can help them to improve their practical ability and innovative ability, which can lay a solid foundation for students to adapt the work of engineering management smoothly after graduation, in addition, it can be better meet the needs of engineering management personnel.

2 Strengthen the Interface between Practice and Theory of Teaching

Engineering management major is highly called for practice for engineering management professionals, so it needs more practical activities to help students to

S. Lin and X. Huang (Eds.): CSEE 2011, Part V, CCIS 218, pp. 11–15, 2011.

understand the theory deep, in order to improve students' learning effects, the practice and theory are arranged should be scientific linkage each other. In this way, not only can students deepen learning and understanding of theories, but also conducive to the improvement of practical ability of students, and can be conducive to train their innovation in practice. For example, a lot of professional courses of engineering management major have strong theoretical basis, in the process of teaching should be based on characteristics of the courses, then students can be arranged for groups, in accordance with the teaching schedule, contrast laboratory teaching equipments to learn deep the theoretical knowledge and principles, then let Students as a team to talk about their views and their own conclusion, and using the results of the students practice to organize class discussion, and encouraging pupils to speak, in discussing process ,continuously discover new problems and new ideas to further consolidate the results of theory teaching, while natural training the students' creative thinking.

In addition, teaching resources can be integrated to enrich teaching methods, make full use of PPT and multimedia simulation software, multimedia courseware, and the network resources etc, which are sinister of he modernization teaching resources, collecting classic case and pictures to increase the teaching of practice and realistic. Focus on the use of cases teaching to train students' abilities of "doing something as follow what they have learn "and "learning form what they do", and effectively improve their theoretical knowledge and practical ability.

3   Strengthen the Cooperation between Industry and University

Engineering management professional, in the teaching staff, laboratory and experimental base construction, talents cultivation mode and revolution and innovation etc should achieve comprehensive and substantive school-enterprise cooperation, to create a good training environment and conditions to improve the quality of engineering management professionals. Engineering management students through direct contact with excellent engineering teams of large-scale engineering companies, the real operation objects of engineering management and projects operating environment, and the evolving engineering market, and learn the latest equipments, technology, Technical, technological updates, the latest high-paying information technology application development of engineering firms.

For example:

Steering committee of engineering management can be set up by the company and the school teachers, which can provide a guidance to the students of engineering management professional, and they also can fund excellent students to successfully complete their education, a number of graduate students funded by the subsidy directly to the engineering enterprise to work as a staff , achieving production and research cooperation to train talents closely.

We can employ a number of extensive practical experience persons from engineering companies as guide teachers to guide practice teaching, responsible for training the students of engineering management professional, guided practice, training and graduation design.

According to the teaching needs, the school sent students to engineering company to work as a internship at appropriate real-time, with the help of cooperation companies' the equipments, facilities, projects, training of personnel to guide students; on the other hand, students can also use the alumni association and other social relations resources to actively explore ways to be a internship by contact your professional counterparts in the engineering business

School should be encouraged to contact with the enterprises to organize the students for the engineering construction design contest, and asked teachers to provide the related design guidance on theory and practice so that enable students to work actively in-depth investigation unit actual operation, make full use of their learned major knowledge to solve practical engineering problems, then bold and innovative to solve the problem they are facing, and carefully confirm the result. The design competition can arouse passion of students and stimulate students to develop innovation in practice, give full play to the main part of students.

4   Strengthen the Laboratory Constructing and Undertaking the Experimental Projects

Practice teaching aim at improving practical ability to master basic skills and methods of testing as main line, and mastery of scientific knowledge, promote scientific thinking and creative thinking as the main teaching objectives. Therefore, in engineering management teaching should attach great importance to the construction and experimental teaching laboratory. Before experimental activities, you should require students to use information technology to learn the relevant laboratory equipments' performance and usage, independent design practice and the experiment contents, when they have the experiment they can test the feasibility and practical results of innovative content. Encourage teachers to undertake school out construction projects and make efforts to transfer the items into laboratory projects, which are more practical and feasible, students want to complete these projects, they must learn to access information, testing by them. With these experiences, students adapt to their work quickly after employment, employers are also very welcome such graduates. Moreover, it may solve a problem faced by the students: In the past, in the library and study room school only can learn abstract theoretical knowledge, often couldn't understand well, unable to resolve the real problems, in the learning process, thoughts and ideas generated by can not in practice, but in the laboratory, they can try these ideas ,it can not only inspire students to study and explore new things of interest, but also train the students in the innovative spirit and practical ability.

5   Strengthen the Construction of Laboratory Teaching Team

The key to a good teaching is teacher, for engineering management professional; teachers, especially, should pay more attention to their own hands-on ability. Laboratories should actively select outstanding teachers and laboratory assistants to participate in the training of senior project management skills to continuously improve their professional level, to meet the needs of innovation engineering management theory and practice of professional teaching; at the same time, the laboratory actively create opportunities for teachers to participate in self-development projects Software and the work of home-made experimental apparatus, which allows teachers to be well in practice and innovation training, also can provide opportunities to talent students to develop creativity. In addition, "internal training" should be teachers enhanced for teachers, such as teachers' basic functions of training should be carried out, experimental teaching demonstration, experiment ability contest of teachers, to encourage teachers to participate in compiling professional teaching materials, through a series of activities to enhance the abilities of teachers about the theory and practice innovation.

6 Design Competition Will Help Train Students' Abilities of Independent Learning and Exploring

Engineering Design Competition adopts a semi-open proposition to allow students to analyze real problems for enterprises and put forward the solutions, which requires students on the basis of mastering the professional knowledge they have been learned to go to enterprise to research the actual operations of them, and then can they make a preparation for an optimal solution. In addition, in order to make their design can be stand out, each team member have to spend a lot of time to self-learning and exploration, while discussing and ask for advice from professional teachers, and then learn a lot knowledge never have learned before but it's very important to make programs, for example, some students in process of the use the "save mileage method "to optimize the design mastered Matlab, which inspired them to learn the engineering knowledge and master skills and build up a interest in the engineering, the whole process of design the students as main parts to participate, which enable students to truly become a learning center, and students heuristic scientific way of thinking, stimulate their learning motivation and creativity. Participating students through practice and training, to develop new ideas, explore new ideas, new designs, new technologies and new products, to develop their skills of creative thinking and innovation.

7 Engineering Design Competition Has Greatly Promoted the Development of Engineering Education

Engineering solutions design features with case studies and thinking, that's mean this case is used as a supplementary of he theory of engineering teaching , the use of actual cases through a variety of organizations and disciplines to enable students to study the case they have faced ,at the same time ,they seek for information and application the knowledge they have learned to solve problems, thus contributing them to form a more extensive, systematic and integrated knowledge system, thereby achieving the training requirements and to achieve the goal that higher education has settled that the theory is "enough" to use . Meanwhile, in the process of engineering Design Competition engineering, can make full use of enterprises' resources to achieve between business and universities to effective communication and to overcome the problem of lacking of university laboratory software and hardware; In addition, through contact with the actual engineering business case so that students do not have a passive learning foreign business case, but to really understand the actual software and hardware conditions of the domestic engineering enterprises and their operating conditions, which can provide practical and useful reference information and experience for their future work.

8 Conclusion

Practical education is an important part of engineering management professional teaching, the spirit of innovation and practice is the key and foundation to convey the eligible talents to society. Strengthen the training of the engineering management professional students on the abilities of innovation and practice is a significant and long-term project, which requires us to continually improve teaching methods and ideas. Only in this way can we meet the requirements of modern higher education in order to train personnel to meet the needs of society, in order to make contribute to the development of China's construction industry.

References

1. Tan, H.: Vigorously carry out cooperative education, and actively explore the application of personnel training. China's Higher Education Research (July 2008)
2. Luo, Z.X.: Both theory and engineering practice to cultivate creative talents. Test Technology and Management 23 (February 2006)
3. Zhang, Y.: Develop students' creative and practical ability of the experimental teaching model. Electrical & Electronic Education (July 2008)
4. Cheng, J., Liu, J.: Carried out traffic management professional practical teaching according to grass-roots demands. Yunnan Landscape Institute (January 2007)

Emphasizing on Curriculum Features: The Key to General Technology Multimedia Design

Weiqiang Chen

Center of Basic Education Research, Zhejiang Normal University,
321004 Jinhua, Zhejiang, China

Abstract. Evidence suggests General Technology instruction should emphasize on three curriculum features of General Technology curriculum in the process of multimedia design. Three typical features of General Technology curriculum ought to be taken into concerns. First, "learning-by-doing" and "doing-by-learning", namely, teacher must lay stress on curriculum creativity and make students have a profound understanding about the spirit of "mind and hand", afterwards, multimedia should be taken as a medium between "learning-by-doing" and "doing-by-learning" . Second, "life-stylized", namely, there must be a tight integration between multimedia design and real life; emphasis must be laid on exploiting "life-stylized" multimedia teaching resources. Third, "personalized", multimedia design must implement the "personalized teaching concept", effective individualized teaching strategies must be adopted in teaching contents, teaching models and teaching approaches.

Keywords: General Technology, multimedia design, curriculum features, effective instruction.

1   Introduction

It is witnessed General Technology curriculum, as one of the most innovative procedure in China New Curriculum Reform, is implemented vigorously all over China [1]. Over the past years, multimedia teaching is gaining popularity to an extensive extent nationwide in the General Technology instruction in China. However, a crucial issue is neglected during multimedia design for some instructors, i.e. those multimedia designs did not reflect the curriculum features commendably.What curriculum features should be reflected in the process of General Technology multimedia design? It is suggested that three key points should be emphasized.

2   "Learning-By-Doing" and "Doing-By-Learning"

Although multimedia teaching has been prevalent nationwide, the presentation of multimedia merely reduplicates the content of teaching material, which results in inert classroom and dizzy students and it runs counter to the curriculum feature of "learning-by-doing" and "doing-by-learning". And it goes against to the social

S. Lin and X. Huang (Eds.): CSEE 2011, Part V, CCIS 218, pp. 16–21, 2011.

development and New Curriculum Reform and discourages students [2]. How should teachers' multimedia design embody the concept of "learning-by-doing" and "doing-by-learning"?

2.1 Multimedia Ought to be Taken as a Medium between "Learning-by-Doing" and "Doing-By-Learning"

"Learning-by-doing" and "doing-by-learning" is an indispensable procedure for human cognitive development. The development of human cognition is a process of "simpleness to complexity" "inferiority to superiority", nonetheless, cognitive development of middle school students manifests an essential feature of "specific image thinking" gradually transit to "abstract thinking", however, so-called "abstract thinking" associated to experience directly and demands specific vivid image to a large extent. Moreover, the optimal source of the specific vivid image comes from the students' direct experience. First, investigation takes priority, and investigation can verify perceptual direct experiences. Second, conversion from specific thinking to abstract thinking must be achieved.

2.2 Stress Must Be Laid on Specialty of Curriculum Creativity

Creativity is the essence of technology. General Technology curriculum is a creativity-focused curriculum. The primary goal of General Technology curriculum is displaying students' creativity and cultivating students' innovative spirit and practice ability in the process of information obtaining, processing, managing and communicating and by the way of General Technology designing, manufacturing, assessing and application of concrete methods and practical problem-solving. The best solution to achieving this goal is making students experience personally. Consequently, first, teacher must make full use of multimedia as a medium and create concrete situation for students. for instance, in the process of "design a practical, good-looking, personalized and functional pen container", via the multimedia, teacher can organize students to make analysis and discussion on the information that has been collected and the typical example of case. Second, teacher must make appropriate use of students' achievements. Teachers can display students' design achievement using multimedia, for instance, teacher can display a model of a certain simple product which was designed by student, then let students have a discussion about the fundamental issues in product design. It can conduct students to make discussion about technology design, methods and originality. All this process embodies the concept of "learning-by-doing" and "doing-by-learning" and reflects the quality of curriculum creativity, and that, overall it can stimulate peer-interaction and make cooperation and resources allocation an Art [4].

2.3 "Mind and Hand"

The key to technology acquisition is combination of intellectual skills with practical skills and integration of theory with practice. Knowledge acquisition is an organic, integrative process of brainstorming, activities and reflections after class. This training way of "Hands-on" enhances students' technology ability, problem-solving ability effectively, and that, it is no doubt that the best way to intensify students' ability of "Mind and hand" and practice ability is to integrate "learning-by-doing" with "doing-by-learning". Hence, in process of multimedia design should be in accordance with the concept of "learning-by-doing" with "doing-by-learning" and make the concept of "valid integration between innovative curriculum and brilliant teaching contents" [6]. And then teachers should strive to create specific situations that reflect all these two concepts. Situation creation should include comprehensive contents and concrete methodologies. First, teaching medium should have great pertinence, i.e. it is in accordance with the scientific principle and satisfies the teaching demands, reflects the demands of heuristic teaching and is beneficial to the problem-solving and it can stimulate students to use their mind and enhance the flexibility and creativity of their mind. Second, the situation creation is required to conduct students to practice personally. The object of the practice is improving students' technical ability. All these created situations should be vivid, visualized and effective, and create an astrosphere which stimulates students to practice. The situation creation should combine the mind experience with practical experience. Only through all those ways, students' practice ability can be enhanced.

3 Life-Stylized

It is presumed by a great portion of teachers that General Technology teaching is a hard nut to knock and General Technology study is believed to be boring by a great number of students. The fundamental reason for this problem is there is a large gap between teaching and real life. Confronted with the problem of "life-stylized", here are some suggestions.

3.1 Inexhaustible Source for Multimedia Teaching Material: The Practical Life

There are three reasons why the "life-stylized" instruction is emphasized. First, General Technology curriculum covers an extensive knowledge scope and manifests to be general, concise, profound, and abstract theoretically. Second, life is the inexhaustible source for multimedia teaching material. For one thing, life is a live teaching material. Therefore, curriculum must be endowed with characteristics of the age. Only if it is mixed with real life, General Technology curriculum would be powerful and effective and, realize the curriculum value. For another, practical life catalyzes students' technology study. The aim of technology education is colorizing students' future and laying foundations for the tomorrow. Only if multimedia design is life-stylized, and is adjoined to the practical situation, can enhance students' enthusiasm and independence and achieve the goal of New Curriculum. Moreover, practical life is the basis for curriculum' existence and development. Technology teachers should have an active mind and keep step with the age. In the process of multimedia design, teacher should be observant and conscientious, start from students' real life and extend to the innovative and high technology, and attract students' interest by introducing brand-new achievements and future trends. Life-stylized classroom is most impressive to students, and multimedia itself attracts students, then students will enjoy the technology study.

3.2 Multimedia Design Should Explore Life-Stylized' Teaching Resources

First, construction of multimedia curriculum should be students-oriented, i.e. it should be start from students' interest, ability, need, previous experiences and meet up with students' physiological and psychological and cognitive development patterns. Second, construction of multimedia curriculum should be good at capturing "generative" teaching resources in the teaching process. Generative teaching resources are not the static teaching resources that teacher has prepared, but it generates from mutual communications between students and teachers or peer-collaboration or peer-communication based on multimedia. This kind of teaching resources is reflections of students' authentic experience, and it is transient and precious If multimedia teaching contents were enriched by revised, improved "Generative" teaching resources, General Technology education would be active and energetic.

4   Personalized

Psychologically, personalized is a process of individuals' cognition growing and developing and gradually being different from others' cognition pattern, including the formation of personality, self realization and emotional maturity, etc. If this process is delayed, it results in immature personality [8]. General technology curriculum emphasizes on promoting students' personality development, its essence is to exploit students' inner potential, promote the formation of mature personality. But it is discovered that in multimedia design teachers have not promoted students' personality development effectively. Then, how to fulfill personalized education successfully? Here are four recommendations as follows:

4.1   Persistent in the "Personalized" Educational Ideas

In the process of multimedia design, teachers ought to take curriculum features into concern, make the personalized education reinforced, and in the practicalconduction, teachers should provide colorful, rich-in-content, unique teaching situations in the multimedia design based on the personslized approach. Teachers should strengthen students' advantages, and improve students' disadvantages and make students enjoy the study.

4.2   Exploiting Personalized Teaching Contents

Personalized, diversified teaching contents require teachers should give a comprehensive, selective and generative multimedia design. Because teaching contents exert great influence on knowledge acquisition and construction, the authentic design of interactive activities should be instant, dynamic, mutual exchanges between teaching system and learners. Teachers should encourage students to choose some elective course, by acquiring different teaching contents, which will be benefit for students to form an internal, stable and effective cognitive structure and behavior pattern. Besides,

Teachers would take the needs of social development and require of cultivating personalized students into consideration. And then they can meet the needs of diverse individuals.

4.3 Constructing Personalized Teaching Model

Personalized teaching model requires mixed, various teaching approach. Teachers should abandon the spoon-feed approach, but use various kinds of teaching approach, like acceptive learning, exploratory learning, experience-oriented learning, inquiry learning, practical learning. Moreover, teachers should create a comfortable, harmonious studying atmosphere and in the activities of emotional-experiencing, atmosphere-experiencing, error-correcting, students can find their advantages and disadvantages and where their interests lies in , and all those process will create a live and peer-cooperative phenomena, and effective technology studying will be achieved and students' personality will be well-developed.

4.4 Adopting Personalized Teaching Approaches

Personalized teaching approaches emphasizes on "returning to life", i.e. students are immersed in the atmosphere of "learning for life" and "learning from life", and individuals' innate temperament characteristics can be diffused in life constantly[9]. Therefore, in the multimedia design, teachers should discard the concept of "curriculum-based" teaching approach. Teaching is not only a process of curriculum conduction or implementing, but also a process of innovation or exploiting of curriculum. If teachers give considerations to curriculum implementing and curriculum innovation, then integrate teaching to life and exploit school-based curriculum, the personalized teaching approaches will be attained in the near future.

5 Conclusion

Three significant features of the General Technology curriculum should be taken great concern in the process of multimedia design; those three features may contain diverse connotations, but it doesn't mean that they are independent to each other, but connected to each other and make an integrative system. Instructors should regard these three features as organic system. The implementing of General Technology curriculum certainly will be rely on the development of multimedia technology, so instructors should make a good use of this effective teaching aid. Guided by the concept of New Curriculum Reform in China, instructors should have a comprehensive view and solve the significant issues and accumulate experience of multimedia design [1]. Finally, it is believed that all the theoretician, instructors and learners will find the best way to express their educational beliefs and share their experiences, ideas of teaching and learning, and the effective method to achieve the education goals of persistent development [10].

Acknowledgements. I show my sincere gratitude to China's National Education Science "Eleventh Five-Year Plan" of Ministry of Education（DHA100246), The project of Teacher Education Research of Zhejiang Province" The Model for Professional Development of General Technology Teachers in High Schools" (2010(78)), and the research of "Effective Strategies for Professional Developments of General Technology Teachers in High Schools" for their great supports.

References

1. Chen, W. q.: The key issues in the implementation of general technology curriculum. China Educational Technology 11, 84–88 (2010) (in Chinese)
2. Zhou, X.-l.: Group Presentation in College EnglishTeaching: Practice and Reflections. Journal of Zhejiang Normal University (Social Sciences) 35(3), 108–112 (2010) (in Chinese)
3. Frith, V., Jaftha, J., Prince, R.: Evaluating the Effectiveness of Interactive Computer Tutorials for an Undergraduate Mathematical Literacy Course. British Journal of Educational Technology 2, 159–171 (2004)
4. Liu, Y.-c.: RationalAnalysis of andOutlook for"Team Teaching. Journal of Zhejiang Normal University (Social Sciences) 35(3), 113–117 (2010) (in Chinese)
5. Barker, P.: Designing Interactive Learning Systems. Educational and Training Technology International 27(2), 125–145 (1990)
6. Tong, A.-l.: On the Teaching Reform of Teacher Education Courses inTeachers Colleges. Journal of Zhejiang Normal University (Social Sciences) 34(4), 122–124 (2009) (in Chinese)
7. Miao, X.-h.: On Rousseau's Understanding of the Nature of Child's Lif. Journal of Zhejiang Normal University (Social Sciences) 35(3), 32–37 (2010) (in Chinese)
8. Jonassen, D.H.: Objectivism versus constructivism: Do we need a new philosophical paradigm. ETR & D 39, 5–14 (1991)
9. Jun, R.: Correlation of Zone of Proximal Development with Emotional Changes. Journal of Zhejiang Normal University (Social Sciences) 35(1), 77–84 (2010) (in Chinese)
10. Zhu, X.-g.: Environmental Education, Sustainable Development Education and Their Mutual Relations. Journal of Zhejiang Normal University (Social Sciences) 29(2), 81–84 (2004) (in Chinese)

Research on Teaching Reform on Environmental Biochemistry Based on Teaching Materials

Yun Qi, XianHua Liu, YiRen Lu, and Lin Zhao[*]

School of Environmental Science and Technology, Tianjin University,
Tianjin 300072, China
{qiyun,lxh,luyiren,zhaolin}@tju.edu.cn

Abstract. Environmental Biochemistry is an important basic course of Environmental Science and Engineering. Based on the current undergraduate teaching characteristics and the actual teaching situation and existence problems of Environmental Biochemistry, the teaching model is discussed. Some reform about teaching model, including selection of teaching material, teaching method and experiment teaching were proposed in this paper. New teaching model is exploring, so as to improve teaching quality as well as cultivate innovative and application-oriented environmental talents.

Keywords: Environmental Biochemistry, Environmental science and engineering, Teaching reform.

Introduction

During the last decade, it has become obvious that the teaching-learning process is undergoing a continuous evolution. Most students do not develop learning skills spontaneously. Therefore, they should be taught explicitly in a well-planned way [1].

The specialized core courses of the biochemistry program are taught within both the Departments of Chemistry and Biology. Environmental Biochemistry is an important core courses in engineering colleges. Tianjin University is a comprehensive university with environmental engineering⬚ chemical engineering as well as other engineering courses in China. In most of the scientific and technological school of Tianjin University, biochemical has been listed as one of the basic and core courses for environmental science and engineering.

Biochemistry concern complex and abstract concepts, involves many complicated molecular structure and chemical reaction in the living organism. All of these characters make biochemistry particularly difficult for student to grasp. The rapid growth and inter- and multidisciplinarity of biochemistry science increased the difficult for student. Meanwhile many of the students have not studied biology in 6 years caused unique difficulties to educators. As a result, most students can hardly catch the principles of biochemistry and lose confidence in study. Although most students can pass the examination, they have no ability to use the principles in further research. That is far from our demand for higher education.

---

[*] Coeresponding author.

S. Lin and X. Huang (Eds.): CSEE 2011, Part V, CCIS 218, pp. 22–25, 2011.

The educators of biochemistry must have a broad acquaintance with a great deal of modern science, from physics to chemistry [2]. But most important for educators is to use some methods so as to improve the interesting⬚ confidence and science thinking of students.

Combining with the characteristics of biochemistry and environmental science, this paper gives a discussion and appropriate adjustments for environmental biochemistry teaching content and style. And some new curriculum reform to improve the teaching effectiveness is proposed to develop student's abilities of science thinking and practice.

1 Which Teaching Materials Should Be Used?

Contemporary textbooks include a large number of topics and concepts but the depth of coverage for each concept is varies from each others. In fact, there is a large gap between what is known by practicing biochemistry scientists and what is taught about the domain in secondary schools and universities [3]. The comprehensive biochemistry texts used in most courses are becoming thicker and more intimidating with each new edition for the students. As a result, there are a large number of heavy textbooks wrought with numerous disconnected scientific facts and activities, making it difficult for students to grape the basic content and develop meaningful understanding of the science.

There are various biochemistry teaching materials available for teachers. Different colleges or universities choose different materials in China. The Chinese-materials included the Biochemistry edited by Wang Jing-yan [4]; Simple Course in Biochemistry edited by Nie Jian-chu [5]; Course in Biochemistry edited by Shen Ren-quan [6] and General Biochemistry edited by Zheng Ji [7];The Biochemistry edited by Wang Jing-yan is the most used materials in many comprehensive universities. In this textbook, the theoretical system is more perspective and more deeply. As its need much more course time to elucidate, this textbook is suitable for the biological sciences students. Simple Course in Biochemistry, edited by Nie Jian-chu, concise summary the elements of biochemistry, which is practice for universities of engineering. Some university also use English original teaching materials, such as Instant Notes in Biochemistryedited by Hames[8] and Principles of Biochemistry edited by Lehlinger [9]. Those English original materials is much more difficult to understand for beginner, and much more expansive.

Considering the characteristics of biochemistry and environmental science, we chose the Simple Course in Biochemistry which is edited by Nie Jian-chu as teaching material in Tianjin University, combining with Biochemistry edited by Wang Jing-yan and Instant Notes in Biochemistry edited by Hames as aids materials.

2 Multimedia Teaching, Use or Not?

We all know that students learn by various ways -- with their ears, with their eyes, with their hands, and so on. So we should use a variety of ways of teaching to stimulate the senses.

Along with the expanding from technology to the field of education at the present age, the multimedia has applied more and more in education. All biochemist educators would readily agree that visualization tools are essential for understanding and researching the biochemistry. Since, for teachers, interactive tools may help to explain complex concepts more easily than a textbook [10]. We often told our students a picture is worth a thousand words. The modern biochemistry textbooks are overflowing with colorful pictures. These pictures are helpful to our students and can be used in courseware. Pictures shown in the courseware made it easy to understand the structure of molecules and the relation between the structure and function of molecule. However, many aspects of biochemistry are dynamic, from how to use a piece of apparatus to visualizing a complex process such as the DNA replication, transcription and translation. Video ought to provide the ideal way of showing such dynamic processes. The result of the multimedia teaching is deepen of scientific understanding, increased student interest, and subsequently, high attainment scores.

However, we should note that the video programs do not stand alone. We can compare video with TV. When children watch several hours of TV a day, they will not be impressed with poor quality material, and they do not take programs very seriously and do not necessarily remember very much [11], the same with the video. When we used the video, we should tell students what they are going o see, and remind them of what they've seen, so as to impress the detail of biochemistry.

It is important to highlight that we did not want to substitute the traditional means, but rather their function was to supplement it and to reinforce the work where traditional means do not satisfy the necessities under which the teaching-learning process is developed at present.

With the textbook and PowerPoint-based multimedia courseware offered to students, the information on essential concepts and principles was transferred to the students effectively. So the students can acquire the appropriate knowledge on studied subjects with the minimum possible effort.

3 Experiment Courses, Is It Important?

Biochemistry experiment course is an important part of teaching of biochemistry. By the experiment, the teacher can actively develop student understanding of science by combining scientific knowledge with reasoning and thinking skills [12].

The complete laboratory experiment course is organized in 8 sessions of 4 hours each in Tianjin University. Most of the students enrolled in this course have no background in scientific subjects, and they have never been in contact with a laboratory of biochemistry. As a consequence, the experiment includes an initial session. In this session students are familiar with basic laboratory techniques and apparatus, as well as the laboratory safety rules. The other sessions are comprehensive and creative biochemistry experiments. Students are separated into several groups. Each group has to make them on their own. Group is responsible for designing testable questions, designing investigations, analyzing data, construction explanation, discussing ideas to others, etc. After the laboratory experiment course, the students can gain valuable problem-solving skills, improve the quality and authenticity of science teaching and thereby increase student interest and achievement in science [13].

4   Conclusion

It is our opinion that only set up the new engineering education idea, then can increase the college's running level and fostering quality in talented person. And then the students can suit the needs of the society and talented person market.

Acknowledgement. This work is supported by Quality Reform of Engineering Education in Tianjin University and Practice Teaching Reform on Undergraduate in Tianjin University.

References

1. Spektor-Levy, O., Eylon, B., Scherz, Z.: Teaching and Teacher Education 24, 462 (2008)
2. Woods, E.J.: Biochemical Education 18, 170 (1990)
3. Howitt, S., Anderson, T., Costa, M., Hamilton, S., Wright, T.A.: Australian Biochemist 39, 14 (2008)
4. Wang, J.-y.: Biochemistry. Higher Education Press (2007)
5. Nie, J.-c.: Simple Course in Biochemistry. Higher Education Press (2009)
6. Shen, R.-q.: Course in Biochemistry. Higher Education Press (1993)
7. Ji, Z.: General Biochemistry. Higher Education Press (2007)
8. Hames, B.D., Hooper, N.M.: Instant Notes in Biochemistry. Bios Scientific Publishers (2000)
9. Lehlinger.: Principles of Biochemistry. Freeman and company, W. H. New York (2000)
10. Schönborn, K.J., Anderson, T.R.: Biochemistry and Molecular Biology Education, vol. 34, p. 94 (2006)
11. Wood, E.J.: Biochemical Education, vol. 20, p. 19 (1992)
12. National Research Council. National science education standards. National Academy Press, Washington, D.C (1996)
13. Silverstein, S.C., Dubner, J., Miller, J., Glied, S., Loike, J.D.: Teacher's participation in research programs improves their students achievement in science. Science 326, 440–442 (2009)

Reformation and Practice on Curriculum System and Teaching Model of Coordination Chemistry for Postgraduates

Guoqing Zhong

State Key Laboratory Cultivation Base for Nonmetal Composite and Functional Materials,
Southwest University of Science and Technology, Mianyang, Sichuan, 621010, China
zgq316@163.com

Abstract. Cultivation of the postgraduate creativity is the core content of postgraduate education. The reformation of postgraduate curriculums should lay stress on cultivating of innovation ability as the main purpose, update the educational concepts, reinforce teaching reforms, optimize the contents of curriculum structure, and carry out a great diversity of teaching organizational modes. Studies on coordination chemistry have been one of the most vigorous fields in chemistry. In order to strengthen innovative ability for postgraduates, the curriculum system, teaching contents, teaching methods and examination methods for coordination chemistry were reformed, and obtained better effects.

Keywords: Postgraduate education, Coordination chemistry, Teaching model, Teaching reformation, Innovative ability.

1 Introduction

As a main source of technological innovation and form of high level personnel training, postgraduate education is closely associated with national economic and cultural development. The postgraduate curriculums teaching is carried out not only to meet the requirements of passing on knowledge, but also served as necessary means of cultivating their innovative ability. Its goal is not just to make them master basic theory and professional knowledge, more importantly, also to cultivate innovative ability through innovative curriculum teaching [1]. Curriculum teaching plays a key role in training postgraduates, that is, basing on consolidating and reinforcing basic theory and professional knowledge, it is used to train ability of active learning and knowledge application, also to promote formation of scientific spirit and critical thinking. Curriculum teaching process, which is process of exploiting and reserving for postgraduate intellectual resources, may lay foundation for developing and writing of dissertation work, and provide long-term academic support force in future scientific research. Reformation of postgraduate curriculums should lay stress on cultivating of innovation ability, put teaching focus on training their innovation ability, scientific thinking and quality.

Coordination chemistry is an important curriculum for chemical specialties postgraduate education in our school, with 36 teaching hour. How to maximize supply

S. Lin and X. Huang (Eds.): CSEE 2011, Part V, CCIS 218, pp. 26–31, 2011.

of frontier knowledge and latest development trend of coordination chemistry in limited hours, enable teaching contents to obtain more supplement and renewal, increase their further awareness of the subject and identify the importance of coordination chemistry, are issues worthy of attention and to be resolved. Coordination chemistry has developed rapidly, and new contents, knowledge and achievements have emerged constantly. We should pay attention to adding some of latest research achievements to teaching contents in time, so as to broaden students' knowledge, and cultivate their innovative ability and scientific literacy.

2 Optimizing Curriculum System and Updating Constantly Teaching Contents

Since its creation, coordination chemistry has been mainstream in research fields of inorganic chemistry all the time. Research contents and scopes of modern coordination chemistry has gone far beyond traditional areas of inorganic chemistry, has gradually formed a new chemical second-level discipline, and has been in the centre of modern chemistry. Close connection and interpenetration lies between coordination chemistry and all chemical second-level disciplines, as well as first-level disciplines such as material, life and environment. Professor Xu used the following metaphor [2]: if chemistry of the 21st century was compared to a man, then physical, theoretical and computational chemistry was his head, analytical chemistry was his eyes and ears, coordination chemistry was his heart, inorganic chemistry was his left-hand, organic and polymer chemistry was his right-hand, material science was his left leg, and life science was his right leg. Coordination chemistry is a bridge between inorganic and organic chemistry, bonding agents of inorganic-organic hybrid and composite materials, and intersection of basic and application research. Coordination chemistry has derived a number of interdisciplines, such as solid state coordination chemistry, solution coordination chemistry, functional coordination chemistry, interface coordination chemistry, organometallic chemistry, coordination polymer chemistry, coordination electrochemistry and so on. Through learning of the curriculum, basic knowledge of coordination chemistry, means of synthesis and characterization, related applications of complexes, the methods of scientific thinking should be mainly mastered.

Curriculum contents which is carrier of implementing teaching, should be basic, advanced and comprehensive. The teaching contents of traditional coordination chemistry is old, and its teaching system could no longer adapt to rapid development of the subject and demands of cultivating postgraduates. To strengthen education for all-around development and cultivate innovative talents, it is necessary to carry out continually reformation and construction of the curriculum system, teaching contents and examination methods. Taking reformation of teaching contents and methods as breakthrough point, with the purpose of strengthening cultivation of students' scientific thinking and innovative ability, we construct a new system of coordination chemistry, which is able to fully embody modern education idea, that is, taking knowledge as basis, capacity as focus and quality as fundamental. Teaching contents should be selected to be beneficial for training and improvement of scientific and creative thinking, as well as to own properties of advanced, researchable, professional and dynamic. Postgraduates take curriculums not only to learn basic theory and professional knowledge, but also to stimulate learning motivation, develop potential high-level thinking ability, analyze and explore complicated issues dialectically and omnidirectionallly, and use theoretical knowledge creatively to solve all kinds of specific problem in scientific discovery and technological invention, during the learning process of complicated and advanced professional theoretical knowledge [3].

In order to adapt to development of coordination chemistry, it is required to adjust curriculum system, update teaching contents and set new syllabu. The teaching contents of coordination chemistry should be made according to requirements of strengthening basic theory, training scientific thinking, improving quality and ability of scientific research, and emphasizing innovative level of science and technology, so as to retain contents of basic theory, emphasizes application and practice of theoretical knowledge, and handle relationship between tradition and frontier, basic and application. Coordination chemistry has opened up many new research fields, such as functional complexes, macrocyclic complexes, supramolecular chemistry, fullerene complexes. As deep-going and development of research on supramolecular chemistry, non-bonding weak interaction of C−H···π has drawn more and more attention in fields of crystal engineering, molecular recognition, host-guest chemistry, self-assembly supramolecular systems and interactions between biological macromolecules and ligands [4]. Therefore, suitable contents of novel complexes, such as macrocyclic complexes, molecular hydrogen complexes, π-acid ligand complexes, π complexes and supramolecular chemistry, as well as organometallic compounds, bioinorganic chemistry, application of complexes in catalyst and medicine field, should be added. The contents of common analysis and characterization means such as UV-Vis, IR, MS, NMR, EPR, TG-DTA, XPS, X-ray structure analysis should be introduced by example.

Progress of discipline frontier knowledge is to be increased, so as to expand scientific thinking and vision field of postgraduates. Since 1970s, study on anti-cancer complexes has arouse chemists great attention, in particular study of new anti-tumor complexes such as platinum and ruthenium, which has drawn wide concern from chemists. The cisplatin is the most widely used inorganic anticancer drug up to now. As some compounds of arsenic, antimony and bismuth have important drug functions and biological activities, they have been used in medical fields for a long history. In recent years, we have carried out study of synthesis, characterization and related properties of biofunctional complexes from arsenic, antimony and bismuth, expecting to obtain antitumor drugs with well effect and low toxicity. Therefore, combining with our own research direction and main results, and enriching teaching with latest development of discipline in time, can stimulate students' interest and desire in learning.

3 Reforming Teaching Methods and Emphasizing Cultivation of Innovative Ability

To strengthen cultivation of scientific thinking method and innovative ability of postgraduates, teaching modes should be reformed and researchful teaching should be introduced. Teachers are not only organizers and executors of teaching activities, but also researchers and developers of contents for teaching materials, copartners and participants who can improve their research together with students. Many students own a wealth of theoretical knowledge, but do not have their own ideas, so that teachers should focus on widening students' eyeshot. The innovative ability is the bottleneck that restricts quality improvement of postgraduate cultivation. Postgraduate education should always keep original innovation as a goal, and focus on cultivation of originality ability of developing knowledge and solving problems and formation of exploration spirit of students. Traditional teaching mode limits cultivation of student' expansive and critical thinking, teachers' teaching and students' learning should be transformed so that teaching and learning are autonomous, collaborative, researchable and interactive. To improve cultivation quality of postgraduate, it is necessary to change traditional education thoughts and teaching modes, take active action to carry out the teaching reformation and explore new methods of postgraduate teaching. Key points of lectures should be placed on making problem clear in aspects, such as origin, background, concept, analysis thinking, research approachs and methods, latest progress and related research hotspots and so on, so as to introduce students to frontier science and technology of discipline, absorb lots of new concept, thought, methods, process, technology, new hotspots, progress and problems to be resolved into postgraduate education, guide students to think and discuss actively following teachers' explanation, change students from passive listener to active explorer, which can enlighten thinking, train ability and deepen knowledge understanding. As research topic of each postgraduate varies in direction, it is great important to impart thinking method, design and skill of scientific research according to specific instance in teaching. Diversity teaching mode, in which teaching method of heuristic, discussional and researchable, postgraduates doing report combining with teachers' comment and discussion, will be used so as to emphasize students' subject status, make students participate more in academic discussion and report, stimulate students' potential of being ready to question, willing to explore and good at innovating , train students attitude of insatiable and pursuit of excellence, as well as ability of discovering, raising and solving questions, change gradually students' habits of depending on classroom teaching and teachers, form habits and routes of obtaining knowledge out of classroom, and blend scientific thinking and method organically into curriculum teaching. Benign interaction between teaching and scientific research will be of great benefit for improving teaching quality, so that teachers should improve themselves in both teaching and scientific research, and realize facilitation of teaching and research work, in order to pass on latest research achievements and cutting-edge scientific information to students.

Reformation and construction of classroom teaching means and teaching methods are crucial links that can influence teaching quality. The contents of coordination chemistry are rich, but class hours are less, in order to make full use of classroom time, multimedia courseware are adopted for teaching, which can strengthen students' perceptual knowledge, meanwhile save class hours and improve classroom teaching effect. Spatial structures of complexes are more complicated, and it will make teaching contents that are difficult to understand more lively, intuitive and vivid by using multimedia courseware when they are shown to students. While using multimedia in teaching, it is worth noting that text in courseware should avoid excessive, which generally includes headlines and subtitles, important concepts, formulas, charts, summary descriptions and emphasized parts, meanwhile the courseware contents are updated constantly, and new concepts, achievements and developments are replenished in time. In teaching process, it is necessary to spell out not only connotations of basic concepts and principles, but also their practical application. Combining theory with practice will help students to have a clear learning aims, and arouse learning interest and enthusiasm of students, so that they would not felt the learning contents bored, vacuous and abstract. Holding academic lectures according to scientific research experiences, teachers can enable students to understand and master knowledge by relating theory with practice, increase the ability to analyze and solve problems, as well as enhance resonance between teachers and students, so as to achieve better teaching effect.

4 Innovating Examination Methods and Cultivating Creative Ability

As an index of appraisal system, the examination plays an important guiding role in both students' learning and teachers' teaching. Traditional examination is used to test students' mastery of book knowledge, in which it is difficult to check and cultivate their ability of using knowledge to solve practical problems. As a mean but not purpose of teaching evaluation, the task of examinations is to test students' grasping level of basic theory and fundamental knowledge, find out problems existing in teaching, detect students' learning effect, urge students to study, and its purpose is to test implemental degree of teaching target, ameliorate teaching work, enhance teaching quality, and heighten ability and quality [5]. The targets of reforming the examination methods are: making students be more interested in learning, enhancing their enthusiasm, independence and autonomy of learning, as well as changing them from passive learning to active learning, and from receptive learning to researchful and innovative learning; training and improving their ability of independent thinking, analyzing and solving problems; prompting teachers to heighten their professional skills, as well as improving teaching quality and level as a whole.

Writing review papers of curriculum and doing report, is the best way to test innovative thinking ability of students, is the important mean to raise ability of self-study, obtaining information and utilization of information, train their innovative consciousness and thinking ability, is the important and requisite link to exercise them on collecting, analyzing, processing, transferring and applying of information. In the first lecture, what to be introduced to students are teaching contents, references, requirements, meanwhile the basic knowledge of aspects such as academic thesis writing, academic report, symbols and terms of science and technology and so on should be explained. This curriculum requires that review papers concerned with coordination chemistry should be written, full text of not less than 5000 characters, and references of not less than 30 piece. Meanwhile it is required to translate an English article concerned with coordination chemistry into Chinese. Through writing review papers of curriculum, students' learning enthusiasm can be aroused, their competence of acquiring knowledge can be increased, and the ability of writing paper can be improved. Every postgraduate is asked to make one academic report in PPT form in class, which takes about 15 minutes, then it takes about 10 minutes to allow other students or teachers to ask reporter questions, present their own different ideas towards proposition of report, point out the errors existing in report, or require the reporter to explain or express views on some content, finally, the teacher is to give comments on the special topic and summarize the discussion briefly. Such teaching mode can fully develop their competence of organizing language, expressing, reacting and understanding knowledge thoroughly. We have established an assessment reform program to evaluate curriculum grade comprehensively, which comprises curriculum paper (40%), English translation (25%), special report (25%), note-taking (5%) and attendance (5%). After years of practice and continuous improvements, such good effect has been achieved that postgraduates' competence on consulting literature of Chinese and foreign, as well as writing skills and ability of technology papers are greatly improved, and annually curriculum papers completed by students have been published above core journals, some of which are indexed by SCI.

Acknowledgment. This work is supported by the Postgraduate Education Reform Project of Southwest University of Science and Technology (No. 09xjjg06).

References

1. Jian, X.: China Higher Education Research (12), 38 (2008)
2. Xu, G.: Acta Scicentiarum Naturalum Universitis Pekinesis (2), 149 (2002)
3. Han, R., Hu, L.: Journal of Military Economics Academy (4), 66 (2010)
4. Guo, H., Tao, Z., Zhu, Q., Xue, S.: Chinese Journal of Inorganic Chemistry (5), 435 (2002)
5. Zhong, G.: Education and Teaching Research (10), 100 (2010)

An Applied Research of Conjunction Cohesion in EFL Writing Teaching Based on Data Analysis

Yao Fu and Xin Chen

Foreign Languages College of Changchun University of Technology
Foreign Languages Section of Teaching Center of Basic Courses,
Jilin University Heping Campus,
No. 17 Yan'an Street, Changchun, Jilin Province, China P.R. 130012
fuyao_ccut@foxmail.com

Abstract. The present study investigates the use of conjunction cohesion in writing on the basis of text analyses and global scoring of 70 compositions. It analyzes the contrast of scores in pretest and posttest and the overall uses of conjunction cohesion in compositions, and studies the relationship between the frequencies of conjunction cohesion and writing quality. The research result reveals that there is a certain correlation between English learner's frequency of using conjunction cohesion and his writing quality.

Keywords: cohesive device, EFL writing, conjunction, coherence.

1 Introduction

Since 1990, English writing teaching has not been paid much attention so that the scores of writing tasks in CET-4 have been relatively low for a long time. These years, more stresses on cohesion and text analysis were placed on EFL teaching, especially on EFL writing teaching. It has become a focal problem in discourse analysis in the recent two decades because discourse coherence is one of the most difficult and complicated topics of discourse analysis, which is also vital in EFL listening, reading and speaking teaching. However, more studies should be conducted to examine the developmental trend in the use of cohesive devices in the context of ESL learners of China. Therefore, this study attempts to conduct an experimental research on the usage and teaching of conjunction cohesion in EFL writing and provide evidences for further discussion on conjunction cohesion training.

2 Conjunction Cohesion

In 1976, Halliday and Hasan published Cohesion in English, in which they made the definition of cohesion: "The concept of cohesion is a semantic one; it refers to relations

S. Lin and X. Huang (Eds.): CSEE 2011, Part V, CCIS 218, pp. 32–37, 2011.

of meaning that exist within the text, and that define it as a text. Cohesion occurs where the interpretation of some element in the discourse is dependent on that of another. The one presupposes the other, in the sense that it cannot be effectively decoded except by recourse to it. When it happens, a relation of cohesion is set up, and the two elements, the presupposing and the presupposed, are thereby at least potentially integrated into a text" (1976: 4).

Conjunction is one of the cohesive devices. In Oxford Concise Dictionary of Linguistics, the definition of conjunction is a word, etc. which joins two syntactic units. And the examples are showed is "and" and "but". For example, "He came but didn't stay." The second meaning of it is logicians' term for a proposition of the form p & q which is true if and only if both p is true and q is true. For example: "You and your sister in I saw you and your sister" (2000: 68). In Longman Dictionary of Language Teaching and Applied Linguistics, conjunction is also connective. The first meaning is it is a word which joins words, phrases, or clauses together, such as but, and, when. For example: "She sings but I don't." The second meaning is that it is the process by which such joining takes place, using as coordination and subordination. For example: "It is rained, but I went for a walk anyway." For another example: "Unless it rains, we'll play tennis at 4" (2005: 137). In Halliday and Hasan's view, conjunctions are on the borderline of the two: mainly grammatical, but with a lexical component. In the book Cohesion in English, Halliday and Hasan (1976) categorized conjunctions into four types: additive, adversative, causal and temporal.

In conclusion, Halliday and Hasan's (1976) concept of conjunction cohesion and the well-developed taxonomy of cohesive devices should be adopted as the framework, which may provide the objectivity and reliability of the future relevant studies. As we can see, it was adopted by many former researchers. There is still a lot to investigate in the teaching of English writing of Chinese college students, with the efficient approaches teaching in class. The analysis of the organizational pattern and the use of conjunction cohesion in the quantitative and qualitative methods might be of great importance in the improvement of writing quality researching.

3   Research Design

3.1   Research Questions

The purpose of the case study is to summarize the frequency of conjunction cohesion in EFL writing and explore the feasibility of applying conjunction cohesion in EFL writing teaching which can be applicable in the current EFL writing teaching effectively. This study is further conceptualized in terms of the following three questions.

(1) How frequently are conjunctions used in the samples before teaching conjunction cohesion?

(2) What will be the effect on English writing quality after teaching conjunction cohesion?

(3) What are the common features in the students' writing in the use of conjunctions?

3.2 The Participants and the Teacher

This study investigates the use of conjunction cohesion in writing on the basis of text analyses and global scoring for 70 compositions, 35 of which are written by the freshmen who are majoring in Computer Science in Changchun University of Technology, the other 35 of which are written by the freshmen who are majoring in Agronomy in Jilin University. The 70 subjects are of a similar age, ranging from 19 to 20 years old. They are Chinese students of English as the foreign language. At the time of the research they had been studying English for at least 6 years before entering university including 3 years' English education in Junior High School and the other 3 years' in Senior High School. The English teacher is the author of this thesis, with seven years' experience of teaching college English. The text book which was learned by the subjects is College English (Integrated Course Book I) published by Shanghai Foreign Language Education Press. The subjects received a series of planned conjunction device training and were required to write one composition in the same limited time in the end of the semester. Finally the 70 selected written compositions can offer the primary data to be collection work.

3.3 Research Procedure

The experiment was conducted in the first semester of the school year of 2009-2010, lasting about 17 weeks. It consisted of three steps: the pretest, the class teaching and the posttest. Before teaching the conjunction cohesion the subjects were asked to finish one questionnaire. It is to investigate whether the subjects learned to use conjunction cohesion in writing before entering into university or they have got the particular writing training before. Also from the questionnaire it can be made clear that the subjects are interested in improving writing.

The pretest is necessarily carried out at the very beginning of the experiment because only if in the pretest the subjects are identified as equivalent ones which had no obvious difference in writing proficiency before the experiment. Then the results of the experiment can be guaranteed.

Later in this semester the various teaching approaches were adopted and different performances are presented to teach conjunction cohesion in the EFL writing instruction. First the researcher teaches the students to learn the usage and function of conjunction cohesion. The conjunctions are taught in the framework and classification of Halliday and Hasan's. And then there are class activities to enforce the understanding and using of conjunction cohesion.

The other writing test, that is posttest, was held at the end of the experiment, with the purpose of testing whether this teaching model of conjunction cohesion is more effective in improving the students' EFL writing compared with the previous condition.

4   Results and Discussions

4.1   The Contrast of the Scores

The minimum score is 4 in the pretest but 6 in the posttest. And the maximum score is 10 in the pretest but 14 in the posttest. The mean score is about 7 in the pretest and about 10 in the posttest. It is clear that it is the improvement in the scores in the pretest and the posttest. It is shown in the following descriptive table:

Table 1. Descriptive Statistics

	N	Minimum	Maximum	Mean	Std. Deviation
Pre-test Score	70	4.00	10.00	7.8286	1.36171
Post test Score	70	6.00	14.00	10.2143	1.77660
Valid N (listwise)	70				

4.2   Overall Uses of Conjunction in Subjects' Compositions

Then, a thorough and detailed study of the effect of the amount of conjunctions use on the quality of compositions will be presented.

In order to have a comprehensive understanding of how conjunctions are used in subjects' compositions, we can analyze the following items: the total number of conjunctions, the number of each kind of conjunctions, the kind of conjunction which is highest frequently used and the certain conjunction which is highest frequently used. Statistical results are shown in Figure 1 and Figure 2:

Fig. 1. The Distribution of Conjunction

Var. 2 is the additive conjunction, Var. 3 is the adversative conjunction, Var. 4 is the causal conjunction and Var. 5 is the temporal conjunction. Here from the Figure 1 it is apparent that the additive conjunctions are most frequently used in the samples. The causal conjunctions come the second. And the adversative ones are the least used.

Fig. 2. Var. 6 = "and", Var. 8= "because", Var 10= "but", Var. 7= "so", Var. 9= "first…"& "firstly…"

Among the conjunctions, "and" as an additive conjunction appears most frequently almost in every subject's compositions. "so" as a causal conjunction comes the second. The number of "because" and "so" are almost the same used in the compositions. "but" which is used as an adversative conjunction follows the "because". Temporal conjunction "first…" as well as "firstly…"is utilized the least frequently. The chart shows the easiest conjunctions are of more frequency in the compositions. The causal conjunctions are relatively easy to use in the compositions.

5 Summary

It could be obviously seen that after the conjunction cohesion training, this type of cohesive device is more frequently used in the students' writings. It could be apparently seen that the students' writing performance is improved on textual level by regarding this increase of using of cohesive devices, because the samples with more conjunctions gained higher scores.

The research results reveal that there is a correlation between the non-English majors' frequency of using conjunction cohesion and writing quality. Although the frequency of the use of conjunction cohesion isn't in the direct proportion to the scores of essays written by the subjects, the compositions with the higher scores in the posttest really contain more conjunctions, especially formal and various types of conjunctions.

From the present research, as a competent English teacher, one should be clear that it is not enough to make grammatical analysis on the sentence level. We should extract every useful theory from text linguistics and apply it into our teaching practice so as to shift our focus from sentence to text.

References

1. Beaugrand, Dressler, W.U.: Introduction to Text Analysis. Longman, London (1981)
2. Brown, Y.: Discourse Analysis. Cambridge University Press, London (1983)
3. Cook, G., Seidlhofer, B.: Barbara Seidlhofer: Principles and Practice in Applied Linguistics. Oxford University Press, Oxford (1995)
4. Hyland, K.: Teaching and Researching Writing. Foreign Language Teaching and Research Press, Beijing (2005)

5. Ede, L.: Work in Progress: A Guide to Writing and Revising. St. Martin's Press, Inc., New York (1989)
6. Halliday, M.A.K.: An Introduction to Functional Grammar, 2nd edn. Foreign Language Teaching and Research Press, Beijing (2000)
7. Halliday, M.A.K.: Language as Social Semiotic: The Social Interpretation of Language and Meaning. Foreign Language Teaching and Research Press, Beijing (2001)
8. Halliday, M.A.K.: Ruqaiya Hasan: Cohesion in English. Foreign Language Teaching and Research Press, Beijing (2001)
9. Fu, Y.: Application of Conjunction Cohesion in EFL Writing for College Non-English Majors. Jilin University (2009)

A Probe into the Intervention of College Students' Anxiety in Interpersonal Communication by Means of Group Guidance

Yun Zhao

Department of Sociology, Guangxi University of Technology, Liuzhou, P.R. China
Free_bird2000@163.com

Abstract. The anxiety in interpersonal communication among college students is a quite common psychological problem in college, and stands relatively high ratio in kinds of psychological problem. To solve college students' problem in interpersonal communication becomes an important task for psychological instructors. As there are quite a number of college students who suffer from anxiety in interpersonal communication, group guidance is an effective and efficient means to intervene and solve the problem in colleges. In view of anxiety in interpersonal communication, a series of intervening group guidance such as cognitive reconstruction, relaxation training, demonstration exercises, and self-monitoring training can effectively reduce college students' anxiety in interpersonal communication, and improve their communication skills.

Keywords: Group Guidance, College Students, Anxiety in Interpersonal Communication.

1 Introduction

College students' anxiety in interpersonal communication refers to the contradictory and painful emotional experience caused by having difficulties, feeling afraid and lonely in interpersonal communication. Anxiety is an emotional experience caused by individual's being anxious and worried[1]. People may experience anxiety when in the face of dangerous situations which they can't handle with. In a sense, it plays a very important role in human being's survival and development. However it may become psychological problem when anxiety becomes too serious or when it doesn't go with the real situations.

College students' anxiety in interpersonal communication is one of the most common psychological problems among college students. Compared with children's anxiety problems, college students' anxiety in communication doesn't have such a frequent incidence rate, long duration and high co-morbidity rate. However college students' anxiety in interpersonal communication might do more harm, exerts more influence to their life and study. College students' anxiety can be cured and intervened by group guidance. On the one hand, group guidnace can improve efficiency of intervention, and can guide and intervene several or even dozens of students at the same

S. Lin and X. Huang (Eds.): CSEE 2011, Part V, CCIS 218, pp. 38–42, 2011.

time. On the other hand, group guidance can provide students who suffer from communication anxiety with some bad and good lessons to learn from. Also students' desire and courage may be aroused to communicate with others in a group.

2 The Function of Group Guidance in Intervening College Students' Anxiety in Interpersonal Communication

2.1 Experiencing and Developing Fine Interpersonal Relationship

For college students, fine interpersonal relationship needs to be gained by socially study. So learning how to build up fine interpersonal relationship is a very important learning process. Comparing with individule guidance, group guidance can develop college students' communication skills in a more effective way. In a team or group activites, college students can watch, and experience how the interpersonal relationship is formed and how the interpersonal communication is going on among teacher and students through a series of interactive activities among group members. In this process, students learn the skills of interpersonnal communication through watching kinds of subtle commnucation response, and so build up and enhance a good interpersonal relationship with others.

2.2 Enhancing the Individual's Social Belongingness

The person who suffers from poor interpersonal communication often experience little belongingness, and feel hard to find position in a group. In group guidance, with the carrying out of the activities, the group cohesion is gradually formed and enhanced, and the group member will develop a strong sense of belongingness and acceptance[2]. Each individual in a group can clearly realize ones' belongingness and desire to keep consistance with the group. They learn to attach much importance to the group's interest and uphold the group's image and honor, and maintain the group interest together. These senses of acceptance and belonging can be formed through group guidance, which is a very important experience to boost the communication passion and to raise the successful communication rate among the college students suffering from interpersonnal communication anxiety.

3 Experiencing Mutual Assistance and Mutual Benefit

The interpersonal communication among college students is a part of social comminucation. It needs unselfish help as well as mutual benefits. They supplement each other. Group guidance can help college students experience these affection and process. Group activities require each individual to help each other, support each other, brainstorm, share duty and pains. They can experience positive mood of aid and being needed. These experience help college students who suffer anxiety in interpersonal communication to realize one's value, and gain the psychological sense of happiness and satisfaction to heighten confidence of communication. Mutual assistance and mutual benefit is a positive experience in group guidance, also it will extend to their future life and makes them actively shoulder responsibilty and keep helping others.

4 Learning from Good Examples and Developing Fine Interpersonal Communication

In group guidance, good examples intentionally provided by instructor are the sighting of college students who suffer from communication anxiety. These students can mend their incorrect ways of communication by copying others' successful examples. That's one of the superioroties of group guidance and which makes it different from individule guidance. In individule guidance, visitors can't see the interpersonal communication, but to learn from the consultant. While in group guidance, besides instructor, they can copy and refer to other member's behavior. Group guidance can offer group members chances to receive feedback from others. Suggestions, reactions and remarks from other members are usually quite valuable[3]. Group members have more chances to hear other's comments on themselves in group guidance which can effectively change their incorrect behaviour and develop approprite behavior.

5 The Group Guiding Contents to Intervene College Students' Anxiety in Interpersonal Communication

5.1 The Cognition Restructure

In group guidance, making use of cognition restructure to guide those who suffer from social communication anxiety to have self-guiding training. Students with interpersonal communication anxiety usually have declination in their cognition. Through cognition restructure in group guidance, they can reanalyze those vague stimulating situation in a harmless way. Cognition restructure is in fact a kind of cognition therapy. Among the treatments of communication anxiety, cognition restructure is a very important link. They can be practiced in different ways. Sometimes they can even be applied to students' parents. In the intervening joined by the parents, parents need to learn the steps to restructure the cognition, and learn to remind their children to take strategy to restructure their cognition. After college students have learned how to use the strategy to restructure the cognition efficiently, the instructors should help them to reinforce them in time.

5.2 Relaxation Training

In the practice of offering psychological consulting, relaxation training is a fundamental link and measure. It is an effective way to deal with anxiety. At present, the main relaxation skills used in psychological practice mainly include muscle relaxation, deep thought, breathing deeply, guiding envision ect. They are all suitable for group guidance. Among them, the most popular way is to relax muscle gradually[4]. While having the relaxation training, every group of muscles should be kept tight or relaxed to a maximum extent and practiced repeatedly till the students can experience a sense of relaxation, one group of muscle after another, till all groups of muscles are relaxed. In group guidance, before and after relaxation exercises, the instrutors should evaluate students' relaxation status according to the 5, 7 or 10 scale , from relaxing completely to extremely anxiety, and give them positive evaluation and encouragement every time after they have finished relaxation training.

5.3 Demonstration Exercises

Bandura, an important representative of Behaviorism, strongly emphasizes imitation learning in his Social Learning Theory. He holds that lots of human beings' learning are not from direct experience, but from observing others' behavior and the result from it. Therefore, providing demonstration exercises for those college students suffering from interpersonal communication anxiety is very important. By showing successful examples in social communication, the students can learn by imitation, eliminate their own anxious and perturbed feeling, and so in this way, stimulate their desire to communicate with others. Practice proves that demonstration training is especially effective to improve social communication skills. Most college students who have bad habits in interpersonal communication can benefit a lot in taking demonstration exercises.

5.4 Self-monitoring

Self-monitoring, also called self-management, self-control, self-adjustment, self-discipline management, is an important element of self consciousness. Those who can monitor themselves efficiently show great adaptability in adjusting their own behaviors to the external environment. They are sensitive to environmental elements, and tend to take different behaviors in response to different situations[5]. College students with anxious response are insufficient in self-controlling, which results in their failure to make any adjustment to their own terrible behavior in interpersonal communicating. Self-monitoring helps college students to recognize the anxious response in themselves, and so help them to change or abandon harmful thoughts and behaviors. The students having learned how to monitor themselves will be able to use this skill in their lives permanently, and help them change all kinds of bad habits.

6 The Methods Used in Group Guidance to Intervene College Students' Anxiety in Interpersonal Communication

The process to take group guidance on those communication anxiety college students can be divided into 6 stages:

The first stage: Getting to know each other. At this stage, let members in the group get to know each other, create a harmonious atmosphere, strengthen the team cohesion. The second stage: Having further contact with others and accepting others. Promote the sense of trust and amity among the group members basing on the first stage. Building up an atmosphere of trusting and accepting each other, every individual can experience concern from others, and so heighten self-confidence. The third stage: Self-exposal. Group members are guided to expose themselves based on mutual understanding and trusting, to open their mind, have better understanding of themselves in exposing themselves, and realize their own problems in interpersonal communication. The fourth stage: Sharing with each other. At this stage, every one talk freely about their own problems and what they have got and learned in group guidance, sharing with each other their experience and understanding. The fifth stage: Problem solving. Situations of interpersonal communication are introduced. By role-playing, the group members help each other to solve the anxiety in interpersonal communication, increase their self-confidence, improve successful rate in communication. The sixth stage: Developing new behaviors. Try in the group and in their daily life the new behavioral paterns they have learned like attitude, skills in interpersonal communication.

7 Conclusion

Group guidance can help college students to have a better understanding of themselves and shape a positive self-image. In the group guidance, activities like "Brainstorm of Advantages" can be used to increase college students' self-confidence, helping them to realize their own advantages, experience attention and respectation from others. The formation of good behaviors in interpersonal communication is a prpcess of recycling of "perceiving, understanding, persisting, and practicing". To most college students, they are accustomed to "perceiving" of the good qualities of communication. What they are need is the adjustment of "understanding" and "persisting". Group guidance, which pays attention to emotional experience and the sharing and deepening after the activities, plays an adjusting role in forming the students' proper communicating behaviors.

Acknowledgement. This research was supported by the Youth Foundation of Guangxi University of Technology "A study of intervening strategies of interpersonal interaction anxiety among college students" under Grant 030207.

References

1. Li, X.X.: A Study on the Application of Group Guidance on Improving Self-confidence of Elementary Students, Master's thesis (Southwest University) (2010)
2. Kong, Z.G.: The Common Communicating Barriers for College Students. Journal of Shengli College China University of Petroleum 3, 61–63 (2010)
3. We, S.: The Psychological Barriers and Elimination of them in College Students Interpersonal Communication. Journal of Southwest Agricultural University (Social Science Edition) 4, 101–102 (2010)
4. Wang, S.Y.: Mental problems and Countermeasures of College Students Intercourse. Journal of Guizhou University of Technology (Social Science Edition) 4, 173–175 (2007)
5. Zhang, Q.M.: A Brief Analysis in University Student's Interpersonal Communication Barriers and Countermeasures. Journal of Henan Polytechnic University (Social Sciences) 4, 337–341 (2009)

An Exploration of Vocal Music Teaching in College Based on Social Learning Theory with Information Technology

ZhuWen Tan[1], Yuan Tian[2], YingZhen Deng[3] and ZhenGuo Wu[1]

[1] Guangxi University of Technology, Liuzhou, P.R. China
[2] Huazhong Normal University, Wuhan, P.R. China
[3] Liuzhou City Vocational College, Liuzhou, P.R. China

Abstract. Vocal music teaching is an important part of art education in college. For many college students, vocal music learning is very artistic. Learning theories of imitating, behaviors and skills has valuable directive significance in vocal music teaching in college. Social learning theory should be fully taken advantage of in vocal music teaching in college: observational learning should be used to help students get right singing methods and skills; teachers' modeling effects in vocal music teaching should be given due attention; students' self-regulation should be emphasized; help college students understand vocal works style correctly; teachers should be confident in students' vocal music learning in order to help them get better learning effects.

Keywords: social learning theory; college; vocal music teaching.

1 Introduction

Vocal music is also known as artistic singing, which is a music performance art, combing artistic language (singing language) and scientific singing methods (artistic voice) to build vivid and beautiful hearing images, showing lyrics that are highly condensed and classified and emotionalized tunes, expressing feelings and do the second creation.

Therefore, for college students, it's possible for them to learn vocal music well as long as appropriate methods are used because vocal music is in fact an expression language that uses different singing language and words to express own feelings. In teaching activities, teachers should teach students according to their specific situations so that better results can be got. In this field, social learning theory can provide us with theoretical foundations.

2 Basic Points of Social Learning Theory

2.1 The Individual Expectations of Success

A man's expectation on the success is generated by three factors: the first one is the last experience a man gained in a particular environment; Secondly, if the individual has no

S. Lin and X. Huang (Eds.): CSEE 2011, Part V, CCIS 218, pp. 43–47, 2011.

`related specific experience, previous experience will be an impact; finally, the individual produce a particular perception of task characteristics [1].

For an individual to complete the task characteristics, social learning theory pay attention to skills related with concerns and opportunities. It believes that in the skill task, if the result is decided by a person's ability and efforts, expectation will increase after the success and reduce after the failure. When the task is determined by opportunities, regardless of succeed or not in the past, the expectation for the next will not change. Then the famous theory of the control points is put forward. The main point is that a person with internal controls fells that they should be responsible for their own behaviors and all the reinforcements. But the person with the external control believe that the powerful others, luck or circumstances beyond the control of her own behavior should be responsible. Who has the internal control points have a more adaptive motivational state, proper internal control and outcome expectations will be easy to get better results.

2.2   The Acquisition of Behavior

Bandura believes that human behavior, especially complex behavior is mainly learned. Behavior is well received by the acquisition of genetic factors and physiological factors, but also by the acquired experience and the environment. Physiological factors and acquired experience interact on determining one's behavior [2]. There are two different processes of behavior learning: one is through direct experience to obtain the process of behavioral response patterns, Bandura named this process as "the result of reaction carried out by the study," that is usually said direct experience of learning; another example is to observe the process and learn behaviors, Bandura called it "the study conducted by example", which is indirect experience of learning.

The social learning theory of Bandura emphasizes on observational learning or imitative learning. The individuals acquire their model's representation through observational learning, meanwhile, if the teachers can appropriate guide or operate during this process of modeling, the effect of observational learning will be much better. The observational learning is divided into four stages: The first is attentional process, which is the beginning of the observational learning. The second is the maintenance. The third is reappearance. The forth is motivation, which can represent the model behavior, whether the observers can always show the influence from the consequence of the behavior on the model behavior. The consequence of the behavior includes external reinforcement, internal reinforcement and vicarious reinforcement.

2.3   Self-control and Self-efficacy Theory

Self-control is an important point in social learning theory, which is the reinforcement process within the individuals. The individual regulates his own behavior by the comparison with the planning and expectation of his bahavior and practical consequence of the behavior. The individual can regulate his own behavior by his self-established internal standard, and the self has the ability of providing the cognitive framework, perception, evaluation and regulation of behaviors refered to the mechanism [3]. The social learning theory emphasizes that the behaviors are influenced by both external factors and self-established internal factors. Self-regulation is consisted of self-observation, self-judgment and self-response, from which the individual acquire their regulation over his own behavior.

Self-efficacy is another important point in social learning theory, which means the individual experience of capability and confidence in completing a task in a certain level. In another word, this is about the experience of confidence, self-care self-esteem and other aspects when facing a task. It is an important factors that affect the individual learning effect. If you want to increase the level of learning effect, you have to increase the learners' self-efficacy.

3 The Vocal Music Teaching in College Based on Social Learning Theory

3.1 Use the Observational Learning to Help Students Acquire the Right Sing Methods and Skills

This kind of theory holds the idea that most behaviors of human beings are acquired through observing others' behaviors and their consequences. A large number of behavioral model can be acquired quite soon through observational learning. The vocal music learning, as it emphasizes on skills, especially the observation plays an important part. During the learning process, the teachers must act as a behavioral model to provide with the students, especially in the teaching of vocal , the teachers must make sure the performing function and the use and collaboration of each part, Such as respiratory organs, resonance organ, the pronunciational and enunciation organs. The students can have an understanding on its theory, and the teachers should pay more attention in the skills training in order to let the students have a clear observation over these skills, specific to the the breathing method in singing, resonance adjustment, throat opening and so on. By helping the students practice vocal exercises , they can use their right conceptual regulation of the muscles, mouth, and part of the singing organ into their specific perform. Under the right voice concept guidance, the students can experience and take into use of the specific singing organs in the vocal exercises. This process is the basis of the right sing method for students.

3.2 Value Teacher's Demonstrative Singing in Vocal Music Teaching

The social learning theory emphasizes that performance can be acquired through the process of observation and learning. However, what kind of behavior will be acquired and the performance of the behavior depend on the role model. The vocal music theory is easy to be obtained for undergraduates. However, teacher's "singing demonstration" plays a key role in helping students to sing well, tap their potential, learn the real skills in singing, and use the skills of singing practice into singing of songs. During this process, although students get some correct knowledge about vocal theory, they are still interfered with their old singing habits when using these theories. It's hard to achieve a natural and balanced state in real use[4]. The music master Ryan stressed that "at the initial stage of learning singing, the learners need a model to follow, just as the painters and sculptors need models. This process continues until they can work independently." Therefore, when the undergraduates first learn to sing, teachers become their "models" to provide standard and scientific "demonstrative singing". Teachers should not only let students understand the use of methods and skills in singing songs through the "demonstrative singing", but also guide them according to everyone's own vocal characteristics and sound features, help them find similar singers to imitate, and provide them with proper target models.

3.3 Emphasize on Undergraduates' Self-regulation Roles in Singing Learning

People's behavior is not only influenced by the results of external behavior, more importantly, it is influenced by the self-produced behavior results, i.e. self-regulation. Self-regulation regulates behavior mainly through motivational functions which are produced by goal establishment and self-assessment. Undergraduates' internal motivation and confidence play important role in leaning singing. Seen from the practice, those who can regulate themselves well, use their internal positive factors to study will often better overcome bad attitudes in singing learning and correct problems occurring in the process. They are good at setting their study goals, doing self-monitoring and self-assessment in the process. The confidence degree one has in dealing with all kinds of situations plays a key role in people's active function. It determines whether one is willing to face difficult situation, the degree of difficulty one can cope with and the durability in facing difficult situation. If one has high expectation for his ability, he will always face difficulty with courage, try hard for it, and persist for longer time. On the other hand, if someone lacks confidence, he will often be anxious and escape. Therefore, it is important to change people's avoidance behavior and establish high confidence.

3.4 Help College Students Understand the Styles of Vocal Music Works Correctly

Social learning theory emphasizes on individual's learning experiences and the environmental effect which are the important factors in affecting learning effect. And the vocal music works are characterized with strong individual styles, because of the different living environment, individual experiences and characteristics, every composer chooses differently in creating and selecting songs' materials, using various performance skills. In the course of teaching, teachers should actively guide students to understand first the historical background in creating the work, the motivation and personal styles and let students know about related knowledge by observing on site, listening to the audio materials, watching video, etc. In this way can students understand the significance of the work, lay solid foundation for understanding music works. The "imitate" characteristic style of works and musical performance of the works is an important mean of teaching. Our famous signer, Peng Liyuan once said in her memory of music learning: "When I was a student in China Conservatory of Music, and we had lessons of folk music, during that time we heard a female voice singing Xin Tian You, and the tune was 'The chicken is crying, and the dogs are barking, the brother is coming back, back... '. This is it, this is the style of the song, which is the basis of your imitation. If you understand the style of the song, you can better understand the content and its singing way, and this is the basis of learning music.

3.5 The Teachers Should Look Forward to the Vocal Learning in College

The music education is full of emotional factors. No matter the thoughts and feelings from the teachers through model singing or the expectational emotions from the students, incessantly influence the enthusiasm and learning effect. Former Soviet Union educator Holme Linsky once said:"A real teacher not only teaches people, but also improves the people by his great confidence over them. " Each teacher must understand and have confidence over his students, believe that the students have positive requirements, self-improved wishes, and adaptive capacity of self-control and regulation. Teachers should help students tap their potency which shines with its unique brightness. Only in this way can the students and the teachers acquire mutual recognition, mutual acceptance to form the real educational interaction, which has a great influence on the efficiency of the expectational effect results.

The expectation of the teachers on students will be transferred into great internal power to improve the students' hard-working, enthusiastic exploration and the teacher will get repaid by his students' hundred time's pay. Especially to those experienced, knowledgeable and emotion-rich students, the expectation from their teachers can just meet the needs of their ever increasing esteem and self-confidence. The trust from the teachers can greatly result in the increase of their self-confidence, the cultivation of the self-efficacy, formation of their good learning emotion, and arousal in their cells of vocal learning. As the Former Soviet Union educator Holme Linsky once said:"In the most secret corner of each student, there is always a unique string, once plucked, it will make an unique sound." During the vocal learning, the mutual understanding and trust is the basis of the harmony education.

Acknowledgement. This research was supported by the Teaching Reform Research Foundation of Guangxi University of Technology "Study and practice of vocal teaching model reform based on local engineering course university" under Grant J1020.

References

1. Tang, J.: The theoretical learning and practice of the contemporary vocal music. Literary Theory 11, 71 (2010)
2. Zhang, J.X.: The emotional features and its ability cultivation in vocal learning. The Journal of Anshun College 8, 41–43 (2010)
3. Xu, X.Y.: Vocal singing and teaching. Shanghai Music Publishing House, Shanghai (2002)
4. Zhang, X.X.: The value and role of expectational effect in vocal teaching. The Journal of Xi'an Academy of Music 6, 91–93 (2010)

The Discussion of University Art Education Training Based on College Students' Employability in Mordern Information Age

ZhuWen Tan[1], Yuan Tian[2], YuHang Wei[1], and Rui Deng[1]

[1] Guangxi University of Technology, Liuzhou, P.R. China
[2] Huazhong Normal University, Wuhan, P.R. China

Abstract. College students' employability is the comprehensive quality and the potential system including discipline knowledge, ability and psychological quality. The art education should exert its unique function as an important part of the over-all development education. Around the employment of college graduates force developed, we should take active measures widely developing a variety of art education to enrich students' knowledge. Strengthen emotional factors help to promote college students' emotional development. We should also permeate professional ethics education. Pay attention to the creativeness of art education and stimulate it. In addition, we should actively promote the development of college students' personality, develop its harmonious interpersonal relationship, and comprehensively advance college students' employment.

Keywords: Employability; Art education; Emotional factors.

1 Introduction

At present, our university student's employment question has becomes the focus of attention of the whole society. How to solve the employment of college graduates problem is the social outstanding problems should be solved. But, it can't be really solved simply rely on the government. Colleges and universities should actively explore how to improve the quality of the students, to adapt to the social development and unit of choose and employ persons' needs. Art education can play an important role as an important part in promoting the over-all development in college. Art education not only can edify sentiment, improve quality, but also help develop intelligence, even has an irreplaceable function to promote the comprehensive development of students, which was indicated by the state council of the communist party in "About deepening education reform promoting quality-oriented education decision".

In 2006 national common universities public art course guidelines", its spirit clearly points out," Art course is established for cultivating socialist modernization needs of high-quality talents. It is irreplaceable in improving college students' aesthetic quality, developing students' innovative ability and practicing ability, shaping a good personality." Therefore, colleges and universities of art education should actively conform to the demand of social development. According to the need of society and the

S. Lin and X. Huang (Eds.): CSEE 2011, Part V, CCIS 218, pp. 48–52, 2011.

enterprise unit of choose and employ persons. Closely combined art education with quality employment required. Comprehensively promote the development of students.

2 Overview of College Students' Employability

2.1 Definition of College Students' Employability

Employability is a rising research field in recent years, there is no unified concept. British scholar Hillage·Pollard defines it as "have the ability to finish first employment, can maintain current position and get the next post demand when necessary." They think the employment of college graduates with the level of the ability of employment market and graduates have knowledge and professional skill closely related. British scholar Brown·Duguide thinks "Employability is able to obtain and maintain different employment of relative opportunity". His definition is mainly from graduate personal level, is a kind of ability revealed when graduates show their personal advantages to employing unit. Knight's definition is: "employability is a series of achievements, understanding and personal qualities that can promote individual successful employment and career choice." Little thinks "Employability is a complex structure of person's ability and operation skill and professional knowledge". To sum up, college students' employability is the comprehensive quality and the potential system including discipline knowledge, ability and psychological quality, which adapt to the social requirements and the college students obtained in the learning process.

2.2 Structure of College Students' Employability

The UK experts Peter TKnight & Mant Yorke puts forward employability structure model, namely USEM model, through the huge investigation to job unit human resource department and staff. The USEM model consists of four elements: comprehension of professional knowledge (Understanding); general and specialized skills must have in work (Skills); individual's self-efficacy (Efficacy); meta-cognitive which can reflect various thoughts and cognition (Meta-cognition).

   At present, the employability studies is just at the beginning. And for the employability issues, different researchers have no unified understanding. Generally speaking, mainly involving the following aspects: Discipline knowledge; Factors of ability; Psychological quality.

3 Higher Art Education Based on College Students' Employability

3.1 First, Developing a Variety of Art Education Widely and Enriching Students' Knowledge

On practice, university graduates have comparative sufficient of their work and development in the future, which have a huge potential for development. The reason is the comparatively rich knowledge that university students have, which provide the solid foundation for the development of its ability. Art education in college can advocate diverse activities widely from the form and content of two sides, combined with the cultivation of students' employability. We should put together with the art, music, calligraphy, photography, drama, Chinese folk art forms, literature, recitation, all sorts of good folk art content and so on. Even the sketch, language kind aspects art can be a part of it. So our students have full access to understand the art content at home and abroad. Then broaden their vision, improve their art taste. Carry out various art salon, and various forms of the party. Contemporary college students have high scientific and cultural level and higher aesthetic consciousness and enthusiasm. So we should give full play to students in art education process self education's enthusiasm, especially the function of the student communities and organizations. Then strengthen and improve them. To establish various art community organization under the guidance of professional teachers, such as chorus, band, wanshun, photography club, poetry society, literature salon, etc. Carry out healthy and various forms of aesthetic activities, such as Karaoke concerts, poetry slams, toastmasters, calligraphy exhibitions, art exhibition, etc. Guide more students to attend art education activities, edify them imperceptibly by beauty edification in the rich and colorful campus cultural activities. Through various forms of art education like this, the students can aspect much better influence in literary and artistic in the school, and expand their knowledge base, become more easily to adapt to society's demands, improve their employment force.

3.2   Second, We Should Strengthen Emotional Factors, Promoting College Students' Emotional Development in Art Education

Lenin said: "If missing human emotion, it is impossible for someone to pursue truth." Art is the embodiment of people's emotion, thus it is a particularly significant role for human emotion's raise and the enhancement. Educators should attach great importance to the cultivation effect of art in edifying person's feelings and individual character, because it can cultivate individual good emotion and personality, building up a perfect personality. Art have strong appeal and shock strength to people, which completely from its rich emotional factors. Therefore, colleges and universities should make full use of the rich and excavate the emotional factors to inspire the students during the art education, raising the students' good emotions, let them become compassionate and responsible. Then they can serve their own businesses better. Only a person has good thoughts and feelings can truly understand the experience of life and work with the happiness and share this happiness with others. Sukhomlinski, a famous educationist, said:" The best self education can understand and feel beauty .And beauty is a mirror, people can know how to treat themselves through beauty. Beauty is also a kind of heart gymnastics, it can model the human spirit, conscience, beliefs and emotions. "So we can say that beauty is the peak of life, from the top of the hill we can see those we never have felt and understood , can see the beauty and goodness which were unaware in the past. Beauty is the light to light the world, through which you can see the truth and kind. "Art can make excellent talents become more sensitive, their vision also will be more open. As young intellectuals, college students have extensive knowledge, the emotion and beauty of art can give them great power, promote them a better development, become better adapt to the social requirements. Art is also an important mean to develop their brains potential to understand the human experience throughout history; learn to appreciate, taste, drawing; respect other people's way of thinking and working and mode of expression. It's also a mean to develop the students' capabilities of expression, analysis, development and dealing with various kinds of practical problems through art.

3.3 Third, the College of Art Education Process of Infiltration Professional Ethics Education

"Having both ability and political integrity" is the target and requirement of the employing unit for talents. Modern enterprise especially requires staff must have good occupation morals. Contemporary undergraduate, especially college students after 80, after 90, tend to think more about their own feelings, optional job-hopping phenomenon for small things can be found everywhere. It has a serious influence for enterprise to conduct its work orderly. So we should increase and penetrate professional ethics education by the model role from a variety of art image during the art education in colleges. Teach students how to behave, especially learn to be a responsible person. Strengthen college students' professional responsibility and education of loving their job. Cultivating students' positive working attitude whatever they do in the future. Motivate them to be responsible for their job, be filled with occupational honor and mission. Make them understand that responsibility is the necessary ideological quality. Be honest, it is not only the traditional virtue of Chinese, but also the basic content of university students' moral education. Teachers should set themselves as model, the school also should emphasize its seriousness such as in the exam links. Let the students have a deep understanding and experience about that honesty is one of the most important virtues. Honesty is the base, the most basic request a society for talents. So we should be honest in employment and work in the future.

3.4 Fourth, Pay Attention to Creativity in Art Education, Stimulate College Students' Creativity

Someone said that art is a visual thing, which is difficult to make person creative. But, on the contrary, both art and work of art are creative products. Science and art always like the positive and negative sides of a coin. Without art, human's imagination can't create a new road of science and can't reach the peak of scientific development. However, without cognition of the world and social scientific, human emotion also can't rise to beautiful realm. In today's society, any state, nation or enterprise needs human creativity if it wants to develop, and it is our foundation of survival and sustainable development. Art education not only means teaching students singing, painting, the more important thing is to teach students to observe, to think standing at a higher level, with more wide Angle, and cultivate their critical thinking skills. The great scientist Albert Einstein once said: "imagination is more important than knowledge." He benefited a lot from music, "Many of my scientific achievements are inspired music." You may say, the process of artistic creation and art appreciation itself is the process we actively involved in creating the world. We should attach great importance to inspire their potential when conducting college students' art education. As Maslow, a humanism psychologist, said, "Pedestrian innately has ego transcendence, healthy people's desire would naturally to find more broad vision after it is met in a certain extent. Seek farther things rather than more recent things. Quality like beauty and kindness, are human nature reveal to a certain extent". The requirement of modern society for talents' quality enhances unceasingly. Not only require good professional knowledge, but also require certain creativity .From actual, contemporary college students gain varied source of knowledge because they come in contact with all sorts of mass media. They are knowledgeable in knowledge tend, what they lack most is creativity and the ability to solve practical problems. Therefore, colleges and universities should value its creativity in developing the art education. The teacher must cultivate students' creativity to adapt to the need of the society. Inspire them to explore the creation factor, and cultivate their create cells during the process of art creation works.

4 Conclusion

Artistic education is an important part of quality education. We can't imagine a society without art. Similarly, a college student without artistic accomplishment also isn't a real college student. Higher education should strengthen the art education for college students, exert the function and education value of art, promote and optimize the development of human nature.

Acknowledgement. This research was supported by the Research Foundation of "study on university undergraduate employment competition ability cultivation in context of economic crisis" under Grant 200911LX177 and "Study on meeting mechanism between Guangxi cultural market development and art personnel cultivation under Grant 08FSH003.

References

1. Guo, Z.W., Hector, B.I.J.M.: Employability in borderless career era of: A new kind of psychological contract. Journal of Psychological Science 2, 485 (2006)
2. Wang, J.G.: The innovation of talent cultivation mode from the current college students employment difficulties. Chinese Power Education 25, 10–12 (2010)
3. Guo, Z.W., Song, J.H.: Employment ability research: retrospect and prospect. Journal of Hubei University (Philosophy and Social Science Edition) 11, 90–91 (2007)
4. Peng, H.: Thinking on strengthen the art education of student in science and engineering university. Guangdong University of Technology (Social Science Edition) 7, 28–29 (2008)
5. Tsou, H.: The discussion of university art education's significance. Three Gorges University Journal (Humanities and Social Science Edition) 7, 99–102 (2007)

The Application of Learning Organizational Theory in Agricultural College English Education Based on Broad Web Resources

Shi-de Li and Jian Tian

Tianjin Agricultural University

Abstract. For the sake of change our country the irregularity of the common high school English traditional teaching mode, improve a teaching target in the teaching, well embody the student's corpus position, relocate relation of teacher and pupil, build up the team study mode, development aware of self study, ego control, ego management of behavior habit, this text to study type organization theory the usage carried on a viability assessment at the teaching process and put forward to is the speculation of study of study type organization the study change of classroom.

Keywords: Learning organizational theory, English teaching, the team studies mode, application.

1 Theoretical Base on Setting Up Agricultural Colleges English Learning Organization

Currently, educational reform and innovation are the hot topics in colleges and universities. During the process of educational reform, not a few teachers borrow teaching ideas from higher education and educational psychology, getting the good teaching achievement. But, in fact, the experiences and theories on educational reform we can use are not only limited in the fields of education. The learning organization theory in the field of management caters to the improvement of students' passive and objective role in the traditional classroom teaching and the need of improvement of teaching efficiency. It also supplies an effective way on how to train students' teamwork consciousness and ability, as well as the sustainable development in learning ability. The theory of learning organization appeared in western scholar Hutchins's Learning Society, published in 1968 at the earliest and then finally was formed in The Fifth Discipline---Art and Trend of the Learning Organization, written by American managerialist Peter M. Senge. The five disciplines of learning organization refer to personal mastery, improvement of mental models, building shared vision, teamwork learning and system thinking. The personal mastery means organization is made up of several individuals engaging in the continuous creations. The shared vision means to unite the different people with different personalities through the shared will, value and mission, gradually breaking through the toplimit in organization members' personal ability growing in order to make progress for the shared aim. To improve mental models is to breach the traditional thinking patterns to the disadvantage of the

S. Lin and X. Huang (Eds.): CSEE 2011, Part V, CCIS 218, pp. 53–58, 2011.

development of organization and to overcome all factors influenced organization activities efficiency. Instead, it aims to improve organization activities efficiency by use of new ideas and ways, methods in favour of its development. The feature of teamwork learning breaks through the individual's being enclosed learning state and organizes the active discussion in members for the purpose of making progressing together. The system thinking requires the notice of the interaction among all factors. It requires one should not take link between the learning organization and other organizations one-sidedly, regarding the links in learning organization activities as the isolated states. It is a kind of beneficial attempt to apply the learning organization to colleges and universities' educational reform especially to the teaching reform in English major.

2 Analysis of Applicability of Learning Organization in the English Teaching among Institutions of Higher Learning

In modern society, the need for the talents specialized in English is not limited to the professionals of a single English, on the contrary, those versatile talents who have a better understanding of the expertise and possess related organizational abilities are really favored by the society. Therefore, for students who are specialized in English, it's equally important to foster the creative and organizational ability as well as the teamwork spirit besides leaning professional skills and theoretical knowledge.

2.1 Particularity of English Teaching Is Beneficial to Operation of Learning Organization Theory in Teaching

Particularity of English lies in: first, the English major courses are divided into two parts: theory and practice lesions with the majority in practice lessons. Second, the learning combines static and dynamic and the former gives priority to the latter. Third, it takes the English exercise as the principle thing in learning content and it has less extracurricular work. Thus, there is abundance of free time. At present, the teaching from, the two-classes successively is used in colleges and universities' English teaching. Within the limited 90 minutes, students can only get English exercises, but the training for their cooperation, creativity and consciousness is relatively rare. If some practice lessons are properly arranged to students, it is good for students' realization to teaching content improvement from perceptual level to the rational level. If some practicable operations such as match, holding the post of judge and teaching practice and organized for students in teaching process, it can make students experience the whole process in which theory knowledge and techniques are applied to the practice. It will get the incomparable effect beyond the simple lecturing. It is urgent affairs to take a way to combine the class and extracurricular lessons, individual and community lessons. Once such organization which has cooperative, focus on teamwork learning and shared knowledge is set up, the whole teaching process becomes the process of collective exploration and studying on the basis of mutual inspiration and thinking. It can bring up a kind of relation that teaching benefits teachers as well as students. This process can benefit for the product of innovative thinking.

2.2 The Modern Teaching Development Provide the Convenient Conditions for Carrying Out Learning Organization Theory

The application of the multi-media in teaching can widen teachers and students' knowledge vision and can provide them with rich and teaching-related information source and learning materials, saving time for their material and information searching. At the same time, it can supply an exchange platform between students and teachers, students and students so that the exchange can not be limited in space and time. As a result, people can learn from each other and solve their common problems in groups, breaking down the bounds between class and outside of classroom. After the building up of learning organization, teachers, just as students, become the members in the organization. Thus, teachers can change their identity in thinking and can realize what students really want in teaching, making their teaching objective more directed to demand students' need in learning. In addition, their teaching efficiency can be improved greatly. These fit into the modern teaching theory.

3   Application of Learning Organization in Agricultural College English Teaching

3.1 Cultivating Cooperative Consciousness and Summarizing and Improving Teaching Method

Combined with the first practice—personal mastery, the teacher should firstly propagate the advantage of learning organization and mobilize students to join the organization. Competition in class, election of the representatives of subjects, comparing and appraising of groups, setting up progress award and other activities should be held. Its purpose is to place students in dynamic environment and to make the members of class, representatives of subjects; groups and organizations surpass themselves and progress constantly. The second purpose is to make the members of organization process collective honor and the achievement and pride of conquering themselves. The third purpose is to give students inexhaustible motive of study by continuous self-motivation and stimulation of external condition. What's more, by combining the second practice to improve the mental model, English education teachers' traditional managing modes and teaching ideas should be alter in studying-type class. The theory of learning organization focuses on giving full play to the positivity, initiative and creativity of the members. It also emphasizes humanism, because human is both the production factor and the factor different from other material form, highlighting that people are a kind of living elements. Teacher as the organizer and guides of the organization is the supervisor of executing the decision and provides the time and space guarantee for organization learning. Teacher should ensure that the information of organization learning is unblocked, try to communicate with students, develop the communication among students and timely praise progressive students. Teacher and students should be together to question the problem in English teaching and investigate and find the solutions.

3.2 Defining the Learning Goals and Establishing Shared Vision of Teachers and Students

Shared vision is an important feature of learning organization. The goal of learning organization refers to that the learning subject should specially describe the goal he or she wants to realize. It is not an external standard, but the internal forming. It is the common vision of both parties of teacher and students. When processing the common vision, the members of origination will strive for the common goal.

Concerning with teaching practice, establishing the corporate vision actually requires teacher to formulate the teaching goal of applying to the teaching features of PE major, combining the different demands and the mental features of every students. Students have the strong desire performance and yearn for the recognition and approval of college and teachers. At the same time, PE major students' self-consciousness and independence formed in the competition are more obvious than students' of other majors. They will affect the character formation of modesty and tolerability. Thus, as long as they meet the problems, they will have the improper actions and destroy the harmonious development of class under the influence of self-consciousness. Therefore, to make students establish the clear learning goals and plans is good for students, who can have guide to action. Thus, students can work hard toward the common goal that includes both short-term and long-term goals.

3.3 Reorientation of Relationship between Teachers and Students to Establish Team Learning Model

Team learning is a process that members of team work hard and actively and coordinate with each other to realize the goal of team under the guidance of common vision and that all the members change the common vision into its individual ideal. Learning organization focuses on stimulating members to create new knowledge by learning ability of collective intelligence, based on group learning to pool collective wisdom and rational communication and assistance to share the learning experience. Thus, the efficiency of individual learning is much poorer than group learning.

3.4 Reorientation of Relationship between Teachers and Students

To build mode of group learning requires the new orientation of role of teacher and students. In traditional teaching mode, teacher is the only subject and students are just the objects to learn passively. Thus, students can not study initiatively and there is not enough communication between teacher and students and among students. At present, the classes of college and university are typical individual learning and leaning efficiency is low. Therefore, in the process of building organization learning, teacher should be not the subject of teaching and students not the object of teaching. Traditional relationship between teacher and students should be changed to be more equal like the members in a group. Through the role transformation, teacher should be the guider and partner of students in the process of class teaching. Namely, both teacher and students should be the subjects of class teaching. Thus, teaching method in class is not to emphasize teacher' lecture but to concern with students' discussion and practice in line with such requests. In class, teacher should not just encourage students to express their opinions, but also guide them to obtain actively truth from their practice. In the entire stage of learning, teachers should pay attention to grasping the overall situation and coordinating relation. In English education, students' minds are excited so that the little thing may cause the great conflict. Teacher should use aptly the conflict and guide students to change the conflict into inflection and discussion of skills and actions. Thus, conflict can become the learning motivation and a chance to increase the friendship of students.

3.5 Establishing Mode of Group Learning by Reasonable Grouping

Reasonable grouping is an important step of implementing the learning organization theory. When students are simply divided into several groups and each group has the same task, teaching task can not be distributed reasonably and students' learning enthusiasm and initiative can be fully mobilized, based on the grouping. In addition, because students have no positive interaction, the expectant goal can be achieved. Therefore, groups should be classified by students' common interests or specialties. On the premise, there should be diversity and complementarily of students' learning foundation, learning style, grade, gender, personality and other aspects. It is a method of combining similarity in a group with difference among groups. Based on the grouping, teaching task should be assigned and teacher should guide students to think actively and explore bravely so as to give full play to groups' wisdom and creativity. When steering the groups to communicate and share the knowledge, the difference of members' receiving ability should be considered. Thus, everyone in a class should be stimulated to improve overall and progress together. Before carrying on the activity of learning organization, teacher should elaborate the learning content and goal, rule of active and main methods and evaluation standards of completing learning task so that students can understand them clearly.

3.6 Cultivating the Ability of System Thinking

System thinking is the core among the five disciplines in realizing the learning organization. System thinking enables people to get a complete picture of the problem and comprehensively consider the interactive relation of various factors, rather than one-track thinking. In terms of the teaching practices of English education in colleges and universities, most students cannot relate different aspects of learning and they don't know how to integrate the knowledge of each teaching unit together, neither do they know how to connect each course laterally into a whole so as to make a systematic study.

4 Conclusion

Presently, English teaching in China's institutes of higher learning exist a lot of disadvantages, for example, teaching methods are single and outmoded, course contents break away from practice and teaching arrangements lack the links of practices, etc, the cause of which is that students lack the study enthusiasm and therefore the teaching effect is not that favorable. However, the Learning Organization Theory has a strong objective, which, specifically, can not only enable the teachers to become the organizer, guider, regulator, decider, instructor and participator instead of the role as an authority in an activity so that teacher objectively treats students' individual difference and teaches them according to their aptitude, but also stimulate students' learning enthusiasm and initiative to better excavate students' potential so that students constantly break limitation of ability to improve their learning efficiency.

Acknowledgment. The paper is supported by Research of the Solutions to the Problems of Service Quality of Higher Agricultural Education in the New Countryside Building Process National Education and Science. The Project is supported by the Youth Foundation from the Ministry of Education (Grant No. EIA100407).

References

1. Senge, P.M.: The Fifth Discipline—Art and Trend of the Learning Organization. Shanghai San Lien Book Store (1998)
2. Senge, P.M.: The Fifth Discipline—Strategies and Methods of Establishing Learning Organization. Orient Press (2009)
3. Haiqin, C.: Analysis on Learning Organization's Value of Improving Teaching Quality in Colleges and Universities. Suzhou S&.T University Journal (Social Science Edition) (4) (2004)
4. Jianmin, T.: Practice Strategy of Constructing Learning Organization with Analysis of Class Teaching Cases as the Carrier. Jiangsu Education (1) (2004)
5. Fanhua, M.: Constructing Learning Organization of Modern Schools. Research on Comparative Education (1) (2002)

Research of the Distributed Heterogeneous Database Conversion Mechanism

ZhenYou Zhang[1], WeiLi Wang[2], and Rui Zhang[3]

[1] The College of Information Engineering, Hebei united university,
No 46 Xin Hua Xi street, Tangshan, Hebei, China
youzhenadd@163.com
[2] The College of Information Engineering, Hebei united university,
No 46 Xin Hua Xi street, Tangshan, Hebei, China
tsWangweili2007@163.com
[3] School of science, Xi'an jiaotong university, No28 xian ning xi street, Xi'an, Shanxi, China
Zhangrui2011@stu.xjtu.edu.cn

Abstract. Between each node database there must be all different in the distributed heterogeneous database , so how to resolve these differences(It's said that realize the mutual transformation between heterogeneous databases) was an basic problem in the heterogeneous database integration, synchronous and optimized.This paper analyzes the conversion mechanism for the distributed heterogeneous database between node databases and the realization of the conversion module theoretical includeing the conversion information extraction module, structural conversion module, structure formation module and put forward a concrete realization solutions.

Keywords: Heterogeneous database, conversion mechanism, single mode, the structure transformation.

0 Introduction

Research of the distributed heterogeneous database system was integrate many different types of database system, thus the user can visit different qualitative database system. But study the structure convert of the different database was the basic research in the heterogeneous database access, data synchronization transparent. Conversion can make the user data table in each site of the heterogeneous database system,can be reconstructe according to the user's requirements in another heterogeneous database.So that it can put data in some user data table in the heterogeneous node database into a system database, and thus get total set for data synchronization.

1 Theoretical Analysis of the Transformation Mechanism of Distributed Heterogeneous Database

The fundamental purpose of the data synchronization of the heterogeneous database was made in different nodes of different types of databases to keep same of the data same in the table . Because of the autonomy of the heterogeneous database system, so

S. Lin and X. Huang (Eds.): CSEE 2011, Part V, CCIS 218, pp. 59–64, 2011.
© Springer-Verlag Berlin Heidelberg 2011

the system makes each heterogeneous database data maintain consistency only by third party system to synchronize data transmission.

The essence of the transformation in heterogeneous database was put a node database user data table and data into anther heterogeneous databases include the table structure and data.

It's used specification type to define field type in the database system development for the different manufacturers. The field types of Mysql, Sybase SQLServer and Oracle database shown in Table 1.

Table 1. Field type of Mysql,Sybase,SQLServer and Oracle

Mysql	sybase	SQLServer	oracle
Int type			
bigint	N/A	bigint	number
int, integer	int	int	
smallint	smallint	smallint	
tinyint	tinyint	tinyint	
mediumint	N/A	N/A	
Character type			
Char(n)	char(n)	char(n)	char(n)
varchar(n)	varchar(n)	varchar(n)	varchar(n)
N/A	nchar(n)	N/A	N/A
N/A	nvarchar(n)	N/A	N/A
N/A	unichar(n)	nchar(n)	nchar(n)
N/A	univarchar(n)	nvarchar(n)	nvarchar(n)

Realizing the transformation between heterogeneous databases, first acquisition to convert database user data tables of information, such as table structure, table structure of storage location and other information. And then conversion a database structure to another heterogeneous database , and last it's replication the user data.

The basic of the switching mechanism of heterogeneous database was collection the conversion information. In order to acquisited the information of user data table structure of from node database,this study adopts metadata programming way, namely according to different characteristics of heterogeneous database, read the table structure information of the user data table. This is the premise of data transformation.

The key of the transform mechanism of heterogeneous database table was the structure conversion between heterogeneous databases . It is well known that the table structure column type of presentation between heterogeneous databases was not consistent different. Because of the type of heterogeneous database is varied, how to transformation in different between heterogeneous databases conversion was a complicated problem. Usually there are three conversion ways, one was opposite each other, this way was the most complex conversion. Another way to convert structure to the SQL statement for undertake unity, as a result of each database SQL language has manufacturer to expand, making the changeover job more difficult. Another way is converted into an intermediate database undertake unity, although look more complex, but is a practical method.

The final phase of the conversion of heterogeneous database was copied or mobile the data. Because of the data processing between heterogeneous database ,so it can only through the relevant procedures to transfer the single data record.

2 Design and Implementation of the Transformation Mechanism for the Distributed Heterogeneous Database

There are three modules in the conversion system for the distributed heterogeneous database .It's structure information acquisition module, structural conversion module and data migration module. The function of structure information acquisition module was the structure information extracted on node database table.The function of structural conversion module was conversion some type of table structure information to the middle type database table structure information. Data migration modules of the system is based on the table structure information among types in another node database created a new table structure information, and data copied to the new table.

2.1 Design and Implementation of the Structure Information Acquisition Module

This module mainly realizes from each node database to extract the structure information of user data table that had to convert, also was each field types information of the user table. Because of the heterogeneity of the heterogeneous databases,it has differently method from the different database. Extraction of flow chart as figure 1.

Here in SQLServer2000 and Mysql5.0 as an example to illustrate the key SQL statements to extract table structure information.

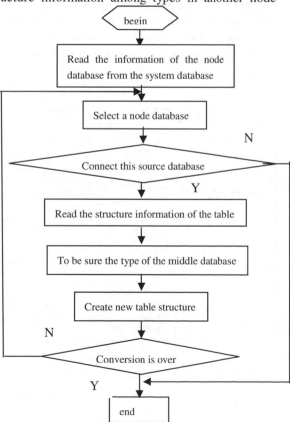

Fig. 1. Extract the structure from user table

For SQLServer2000 relational database, the user data table structure information stored syscolumns system table and systypes system table in the user database. Specific SQL statements for:"select syscolumns.name, systypes.name, syscolumns. isnullable,syscolumns.length from syscolumns, systypes where syscolumns.xusertype = systypes.xusertype and syscolumns.id = object_id('"+users table name+"')"

For Mysql5.0 database, its user database table structure information stored in columns system tables in the Fig. 1 extract the structure from user table information database information_schema.First information_schema database must be connected, and then read the table structure information. Specific SQL statements: "select column_name, data_type,character_maximum_length, is_nullable   from columns where table_schema= '"+database name+"' and table_name='"+users table name+"'"。

Because the expression list structure information different,these information need corresponding conversion for show the users.

2.2   Design and Implementation of the Structure Conversion Module

This module mainly realizes structure conversion of the user table. In extracting the original structure information of the user table from the database users table ,it has to conversion the field data information structurethe in user table to middle type data types, and database structure for some without the corresponding data types require special treatment. Specific conversion process figure2.

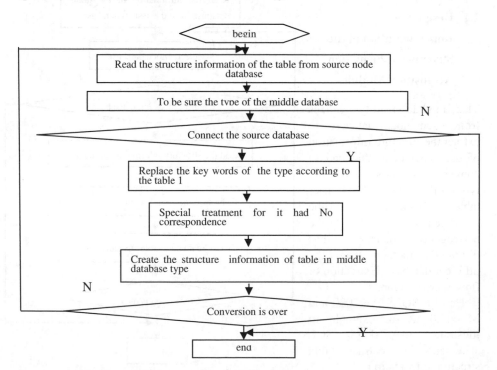

Fig. 2. Conversion the structure information from user table

2.3 Design and Implementation of the Data Migration Module

In data migration module, it generate a new table structure information according to the middle type of database,and also it copied the original node database data to the new type database. Specific process as shown in figure 3.

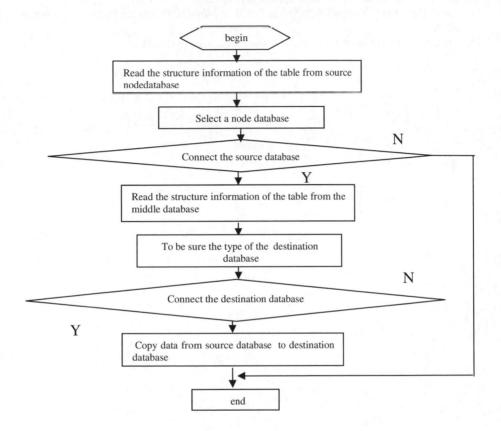

Fig. 3. Copy data from source database to destination database

3   Summary

Conversion between the distributed heterogeneous database was currently an important problem of information management, the traditional database duplication technology has many shortcomings. This paper puts an mechanism for resolving the dynamic extraction, and choose a application database as conversion intermediation, it improved the system practicability. The study hopes to provide some new ideas in data conversion of heterogeneous database.

References

[1] Kong, X.: Computer Application Research, vol. 4, p. 20 (2006)
[2] Zhang, S.: Computer Application Research, vol. 1, p. 22 (2000)
[3] Zhang, S.: Computer Application Technology, vol. 5, p. 54 (2007)
[4] Sams, B.F.: Teach Yourself SQL Server T-SQL in Minutes. Wordware Publishing, America (2006)
[5] Tamer, M.: Department of Computer Science, vol. 4, p. 19 (2008)

Research in Synchronization Optimization of the Distributed Heterogeneous Database Data

ZhenYou Zhang[1], LiHong Liu[2], and Rui Zhang[3]

[1] The College of Information Engineering, Hebei united university, No 46 Xin Hua Xi street,
Tangshan, Hebei, China
[2] The College of Information Engineering, Hebei united university, No 46 Xin Hua Xi street,
Tangshan, Hebei, China
[3] School of science, Xi'an jiaotong university, No28 xian ning xi street, Xi'an, Shanxi, China
youzhenadd@163.com, 175550389@qq.com,
Zhangrui2011@stu.xjtu.edu.cn

Abstract. The data synchronous of the distributed heterogeneous database was one of the important research for the heterogeneous databases. So, the research for improving the efficiency of data synchronization of the heterogeneous database had an important meaning. This paper analysied the data synchronization optimization mechanism of the distributed heterogeneous database and realized the theoretical of the data synchronization, and put forward a concrete realization solutions.

Keywords: Synchronous optimization mechanism, data changes set, minimal changes set, minimal changes update sets.

0 Introduction

Research of the data synchronous distributed heterogeneous database was together multiple heterogeneous database system to realize the synchronization between them. The so-called synchronous refers to the node database in different between user data tables keep data in the agreement. Because the autonomy of heterogeneous database system, this synchronization cannot affect the original database of all kinds of user operation. It also realize the share data in multiple node database.

1 Theory Analysis of the Data Synchronization Optimization in Distributed Heterogeneous Database

Heterogeneous database data synchronization essence was the user data table in a period of datain a node database, make other heterogeneous database also did the same change.

There was three stages for realization the data synchronous of the heterogeneous database. The first stage was to collect the data of change in the table in a user table in

S. Lin and X. Huang (Eds.): CSEE 2011, Part V, CCIS 218, pp. 65–69, 2011.
© Springer-Verlag Berlin Heidelberg 2011

node database. The second stage was the concentration of these changes data. The third stage was updateing the user data table in the destination node database.

Assuming node database in the heterogeneous database system such as shown in table 1.

It used trigger mechanism to realize the data acquisition. According to the working principle, system created two triggers for each user data table ,Insert action triggers (Insert) and Delete action triggers (Delete). Whenever the user data table that had two triggers when operating, trigger will be triggered. System can be found those changes, in which the data collection called single database changes. These data changes to store in table 2 named data table. These data table and user data table have the same table structure, but plus a field named insert time field. When there was data.

Table 1. Node database

No	Node name	Database type	Table name	Field ncount	Size of recorde
1	node a	SQLServer	user	5	60
2	node b	Oracle	user_inform	5	75
3	node c	Mysql	amdin	5	45

Insert user data table, Insert trigger action. When there was data Delete a user data table, the Delete trigger action. When there is data update, Insert trigger action and Delete triggers actions. Execute actions, the changes data in user data table will be added to the data table shown in the table 2.

Table 2. Changes data concentrated in node database

No	Table name	Table name create by Insert trigger	Table name create by Delete trigger
1	user	user_Insert	user_Delete
2	user_inform	user_inform_Insert	user_inform_Delete
3	amdin	user_Insert_Insert	user_Insert_Delete

Change data concentrated stages was an important stage of synchronous data optimization. This phase is divided into three steps, the first step was to concentrate from a single database changes set to the system database. The second step was to change collation,and get tiny collection of change. In the process of change set finishing the collection was the process of optimizing synchronous data, the sorting process greatly reduces the amount of data synchronization transmission efficiency, and improved synchronization. The third was to use tiny changes the inclination and a single database changes the difference to get integrating tiny update set in a single node.

Updates the user data table in the destination node database was to used tiny update set to update the various heterogeneous database in the process data table.

2   Research and Implementation of the Synchronous Optimization Mechanism of Heterogeneous Database

2.1   Concentration from an Single Database Changes Sets

It was optimized foundation that the change of the user table had to integrating. Because of individual database changes sets in each node database, in order to focus them, first stage was established the corresponding user data table in the system's database, then copy the data in user data table to system database. Such data were all concentration changes to system database. But such concentration was a global user data table name for corresponding relationship, that is to say, with the same structure of the same global name in the user data table data were focused.

If it put the three use table in the three node database to the system database, the first stages will check the user table compatibility, namely three table fields type whether incompatible, if incompatible data table can proceed the concentration. In order to perform the synchronous optimization put these user data schedule uniformly to a user global table.

Its such as shown in table 3 after reunification information.

The user table name in table 3 was a node database user list the name in system database. While the global user table name was symbol that allowed synchronous in this distributed heterogeneous database.

Table 3. Table name after reunification information in system database

No	Global user table	Node name	User table name
1		Nodea	user_Nodea_user_Insert
2	user_Insert	Nodeb	user_Nodeb_user_inform_Insert
3		Nodec	user_Nodec_amdin_Insert
4		Nodea	user_Nodea_user_Delete
5	user_Delete	Nodeb	user_Nodeb_user_inform_Delete
6		Nodec	user_Nodec_amdin_Delete

Uer_Insert user data collection concentration process changes as shown in figure 1.

2.2   The Tiny Change Set Collection Generated

The main function of the module of the tiny changes set collection was processing the generated by synchronous set each heterogeneous database data,delete redundancy.Insert collection set in the tiny changes set of the total concentration generative process as figure2.

According to the same process could generate the delete sets and update sets, both of them was the minimal update sets of individual heterogeneous database. The minimal update sets in written back to the corresponding each node database can complete the heterogeneous database data Synchronization.

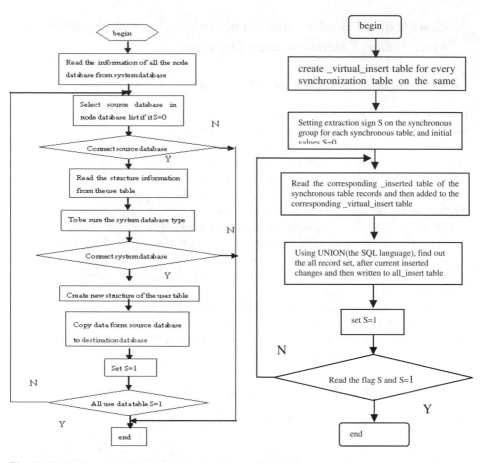

Fig. 1. Uer_Insert user data collection concentration process

Fig. 2. Insert collection set in the tiny changes set of the total concentration generative proces

2.3   The Tiny Update Set Collection Generated

Tiny update collection set was generated in the system's databases,it used to update the user data tables in node databases.The main idea was the tiny change in a single database changes collection and the differ set to get integrating a user data table of minimal update sets for node database. The processing of the insert sets in the minimal update sets as figure3.

3   Summary

Data synchronization problem is currently an important problem of information management, if the traditional database replication technology has many disadvantages. In this paper the proposed synchronization mechanism solved data extraction and data update, and the minimal change sets can reduce synchronous data through put, and improves the efficiency of system. So it hoped some ideas for the heterogeneous database data synchronization study.

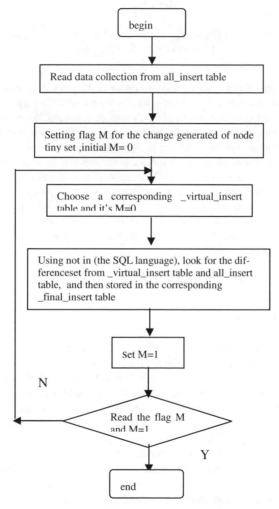

Fig. 3. The processing of the insert sets in the minimal update sets

References

1. Zisman, A., Kramer, J.: Network Management, vol. 29, p. 44 (2007)
2. James, A.P.: ACM Computing Surveys, vol. 11, p. 12 (2008)
3. Li, S.P.: Journal of Chinese science and technology information 16, 33 (2008)
4. Ye, G.Q.: Office Automation, vol. 6, p. 55 (2010)

On Innovation of the Academic Library Services from the Information Service Equalization

Mei Zhang

Library, Linyi University, Linyi, Shandong, 276000, China
zhangmei7596@163.com

Abstract. Information service equalization is an important component of public services equalization. It is one of the vital conditions for achieving information service equalization to eliminate poverty, promote economic development and build a harmonious society. Academic library is an important component of social information system, and it is the base of university and social infomationization. Therefore, the academic library should base on universities, face society, serve the nation and take responsibility of information service equalization. This paper analyzes the nature of the information service equalization and influence of promoting information service equalization by digital gap, explores the advantages for academic library to promote the equalization of information, finally proposes the measures of propelling information service equalization.

Keywords: Academic library, Information service, Equalization, Digital gap.

1 Introduction

The government of China proposed to gradually achieve the equalization requirements of basic public services for the construction of service-oriented government in the fourth collective study of CPC Central Committee Political Bureau in February 23, 2008. It is the needs to protect people's fundamental interests, expand domestic demand, accelerate economic development and change needs of the socialist market economy, and perform government functions and significance of the task to actively promote the equalization of basic public services [1]. The so-called basic public services, is based on certain social consensus, to provide the public service of basic social conditions which is to protect personal right to existence and development according to economic and social development and overall level by the government. It emphasizes the core of equal opportunities and results, rather than simply average and undifferentiated. Information service, as an important component of public service, exists serious non-equalization between inter-regional, urban and rural areas and different groups, which is another important area concerned by the library and the community after basic education, public health, social security and other basic public services.

2 Nature of Information Service Equalization

The essence of information service equalization is information equity. Information equity, in essence, is the main information activities, including a country, a region, a

S. Lin and X. Huang (Eds.): CSEE 2011, Part V, CCIS 218, pp. 70–75, 2011.

group or individual, to achieve information resources and reflect the state of balance and equity in the process of distribution of information resources[2]. Information equity includes equity of information access and distribution. The society of information equity should be that the subject can unrestrictedly, freely and equally access, use and share information resources. Professor Yongfu Jiang, a well-known scholar in China, believes that information equity must follow three principles, information freedom, information equity and information sharing.

3 The Principle of Information Freedom

Information freedom is the free station that people have required activities under the situation of no or less external restriction. It emphasizes that information right of a citizen is not violated and forced by information power, because from the legitimate relations of power and right, power is conferred by rights, and the task of power is to protect rights. It is the most basic prerequisite of information equity to protect full enjoyment of information freedom within the limits of the law.

4 The Principle of Information Equality

Information equality, which is human equality ideal reflected in the field of information activities, refers that the information subject is in the station of equal rights, equal opportunity and equal distribution scale in the information activities. Equality of information rights refers that everybody is equal before information [3]. Equality of information opportunity refers to opportunity equality of access to information, that is all information resources and services should be opened and provided to those who have the ability to obtain information, and regardless of differences of natural endowments and social conditions. Equality of information distribution scale refers to treat all demanders equally, rather than take discrimination. Information equality opposes information discrimination. Equality is a basic measure of fairness. Therefore, there will be no information equality without information fair.

5 The Principle of Information Sharing

Information sharing refers that the people share specific information resources. In other words, people who do not have certain information right will not have qualifications of sharing specific information. Information sharing is the opposite of information monopoly. Information monopoly, as an exclusive act, is bound to violate rights of other people. Therefore, in order to ensure the information fair, we must do the follows. All the public information resources must be equally open to the right people, and all people have the right to share all the public information resources. The higher level information technology and information resources share, the higher degree of social justice.

5.1 Influence of Promoting Information Service Equalization by Digital Gap

In real life, digital gap refers to extreme information disparity between the rich and the poor, different countries or regions, urban and rural, different industry, enterprises and groups because of development level and application level of information technology and network technology.

5.1.1 Break the Fairness of Information Society

Academic library, as the academic institutions, only focus on providing information service for teaching and research of university, not make full advantages of information resources to achieve maximum openness and resources sharing, and it is not commit the function to maintain information fair of all society[4]. Some service of the library is the agency service, to a certain extent and scope, causes the library to its monopoly business and exacerbates the digital gap. For example, readers copy the literature only in the library, the library has the monopoly of copy price. Readers are not allowed to bring related reference books and bags, also breaks its fairness.

5.1.2 Break the Rational Allocation of Information Resources

Academic library service is targeted at all teachers and students of the university. Different economic capabilities, status and many other factors, makes academic library exist many inequalities of information resource allocation, for example, readers are divided into different types, provided with different borrowing numbers, reading room are divided into different levels or different reference materials are borrowed by different people. All these phenomena seriously affect the full utilization of information resources, and information resources can not be reasonably and effectively configured.

5.2 Advantages for Academic Library to Promote the Information Equalization

Academic library is the information center of the region, and it has advantage that other information agencies can not be compared in bearing, organizing, developing, delivering information. It has a wealth of information resources, full disciplinary professional database, thematic literature database, network electronic resources and a variety of document collections. Academic library has high-quality information management personnel, who use the advanced information technology to not only science, effectively and quickly manage and deliver the information, but also creatively process and refine the information, and provide personalized and specialized information services. Academic library has superior consciousness in the the application of new technologies and information service has high level of systematic, automation and networking, which makes the ease and rapidity of information transferring realize. All these advantages of academic library are the material basis to expand its services and promote the equalization of information service.

5.3 Measures for Academic Library to Promote Information Service Equalization

Academic library is an important component of social information system, and it is the base of university and social infomationization. Article 19 of General Academic Library Regulation, states that academic library should protect the rights of readers to legally and fairly use library. It should provide convenience for the disabilities and other special readers. It has become an important subject for academic library to maintain the rights of readers and advocate information equality. It held *China University Curator Forum* in Wuhan University in July 8, 2005, and more than 60 delegates signed *the Library Cooperation and Information Resources Sharing, Wuhan Declaration*. The Declaration states that university is the institutional arrangements for the government to protect civil liberties and equal access to information and knowledge[5]. It is the bounden duty of the library to maximally satisfy every reader on information and knowledge needs. University libraries must practice the spirit of public libraries, change the past model that only focus on providing information service for teaching and research, give full play to the advantage of information resources, actively explore new mechanisms and model for social information service, radiate the advantages to the entire community, break information barriers, to achieve maximum openness and sharing, highlighting the people-oriented, democratic and free spirit of a century library, and undertake the functions of maintenance social information equalization.

5.3.1 Update Service Concept and Advocate Universal Reading

Academic libraries should base on universities, face society, serve the nation, increase publicity of education, actively guide for national learning, lifelong learning, and promote knowledge innovation, technological innovation to save energy for sustainable development of the whole society. Academic libraries should set the person - oriented concept, carry out humanistic education for education, and play the front role of social education in building a harmonious society. Harmonious society needs everyone to participate and work together, so librarians should continuously improve their cultural accomplishment and moral standards. Only update the service concept, innovate services, expand service areas and enhance service function, change passive service to active service, static service to dynamic services, vigorously carry out education campaigns, it can provide an inexhaustible spiritual power for the social development and human progress, stimulate citizen interest in learning, sprit of forging ahead, to make everyone be a learning person, the society be study society, and ultimately realize the harmonious development of human and social.

5.3.2 Establish a Service System of Multi-level, Comprehensive and Three-Dimension

The information service of modern library gradually go from museum to broad social market, participate in government decision-making and economic activities, expand their business and service targets, and deepen in these aspects, such as digital of service, network of information transmission method, extensive of service range, diversification of products, marketization of service object[6]. In addition to providing services for our readers of university, academic library should provide maximum equal services for the community, government, enterprises, hospitals and other institutions. The academic library can also issue library cards to the community, organize popular science lectures, book reports, academic salon, to strengthen information education of social users. We can establish branch libraries in the community, or collaborate with the local public library and agencies of information science and technology, establish cooperation network of resource sharing. Academic libraries should open to the public without changing the existing subordinate system of library resources and under the premise of respecting intellectual property, and their responsibilities of information security.

5.3.3 Concern about the Disadvantaged Minority and Bridge the Digital Gap

The disadvantaged minority loses the right of equally access to knowledge and education because of their economic distress and lack of public resources. As a part of social knowledge security system, the academic library has its irreplaceable role in concerning about the disadvantaged minority and improving their living conditions, such as the project of sending books to the countryside, the National Cultural Information Resources Sharing Project. Academic libraries will extend their services to the community, site, hospitals, prisons, and run labor schools, Technology Functional training and so on. To some extent, all these make up for the digital gap, and thus promote the harmonious development of society. However, the process of building a harmonious society is long, and the academic library should make unremitting efforts for the disadvantaged groups.

5.3.4 Complete the Network Services and Improve Information Literacy of Readers

The Internet is the world's largest computer network, spreads rapidly and forms the largest information systems. The Internet provides readers with e-mail delivery, Internet chat, information retrieval and many other features, and any user can obtain the necessary information online, so it is an effective way to bridge the digital gap. Using network technology, we establish a sound consulting services window, carry out SDI service and latest literature report, and provide readers with the second or third document service, so as to provide the desired service anywhere and anytime. We can develop distance education to make the backward areas share the advanced educational philosophy and resources. We can create the electronic reading room to provide CAI services, various multimedia video with maps, text and audio, Chinese and English typing and learning software of computer application, enable them to master the basic skills of computer use.

6 Summary

In short, it is a long and arduous process to promote the equalization of information services. It can help eliminate the information gap, achieve information equity, thereby eradicate poverty, promote economic develop and build a harmonious society. As one of the main carrier of information resources, academic library should take positive action, combine with all social forces, and devote to the protracted and tough fight of information services equalization.

References

1. Yu, L., Qiu, G.: Towards the Age of Universally Equal Services: On the Construction of a Public Library Service System in China. Journal of Library Science in China (3), 31–34 (2008)
2. Dong, M., Wu, Q.: The Roles and it Strength of Library in Social Information Fairness. Information Science (6), 820–823 (2009)
3. Xiao, A.: Discussion on the Advantages and Tactics for the Academic Libraries in the Process of Information Service Equalization. Library Work and Study 27(3), 12–15 (2009)
4. Chinese Academic Library Directors Forum: Wuhan Declaration for Library Cooperation and Information Resource Sharing. Journal of Academic Libraries 6, 1–4 (2005)
5. Li, K.: Innovation of the University Library Readers Services Mechanism from the Information Fairness. Academic Library and Information Service 8(1), 20–23 (2009)
6. Song, H., Zeng, W.: On the Public Library Service Innovation to Ensure Equal Access to Basic Public Services between the City and Countryside. Library (3), 27–29 (2009)

Situation Analysis and Countermeasure Study on Rural Vocational Education and Training for Modern Farmers' Cultivation Based on Information Technology

Chunying Weng[1] and Renyuan Yan[2]

[1] Faculty of Business Zhejiang Business Technology Institute, Ningbo, China
grace1808@yahoo.cn email
[2] Faculty of Business Ningbo University, Ningbo, China
ppoxiaogeda@126.com

Abstract. Farmer is an essential part of modern agriculture development and new countryside construct. The rural vocational education and training plays an important role in cultivating farmers' capabilities such as "knowledge, technology and management skill". Based on the investigation on the farmers engaged in agricultural production in rural areas in Ningbo, this paper makes a situational analysis on rural vocational education and training for modern peasants, and finally relative countermeasures are suggested to further develop rural vocational education and training, that is, the vocational education in rural areas should be positioned to meet the real demands of modern farmers.

Keywords: modern farmers, cultivation, rural vocational education and training.

1 Introduction

Farmers are the principal part of both developing rural society and modern agriculture. Therefore, modern farmers equipped with high capabilities can play an important role in promoting development of modern agriculture and construction of socialist new countryside effectively. However, the low capabilities of the farmers have become a great barrier to develop modern agriculture and the construct new socialist countryside for the time being. Therefore, how to improve the quality of farmers is on the top agenda [1]. The development of rural vocational education is able to improve the quality of labors. It is not only an important way to equip farmers with capabilities such as "knowledge, technology and management skill" but also an important measure to promote economic and social development in rural areas [2].

From the perspective of cultivating modern farmers and taking Ningbo as an example, this paper makes an analysis and study in order to explore the relative problems about vocational education and training in rural area in the process of cultivating modern farmers.

S. Lin and X. Huang (Eds.): CSEE 2011, Part V, CCIS 218, pp. 76–80, 2011.
© Springer-Verlag Berlin Heidelberg 2011

2 Situation Analysis

Nurturing new farmers is the most essential and core content of constructing new countryside. It is so important that it is on the top agenda of it. Ningbo is a relatively high industrialized and urbanized area. Under the leadership from Ningbo municipal government to " highly develop rural vocational education and training, the training system should be suitable for the social development of Ningbo city and industrial development as well and it should be developed with service-oriented regional characteristics," great changes have taken place in rural vocational education and training in recent years. Works on rural vocational education and training have been vigorously strengthened and well-planned rural vocational education and training have been carried out. More than 400 million Yuan has been invested cumulatively in farmer training from financial facilities at all levels since 2003. And the great joint efforts have led to rural vocational education and training system with Ningbo feature.

But compared with the goal of cultivation of modern farmers to equip them with capabilities such as "knowledge, technology and management skill", there still exists relatively big gap. Based on the questionnaires and interviews with 112 farmers who are living in Ningbo suburban area and who are engaged in agricultural production, we found that there are still some problems about vocational education in rural areas of Ningbo for the cultivation of new farmers after a careful analysis of the survey results. Main features are as follows:

1. The popularity of vocational education and training is not enough.

Farmers' proportion being surveyed in the vocational and technical training is significantly low. More than half farmers did not participate in vocational and technical training. Only 7.8% respondents took regular participation in it. The remaining 37.4% of farmers only participated occasionally. The above data shows more farmers in the countryside around the city of Ningbo need to take part in vocational education and training and needs to go there more frequently.

2. The traditional agricultural technical training should be further strengthened.

The survey found farmers' mastery for traditional agriculture-related technology is unsatisfactory. Approximately 59.6% of the surveyed farmers did not fully grasp the traditional agriculture-related technology which have already been applied and promoted in rural areas for many years. For example, they don't know how to select good varieties and make reasonable and rational use of fertilizer. One reason is that the respondents at home are relatively old and less educated and they find it difficult to accept and it takes time for them to master the relevant agricultural technology. The other reason is that those relatively young farmers are working in the local township and village enterprises accounting for 61.2% of the total respondents. They are relatively weak in mastering agricultural technology. It is necessary to further strengthen traditional agricultural technology training for farmers working at countryside.

3. The current contents of rural vocational education and training can not meet the diversified needs of the farmers.

Currently, the non-agricultural income is increasingly becoming an important part of the whole rural household income. Based on the survey "the most expected contents that farmers expect from vocational technology education", farmers are eager to have vocational education for food, beauty, hairdressing, accounting, agricultural products processing, storage and other non-agricultural aspects, which accounts for 95.61%. Among farmers' expectation for agriculture-related technologies, farming and breeding industry training reach as high as 87.96%. Most respondents believe that the current training content is not appropriate or not practical accounting for 68.36% and 79.45% respectively. It shows that rural vocational education and training is not well-targeted.

4. Resources of the rural vocational education and training available are not substantial and less advanced.

In the survey we found that resources of education and training in some rural areas are not well-integrated and that the resource advantages have not been fully realized. Many rural training facilities are in poor conditions. Some of the training bases are in great shortage of internship sites. It is difficult to carry out higher level or modern technical training because training teachers are not qualified in some training bases. About 92.52% of the respondents think that they would not attend vocational training because there are no local vocational training schools. More than half (51.2%) respondents believe ineffective organization and unreasonable guidance are a big problem for vocational training at present. At the same time, some of those surveyed (27.68% of the total number) believe that training teachers are not qualified, which makes it difficult to carry out higher-level technical training and modern new technology skills training. All in all, there are still some aspects being neglected. Lack of training entities and effective resources in rural areas remains a constraint for sustainable development of the vocational education and training in rural areas in the process of cultivation of modern farmers.

5. Channels for technology promotion and education and training services should be broadened.

According to the 112 respondents, agricultural technology that 60.56% of the farmers of are using come from the agricultural sector and professional associations, and part are from television, radio, newspapers, magazines, books, etc., which shows that the agricultural sector and professional associations are still the main sources where farmers accept and master agricultural technology. So, channels to help farmers to accept new technology to improve their qualities should be broadened and modes for technology promotion and education and training services should be diversified.

3 Countermeasures to Further Promote Vocational Education and Training for Rural Areas in the Process of Cultivation of Modern Farmers in Ningbo

The survey and analysis of the status quo of the vocational education and training for farmers engaged in agricultural production in suburban areas in Ningbo show that it is a complicated and systematic project to cultivate modern farmers. Through effective training, farmers can be equipped with new qualities such as "knowledge, technology and management skill." Only modern farmers with these new capabilities can provide a more effective intelligence support and personnel security for the development of modern agriculture and construction of new countryside. Therefore, it is essential to promote cultivating project for modern farmers by reconsidering the system, methods and contents of vocational education and training and adjusting its focus in rural areas accordingly.

1. Further strengthening the construction of agricultural training system

Because of the fact that rural labor force are low-educated, it is necessary to offer scientific and technical training for farmers to further improve the cultural and scientific accomplishment of farmers. Therefore, it is of utmost importance to cultivate modern farmers to improve their knowledge on culture, technology and management skills by strengthening the construction of agricultural training system and integrating education and training resources of agricultural sector so that the agricultural sector and professional associations can give full play to promote agricultural technology.

2. Improving mode of vocational education and training

Because farmers' demands towards vocational education and training are diversified, a more flexible mode should be adopted by improving the level, time and mode of vocational education and training. Take training venue for example, vocational training can be located in village, township and town where farmers live. As for training method, besides formal class teaching, face-to-face lectures and on-site training will be more effective. And "one issue one solution" training and short-term training will meet farmers' demand for skills training which are short, fast and direct. And the customized training will improve efficiency and effectiveness of training.

3. Adjusting the key point of rural vocational education and training under the new situation of construction of new countryside.

It is necessary to adjust the key point of it under the new situation of construction of new countryside. Firstly, as modern agriculture is developing very quickly, construction of new countryside asks for more qualified farmers, therefore, rural vocational education and training later on should adjust their working focus and pay more attention to the improvement of the capabilities of farmers. Secondly, multi-skilled and multi-profession training should be recommended for farmers step by step to help them gain more work chance. More types of training can improve the job options for farmers. Therefore, vocational education and training of farmers need to focus on practical technical training and vocational skills training as its main types.

4. Promoting construction of rural vocational education and training bases

We suggest establishing rural vocational education and training bases under the guidance of the government policy. Educational resource in counties (cities) should be integrated in the region to build integrated rural county-level vocational education and training base. Under the guidance of the base model of county-level vocational education and training in rural areas, each rural township should set up a township-level vocational education and training base. Meanwhile, the relatively large villages should rely on schools and other educational resources to build a number of village-level rural vocational education and training bases. Various vocational education and training programs planned by different government departments can be implemented by different levels of rural vocational education and training bases once the bases at all levels are established, thus a top-down vocational education and training bases management network can work effectively.

5. Strengthening the education and guidance to fully encourage the farmers to participate in vocational education and training

Farmers would be encouraged take part in vocational education and training voluntarily and it will create a good learning atmosphere. Moreover, incentive mechanisms and policies should be developed appropriately, for example, farmer can be granted with certain subsidy or certain benefits in loans or taxes if they obtain "professional qualification certificate" or professional title from vocational education and training.

6. Increasing government support and reduce peasants' burden

Government should pay attention to reducing training costs while providing paid training for farmers. It is of great significance to further develop rural vocational education and training for modern farmers by increasing government support, establishing and improving of investment mechanism in vocational education in the rural area, optimizing public finance support mode for rural vocational education methods.

4 Conclusion

Based on the investigation on the farmers engaged in agricultural production in rural areas in Ningbo, this paper makes a situational analysis on rural vocational education for modern peasants, and finally relative countermeasures are suggested to further develop rural vocational education and training, that is, it should be positioned to meet the real demands of modern farmers.

The objects of rural vocational education should include more than farmers engaged in agricultural production. Those who are migrant workers or people finished compulsory education should also be included in the occupational skills training and vocational education programs. Therefore, future research work will include further expanding the scope of the survey area and further investigation and analysis of vocational training for migrant workers and the offspring of farmers who have completed compulsory education and facing the choice of their job, rather than merely focusing on farmers engaged in agricultural production.

Acknowledgment. It is a project supported by Zhejiang Research Institute of Education Science under (SCC361).

References

1. Haiqing, G.: Modern farmer cultivation research from the perspective of adult education in rural areas. Rural Economics 2, 110–113 (2010)
2. Xiangrong, L.: Cultivation of new farmers in developing modern agriculture. Hubei Social Science 10, 52–54 (2010)
3. Qiuyue, L.: Studies on rural vocational education in constructing new countryside. Modern Rural Technology 3, 62–63 (2011)
4. Jieling, X., Wenxiang, W.: Farmers' quality status and cultivation of modern farmers from the perspective of new countryside. Anhui Agricultural Science Bulletin 37(13), 3176–6178 (2009)
5. Deyin, F., Xudong, Z.: Confusion and path selection for rural vocational education in constructing new countryside. Vocational Education Research 3, 52–56 (2009)

An Appraisal Method of the Interoperability of Architecture Based on DoDAF

Fabin Guo, Mingzhe Wang, and Ani Song

Dept. of Control Science & Engineering, Huazhong University of Science & Technology,
Wuhan 430074, China
{Guofabin,songani}@163.com, wangmzhe@netease.com

Abstract. An important factor in the Joint Operation, interoperability is regarded as the key to win a battle. This study proposes a quantitative method to assess the system interoperability at architecture level based on DoDAF (Department of Defense Architecture Framework). The proposed method works by extracting the systems and their interoperability features from the DoDAF model and by referring to the appraisal method of system similarity. The NMD (National Missile Defense Systems) is taken as an example to illustrate the proposed appraisal method.

Keywords: Interoperability similarity DoDAF architecture.

Introduction

The combat mode of modern battles has experienced great changes. Multi-Services and Arms Cooperation and Joint Operations between several countries have become the prevailing mode of modern battles. Consequently, great importance has been attached to improving the information exchange and utilization capability between cooperation units and strengthening the interoperability of combat effectiveness. In 1998, the C4ISR architecture working team of U.S. Department of Defense (USDD) proposed the DoD Levels of Information Systems Interoperability Model (LISI)[1], providing a general framework for defining, evaluating and measuring system interoperability. Several models or methods were proposed based on that model, such as the Organization's LISI-extending Operational Interoperability Model (OIM) by Clark and Jones[2], the Levels of Conceptual Interoperability Model (LCM) by Tolk and Muguira[3], the Carnegie Mellon System of Systems Interoperability Model (SoSI) by Morris[4], the method of measuring interoperability by questionnaire by Noelia Palomares[5], and the maturity model for digital government by Petter Gottschalk[6], etc. These models or methods, however, failed to carry out the quantitative evaluation on system interoperability, due to their excessive dependence on experts' or respondents' knowledge about the system. The Interoperability Score (i-Score) proposed by Ford and its optimized versions were only applicable to single-threaded systems[7,8], unable to measure and evaluate concurrent systems.Currently there is no perfect and widely applied method to appraise the interoperability due to the heterogeneity of system and system interoperation. Based on DoDAF, this study

S. Lin and X. Huang (Eds.): CSEE 2011, Part V, CCIS 218, pp. 81–87, 2011.

proposes a method to appraise the system interoperability at the architecture level. First, a system architecture model is established, from which the interoperating systems and their features are extracted, meanwhile the appraisal method of system similarity is used as a reference. Based on this, a quantitative measurement on the interoperability of a heterogeneous set of systems is achieved. The proposed method is widely applicable and highly flexible.

1   The Appraisal of Interoperability

The architecture framework provides the general procedure and product description standard for the integrated architecture design. The DoDAF, which is recognized as the most authoritative architecture framework in the world, provides a detailed description of the system architecture using 26 products from four views: All View(AV), Operational View(OV), System View(SV) and Technical View(TV). The description of DoDAF has been accepted as the standard for all integrated systems [9]. In this paper, first, the operational process of the system is modelled based on DoDAF, from which the interoperation features between systems are extracted. Then, the eigenvalues of the interoperability features between systems are defined, and the appraisal of system interoperability is carried out according to the interoperability appraisal function.

1.1   The Extraction of System Interoperation Features

After the model of system architecture is built based on the DoDAF standard, the interoperating systems need to be located and the interoperation features of systems need to be extracted. First, extract all the component systems according to SV-1 (Systems Interface Description) in DoDAF model. As SV-1 defines the interface between combat support systems, as shown in Fig. 1, all the systems can be directly extracted via SV-1. Then, determine the interoperability features between systems, i.e. specific interoperation activities, which can be defined mainly by three products in the DoDAF model: OV-2(Operational Node Connectivity Description), OV-3(Operational Resource Flow Matrix) and OV-5(Operational Activity Model).

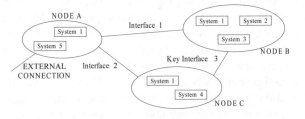

Fig. 1. The Representation of SV-1 in DoDAF Model

OV-2 in DoDAF model graphically visualizes the demand for information exchange and transfer among operational nodes (organizations) through needline, as is shown in Fig. 2. The physical realization of OV-2 is depicted by SV-1 and the operational nodes in OV-2 correspond to the system nodes in SV-1.

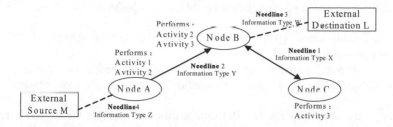

Fig. 2. The Representation of OV-2 in DoDAF Model

OV-3 identifies the information elements in information exchange and the properties relevant to them. It also links the information exchange with the operational nodes and operational activities that produce or consume information. Information exchange, as its name suggests, refers to the information-switching action between two operational nodes, and it corresponds to the needline of operational nodes in OV-2, while the exchange of each information element is related to the bottom operational activities (from OV-5) in which the information elements are produced and consumed. OV-5 not only depicts various kinds of normal activities operated for fulfilling a task or a goal and the input/output flows generated between these activities, but also depicts the input/output flows generated in activities beyond the scope of architecture. Being closely related to the information elements in OV-3, the input/output flows of operational activities can be described in a more detailed manner with the properties of information exchange in OV-3. Therefore, the process of identifying system interoperations and determining system interoperability features can be described as follows: first match the system nodes in SV-1 with the operational nodes in OV-2, then match the needlines of operational nodes in OV-2 with the information exchange in OV-3, finally match the information exchange in OV-3 with the operational activities in OV-5. It should be noted that the information elements in OV-3 matrix are not all in a one-to-one correspondence with the input/output flows in OV-5 that connect the operational activities, sometimes there might be one-to-many or many-to-many correspondence.

1.2 The Appraisal of System Interoperability

System similarity refers to the similarity degree between the features of two or more systems [10], and the similarity appraisal is a measurement of the similarity degree of the features of different systems. System interoperability represents the interoperation ability among systems, in another word, it reflects the similarity of interoperation performance among systems. So, when only the interoper-ability features are taken into consideration, the appraisal of system interoperability can be converted into the appraisal of similarity of system interoperability features.

Axiom: if only interoperability features among systems are taken into consideration, then the similarity of interoperability features can be taken as a reflection of the interoperability among systems.

Definition: a similarity appraisal function can be regarded as an interoperability appraisal function as long as it satisfies the following conditions:

1) Acquire value among [0, 1], in which 0 means no interoperability at all while 1 means perfect interoperability.
2) Reward shared interoperability features while punish the independent features.
3) The higher the degree of shared interoperability features, the more reward.

Based on the above Axiom and Definition, this study adopts the function in Eq. 1 as the appraisal function to appraise system interoperability. Assume that interoperation exists between system σ' and system σ'', and $\sigma'(i)$ denotes the eigenvalue of interoperation features xi of system σ', then the interoperability between system σ' and system σ'' can be appraised by Eq. (1):

$$ I = \left[\frac{\sum_{i=1}^{n} \sigma'(i) + \sum_{i=1}^{n} \sigma''(i)}{2nc_{\max}} \right] \left[1 - \left(\frac{1}{\sqrt{n}} \right) \left(\sum_{i=1}^{n} b_i \left(\frac{\sigma'(i) - \sigma''(i)}{c_{\max}} \right)^r \right)^{1/r} \right] \quad (1) $$

where $b_i = \begin{cases} 0 & \sigma'(i) = 0 \ or \ \sigma''(i) = 0 \\ 1 & esle \end{cases}$, $c_{\max}$ denotes the maximum eigenvalue, r denotes the

Minkowski constant, for which 2 is usually taken.

The study rates the eigenvalues corresponding to various system interoperation features into 3 grades {0, 1, and 2}. If the system is directly involved in a certain interoperating activity, then the corresponding eigenvalue is 2; if the system is indirectly involved in a certain interoperating activity (e.g. via other system or media), then the corresponding eigenvalue is 1; if the system is not involved in any interoperating activity at all, the eigenvalue is 0. Following the method described in section 2.1, define the eigenvalues in each case and substitute them into Eq. (1) to appraise system interoperability. In the following section the NMD system will be taken as an example to illustrate the application of this method.

2   The Measurement of Interoperability of NMD System

First, the architecture of NMD system is modeled based on the standard of DoDAF. Then, with the abovementioned methods and based on the SV-1 of DoDAF model of the NMD system architecture, five systems are identified, that is the EWS(early warning satellite) system, UEWR(upgraded early warning radar) system, X-Radar system, GBI(ground-based interceptor) system and BMC3(battle management, command, control and communication) system. Match all the systems with the corresponding nodes in OV-2, for example, match the EWS system with the operational nodes of EWS.The OV-3 model of NMD system architecture (part of) is shown in Table 1. The exchange information between nodes can be obtained by matching all the needlines of operational nodes in Fig. 3 with OV-3. For example, C1 corresponds to the information exchange between BMC3 nodes and UEWS nodes. The information being exchanged is UEWS Direction, etc.

Table 1. OV-3 Model of NMD System (part of)

Needline Identifier	Information Exchange Identifier	Information Element Information Element Name	Description Content	Producer Sending Op Node	Consumer Receiving Op Node
		...			
C1	C1	UEWS Direction	...	BMC3	UEWR
C2	C2	X-Radar	...	BMC3	X-Radar
C3	C3	GBI Direction	...	BMC3	GBI
		...			

The OV-5 model of NMD system architecture (part of) is shown in Fig. 3. By matching the UEWR guiding instruction in Table 1 with OV-5 in Figure 3, it can be learnt that the activity corresponding to the UEWR Direction is Guide.UEWR. Therefore the Guide.UEWR can be identified as the system interoperating activity, namely, the system interoperation feature. Other interoperability features can be identified in the same way. So, a set of interoperability features can be eventually decided for NMD system, which constitute set X: {Comm, C2.EWS, C2.UEWR, C2.X-Radar, C2.GBI, Guide.UEWR, Guide. X-Radar, Guide.GBI}

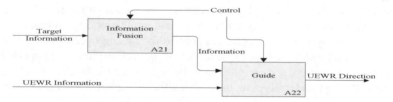

Fig. 3. OV-5 Model of NMD System (partly)

According to the scaling of interoperability eigenvalues in section 2.2, it can be found that: if BMC3 system can directly guide the Prewarning Radar, the corresponding eigenvalue would be 2; if the Prewarning Satellite guides the Prewarning system via BMC3 system instead of directly guiding it, the corresponding eigenvalue would be 1; if the Prewarning system can not guide Interceptor at all, the corresponding eigenvalue would be 0. The eigenvalues of interoperability features corresponding to all the systems are shown in Table 2.

Table 2. The eigenvalues of interoperability features corresponding to all the systems

	EWS	UEWR	X_Radar	BMC3	GBI
Comm	2	2	2	2	2
C2.EWS	2	0	0	2	0
C2.UEWR	0	2	0	2	0
C2.X-Radar	0	0	2	2	0
C2.GBI	0	0	0	2	2
Guide.UEWR	1	2	0	2	0
Guide. X-Radar	0	1	2	2	0
Guide.GBI	0	0	1	2	2

Table 3. The interoperability of NMD system

	EWS	UEWR	X-Radar	BMC3	GBI
EWS	0.312	0.309	0.375	0.54	0.438
UEWR	0.309	0.438	0.36	0.592	0.406
X-Radar	0.375	0.36	0.438	0.592	0.334
BMC3	0.54	0.592	0.592	1	0.687
GBI	0.438	0.406	0.334	0.687	0.375

With the eigenvalues in Table 2 and Eq.(1), the interoperability of NMD system can be obtained as shown in Table 3.

It can be seen from the Table 3 that the interoperability appraisal value of BMC3 system is high, which indicates that this system requires strong interoperation with other component systems. Based on the analysis of the system architecture model, it can be learned that BMC3 plays a central and coordinating role in the whole architecture. So to guarantee its connection, communication and interoperation with other component systems is of great importance for raising operational effectiveness. As we can see, analyzing the appraisal results of the architecture's interoperability can help both policy makers and developers to have a better planning and adjustment of the combat strategy and procedure, thus raising the effectiveness of the system.

3   Conclusions

As combat pattern changes, the appraisal requirements for system interoperability become more and more demanding. However, there is no perfect method to appraise the system interoperability due to the heterogeneity of systems and system interoperations. The system interoperability reflects the similarity of the interoperation performance among systems. In this paper, a system architecture is first modeled on the basis of DoDAF. Then, the interoperating systems and the interoperability features are extracted from the architecture model, and the interpretability of system architecture is quantitatively appraised by referring to the similarity appraisal method. The proposed method is applicable to various kinds of systems. The National Missile Defense system is taken as an example to illustrate the application of this method.

Further research still needs to be done to analyze the possibility of incorporating combat effectiveness into the appraisal of system interoperability.

Acknowledgment. This work was supported by a grant from the National Natural Science Foundation of China (No. 60874068).

References

1. C4ISR Interoperability Working Group. Department of Defense Levels of Information Systems Interoperability (LISI), Washington (1998)
2. Thomas, C., Robson, J.: Organizational Interoperability Maturity Model for C2. In: The 4th International Command and Control Research and Technology Symposium, Washington (1999)
3. Tolk, A., Muguira, J.: The Levels of Conceptual Interoperability Model. In: 2003 Fall Simulation Interoperability Workshop (2003)
4. Morris, E.: System of Systems Interoperability(SOSI), Final Report. Carnegie Mellon University, Software Engineering Institute, Pittsburgh (2004)
5. Palomares, N., Campos, C., Palomero, S.: How to Develop a Questionnaire in Order to Measure Interoperability Level in Enterprises. Enterprise Interoperability IV (2010)
6. Gottschalk, P.: Maturity levels for interoperability in digital government Government. J. Information Quarterly 26, 75–81 (2009)
7. Ford, T., Colombi, J., Graham, S., et al.: he Interoperability Score. In: Proceeding CSER (2007)
8. Ford, T., Colombi, J., Graham, S., et al.: Measuring System Interoperability. In: Proceeding CSER (2008)
9. DoD Architecture Framework Working Group. DoD Architecture Framework Version 1.5, vol. I, II. Department of Defense, The United States (2007)
10. Guan, Y., Wang, X., Wang, Q.: A New Measurement of Systematic Similarity. J. IEEE Transactions on Systems, Man, and Cybernetics—Part A: Systems and Humans 38, 743–758 (2008)

An Image Encryption Algorithm for
New Multiple Chaos-Based

XiaoJun Tong[*] and Yang Liu

School of Computer Science and Technology, Harbin Institute of Technology,
Weihai, 264209, China
tong_xiaojun@163.com

Abstract. An image encryption scheme based on high-dimensional dynamical multiple chaotic maps are proposed in this paper. In order to produce fast encryption and more avalanche effect, the circular shift algorithm is utilized to permute the positions of the image pixels in the spatial domain. The experimental results show that it is more efficient than traditional encryption schemes and it provides an secure way for image encryption.

Keywords: Image encryption, Dynamical Multiple chaos, Circular shift algorithm.

1 Introduction

In recent years, using chaotic theory to design encryption algorithm is a new research in cryptography, because chaotic systems are characterized by ergodicity, sensitive depend on initial conditions and random-like behaviors. These properties are of great importance in permutation and substitution process [1]. So encryption algorithms based on chaotic map are widely applied in cryptography frontier. In 1998, Baptista publicly published a paper about chaotic encryption algorithm. Many researches are carried based on this paper, a large number of experiments based on his proposed method started and some improved methods were proposed. At the same time, aimed at finding a safe and efficient image encryption method, many image encryption algorithms based on chaotic map had been extensively studied [2]. And chaotic maps are widely used in the algorithms such as Logistic map, Arnold cat map, Baker map, Standard map and Lorenz map [3].

However, the most serious problem in chaotic encryption algorithm is the finite precision effect [4]. Due to the limitation of computer finite precision, the finite precision effect may cause an existing sequence of infinite cycle into a sequence of short period. Tao Yang uses neural network to decrypt low-dimensional chaotic system, some academics have also decrypted simple one-dimensional multiple-chaotic system [5, 6].

So a high-dimensional multiple-chaotic map encryption algorithm is proposed in this paper, which based on Devaney [7] chaotic theory, to improve the security and confidentiality of the chaotic system.

---

[*] Corresponding author.

S. Lin and X. Huang (Eds.): CSEE 2011, Part V, CCIS 218, pp. 88–93, 2011.
© Springer-Verlag Berlin Heidelberg 2011

2 The Proposed Encryption Algorithm

The proposed encryption algorithm includes two parts: firstly, the values of the pixels are encrypted by multiple-chaotic map; secondly, the positions of the original image pixels are permuted by Circular shift algorithm.

Dynamical Multiple Compound chaos algorithm. The dynamical multiple-chaotic sequence that used in this encryption algorithm is generated according to the following rules:

$$
\begin{cases}
f_0(x_{n-1}) = 2x_{n-1}^2 - 1 \\
f_1(x_{n-1}) = 8x_{n-1}^4 - 8x_{n-1}^2 + 1 \\
x_n = F(x_{n-1}) = \begin{cases} f_0(x_{n-1}) & , x_{n-1} < 0 \\ f_1(x_{n-1}) & , x_{n-1} \geq 0 \end{cases}
\end{cases}
\tag{1}
$$

where $x \in I = [-1,1]$, mark $f_0(x) = 2x^2 - 1$, $f_1(x) = 8x^4 - 8x^2 + 1$. The system takes $f_0(x) = 2x^2 - 1$ or $f_1(x) = 8x^4 - 8x^2 + 1$ as the generator of the current chaotic random sequence dynamically. If the result generated by $f(x_{n-1})$ is less than zero, the system takes the output of $f(x_{n-1})$ as the input of $f_0(x)$, while if the result is greater than zero, the system takes the output of $f(x_{n-1})$ as the input of $f_1(x)$. So this key stream is more random than it just generated by one chaotic map. Formula (1) is passed chaos proof by Devaney's definition of chaos and has good randomness [8, 9].

Substitution algorithm of image. chaotic random sequence is generated by multiple-chaotic map given by formula (1), the steps are shown in Fig.1:

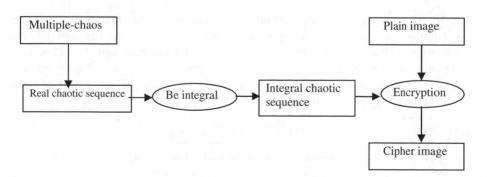

Fig. 1. Multiple-chaotic map encryption

Conduct to be integral is a produce that dividing chaotic domain $[-1,1]$ into N=256 parts sub domain π_i, i=0,1,...,N-1. $\pi_i = [t_i, t_{i+1})(i = 0,1,..., N-2)$, $\pi_{N-1} = [t_{N-1}, t_N]$. Where t_i is described as formula (4):

$$t_i = -\cos(\frac{i}{N}\pi), i = 0, 1, ..., N-1 \tag{4}$$

Mark the 256 parts sub domain as 0,1,…,255 from left to right and make real chaotic sequence $\{z_k\}_{k=1}^{\infty}$ into integral chaotic sequence $\{S_1(k)\}_{k=1}^{\infty}$ using formula (5), where $S_1(k)$ is described as formula (5):

$$S_1(k) = \begin{cases} \left\lfloor (1 - \arccos(z_k)/\pi) \bullet 256 \right\rfloor, & \text{if } z_k \in [-1,1) \\ 255, & \text{if } z_k = 1 \end{cases} \tag{5}$$

Permutation algorithm of image. The detailed process is that: First, we name the width of the pixels of each row as W and assign what input to initial values are x_0 and y_0. x_0 and y_0 are the first iteration values using formula (1). Second, we take the output of formula (1) to formula (5), using formula

$$S_2(k) = \begin{cases} \left\lfloor (1 - \arccos(x_{0k})/\pi) \times part \right\rfloor, & \text{if } x_{0k} \in [-1,1), \\ part\text{-}1, & \text{if } x_{0k} = 1. \end{cases}$$ we get a digit value named as $S_2(1)$. Third,

we make the first row of image shift $S_2(1)$ steps circularly. Using dynamical multiple compound chaos algorithm and formula (5), the remnant rows of the cipher will be permuted similarly. After we permute all the rows, we permute the entire columns with the same method.

3   Experiment Results and Security Analysis

Experimental parameter: multiple-chaotic map is given by formula (1), key pairs are (0.124758634526796, 0.57846325988644), the image is "24bit Lena" with size 256×256.

Sensitivity analysis. A good encryption algorithm should be sensitive to the secret key and the plaintext [12]. If the algorithm is sensitive to the secret key, and then use another key with only small different for image encryption; the results should be very different. The sensitivity to the secret key can be quantified by correlation coefficient given by formula (6), Where x_j and y_j are the values of two adjacent pixels in the image and N is total number of image pixels.

$$C_r = \frac{N \sum_{j=1}^{N}(x_j \times y_j) - \sum_{j=1}^{N}x_j \times \sum_{j=1}^{N}y_j}{\sqrt{(N \sum_{j=1}^{N}x_j^2 - (\sum_{j=1}^{N}x_j)^2) \times (N \sum_{j=1}^{N}y_j^2 - (\sum_{j=1}^{N}y_j)^2)}} \tag{6}$$

Two key pairs KEY1=(0.124758634526796, 0.57846325988644) and KEY2= (0.124758634526797, 0.57846325988645) which have only 10^{-14} different are chosen. The experimental results in Table 1 show that the proposed scheme is sensitive to the secret key.

Table 1. Sensitivity of secret key

Testing Content			Testing Results
Sensitivity of cipher to key (difference level of kye is 10^{-14})			-2.7146954005677062e-003
Sensitivity of cipher to plaintext testing (plaintext change 1 bit)	NPCR	Blue component	0.995941162109375
		Green component	0.9960479736328125
		Red component	0.995941162109375
	UACI	Blue component	0.33560300340839461
		Green component	0.33653211406632966
		Red component	0.33632662904028798
		Avalanche effect	0.499500527465820313

Statistical analysis. Many cipher texts have been successfully analyzed with the help of statistical analysis and an ideal cipher text should be robust against any statistical attack. The experimental results that are shown in histograms have proved the robustness of the proposed image encryption scheme.

An image-histogram illustrates how pixels in an image are distributed by graphing the number of pixels at each color intensity level. Using the scheme which mentioned in Section 2.2 to the image "Lena" with size 256×256, the histograms are shown in Fig.2, key pair is (0.124758634526796, 0.57846325988644).

 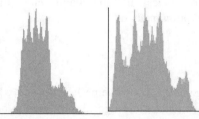 

   (a) plain text   (b) blue component (c) green component (d) red component

 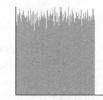 

  (e) Cipher text   (f) blue component (g) green component (h) red component

Fig. 2. Statistical analysis tests

Entropy Testing. Message entropy formula is as follows:

$$H(S) = \sum_{S} P(s_i) \log_2 \frac{1}{P(s_i)} bits \tag{7}$$

where $P(s_i)$ indicates that the probability of each symbol appearance. A statistical unit is 8 bytes, if the probability of every symbol in accordance with uniform distribution would be 1/8, so the entropy should be 8. But because of actually the probability is not in the same, a good encryption algorithm should make the entropy to 8 as close as possible. The entropy of experimental results is 0.7172870452731786.

Compare of encryption speed. The results of each encryption scheme are shown in table 2.

Table 2. Encryption speed of each scheme

Image for	DES encryption time	Multiple-chaotic map
encryption	(unit: s)	encryption time
House 8 bits	0.78714529360575158	0.54613326649979166
Lena 24 bits	4.7489820633628019	1.5843895025391523
Lena 8 bits	1.5772688987008125	0.53945983377245055

Compared with DES, dynamical multiple-chaotic encryption scheme has higher speed than traditional encryption methods.

4   Conclusions

In the paper, an fast image encryption scheme is proposed which utilizes dynamical multiple-chaotic map. The circular shift algorithm is used to permute the positions of image pixels in the spatial-domain and the mixing of confusion and diffusion can produces more randomness. The experimental results demonstrate that he precision of cipher is sensitive to the secret key approach to 10^{-14} and the proposed image encryption technique has advantages of high-level security.

Acknowledgements. This work was supported by the National Natural Science Foundation of China (Grant No. 60973162), the Natural Science Foundation of Shandong Province (Grant No. ZR2009GM037), Science and technology of Shandong Province of China (Grant No.2010GGX10132), the Scientific Research Foundation of Harbin Institute of Technology at Weihai (Grant No. HIT(WH) ZB200909), and the Key Natural Science Foundation of Shandong Province of China (Grant No. Z2006G01).

References

1. Zhang, L., Liao, X., Wang, X.: An image encryption approach based on chaotic maps. Chaos, Solitons & Fractals (24), 759–765 (2005)
2. Fridrich, J.: Symmetric ciphers based on two dimensional chaotic maps. Int. J. Bifurcat Chaos 8(6), 1259–1284 (1998)
3. Fu, C., Zhang, Z.C., Cao, Y.Y.: An Improved Image Encryption Algorithm Based on Chaotic Maps. In: IEEE Proceedings of the third International Conference on Natural Computation (ICNC 2007), Haikou, China, vol. 3, pp. 189–193 (2007)
4. Kwok, H., Tang, W.: A fast image encryption system based on chaotic map with finite precision representation. Chaos, Solitons & Fractals 32, 1518–1529 (2007)
5. Chen, J.C., Guo, J.I.: A new chaotic key based design for image encryption and decryption. In: Proceedings of the IEEE International Symposium Circuits and Systems, vol. 4, pp. 49–52 (2000)
6. Wei, J., Liao, X.F., Wong, K.W., Tao, X.: A new Chaotic Cryptosystem. Chaos, Solutions & Fractals 30, 1143–1152 (2006)
7. Xiang, T., Liao, X.F., Tang, G., Chen, Y., Wong, K.W.: A novel block cryptosystem based on iterating a chaotic map. Phys. Lett. A (349), 109–115 (2006)
8. Tong, X.J., Cui, M.: Image encryption with compound chaotic sequence cipher shifting dynamically. Image and Vision Computing 26(6), 843–850 (2008)
9. Tong, X.J., Cui, M.: Image encryption scheme based on 3D baker with dynamical compound chaotic sequence cipher generator. Signal Processing 89(4), 480–491 (2009)

Design and Application of the PID Control System of IMC^{*,**}

Minghui Li and Xiankun Meng

Shannxi University of Science &Technology, Xi'an, China
liminghui1972@126.com, mengxiankun668@qq.com

Abstract. Through analyzed and researched the respective advantages of PID and IMC system, and integration of the advantages of both, combined with the realization question of IMC based on its structure, proposed a method of PID parameter tuning based on thoughts of IMC, compared internal (model controller with the traditional PID controller to determine each parameter values of PID control system of IMC,designed the PID control system of IMC. Practical application shows that ,in the case of disturbance and mismatch in the parameters, this system can still obtain better control effect, beneficial in engineering applications.

Keywords: IMC, Filter, Model error, Decay curve, Robustness.

0   Introduction

Internal model control (IMC) is a very practical control methods, since its has been formation, it get a lot of applications in the slow response of process control and achieved more superior effect than PID in the fast response of the motor control. Traditional PID control algorithm has the advantages: Low requirement on the model, Simple Controller, being easy to implement, Fewer adjustable parameters, being easy to operators' Online regulation, better Control effect [1]. But in the field of industrial process control, many of the mechanism of the controlled process is more complex, have the characteristics of highly nonlinear, time-varying and pure delay etc. For the existence of uncertainty factor which is parameter changes、 interference etc. The parameters of conventional PID tuning is difficult to adapt to a wider range of uncertainty of the system and obtain satisfactory control effects. When the parameter changes of controlled objects is beyond a certain range, robustness of conventional PID controller is poor, which should be avoided during Industrial production. The main characteristic of IMC are simple structure、 easy and intuitive design、 fewer adjustable parameters online, and the policy of adjustments is clear and adjustments are easy, especially for the improvement of the robustness and immunity and the

---

 * Shaanxi University of Science and Technology Foundation projects of research and innovation team (SKTD10-02).
** This project was supported by the Graduate Innovation Fund of Shaanxi University of Science and Technology.

S. Lin and X. Huang (Eds.): CSEE 2011, Part V, CCIS 218, pp. 94–99, 2011.

control of large delay system, the effect is particularly significant, this makes it gain more and more applications widely during the Industrial process control [2].The design combines the advantages of both, designing PID control system of IMC can enhance the level of design of PID controller ,and are better than the strategy of traditional PID control In terms of both immunity and robustness performance in system.

1   Principle and Structure on IMC

IMC is a new control strategy Which is based on a mathematical model of process to carry on the design of the controller,when modeling errors or disturbances happen, filter will play a role to restrain interference or model mismatch that leads to the difference of actual output and model output. The structure of IMC is shown in Figure 1, it was generated through the transformation based on the traditional feedback control [3]. In the actual control system,the mathematical model of controlled object can be regarded as first or second link with pure delay, after the link with pure delay is used by Pade approximation ,IMC can be converted into a conventional unit feedback control ,which can make the design of internal model controller more simple and practical.

In Figure 1,G_{IMC} (S) is the internal model controller,G (s) is the control object,G_m (s) is the plant model,R (S) is the reference input of system , E (s) is the control error , U (s) is the control output , Y (s) is the output of system , D (s) is unknown disturbances that affects the system ,F (s) is the feedback signal . G_{IMC} (S) and G_m (s) Surrounded by dotted line part combine into a box and get a classic feedback control system G_c(s),and feedback signal: F(s)=[G(S)-Gm(s)]U(s)+D(s),Among them, G_c(s) is the PID feedback controller.

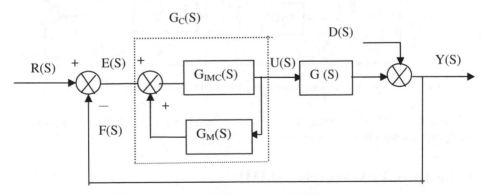

Fig. 1. Classic equivalent mode of IMC structure

From figure 1 can obtain:

$$G_c(S) = \frac{G_{IMC}(S)}{1 - G_{IMC}(S)G_m(S)} \tag{1}$$

Figure 1 change into the form shown in Figure 2,in the figure what surrounded by dotted line part is an internal model controller, that is:

$$G_{IMC}(S) = \frac{G_C(S)}{1 + G_C(S)G_{m-}(S)} \qquad (2)$$

$$Y(S) = \frac{G_{IMC}(S)G(S)}{1 + G_{IMC}(S)[G(S) - G(S)]} R(S) + \frac{1 - G_{IMC}(S)G_m(S)}{1 + G_{IMC}(S)[G(S) - G(S)]} D(s) \qquad (3)$$

If G_m (s) = G (s),the system's dynamic characteristics are determined by G_{IMC} (s) G (s),for G (s) is a inherent function of physical system and does not change, but manual intervention can affect the G_{IMC} (s),so it can change the response of output .

If G_{IMC} (0) G_m (0) = 1, system has no stable bias of constant disturbance.

If G_m(s) =G (s) and D(s) = 0, then the output of model and output of process Y(s) are equal, at this time the feedback signal is 0, under the condition of no uncertainties of model and no unknown input, the system of IMC have open-loop structure, which shows that in terms of open-loop stable process the purpose of the feedback is to overcome the uncertainty of the process.

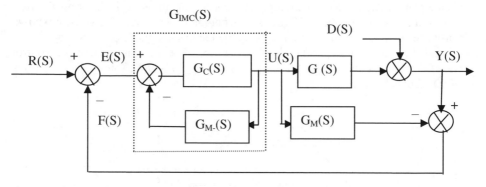

Fig. 2. IMC equivalent structure of classic mode

When G_m (s)≠G(s), selecting G_{IMC}(s) can realize parameters of factors to improve the dynamic characteristics of system.

2 Design of PID Controller of IMC

Equation (2) shows, to realize the system's "ideal control" and restrain interference, must meet that GIMC(s) is the reciprocal of transfer function of the model about actual system—Gm^{-1}(s), but gaining the full reciprocal of the transfer function on actual system can not be achieved for the restrictions of the terms , internal model controller can not be taken as G_m^{-1} (s).

The core question of PID control system design of IMC is how to process model combined with internal model controller, and combined with the PID controller design. to solve the problem, First, do decomposition of the actual object prediction model:

$$G_m(s) = G_{m+}(s)\, G_{m-}(s) \qquad (4)$$

In the equation, $G_{m-}(s)$ means the smallest phase characteristics part of prediction model $G_m(s)$, $G_{m+}(s)$ means not the smallest phase characteristics part of prediction model $G_m(s)$, like the zero dote in right half plane or pure delay etc, define : $G_{m+}(0)=1_o$ If take the internal model controller $G_{IMC}(s) = G_{m-}^{-1}(s)$, then:

$$G_C = \frac{G_{IMC}(S)}{1 - G_{IMC}(S) G_{m-}(S)} \qquad (5)$$

Usually, model error easily lead to instability in this system, the system is very sensitive to modeling errors. In order to solve this problem, can extend a low-pass filter f (s) on G_{IMC} (s) in order to achieve the robust stability performance of the closed-loop system, define: $f(s)=1/(\lambda s+1)$, now the form of the structural internal model controller is shown below:

$$G_{IMC}(s) = G_{m-}^{-1}(s)\, f(s) \qquad (6)$$

For the process with time delay , in order to get a PID equivalent form of controller, pure delay time needs do first-order Pade approximate, namely: $e^{-\theta s} = (1 - 0.5\theta s) / (1 - 0.5\theta s)$, so do first-order Pade approximation in delay time, have:

$$G_m(s) \approx \frac{K_p(1 - 0.5\theta s)}{(Ts + 1)(1 + 0.5\theta s)} \qquad (7)$$

Get its minimum phase part, designing the form of internal model controller below:

$$G_{IMC}(s) \approx \frac{(Ts + 1)(1 + 0.5\theta s)}{K_p(\lambda s + 1)} \qquad (8)$$

Substitute equation (8) into equation(6), available:

$$G_{PID} = K_C \left(1 + \frac{1}{T_i s} + T_d s\right) \qquad (9)$$

Compared with the form (9) of the actual PID feedback controller, available:

$$K_C = \frac{T + 0.5\theta}{K_p \lambda}$$

$$T_i = T + 0.5\theta \qquad (10)$$

$$T_d = \frac{0.5T\theta}{T + 0.5\theta}$$

In the equation, KC is proportionality constant; T_i is integral constant; T_d is differential constant. Then will do configuration in the control algorithm of DCS according to equation (9), and design the parameters of PID controller according to equation (10), just complete the task of the PID control system of IMC.

By using Pade approximation, this means filtering factor can't take any small, because Pade approximate cause model with uncertainty, suggest take $\lambda \geq \theta$ [4]. Usually, adjustment of filter parameters according to the error constantly choice. Feedback filter λ is larger, the response more slowly, while the less sensitive to model error; conversely, fast response but lack of robustness, easy to cause oscillation [5]. When the error is larger, to make the error decreases rapidly and output tends to the settings value in the fastest speed, λ should take a smaller value, along the error gradual decreases, value of λ is also growing larger; When the error is smaller, if the system response will have appeared overshoot tendency, in order to prevent output produce overshoot and appear oscillation, λ should take larger values. If the system response is slowly tends to the setting value, in order to accelerate the response transition process, but to prevent overshoot, λ should take moderate values.

3 Example Applications

Now simulating specific process of first order and time delay, according to mathematical model $G(S)=\dfrac{1.2}{5s+1}e^{-3s}$ about the control system of Total pressure of the Hydraulic headbox on a paper machine. respectively, can carry on simulation study with Z-N Tuning,Decay curve, IMC controler and IMC-PID controler.

Z-N Tuning: through the composition of pure proportional controller, get the oscillation curve of equal amplitude, based on the actual, K_P=2.74,T_C=10. According to Tuning formula of Z-N critical proportion degree, K_C=1.64,T_i=5.0,T_d=1.2.

Decay curve: proportional band adjust from big to small,when the curve appears 4:1 decay curve Write down the value δ and period Ts. According to the actual experience and PID tuning formula have : K_C=1.26,T_i=0.25,T_d=1.

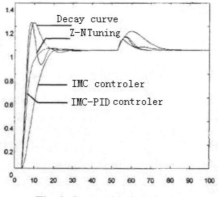
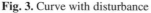
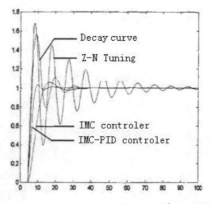

Fig. 3. Curve with disturbance   **Fig. 4.** Perturbed cage of K+20%, T-20%, 0+10%

IMC-PID parameter tuning: according to mathematical model about the control system of Total pressure of the Hydraulic headbox, T=5, K_P=1.2, θ =3, Filter: $f(s)$ =1/(λs +1),In which to take λ =5.5,substituting (10) can be have: K_C=0.984, T_i=6.5, T_d=1.154.

In SIMULINK, establishing simulation model of the PID control system of IMC, and comparing with the adjustments of internal model and the traditional PID, Figure 3, 4 as part of the simulation results.

Application of total pressure control system of Hydraulic headbox on paper machine shows that in the case of 20% increase in the gain K,20% reduction in time constant T,10% increase in delay, Respectively, the PID control system of IMC have better moderating effect and stronger ability of anti-interference and a certain robustness.

4   Conclusion

PID control system of IMC have being designed maintains the characteristics of traditional PID control and has all the advantages of IMC, Its structure is simple, being easy to tune, taking into account the system robustness and the performance of the system control, it can transformed internal model controller into the PID parameters and can be directly applied to existing installations without any adjustment of hardware, the form of its PID is easy for the engineers and technicians to accept and understand, easy to implement and upgrade existing control systems. After using the first order Pade approximation in the link of pure delay, the control system, using principle of IMC can obtain tuning values of parameter of PID controller. This way has obtained more satisfactory control performance, it has some significance in better research on the control of uncertain large delay and nonlinear system objects.

References

1. Yang, Z., Yihua Huang, H.Z.: Controller design and summary of parameter tuning method. Automation and Instruments in Chemical Industry 32(5), 1–7 (2005)
2. Gong, X., Gao, J., Zhou, C.: The expansion of IMC Tuning Method in PID controller with Time Delay Systems. Control and Decision 13(4), 311 (1998)
3. Wang, W., Pan, L., Kongand, D.: Robust controller design of IMC-PID and its application in distillation unit. Journal of beijing University of Chemical Technology 31(5), 93–95 (2004)
4. Controller. Computer Engineering and Applications 44(32), 220–222 (2008)
5. Pan, X., Zhong, Y.: Design and Realization of PID Control Based on IMC. Computer Simulation 22(8), 80–82 (2005)

The English Teaching Model of Cooperative Learning in the Network Environment in Higher Vocational Education

Jianwei Song and Hui Wu

Shijiazhuang Institute of Railway Technology, Shijiazhuang, Hebei, China
happypuppy999@126.com, huihui801121@126.com

Abstract. Cooperative leaning techniques have their own unique advantages for the teacher and the students. This paper is to discuss the English teaching model of cooperative learning in the network environment in higher vocational education based on theory of cooperative learning and theory of computer-assisted cooperative learning. First, it introduces the characteristics of the computer-assisted cooperative learning, and then it analyzes the process of the English teaching model of cooperative learning in the network environment. Furthermore, it discusses the specific contents of each element of cooperative learning in the network environment. At last, it gives its advantages and future development.

Keywords: Cooperative learning teaching model higher vocational English network.

1 Introduction

Cooperative learning refers to "a set of processes which help people interact together in order to accomplish a specific goal or develop an end product which is usually content specific" (Ted Panitz, 1997). Recently research has shown that cooperative learning techniques can promote students' learning and academic achievement, enhance students' satisfaction with their learning experience, improve students' retention, develop students' social skills, help students develop skills in oral communication, help to promote positive race relations and promote students' self-esteem and so on. Therefore, in higher vocational English instruction model, we should integrate the cooperative learning strategies with modern technology. In the English teaching model of cooperative learning in the network environment, each member of the group will achieve the same study target by working cooperatively. And each member can share information and learning materials during the course of exploration and discovery with other members, other groups even with all classmates.

2 The Computer-Assisted Cooperative Learning

The computer-assisted cooperative learning includes two aspects. One is cooperative learning, the other is the tools supporting cooperative learning such as multimedia and

S. Lin and X. Huang (Eds.): CSEE 2011, Part V, CCIS 218, pp. 100–104, 2011.

network technology. The computer-assisted cooperative learning has the following characteristics:

Firstly, it has the character of openness in the space. It breaks through the richness of the world and the net spatiotemporal bounds. The learning, communication and cooperation activities can proceed in an even wider scope of time and space.

Secondly, it has the character of verities in the content. A wide varieties of multimedia teaching resources can create an authentic cooperation circumstance and arouse the students' learning interest.

Thirdly, it has the character of interactivity in the interface. The interface is friendly to both teachers and students and there are plenty of interactive forms. The interactive tools can make the different cooperation and communication easy for the learner from the different positions thereby the construction of knowledge will be realized to some extent. Meanwhile, in the "learning centeredness" of the higher vocational English instruction model, there is a more harmonious relationship among teachers, students and learning process and the interoperability will be more strengthened.

Fourthly, it has the character of humanism in the organization. The organizational ways of hypermedia for the resources can arouse students' enthusiasm and develop creative thinking out of the students. Furthermore, they can stimulate and lead students to explore knowledge actively and individually.

3   The Cooperative Learning of Higher Vocational English Instruction Model in the Network Environment

The cooperative learning in the network environment refers to the fact that computer and network can offer various kinds of learning conditions to support the learners to learn individually and encourage them to communicate and cooperate with one aother in order to accomplish the learning tasks. This kind of virtual environment includes video session, chatting room, message board, E-mails, blog, twitter and so on. With the network, the teacher can store the learning resources into the resource library of the campus network where the students can search and find the materials they needs. At the same time, the teacher should integrate the learning resources, design and offer the efficient searching methods in order to promote the students' operation of the learning strategies and increase learning efficiency. On the other hands, students can learn from the resources individually, explore knowledge cooperatively and construct new knowledge constantly thus cultivate their awareness and self- learning ability. The following (Chart 1) will display the model of cooperative learning of higher vocational English instruction in the network environment.

The activities of cooperative learning mainly start with questions and will take different types according to different questions. First, the theme will be set and each group is assigned an exclusive task. Then, each student in the group should collect and reorganize materials, communicate with other members, learn together and reach an agreement. After that, each group can share learning resources and exchange experiences. If they have difficulty which they couldn't solve in their discussion, they can publish it in the BBS for help. At last, each group will present their learning outcomes.

Chart 1 the cooperative learning of higher vocational English instruction model in the network environment

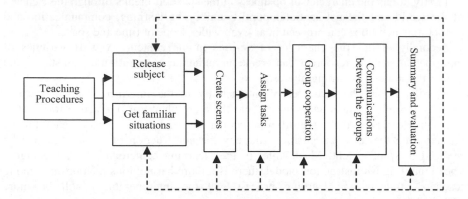

In order to ensure the efficiency of cooperation learning, the teacher should guide the students timely in case they couldn't solve certain problems. And he should organize, manage, supervise and coordinate during the instruction. Of course, the activities of cooperative learning should include the teacher's activities and the groups' activities. The following (Chart 2) will display the process of cooperative learning in the network environment.

Chart 2 the process of cooperative learning under the network

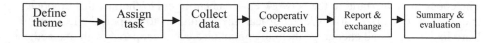

The Elements of Cooperative Learning in the Network Environment

According to the above discussion, the cooperative learning in the network environment should include the following elements.

Learning target. The teacher can help his students find right orientation and methods of study by setting learning goals. Furthermore, the teacher can help them analyze the goal and confirm the learning theme in order to motivate their learning desire and promote their learning interest and enthusiasm. In this way, learning is becoming a need to students who are more likely to participate. This innovative teaching method makes the students shift from "being forced to study" to "being willing to learn ".

Students. As students are the main body of learning, the teacher should fully know his students from different aspects such as their cognitive ability, psychological characteristics, cooperative learning ability with others and so on. In the network environment, students can act as different roles, such as individual learner, group member, cooperator in the group and other roles. each role will build up different abilities.

Network environment. Multimedia network classroom is the hardware platform of the cooperative learning in the network environment which is based on the local area network (LAN) and at same time it is equipped with the function of processing multimedia Input and Output. In the classroom of this kind, teacher's teaching and students' learning can flow in two ways. The hardware of the Multimedia network classroom should include dedicated server, network switching equipments, multimedia processing equipments (MPE) and so on while the software should include network operating system (OS), reciprocal teaching software, multimedia computer assisted instruction (MCAI) software and so on. The MCAI software should be open and modularized in order to expand its function easily.

Projects and tasks. The projects and tasks are the core elements in cooperative learning. The teacher gives the students relevant learning projects and specific learning tasks according to the learning target. The topics should be convenient for students' thinking from different angles. Only if the students know the learning tasks clearly, they can start learning activities efficiently.

Strategies and techniques. While implementing the cooperative learning in the network environment, we should choose proper strategies and techniques such as construction strategy and its teaching method which usually includes three teaching methods, that is, scaffolding instruction, situated or anchored instruction and Shorthand instruction.

Learning group. If students learn in well-organized groups, the effect will be better than in the traditional class. Whether learning groups are well-organized will directly affect the quality and the effectiveness of learning. In a well-organized group, the learners have an organic relation. On the one hand, the learners should finish the task individually. On the other hand, they should communicate with each other to accomplish the whole learning target. In group organization, the following factors should be considered: the same learning desire and similar individuality of the learners. The learning groups in the network environment include the following: discussion type, partnership type, collaborative type, competing type and role-play type and so on.

The teacher. The teacher should integrate all resources and design the learning activities during the cooperative learning. At the same time, he should not only play the role of transmitter of various kinds of information, but also the organizer of the students' study activities. Furthermore, he should guide and help the students timely and evaluate the learning process and learning outcomes.

Learning outcomes. The learning outcomes can be reports, papers and so on. The teacher should control this process and summarize the advantages and disadvantages, then give every student a proper evaluation. The evaluation of the learning outcomes will include the following four aspects: testing objectives, self-evaluation, evaluation of the group, and evaluation from the teacher. In this model, we should evaluate not only the learning outcomes, but also the learning process.

4 Conclusion

The cooperative learning in the network environment will play an important role gradually among all the learning models for its distinct superiorities. In this learning model, the teacher and the students, the students and the students, the students and the groups will interact with each other and the students' abilities, behaviors, emotions and experiences will be enhanced greatly. With the development of computer and network technology and the increase of students' demands on knowledge, single classroom teaching couldn't satisfy the students' needs. Therefore, developing the cooperative learning in the network environment is of profound significance in higher vocational English instruction model.

References

1. Panitz, T.: Collaborative versus Cooperative Learning: A Comparison of the Two Concepts Which Will Help Us Understand the Underlying Nature of Interactive Learning. Cooperative Learning and College Teaching 8(2), 13 (1997)
2. Kagan, S.: Cooperative Learning. Kagan Publishing (1994)
3. Jolliffe, W.: Cooperative learning in the classroom: putting it into practice. Paul Chapman (2007)
4. Slavin, R.E.: Cooperative learning: theory, research, and practice. Allyn and Bacon (1995)
5. David, M.: Implementing Computer Supported CO-Operative Learning. Routledge, New York (2000)
6. Schwartz, L.M., Willing, K.R.: Computer Activities for the Cooperative Classroom. Stenhouse Publishers (2001)
7. Wolfvilw, N.S. (ed.): ICCAL 1992. LNCS, vol. 602. Springer, Heidelberg (1992)
8. Thompson, J.: Cooperative Learning in Computer-Supported Classes. VDM Verlag (2008)

Research on the Curriculum System Reconstruction of Physical Education in Colleges and Universities with Information Technology—Based on Physical Education Club Mode

Dinghong Mu[1], Jian Liu[2], and Xiaobing Fan[3]

East China Institute of Technology, Jiangxi Nanchang, 344000
dhmu1970@sina.com

Abstract. By methods of the documentation, generalization and extension, logic and analysis, the paper, based on physical education club mode, proposes the course system reconstruction of PE in coping with the shortcomings of PE course system such as, the course system deviating from objective reality, neglecting the dialectical unity of course system and goals, teaching mode and college students' physical and psychological features.

Keywords: Colleges and universities, physical education course system, reconstruction, PE club, teaching mode.

1 Introduction

The main goal of PE in Chinese colleges and universities is "efficiently do exercise, to promote the normal development of college students, to develop the body shape and physiological function of college students, to improve the physique". [1] An Outline of National Ordinary College Sports Teaching Instruction (Physical and Art Education [2002] 13) claims that PE is a common compulsory course, taking physical exercise as the main method, through reasonable sports education and scientific physical fitness to improve the physique, strengthen health and develop the sports and cultural qualities; a crucial section of college course system; the key link of PE work in colleges and universities. However, during the PE course implementation, people always pay attention to the research and practice of single segment, neglecting the dialectical unity of sports aim, course system, teaching mode and college students' physical and psychological features, which leads to the fact that the effect of PE course implementation is not good, such as the decreasing of students' physical physique, the increasing appearance of mental obstacles, the impaired social adaptability and so on. Based on the current common club-teaching mode, the paper proposes an assumption on PE course system reconstruction in colleges and universities for the relative researchers and personnel for reference only.

2 The Concept and Features of PE Club Mode

Based on the combination of students' consciousness, stadiums and gymnasiums on the campus and a sports event, PE club mode is a sports teaching mode, by means of

S. Lin and X. Huang (Eds.): CSEE 2011, Part V, CCIS 218, pp. 105–111, 2011.

club organization, to combine sports teaching, extracurricular sports, sports training and mass games as a whole. [2]It means to inspire and induce students to learn and do exercise with their own intelligence and ability, which shows students' subject consciousness of PE learning, cultivates students' interests in sports as well as arouses the enthusiasm of teachers; the introduction and regulation on students' sporting life develop the coherence and consistency of sports teaching and extracurricular physical fitness; to extend the sports teaching far around the whole education in colleges and universities by throwing convention on course schedule; to promote the construction of campus culture and improve sports competition skills; [3] to strengthen students' sports consciousness, cultivate the sporting habits and activate the campus sports cultural atmosphere; to develop sports activities by means of PE clubs, which is beneficial to cultivate backbone for mass sports and to promote campus sports culture construction. [4]

3   Thinking on PE Course System Reconstruction in Colleges and Universities

An Outline of National Ordinary College Sports Teaching Instruction defines Chinese college PE course objective as follows, sports participation, sports skills, physical fitness, psychological health and social adaptability. The construction of course system is bound to on the basis of course objective. In the view of the structure theory principle, the entire PE course should contains guideline, content system, teaching material system, assessment system and management system, which are interconnected, complementary to each other and neither is dispensable. According to the basic feature of PE course system "element—structure--function",[1] on the basis of each element optimization, people should grasp and integrate all elements, making the maximal relevance to course objective together (see figure 1).

Fig. 1. System reconstruction diagram on PE course objective in colleges and universities

Based on the integration of the relevance between course elements and course objective, by means of systemic method, people can select guideline system, content system, teaching material system and assessment and management system as the four main variables from the mass variables among course system, building up and improving course frame to reach the entire optimization of the course (see figure 2).

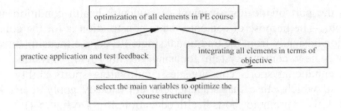

Fig. 2. Thinking on PE course system reconstruction in colleges and universities

4 Reconstruction Assumption on All Elements in PE Course System in Colleges and Universities

Guideline system of course objective. The transformation of sports course from single function to comprehensive functions requires: First, to absorb and embody the education functions as healthy education, cultural education and lifelong education. (1) to combine health education and sports education as a whole. (2) to cultivate students' positive attitude and understanding on sports through the teaching transmission of sports culture. (3) to cultivate students' lifelong consciousness of physical fitness and to learn the practice process on lifelong sporting. Second, taking "to improve students' subjective development through course teaching" as the main clue of teaching, people can accept and absorb the concept of "to improve the all-round development of students' physiology, psychology and social adaptability" to create the practical and creative experiences for students through teaching. Figure 3 shows PE course multi-function transforms to the course objective through organic integration.

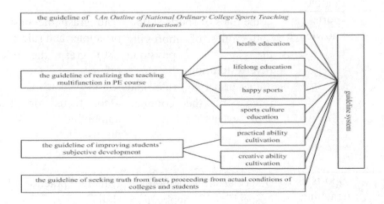

Fig. 3. Thinking on PE course guideline system in colleges and universities

The reconstruction of PE course content system. The PE course content in colleges and universities should adapt to the development of the current modern education concept and social requirement. The selection and organization of sports course should tend to the development orientation on integration, systemic and scientific, which can embody not only the function and comprehensive value of sports teaching but also on the part of the improvement of students' health condition and lifelong sporting habits. The purpose of content system construction is for the content system transformation basically from the traditional single PE course focusing on sports skills teaching to a new content system focusing on improving physique, developing personality, enhancing sports consciousness, cultivating sports ability and lifelong sporting habit, which cause that students can consciously apply sports knowledge, method and skills to promote sports health education. [5] (see figure 4)

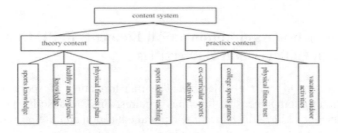

Fig. 4. Thinking on the construction of the new PE course content system

According to the train of thought in figure 4, the new course content in colleges and universities can be list as follows (see table 1).

Table 1. The basic frame of the new course content system in colleges and universities

content system	content module	course content frame	basic requirement of course content
theory content	sports knowledge	①the rules of sports skills; ②the rules of improving the physique (overrestoration); ③the principle, rule and referee of the common sports events; ...	①to grasp the basic sports principles and rules; ②to grasp the rules and referee of the common sports events; ③to focus on teaching, combining students discussion. ...
	...	...	...
practice content	Sports skills teaching	①special skills method ②special skills application ③special strategic application ...	①more practice for the skills ②fewer but better for the skills (focus on the key link of sports skills system) ③the skills are simple but practical. ...

Systemic reforms for the college sports course assessment system. The assessment concepts are changed from discrimination embodiment, function selection to encouraging enhance and function development; the assessment content extends from the single "biology" field to "biology, psychology and sociology"; the assessment standard changes from quantification, absolute assessment to the combination of quantitative and qualitative, relativity and absolutity; the assessment method transforms from a teacher assessment to the assessment by students themselves, by each other, by the combination of teacher and students, process assessment and results assessment.

During the assessment system, the content should focus on weight of skills grasping and sports participation, and pay attention to the knowledge master of health. The sporting skills level usually determines the physical fitness persistence of students. The lifelong sports habit is on the basis of certain sports skills to a great extent. The sports participation weight in assessment can efficiently guide students (esp. students in a bad physique) to take part in sports, which can be an effective measure for students to grasp the sports skills and to inspire the sporting interest. The health knowledge is the fundamental prerequisite for students to know their own physical problems, induce the physical fitness demand and do exercise in a scientific way. Based on the above concept, during the course reforming, the assessment system can be made as follows. (see table 2).

Table 2. Basic frame of college PE course assessment system

check content	assessment content	assessment method	Weight (%)
skills master	① special skill assessment ② special skill proficiency assessment ③ special skill application assessment	quantitative and qualitative assessment in terms of the skill mastery and application condition	40
learning attitude	①attendance records ②participation records ③ex-curricular sports records	the combination of quantitative and qualitative assessment based on attendance records, classroom record and physical fitness registration card	30
basic theory knowledge	①basic sports knowledge ②health and hygienic knowledge ③to make individual physical fitness plan	Through the method of ex-curricular work and testing in the class to make assessment	20
fitness test	to select the testing content for fitness test	Quantitative assessment in terms of "physique health test standard"	10

Course teaching material system. The teaching material directly reflects the education objective and cultivation objective, which is the key link for training qualified people and improving educational quality and is the subject of PE course construction as well. [6] In order to implement the college education concept of "health first" and "people oriented", to adapt the teaching mode and college students' physical and psychological development, people should reconstruct the teaching material system for the ordinary college PE course, which should break the restrictions of traditional concept and abandon the narrow-minded knowledge of sports to extend the attention to the future and lifelong fitness demand. Proceeding from human "overall development", people should take students sports consciousness improvement, lifelong sporting concept building, sports habit cultivation and sports practical ability as the main content of new teaching material system. [7] At the time of pursuing physical fitness, practical, entertainment, culture and interest of teaching content, people also should focus on system design, scientific selection and promotion as a whole, which means people should develop the various features during teaching material construction based on the common function pursuing. In order to make lifelong sporting concept run through the whole PE course system, people should develop the imperceptible influence of sports teaching on college students quality and make a closer combination of teaching material system and health education.

Develop and improve college PE course management system. The paper argues that the ordinary PE course management system consists 3 system branches (see figure 4). The teaching management system should include theory teaching, practice teaching, sports instruction after class (or sports club), sports training and games; PE course management support system should contain teaching condition, course assessment, scientific research and faculty training; students sporting file management system can be divided into students PE course results management and students physique health database. The improvement of teaching management and teaching quality is the key point and difficulty of PE course reform in colleges and universities, and the advanced project for continuously exploring and developing. Therefore, people should take fully use of the modern technology and management concept and update them in time, improve the management system to realize the normalization, scientific and modernization of the course teaching management and teaching quality management. (see figure 5).

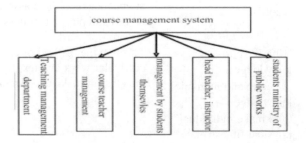

Fig. 5. Thinking on new PE course management system construction

5 Conclusion and Suggestion

In order to realize the college sports teaching and complete the course objective, on the premise of the combination of course system and object, teaching mode and students' physical and psychological features, the system construction should make all the elements optimized, connected and integrated, which means the course can be entirely optimized; the college PE course system gradually exerts into the local culture and the school character, so the characteristic of each school becomes increasingly prominent. Based on subjective and objective factors, each college should construct the PE course system according to the college characteristic by means of theory and practical research; the development and improvement of PE course system should take use of the scientific method "application, check, feedback, regulation" to maintain.

References

1. Maoyuan, P.: Newly Organized Higher Pedagogy, vol. 8(2), p. 194. Beijing Normal University Press, Beijing (2009)
2. Guixin, W., Guixin, W.: Literature Review on Sports Teaching Club Research in Colleges and Universities. Journal of Beijing Sport University (2), 232–234 (2005)
3. Yuwu, Y., Dawei, Z.: Research Review on College Sports Club. Journal of Tianjin University of Sport (3), 34–37 (2000)
4. Haixiao, C.: Research on Club Teaching Mode in Colleges and Universities. Journal of Sports and Science (3), 60–63 (1998)
5. Zhengxian, L.: Research on PE course system in Colleges and Universities. Sports Culture Guide (7), 70–76 (2010)
6. Yan, L., Peng, C.: A Tentative Research on the Reform of Sports Teaching Material System and Content. Sport Science (1), 30 (1999)
7. Guanghui, J., Yanyang, J.: Research on Chinese College Sports transforming to fitness education. Journal of Physical Education (4), 12–14 (1998)

The Determinants and Impact of Customer Base in Modern Information Age: A Competence-Based Approach

Bau-Jung Chang

Department of Business Administration, Feng Chia University, Taichung, Taiwan
changbj@fcu.edu.tw

Abstract. Based on competence-based view and network economics, this study intends to explore the determinants and the impact of customer base of Internet-based firms. This study suggests that the types of firm capabilities (technological versus marketing) are determined the customer base, and the customer base and firm capabilities impact on firm performance as well. Drawing on website traffic data and stock price data of Internet-based firms, this study highlights the roles of firm capabilities and customer base of the Internet-based firms. This study may contribute to competence-based view and enrich our understanding on Internet business in strategic and information management fields.

Keywords: Competence-based View, Customer Base, Internet-based Firms.

1 Introduction

This study intends to explore *how firms compete on the Internet market by amassing customer base and creating firm value*. To explore the question- *how does a firm create firm value*, the competence-based view provides rich grounds for the references. The competence-based view explores the role of key resources which identified as tangible and intangible assets, and capabilities in creating competitive advantage and superior performance [1,10,11,12]. To a great extent the conceptual analysis and empirical research within the competence-based view has focused on the firm's perspective of firm capabilities and the value to the firm of these capabilities. However, only a few studies explore on firm capabilities and the value they provide to the customer. For example, Prahalad and Hamel [10] argue the critical task for management is to create organizational capability of creating product which customers *need* but have not yet even imagined. Whether the key resources and capabilities hold value for the customer also hold value for the firm is still unknown. Therefore, we argue that *value of the firms* and *value of customers* should be discussed separately and investigated the relationships. As a result, this study employs competence-based view as the theoretical underpinning, and intends to separate value for firms and for customers and explore the linkage among firm capabilities, customer base, and firm performance.

S. Lin and X. Huang (Eds.): CSEE 2011, Part V, CCIS 218, pp. 112–117, 2011.
© Springer-Verlag Berlin Heidelberg 2011

2 Literature Review and Hypotheses Development

The competence-based view, developed among others by Barney [1], Teece, Pisano, and Shuen [11], and Winter [12] offers undoubtedly a promising theory of sustaining competitive advantage in strategic management. Capabilities, or competences, are the result of a cumulative process based on learning through experience and of firm-specific problem solving activity through trials, errors and incremental adjustments. Following the deliberations of Teece et al. [11] and Winter [12], dynamic capabilities are those firm-specific processes or routines that integrate its activities, promote learning, and help firms build, reconfigure and transform its asset/resource positions (tangible and intangible), processes, and structures in order to deliver products and services that are of value to all stakeholders, both internal and external. Rejecting optimal and universal responses in the face of new technology impact, competence-based view provides a framework that explains why some firms are more capable of responding than others. As a result, this study proposes two types of capabilities: *technological capability* and *marketing capability* as the firm-level heterogeneity and explore the linkage among firm capabilities, customer base, and firm performance.

Technological capability encompass the system of activities, physical systems, skills and knowledge bases, managerial systems, and values that create a special advantage for a firm [4]. In information system research, informational technology capability has been recognized an important role in firm effectiveness and sustained competitive advantage [2,9]. Bharadwaj [2] defines information technology capability as its ability to mobilize and deploy IT-based resources in combination with other resources and capabilities. Internet-based firm reveals its technological capability in technology platform, Internet infrastructure, hardware, software, networks, and data processing architectures [13]. Technological capability reveals the back-end infrastructure and how information the firms transfers to customers in the front-end. When firms occupy in higher technological capability, they are able to perform better website infrastructure and transit information to users more efficiently, thus attract more visitors to use the website. Furthermore, firms with higher technological capability also indicate they may obtain better performance than rivals. As a result, this study hypothesizes:

Hypothesis 1: Technological capability of the firm is positively associated with number of customer base.

Hypothesis 2: Technological capability of the firm is positively associated with firm performance.

Marketing capability of a firm is reflected in its ability to differentiate its products and services from competitors [8]. These capabilities enable firms to compete by predicting changes in customer preferences as well as creating and managing durable relationships with customers and channel members [3]. A firm that spends money on advertising and promoting its product and services can increase new customers to switch to their brand or enhance the loyalty of existing customers. The capabilities are complex bundles of skills and accumulated knowledge which exercised through organizational process enable firms to coordinate activities [11], thus a firm with knowledge about customers' demand can be regarded as possession of an intangible asset.

Marketing capability of Internet-based firms encompass how firms use and integrate related marketing resources to enhance the objective of the firm. Day [3] has noted that market-driven organization have superior market sensing, customer linking, and channel bonding capabilities. Marketing capabilities are those that provide links with customers, and firms with higher level marketing capability are able to understand what customer wants and provide it more efficient, thus may attract more users to link and use to the website. Hence, this study hypothesizes:

Hypothesis 3: Marketing capability of the firm is positively associated with number of customer base.

Hypothesis 4: Marketing capability of the firm is positively associated with firm performance.

Firm performance may be created by amassing customer base, for the following reasons. First, attributes of increasing return on Internet market may induce user enjoy more network externalities the larger is the number of site users [6, 7]. Second, great popularity of a website enables the firm to spread fixed cost, decreasing average cost per user and increasing cash flows and profits. Third, popular websites are able to charge higher advertising prices, and are able to enjoy higher advertising revenues. Finally, the most popular websites enjoy brand name recognition, higher switching costs for users, and the momentum in recruiting new users, and often a large market share. As a result, this study hypothesizes:

Hypothesis 5: The number of customer base of the firm is positively associated with firm performance.

3   Methodology

This study defines an Internet-based firm as one drives its revenues from transactions conducted over the Internet. The sample, Internet-based firms, is collected by *Dow Jones Internet Index* and *USA Today*. Because this study focuses on firms who operate and earn profit through the Internet, Internet service firms on the lists are excluded in the sample. The final sample includes 40 Internet-based firms. In addition, this study also uses data in the alexa.com website and Mergent database.

Technological Capability. When customers browse the websites and decide whether to fulfill the transactions in the website, *speed of a website* is the most revealed and perceived component for customers. As a result, speed of the website is the proxy of technological capability in this study. Speed of the website, in terms of average load time and measured in seconds, is grabbed from *Alex.com*. The higher the speed of the website, the lower the technological capability the firm occupies.

Marketing Capability. The variable *sites linking in* is a measure of a website's reputation, which count the number of sites linking to the website. Multiple links from the same site are only counted once. Sites linking in are calculated on a *site to site* basis. This means that if ten sites have links to the focus site, that is ten sites linking in. But if one site has ten links to the focus site, that is only one site linking in. This statistic is updated quarterly.

Customer Base. Number of visitor is used to measure the customer base of the firm. Number of visitor is calculated by *reach* which obtained in Alexa Web Information Service. Reach measures how many people the website reaches per million. This statistic is updated daily.

Firm Performance. This study uses stock price as the proxy of firm performance. Because the foregoing data were obtained on April 24, 2009, the stock price is obtained on the next stock transaction day, April 27, 2009. Stock price data is obtained by Mergent database.

The model in this study is estimated by Structural Equation Model (SEM) using AMOS 5.0.

4   Results

According to Jŏreskog and Sorbom [5], four usually used statistics of goodness of fit are Chi-square, CFI (comparative Fit Index), NFI (Normed Fit Index) and RMSEA (Root Mean Square Error of Approximation). The Chi-square ($\chi 2$) of this model is 1.23 ($p>0.05$), the values of CFI (*CFI=0.997*) and NFI (*NFI=0.987*) are both above 0.95, and the value of RMSEA (*RMSEA=0.077*) is under 0.1. These measures of fit suggest that the hypothesized model fit the data well.

Fig. 1 presents the path coefficients of the path model. According to the statistics, Hypothesis 1, Hypothesis 2, and Hypothesis 5 are not supported, but Hypothesis 3 and Hypothesis 4 are supported by the estimated path model.

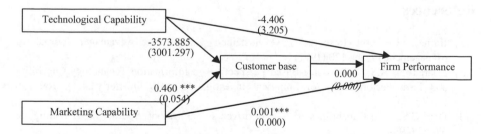

Fig. 1. Estimated model of firm capabilities, customer base, and firm performance (***p<0.01; standard errors are shown on the brackets)

5   Discussion and Conclusions

According to competence-based view and network economics theory, this study proposes several hypotheses to explore whether technological capabilities and marketing capabilities of a firm may attract more customer base, and the impact of customer base on firm performance. The results of the estimated path model partly support the hypotheses. The coefficients of Hypothesis 1 and 2 are negative, which partly support the positively relationship between technological capability and customer base of a firm, but do not reach significant level. This study encountered difficulty in collecting data on back-end Internet infrastructure and technology-related information. Future research may collect data, such as human IT human resources or investment of information technology, to measure a website's technological capability comprehensively. Furthermore, the results of the estimated path model support Hypothesis 3 and 4. Marketing capabilities are those that provide links with customers, and firms with higher level marketing capabilities are able to understand what customer wants and provide those more efficient, thus may attract more users to link and use to the website and induce more profit.

Although the coefficient of Hypothesis 5 is positive but fail to reach significant level. Firm performance may be created by amassing customer base for network externalities that users enjoy, higher switching costs for users, fixed cost sharing, and higher advertising prices charge. Owing to fulfilling the daily and quarterly data of website monitoring, this study employs daily stock price as the proxy of firm performance. Future research may extend longer data collection period.

In conclusion, this study contributes to the competence-based view and network economics on understanding of the firm capabilities, customer base, and firm performance on Internet-based firms. Specifically, this study argues that *value of the customer* and *value of the firm* should be discussed individually, and this study may supplement the competence-based view of exploration of the relationship among firm capabilities, customer base, and firm performance. This study enriches our understanding on Internet business in strategic management and information management fields.

References

[1] Barney, J.: Firm Resources and Sustained Competitive Advantage. Journal of Management 17, 99–120 (1991)
[2] Bharadwaj, A.S.: A Resource-Based Perspective on Information Technology Capability and Firm Performance: An Empirical Investigation. MIS Quarterly 24(1), 169–196 (2000)
[3] Day, G.S.: The Capabilities of Market-driven Organizations. Journal of Marketing 58, 37–52 (1994)
[4] Holstius, K.: Cultural Adjustment in International Technology transfer. International Journal of Technology Management 10(7/8), 676–686 (1995)
[5] Joreskog, K.G., Sorbom, D.: LISREL VI; Analysis of Linear Structural Relationships by Maximum Likelihood. Instrumental Variables, and Least Squares. University of Uppsala, Uppsala (1985)
[6] Katz, M.L., Shapiro, C.: Network Externalities, Competition, and Compatibility. The American Economic Review 75(3), 424–440 (1985)
[7] Katz, M.L., Shapiro, C.: Technology Adoption in the Presence of Network Externalities. The Journal of Political Economy 94(4), 822–841 (1986)

[8] Kotabe, K., Srinivasan, S.S., Aulakh, P.: Multinationality and Firm Performance: the Moderating Role of R&D and Marketing Capabilities. Journal of International Business Studies 33(1), 79–97 (2002)

[9] Mata, F.J., Fuerst, W.L., Barney, J.B.: Information Technology and Sustained Competitive Advantage: A resource-based Analysis. MIS Quarterly 19(4), 487–505 (1995)

[10] Prahalad, C.K., Hamel, G.: The Core Competence of the Corporation. Harvard Business Review 68(3), 79–92 (1990)

[11] Teece, D., Pisano, G., Shuen, A.: Dynamic Capabilities and Strategic Management. Strategic Management Journal 18(7), 509–533 (1997)

[12] Winter, S.G.: Understanding Dynamic Capabilities. Strategic Management Journal 24, 991–995 (2003)

[13] Zhu, K.: The Complementarity of Information Technology Infrastructure and E-Commerce Capability: A Resource-Based Assessment of Their Business Value. Journal of Management Information Systems 21(1), 167–202 (2004)

A Context-Aware Method for Service Composition in Pervasive Computing Environments

Chunmiao Gu[1] and Yongsheng Zheng[2]

[1] Electrical Engineering and Information, Changchun Institute of Technology, China
GU_chunm@163.com
[2] College of Information Sciences and Technology, JilinUniversity,
Changchun, China School of
Win_shbshb@163.com

Abstract. In pervasive computing, it is the physical environment that provides medium to satisfy user requirements. A context-aware approach of service composition in pervasive computing environments is proposed. Services are represented by autonomous mobile agents, and they establish relationship network based on affinity to provide service composition. Affinity adjustment depends on three factors, namely, the matching strength of mobile agents, the service quality score, and the trust. In this way, the method completes a series of work from composition to management autonomously. It adapts well to the changes of dynamic environments.

Keywords: context-aware, service composition, pervasive computing, agent.

1 Introduction

Pervasive computing environments involve a variety of smart devices, which tend to overcharge humans with complex or irrelevant interaction. The true potential of services can only be achieved if services are used to dynamically compose some new services that provide more sophisticated functionalities compared to existing ones. Pervasive service composition architectures should be able to utilize the spatial distribution of services to optimize service composition and execution. Fault management strategy has to take into consideration network level disconnection, service discovery failures, and service execution failures. These issues call for an alternate design approach of service composition systems for pervasive environments. Traditional approaches have not addressed all above challenges [1]. The latest research indicates that the future Internet environment will be an autonomous and intelligent system [2]. It will gather and organize resources into semantically rich forms that both machines and people can easily use. The next generation service systems have the hallmarks of complex systems, namely, evolution, adaptation — no one designs the whole service processes within users and resources. Agent-oriented computing [3] provides a big possibility of implementation for this solution.

Based on bio-network service platform [4-6], a novel self-evolutionary method is proposed. Mobile agents are designed to represent pervasive services. Each service is described as an OWL-S with QoS attributes to allow a user to perform a task on the

S. Lin and X. Huang (Eds.): CSEE 2011, Part V, CCIS 218, pp. 118–122, 2011.

fly. Mobile agents establish relationships based on affinities to provide the composite services [7,8]. Such affinities promote self-organization of mobile agents reflecting user preferences and service usage patterns. The strength of the affinities indicates the usefulness of the relationship. The measure of affinity is based on the matching strength of mobile agents, service quality score of agent, and the trust. As relationships develop, mobile agents narrow down the number of mobile agents to interact with based on matching strengths of affinity. As relationships grow, mobile agents self-organize to present service composition with evolutionary adaptation.

2   A Context-Aware Method of Pervasive Service Composition

Service composition is the result of negotiation among mobile agents in BNSP. Obviously, the service composition is not directly achieved by mobile agents, therefore, a self-evolutionary method and negotiation rules must be provided. We designed a self-evolutionary method of pervasive service composition. Self-evolution is derived from natural selection through dynamically adding and removing mobile agents based on the affinity. Natural selection is at the mobile agent. The measure of affinity includes three parameters to be taken into account, the matching strength, the service quality score, and the trust. Service composition is a chain composition service through interaction among mobile agents according to the matching affinity. The Ontology Web Language for Services (OWL-S) is applied to describe pervasive services. The specification describes a service by functionalities and non-functional attributes. The functionalities include inputs, outputs, preconditions, effects, and exceptions. The non-functional attributes can provide QoS describe precisely. This method provides the necessary flexibility and robustness.

The matching strength $MS^{ws}_{bio-entity}$ is defined as the similarity of pervasive services represented by mobile agents. Ws is a pervasive service, $Ws = \langle In_{req}, Out_{req} \rangle$ has a set of provided inputs In_{req}, and a set of expected outputs Out_{req}.

For two pervasive Services $Ws1 = \langle In_{req1}, Out_{req1} \rangle$ and $Ws2 = \langle In_{req2}, Out_{req2} \rangle$, Out_{req1} is also described as $Out^{Ws_1}_{req1}(C_1, C_2, C_3 .... C_i)$ and In_{req2} is $In^{Ws_2}_{req2}(C_1', C_2', C_3' ...... C_j')$, C_i and C_j' represent the relevant concepts which are composed interface.

$MS^{ws}_{bio-entity}(W_{s1}, W_{s2})$ is given by the similarity of between Out_{req1} and In_{req2}, which relies on the concept similarity C_i and C_j' in ontology. $SM(C_1, C_2)$ is defined as the similarity of two concepts C_1 and C_2, measuring two concepts' similarity in ontology[9]. Concept C_1 is in level L_1, concept C_2 is in level L_2. The level corresponds to the shortest path from the concept to the imaginary root. The minimal distance between two concepts in the concept hierarchy built by WordNet and HowNet. Let $Dis(C_1, C_2)$ be the distance between two concepts.

$$SM(C_1, C_2) = \begin{cases} 1 & C_1 = C_2 \\ SM_{con}(C_1, C_2) & C_1 < C_2, C_1 > C_2 \\ 0 & C_1 \neq C_2 \end{cases} \qquad (1)$$

$$SM_{con}(C_1,C_2) = \frac{\beta \times (L_1 + L_2)}{(Dis(C_1,C_2) + \beta) \times Max(|L_1 - L_2|, 1)}$$

Where, β is a constant and can be set to the distance when the similarity of two words is equal to 0.5.

Four distinct scenarios can occur: $C_1 = C_2$ (the concepts are the same), $C_1 > C_2$ (the concept C_1 subsumes concept C_2), $C_1 < C_2$ (the concept C_2 subsumes concept C_1) and $C_1 \neq C_2$ (concept C_1 is not directly related to concept C_2). Therefore, the matching strength of mobile agents $MS_{Bio-entity}^{ws}$

$$MS_{bio-entity}^{ws}(W_{s1},W_{s2}) = \frac{1}{n}\left[\sum_{j=1}^{n}\max_{i=1}^{m}(SM(C_i,C_j'))\right] \tag{2}$$

$$MS_{bio-entity}^{ws}(W_{s1},W_{s2}) \in [0, 1]$$

Service quality score depends on three factors, Latency, Availability, and Cost. $Q_{bio-entity} = (Q_1(Latency), Q_2(Availability), Q_3(Cost))$. Given a process in a service composition, there is a set of candidate mobile agents, which represent pervasive candidate services $S_{bio-entity}j = \{s_1j, s_2j......s_nj\}$ that can be used to execute this task. By merging the quality vectors of all these services, a matrix $Q_{bio-entity} = (Q_{ij}; 1 \leq i \leq n, 1 \leq j \leq 3)$ is built, in which each row Q_j corresponds to a service s_{ij} while each column corresponds to a quality dimension. A Simple Additive Weighting (SAW) [10] technique is used to evaluate service.

There are two phases in applying SAW. Some of the criteria could be negative, i.e., the higher the value, the lower the quality. This includes criteria such as time and cost. Other criteria are positive, i.e., the higher the value, the higher the quality. For negative criteria, values are scaled according to (3). For positive criteria, values are scaled according to (4).

$$P_{ij} = \begin{cases} \dfrac{Q_j^{max} - Q_{ij}}{Q_j^{max} - Q_j^{min}} & \text{if } Q_j^{max} - Q_j^{min} \neq 0 \\ 1 & \text{if } Q_j^{max} - Q_j^{min} = 0 \end{cases} \tag{3}$$

$$P_{ij} = \begin{cases} \dfrac{Q_{ij} - Q_j^{max}}{Q_j^{max} - Q_j^{min}} & \text{if } Q_j^{max} - Q_j^{min} \neq 0 \\ 1 & \text{if } Q_j^{max} - Q_j^{min} = 0 \end{cases} \tag{4}$$

Where $Q_j^{max} = Max(Q_{ij}), 1 \leq i \leq n$. $Q_j^{min} = Min(Q_{ij})$, $1 \leq i \leq n$. By applying these two equations on Q, we obtain a matrix $P = (P_{ij}; 1 \leq i \leq n, 1 \leq j \leq 3)$ In which each row P_j corresponds to a agent s_{ij}, while each column corresponds to a quality dimension. The following formula (5) is used to compute the overall quality score for each agent,

$$S_{Bio-entity}(s_i) = \sum_{j=1}^{3}(P_{ij} * W_j) \tag{5}$$

Where $W_j \in [0,1]$ and $\sum_{j=1}^{3} W_j = 1$, W_j represents the weight of criterion j.

Trust-based reconstruction of relationship makes the necessary preparations for a more efficient service composition. The adjustment of trust indicated by a user received the service. Whenever a service is provided, mobile agents adjust the trust with their interaction partners based on the level of user satisfaction or happiness. If the user is satisfied (not satisfied) with the service, the trust is strengthened (weakened).

A trust could be a reward or a penalty, which indicates that the degree of a user's preference to emergent service. This message is propagated through the same path where the discovery service has been originally forwarded. When an intermediate agent on the path receives message, it adjusts the trust value of the relationship that has been used to forward the original discovery request. Trust value is increased for a reward, and is decreased for a penalty.

Given a value $R \in [-\frac{1}{2} \leq R \leq 1]$ that contains in a defray message, the agent ΔS updates the trust value of $Trust_{ij}$ using the formula (6).

$$Trust_{ij} = Trust_{ij} + \Delta S \tag{6}$$

$$\Delta S = \begin{cases} (1 - Trust_{ij}) * R^2 & R \geq 0 \\ Trust_{ij}(1 - \frac{1}{1+R}) & R < 0 \end{cases}$$

$$R \in [-\frac{1}{2} \leq R \leq 1]$$

Where $Trust_{ij}$ is a number in [0, 1] that represents relationship value. Correspondingly, ΔS is calculated based on the $Trust_{ij}$ and R. We have chosen the above formula with the purpose of remarking ratings rise slowly and fall quickly.

The affinity between two mobile agents is calculated based on the matching strength $MS_{bio-entity}^{ws}$, service quality score $S_{Bio-entity}$ and trust $Trust$ of mobile agents. It define as

$$Aff_{bio-entity} = (1-\alpha)MS_{bio-entity}^{ws}(W_{s1},W_{s2}) \cdot S_{Bio-entity}(s2) + \alpha \cdot Trust \tag{7}$$

where $\alpha \in [0,1]$ is a weight to affinity. The optimal local affinity can help agent decide where to forward.

If request service is W_{req}, according the rule of optimal local affinity, a service composition is composed a set of mobile agents, such as $W_{s1}, W_{s2}, W_{s3}....W_{sn}$, $Aff_{emergence}$ is the satisfaction value of service composition (the affinity strength of service composition)

$$Aff_{emergence} = Aff_{bio-entity}(W_{req},W_{S1}) \cdot \prod_{i=1}^{n-1} Aff_{bio-entity}(W_{Si},W_{Si+1}) \cdot Aff_{bio-entity}(W_{Sn},W_{req}) \tag{8}$$

A threshold of service composition θ will be specified ($0 < \theta < 1$). If $Aff_{emergence} > \theta$, service composition is successful.

3 Summary

We have originally designed the dynamic self-evolutionary approach for service composition. Mobile agents may establish relationship with interaction partners to form a group to provide a service based on the matching strength, the service quality score, and the trust. The method can well adapt to different scenario, including the changes of dynamic environments as well as partial failure of mobile agents and nodes. Usually, the amount of the available service s and the size of ontology models are huge. Therefore, it is necessary to reduce the search space during problem solving. In addition, more experiments will be designed to evaluate the self-evolution method in service composition and management.

References

1. Maric, D.M., Meier, P.F., Estreicher, S.K.: Mater. Sci. Forum 83-87, 119 (1992)
2. Grady, M.J., Hare, M.P.: Mobile devices and intelligent agents—towards a new generation of applications and services. Information Sciences 171(4), 335–353 (2009)
3. Zhuge, H.: The Future interconnection environment. IEEE Computer 38(4), 27–33 (2005)
4. Jennings, N.R.: An agent-based approach for building complex software systems. Communications of the ACM 44(4), 35–41 (2001)
5. Jerne, N.K.: Towards a network theory of the immune system. Annual Immunology 125C, 373–389 (1974)
6. Ding, Y.S., Ren, L.H.: Design of a bio-network architecture based on immune emergent computation. Control and Decision 18(2), 185–189 (2003) (in Chinese)
7. Gao, L., Ding, Y.S.: A novel ecological network-based computation platform as grid middleware system. Int. J. Intelligent Systems 19(10), 859–884 (2004)
8. Gao, L., Ding, Y.S., Ying, H.: An adaptive social network-inspired approach to resource discovery for the complex grid systems. International Journal of Intelligent Systems 35, 347–360 (2006)
9. Itao, T., Tanaka, S., Suda, T.: A framework for adaptive Unicom applications based on the jack-in-the-net architecture. Wireless Network 10, 287–299 (2004)
10. Cardoso, J., Sheth, A.: Semantic e-workflow composition. Intelligent Information Systems 21(3), 191–225 (2003)
11. Zeng, L.Z., Benatallah, B., Ngu, A.H.H., Dumas, M., Kalagnanam, J., Chang, H.: QoS-aware middleware for Service s composition. IEEE Transactions on Software Engineering 30(5), 311–327 (2004)

A Study on Online-Scoring-System-Based Educational Examination and Measurement

Deling Yuan, Guang Xiao, and Huiling Chu

No. 500 South Qinzhou Road, Shanghai, PRC
aurie9960@sina.com, leoxiao@8163.net.cn,
chu12883@hotmail.com

Abstract. Examination is one of the most important methods to evaluate the educational quality, but it is very necessary to control well the errors related to an examination to obtain results with high reliability and validity. Moreover, attentions must be paid to the subjective test items' scoring which leads to errors more often. So, in mass educational examinations' scoring, online scoring system is used to reduce the bad influence which is common in paper-based scoring that scorers can see the previous mark of an item and be affected by it. This paper introduces the stages of online scoring, the methods to control the quality and the system's functional modules to finish this work; an analysis on errors of scoring results to guide the system parameters' setting to improve scoring quality is also mentioned.

Keywords: online scoring system, educational examination, educational measurement.

1 Introduction

Education is a great issue related to the society's development and humans try their best to improve educational quality, and to seek effective methods to measure it. Examination is the most common one in those many measurement methods and a test designed delicately basing on scientific educational theories has many functions, such as diagnosis and feedback, that is, to detect students' knowledge study level and capability, and then to provide information for students and teachers to improve study and teaching [1].

An examination is a systematic procedure of searching enough validity proofs to support the test's results under the direction of educational measurement theories, which includes the processes of overall planning and description, content specification, items writing & arrangement, scoring, level classification, and results' reporting [2]. As a kind of measurement, an examination does bring errors which are rare in those periods such as content specification and items writing & arrangement thanks to a few and outstanding involved experts, but common in the period of scoring due to huge amount test papers, a tight schedule, and the needs of a lot of scorers who probably comprehend the marking criterions in diversity. In mass educational examinations, there are two types of items, the subjective and the objective. The latter is an item of identifying the right answer and Optimal Mark

S. Lin and X. Huang (Eds.): CSEE 2011, Part V, CCIS 218, pp. 123–127, 2011.
© Springer-Verlag Berlin Heidelberg 2011

Reader can score it automatically, while the former is for measuring more complicated behavioral objectives, answered by words, numbers and charts, and usually scored through manual labor. It is very hard that every scorer comprehend the criterions exactly the same, so errors appear in scoring process, which must be controlled well to strengthen the test results' reliability, interpretation, and practicable validity.

Online scoring is applied more and more usually in mass educational examinations to reduce the interference caused by scorers' different comprehension on grading criterions. Rather than traditional scoring mode, in which lots of scorers and huge amount test papers are centralized in a special place for sequential manual work, the latter scorer can see the former marks on test papers so it is hard for them to grade separately, and a heavy load with a tight schedule leads to more errors, the online scoring mode overcomes these disadvantages with the aids of computer software. It is a new scoring method, that scorers watch the electronic images of test papers which are scanned by a scanner in advance and grade them through the computer network. With the combination of plentiful experiences accumulated in manual scoring and the modern high technology, the most outstanding advantage of online scoring is an easy control of errors to guarantee reliability, equity and justness as far as possible.

Developed countries implement online scoring very early and many organizations have mature online scoring systems even computer-based auto scoring systems, such as ETS in USA and UCLES in UK, Whereas China begins as late as in 1999 [3]. However, from then on, the online scoring's development in China is so rapid that it is applied widely in mass educational examinations such as the national college entrance examination and the high school entrance examination.

This paper summarizes the practical experiences of online scoring of mass educational examinations' subjective items in Shanghai in recent years, brings a brief introduction to a series of stages of online scoring, and discusses some ways to control quality, as well as illustrates the functional modules of a online scoring system and its development direction. It also sheds some light on the measurement theories of the online scoring's quality.

2   Stages of Online Scoring

Just as manual scoring, online scoring also includes stages of sampling, test scoring, real scoring and anew scoring, but under the control of computer software, many good practices which cannot or hard to be executed in the past, are implemented now to improve the scoring quality and review the tasks of scorers.

In the sampling stage, the scoring committee picks up test items at random and set a few typical samples for scorers' reference at the stage of test and real scoring.

In the test scoring stage, papers will be distributed randomly to all scorers by the system for test grading. Scorers will be familiar to the system and the marking criterions through this stage, and these marks are just for a trial, that is, not the students' real scores.

In the real scoring stage, papers will also be distributed randomly to all scorers by the system, and through the system's error control mechanism, final scores will come out generally.

In the anew scoring stage, some special test papers are confirmed again, such as the zero and the full paper.

For the sake of high quality, the real scoring stage is divided into three small ones: learning, testing, and grading. While learning, scorers learn the samples to comprehend the criterions. And while testing, some standard papers set by the scoring committee will be distributed to scorers secretly to test their quality and constancy, and to evaluate their abilities to do the real scoring. Besides, in the real scoring stage, some papers graded by a scorer will be sent to him or her again for a second grading to test the constancy.

3   The Quality Control Methods during Online Scoring

Random Distribution & Minimum Reading Time. Before the online scoring, administrator uses the system to package records item by item randomly or in some rules but without students' private information, and inserts them to database. While scored, item records are distributed to scorers randomly. Otherwise, in manual scoring, test papers are put and exchanged orderly for easy administration, so private information may probably leak out.

Generally, subjective answers, such as writing and essays, need some minutes for reading. In manual scoring, it is hard to supervise everyone and let them obey the rule of minimum time for such items. However, in the online scoring system, a minimum time parameter is set for this kind of subjective items to force scorers reading the answers at least for some time else they cannot submit marks. This way may guarantees the scoring quality to some extent.

The Roles of Sample Paper, Standard Paper, and Self-inspect Paper. As mentioned before, sample papers are generally set by the scoring committee in the sampling stage, as well as in the real scoring stage according to students' real scores, and their standard marks are visible for all scorers for reference.

However, standard papers' standard marks are invisible to scorers and distributed randomly to "seduce" them into an improper mark. This method is used to test scorers' proficiency and stability, and if data shows a scorer's instability, the scoring committee may let him or her learn the scoring criterions again.

The self-inspect paper is sent to a same scorer for a second grade, and the distribution frequency is set by the system administrator according to the scoring committee's opinions. The system can provide statistical data for supervision.

The Quality Control & Inspection Group. This group's members are professionals who participated in assigning questions and are very familiar to the scoring criterions. During the online scoring process, this group may do selective check with the system at any time, and improper marks will be challenged for a second judge by the scoring committee only. The quality control & inspection group can also make fully use of the online scoring system's functions to observe the overall situation or compare scorers' work, such as the scoring progress, marking history, average score, scores' distribution, scorers' workload, errors' detail, and adjust some control strategies relying on these observations [4].

4   Framework of the Online Scoring System

Generally speaking, online scoring system's users consist of administrator, scoring committee, quality control & inspection group, scorer, and so on. Administrators, who are good at Information Technology and database knowledge, are supporters responsible for system's preparation and maintenance. The scoring committee is in charge of organization, coordination and management with the goal of completing all the scoring work on schedule with an acceptable quality, and they need to settle the puzzles and difficulties. The quality control & inspection group is responsible for checking the work quality of scorers. And scorers are divided into two types, one is team leader, and the other is common scorer responsible for the common first or second judge. Team leaders grade those test items that exceed the common judges' difference threshold value, and monitor the scoring progress of the team.

To meet all the needs of the above mentioned roles, online scoring system usually includes two parts, the managing part for administrators and the client for the other roles. Administrators use managing part to do things as follows:

Preparation. Configure the network; install and set up Database Servers, Web Servers, and File Servers; deploy the scoring system on corresponding servers; build data tables, subject's structure, parameters; import information of examinees, scorers, and subjects; import data for sampling and test scoring; build accounts and authorization; packaging sampling tasks.

In Sampling Stage. Set the system to sampling status; after sampling finished, arrange and check the sampling data.

In Test Scoring Stage. Set the system to test scoring status; monitor the system's running station and respond in time.

In Real Scoring Stage. Set the system to real scoring status; monitor the system's running station and respond in time; change scorers' role and privilege according to the scoring committee's requests; at the ending period, retrieve the remains and resend them.

Other roles use the client to do things as follows: score; mark item to be problem; refer to sample and standard papers; monitor the statistical data and scoring progress; show grading records, workload, records' distribution, errors; deal with puzzles and problems, and so on. Fig. 1 and Fig. 2 illustrate the functional structures of the managing part and the client.

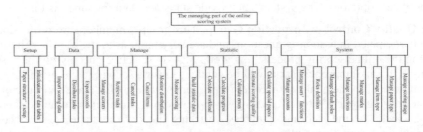

Fig. 1. The functional structure of the managing part of the online scoring system

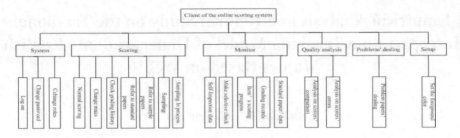

Fig. 2. The functional structure of the client of the online scoring system

5 Conclusions

The online scoring system's application in mass educational examinations is one of the best methods to reduce subjective test items' scoring errors and improve examinations' reliability and validity. The scoring task could be completed quickly with a high quality through an effective organization and the aids of the online scoring system. However, rather than the traditional manual scoring, the online scoring's errors cannot be eliminated though reduced. And these errors should be measured based on the educational theories, such as CCT (Classical Test Theory), GT (Generalizability Theory) and IRT (Item Response Theory). A statistical analysis on the scoring results can help us estimating whether errors are acceptable and where they come from, further seting up the system parameters better to improve the scoring quality in the future. Moreover, we could develop auto scoring systems for some specific test items and papers to counter the errors brought by scorers' different comprehension on the criterions.

Acknowledgement. We are grateful to the financial support from 2008 Educational Scientific Research Program "A Study on the Development and Application of Online Scoring and Related Issues" (ID B08076).

References

[1] Information, http://www.pep.com.cn/rjwk/cxyuwen/022/xy/201101/t20110114_1015177.htm
[2] Chu, H.L.: Examinations Development and Related Issues. Science 9 (2009)
[3] Luo, Y.H., Liu, T.M.: Review of Online Marking Research. China Examinations 11, 34–37 (2009)
[4] Xiao, G.: Application and Thought of Online Scoring in Mass Educational Examinations. Educational Measurement and Evaluation 9, 48–50 (2009)

Empirical Analysis and Reform Study on the Tradional Interpretation Teaching Model of Undergraduate English Majors Based on Web

JinBao Cai[1] and Ying Lin[2]

[1] Jiangxi University of Science and Technology, Ganzhou City,
Jiangxi Province, P.R. China, 34100
caijinbao@yahoo.com.cn
[2] Gannan Normal University, Ganzhou City, Jiangxi Province,
P.R. China, 34100

Abstract. The interpretation course is set up to improve students' interpretatiing skill and communicating ability, but traditonal teaching model of interpretation course can't easily meet with such a teaching goal. This paper, based on the empirical analysis of traditonal interpration teaching model and introduction of overseas advanced teaching model and method of interpretation course teaching, is aimed at establishing a comparatively reasonable interpretation course teaching model from educational internationalization prospect.

Keywords: Undergraduate English Major, Interpretation Course, Teaching Model, Empirical Analysis & Reform Study.

1 Introduction

With the development of Chinese economy and enhancing of China's national comprehensive strength, more and more foreigners come to China to do business, cultural exchange and other international activities, and international conferences are increasingly held in China. Meanwhile more and more Chinese go abroad to do international exchange in various fields. So market requirements for qualified interpreters rises. In order to meet with the requirements, interpretation course is set up in most universities of China. For the reason that interpretation course is a comparatively new course established at the uniersities, traditonal teaching model is wrongly adopted in classroom, which means that oral course method is used to teach interpretation course. Under the instruction of this method, interpretation course teachers plays an active role in classroom whereas the students are put in a passive situation, which can not help students to be trained in a classroom similar to real conference situation. According to metacognition theory, students can not improve their interpretation skill by correcting their own mistakes of course study cognition. Thus, students can not master advanced interpretation skills including facial expressions, gesture, volume, logic of expression, speaking, eye contact, speed, message completeness, grammar, terminology, expression smoothness, intonation and pronunciation and so on. This paper, based on the empirical analysis of traditonal interpration teaching model and introduction of overseas advanced teaching model and method of interpretation course teaching, is aimed at establishing a comparatively reasonable interpretation course teaching model from educational internationalization prospect.

2 The Introduction of Interpretation Teaching Model Used by the University of Westminster in Britain

The University of Westminster is one of the fifteen members of EMCI founded in 2001. Profession qualification certificate awarded by EMCI is authoritative in European Union, which means the bearers of the certificate is qualified to work as an interpreter in the countries of European Union. The interpretation course provided by the University of Westminster is also admitted by AIIC. The interpretation programme majors at the University of Westminster can be easily employed by interpertatiom market. From this part, the interpretation teaching method adopted by the University of Westminster is worthy of being learned by us. The author, who studied in the University of Westminster, also hopes the introduction of the teaching model in this paper can benefit interpretation learners and teachers at the universities in China.

According to cognition theory and psycholinguistics theory, skill is obtained by repeated and special training, which indicates interpretation skill is mastered only by a lot of practice but not by taught in class. So teachers can only play a role in organizing,assisting and directing in class, which means that the acitive role should be played by the interpretation learners. Specifically speaking, the University of Westminster has adopted this method to teach interpretation trainee as follows:

(i) How to make interpretation preparation is the first skill taught by teachers. It includs long-term preparation and short-term preparation. Long-term preparation means that interpreters shall prepare every day for the potential interpreting tasks, which requires students to equipe themselves with: (1) a strong sense of duty;(2)a high level of linguistic proficiency;(3) wide encyclopedic Knowledge;(4) A Good Mastery of Interpreting Skills. In contrast, short-term preparation is more direct and efficient. It refers to the job that can only be prepared shortly before the task is taken. Such preparation is highly necessary for the successful accomplishment of a certain interpreting task. Specifically, the interpretation learners should grasp interpreting skills.

(ii) Topic and topic backgroud are handed out to interpreation trainees in advance in order to train interpretation learners with short-term preparation skill by teaching them how to prepare related documents and glossary lists through asking WH(what/who/when/where). Thus, skill training becomes the main task in class. The impact of language and background knowledge in class is weakened by pre-preparation.

(iii) In class, teaching efficiency is improved by group training based on the multi-media means. The trainees are divided into two groups: one group is acted as speakers and the other group is acted as interpreters. Under the simulation situation, the pre-designed speech is delivered by the speaking group whereas the interpreting group takes the interpretation task. At this time, teachers play a role in controlling the time and recording the students' presentation. Thus the students can experience the similar pressure of interpreting activities and improve the familiarity degree of interpreting activities. After that, by watching the recorded video, the students can correct their unsatisfying presentation including facial expressions, gesture, volume, logic of expression, speaking, eye contact, speed, message completeness, grammar, terminology, expression smoothness, intonation and pronunciation and so on. On the other hand, the students of speaking group can aslo benefit by thinking how to be a qualified interpreter on the position of speaker.

(iv) After class, the students can improve the interpreting skill through various means. First, the students can, based on the integrated platform of teaching and learning, file the relevant material of the topoic including terminology, knowledge of the topic background and interpreting skills, which can be used by the interpreting trainees to do more studying after class. In addition, the integrated platform has been input many video of different topic presented by professional interpreters. The students can also improve the inpterpreting skill by watching these videoes.

(v) The integrated platform of teaching and learning is also a communication platform between teachers and students. It forms a unified effective training system of in-class teaching and after-class learning. Based on the system, the students can be directed by the teachers in time and avoid ineffective practising. In addition, the teachers can improve their teaching methods by the feedback from the students. Futhermore, based on the platform, the teachers can set up a file for the students by the presentation of the students and teach the students how to correct it.

3 Empirical Analysis Based on the Integrated Teaching Model

In order to check the teaching effect of the integrated platform of teaching and learning more objectively and practically, the writer has made one contrast test at Jiangxi University of Science and Technology. The test result can illustrate the effect of the teaching model. It can aslo help the reform of interpretation course teaching model. The test is as follows:

(i) The Participants of the Test

20 undergraduate English majors enrolled in 2007 at Jiangxi Uinveristy of Science and Technology were selected out as the participants of the test. They have studied the interpretation courses for two semesters up to 72 learning hours. They were divided into two groups and the English language proficiency is almost at the same level.

(ii) The Means of the Test

Group one were trained by the integrated teaching model whereas Group two were trained by traditional teaching model. The in-class topic and background framework are almost the same.

(iii)   The Process of the Test (GROUP ONE)

Step(1): The topic and the backgound framework was handed out to the students through the intergrated platform. Then, the students were directed on how to make short-term preparation including how to use internet to get topic related information including terminology.

Step(2): In class, other students were invited as audiences. Goup one is divided into two groups acting as speaking group and interpreting group.

Step(3): In class, the speaking group acted as the speaker of the given topic whereas the interpreting group acted as the interpreters of the speaker. At the same time, the teacher played a role in being a controller of the class, teaching students how to improving their interpreting skill.The presentation in class was recorded.

Step(4): After the presentation, the video recorded in class was shown to the students. Based on the video, the teacher advised the students how to improve the skill from the part of the facial expressions, gesture, volume, logic of expression, speaking, eye contact, speed, message completeness, grammar, terminology, expression smoothness, intonation and pronunciation. Then the students watched the video presented by professional interpreters and were required to self-correct their mistakes. Finally, the teacher required the students to summarize their presentation and file the topic related materials including terminology, topic background knowledge and topic related video.

(iv)   The Process of the Test (GROUP TWO)

The Group 2 was trained by tradional teaching model, which means that the teacher played a role in being a speaker whereas the student played a role in being a interpreter. Then the teacher made an analysis of the students presentation. After that, the teacher gave some background knowledge and related words to the students.

(v) One week later, the two groups were invited to attent another topic's conference, and their presentation was analyzed carefully.

(vi)   Results analysis

The students' presentation was evaluated by the criteria as follows: facial expressions, gesture, volume, logic of expression, speaking, eye contact, speed, message completeness, grammar, terminology, expression smoothness, intonation and pronunciation and alternative interpretation strategies adopted. The full point is 10 for each, and total point is 140. The result is as follows:

序号	Criteria	Group 1	Group 2	Explanation
1	Facial expressiong(10')	8	6	
2	gesture(10')	8	6	
3	volume(10')	8	6	
4	logic of expression(10')	8	6	
5	speaking(10')	8	6	
6	eye contact(10')	8	6	
7	speed(10') (10')	8	6	
8	message completeness(10')	8	6	
9	expression smoothness(10')	8	6	
10	Interpretation strategies(10')	8	6	
11	grammar(10')	8	6	
12	intonation(10')	8	8	The same level
13	pronunciation(10')	8	8	The same level
14	terminology(10')	8	7	

From the above table, it can be clearly seen that Group One, who was trained by the integrated teaching model, has done a better presentation than Group Two ,who was taught by tradional teaching model, based on the fourteen criteria. The two groups are on the same level only in intonation and pronunciation. More importantly, Group One has demonstrated better in the fields of non-linguistic skill. The two show they have the same ability in the fields of linguistic skill.

4 Conclusion

With the development of Chinese economy and enhancing of China's national comprehensive strength, more and more foreigners come to China to do business, cultural exchange and other international activities, and international conferences are increasingly held in China. Meanwhile more and more Chinese go abroad to do international exchange in various fields. So market requirements for qualified interpreters rises. The interpretation couse set up for the undergraduate English majors is to improve students' interpretatiing skill and communicating ability so that the students can finish the interpretation task with high quality when they graduate from uninversity. The test has proved that the traditonal teaching model of interpretation course, in comparison with integrated interpretation course teaching model, has demonstrated low efficiency in equiping students with interpreting skill. So the current teaching model should, based on learning from the advanced teaching model of overseas universities, be reformed urgently. In order to implement the integrated interpretation course teaching model easily, the teachers should aslo equip themselves with more practical interpreting experience. This paper, based on the empirical analysis of traditonal interpration teaching model and introduction of overseas advanced teaching model and method of interpretation course teaching, has discussed the possiblity and feasibility of establishing a comparatively reasonable interpretation course teaching model from the prospect of teaching reform.

References

1. Nolan, J.: Interpretation: Techniques and Exercises/Multilingual Matters LTD (2005)
2. Jones, R.: Conference Interpreting Explained /St Jerome Pbulishing (2002)
3. Pochhacker, F.: Introducing Interpreting Studies/Published by Routledge (2004)
4. Skrinda, A.: The challenge of language teaching: Shifts of paradigms (2004)
5. Gile, D.: Basic Concepts and Models for Interpreter and Translator Training. John Benjamins Publishing Company, Amsterdam (1995)

Research on Opening Modular Experiment Teaching in Pyrology Elements Based on Network Resources

Bin Zheng, Yongqi Liu, Ruixiang Liu, and Jian Meng

School of Traffic and Vehicle Engineering, Shandong University of Technology,
Zibo, Shandong, 255049, China
sdutbin@163.com, sdutzb@163.com

Abstract. Cultivating innovative talents is an important task of colleges and universities. It is the trend of higher education development and the need of social development. Experiment teaching is an important link to develop students' practice ability as well as innovative ability and the opening modular experiment teaching is an effective way to train innovative talents. The content, conduct, effect and significance of opening modular experiment teaching were studied in detail basicd on modular experiment course of pyrology.

Keywords: Opening Modular, Experiment Teaching, Pyrology Elements, Practise Ability, Innovative Ability.

1 Introduction

With the highly development of our nation economy, the competition between foreign corporations and domestic corporations, and the competition among domestic corporations become more and more fierce. The master of the same industry advanced technology is the basic of each corporation development. Creative ability of technology is the road of each corporation development. Therefore, the graduates who have innovation consciousness, innovation ability, creative ability and practice ability is the need of each corporation. With China's higher education continuously reform and the needs of the employing corporations, basicd on training students' innovative spirit and practice ability has become one of the main development direction of China's higher education. It is the demand of social development, universities development and the discipline development. It is the need of students' own development.

Practical teaching segment is an important link for training students' practice ability and innovation ability, and experimental teaching is one of the important parts. Experiment teaching can give the human by the scientific knowledge and technology, and cultivate students' teaching practice and innovation consciousness which can't achieve in theory. The traditional experimental teaching which is mainly instruction and demonstration by teachers t now have not adapted to the talent training requirements. While open modular experiment teaching model accord with new teaching mode of the innovative talent training, which can realize the opening of the centralized modular of the professional knowledge, experimental site, experimental

S. Lin and X. Huang (Eds.): CSEE 2011, Part V, CCIS 218, pp. 133–138, 2011.

instruments, experimental time, and realize students' as the core of the experimental teaching [1-6].

Automobile has gradually become an indispensable tool in life. Mastering certain automobile specialized knowledge has become necessary in people's life. Pyrology is a important part of automobile specialized knowledge. The open courses of pyrology open modular experiment teaching not only meet the student demand for pyrology expertise, but also develop practical and innovative ability of students, meeting the needs of creative talents. The content, conduct, effect and significance of opening modular experiment teaching were studied in detail basicd on opening modular experiment course of pyrology elements.

2   The Content of Open Modular Experiment Teaching in Pyrology Elements

Open modular experiment teaching is a kind of teaching organization form which students can choose their experiment content, experiment time and experimental teachers. Opening modular experiment course of pyrology elements is applied this teaching mode. Pyrology modular experiment class is a public elective course which is opened by Shandong University of Technology. It is an elective course to each students of university. The class consists of 10 professional experimental composition of pyrology speciality. It has features of experiment content modular and experimental process opening.

The modular of pyrology modular experiment class. The content of pyrology modular experiment class includes many courses' experiments of the pyrology professional direction. In order to make students master relevant knowledge faster and easier, the method of teaching is opening modular experiment teaching. Modular of experiment is shown in Fig.1. The content of course is divided into professional knowledge teaching module and professional experiment teaching module. Professional experiment teaching module is divided into basic experiment module and comprehensive experiment module which are basicd on the difficult of experiment and the different requirements of the students' practical ability. This course is to each students, students haven't basic knowledge of pyrology. Therefore the purpose of professional knowledge teaching module is added professional knowledge for students with corresponding professional basis and laying good foundation knowledge of their experimental operation.

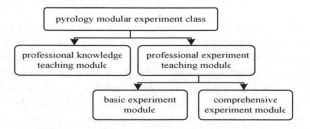

Fig. 1. Modular schematic diagram of experiment

The content of course comprise 10 typical experiments. According to the guiding ideology of progressive approach, content is divided into basic experiment module and comprehensive experiment module. Basic experiment module consists of four experiments. Comprehensive experiment module consists of six experiments. Experiment module is vertical model arrange. Basic experiment module is finished firstly. Comprehensive experiment module is finished lastly. Thereby realize the knowledge from shallow to deep, from simple to complex, benefit students understanding of knowledge. Practice ability of students is improved gradually. This course experiments includes the key experiment of backbone course instructor on pyrology, which can provide a platform for students to fully understand and master the pyrology relevant knowledge.

The opening of pyrology modular experiment class. Pyrology modular experiment class is a public elective course which. It realizes opening at class object, experiment content, experiment time, experimental teachers, etc.

① The opening of class object. The traditional major experiments are only for this specialized student, while other major students who have interested in pyrology experiments can't participate. Pyrology modular experiment class open to each students. It has achieved the opening of class objects, provided a platform for other major students who have interested in pyrology experiment, and improved the utilization of experiment resources.

② The opening of experiment content. Experiment content is divided into basic experiment module and comprehensive experimentmodule. Different modules use different opening forms. Basic experiment module is certain of basic professional experiments carefully selected by teachers. So the students can master the basic knowledge of necessary, the operation and using of common instrument, and the basic method and debug skill of experiment. This part is all required by the students, the goal is to get students to master necessary experiment skill. Comprehensive experiment module is strong comprehensive, research and design ability. According to their own interesting, the students can choose 4 experiments among the 6 experiments. The opening of experiment content can arouse student's enthusiasm effectively, and benefit the cultivation of practice ability and innovation consciousness.

③ The opening of experiment time. Without disturbing the normal experiment teaching, the opening time of laboratory room arrange in the evening and weekends. The experiment time of this course implement two method. One method is the opening of choosing experiment time. This is to say students can do experiments at any opening time by making an appointment. Every student can do experiments according to their own conditions. Thus achieve efficient use of time; the other method is there is no limit on the single experiment in the time length and test times. Students can finish the experiment with different duration according to their ability and do experiment operation many times. To achieve the purpose of the experiment as a standard. And make every student can effective improve their own abilities.

④ The opening of experiment teachers and teaching methods. The opening experiment teaching put forward higher requirement to teachers. The teachers' main task is guiding students by using elicitation teaching mode and take student's thinking primarily and provide guidelines to students. Thus develop the students' each kind of ability as much as possible. The experimental process follow after first, make students gradually deepens, and enables the student to master the ideas to solve problems. After experiments, the students should think and summarize the experimental process of valuable content which can cultivate students' ability of summarization.

⑤ The opening of experiment teaching management. A great deal of modern education technology are used in Pyrology modular experiment class. such as electronic courseware, experimental video, etc. It effectively improve the utilization of electronic resources. Meanwhile, the management also realize opening. At the beginning of each semester the school will arrange the elective to all students. Students can appointment the course with their interesting. Each experiment also realizes the electronic appointments which save the time of both teachers and students. This is easy to manage and scientific.

3   The Implementation and Results of Open Modular Experiment Teaching in Pyrology Elements

The implementation of open modular experiment teaching in pyrology elements. The open modular experiment teaching is not simply opening the door of laboratory. Experiment teachers have done a lot of work for this course can realize the real opening. Firstly, they have collected lots of information through kinds of ways and communicated with numbers of famous university professional experiment teachers. By using all of these ways, they put forward vertical model experiment modular teaching method and the elective model which the experiment content is full opening. Secondly, according to the new course content and class objects, the teachers have specially written experimental outline, experimental procedure, test report and so on. Besides, they have made electronic courseware, experimental video and other teaching materials. The course has realized whole school elective and electronic appointment of experiment, and got the acceptation of university functional department.

The results of open modular experiment teaching in pyrology elements. From the offering of pyrology modular experiment class, every semester we can begin our class, and each time the number of elective course selection number has reached the upper limit. Thus we can see great interesting to this course content among students. And they have high approval degree to this mode of course. In the feedback information of opening experiment teaching modular, Students thought highly of this course. The satisfaction rate is 98%. The students generally deem that this course let them know how to think and explore on their own. They can gain experience from the failure of the experiments, and gain achievement from the success of the experiment. As a result, they can effectively improve their ability of overcoming difficulties. Through this course students thought that expand their own aspect of knowledge, master the methods to solve the problems, improve their innovation consciousness, and give great help to the development of themselve and the study of other courses.

The Significance of Open Modular Experiment Teaching in Pyrology Elements. Pyrology modular experiment course provide all new knowledge. For better finishing and mastering the experiment, the students should self-study the relevant knowledge, consult plenty of dates, then work out the best experiment plan. Besides, they need to hands-on experiment design and experimental operation. Therefore, it contributes to cultivate the students' self-learning ability, practical ability and expand the scope of students' knowledge.

The goal of the opening modular experiment is to reach the purpose of experiment. It needs students to design the whole experiment process. This contributes to cultivate the students' the ability of solving problems. Through the careful observation, analysis and summary in experimental process, the students can expand their thinking ways which makes the solution of the problem diversity. Thus it contributes to cultivate the students' innovation consciousness.

The open modular experiment teaching is a kind of new teaching mode which has a certain requirements to teachers. It requires the teacher not only need a solid theoretical knowledge and rich practical experience, but also must be continually updated knowledge, and consciously accelerate knowledge update, improve their comprehensive quality. Meanwhile, new teaching mode has reached the real goal of the experimental teaching which makes the experiment teaching quality obviously improved.

The open modular experiment teaching pays attention to develop students' subject position in the experiment teaching. Make sure that the students can give fully play to its enthusiasm, subjective initiative in experiment teaching. Meanwhile, it is group cooperation during the experiment process. The teachers encourage discussion among students and cultivate their team spirit.

4 Conclusions

It is a significant task for university and higher education development trend and the demand of social development to cultivate talents with innovation consciousness, innovation ability, creative ability and practical ability. Experimental teaching is an important link to cultivate students' practice ability and innovation ability. The open modular experimental teaching mode is the effective way of training innovative talents. We should promote the reform of the opening modular experiment teaching, vigorously inspire students' interest of experiment, active students' thinking, and cultivate the students' practical ability and creative ability. Finally enhance the comprehensive ability of the college graduates.

Acknowledgment. This work was financially supported by Shandong University of Technology Teaching Innovation Foundation (No.107035 and No.108009).

References

1. Wang, M., Li, J., San, X.M.: Journal of Chongqing Institute of Technology (Natural Science Edition) 21, 169 (2007) (in Chinese)
2. Luo, H.B., Yao, H., Lin, X.H.: Journal of Fujiun Medical University (Natural Science Edition) 9, 34 (2008) (in Chinese)

3. Su, R.: China Science and Technology Information 2, 268 (2009) (in Chinese)
4. Zhu, H.B., Dai, W.Y., Li, J.: Journal of Ningbo University(Educational Science Edition)
   30, 107 (2008) (in Chinese)
5. Wang, J.H., Zhang, D., Cang, J.: Journal of Northeast Agricultural University(Social
   Science Edition) 5, 69 (2007) (in Chinese)
6. Deng, J.Z., Zhang, Z.Y., Li, Z.L.: Journal of East China Institute of Technology(Social
   Science) 26, 76 (2007) (in Chinese)

Research on Knowledge Management with Innovation Performance Based on Information Technology– Organizational Culture Perspective

Chiung-En Huang[1], Yi-Chun Chen[2], and Fuh-Gwo Chen[3]

[1] 70-11 Pei-Shin Liao, Matou, Tainan 721, Taiwan, R.O.C
a3126747@gmail.com
[2] No 11, Gongye Rd., Dali City, Taichung County 412, Taiwan, R.O.C
jeniffer960@hotmail.com
[3] No.34, Zhongqi Rd., Shalu Dist., Taichung City 433, Taiwan, R.O.C
fgchen@gmail.com

Abstract. The prerequisite for successful KM is to understand the employees, and to transfer their mindset, cultivate the culture of knowledge sharing, and integrate knowledge sharing with the entire organizational process, in order to utilize the human potential in organizations based on the transformation of organizational culture. This study investigated the influence of KM, organizational culture and innovation on the technology manufacturing industry. The research results indicated that KM has a significant positive influence on organizational culture, organizational culture has a significant positive influence on innovation performance, KM has a significant positive influence on innovation performance.

Keywords: Knowledge Management (KM), Organizational Culture, Innovation Performance.

1 Introduction

The environment of the knowledge-based economy era is highly competitive, which rapidly transforms technology and shortens product life cycle, and enables worldwide manufacturers to easily obtain the same manufacturing technology, raw materials, and resources [1]. In order to be competent in a competitive environment, enterprises have to retain their status through "innovation" and make innovation performance the key factor to gain a competitive edge [2]. Knowledge is the foundation of innovation. KM can help enterprises to respond to the constantly changing environment and enhance their competitive strengths to develop business strategies. In addition, it can assist them in the self-review process of the coordination among internal departments. It is an important asset for enterprises to survive and maintain competitiveness, as well as a power resource for sustainable innovation [3].

Although the importance of knowledge has been widely acknowledged, to properly manage and control it to create new capacity is subject to the form and skill of

S. Lin and X. Huang (Eds.): CSEE 2011, Part V, CCIS 218, pp. 139–143, 2011.
© Springer-Verlag Berlin Heidelberg 2011

management, which also has an influence on enterprises. The internal culture of an enterprise varies with the difference in the enterprise nature and mode of operation, and thus the adoption and application of knowledge may vary as well. Therefore, how to combine the application of KM with enterprise culture to create profits is an issue worth investigating.

Based on the research background and motivations above, the main purposes of this study are to investigate the influence of KM, organizational culture, and innovation performance.

2   Literature References

Knowledge Management and Organizational Culture
KM can provide members with correct knowledge in time to help them take precise actions to increase the sustainable organizational performance [4]. [5] suggested that organizational culture is a model for sharing values and beliefs in organizations, which can be viewed as the criterion for regulating corporate behavior. [6] survey on the application of KM indicated that most successful knowledge sharing experiences as well as KM in organizations are associated with organizational culture. Therefore, successful KM is subject to the cooperation of culture, management and organizations. [7] found in a study on the learning of knowledge workers that organizational culture can affect individual learning. Therefore, it is necessary to create a culture that encourages learning when organizations promote KM. In addition, an organizational culture that encourages and supports learning can help capture knowledge [8]. Therefore, Hypothesis 1 is proposed as follows.

H1: KM has a significant positive influence on organizational culture

Organizational Culture and Innovation Performance
[9] proposed the idea that innovation is achieved by the combination of creativity and organizational culture. When creativity is implemented in appropriate organizations, innovation will be generated. Therefore, only when enterprises offer appropriate environments can individual innovation in organizations be triggered. [10] suggested that enterprises with good performance possess a prevailing organizational culture. They also pointed out that a strong and powerful enterprise culture is the main cause for enterprises' better organizational performance. [11] conducted an empirical study on organizational culture, which proved that contributing factors such as organizational encouragement, supervisors' support, work team support, and challenging work, are positively correlated with the implementation of individual creativity in an organization and organizational productivity. In addition, [12] suggested that organizational structure, organizational culture, and human resource policies are the important factors triggering innovation. Therefore, Hypothesis 2 in this study was deduced.

H2: Organizational culture has a significant positive influence on innovation performance

Knowledge Management and Innovation Performance

[13] indicated that knowledge creation is the key to enterprises' sustainable innovation. One of the characteristics of knowledge work is innovation [14], and workers with KM capacity will be the most valuable and important assets for the enterprises' survival. Therefore, employees' KM capacity is helpful for organizational innovation [15].

[16] suggested that the process of employees' development of KM, as well as their objective to have a thorough understanding of products and procedures, contribute much to enterprise innovation. When employees can freely use knowledge, knowledge will become more valuable. If employees can appropriately transform existing knowledge into new concepts, not only productivity can be increased, but creativity can be triggered as well [17]. [18] found that KM capacity has a positive influence on organizational performance, such as company innovation, product improvement, and employee improvement. Therefore, Hypothesis 3 in this study was deduced:

H3: KM has a significant positive influence on innovation performance.

3 Research Methodology

Data Collection and Sampling

The subjects for the questionnaires were large-scaled technology companies among 500 major manufacturing industries in Taiwan, which had all implemented KM. A total of 121 effective questionnaires were returned.

Measures

To improve the questionnaire's content validity, five academic experts and five firm executives were invited to participate in the discussion. Empirical studies were conducted the technology manufacturing industry in Taiwan in order to find out on the influence on three aspects, namely the implementation of KM organizational culture, and innovation performance. For the aspect of KM included 12 items, with a Cronbach's α coefficient of 0.949 and a cumulative explained variance of 65.207%.For the aspect of organizational culture included 23 items, with a total Cronbach's α coefficient of 0.946 and a cumulative explained variance of 66.581%.For the aspect of innovation performance included 21 items, with a total Cronbach's α coefficient of 0.977 and a cumulative explained variance of 75.979%.

4 Analysis and Results

The data were analyzed with SPSS for Windows 15.0. Regression analysis was conducted to investigate the influence of KM on organizational culture, the influence of organizational culture on innovation performance, and the influence of KM on innovation performance.

The F value of the hierarchical regression model for analyzing the influence of KM on organizational culture is 76.319 ($p<0.001$) and the β coefficient is 0.809 ($p<0.001$), suggesting that KM has a significant positive influence on organizational culture. The organizational culture and values formed for the efficient and effective KM of organizations imperceptibly triggers organization members' spontaneous devotion to knowledge activities. Such a viewpoint is consistent with that proposed by [19].

The F value of the regression model for analyzing the influence of organizational culture on innovation performance is 19.267 ($p<0.001$) and the β coefficient is 0.561 ($p<0.001$), suggesting that organizational culture has a significant positive influence on innovation performance. Such a viewpoint is consistent with that proposed by [20]. Organizational culture is a form of enterprise atmosphere, which imperceptibly helps trigger groups' spontaneous knowledge creation, learning and diffusion.

The F value of the regression model for analyzing the influence of KM on innovation performance is 11.638 ($p<0.001$) and the β coefficient is 0.463 ($p<0.001$), suggesting that KM has a significant positive influence on innovation performance. Such a viewpoint is consistent with that proposed by [18] and [21]. The purpose of KM is to apply knowledge, in order to improve the performance of technology, products, service innovation, and organizations' external competitiveness.

5   Conclusion

The key to successful KM relies on a well-established organizational culture
The results in this study indicated that KM has a significant positive influence on organizational culture, namely, organizations should establish trust and cooperation and re-cultivate interpersonal relationships through various mechanisms and approaches, as well as the exchange of encouraging experiences.

KM plays an important role in innovation performance
The results in this study indicated that KM has a significant influence on innovation performance. The purpose of KM is to apply knowledge to improve the innovation performance of technology, products, and services, as well as to increase organizations' external competitiveness. [13] also suggested that KM is the key to enterprises' sustainable innovation, which is consistent with the conclusion obtained from this study.

A well-established organizational culture has a decisive influence on innovation performance
The results in this study indicated that a well-established organizational culture has a decisive influence on innovation performance. The promotion of a culture of sharing, a positive attitude towards the establishment of non-standard practical groups and social exchange activities, attention from senior supervisors, and proposals for interpersonal relationships and organizational promotion systems all will affect organization members' willingness to share knowledge. In addition, they will help increase enterprises' overall innovation efficiency. Therefore, organizational culture plays an important role in innovation performance.

References

1. Porter, M.E.: Competitive advantage: Creating and sustaining superior performance. The Press, NY (1990)
2. Leskovar-Spacapan, G., Bastic, M.: Differences in organizations' innovation capability in transition economy: Internal aspect of the organizations' strategic orientation. Technovation 27(9), 533–546 (2007)

3. Beckett-Camarata, E.J., Camarata, M.R., Barker, R.T.: Integrating internal and external customer relationships through relationship management: A strategic response to a changing global environment. Journal of Business Research 41(1), 71–81 (1998)

4. O'Dell, C., Grayson, C.J.: In Only We Know What We Know. The Free Press, New York (1998)

5. Osland, J.S., Kolb, D.A., Rubin, I.M.: Organizational Behavior: An Experiential Approach, 7th edn. Prentice Hall, Englewood Cliffs (2004)

6. Alavi, M., Leidner, D.E.: Knowledge management system: issues, challenges, and benefits. Communications of the AIS 1(7), 1–37 (1999)

7. Kimball, F.: Shedding light on knowledge work learning. The Journal for Quality & Participation 21(4), 8–16 (1998)

8. Kulkarni, U.R., Ravindran, S., Freeze, R.: A Knowledge Management Success Model. Theoretical Development and Empirical Validation. Journal of Management Information Systems 23(3), 309–347 (2007)

9. Higgins, J.M.: Innovation: The core competence. Planning Review 23(6), 32–36 (1995)

10. Deal, T.E., Kennedy, A.A.: Corporate cultures. Common Wealth Publishing, NY (1984)

11. Amabile, T.M.: Assessing the Work Environment for Creativity. Academy of Management Journal 39(5), 59–1162 (1996)

12. Robbins, S.P.: Organization Behavior, 9th edn. Prentice-Hall Inc., N.J (2001)

13. Nonaka, I., Takeuchi, H.: The Knowledge-Creating Company. Oxford University Press Inc., NY (1995)

14. Zidle, M.: Retention hooks for keeping knowledge workers. Manage. 50(1), 21–22 (1998)

15. Liu, P.L., Chen, W.C., Tsai, C.H.: An empirical study on the correlation between the knowledge management method and new product development strategy on product performance in Taiwan's industries. Technovation 25(6), 637–644 (2005)

16. Forcadell, J.F., Guadamillas, F.: A case study on implementation of a knowledge management strategy oriented to innovation. Knowledge and Process Management 9(3), 162–171 (2002)

17. Davenport, T.H., Prusak, L.: Working knowledge: How organization manage what they know. President and Fellows of Harvard College, Boston (1998)

18. Kiessling, T.S., Richey, R.G., Meng, J., Dabic, M.: Exploring Knowledge Management to Organizational Performance Outcomes in a Transitional Economy. Journal of World Business 44(4), 421–433 (2009)

19. Palanisamy, R.: Organizational Culture and Knowledge Management in ERP Implementation: An Empirical Study. Journal of Computer Information Systems 48(2), 100–120 (2008)

20. Tushman, M.L., O'Reilly III, C.A.: Ambidextrous Organizations: Managing Evolutionary and Revolutionary Change. California Management Review 38(4), 8–30 (1996)

21. Talisayon, S.D.: Knowledge and People. Business World 2(3), 1–5 (2002)

Quality of Personnel Training of Higher Education: Problems and Solutions Research with Modern Information Technology

TingYan Bi

Weifang University, Weifang 261061, China
btylook@163.com

Abstract. After entering the post-mass period, higher education in China was facing a very good opportunity of raising the training quality, meanwhile it would also encounter many difficulties and problems. According to the national Education Plan and the requirements of education conferences, the top priority of the present education theory and practice of China's higher education will be to carefully analyze the opportunities and challenges in the process of transforming from a mass higher education country to one with powerful higher education, actively explore and comprehensively improve the quality of the training of higher education strategies and methods.

Keywords: talent, quality of personnel training, higher education.

1 Introduction

Training refers to the process of personnel education and training. The specific requirements of personnel training are different in all walks of life, but the overall goal is to achieve moral, intellectual and physical development. In the past 30 years, the development of China's higher education has made remarkable achievements and has achieved a historic leap. Socialism with Chinese characteristics, the initial formation of the higher education system, economic and social development in China provides a strong intellectual support and personnel security. As a higher power, the total scale of China's higher education ranks first in the world, and the total number of employees with higher education ranks second in the world. But compared to the new demands of China's development and people's new expectations, low quality of personnel training, weak international influence and less competitive ability do not meet the economic and social development needs. Studying and solving these problems is the core mission of higher education in China.

Quality of the personnel training is an eternal theme, but also the practical problem facing higher education in China. Education carries the hope of the country and nation, entrusted with the hundreds of millions of people's hope for a better life, so it is a noble mission and important responsibility to prompt the education reform and development. [1] Prospection of Goal 2020: it is to basically modernize education, bring a learning society into shape, and turn China into a country rich in human resources (*As is shown in table 1*).

S. Lin and X. Huang (Eds.): CSEE 2011, Part V, CCIS 218, pp. 144–148, 2011.

Table 1. Prospection of China's Higher Education in 2020

Year	2009	2015	2020
H. E. Learners in total (million)	29.79	33.50	35.50
HEI Students in total (million)	28.265	30.80	33.80
in which: Postgraduates	1.405	1.7	2
Regular undergraduates	21.45	29.1	31.8
Adult undergraduates	5.41	-	-
Gross enrolment rate in Higher Education	24.20%	36%	40%
Number of people with higher education	98.3	145	195
Percentage of those having received higher education in the working-age(20-59 years old) population	9.90%	15%	20%

2 Problems and Analysis

Chinese higher education meets sound development opportunities while in the training of personnel it is also faced with many difficulties and problems. For example, the concept of education is relatively backward: it has not become a society-wide consensus that it is necessary and urgent to improve the personnel training quality of higher education; the government has not yet been aware of that it is required to build the appropriate legal mechanisms, policy mechanisms and economic mechanisms and other effective measures to regulate and guide the behavior of institutions; universities emphasize specialty but light basis, emphasize theory but light practice, emphasize marks but light ability and emphasize teaching but light guiding on how to train creative talents; it is required to further deepen the educational reform; teaching staff need to be improved and it is urgent to develop a number of high-level personnel; management system and operational mechanism need further innovation and improvement; the defects of creative talent evaluation and selection mechanism for creative talents are imperfect, and so on. These problems need be carefully analyzed and solved with effective measures.

OrtegaY. Gasset, a famous Spanish thinker and social activist in 20th century thinks that people should directly and clearly answer to what the university is and what the university should do, which is directly related to university reform. People don't know how to run universities and can't run them well without thinking about the basic attributes and mission. In his famous book Universities' Mission; he points out "It is important for universities to re-understand their mission and the university activities can really play out the power." [2] Teaching level of teachers is a key factor in the quality of teaching. Problems of Chinese university teachers' teaching level are very prominent, because most university teachers do not receive specialized training in teaching methods and many teachers directly go onto the podium after taking a master's degree or a PhD. As for how to prepare lessons, how to use teaching methods, how to effectively guide students, how to create a classroom atmosphere, how to efficiently do teaching, they are not trained and entirely go to explore by themselves, which is a common problem. This problem didn't just appear today, and it is practice for college graduates, postgraduates and doctoral graduates directly to go to the podium. [3] The American College Teacher survey shows that American university teachers for some of the main objectives of undergraduate education are actually quite common: to help students develop thinking skills of judgments and master the knowledge of specific subjects; to teach students how to identify the quality and reliability of information; to train writing skills of students. The survey of Higher Education Research Institute of University of California at Los Angeles also shows a trend of long-term effects, namely teachers in the United States institutions of universities, particularly for young teachers, tend to reduce the lecture-style teaching and to be in favor of student-centered teaching methods. [4]

China's training capacity of top creative talent is weak. Universities lack a large number of high level talents which directly affects the improvement of education quality and the training of innovative talents. Education budget of students of national colleges paces up and down on the lowest level for many years, and the province of the highest budget is from six times to eight times more than the province of the lowest one (*As is shown in table 2*).

Table 2. Budgetary expenditure per student in Regular HEIs (RMB Yuan)

Year	2003	2004	2005	2006	2007	2008
Avg.	5772.58	5552.5	5375.94	5868.53	6546.04	7577.71
Max	15806.43	15809.95	17036.5	18228.36	21431.73	24380.4
Min	2040.77	1946.3	2076.09	2219.41	3125.25	3713.46
Max/Min	7.75	8.12	8.21	8.21	6.86	6.57

China's university graduates' entry level salary is still proportional to their education level, but the expected starting salary level of graduates is not very high. Although the implementation of Labor Contract Law pulls up the entry point after the implementation of pulling up, it is very different in different regions, because of the effect of the international financial crisis; a certain degree of structural employment problem appears. Each year university graduates have passed half of the city and town's new jobs of that year. The original aim of higher education to pursuit greater benefit turns to ensure a smaller loss, which leads to the further increase of social needs for higher education level and is bound to raise new demands for personnel training and using segment. [5]

Education system mechanisms are inadequate and the schools lack vitality, which are major changes for education development of China and directly affect the improvement of the quality of training. The main source of the problem is the actual existence of administrative philosophy and system in the field of education for a long time. Whether the administration can be eliminated lies in the government's policy and action. If the blueprint and path of plan can be implemented, the good relationship of modern university, government and society will be established, educational situation full of vigor and vitality will occur and the grand goal of power in higher education and human resources will come true possibly at an early date. [6]

A systemized education is used in China, which leads to the people's curiosity being ignored and even being gradually denied in the way of explicate or potential force and discipline. In the simple access to the knowledge and its understanding it is perhaps not bad and even good. However, it may be the most fail in the development of various kinds of human potential and the training of all kinds of creative talents. This is my basic judgment of school education in China on the missing of cultivation of innovative talents. [7] To improve the quality of Chinese higher education personnel training, deep society conflicts are inevitable to be exposed to be the shortage of critical resources, basic resources, dynamic resources and developing resources that exist generally in universities. Resource constraint is the specific character of institutional barriers. The specific performance is the shortage of critical resources, basic resources, dynamic resources and developing resources. [8]

3   Main Content, Strategy and Suggestion of Personnel Training

Unswervingly adhere to the center status of personnel training. Universities are educational institutions and academic organizations which aim to explore knowledge and are responsible for guiding social values and standardizing the social behaviors from the level of moral spirit. Universities have significant irreplaceable public influence and driving force to the improvement and enhancement of human's quality and the development and progress of social civilization. Besides, universities are the world to the growth of the new. [9] Chinese higher education should firmly establish the primary responsibility of teaching and educating people for university teachers.

Optimize Training Structure. Western countries' higher education emphasizes profession's important position in the life, focusing attention to the students' overall development and lifelong development, which encourages students to rationally plan for the future, and strive to consciously improve the learning process consciously employability and career management in the learning process. [10] China's higher education personnel training should focus on expanding the training scale of variety of application talents, compound talents, and skilled talents.

Perfect the assurance system of personnel training quality. From the perspective of international comparisons in the construction of higher education quality assurance process with Chinese characteristics, it is required to involve more community people involved in other sectors, to further increase the transparency and performance of university education to establish and perfect the institutions internal quality assurance mechanisms, to strengthen international cooperation and to pay attention to the international dynamic development. [11] It is also required to actively promote "comprehensive reform of higher education." We should focus on co-ordination, planning, layout and management of higher education in the region to determine the number, level and type of colleges and universities in the region, and to build regional higher education system. Iran, starting from the internal management of the University, the appointment and election of university president fully embodies the "politics" to elect university pricipals is not elected by the school, but appointed by the Ministry of Higher Education, with vice-president being appointed by the president. Whenever the president election, there will be a large number of principals to be replaced. That is to say, all of the current university presidents are the supporters of Nejad. [12]

4 Summaries

Personnel training is the historic mission of higher education. Colleges and universities should unswervingly adhere to the personnel training center. Around the center of personnel training, positive and effective measures should be taken to change the education concept, to deepen teaching reform, to optimize the talents' team structure, to improve the quality of teachers, to increase the input of fund, and to improve assurance mechanism of personnel training quality to comprehensively improve the quality of the training of higher education. Mechanism and atmosphere should be constructed to train several of creative talents with the core of training students' social responsibility, innovative spirit and practical ability. Tens of millions of highly qualified professionals and a large number of top creative talents can be developed, which makes the personnel training of China's higher education is more responsive to economic society's development needs.

Acknowledgement. The research projects have been funded by Social Science Planning Office of Shandong Province (No. 09CJGJ48).

References

1. Liu, Y.-d.: Summary Speech in National Education Work Conference. China Education Daily (September 20, 2010) (in Chinese)
2. Gasse, O.: Universities' Mission, pp. 4–5. Zhejiang Education Press, Hanghou (2001)
3. Mishing, Y.: Diffusion Processes in Advanced Technological Materials. In: Noyes, D.G. (ed.). Publications/William Andrew Publising, Norwich (2004)
4. America. gov. [J/OL][October 06, 2009],
   http://www.america.gov/st/diversity-chinese/
5. Zhang, L.: Massfication of Higher Education in China: Analysis on Several Policy Trends. China's higher education BBS, Finland (May 2010) (in press)
6. Chen, X.-f.: Eliminating Administration of Universities: Key Lying in Government. Exploration and Free Views, 63–65 (September 2010) (in Chinese)
7. Yan, G.-c.: Caring People's Curiosity Being in Need to Train Innovatory Talents. Exploration and Free Views, 5–7 (March 2010) (in Chinese)
8. Lu, G.-l.: Reunderstanding Improvement of Personnel Training Quality of Higher Education. Modern University Education, 81–86 (May 2010) (in Chinese)
9. Sui, Y.-f.: Defending University with Reason: Responsibility of Higher Education Theory. Tsinghua Journal of Education, 14–19 (April 2010) (in Chinese)
10. Bi, T.-y.: New Discussion of Career Development of University Students. Chinese Science and Technology Publishing House, Beijing (2010)
11. Huang, F.-t.: International Trend and Chinese Choice of Higher Education Quality Assurance. Peking University Education Review, 114–124 (January 2010) (in Chinese)
12. Wu, D.-g.: Uncovering mystery of society and higher education of Iran- Sidelight Being in Iran. Modern University Education, 100–105 (January 2010) (in Chinese)

Improve Modern University System: Challenges and Experiences

TingYan Bi

Weifang University, Weifang 261061, China
btylook@163.com

Abstract. After the popular stage in higher education, to improve the modern university system with Chinese characteristics was put forward as a major strategic issue accompanied by deepening the reform of higher education. In the field of system construction of modern university, many western countries have accumulated a wealth of practical experience which we should learn from. Newly issued Education Plan made it clear that the main elements of China's modern university system construction are to improve governance, strengthen the constitution-building, expand social cooperation and promote the professional evaluation. This will help establish the goals and tasks of establishing and further perfecting a sound and modern university system with Chinese characteristics.

Keywords: Modern university system, governance structure, university regulations, specialty evaluation.

1 Introduction

From 2000 to 2010, the average annual increase rate of college graduates in Mainland China is about 20%, which leads to a difficult employment situation (*As is shown in Figure 1*).

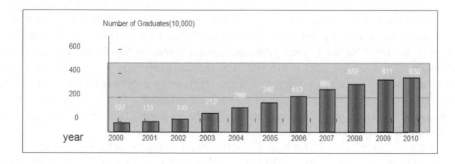

Fig. 1. Status quo in China

S. Lin and X. Huang (Eds.): CSEE 2011, Part V, CCIS 218, pp. 149–153, 2011.
© Springer-Verlag Berlin Heidelberg 2011

Higher education system construction level revealed more and more problems after the post-basification. Qiu Chengtong, a famous scholar, thinks that higher education system lacks creative young academic leader; evaluation system is not perfect, which leads to the intricacies of the academic politics, or seemingly objective quantity standard; senior scholars' administrative task is arduous, and the government-owned standard ranking thought haunts. Lao Kaisheng, an education legal science expert thinks that the relationship between the government and colleges still has the color of planned economy system, whose main characteristic is still the higher school's dependence on the government, and higher school's actual status hasn't changed substantially. Wang Yingjie, a comparative higher education expert thinks the conflict between academic authority and administrative power is increasingly sharp. The academic power is continuously extruded, and the administrators become employers and dominators of universities which increasingly become bureaucratic institutions. The phenomenon of government power rent-seeking by a few teachers who hold administrative power or administrators who occupy the teacher resource, ruins and corrodes the traditional college culture. Wu Daguang thinks the flaw of the modern university system in our country, as a matter of fact, is the lack of university ideas; the confusion in constructing the modern university system is actually the confusion of university ideas. [1]

2 Perfect University's Governance Structure

To perfect university governance structure, we must focus on the fundamental problem of "what people to be cultivated and how to cultivate people ", which must be beneficial to advance the reform of the education and teaching, must be beneficial to arouse the creativity enthusiasm of teachers, must be beneficial to the students' development in an all-round way and quality improvement, must be beneficial to the cross and fusion of disciplines, must be beneficial to the formations of the good academic atmosphere, and must be beneficial to the formation of the good style of study, the school spirit and work style. [2] Perfect the university's external governance structure. The common characteristic of external management in western countries' universities is: separating the functions of government and school autonomy. Governments don't manage the university directly. The university's internal affairs are managed by itself. Perfect the university's internal governance structure. University internal management means the establishment, subordinate relationship and purview division of the university internal organization, reflecting the static side of university internal system. University operation mechanism refers to the forms and operation principle of the relationship, interaction and mutual restrict between each subsystem and each factor of university internal system, reflecting the dynamic side of university internal system. Perfect the university operation mechanism. The highlight of foreign universities' internal operation mechanism is the colleges' two levels management system, and to say specifically is college system construction.

France is the world's birthplace of University College system, the University of Paris which is called the "Mother of European Universities" is the most comprehensive university in the history of School System. The internal operation mechanism of overseas universities enlightens us that a reasonable system plays a very important role in the formation of college running characteristics which is possible with a reasonable system, but a set of mature operation system of the university is also needed to make it come true. [3] (*As is shown in Figure 2*).

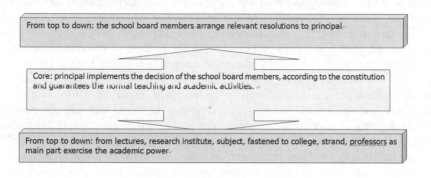

Fig. 2. University internal governance structure model

3   Establish and Perfect University Charter

Formulating university charter helps to make the modern university organization system characteristics clear. However, in order to construct the modern university system with Chinese features how to shows the advantage of Chinese university charter in the implement level, and how to make power clear, balance power and work efficiently are unavoidable questions to answer and solve. Different universities through the formulation of regulations know their own nature, mission and purpose, university internal power structure, organizational system, department functions and permissions etc, which are the important prerequisites for university to establish independent legal status and realize the aim of running independently. The charter of British university has a long history. Though the United States university charter has a history of only 200 years, the university charter has developed to a mature level. And the United States was once a British colony; so many places of both Britain and the United Kingdom university charter are interlinked. [4]

University charter is the standard about the basic organization and the fundamental rights that a university set up, it stands for the common determination of staff and students. Once approved by, it becomes the basic law of standardizing school behavior, and plays an extremely important role in the college management. According to the provisions of the laws of Japan, each Japan University has its articles of association. [5]

4   Perfect and Expand Social Cooperation System

The modern university should adhere to the promoting open reform and development. In order to give full play to the role of universities to perfect national innovation system, the government needs to formulate the corresponding policy encouraging the R&D collaboration between colleges and transnational corporations. Colleges and universities should pay attention to and promote the technological overflow in cooperation and strengthen the formal academic exchanges and the flow of human capital; expand staff exchanges especially college R&D personnel to multinational companies R&D institutions involved in research and development activities to develop the function of benefits from demonstration and imitation to university scientific research ability. [6] However, the technical cooperation between universities and enterprises exist certain risks in the process of technical innovation, which affects the results of school-enterprise cooperation technological innovation. Universities and enterprises must pay more attention to technical project risky factors in the cooperation process, and actively learn successful experience from enterprises' technological innovation on the project technology to avoid the school-enterprise cooperation going into erroneous zone in the process of technological innovation; actively walk the path of combining study, fully mobilize large number of scientific research personnel's enthusiasm, emphatically strengthen project technology improvement; pay more attention to development state; timely give feedback of adverse impact on project technology, then give new vitality to   the project technology. [7]

5   Perfect Specialty Evaluation Systems

Specialty evaluation aims to fully excavate teachers' potentiality, promote in-depth and meticulous analysis and reflection, and finally to achieve the purpose of self-improvement. Specialty evaluation is comprehensive, circulating and improvable, whose contents include providing comprehensive and effective feedback for the extension of specialty designers enabling them to make right decisions which can improve specialty; revealing specialty teaching's influence and contribution to talents' development for teachers, teaching assistant personnel, students and other social personage; providing performance information for the school educational administration department and external certification institutions, which mainly reflects the students' development status in cognition, emotion and skills. [8]

The professional evaluation of American college is different from the conventional external evaluation organized by the superior education administrative department or specialized organization, but a kind of internal evaluation which is carried out specifically by departments according to schools' uniform requirements and department. This evaluation is hosted by a special group, whose members include the school personage, professional teachers, students, parents and related community personals. One senior professor work as team leader to organize and coordinate the evaluation, and the other teachers are the main strength to carry out evaluation. In order to make the process and result of the evaluation reliable and to avoid factitious or administrative factors' interference, many schools' leaders make the rule that school leaders don't attend school evaluation and they only provide information that the evaluation need.

Chinese universities should pay attention to specialty evaluation. According to the practical needs of the national economy and social development to update specialty structure, perfect the curriculum and teaching modes, and make students' expertise and comprehensive ability keep up with the pace of the times. To maintain excellent education quality, universities should constantly monitor and evaluate internal specialty to find advantages and disadvantages of each major, and then make timely adjust and reform. Specialty evaluation makes a big difference in the healthy development of specialty and the improvement of school's overall quality.

6   Conclusions

To perfect governance structure of the university, specifically speaking, that is to perfect the university's internal governance structure and operation mechanism, to establish and perfect university charter, to establish a modern university system. To set up a modern university system, professional evaluation system construction need be promoted actively. We should encourage the specialized agencies and social intermediary organizations to evaluate the level and quality of university subjects, specialties and courses; establish scientific and standard system of evaluation system; explore cooperating with international high level education evaluation institutions, in order to form university evaluation mode with Chinese characteristics and establish annual report release system of higher school quality.

Acknowledgement. The research projects have been funded by Social Science Planning Office of Shandong Province (No. 09CJGJ48). Shihua Song, Wenfang Yang of Weifang University participated in the revision and translation of the article, here thanks to all of them.

References

1. Ma, L.-t.: Modern University System Building and Innovation Personnel Training. Chinese Higher Education (May 2010) (in Chinese)
2. Gu, H.-l.: Theoretical Guidelines. Improve Internal Governance Structure of Construction of Modern University System. Chinese Higher Education, 15–16 (2010) (in Chinese)
3. Hu, R.-d., Zhang, Z.-m.: System and Mechanism: American Universities School-running Features of Formation. Coal Higher Education (March 2010) (in Chinese)
4. Cao, Y.-j., Wang, H.-z.: Characteristics of American University Regulations. Gan Nan Teachers College (February 2010) (in Chinese)
5. Chen, L.-p., Liang, Y.-y.: University Charter Construction of Japan. Chinese Higher Education 17 (2010) (in Chinese)
6. Cui, X.-j., Kong, L.-l., Zhang, T.-q.: Spillovers Way of Multinational Company and China University of R&D Cooperation Technology. Technology Policy and Management (11) (2008) (in Chinese)
7. Ling, Z., Liu, T.-X.: Technological Innovation Risk Evaluation of Universities and Enterprises Cooperation. Science Economy Society (3) (2010) (in Chinese)
8. Min, C.: American College of Professional Evaluation of Implementation Strategy. Foreign Education (September 2010) (in Chinese)

Research on Expert System of Automatic Scoring for Computer Basic Course Examination

Jie Zhang and Junhong Feng

Department of Computer Science and Technology, Guangzhou University SonTan College,
Zengcheng, Guangzhou, Guangdong, P.R. China
290813268@qq.com, 376915877@qq.com

Abstract. The purpose of this paper is to develop expert system of automatic scoring and apply it to the exam of the computer basic course. Structures and designing of the system are described in detail.

Keywords: Expert System, Automatic Scoring, Computer Basic.

1 Introduction

An expert system is a kind of intelligent programming system on the basis of expertise and experience, which can resolve complex issues by simulating the thought processes of experts [1]. The applications of the expert system are always hot issues. A fuzzy expert system is adopted to diagnose medical conditions such as diabetes and heart disease [2]. Theories of expert system are applied to solve the problem of fault diagnosis in the aircraft fuel system [3]. An expert system is applied to soil erosion in the traffic engineering [4]. An expert system is used to detect the malware [5].

The automatic scoring plays a key part in the OA (office automation). It is worth studying matters how to combine the expert system with the automatic scoring. This paper presents the expert system of automatic scoring for computer basic course.

The remainder of this paper is organized as follows. Section 2 describes the structure of expert system. In sections 3 the development platform is summarized and chosen. How to build the knowledge bases is described in Section 4. Section 5 shows the design of reasoning machine, and finally this paper is concluded in Section 6.

2 The Structure of Expert System

According to the general structure, we design the structure of the expert system of automatic scoring for computer basic course, as is shown in fig1.

The basic parts of the expert are human-computer interface, knowledge base, reasoning machine, interpreter, maintenance program and integrative database. The function of every part is described as follows.

S. Lin and X. Huang (Eds.): CSEE 2011, Part V, CCIS 218, pp. 154–159, 2011.

(1) expert: It provides the basic knowledge of the computer basis, the experiential knowledge of experts, and the newly knowledge in the area and so on. This knowledge is applied to constitute rich knowledge base. (2) user: It is used to go over and score examination papers, and test by the expert system. (3) human-computer interface: It is responsible for the dialogs of the system and user, the system and the experts. (4) reasoning machine: It is an important part of the expert system, and mainly carries on the reasoning processing of the system. For example, when a question is asked by a user, it will utilize the

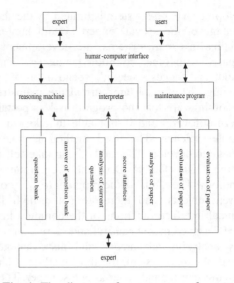

Fig. 1. The diagram of expert system for automatic scoring

knowledge of the knowledge base to successively reason and acquire the correct answer which is then told the user.(5) Interpreter: It is mainly in charge of interpreting the reasoning process of the system. For the foregoing example, when a question is asked by a user, how to draw a conclusion in each reasoning and what are features of the conclusion and so on. To put it simply, the interpreter is the reason of the answer.(6) Maintenance program: It is mainly in charge of management and maintenance of the knowledge base and the reasoning machine. The creating, altering, and deleting of question base in the knowledge base are all belong to maintenance.(7) Integrative database: It is mainly in charge of storing the temporary data of the system. (8)knowledge base: It is comparatively complex, but it isn't disordered. According to requirements and functions in the process of going over examination papers, the knowledge of the knowledge base is divided into different modules, such as the module of the question base, the module of the answer base, the analytical module of the current question, the statistical module of the score, the analytical module of the paper, and the evaluating module of the questions and so on. This is one hand of that the expert system is different from the other general program. There is different module in the knowledge base for different type question. The knowledge base concentrates the essence and the wisdom of the experts. It almost includes all knowledge of the computer basis, and is one of the core parts in the expert system.

3   Choices of Development Platform

There are three major methods in the expert system development. The first method is take advantage of the shell system having already designed to develop. The method is easy to operate, and the developers need not understand too many knowledge of an expert system. Its shortcomings are that the current available shells are very little, and developing an expert system is limited by the shell system. The second method is take advantage of the special expert system languages to develop. Because languages specialize in expert systems, the development process therefore can be simplified compared with other common languages. These languages often provide a logic method, and the user needn't spend a lot of effort for the development of logical reasoning, therefore, it are current the mainstream of designing expert systems. Its shortcomings are that the program is less portable, do not meet the popular trend of modern software, and is not able to take full advantage of the newly benefits of computer science. The third method is take advantage of the common variant language to develop. The method can take full advantage of the database technology and the OOP (Object Oriented Programming) technology in modern computer technology. These enable the program to carry out different functions according to the different objects, and therefore get a high flexibility. Because of the powerful graphical interface functions of the common language, the interfaces of the program can be designed more beautiful and more operational.

By analyzing advantages and disadvantages of the above three development method of expert system, the third method is chosen to develop the expert system of automatic scoring and generating test paper. The pattern of VB+LISP is chosen as the development platform, which the operational interfaces are designed by VB, and the internal reasoning is carried out by LISP.

4   Building of Knowledge Base

All possible knowledge points that can be examined are almost stored in the knowledge bases of the expert system of automatic scoring for computer basic course. The methods of knowledge representation can be roughly divided into two categories in expert system [6], namely the narrative knowledge representation and the procedural knowledge representation. Common knowledge representations include logical representation, production representation, semantic networks representation, frame representation, and characteristic representations, which basically all belong to the narrative knowledge representation. This paper adopts the most widely used knowledge representation in expert system, namely rule-based production representation.

The knowledge in the knowledge base is divided into several modules according to various knowledge points. The knowledge in each module adopts the pattern of many base organizations according to various ranks. Many base includes data base, fact base and rule base. This can not only improve the system efficiency, but also facilitate the search of knowledge. Each base is each other independent. Updating of a base will not affect the other bases.

5   Design of Reasoning Machine

After knowledge base has been built, the design of reasoning machine directly affects the speed, completeness and correctness of reasoning in expert system. A good reasoning machine can not only help users to deduce the correct result, can but also enable users to understand the process of reasoning in the process of deducing. It is in the process that the expert knowledge is acquired by the expert system.

The reasoning of the expert system of automatic scoring employs the fuzzy theory to deal with model building and knowledge reasoning. The interaction between systems and users is fully considered in the designing process, which make reasoning more accurate and transparent.

Many complex expert systems is often incomplete, fuzzy or uncertain, therefore, the uncertain calculation or reasoning is often used when using the structure of productive system or expert system. There are two kinds of uncertainty, namely the uncertainty about the evidence and the uncertainty about the conclusion.

6   Choices of Reasoning Mechanism

The reasoning way of the reason machine for productive system can be divided into three kind, namely the forward reasoning (FR), the backward reasoning (BR), and the forward & backward hybrid reasoning (FBR).

(1) Forward reasoning
The forward reasoning is a kind of reasoning based on the known facts as a starting point, is also called the data-driven reasoning, the forward chain reasoning or the antecedent reasoning, etc. The most important issue to consider in forward reasoning is how to choose available knowledge from the knowledge base, which has greater influence on reasoning speed. The main advantage of the forward reasoning is that it can make full use of the information provided by the users. Therefore, the system can quickly respond to user's input. Its main disadvantage is that it has a "blind reasoning" tendency. One way to reduce blind reasoning is to select an appropriate control strategy.

(2) Backward reasoning
The backward reasoning is a kind of reasoning based on a certain hypothesis target as a starting point, is also called the goal-driven reasoning, the backward chain reasoning or the consequent reasoning, etc. The basic ideas backward reasoning is as follows. A hypothetical target is first selected, and then look for the evidence to support the hypothesis. If the required evidence can be found, then the hypothesis is turned out to be relatively correct. If we can't anyway find evidence, then the hypothesis should be wrong, and need to make another new hypothesis. If the required evidence can be found, then the original hypothesis is testified to be correct, and if the required evidence in any case can not be found, then the original hypothesis is testified to be incorrect. At this moment, a new hypothesis is need to make.

(3) Hybrid reasoning
Forward reasoning possesses blind and low efficiency drawback. The disadvantage of backward reasoning is that if the hypothesis doesn't accord with the fact, the efficiency of the system will be reduced. In order to solve these problems, the forward reasoning and the backward reasoning can be combined, and complement each other. The reasoning such as possess both the forward reasoning and the backward reasoning is called the forward & backward hybrid reasoning, also called two-way hybrid reasoning two-way hybrid reasoning. The so-called hybrid reasoning is that the forward reasoning first carried out according to the given original data or evidence (such data or evidence is often not sufficient), and draw diagnostic

conclusions that are possibly correct. Then, such conclusions are regarded as the hypotheses, and backward reasoning is carried out to look for the facts or evidences supporting these hypotheses. There are two kinds of hybrid reasoning, which is described as follows.

① first forward and then backward reasoning. The forward reasoning is firstly carried out to help select a target, and some results are deduced from the known fact. The backward reasoning is then carried out to confirm the target or enhance its confidence level.

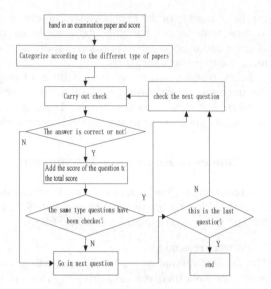

Fig. 2. The reasoning graph of checking

② first backward reasoning and then forward reasoning. A target is firstly supposed to carry out the backward reasoning. The information acquired in the backward reasoning is then employed to carry out the forward reasoning so as to acquire more conclusions.

The integrated reasoning mechanism is adopted in the paper. The result is first judged whether it is accord with the answer or not. If they are accordant, the process of solving question is further judge. The process of scoring and reasoning is shown in fig2.

According to the content of the theme, the key point and question type, the system will categorize the items of test. The different reasoning mechanism will be adopted to score in the light of the different question types and the key points. For example, to the choice questions, the forward reasoning is directly employed. To the construction problem in Excel this paper adopt the method of the first backward reasoning and then forward reasoning. As a detail example is described as follows.

In the sheet named "student score table" , employ a columnar cluster graph to represent the score of the three course about "advanced mathematics", "English", and "computer", and store the graph in the area "H10:H25".

The reasoning procedures of the examination question are described as follow. ① If there exists a worksheet whose name is "student score table" in Excel, then turn procedure ②; ②If there exists a graph in the areas "H10:H25", then turn procedure ③; ③ Judge whether the graph is columnar graph or not. If it is yes, then turn procedure ④; ④ Judge whether the columnar graph is the columnar cluster graph or not. If it is yes, then turn procedure ⑤; ⑤ Judge each data are produced whether according to the requirements or not. If it is yes, then turn procedure⑥; ⑥Draw the conclusions that the operating of the examination question is correct, and then turn procedure ⑦; ⑦ The score of the examination question is added up to the total score, and then Exit.

The backward reasoning is employed in procedure ① to ④, and the forward reasoning is employed in procedure ⑤. In practical applications, each examination question needs to choose suitable reasoning mechanism according to the specific situation.

7 Summary

The system applies the expert system to the automatic scoring for the computer basic course, which make subjective questions be mark more intelligent and accurate.

References

1. Bo, W., Ma, Y.-x.: Expert system, vol. 9, pp. 9–10. Beijing Institute of Technology Press, Beijing (2003)
2. Lee, C.-S., Wang, M.-H.: A Fuzzy Expert System for Diabetes Decision Support Application. IEEE Transactions On Systems, Man, and Cybernetics — Part B: Cybernetics 41(1), 139–153 (2011)
3. Long, H., Wang, X.: Application of Aircraft Fuel Fault Diagnostic Expert System Based on Fuzzy Neural Network. In: 2009 WASE International Conference on Information Engineering, Shanxi, China, pp. 202–205 (2009)
4. Xing, K., Zhou, B., Yong, Y.c.: Application of an expert system in the environment impact assessment for traffic engineering. In: 2010 2nd Conference on Environmental Science and Information Application Technology, Wuhan, China, pp. 667–669 (2010)
5. Zhou, R., Pan, J., Tan, X.: Application of CLIPS expert system to malware detection system. In: 2008 International Conference on Computational Intelligence and Security, Suzhou, China, pp. 309–314 (2008)
6. Daoping, W.: Study on the Classification and Disposal of Uncertain Knowledge in Intelligent Fault Diagnosis Systems. In: Proceedings of the third WCIIC&A, Heifei, China, pp. 126–129 (2000)

Four Critical Points of General Technology Curriculum Implementation Propelled by Administration: A Case Study of Zhejiang Province

Weiqiang Chen

Center of Basic Education Research, Zhejiang Normal University,
Jinhua, Zhejiang, China

Abstract. It is presumed that New Curriculum Reform all over China is a tough and complicated process. Some successful experiences inspired that implementation of General Technology curriculum relies on the mighty support of the administration. Therefore the educational administrative departments are obliged to alter of ideologies and concepts firstly, guarantee the policies secondly, and participate in the concrete work thirdly and provide evaluation guidance fourthly.

Keywords: New Curriculum Reform; general technology; administrative force; critical points.

1 Introduction

The Complexity Theory acknowledges the complexity of surroundings of mankind and the practical activities [1]. Undoubtedly, implementation of New Curriculum Reform is a complex and systematic process; it touches upon issues with both complexity and multiplicity, moreover, General Technology curriculum is one of the most innovative and unprecedented procedure in the process of the New Curriculum Reform, therefore though the executors manage to do abundant and concrete work painstakingly, when it comes to the instance of executors' incompetence, effective administrative force turns out to be necessary. Evidence shows that in the process of the implementation of general technology curriculum, educational administrative departments ought to not only supply with guidance and conductions, but also participate and propel the operation of it.

2 Altering of Ideologies and Concepts: Core of Curriculum Implementation

The Reform and Opening-up Policy converts the destiny of education. Ideological emancipation and concepts renovation is the forerunners for the successful curriculum reform [2]. Educational administrative departments are required to alter mind and concepts, unify thoughts and reinforce the origin of force for curriculum implementation. Specifically, first, educational administration should identify its own

S. Lin and X. Huang (Eds.): CSEE 2011, Part V, CCIS 218, pp. 160–166, 2011.

position and obligations. Educational administrators should adjust themselves to the modified surroundings, the implementation of the general technology curriculum is a scientific and systematic process, and it requires efficient and competent administration. Conversely, neglect and dereliction will leads to inefficient operation of the implementation of curriculum. Second, educational administrators should deepen their understandings. In any educational reform, executors' understandings about the reform exert great influence on the results of the reform. Therefore the administrators' attitudes and solutions to the problems make significant sense in the process of the curriculum reform. The connection between the government and basic education should be strengthened in various ways, and more attention should be paid to the tendency of the basic education reform [3]. Third, the administrators ought to put the reform into practice. Alteration of the ideologies and concepts does not mean visualized theoretical transformation, but specific and authentic practice, which requests discard of indulging in empty talk, reformative operative scheme and modified measures.

Regarding to the issue of enhancing the origin of force, educational administrative departments set a favorable example. In the preliminary stage of implementation of general technology curriculum, a seminar for implementation of general technology curriculum in ordinary high school was held by the educational administrative departments [4]. The seminar unified the ideology and concepts of the district educational administration. Also, the seminar demanded the district educational administration to take the initiative to alter the concepts about implementation of general technology curriculum. Specifically, the district administrative departments should elevate understandings and engrave their mission and strengthen their sense of responsibility. It elevated the attitudes towards the general technology curriculum to a height and regarded it as the criterion to value whether it is "genuine curriculum reform" or "artificial curriculum reform". Second, district educational administrators should secure ideals and fortify faith and build a strong concept of honor and discard the concept of pursuing enrollment quotas. Third, district administrative departments should integrate wisdom and inspirations into the process of the implementation of the curriculum and be enthusiastic and vigorous, and overcome the feeling of fear and take a broad and long-term view and be confident about the future.

3   Policy Guarantee: Key to Curriculum Implementation

Policies guide the practice and conduct supervision and administration. Valid and reasonable policy guidance impels the curriculum reform. As a result, appropriate systematic and political macro-control becomes necessary [5]. Therefore educational administrative departments are required to take effective policies and strategies, implement feasible and effective administrative management, which will make the general technology curriculum implementation develop in a healthy and smooth way. Specifically, first, educational administrative departments should release relevant policies promptly, i.e. policies should be scientific and distinct and congenial to the concepts of curriculum reform. Also, policies should be correspond closely with the practical, and be specific to the details and feasible. Policies should be adjusted according to local conditions, carried out and consummated step by step. Also a case-by-case review system should be built, and an integrative educational system formed. Second, educational administrative departments should take the initiative to carry out the policies and provide conductions and guidance. The district educational administrative departments are not only the organizers, impellers, conductors, but also the propagandists, executants. Therefore, district educational administrative departments should take the initiative to make the policies take effect and function into full play and make the policies efficacious and thoroughgoing. Moreover, in the process of general technology curriculum implementation, provincial education administrative departments take charge of deploying and organizing the preoperational work for the implementation of the curriculum reform, designing and coordinating the implementing scheme. Also, provincial education administrative departments should provide conductions, evaluations and supervisions for the lower administrative departments. District educational administrative departments should fulfill the spirit upper departments' conductions and elaborate on the implementing scheme and provide specific, appropriate organizing and working plans. Third, educational administrative departments should do investigations and research and make timely adjustments to its policies in accordance with the changed situations. Education administrators at all levels should dig into the concrete classroom teaching research and be acquaint with the concrete problems which students and teachers encountered in the process of general technology curriculum implementing and provide congenial solutions and provide professional assistance and propel the implementing of general technology curriculum.

Educational administrative departments of Zhejiang province release a series of policies to propel the implementing of general technology curriculum [4]. First, Educational administrative departments of Zhejiang province founded leadership organizations and develop leadership teams. In the February of 2006, Department of Education of Zhejiang Province promulgated an official notice for "Member List for the Basic Education Curriculum Reform Organizations of Zhejiang Province" and developed a leadership team for curriculum implementing. Second, the government released a series of policies on curriculum management and promulgated "Practice Advisory of General Technology Curriculum Implementing". In May of 2007, Department of Education of Zhejiang Province promulgated officially "Practice Advisory for Ordinary High School in General Technology Curriculum Implementing", which provided detailed instructions, regulations, and operational guidelines. Third, Educational administrative departments of Zhejiang province released policies on construction of teaching equipments and promulgated standards on constructions of the practice bases. In July of 2007, Department of Education of Zhejiang Province promulgated "Zhejiang Province Ordinary High School General Technology Teaching Equipments directory (trial)", which provide explicit instructions and regulations on the practice bases constructional requirements, curriculum requirements, equipments standards. Fourth, Educational administrative departments of Zhejiang province released policies on curriculum evaluations and promulgated Practice Advisory on curriculum evaluation implementation. In December of 2006, Department of Education of Zhejiang Province promulgated "Practice Advisory for Adhering to and Consummate High School Graduate Test

System by Department of Education of Zhejiang Province", which recommended bringing general technology into the High School Graduate Test and students' Synthetic Quality Evaluation System and regulated that methodologies for students' portfolio assessment and synthetic quality evaluation should be "Realistic Evaluation plus Gradation Evaluation".

4 Participation into Concrete Work: Fundamental Requirement of Curriculum Implementation

It is regarded that Educational administrative departments are not only the leader of New Curriculum implementing, but also the participator. Effective participation and cooperation of educational administrations can impel the implementation of New Curriculum. And that, education administrative department itself assumes the responsibilities of Curriculum Reform. Moreover, educational administrative departments should not be "remote-controllers" whose tasks are merely issuing orders, but frontline participants. First, they should participate in investigation and research and suit policies and measures to differing conditions in terms of locality, time, issue and persons involved. Also, they should dig into the frontline practice and elaborate on the key points and problems encountered in the process of curriculum implementation and accumulate feasible, effective experience and adjust the measures and policies to the altering situations and they should be insurance of having sound regulatory rules and make the process of curriculum implementation systematic, standardized, well-organized. Second, they should participate into resources constructions and coordinate balance of urban and rural education resources. And that, it is no doubted that general technology was taken into the New Curriculum for the first time ever, it is inevitably short of teaching resources. Therefore, educational administrative departments should participate into the constructions of material resources and intellectual resources and integrate various educational resources. The government should encourage social organizations to utilize the already existing education resources, and develop new education resources. Also, it is the fundamental measure that they should identify their primary responsibilities and allocate public educational resources reasonably [6]. And it will realize the balanced development of regional education resources, making the strong much better, and the weak gradually better, also seeking equalities while conducting balanced development [7]. Third, they should participate into the Interaction Adjustment Process and improved curriculum implementation plan. The process of curriculum implementation is a dynamic and progressive process, the administration should emphasize on the interactions and adjustments. Therefore, educational administration should reflect on the problems and reacquaint them in an altered view, them they should adjust policies and measures to the altering situations and improve the curriculum implementation plan. Fourth, they should participate into the assessment and monitoring process and perceive the results of curriculum implementation; they should found evaluation system of curriculum implementation, and carry out regular sampling inspections through specialized monitoring agencies. They should elaborate on supervision of the process of curriculum implementation and evaluation of teaching level, i.e. they should monitor the progress of curriculum implementation and strengthen authoritativeness and effectiveness of the supervision and inspection and improve teaching level and educational quality. Fifth, they should participate into the constructions of research team and exert on enhancing researching level, i.e. educational administrative departments ought to emphasize on the construction of research team and integrate research team at all levels into an alliance, moreover, the teaching research institutions and teaching researchers should act their roles effectively, it is recommended that teaching research should provide support for the construction of research team and discipline construction should be driven by teaching research and teaching researching should propel the curriculum development.

The educational administrative departments participate in the implementation in several aspects as follows: first, educational administrative departments participated into the inspections and managements of the implementation of General Technology curriculum. Curriculum Reform Council built several professional teams and those specialized teams dug into the frontlines of curriculum implementation to do preparation work and also, principals in charge were supervised and urged to fulfill the course-opening work. Second, educational administrative departments participated into the construction of teaching staff, and plenty of related work had been carried out and fulfilled, e.g. one professional teacher was arranged to manage the instructional work of 5 or 6 parallel classes. Third, educational administration participated into the construction of curriculum resources. And then, several achievements were fulfilled, e.g. pedagogical websites for general technology was constructed. Moreover, tens of millions of RMB was allocated in order to build specialized classrooms for underdeveloped areas and island regions. Fourth, educational administration also participated into evaluation of curriculum implementation. Guided by educational administration, High School Graduate Exam and College Entrance Exam, Credits Assessments were carried out all over Zhejiang province and then. Fifth, educational administration departments participated into the pedagogical research. Conducted by the educational administration, specialized teachers were allocated to different regions, with dedicated funds allocated for training of "problem-solving", and Research Topics developed [4].

5 Evaluation Guidance: A Supplementary Means for Curriculum Implementation

Evaluation is the beacon giving conductions for education, without it, education has no secure direction. Therefore, educational administration departments should persist in the evaluation principle of "People-Oriented‖ Promoting Development", adopt innovative evaluation methodologies and principles and establish a evaluation system that meets the needs of Quality-oriented education and provide improvement measures according to the feedback of the result of evaluation [8]. Hence, general technology curriculum evaluation should realize functions as follows: first, it should lead curriculum evaluation to proceed in a right direction; the fundamental purpose of curriculum evaluation system reform is to enhance students' overall qualities and teachers' instructional techniques and guarantee the fulfillment of Quality-oriented education. Second, it should become the conductor for pedagogical development and elevation. Being stick to the evaluation principle of "Multiple Targets, Diverse Channel, and Process-Focused, Individual-Differences-Emphasized", applying mixed methodologies of "Concrete Operation, Achievements Displaying, Self-Assessments", educational administration can cooperate with school to build a comprehensive, dynamic Portfolio Assessment, which can record students' developments and growth, and the purpose of "making teaching benefits teachers as well as students" will be in near future. Third, it ought to take effect of conducting students' integrated developments. It is considered that evaluation not only emphasizes on students' academic credits, but also emphasizing on exploring students' potentials. Moreover, students' requirements should be satisfied, and students should be conducted to build "Self-consciousness, Self-Confidence". Through all those ways, it can be achieved that students developed in an all-round way. Fourth, it should conduct teachers' elevation. Teachers are required to be infused with brand-new teaching concepts in the process of New Curriculum Reform. Guided by evaluation, teachers should analyze and reflect on their teaching behaviors. And then, teachers can acquire various reflections, and teachers' instructional skills will be enhanced and professional teachers can be cultivated. Fifth, it should become the conductor for promoting curriculum developments. It is unavoidable that endless, diverse problems come into emergence in the process of New Curriculum implementation, and it is a right attitude that should be emphasized; only a right attitude can improve the curriculum development. And then, educational administrations are required to inspect implement situation of different schools in a certain period, and an education quality monitoring mechanism should be founded [9].

Educational administrative departments of Zhejiang province attach great importance to the conduction function of evaluation for general technology curriculum. Specifically, first, in order to fulfill the pedagogical targets of the state, High School Graduate Exam was carried out. In June of 2008, it is the first time that general technology was taken as a mandatory course in the High School Graduate Exam of Zhejiang province. Second, educational administration of Zhejiang province brought general technology course into the College Entrance Exam, which encourage students' personality developments. In May of 2008, College Entrance Exam scheme in the context of New Curriculum was promulgated, into which general technology course was brought. And then, a diversifying test and evaluation system for recruitment of students was built and this system should be a trinity system of "academic test, overall qualities evaluation, standardized exam". Third, in order to promote students' all-round development, comprehensive-qualities evaluation system was carried out.

6 Conclusion

It is four critical points of general technology curriculum implementation propelled by administration that is expounded. Those four critical points may contain diverse connotations, but it doesn't mean that they are independent to each other, but connected to each other and make an integrative system, and a systematic view should be held [10]. It is no doubt that general technology curriculum implementation relies on the propelling by administration departments. An idea should be prevalent that curriculum implementation is not only the business of experts and teachers, it is in fact an organic part of the educational reform and even social reform, and working alone is not a way to final success [11].

Acknowledgements. I show my sincere gratitude to China's National Education Science "Eleventh Five-Year Plan" of Ministry of Education⬚ DHA100246), The project of Teacher Education Research of Zhejiang Province " The Model for Professional Development of General Technology Teachers in High Schools" (2010(78)), and the research of "Effective Strategies for Professional Developments of General Technology Teachers in High Schools." for their great supports.

References

1. Kuhn, L.: Complexity and Educational Research: A Critical Reflection. In: Mason, M. (ed.) Complexity Theory and The Philosophy of Education, p. 174. John Wiley & Sons Ltd., West Sussex (2008)
2. Huang, Y.-x.: An Ecological Perspective of Educational Values. Journal of Zhejiang Normal University (Social Sciences) 29(2), 85–88 (2004) (in Chinese)
3. Lei, S.-f.: On Reform of Teacher Education at Teachers Colleges under the Background of New Curricula. Journal of Zhejiang Normal University (Social Sciences) 33(1), 94–97 (2008) (in Chinese)
4. The website of the teaching of general techniques of Zhejiang, http://www.zjpgte.net/index.php?Category
5. Jin, M.-s.: On Further Opening-up of Higher Education and Its Strategies. Journal of Zhejiang Normal University (Social Sciences) 30(2), 96–99 (2005) (in Chinese)
6. Yao, L.: Research on New Countryside County Community Educational Development Pattern: Taking the Community Education of Yiwu, Zhejiang as an Example. ournal of Zhejiang Normal University (Social Sciences) 35(5), 109–117 (2010) (in Chinese)
7. Xie, X.-b.: On Teacher-oriented Policies in the Contex tofBalanced Development of Regional Elementary Education. Journal of Zhejiang Normal University (Social Sciences) 32(1), 116–120 (2007) (in Chinese)
8. Lin, Y.-g.: On System of Teaching-Ability Development for College Teachers based on Reform in Teaching Assessment. Journal of Zhejiang Normal University (Social Sciences) 33(6), 69–72 (2008) (in Chinese)
9. Jin, Y.-L., Li.: Notion and Strategy of Curriculum Reform in Regular Senior Middle School. Journal of Zhejiang Normal University (Social Sciences) 30(1), 6–11 (2005) (in Chinese)
10. Chen, W.: The key issues in the implementation of general technology curriculum. China Educational Technology (11), 84–88 (2010) (in Chinese)
11. Pan, Y.: Aspects in Implementing New Curriculum of Chinese in Senior High Schools. Journal of Zhejiang Normal University (Social Sciences) 31(5), 98–102 (2006) (in Chinese)

An Empirical Research on the Relationship between Corporate Social Responsibility and Performance Based on Data Analysis in Northeastern Provinces of China—A Case Study of Listed Companies in Shanghai and Shenzhen Stock Exchanges

Xu Hong[1], Weidong Li[2], and Xihuai Yang[3]

[1] School of Business Administration, Northeastern University, Shenyang City, China
jenna_qhd@tom.com
[2] Foreign Language Department, Northeastern University at Qinhuangdao,
Qinhuangdao, China
bleewd1225@163.com
[3] School of Business Administration, Northeastern University, Shenyang City, China
cjenna_qhd@163.com

Abstract. According to Stakeholder Theory, the author of the article conducted a research on the influence of corporate social responsibility (CSR for short) on its performance by using the Structural Equation Modeling. On the basis of the research results of available literatures, setting up an assumptive Conceptual Model indicating the relationship between the factors of corporate social responsibility and the factors of its performance, selecting the annual report data of 76 listed companies in Northeastern provinces of China in the 5 consecutive years from 2005 to 2009 as research sample, the author conducted hypothesis testing through the Structural Equation Modeling. The result is that in the 5 consecutive years from 2005 to 2009, CSR for shareholders has a positive effect on a company's performance; CSR for creditors has a positive effect on a company's performance; CSR for government has a positive effect on business performance, and the impact on financial performance was not significant. Generally speaking, CSR causes great effects on a company's performance; namely, the more responsibility for stakeholders, the better a company's performance.

Keywords: Stakeholders, CSR, Performance, SEM, Northeastern provinces of China.

With the increasing promotion companies have played to the rapid economic development, the matter of CSR has accordingly come into being since 20th century, because a company causes a negative effect on the society out of its profit creation [1]. For the definition of CSR has been enriched, a company's status advances on a gradual basis [2]. In recent years, CSR philosophy has drawn wide attention and been attached more importance to, which is proved by the event that China Corporate

S. Lin and X. Huang (Eds.): CSEE 2011, Part V, CCIS 218, pp. 167–174, 2011.

Social Responsibility Summit held in the Great Hall of the People awarded 17 outstanding companies in terms of their social responsibility in 2010. Northeast region is China's old industrial bases and major grain producing areas, but also the window that China opens to Northeast Asia, has significant regional advantages. So, in order to realize constant sustainable development, it is of great significance to study the relationship between CSR and a company's performance in the region.

1   The Theoretical Basis of the Study

Corporate social responsibility means that a company fulfills various positive obligations and duties for its stakeholders via its regulations and behavior. It is beneficial response to market and stakeholders, and an overall index for a company's operational objectives [3]. A company is supposed to take responsibility to maintain and foster public interests, when maximizing profits for shareholders [4].

CSR philosophy was derived from the United States in the early of 20th century as a result of American special system, then urbanization and the mergence of modern companies [5]. Thereafter, many a scholars held heated discussions and in-depth researches, and Stakeholder Theory which was concluded in the western countries after1960s came to become striking. Compared with traditional Shareholder Primacy, Stakeholder Theory emphasizes that a company's progress fail to come true without the participance and devotion from all stakeholders including those who are affected directly or indirectly by a company's operation such as shareholders, creditors, government, employees, clients and suppliers, not simply was confined to the main benefit body [6].

2   Research Hypothesis and Research Design

Research Hypothesis. Available literatures show that the fulfillments of CSR not only can meet stakeholders' interests, but also boost a company's performance, and then maximize profits of shareholders. The following research hypotheses are put forward in the view of definition of a company's social responsibility:

Hypothesis 1: CSR for shareholders is positively correlated with a company's performance.

Hypothesis 1a: CSR for shareholders is positively correlated with a company's financial performance.

Hypothesis 1b: CSR for shareholders is positively correlated with a company's operating performance.

Shareholders are the foundation as well as core for a listed company, and play a role of agents. As investors, shareholders are offered such rights as getting profits, making decisions and appointing corporate leaders in order to promote economic development and improve the efficiency of resource allocations. The main concern from shareholders is the rate of return on investment. Thus, the action that a company takes social responsibility does good to increase credibility and ability to finance which lays a constant and stable financial foundation for a company's development.

Hypothesis 2: CSR for creditors is positively correlated with a company's performance.

Hypothesis 2a: CSR for creditors is positively correlated with a company's financial performance.

Hypothesis 2b: CSR for creditors is positively correlated with a company's operating performance.

Creditors are among important stakeholders for a company. Creditors take more risks because more and more companies are run in gearing, and the gearing ratio and size are enlarged. A company's debt disputes and crises have a bad influence on its fame and reputation, and worsen its operation and profits. So, a favorable credit relationship between a company and its creditors will boost value of creditors and the company itself.

Hypothesis 3: CSR for government is positively correlated with a company's performance.

Hypothesis 3a: CSR for government is positively correlated with a company's financial performance.

Hypothesis 3b: CSR for government is positively correlated with a company's operating performance.

In the market economy, government regulation is a crucial factor to manage economy when the market fails to do so. Government offer corporations public services, share benefits and finance their organs via revenue. When public interests are met, government will provide better public services, such as perfecting market mechanism, improving infrastructure. Government is among stakeholders and its public benefits have a strong connection with a company's performance.

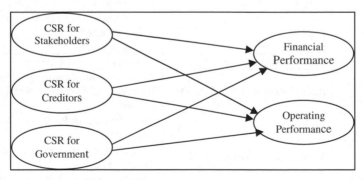

Fig. 1. The Conceptual Model of CSR and Performance

Model Building. The evaluation system of CSR has a broad definition including a lot of qualitative and quantitative indexes. The paper focuses on financial index. According to the above hypothesis and the structural equation model, as is shown in Figure 1, the conceptual model of the study is presented. The model is used to investigate the connectivity between CSR and a company's performance on the basis of Stakeholder Theory. The arrow starts from CSR for stakeholders and ends with a company's financial and operating performance, which indicates the relationship between the two.

Sample Selection. The paper studies those companies listed in the Shanghai and Shenzhen Stock Exchanges from 2005 to 2009 on the basis of their mean financial figures. By the end of 2009, 113 companies from the Northeastern provinces of China have been listed in the two stock exchanges, excluding Trash Stocks and those lack of data (it means that no data has appeared on the regular reports or prospectuses by 2003), 76 of which are qualified and are analyzed. The statistics used in the paper are all from http://www.cninfo.com.cn/ and http://www.cnlist.com/. The descriptive statistics of latent variable index employ SPSS software; confirmatory factor analysis and data processing of Structural Equation Modeling are conducted by using AMOS software; parameters are estimated by Maximum Likelihood Method.

Variable Selection. The paper selects the financial index to evaluate a company's social responsibility for shareholders, creditors and government in the evaluation system of a company's social responsibility. The commonplace financial index appraising a company's financial and operating performance is shown in the Table 1.

Table 1. Variable Selection

Measure Objects	Variable Name	Variable Calculation
CSR for Stakeholders	Return on Stockholders' Equity	After-tax Profits/Shareholder's Equity
	Addition of the value of Assets	Ending Ownership Interest/Beginning Ownership Interest
	Net Return on Assets	Net Return/Net Assets
CSR for Creditors	Quick Ratio	(Liquid Assets-Inventory)/Current Liabilities
	Assets-liability Ratio	General Assets/Total Liabilities
CSR for Government	Net Amount of Taxation Expenditure	Total Expenses of Taxation –Return of Expenses of Taxation
	Staff Number	Staff number
	Total Donation Expenditure	Non-business Expenditure
Financial Performance	Rate of Return on Total Assets	Total Amount of Earnings before Interests and Taxes/Average Total Assets
	net Profit Rate	Total Amount of Profits×(1- Income Tax Rate)
Operating Performance	Total Asset Turnover Ratio	Core Business net Income/Average Total Assets
	Inventory Turnover Rate	Core Business net Income/Average Inventory Balance

3   Analysis of SEM

SEM. Structural Equation Modeling, SEM is composed of such statistical methods as multiple regression, factor analysis, path analysis and simultaneous equations in econometrics. It is used to analyze the inner relationship between variables and variable groups which exist broadly in the fields of sociology, psychology and business management. In SME, those variables which can be directly measured are called Observed Variables, and those which can't be measured directly but can be shown by observed variable linear are called Latent Variables. In the model of Amos, ξ means exogenous latent variables and η represents endogenous latent variables. X indicates external observed variables and Y internal observed variables. Amos model includes two parts:

Measurement Model: reflects the relationship between observed variables and latent variables. The formula is as below:

$$y = \Lambda_y + \varepsilon \tag{1}$$

$$x = \Lambda_x \xi + \delta \tag{2}$$

In the formula, Λ_x and Λ_y represent the coefficient matrix which reflects the intensity degree of the relationship between x to ξ and y to η. It can also be understood as the factor loading in factor analysis. ε and δ represent the measurement error between y and x.

SEM: reflects the relationship between latent variables. The formula is as below:

$$\eta = B\eta + \Gamma\xi + \zeta \tag{3}$$

In the formula, B presents the interact between latent variables. Γ represents the influence of outside latent variables on inside latent variables. ζ is the error term of SE. The relationship between outside and inside latent variables is established through B and Γ coefficient matrix and ζ (error vector). The detail is shown in Figure 2.

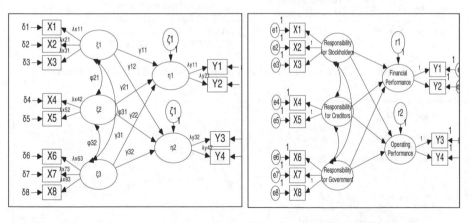

Fig. 2. Schematic diagram of structural

Fig. 3. Path of SEM Indicating the Relationship between CSR and Performance

Initial Model Building. According to the above research hypothesis and the conceptual model, the initial model of the relationship between CSR and performance is set up, which is shown in Figure 3.

Estimation, Evaluation and Modification of Model Parameter. Applying the maximum likelihood estimate program of Amos 7.0, the research conducted the parameter estimate on the initial model. Figure 4 explains the standardized path coefficient.

172   X. Hong, W. Li, and X. Yang

The degree of freedom is 45. The chi-square of the fit of the whole model is 96.499. The significant probability value is p=0.000<0.05, which reaches the conspicuous level of 0.05. The null hypothesis being rejected means hypothesis model and sample data don't agree with each other. These values, including RMSEA value (0.124>0.08), the chi-square DOF ratio (2.144>3.000), AGFI value (0.722<0.900) and GFI value (0.839<0.900), shows that the fit of the whole model is not good enough.

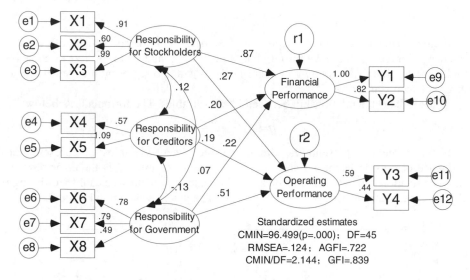

Fig. 4. Path of SEM Indicating the Relationship between CSR and Performance

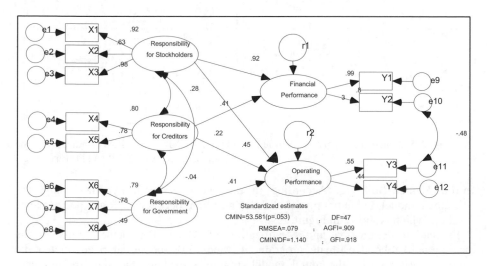

Fig. 5. Diagram of Modification Model Path Coefficient

Table 2. Modification Model Fitting Index

	χ2/df	RMSEA	GFI	AGFI	NFI	RFI	CFI	PGFI	PNFI
Fitting Index	1.14	0.079	0.918	0.909	0.958	0.901	0.942	0.553	0.601

Figure 5 shows the result after modifying the initial model according to the modification value provided by Amos.

In the diagram of modification model, if we suppose that the error terms are not independent, according to the modification value, attention should be paid to the covariant relationship. Finally, no modification values higher than 4 are presented in the model and all the absolute residual values in the standardized covariance matrix are lower than 1.96. The result of the model testing indicates that the C.R. values of all the twelve λ are higher than 1.96, which means all the measurement index parameters reach the conspicuous level of 0.05. The DOF of the model equals to 45. The chi-square of the fit of the whole model is 53.581. The significant probability value is p=0.053>0.05, which doesn't reach the conspicuous level of 0.05. The null hypothesis being accepted means that hypothesis model and sample data agree with each other. It is found that the chi-square DOF ratio equals to 1.140 (lower than 3) and the values of AGFI, GFI, NFI, RFI and CFI are all higher than 0.9 and the value of PNFI is higher than 0.5. As a result, all the values reach the model fitting standard, which means the diagram of modification casual model can be accepted.

Hypothesis Testing and Path Analysis. As already discussed, the modification model displays a great fitting effect. The goodness-of-fit indices all reach the reference value: RMSEA equals to 0.079 lower than 0.8, which indicates the fitting degree between every latent variable and actual data.

The path parameter of CSR for stockholders and the financial performance is 0.92 and the path parameter of CSR for creditors and the company's performance is 0.42. This shows that CSR for stockholders and creditors can increase financial performance, provided that hypotheses 1, 1a and 1b were verified. The path parameter of CSR for creditors and the financial performance is 0.48 and the path parameter of CSR for creditors and the operating performance is 0.45. This shows that CSR for creditors can effectively increase a company's performance, provided that hypotheses 2a, 2b and hypothesis 2 were verified. The path parameter of CSR for government and the operating performance is 0.41, which shows that CSR for government can effectively increase a company's operating performance, provided that hypothesis 3b were verified. Besides, the basic hypothesis that CSR for government has an effect on financial performance is not verified, that is to say the model does not fully verify hypothesis 3. However, generally speaking, CSR has a positive effect on performance, which is in accordance with the previous hypothesis.

4   Conclusion

The conclusion is reached from the empirical study on the relationship between CSR and a company's performance that the former is positively correlative with the latter and there is a conspicuous relationship of cause-and-effect between CSR and a company's performance within the companies in the Northeastern provinces of China. In a word, the fulfillment of the social responsibility of the companies in that region is able to enhance greatly a company's performance, instead of causing negatives. The reason for it is that the fulfillment brings a different and better competitive advantage to the company, despite the increase of cost. Stakeholders, shareholders, creditors and government are affected a lot by a company's performance, so, if their benefits are well protected via a company's fulfillment of responsibility, then a win-to-win situation is coming both for the company and stakeholders.

NOTE: Humanities and social science research project of Department of education in Hebei province.

Project No: SZ2010225.

References

1. Bramrner, Williams, S., Zinkin, G.: Religion and Attitudes to Corporate Social Responsibility in a Large Cross-Country Sample. Journal of Business Ethics 71, 229–243 (2007)
2. Palmer: Multinational corporations and the social contract. Journal of business Ethics 31, 245–258 (2001)
3. Cohen: Socially Responsible Business Goes Global. Business 23, 22 (2000)
4. Adams, Zutshi, A.: Corporate Social Responsibility: Why Business Should Act Responsibly and Be Accountable. Australian Accounting Review 14, 31–39 (2004)
5. Coldwell, D.A.L.: Perceptions and Expectations of Corporate Social Responsibility: Theoretical Issues and Empirical Findings. South African Journal of Business Management 32, 49–55 (2001)
6. Carlisle, Y.M., Faulkner, D.O.: Corporate Social Responsibility: A Stages Framework. European Business Journal 16, 143–152 (2004)

The Design and Implementation of Data Synchronization Mechanism in the Food Tracing System

Xi'an Lou[1], Jia Chen[2], and Pin Yuan[1]

[1] Dalian Maritime University Management Building, Laboratory 204, China
[2] Dalian Maritime University Management Building, Office 118, China
lou_xi_an@126.com, chen_jia8008@sina.com,
yuan_pin_yp@yahoo.cn

Abstract. This paper studies data synchronization mechanism in the food tracing system, ensuring that in the system simultaneous operations and asynchronous operations of data within the databases inter-departmental cross enterprises run successfully. Through the use of the Web Service, the news queue technology etc. we established the corresponding synchronization mechanism, and reach the goal that can reduce data throughput, improve the efficiency, flexibility, security and accuracy of data transmission.

Keywords: Tracing system, database, data synchronization mechanism.

1 Background of Application and Demands

At present many enterprises have had its own internal management information systems, the systems rarely have information exchange with external, so in order to achieve food's traceability, we need within each enterprise establish the enterprise tracing system, through this system the enterprise internal own management information system can realize information exchange, and obtain required information on traceability, and at the same time, we can also upload data by it, that is to say ,we can use the Internet to upload information to the integrated database of tracing system platform. Information exchange and information acquisition mechanism of the tracing system are shown as Fig.1 below.

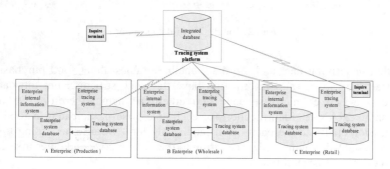

Fig. 1. Tracing system data flow diagram

S. Lin and X. Huang (Eds.): CSEE 2011, Part V, CCIS 218, pp. 175–179, 2011.
© Springer-Verlag Berlin Heidelberg 2011

As shown in Fig.1, the links needed to be realized synchronization in the tracing system can be divided into two kinds: one kind is the synchronization mechanism between the data in the tracing system database within the enterprises(called the underlying data) and the data of integrated database in the tracing system platform (called top data); The other kind is the synchronization mechanism between the data of enterprise internal system database and the data of tracing system database (namely the underlying data). No matter what kind of the data synchronization, they all need to transfer large amounts of data; therefore, in order to ensure the accuracy consistency and timeliness of their transmission, to build a reasonable and steady synchronization mechanism is particularly important.

2   The Design of Data Standard

To realize the data synchronization and information exchange about data within distributed database needs unified data standard as the foundation. Taking food procurement, sales information as an example, we put forward data standard transformation mechanism as Fig.2 shows.

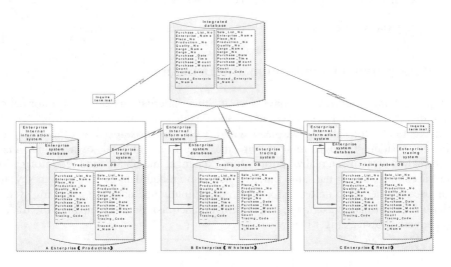

Fig. 2. The design of data standard

Within underlying data and top data, database tables about food purchasing and database tables about sales information have the same structure, but top data table involves retroactive enterprise code and enterprise name, therefore we need to establish an exclusive identification for each enterprise participated in food tracing system, additionally to the each batch purchasing food we also according to certain standards establish tracing code, according to the tracing code and enterprise code we can achieve food traceability.

3   The Design of Synchronization Mechanism

3.1   The Design of Synchronization Mechanism between Integrated Database and Tracing System Database

The synchronization mechanism between integrated database and tracing system database is realized using database replication technology [1].

Before replicating, according to data updating frequency, this paper divides data object in the database into three classes, namely three main groups. This paper defines tracing platform as the main site, namely duplicating terminal, the terminal operational staff should be awarded to administrator privilege. After establishing the connect between underlying database and top database, we define underlying database as branch site, and set synchronous mode as asynchronous, according to the characteristics of main group we set cycle respectively for 24,36,48 hours, then set copying mechanism, synchronous processes begin to run, in order to achieve synchronous data replication between the tracing system and tracing platform.

3.2   The Design of Synchronization Mechanism between Enterprise System Database and Tracing System Database

Enterprise system database and tracing system database's synchronization mechanism adopts the news queue technology to realize.

The enterprise internal information system mainly includes enterprise internal database and the management and maintenance functional module for the database, we in the enterprise internal data table define many kinds of triggers, once the data in the table change (add, modify, delete, etc.), corresponding trigger will send the news to the queue, external listener program from the queue gets news forwarding to tracing system, and cause corresponding change [2]. In order to facilitate transmission of the news about data updating, we need introduce a data exchange center, its main effect is that: on the premise that not change the existing data table structure, through news listener and news transmission, it can deliver timely data updating information to the tracing system, between the two enterprises internal system to realize data synchronization, the system structure of this synchronization model is shown in Fig.3.

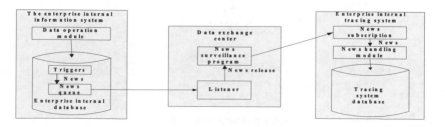

Fig. 3. Main structure of news queues synchronous model

4 The Implementation of Synchronization Mechanism

4.1 The Implementation of Synchronization Mechanism between Integrated Database and Tracing System Database

The Web Service is suitable to solve problems about the system integration and data sharing, so this paper puts forward a solution based on the Web Service to realize synchronization mechanism. The solution is including five parts of each enterprise's tracing system database, data synchronization client program, Web servers, Web Service procedures and integrated database. The core is Web Service procedure, it opens a data synchronization service, and data synchronization service is descripted as follows:

Bool DataSynchronization (Data d, string password). Data synchronization client program is on duty that from each tracing system database extracts synchronizing data and calls the data synchronization service of Web Service. The program periodically and automatically scans triggers form in the all the databases, and extracts the table had been not synchronous data to procedure and according to the specified format encapsulates them well. Web Service program is running in Web server, logically it is put into service interface layer (SIL), business logic layer (BLL) and database access layer (DAL). the data synchronization is carried on, service procedure request information in the client is firstly sent to Web Server, then Web Server transmits it to the Web Service program, after it receives the SOAP request information, Web Service program analyses function calls and parameters format in it, according to document descriptions, it calls data synchronization function defined in business logic layer to deal with. Finally through database access layer it updates synchronize data to the corresponding data table to complete synchronization. Overall system structure is shown as Fig.4.

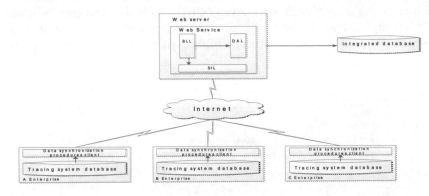

Fig. 4. Main structure of Web Service

4.2 The Implementation of Synchronization Mechanism between Enterprise System Database and Tracing System Database

The realization of the message queue model includes two aspects:①In the enterprise system database sharing data sheet trigger is defined;②Structure of news is defined.

When news is sent to queue, monitor program from the queue work out news and announce it. The news format converses to class files that system code can read.

After the listener release the news, tracing system gets subscribed news by subscription mechanism. Then the news is handed to news handling module to handle, the main work process is as follows: first judge this Then the news by message handling module to handle, the main work process as follows: first judge weather this table corresponding the news is the table that this system needs to keep pace with or not, if not, this system need not to share this piece of table, this news can be ignored, or get Sql_info statement from news body and execute.

5 Summary

This paper expounds data synchronization scheme of the food tracing system, namely giving full security in communication environment, using reasonable structure, it improves the data synchronization's flexibility and accuracy.

References

1. Xiong, Z.: The research and application about data synchronization in distributed database. Huazhong University of Science and Technology (2008)
2. Ozsu, M.T., Valduriez, P.: Principles of Distributed Database Systems (English silverstein), pp. 65–72. Tsinghua University Press, Peiking (2002)

Set Up the Shopping Platform Based on Layout Technology and Animation Mechanism in WPF

ZhenGang Wei, XiaoHua Wang, and Wen Ding

Dept. of Information Technology and Engineering, Ocean University of China,
238 Songling Road, Qingdao, Shandong, China
wzgwzq@ouc.edu.cn, wangxh5407770@yahoo.cn, 19744072@qq.com

Abstract. WPF is the next-generation graphics technology systems. It provides a unified description and method of operation for UI, 2D or 3D graphics, documents, and the media. In this paper, it first researched on the techniques of layout and animation mechanism in WPF. Then, making use of the research, it realized the layout of the first page in the shopping system, and handled the event during the procedure of users' searching for product information .The purpose of the study is just designing a shopping platform with brilliant UI and perfect function.

Keywords: WPF, layout, animation mechanism, shopping platform.

1 Introduction

WPF is a new computer graphics presentation layer technology Microsoft promulgated. As the new design engine of interface in Windows, WPF is mainly used for the Windows' unified display subsystem. In WPF, it provides a unified description and method of operation for UI, 2D or 3D graphics, documents, and the media, so that, developers and designers develop rich client applications, and create better visual effects and provide a different experience for users. The WPF platform appears to us a wealth of features in order to meet the pursuit of people on the user experience and visual impact. As is known to us, the effect of translucent form in Vista system is just due to the emergence and popularity of WPF technology.

Nowadays, with the number of persons shopping online increasing greatly, a variety of shopping sites become more and more numerous and large, and have complete shopping systems. In this issue, the advanced graphics technology WPF will be applied to design a shopping system with C/S structure for users, just in order to build a shopping platform with both complete function and beautiful user interface.

2 Design the User Interface of Shopping Platform

A. Layout the Interface

In WPF, the layout model has a significant improvement, because it introduced a new layout system in which it used such standard as flow-based on layout system during the development of Windows Forms, no longer based on the coordinates of the layout standard. The advantage is that developers can create user interface who is independent of resolution and the window size and can zoom freely when the display changes, also can adjust the content of their own and be well Scaling.

The users are the the main body of the shopping system, so for users, not only the basic functions should be perfect, but also the whole page layout of the shopping platform can meet the needs of users. It should have good effects of shopping platform and the layout forms of the interface is simple but generous for the users, and in addition, the interface can adapt to different sizes of windows.

In order to follow the design principles of the interface layout in WPF, we must first measure the desired size of the elements, and then place the child elements in the right place of the container to arrange the elements. Next, it describes how to layout the user interface according to an example, that is the layout deign of the home page in the shopping platform.

First, we use the Grid to achieve the overall layout of the platform. Grid can be described as a new layout scheme that combines the advantages of the traditional table layout and the coordinate layout. Making use of Grid layouts is enough for us to meet the most layout needs and it provides a very simple way to achieve. In the home page of the shopping plateform, it provides users with a search bar, navigation bar, hot promotion bar, classification column, user login and various navigation buttons. We divide the whole region into different blank Grid forms, and then decide which specific control needs to be placed into the suitable forms.

Secondly, populate appropriate controls in all regions, and automational these controls. As is shown in Figure 1, the blue line is used to divide into different Grid forms, and each Grid is to populate different controls. These controls can not be specified with a fixed width and height so that they won't stretch out as their contents change.

Fig. 1. Overall layout and control settings for home page of the shopping platform

Finally, we use Panel to design the local layout.

During the local layout, the method of adding single control is simple. However, what is worth noting, during the layout, we should ensure that each control can change the size to fit their contents. The reason is that the monitor resolution and the size of the window may change at any time, if the controls were given clear definitions of their size, then when the form changed there would be a large area of blank or missing, or some irregular control list. Therefore, the size can not be set to a fixed value, but should be limited to an acceptable maximum and minimum size. For example, in Figure 1, when setting the search field text box, we can set the maximum number of characters manually entered into the TextBox to 200, that is to say, the value of the parameter "MaxLength" is set to 200. What's more, the value of the parameter "MinLines" that shows the lowest number of rows can be set to 1, the code is as follows :

```
<TextBox          x:Name="textbox_keyword"          MaxLength="200"
MinLines="1" Margin="38.208,6,284,-3" Text="Please enter the keywords..."
TextWrapping="Wrap" Foreground="#FF9B9B9B"/>
```

The above describes the setting method of a single control, then we should consider the need of combining the controls. Following an example to illustrate the partial layout ideas and methods of using the control panel to combine the controls. As is shown in Figure 2, the layout of the labels in the navigation image bar in Hot Promotions just adopts the container named StackPanel to achieve. StackPanel is the most simple layout container, you can simply stack the rows or columns of its child elements.

First, drag a StackPanel onto the window, then with separate contents are "1 ","2 ","3 ","4 ", four navigation lables named lb1, lb2, lb3 and lb4 are placed from left to right orderly. The code is as follows, and the effect can be seen in Figure 1.

```
<StackPanel         x:Name="stackPanel"         HorizontalAlignment="Right"
Margin="0,0,46,-4"  VerticalAlignment="Bottom"  Width="116"  Height="25"
Orientation="Horizontal" Grid.RowSpan="1" Panel.ZIndex="1" Opacity="0.29"
Background="#FFDBC3E0">
        <Label   x:Name="lb1"   HorizontalAlignment="Left"   Margin="8,0,0,0"
Width="20" Content="1" FontWeight="Bold" Cursor="ScrollN" />
        <Label   x:Name="lb2"   HorizontalAlignment="Left"   Margin="8,0,0,0"
Width="20" Content="2" FontWeight="Bold" Cursor="ScrollN"/>
        <Label   x:Name="lb3"   HorizontalAlignment="Left"   Margin="8,0,0,0"
Width="20" Content="3" FontWeight="Bold" Cursor="ScrollN"/>
        <Label   x:Name="lb4"   HorizontalAlignment="Left"   Margin="8,0,0,0"
Width="20" Content="4" FontWeight="Bold" Cursor="ScrollN"/>
</StackPanel>
```

If you want to rearrange the order of these lables, you need to use the "sort" function to achieve instead of simply draging and droping. For example, set lb1 "Bring Forward" or lb2 "Bring Backward" to achieve the exchange of lb1 and lb2.

B.   Implement the Event Handler for Product Search

Product search is one of the most simple way to get product information for users. In this shopping platform, we set up quick search bar in the home page. First set the Click event handler attribute and the name of the event for the "Search" button, the XAML code is as follows:

```
<Button        x:Name="button_search"        HorizontalAlignment="Right"
Margin="0,6,212.463,-3.428"        Width="44"        Content="search"
Background="{x:Null}"        Cursor="Hand"        ClickMode="Press"
Click="btnSearch_Click"/>
```

Then, the next three major parts are need to be operated to achieve:

First, jump from the home page as is shown in Figure 1 to the product search results page, here we use the WPF animation mechanisms to achieve the interface jump.

In WPF, there is an existing animation system, which is an important difference from the WinForm for WPF. Animation is the core part in the WPF model, through which we can create a truly dynamic user interface. To start the drawing board demo using XAML, it should be associated with EventTrigger. EventTrigger is an object that describes what operations would be executed when the specified event occured. Some of these operations can be BeginStoryboard, and you can use this to start a Storyboard.

As is shown in Figure 2, first, add event for the "Search" Button in the trigger management. when the "MouseEnter" event of the button named "button_search" is start off, it will create a new storyboard, and give it the name "OnMouseEnter_button_search". As shown in Figure 2(a), after determining, the the jump animation can be set. Figure 2(b) shows how to set the jump animation. We drag the time line onto the "2" moment, and then the search results page is set to be visible, while, the other pages is set to be hidden:

(a) Add a new storyboard named

OnMouseEnter_button_search

(b) Set the jump animation

Fig. 2. Set the animation in Blend 3

Then, it achieves to obtain the search field, it's necessary to trigger the focus events and keyboard events of the text box named textbox_keyword, and obtain the key words that user input into the text box to be used as the search parameter.

The third step is to access to product information and displays the result page through calling the search interface. In detail, by calling the "btnSearch_Click" method to trigger the search function. In this function, we use keywords obtained in the previous step to be the parameter and call the Top API named "taobao.items.get". After this we will be able to access the image information list of the products, and then control the result page through the corresponding page operations. The implementation of the interface and the page control is not the focus of this paper, so omit it here.

3 Summary

Through this study, we can design a very nice user interface with the help of WPF technology. However, there are more and more design methods and tips in WPF application model, so it is no longer a distant luxury for programmers to develop the cool interface as the Mac. This requires that each programmer go on researching on the development model in depth using WPF technology, in order to explore the more latest WPF features and the more powerful functions. Make full use of this strategy for the next generation of application-level technologies to design more powerful competitive advantage Application.

References

1. Information on,
   http://msdn.microsoft.com/en-us/library/ms754130.aspx
2. Lee, K., Seo, Y.: Design of a rfid-based ubiquitous comparison shopping system, pp. 1267–1283 (2006)
3. Sells, C., Griffiths, I.: Programming wpf. O'Reilly, Sebastopol (2007)
4. Williams, B.: Microsoft® expression blend™ unleashed (2008)
5. C C Commands: Routing events and commands

Exploration in Practice Teaching and Laboratory Operational Mechanism of Digital Media Technology Specialty

Jiangsheng Gui, Shusen Sun, and Yanfei Liu

College of Information and electronic, Zhejiang Sci-Tech university,
Hangzhou, China, 310018
dewgjs@126.com

Abstract. Aim to the features of digital media technology specialty, we combined with our specialty teaching and laboratory operation, Exploration and discusses the pattern of practice teaching for our specialty and appropriate laboratories operating mechanism in order to achieve the objectives of personnel training.

Keywords: Digital media technology, Practice teaching, Laboratory operational mechanism.

1 Introduction

The digital media technology specialty is a technology-based computer, art, supplemented by a combination of technology in the arts complex specialty.In order to train the social urgently needed digit media technology talented person, in recent years, our country the nearly more than 50 institutions of higher learning will have opened the digital media technology specialty in abundance, although the school characteristic varies, but each kind of colleges and universities emphasized " technical and the artistic union in the digital media technology and in the digital media art professional's raise goal ", "the raise multi-skill innovation talented person"; Is realizes as if by prior agreement in the specialized construction process: The digital media specialty is the discipline that need practice, in the curriculum, to increase the strong practical courses to improve practical teaching process to develop a strong practical ability.

2 Existence Question of Currently Practice Teaching

First, the current practice of digital media content teaching arrangements to implement the provisions of a unified course arrangement, generally focus on one week after the scheduled end of the course of time, it is difficult to embody the "student-centered" philosophy of education. This problem is reflected in two aspects: from the timing point of view, the whole class at the same time period, at the same location, the same experiment, so a good foundation for students may be relatively

S. Lin and X. Huang (Eds.): CSEE 2011, Part V, CCIS 218, pp. 185–189, 2011.

spare time, and for Practical ability of the original foundation is weak or poor students may be unable to finish the task. From the experimental point of view the content of the arrangements, there is the same problem, can not be individualized, with different purposes for different students in the practice of teaching. In view of this practice is currently teaching, laboratory and related software systems have made some adjustments, no longer concentrated in one week after the end of the semester, but were scattered in the semester, but this brings new problems, not learning courses End to the practice, you can not give students the knowledge to understand and master the system in practice situations, but also did not address these two issues. Therefore, the content of this unity, focus on the practice of teaching time can not meet the students creative thinking and innovation capabilities.

Second, in the digital media specialized practice curriculum system aspect, various class's practice content from becomes the system, the knowledge is scattered, and does not pay great attention the specialized practice knowledge between the usability and the special course connection. Because my school digit media specialized direction divides into the animation film and television manufacture and the game develops, but this specialized some practice content not very good engagement this specialized direction but imitates the computer specialized practice content, causes to come apart with the following practice course content. Therefore scattered, from becomes system's practice course content to be unable to satisfy under the new situation the personnel training pattern change, is also unable to enhance the utilizing rate of laboratory and instrumentation equipments.

Finally, the laboratory in the school level of staffing, curriculum, identification of the fruits of labor, reward promotion, coordination of interests and there exist many problems, the team instability, laboratory open up much. Therefore, how to stimulate the enthusiasm of teachers experiment, to break the closed-end management, resource sharing goals, the establishment of suitable laboratory operating mechanism is very urgent.

The practice teaching is in the undergraduate course teaching link the very important constituent, regarding raises student's practical ability, application ability and the innovative spirit, has its irreplaceable crucial role, the laboratory has not realized from the teaching practices to the practice teaching fundamental transformation, the practice teaching attaches to a great extent in the theoretical teaching, attaches in the theory curriculum. It is necessary to explore and ponder to the digital media specialized present practice educational model and operational mechanism's innovation.

3   Exploration and Consideration

3.1   The Aspect of Practice Teaching Pattern

To focus on the reform of teaching mode of Unified content at the current time, we can use this advantage lab teacher imprisoned by an open practice teaching, to encourage independent project outside of class time for students to participate in research projects such as teachers, the establishment of a multi-level multi-way system of open Practice teaching, encouraging students to innovation, and fully mobilize the enthusiasm of students and initiative, so that reflects the student-centered teaching philosophy, the implementation of individualized, based on a better solution for students and practical ability of the original foundation is weak or poor students Differences.

The new practice educational mode implementation cannot leave student's positive participation, to arouse student's enthusiasm and the initiative, must adopt the enterprise project development pattern, establishes the project development system, enables the student to be possible to carry on the knowledge under the real environment the practice, also after graduation steps onto the operating post to build the foundation directly, thus may attract the student to participation positively. The project development system's exploration has implemented in 07 level of digital media specialized game programming teaching, groups the student according to the enterprise developmental item form, each group is dividing into the model group, the plan group and the procedure group, and supposes Team Leader, every week progresses through the ppt report, each group does not surpass 5 minutes. This kind of pattern has aroused student's enormous interest, attends class to the class rate, had the enormous improvement extracurricularly in the laboratory independent study's situation, very little appears in the laboratory plays the game to glance over the homepage the phenomenon.

For one year digital media specialty and the laboratory cooperated fully to practice the teaching system to carry on the reform, the conformity optimization practice course content, established the systematic characteristic and the continuous practice teaching system, solved various class practice content from to become the system, the knowledge is scattered, did not pay great attention the specialized practice knowledge between the usability and the special course joining question, to curricula and so on construction of data, application procedure practice no longer imitated the computer department the content, but focused on the game development and the animation design aspect, has made the revision to these two curriculum's practice content, practice contents and so on such following java game design might be no longer redundant, raised test installation's use factor, simultaneously guarantees the practice content the continuity.

3.2 The Aspect of Laboratory Operational Mechanism

The laboratory operational mechanism aspect in view of the new practice educational model, needs a perfect laboratory open system. Believed the electricity institute innovation experiment locellus already to start to attempt the running open, but has not formed one perfect system, also did not have the corresponding system to appraise, regardless of did not have the very good approval to the student to the laboratory teachers, the very great degree has affected the laboratory open effect. Must therefore carry on the consummation to the laboratory opening system, guarantees the new practice educational model implementation.

The open laboratory carries on experimental design's scope is quite broad, the difficulty is relatively big, will have various problems in the experiment process, this will request to instruct teacher's aspect of knowledge to extend, and must renew unceasingly, will know the most recent development tendency promptly. But tested teacher the daily management already to be very arduous, the knowledge renewed slowly, can only carry on some simple instructions at best, they very difficult to deal with to some quite thorough question. Therefore, we adopted to conform to my courtyard to be practical and digital media specialized characteristic opening management form:

(1) Publicity of Laboratory use. In The past, extra-curricular needs of students to laboratory experiments, teachers need to consult the laboratory to the laboratory free time, very inconvenient, and we will use the laboratory for a semester through the bulletin board form walls, the students at a glance, a reasonable Organize their spare time, no longer have to make an appointment to the experimental teachers.

(2) Experiment with the content inside and outside class opening. In the synthesis experiment, unifies the student to study the curriculum, gives 3~5 experiment topics, the student chooses independently, the student may also bring the topic, verifies after the teacher after carries on the experiment. In tests in the curriculum time, the student has not completed the experiment content, for example regards the audio frequency edition experiment, may when the laboratory free time uses regards the audio frequency edition equipment to carry on the experiment, gives the student a bigger flexibility.

(3) Establish quantitative and qualitative evaluation of a combination of approaches. The new practice educational pattern and the laboratory opening need the laboratory personnel's positive participation. In view of present is in the campus two levels of reforms, the policy mechanism drives does not arrive, the experiment teaching troop deficient enthusiasm, the power is insufficient question. Was considering how to stimulate to test the teacher troop the enthusiasm, breaks the enclosed management, realizes the resource sharing goal aspect, we have established the examination means which initially the establishment quantity and the nature unify. The experiment teaching's inspection with is responsible for the experiment teaching work load suspension hook which undertakes, implements the teacher appraisal and laboratory chief appraises the comprehensive appraisal system, the measure results is direct and remuneration for services rendered suspension hook. The instrument service work load's inspection defers to services instrument's quantity and laboratory instrument's integrity quality synthetic evaluation, the measure results is direct and remuneration for services rendered suspension hook. The extra instruction's student experiment and the vacation laboratory opening work load's computation adopts 0.5 standard teaching work load, the student assessment and laboratory chief initially at present appraises the comprehensive method.

4   Conclusion

Practice teaching is an innovative personnel training activities. By practice teaching, not only has raised student's ability, and has inspired their innovative spirit and the innovative ideology. At present we designed the practice teaching to 2007 level of digital media technology specialty game to carry on the innovation practice initially, the effect are good, sharpened student's beginning ability and innovation ability, obtained the animation game to design big game's many award items. The practice of the specialty and laboratory teaching reform of the mechanism is constantly running in practice, there are many areas need further improvement and perfection, for ultimately achieving "student-centered" teaching practice and laboratory operating mechanism.

References

1. Ying, L., Xi, Y.-B.: Exploration and Practice on the Operational and Managerial Mode of Experimental Center. Research and exploration in laboratory 28(4), 88–90 (2009)
2. Wei, W., Wang, C.-C., Li, X.-Y., Liang, M., Ding, S.-F.: Consideration and Exploration on Opening Laboratory Construction. Research and exploration in laboratory 28(4), 272–273 (2009)
3. Chen, Y.-H., Gan, X.-X., Liu, W.-H.: Reflections on the practical teaching of digital media technology. Journal of Hubei Normal University (Natural Science) 29(2), 87–90 (2009)
4. Feng, L., Wang, S.-P.: The research of Practice teaching pattern of Digital media specialiyt. The Computer of Fujian 4, 32–33 (2009)

A Study on Patient Safety and Accident Prevention Measures with Modern Information Technology

Hung-Lieh Chou[1,2], Ching-Hsue Cheng[1], Fuh-Gwo Chen[3], and Jr-Shian Chen[3,*]

[1] Department of Information Management, National Yunlin University of Science and Technology, No. 123, section 3, University Road, Touliu, Yunlin 640, Taiwan
[2] St. Joseph's Hospital, No.74, Xinsheng Rd., Huwei Township, Yunlin County 632, Taiwan
[3] Department of Computer Science and Information Management, Hungkuang University No. 34, Chung-Chie Road, Shalu, Taichung 433, Taiwan
{g9623805,chcheng}@yuntech.edu.tw,
{ronald,jschen}@sunrise.hk.edu.tw

Abstract. The Taiwan Patient-Safety Reporting System, which was designed by the Taiwan Joint Commission on Hospital Accreditation (TJCHA) in 2004, is one of the few national, voluntary, external reporting systems. The systems is built on RRS and publish/subscribe application software, and Message Queue, SOAP, XML technologies are adopted to manage the internal information procedures of healthcare institutions. This study discusses the understanding of medical personnel concerning patient-safety incident prevention measures, from the perspective of trends in reporting of patient-safety irregularities. The results of the study will assist healthcare institutions to better understand their internal errors, in order to design effective strategies for improvement that will enhance the quality of their services, thereby providing safe and effective healthcare to every patient.

Keywords: Patient-safety, educational training, preventive measures.

1 Introduction

In 1999, IOM(Institute Of Medicine) produced the "To Err is Human" Report, which suggested: an accident reporting system that is not based on punishment is the first step to building a safe healthcare system [1]. The Taiwan Patient-Safety Reporting System (TPR) (Fig.1), which was designed by the Taiwan Joint Commission on Hospital Accreditation (TJCHA) in 2004, is one of the few national, voluntary, external reporting systems. The systems is built on really simple syndication (RSS) and publish/subscribe application software, and Message Queue, Simple Object Access Protocol (SOAP), The Extensible Markup Language (XML) technologies are adopted to manage the internal information procedures of healthcare institutions. These define and manage the reporting process and information, using a finite states machine as the basis for undertaking process calculations; analysis and designation of safety incidents adopt rule-based principles, using professional experience and

---

* Corresponding author (J.S. Chen).

S. Lin and X. Huang (Eds.): CSEE 2011, Part V, CCIS 218, pp. 190–195, 2011.

standard operating procedures to undertake analysis and designation in respect of patient-safety incidents. The reporting interface is web-based, and the interface for discussion of proximate and ultimate causes is based on problem management [2].

This study discusses the understanding of medical personnel concerning patient-safety incident prevention measures, from the perspective of trends in reporting of patient-safety incidents. The results of the study will assist healthcare institutions to better understand their internal errors, in order to design effective strategies for improvement that will enhance the quality of their services, thereby providing safe and effective healthcare to every patient. It is hoped that healthcare institutions will participate in the reporting system through advanced information technologies; a sound reporting system will help these institutions to learn from their past mistakes, prevent and detect the occurrence of adverse medical incidents, minimize the possible damage, and thereby ensure the safety of their patients [3].

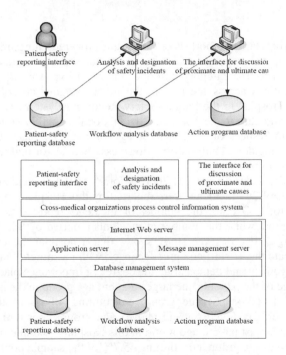

Fig. 1. Taiwan Patient-safety Reporting system

2 Method

This is an exploratory study based on a quantitative approach. Subjects of the study are the 10,419 reports made by healthcare institutions participating in the Taiwan Patient-Safety Program from January 1 until December 31, 2006. The study samples are divided into two mutually independent yet also mutually comprising pools:

1. National samples: This sample pool consists of the number of reports made by healthcare institutions participating in the Taiwan Patient-Safety Program from January 1 to December 31, 2006.
2. Control samples: This sample pool consists of the total number of reports made by this Hospital to the Patient-Safety Reporting System from January 1 to December 31, 2006.

Both sample pools are based on information collected through the Taiwan Patient-Safety Reporting System. All information and data are entered into the database and analyzed using SPSS10.0 packaged software. At this study is exploratory in nature, differential variance analysis will be considered to be mutually symmetric variances and there will be no factor analysis.

3 Results

A healthcare irregularity report is a procedure for recording incidents that are inconsistent with the regular operation of a hospital or patient-care standards (TJCHA, 2004). The first category describes the reporting of healthcare incidents by healthcare institutions across the nation; the latter category describes the incidents reported by this Hospital to the Patient-Safety Reporting System. This study explores the similarities and differences between the national and this Hospital's reporting characteristics, in respect of 6 variances: age of patients, place that the incident occurred, type of incident, analysis of seriousness, analysis of reason for occurrence, and prevention measures.

From January 1 to December 31, 2006, a total of 10,419 incidents were reported nationally; a total of 269 incidents were reported by this Hospital, representing 2.58% of the national total. Overall, the number of incidents reported nationally shows a monthly rising trend, while the number of incidents reported by this Hospital shows a falling trend (Fig.2, Fig.3). The study shows that a hospital must consistently and continue to educate the its staff and give feedback with meaningful analysis, as well as provide encouragement and demonstrate the degree of importance placed on reporting.

In terms of age of the patients, the largest patient age group in the national sample is the adult (aged 19-64 years) age group, constituting 40.6% of the sample pool, followed by the elderly (aged 65 and above) age group, constituting 32.9% of the sample pool. The largest patient age group in this Hospital's sample pool is the elderly (aged 65 and above) age group, constituting 45.7% of the sample pool, followed by the adult (aged 19-64 years) age group, constituting 37.9% of the sample pool.

In terms of the places where the incidents occurred, the national sample and this Hospital's sample are alike in that the greatest number of incidents occurred in public wards, representing around 60% of the total number of incidents.

In terms of the types of incidents reported, the statistical results for this Hospital's sample and the national sample show slight differences. The statistics for the types of incidents reported in the national sample, from highest to lowest, are: falling incidents with 29%, followed by pharmaceutical incidents with 26%, tubing incidents with 11%, and injury incidents with 10%. In the sample pool for this Hospital, the largest number is tubing incidents with 24.9%, followed by falling incidents with 22.3%, pharmaceutical incidents with 20.1%, and medical care incidents with 13.4%.

In terms of analysis of the degree of seriousness, the national sample and this Hospital's sample are alike in that the majority results in no injury, followed by medium degree of injury and then minor degree of injury.

In terms of analysis of the reasons for occurrence of the incidents, both samples show that "physical and behavioural factors relating to patients" occur most frequently, followed by factors "relating to individual staff". In terms of preventive measures, the national sample and this Hospital's sample are alike in that the main prevention measure adopted by the majority of reporters is still "improving educational training", followed by "improving method of communication".

According to results of the study, this Hospital's sample and the national sample differ in terms of statistical results for incident type and age spread of the patients. An analysis of the reasons for such differences show that because the majority of patients involved in incidents in this Hospital's sample are elderly patients, who are more likely to be intubated; if they were not given appropriate medical care, then the likelihood of tubing slippage or pulling out of tubing would also increase. This result demonstrates the necessity for the Hospital to install respiratory care facilities and professional respiratory care staff.

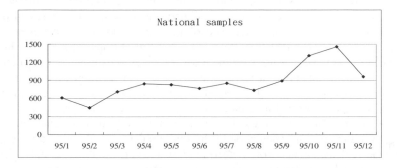

Fig. 2. National the number of incidents report

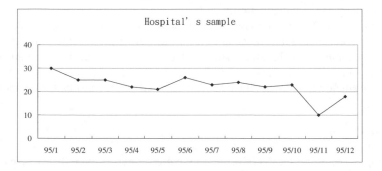

Fig. 3. Hospital the number of incidents report

The national sample and this Hospital's sample are similar in terms of statistical results for the places where the incidents occurred, analysis of the reasons for occurrence, and preventive measures. In this Hospital's sample, when reporters are asked to evaluate preventive measures for preventing reoccurrence of such types of incidents, the reporters still chose "improving educational training". In terms of the top three types of incidents reported by this Hospital and their preventive measures, the results of analysis are as follows: 1).The reason for occurrence of tubing incidents is "physical and behavioural factors relating to patients" (85.2%), and 38.3% of reporters suggest the preventive measure of "improving educational training". 2).The reason for occurrence of falling incidents is "physical and behavioural factors relating to patients" (71.4%), and 41.0% of reporters believe that "improving educational training" will reduce the frequency of occurrence.

The majority of reporters believe that pharmaceutical incidents occur due to "human factors" (92.0%), and 71.0% suggest the preventive measure of "improving educational training".

The percentages of reporters who choose "changing the method of medical care" and "changing administrative management" as preventive measures are both rather low. This shows that the staffs of healthcare institutions around the country still need to be better educated concerning the cause-and-effect relationship between patient-safety reporting, reasons for occurrence of incidents, and preventive measures. A scholar once pointed out that the effectiveness of "educational training" endures for only 3 months, and can be said to be the most resources consuming yet least enduring measure amongst all preventive measures [4]. Many countries are making a considerable investment in the development of integrated drug information management systems to facilitate electronic prescribing and improved safety in drug treatment [1,5,6]. However, there has been extremely limited evaluation of these systems even though implementation of these systems in ambulatory care is expected to provide enhancements for detecting adverse drug-related events. This is particularly true for primary care physicians as they provide front-line health care to patients with a wide range of types and numbers of comorbidities, a common reason for adverse drug-related events. So the Pharmaceutical incident can controls through hospital information system or integrated drug information management systems, and that need for systematic evaluation.

Therefore, in order to effectively prevent occurrence of incidents, it is necessary to ascertain the exact reasons for occurrence of the incidents, besides improving basic educational training for the staff. The chief objective for reporting of patient-safety incidents is in fact to encourage the healthcare staff to undertake systematic review and improvement of the medical care process, based on the reasons for the incidents.

4 Discussion

Reporting is one of the means of promoting patient safety. Given that overseas studies have suggested that the appropriate number of incidents reported by an institution should be double the number of beds, there would seem to be a major concern about the patient-safety reporting undertaken by hospital staff. The results of this study also show that improving educational training is in fact not very effective in reducing the likelihood of patient-safety incidents recurring. In the future, hospital staff should be better guided in discovering the true reasons for occurrence of the incidents, helping them to understand and discover these reasons and then undertake improvements.

The ultimate solution to enhancing patient safety and work safety is in fact through using the information systems to detect and discover patient-safety incidents, at the same time as using other means to involve a greater number of medical group members in discussions and the improvement process, such as through reviews of medical records and discussion of individual cases. Collection of statistics regarding irregular incidents is not merely the collection of data; it is a long-term tracking, pre-warning system for the purposes of analyzing and preventing potential and actual risks, and preventing recurrence of mistakes. Future research should use technology acceptance model survey attitudes of Hospital's user.

References

1. Committee on Quality of Health Care in America and Institute O. Medicine. To Err Is Human: Building a Safer Health System, 1st edn. National Academies Press (April 2000)
2. Taiwan Patient-safety Reporting system, System Introduction (2007),
   http://www.tpr.org.tw
3. Taiwan Joint Commission on Hospital Accreditation, Patient safety definition of the term (2004)
4. Firth-Cozens, J.: Barriers to incident reporting. Quality Safety Health Care 11-1, 7 (2002)
5. eHealth Initiative, Electronic Prescribing: Toward Maximum Value and Rapid Adoption, Washington, DC (2004)
6. Lipton, H.L., Miller, R.H., Wimbush, J.J.: Electronic prescribing:ready for prime time? J. Health. Inform. Manage 17-4, 72 (2003)

Study on the Training Mode of Innovative Postgraduate Students Based on Web Resources

Jie Yao[1], Pei-jun Zhu[2], and Yan Zhang[3]

[1] School of Economy and Management, Northeast Dianli University, Jilin, China
[2] School of Economy and Management, Northeast Dianli University, Jilin, China
[3] School of Foreign Linguistics and Applied Linguistics,
Tianjin Foreign Studies University, China
leeyooab@163.com, zhupeijun007@yahoo.com.cn,
zhangyan_zpj@yahoo.com.cn

Abstract. In recent years, with the rapid social and economic development, China is in great demand for the talents so that the postgraduate student education in China develops very rapidly. The training of innovative postgraduate students is a systematic project, which requires the close integration of all aspects and various elements of postgraduate education. Only by deepening the education innovation can we implement those elements into the practice of training the postgraduates' innovative abilities. By analyzing the basic elements of the postgraduate training mode, this paper puts forward the training mode of innovative postgraduates suitable for our country from the following four aspects------training goal, training process, curriculum arrangement and quality management.

Keywords: Innovative postgraduates, training mode, training goal, training process.

1 Introduction

Nowadays, the training of the innovative postgraduates has great significance in our country. Firstly, the development of our country needs the innovative talents. Facing to the 21st century, the construction of a prosperous, democratic, civilized, modern and socialistic country has an urgent need to train a large number of the innovative talents which are able to take on heavy responsibilities. Secondly, the knowledge economy requires the innovative talents. Since the innovative quality of the labors, especially the innovative abilities of the labors become the key elements of affecting economic development, the development of knowledge economy need to train the talent to be the one who can not only use the scientific and cultural knowledge skillfully but also have innovative consciousness and innovative abilities. Thirdly, training of the innovative talents is an important symbol to measure the education quality of higher school, and it is also an important manifestation of the comprehensive strength of the higher school. Therefore, the vital task of the postgraduate education in China is to train the talents to be of high quality and have innovative spirit and innovative abilities.

S. Lin and X. Huang (Eds.): CSEE 2011, Part V, CCIS 218, pp. 196–201, 2011.

2 Composition of the Postgraduate Training Mode

The training mode of postgraduate students is mainly concerned with two questions which are what kind of people should be trained and how to train these people. The training of the postgraduates involves many aspects, such as admission, instruction, scientific research, graduation design, thesis, degree conferred, and so on. All these aspects are closely related to the establishment of teaching goals, the interaction between teachers and students, the curriculum arrangement, the choice of research projects, the training ways and methods, and the supervision and management of the postgraduate quality. Therefore, the training mode of the postgraduates mainly includes four elements which are the training goal, the training process, the curriculum arrangement and the quality management.

The training goal prescribes the orientation and specifications of the postgraduate training. It is the answer to the question that what kind of people should be trained. The training goal is the starting point and the destination of the whole training, which guides the training process, the curriculum arrangement and the quality management. Based on a certain training goal, the training process aims at improving the knowledge, the quality and the ability of the postgraduates, and makes them become the qualified high-level talents through course learning and scientific research under the instruction of the tutors. Therefore, the training process is the answer to the question that how to train the people. The curriculum arrangement is the carrier of the personnel training. It is the manifestation of the goal and the characteristics of the professional training, which directly affects the quality of the postgraduate training. We can measure the reasonableness of the curriculum arrangement from various aspects which are the depth and the width of the curriculum, the arrangement of the required courses and the selective courses, the distribution of the professional and the cross-disciplinary courses. The quality management is the key aspect of the postgraduate training, which is carried out through the whole process. The essence of quality management is to monitor each stage of the postgraduate training to guarantee the realization of the training goal by using certain methods and taking some measures. The four aspects of the training mode of the postgraduates complement each other and play a decisive role in the training quality of the postgraduates.

3 Constructing China's Training Mode of the Innovative Postgraduates

In recent years, as the social and economic development of China has the increasingly strong demand for the talents, the postgraduate education in China has been developing rapidly. However, the expansion of the number does not equal to the improvement of the quality. What we can not avoid is how to face the new situation, reform the training mode of the postgraduates, and improve the quality of the postgraduates. The study of the training mode of the innovative postgraduates in the universities should mainly focuse on the following four aspects: the first one is to realize the various training goal, and the second one is that the training process should emphasize the training of the postgraduates' innovative abilities. The third aspect is about the optimal design of the curriculum and the reform and innovation of the teaching methods. The last one is to emphasize the strict quality management.

3.1 Realize the Various Training Goal

The postgraduate education should break the traditional and single framework which focuses on the pure science and the pure theory. It should be the manifestation of various training goal. For example, the postgraduate education in America includes the academic degree and professional degree. The main training goal of the academic degree is to train the talents who can create new knowledge and explore the unknown fields. It emphasizes the learning and mastery of the research methodology, the original research, and so on. On the contrary, the training goal of the professional degree is to train the applied talents to learn and master the professional knowledge and skills so as to meet the demands of the society and individual development. Therefore, China's postgraduate education should be in accordance with our country's conditions and aims at the diversification. On one hand, it is necessary for us to strengthen the professional theory and the knowledge learning and pay attention to the improvement of the abilities to analyze and solve the problems. On the other hand, we should decide the different training types depending on the various actual needs, and realize the configuration that the master education regards the applied education as its main part and the doctor education develops the academic education and the applied education simultaneously. Therefore, the postgraduate education can not only train the teachers and researchers for the educational and research department but also transfer the high-leveled applied talents to the society.

3.2 Emphasize the Training of the Postgraduates' Innovative Abilities

Firstly, we should follow the international trend of the postgraduate education, and integrate with the world from the following different aspects such as the education thoughts, the teaching contents, the teaching means, the teaching methods, the teaching conditions, and so on. It is necessary for us to constantly absorb the foreign advanced teaching thoughts and teaching methods, and create more opportunities for the postgraduates to know the international academic trends, and then take a "go out and come in" international road.

Secondly, we should provide the free and easeful academic environment for the postgraduate students and pay more attention to the training of the students' innovative sense and innovative abilities so as to stimulate their imagination and creativity and make them fully play their personality. Thus we can cultivate the thoughtful and bold innovative talents. We should encourage the postgraduates to explore scientific problems and the forefront academic subjects and choose the subjects in the practice as the topics of their thesis. In America, the government advocates the universities to cooperate with the companies. It encourages the universities to reform the training modes of the postgraduates and combine their teaching and research work with the manufacture process so that they can not only actively cultivate all kinds of talents to meet the needs of the industrial and commercial circles but also train the postgraduates jointly through the cooperation with the companies.

Thirdly, the improvement of the postgraduate innovative abilities is also closely related to whether we have own some teachers with strong innovative sense and high research level or not. In China, the scale of the postgraduates, especially the masters, is becoming larger and larger. Moreover, the number of the teachers in the universities is relatively limited, which results in the serious unbalance of the proportion between the postgraduates and the teachers. It has influenced the training quality of the postgraduates seriously. Besides, at present the system of the tutors' individual responsibility has been popular in the training of China's postgraduate students. It is harmful to overcome the contradiction between the time and energy limitation of some teachers and the urgent communication needs of the students. At the same time, it will not be helpful for the students to contact with the various ideas and styles of different tutors. Therefore, the system of tutor group responsibility is the "many-to-one" guidance by the group which is consisted by the tutors from different fields. It is very useful for the comprehensive development of the students and the training of the compound talents.

Lastly, we should pay more attention to the training of the postgraduates' self-study abilities, independent learning and practice abilities in the class. During the class, the teacher should not teach too much. On the contrary, they should arrange the students to read more references after class to improve their self-study ability and independent thinking ability. Meanwhile, in class, we'd better avoid the phenomenon that the teacher is continuously giving lectures. On the opposite, we should encourage the students to develop their imaginations, put forward problems and state their views. It would be useful to build an active classroom atmosphere. Besides, in the laboratory, we should encourage the postgraduates to do the experiment by themselves. And the teachers only play the guiding role during the process.

3.3 Emphasize the Optimal Design of the Curriculum and the Reform of the Teaching Methods

It is universal to carry out the appropriate flexible credit system in the postgraduate education. The flexible credit system is complying with the basic rules of postgraduate education and it is also the basic requirement of ensuring the postgraduate training quality. In the process of the postgraduate training, we should quantify each part like the course selection, the practice and the thesis writing into the corresponding credits. The students who are trained by the flexible credit system can adjust their learning plans depending on their actual situation, so that they can shorten or extend their learning period to some extent which expand their autonomy of learning.

The postgraduate school should provide various courses for the selection. The teaching plan ought to be flexible to meet the students' needs. The postgraduates could select the courses across the disciplines, the departments or the schools and join the study in other departments according their own foundation, characteristics and interests. Meanwhile, the postgraduate school can prescribe a certain number of required courses. It can not only avoid the drift, but also fully play the individual specialties and creativity of the postgraduates. In addition, the postgraduate school should arrange well the proportion of the professional courses and the elementary course and focus on the mastery of the professional knowledge, especially the mastery of the solid theory foundation and the rich humanities knowledge. It should also highlight the intercrossing and the pioneering of the course contents to implement the training goal of the compound talents. Besides, the curriculum arrangement should keep pace with the times, and constantly updating the course content, and reflect the latest developments and needs of the society.

In the aspect of the teaching method, the ways that focus on giving lectures similar to that of the undergraduate teaching can not fully stimulate the postgraduates' activity for learning, which may have a serious effect on the actual performance of the class instruction. We should reform the teaching methods of the postgraduate courses, focus on improving the subjective status of the students and implement the elicitation instruction. We can take different teaching methods such as discussions, speeches, debates and case analysis, which would provide the room for the students to develop their imagination and train their abilities of exploring and solving the problems. These methods are embodied very well in the class of the American universities.

3.4 Emphasize the Strict Quality Management

The postgraduates are the future and hope of our country. They are the high-leveled talents which meet the needs of the social progress and development. Therefore, the control of the postgraduate training quality is much more important. Referring to the whole training process of the postgraduates, different universities have their own set of the regulations. They usually control each layer of the postgraduates' course learning and scientific research though different links such as the examination, the assessment, the opening report, the intermediate inspection, the thesis, and so on. All these are very helpful to achieve the goal of improving the postgraduates' training quality. However, there are still some problems in China's postgraduate management system now. The most important one is that the postgraduate admission is relatively difficult while the management after the admission is looser. It will be bad for the stimulation of the postgraduate autonomy and innovation. Therefore, we should continuously establish and improve the examination system to select the talents and weed out the unqualified postgraduates during the postgraduate students' study period so that it will come to the separate training. At the same time, we should especially teach the students to obey the academic norm and academic morality and resolutely stop the plagiarism of others' results or data. It is necessary to control the quality of the thesis and perfect the system of detection and punishment to the academic misconducts. All these will be helpful for the students to put their energy into the scientific research work and reduce the opportunism so as to improve the academic quality and the scientific level finally.

4   Summary

The training of innovative postgraduate students is a systematic project, which requires the close integration of all aspects and various elements of postgraduate education. Only by deepening the education innovation can we implement those elements into the practice of training the postgraduates' innovative abilities. By analyzing the basic elements of the postgraduate training mode and combining with the guiding ideology, this paper puts forward the training mode of innovative postgraduates which is suitable for our country from the following four aspects, they are the training goal, the training process, the curriculum arrangement and the quality management.

References

1. Pan, W.: The U.S. Self-evaluation System of Graduate Educational Qualities and Its Revelations. Teacher Education Research 2, 78 (2004)
2. Liu, T.: Innovation and Practice of the Evaluation of Graduate Education. International Business 1, 98 (2005)
3. Wang, D., Wang, J.: Analysis on the model of Quality Assurance System of Graduate Education. Journal of Higher Education Research 4, 15 (2004)
4. Cao, J., Huang, Z.: Systematic Comparison of the Graduate Students Training Mode between China and USA. Journal of Technology College Education 4, 39 (2005)

Research on Synchronous BUCK LED Driver Based on IRS2541 CCM Mode with Analysis of Scientific Materials

Peng Wu, Wenju Zhang, Min Xie, and Qian Luo

School of Electronic Information, Wuhan University, Wuhan 430079,China

Abstract. LED, an effective energy saving light source, is becoming a mainstream resource. By analyzing functionality principles of the Synchronous BUCK LED deriver based on IRS2541 CCM Mode, this paper depicts a Synchronous BUCK LED deriver based on IRS2541 CCM Mode. It constructed the mathematical model of BUCK CCM mode and designed a simple and low-cost LED driver.

Keywords: IRS2541, CCM, PWM, LED control.

1 Introduction

LED is known for its effective energy saving and long lasting life span. With the profound influence of "low carbon" and "green life style", LED is becoming highly preferred as a lighting option and will replace filament lamp and daylight lamp eventually. As LED is widely adopted increasing, it faces new challenges. The design that this paper proposes is simple, practical and low-cost, which switches on and off automatically with lighting been adjusted when required. The electric circuit has the advantage of high exchange efficiency as Synchronous BUCK and simple design based on IRS2541, as well as that it has reduced the size and weight of the controller, promoting its functionality.

2 Mathematical Model of Synchronous BUCK CCM Mode

BUCK or BUCK chopper means voltage input is higher or equivalent than voltage output. Figure 1 shows topological structure of Synchronous BUCK converter. It is comprised of switch S1, S2, inductance L and Capacitance C.

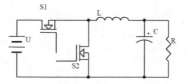

Fig. 1. Topological structure of Synchronous BUCK converter

S. Lin and X. Huang (Eds.): CSEE 2011, Part V, CCIS 218, pp. 202–206, 2011.

Within a switch on and off period T, status of S1, S2 are as follows:

$$\begin{cases} s_1 on, s_2 off \left(0 \le t \le DT\right) \\ s_1 off, s_2 on \left(DT \le t \le T\right) \end{cases} \tag{1}$$

(D applies when PWM signal is not taken into account)

In two different scenarios with the switch on and off, the relationship with the increase of current is as follows:

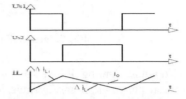

Fig. 2. Shows wave shape of inductance current iL in Synchronous

$$\begin{cases} \Delta i_L + = \int_0^{DT} \dfrac{U - Uo}{L} dt = \dfrac{U - Uo}{L} DT \\ \Delta i_L - = \int_{DT}^{T} \dfrac{U_o}{L} dt = \dfrac{U_o}{L}(1 - D)T \end{cases} \tag{2}$$

And $\Delta i_L + = \Delta i_L - = \Delta i_L$ $L \ge \dfrac{U_o(1-D)}{2i_o}T = \dfrac{U_o(1-D)}{2i_oF}(3)$ With constant current: $\Delta i_L < 2i_o$ (when it is even $\Delta i_L = 2i_0$)

3 LED Driver Circuit Based on IRS2541

3.1 Features of IRS2541

IRS2541 is the chip to control Buck Regulator. It is a high voltage rectifier (600 V half-bridged driver) with high frequency (highest can reach 500 KHz) adopted internationally, utilized to control permanent current. Figure 3 shows the internal functionality structure of IRS2541.

There is a two-way four-diode clamp between the lead pins of VCC and COM in IRS2541. Two-way four-diode prevent from high voltage, as diode reverse breakdown voltage is 15.6 V. The base pins of IFB and ENN are connected internally to resistance comparators respectively, of which IFB is used for Load current feedback. When IFB pin voltage changes, the operating status of chip is as follows:

$$\begin{cases} \text{VIFB>0.5 V, HO is low while LO is high, thus load current decrease} \\ \text{VIFB<0.5 V, HO is high while LO is low, thus load current increase} \end{cases} \tag{4}$$

ENN pin is used to control power, which can be used to adjust LED and open-circuit protection. When ENN pin voltage change, the operating status of chip is as follows:

$$\begin{cases} \text{VENN>2.5 V, chip is inhibited (HO decreases, LO increases)} \\ \text{VENN<2.5 V, chip is enabled} \end{cases} \tag{5}$$

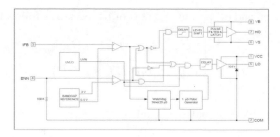

Fig. 3. Internal Functionality Structure of IRS2541

To adjust lighting, PWM wave is input from ENN pin, shows a linear relationship between pulse width and average load current. Dead time generator installed is to prevent Discretion edge power been turned on at the same time. There is a Bootstrap resistor between VB pin and VS pin, providing levitation voltage for High edge gate drive. In order to prevent HO long time buy tall, make both ends bootstrap capacitance discharge high voltage driving voltage grid caused low side which will alternatively lead to high cost because of incomplete circulation of the switch. The design of door keeping timer enables IFB to be forced to decrease when IFB input voltage constantly stay lower than 0.5 V with HO stays up to 20μs. LO stays high, this enforcement maintains input around 1μs, supplying power to bootstrap electric capacity CBOOT.

3.2 Theoretical Base and Structure of Synchronous BUCK LED Driver Based on IRS2541 CCM Mode

Input a.c. voltage 220V±10%, maximum output d.c.voltage 48V, maximum current 1A, maximum output powers 48W are set for the circuit. The circuit comprises EMI filter, full-wave rectification controller, synchronizing step-down rectifier circuit, current feedback circuit and short circuit protection in figure 4.

3.2.1. Theory of the Driving Circuit

When 220V a.c. voltage is input to EMI filter, rectification controller receives approximately 320 V d.c. voltage, which is charged to C1 by R2. When VCC voltage reach starting voltage, the chip starts working, which results in LO remains high and HO stays low. The process charges power to Bootstrap resistor CBOOT, building driving voltage. Then output current can be adjusted by the closed-loop current system to control HO and LO, to achieve consistent output.

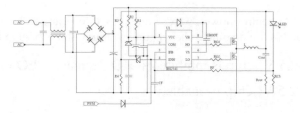

Fig. 4. Circuit of Synchronous BUCK LED Driver Based on IRS2541 CCM Mode

3.2.2 Inductor L and COUT

Compatible inductor L and output COUT will reduce output voltage current wave effectively. Meantime, IRS2541 is based on free frequency; its working frequency is decided by input and output of Inductor L and COUT. d.c. voltage 320 V is input produce output d.c. 48 V. D=48/320=15%.

From formula (3)$L \geq \dfrac{20.4}{F}$ (6) because (2) change current $\Delta i = \dfrac{U_o}{L}(1-D)T = 1A$ (7)

Thus $L = 40.8T$ (8) $L = 1mH$ $F = \dfrac{1}{T} = 40.8kHz$ (9) Output wave voltage:

$\Delta U_o = \dfrac{U_o(1-D)}{8LC}t^2$ (10) Because of (8), (9), (10): $\Delta U_o = \dfrac{T}{8C} = \dfrac{1}{8CF}$ (11) $\Delta U_o = 0.1V$:

$C = 30.6\mu F$, Thus $C = 33\mu F$.

3.3 Principles of the Design of the Circuit and Structure

The functionality of the controlled circuit is to produce PWM wave, with LED been turned on and off by sensing light in the environment. Control circuit by the front-end hysteretic comparator level of PWM generator. When lighting changes, light dependent resistors results the change of V1, the relationships are:

$$V_3 = \begin{cases} V_{OL}, V_1 > \{[1+(R_6 / R_9)]V_2\} - [(R_6 / R_9)V_{OL}] \\ V_{OH}, V_1 < \{[1+(R_6 / R_9)]V_2\} - [(R_6 / R_9)V_{OH}] \end{cases} \quad (12)$$

High V3 enables NE555 and PWM signal to adjust the lighting of LED. Reduced V3 disables NE555, number 3 pin output decreases. Because of the opposite effect of triode, PWM signal output end produce high-level (higher than 2.5 V) to disable IRS2541. LED will go off to achieve LED been turned on and off automatically. When LED is on, it can be adjusted by slide rheostat R5 to change wave width DPWM.

$$D_{PWM} = \dfrac{R_A}{R_A + R_B}(13) \qquad \text{PWM signal frequency:} \qquad F_{PWM} = \dfrac{1.433}{(R_A + R_B)C}(14)$$

RA=R11+R5_1, RB=R10+R5_2

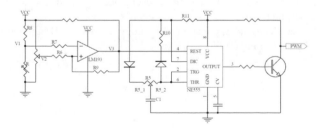

Fig. 5. Structure map

206   P. Wu et al.

4 PhotoFilter of Matlab

The experience is conducted when a.c. input voltage is 220 V. Map 6 and 7 shows inductive current wave and output voltage respectively. Map 6 indicates average inductive current is 1A, the change of current is $\Delta i = 1A$, which is in line with theory. From map 7, output voltage wave $\Delta U_o = 0.1A$, which testified as well.

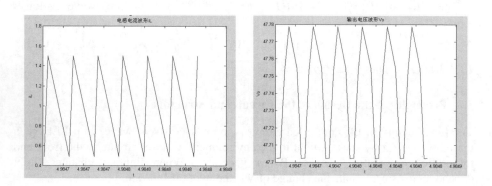

Fig. 6. PhotoFilter of Matlab inductive current wave

Fig. 7. PhotoFilter of Matlab of output voltage wave

5 Conclusion

Synchronous BUCK LED driver based on IRS2541 CCM Mode is simple, reliable, practical and low-cost. It reduced its size and weight without voltage transformer and it can be used both for business and home.

References

1. Three, C.X., Wen, G.S.: High frequency power electronics. China Water Conservancy and Hydropower Press, Beijing (2009)
2. IRS254(o'1)Um BUCK REGULATOR C0N IROL IC, International Rectifier
3. Min, Z., Hua, J.: Led lighting technology and engineering applications, pp. 90–93. China Power Press, Beijing (2010)
4. Linfei, D.: Power electronic application technology of MATLAB simulation, pp. 97–106. China Power Press, Beijing (2009)

Study on the Teaching Methods of Theory and Practice in Communications Principles Course Based on Teaching Materials

Liqun Huang, Guang Yang, and Jie Zhang

Department of Electronic Information, Northeastern University at Qinhuangdao, China
persistent_hlq@sina.com, yangguangneuq@163.com,
zhangjieshr@163.com

Abstract. The currently facing problems of the teaching of communications principles course are summerized and analyzed in this paper. For the teaching of theoretical knowledge, a series of effective measures are taken to improve teaching effectiveness, including organizing appropriate course contents, designing excellent multimedia coursewares, and selecting valid teaching methods. On the other hand, the teaching of practical skills is successfully enhanced by taking full advantage of curriculum experiments, integrated course project for communication systems, graduation design, and so on. Students' practical skills and innovative ability are strengthened by applying EDA tools, such as Matlab and FPGA, to design and implement communication systems and function modules.

Keywords: Communications Principles; Teaching Methods; Practical Skills; Innovation Ability.

1 Introduction

Communications principles" is a major compulsory course for communications engineering specialty, but also it's a graduate entrance examination course for communication and information system specialty. This curriculum has many prerequisite courses, such as "signal and linear system", "probability and random processes", "fundamentals of digital electronic", "high-frequency electronic circuits", and so on. Meanwhile, it is also a prerequisite course for "mobile communication systems", "optical fiber communication systems", and "modern communication network". So "communications principles" forms a connecting link between the preceding and the following courses, and play an important role in the curriculum architecture.

In order to improve teaching quality, we need to reform the teaching methods of communications principles course. The reform aims to make students to have not only a solid theoretical foundation, but also emphasizes the development of students' practical skills and innovation ability, which is beneficial for improving the training quality of communications engineering undergraduates [1].

S. Lin and X. Huang (Eds.): CSEE 2011, Part V, CCIS 218, pp. 207–212, 2011.

2 The Facing Problems of the Teaching in Communications Principles Course

2.1 Difficulties of Theoretical Knowledge Teaching

Communications principles course has a lot of distinguishing features, such as comprehensive knowledge, strong theory, and many abstractive formulas, moreover, there are relatively high requirements for the mastery of prerequisite courses. These features make students difficult to grasp and understand this course. During the teacher-student conversations, many students often said that communications principles course is difficult to learn.

After the expansion of college enrollment, the enthusiasm and the initiative of undergraduates' learning attitude show a greater difference. Current students can be divided into three types: (1) the first kind of students has strong motivation to learn, solid foundation of basic knowledge, and active thinking during class; (2) the second one has no clear learning goals, and completes the learning task only for enough credits. (3) the third one lacks of the basic knowledge of prerequisite courses, loses confidence in learning "communications principles", and even shows the weary emotion of learning [2].

According to the observations and the conversations during the teaching of communications principles, the proportions of three kinds of students are approximately 50%, 35% and 15% in the communications engineering specialty of our school, which is consistent with the survey results of other universities [2, 3].

In addition, "communications principles" is a major compulsory course for communications engineering specialty and electronic information engineering specialty, and the students of each grade are more than 150 peoples for communications engineering undergraduates in our college. Hence, the situation of teaching large classes is unavoidable, which makes teachers difficult to learn about how well every student has mastered the knowledge during lesson. Moreover, It is difficult to effectively supervise few students whose learning falls behind [4], and good interaction often lacks between teachers and students.

2.2 The Limitations of Traditional Practice Teaching

In order to develop and improve the practical skills of each student, and enable students to better understand the theoretical knowledge, our teaching program of "communications principles" arranges experimental courses with 10 class hours. The experimental contents include: the validation of line codes, digital baseband transmission system, digital waveband transmission system, and PCM digital voice transmission. Obviously, all these courses belong to validation-type experiments.

Through the teacher-student informal symposium during the teaching evaluation in the middle of semester, and the observation in the experimental teaching, we find that many students lack of interests and patiences on the validation-type experiments, only operate the laboratory equipments according to the experimental instructions, and observe the oscilloscope waveform without active thinking, moreover, and most students have the strong dependence on experiment teachers. After finishing experiments, a lot of students are still fuzzy and confused on experimental principles, methods, procedures, and the theoretical meanings of experimental results. On the other hand, many students also feel the lack of training opportunities about practical skills.

3 The Improvement of Theoretical Knowledge Teaching of Communications Principles

3.1 The Design of Multimedia Coursewares

We choose the 6th edition of communications principles edited by Fan Changxin as a textbook, which is the eleventh five-year national planning teaching material, and research the electronic lesson plan of the national quality course of communications principles at Xidian university. Considering the course architecture feature of communication engineering specialty in our school, the teaching content of communications principles is carefully optimized, and an excellent multimedia courseware is elaborately designed and compiled, which has received the third prize in the 12th multimedia educational software competition of Hebei Province. In the teaching process, good teaching effectiveness has obtained by using this multimedia courseware.

In the process of compiling multimedia courseware, we should pay attention to the visual effects, for example, the font size is appropriate, and the line spacing is moderate. In order to make the teaching more vivid and intuitive, we should adopt the figures and the tables as many as possible in multimedia coursewares. Meanwhile, using animations and hyperlinks makes the knowledge points to relate and confirm each other. Finally, the multimedia courseware has many advantages, such as clear structures, vivid demonstrations, and outstanding focal points, which is beneficial to enhancing the intuitive impression of students.

3.2 The Improvement of the Teaching Methods

Because communications principles course has comprehensive knowledges, strong theory, and many abstractive formulas, a lot of students find it difficult to learn, and feel difficult to focus their attention on the lectures for a long time. Hence, the following issues should be noticed in the process of theoretical knowledge teaching.

(1) On the basis of ensuring the completeness of course knowledge system, we need to strengthen the teaching of the important chapters of communications principles. For example, Chapter 3, channels and noise, is easy to understand, and suitable for students' self-study. Therefore, we mainly teach the important knowledge points, and speed up the progress of teaching, which is beneficial to heightening student's self-learning ability and learning initiative. However, Chapter 5, digital baseband transmission systems, is one of the key chapters of this course, and the theory of this chapter is difficult to understand. Most paragraphs in this chapter is gradually established around how to effectively solve the inter-symbol interference (ISI) problem, the contextual relationship of theoretical knowledges is very close, which plays a good role in training the thinking ability of students. Hence, we need to teach this chapter in detail.

(2) At the beginning of each class, the main knowledge points taught in the last lesson are simply reviewed and summarized, the knowledge review is helpful in strengthening student's impression, and lay a good foundation for carrying out this lesson. During the process of the teaching, the teaching methods, such as asking questions teaching, heuristic teaching, etc, are often adopted. Due to the constraint of teaching large class, the discussion teaching method is difficult to implement. Simply asking questions often leads students to think carefully in the classroom, inspires the enthusiasm and the initiative of student's learning attitude, and makes the learning atmosphere become active. Through student's answer, teachers can find out in time whether students keep up with the teaching progress, and know how well students have mastered the knowledge that has been taught in the past.

3.3 The Reforms of the Practical Teaching in Communications Principles Course

In addition to theoretical knowledge teaching, our teaching program of "communications principles" arranges experimental courses with 10 class hours. After finishing the curriculum, there is 3 weeks' integrated course project for communication systems. Course experiments mainly belong to validation-type experiments, which emphasizes the combination of theory and experiment. So these experiments are indispensable, and helpful for training student's basic practical skills[5]. In oder to further strengthen student's practical ability and innovation ability, and stimulate their learning enthusiasm, it's necessary to reform the traditional teaching methods of practical skills, and the teaching of practical skills in communications principles course can be put into the integrated course project for communication systems and the graduation design project.

3.4 Carrying out Design-Type Experiments in the Integrated Course Project

The integrated course project for communication systems is arranged as a key practice teaching link for "communications principles", "high-frequency electronic circuits", "FPGA theory and applications", "microcontroller principle and application", and "computer networks", and the purpose aims at training student's ability of practical engineering combined with theory. Through this integrated course project, students are required to master the basic theory of communication systems, utilize Matlab, electronic circuit, microcontroller, FPGA, NS-2 or other technologies to design, simulate and implement electronic systems, communications subsystems, or computer networks, and calculate the basic performance parameters. Finally, their practical ability of integrated design is effectively enhanced.

Communications principles course has strong theory, its study issues involve all parts of communication transmission systems, and many design-type experiment projects with moderate difficulty can be selected from these issues. For example, The performances of analog or digital communication systems can be simulated and analyzed by using matlab, simulink, systemview, or other simulation softwares, and compute the relationship curves between signal-to-noise ratio (SNR) and bit error rate (BER). For various analog or digital signals, their time-domain waveforms and the power spectrums can also be simulated using the same simulation software.

Consequently, these design-type experiment projects make students to have the thorough understanding of theoretical knowledges.

In addition, electronic circuits and FPGA technologies[6] can be used to design and implement AM modems, FM modems, the encoders and the decoders of AMI, CMI, and CRC codes, 2ASK, 2FSK, 2PSK modems, and other communication modules. All these projects are beneficial to improving student's electronic design skills and training their engineering practical ability.

3.5 Further Strengthening Student's Innovation Ability through Graduation Design

During the graduation design and the extracurricular activities of science and technology, we can select the innovation-type experimental projects from communications principles course, and these projects have higher difficulty. For example, the demodulation of digital signals often needs to use carrier synchronization, bit synchronization and frame synchronization. Then, how can we achieve these synchronizations in the actual communication systems? Graduation design topics may include the following projects:

(1) Design and implementation of HDB3 encoder and decoder based on FPGA;
(2) FPGA implementation of M-QAM modulation and demodulation;
(3) FPGA implementation of OFDM modulation and demodulation;
(4) The implementation of digital multiplex system based on FPGA;
(5) Design and implementation of convolutional codes;
(6) FPGA implementation of interleaver;
(7) Design and implementation of early-late gate bit Synchronizer;
(8) Design and implementation of frame synchronization system;

Students search relevant references by themselves, propose and demonstrate the design schemes, and do theoretical and experimental research independently. Finally, Students carry out the implementation of hardware and software, all by themselves. The entire practice process can take advantage of student's initiative, independence and creativity, and enhance their engineering practical ability and innovation ability.

4 Summary

As a connecting link, communications principles course play an important role in the curriculum architecture. This course has a lot of distinguishing features, such as comprehensive knowledge, strong theory, and many abstractive formulas. Thus, these features make students feel difficult to grasp and understand this course. Moreover, due to the serious limitations of traditional validation-type experiments in communications principles course, it's difficult to inspire the learning positivity of students. In this paper, We do preliminary research on the teaching reforms of theoretical knowledges and practical skills. During the teaching of communications principles course, we take full advantage of curriculum experiments, integrated course project for communication systems, graduation design, and other teaching links. On the basis of mastering theoretical knowledges, students' practical skills and innovative ability are successfully enhanced.

Acknowledgment. This work was supported by the Eleventh Five-Year Planning Project of Education Science Research from the Education Department of Hebei Province under Grant No. O8020027. and also supported by the Scientific Research Program from the Education Department of Hebei Province under Grant No. z2005323.

References

1. Zhang, Y., Zhang, X., Ha, C.: Construction of the practical teaching system for feature specialty of communication engineering. Journal of electrical & electronic education 32(3), 106–107 (2010)
2. Zhang, C.: Study and practice of communication principle teaching. Journal of Xi'an University of Posts and Telecommunications 14(1), 167–170 (2009)
3. Chu, W.: Research and practice on the teaching of communication principles based on multi-element integration idea. Journal of Xi'an University of Posts and Telecommunications 15(1), 148–151 (2010)
4. Chuai, G., Wang, W., Qi, Z., et al.: Practice and exploration on innovation of excellent-course of the mobile communication. Journal of Beijing University of Posts and Telecommunications (Social Sciences Edition) 11(4), 85–90 (2009)
5. Xiufang, W., et al.: Reform and practice of training students' innovation ability in the teaching of communication principles. Chinese Modern Educational Equipment 8, 65–67 (2009)
6. Xue, L., Cui, W.: Design practice teaching in communication system based on FPGA. Journal of Electrical & Electronic Education 31(2), 86–88 (2009)

Research on Teacher Training Curriculum Mode Innovation Based on Web

Xilong Tan[1], Huiling Wang[2], and Wentao Tan[3]

[1] Teachers' Quality Training Center of Hubei University of Education, Wuhan, China, 430205
[2] Library of Hubei University of Education, Wuhan, China, 430205
[3] School of Information Management of Wuhan University, Wuhan, China, 430072
65787539@163.com, txl@e21.edu.cn, 676989245@qq.com

Abstract. Teachers should be received specialized training, have higher education workers of professional quality. In order to develop the high quality teacher, teacher training curriculum should focus on professional skills. Our school has to strengthen the professional skills of teachers as a breakthrough in curriculum mode innovation, by enhancing practice teaching in the curriculum, strengthen the ethical culture and teaching ability training to innovate the teacher training mode. Increase the proportion of teacher education practice courses, outstanding teachers "professionalization"; strengthening teachers' professional skills training, outstanding teaching "practicality"; making full use of modern educational technology features, outstanding service a "technicality" for skills training; providing students with a comprehensive range of technical services, outstanding training "autonomy" and other means to have achieved remarkable results. Students' professional identity obvious enhancement, professional qualifications and teaching ability was improved obviously. Graduates of our school were warmly welcomed by primary and secondary schools.

Keywords: teacher training, curriculum setting, curriculum mode, professional skills, teacher professionalization.

Teacher training has been "normal characteristics" and "academic characteristics" debate for a long time. In my view, what is focused on the training mode "academic" or "normal" according to the school level, running tasks and training objectives. Training primary and secondary school teachers is the primary task of Normal College (including Normal College and Higher Normal Junior College). To cultivate culture of educational theory and professional capacity of qualified teachers for the objectives of education. Therefore, the Normal College curriculum mode must focus on "normal characteristics".

Our school has been engaged in the in-service teachers ' training for 80 years. Since 2000, it began to assume the primary and secondary school teachers in pre-service training tasks. In more than 10 years of primary and secondary school teachers in pre-service training curriculum mode in practice, our school has given a "normal characteristics" with a focus on innovative talents training mode. To develop professional skills of teachers as a value-oriented. Increase the proportion of teacher education curriculum, and strengthen the professional skills of teachers, and make full

S. Lin and X. Huang (Eds.): CSEE 2011, Part V, CCIS 218, pp. 213–220, 2011.

use of modern educational technology services; student learning offers a full range of technical services and other means to have achieved significant results, enhances students' sense of professional identity, improve literacy and educational ability in students. The curriculum mode reformation has achieved the desired effect.

1   The Necessity of "Professionalization" Oriented Curriculum Mode Innovation

Our teacher education has existed "normal characteristics" and "academic characteristics" controversy since the 1950's. A view is a teacher-training college for primary and secondary school services, we must highlight normal; and another view is equivalent to the academic level to University, pay attention to the academic. Without taking into account the tasks of the school and training object opinions are plausible under the circumstances. Reality is that there were different levels of University, admissions are different batches. Colleges and universities also have "research university", "research teaching universities" and "teaching universities" category. Participation of teachers' training school focused comprehensive University, Ministry of education subordinate normal university, Undergraduate normal colleges, and Teachers' college at different levels. In my view, aside the status quo of teacher education in general terms to talk about "normal characteristics" and "academic characteristics" are meaningless.

1.1   Highlight the "Professionalization" of Teacher Education Reform Is the Policy Regulation

Teacher training curriculum mode reform must be based on teacher education policy in China, running patterns of teacher education and professional requirements for teachers. Thus, as undertaken tasks of primary and secondary school teachers training, the normal colleges must clear the outline of national medium and long term educational reform and development plan (2010-2020) [1] (hereinafter referred to as "The Outline") on the reform of teacher education: "Strengthening of teacher education, deepen the reform of teacher education, innovation in training mode, enhanced practice, strengthen the ethical culture and teaching ability training, improving the quality of teacher training. "The outline" enhancing practice, strengthen the ethical culture and teaching training "requirement is actually a normal College curriculum and training mode to highlight the "normal characteristics" policies and regulations.

Normal colleges to cultivate specialized talents with a dual character. On the one hand they are a subject of professionals, but on the other hand they are teachers, and teachers itself is a kind of professional, also need special training. "A qualified teacher in addition to study general major beyond, still need a professional training, i.e. about education discipline of integrating theory with practice of specialized training. And this, we should admit that we used to be done very not enough. So, in order to meet the demands of this new era, cultivate higher quality of various disciplines of qualified people's teacher, for normal colleges students it is necessary to further strengthen education specialized training." [2] We must reform teachers professional training mode according to "The Outline" requirements.

1.2 Highlight "Professionalization" Is the Teacher Training Goal Request

Most students don't want to read the normal school, the quality of the new students in normal colleges can not compare with key university's. Furthermore, university is focus on a research-oriented to nurture research talent, and paying attention to the "academic characteristics". The normal colleges are teaching to foster practical, primary and secondary school teachers, it should also focus on "normal characteristics". "The 'normal characteristics' as teachers education of inherent property, general is refers to teachers of education professional characteristics, it is main solution the 'how to teach' problem, it is teachers' professional thought, and ethics, and behavior specification, and professional literacy and professional skills, aspects in school education science and various activities in the concentrated reflect, it is the teachers education difference   other professional education of nature property and particularity is located." [4]

1.3 Highlight "Professionalization" Is the Needs of the Teacher's Professional Development

"Teachers are fulfilling responsibilities of professionals in education and teaching" is the laws and regulations with Teacher Law. Teachers should have received specialized training, has a high professional quality of education professionals. Training with a professional level of teachers has become the goal of the reform of teacher education. Therefore, the new curriculum mode should be used to train teachers in the future. As teachers training as the main task of the normal colleges, must be based on teachers ' professional needs of teachers ' training and innovation mode.

The author believes that training teachers and doctors alike. Training doctors in addition to basic knowledge, it should also focus on clinical teaching. Training teachers to "enhance practice, strengthen the ethical culture and teaching training". Curricula must pay attention to the education professional. Attention to the theory of education and vocational skills training courses for teachers. Provide students with adequate teaching training opportunities. They embark on teaching jobs is a qualified teacher. Because, if an unqualified teachers to go to class, he practices what he faced with hundreds or thousands of student development opportunities. Therefore, we must be based on reality of the normal college students and teachers, highlight on the curriculum of students ' teaching skills. Only to enhance teaching skills training as a breakthrough innovation in training mode, to train qualified teachers.

2 Value Orientation of the Curriculum Mode Innovation

The Outline emphasis: "Deepening the reform of teacher education, innovation in training mode, enhanced practice, strengthen the ethical culture and teaching ability training, improving the quality of teacher training." The policies and regulations clearly emphasize teacher training mode to highlight the "normal characteristics". Therefore, the normal college curricula and reform must be to bring out "normal characteristics" as the value.

2.1   Take the Teacher's Ethics Education as the Foundation

Normal students are the future teachers. In the "rule of law, building a socialist State" up for the country programme in today's society. The platform for "strengthening ethical culture" required by the policy. "Exemplary virtue", "teaching according to law" has become a basic code of conduct for teachers develop teaching activities. So, you must strengthen teacher professional education in moral and legal knowledge of education for the students. Fostering students ' compliance with the code of ethics for teachers, master the education law, establishing the legal concept of education, and legal knowledge with educational guide teaching practice, regulating teaching ability.

2.2   To Develop Teachers' Professional Skills for Emphasis

Primary and secondary school teachers are engaged in teaching practice, the core skills is how to teach students, how to book their own knowledge and expertise through their own teaching skills into students knowledge. Master the "how to teach" of the expertise and professional skills, it is particularly important. Therefore, the curriculum and training mode must focus on the development of professional skills.

2.3   Take the Teaching Ability Training as the Core

Qualified teachers need not only good ethical culture, extensive cultural literacy, a depth of expertise in literacy, and rich culture of educational theory, and even master teaching skills. Students ' educational skills need them hands-on teaching practice, recurrent training can master in teaching skills. Therefore, the students ' training must, like doctors "clinical experience" training teachers of "classroom experience". To this end, the curriculum must increase the proportion of practical teaching, training mode must be beneficial to develop students ' practical skills.

2.4   Take the after Duty Trains Experience as the Supplement

UNESCO stated: "towards an integration of education and training mode in teacher education, pursued by all over the world. "[5] The integration of education and training in teacher education mode makes teachers college issues found in the training of teachers, to participate in in-service teacher training with learning. Therefore, teachers college training modes of both primary and secondary school teachers in pre-service training, but also to primary and secondary school teachers ' in-service training, give full play to on-the-job training experiences for pre-employment training services.

3   The Teacher Training Curriculum Mode Reform Practice

The teacher professionalization requests the teacher to master skilled professional skills. Our curriculum reforms highlight the training mode "professional", "practicality", "technicality", "autonomy". Curriculum mode reform to meet the quality of teachers need as the basis.

3.1 Increasing Teacher Education Courses, Stressing the "Professional"

Curriculum mode reform of primary practices is to increase the proportion of teacher education programmes, and to lay a solid teachers' ability foundation for the students. The courses are divided into general education courses (50 credits). Basic and professional development courses (60 credits). Teacher education course (50 credits). Total credits shall be not less than 160 graduate credits.

Teacher education courses are formed by theoretical courses (20 credits) and practical courses (30 credits) two modules. Theoretical courses are divided into teacher education compulsory courses (12 credits), and elective courses (not less than 8 credits in total) in two parts (the curriculum see table 1). The teacher education practice courses is divided into practice teaching, autonomous practice and guiding practice in three parts. Compared with traditional teacher education curricula, through theory and practice in teacher education courses to enhance the teachers' professional basis. It fully reflects "professional" of the teacher training curriculum mode.

Table 1. Teacher education theory curriculum checklist

Curricul-um type	Curriculum name	credits
Compulsory courses	Educational Principles	3
	Psychological development and education	3
	Subject didactics	2
	Information technology and multimedia prepare lesson	2
	Virtue and education law culture	2
Elective Courses	The new curriculum standard and new materials	2
	Classroom teaching psychology application	2
	Teaching essence and efficient teaching	2
	Psychological problems and education	2
	Analysis of teaching cases	2
	Essentials of Chinese and foreign history of education	2
	Famous masterpieces of Chinese and foreign education review	2
	Teachers "Five Course" capability	2
	Educational Research and Thesis Writing	2
	Education research statistics software and application	2

3.2   Strengthening Professional Skill Training, Highlight the "Practicality"

Traditions teacher pre-service training focus on theoretical courses of instruction, not enough focus on the professional skills training, not Strengthening the professional skills laboratory construction, lack of professional skills of teachers and teaching facilities. The students' teaching skills training has focused on internship in short time, the effect is poor.

Professional skills required for students in the practical training in repeatedly to master. Students only in the recurrent practical training can only be familiar with professional skills. Therefore, the teacher training must strengthen "practical", like training doctors "clinical experience" training teachers "classroom experience". So, we have a substantial increase in the proportion of teacher education courses. We opened practice teaching (11 credits), independent practice (5 credits), guiding practice (14 credits) three practice courses (courses see table 2), aims to develop students' ability to practice skills.

Table 2. Teacher education practice curriculum checklist

Curricul um type	Curriculum name	credits
Practice teaching	The micro-standard teaching training	3
	Class management practice	2
	Oral expression and Mandarin training	2
	Group and individual counseling	2
	Teachers etiquette and teaching art	2
Independent practice	Calligraphy and stick figure training	2
	Social practice and education investigation	3
Guide practice	Watching teaching and apprentice	2
	Education internship	6
	Graduation thesis	6

3.3   Making Full Use of Modern Education Technology, Highlight "Technicality"

Since 1999, the number of students increased rapidly. Many colleges and universities are out of the classroom, course teacher shortage, and so on. Limited classroom, teacher limited, limited compulsory courses, but online education services function is huge. In order to enrich the students' learning content, we make use of modern educational technologies to develop over more than 100 online courses. Linking a large number of online learning resources. Students' can independent study on campus network anytime, anywhere.

We make use of modern educational technologies to build online teaching resources and management platform. More than 100 video course of lectures are placed on the platform. Students can choose courses through the network, they can arrange learning time and learning processes independently. The learning problems can be posted online in the discussion. Instructor arrangements 2 times a week answering time on the Internet. In order to ensure the learning experience, each course is building an online question bank. Student exam can apply for online examination in the exam room within a exam week. Students can start examinations online as soon as the they enter the name and the student ID. Examinations end instantly displays test scores, candidates upon confirmation directly included in the students' files. If the student does not pass the exam or his exam results are not satisfactory by himself, He may apply to retake the exam once in the exam week. Through the use of modern educational technologies that not only facilitates student learning, has also been a significant reduction in the workload of teachers.

3.4 Providing "Round-the-Clock and Self-service", Highlight the "Autonomy"

In order to facilitate the systematic vocational skills training for the students, We started to build "teacher quality training centre" in 2003. After several years of development, it was named "College experimental teaching demonstration centers in Hubei Province" in December 2008. This is the first "teacher quality training centre" named "the provincial-level experimental teaching demonstration centers" in China. In order to give full play to "teacher training centre", provide students with a full range of technical services. We strengthen the professional skills of teachers training lab-building. We invest more than 3 million Yuan to build a modern educational technology labs to meet the needs of professional skill training.

In order to make full use of modern educational technologies automation services, we provide "round-the-clock and self-service" for the students. The so-called "round-the-clock services" refers to laboratory equipment is open all the day, students would be free to laboratory training. The so-called "self-service" contains the following three areas: One is the pilot project initiative. Students can independently selecte pilot projects according to their own needs. Second, experimental process can control independently. Experimental equipment can be used independently. Students can wrote experiment procedure. Experimental process video can copy taken away from the laboratory. Third, Experimental results independent evaluation. Experimental procedure can instant video recording, replay, continuous improvement, until you feel satisfied. Modern laboratories with modern educational technology services, improving the effectiveness of the professional skills training. Student qualifications increasing rapidly, students in the province of teaching skills competition in 2010, participating students of our school won medals.

4 Closing Remarks

We have been committed to the teacher training curriculum mode reform for a few years, we strengthen the professional skills as a breakthrough, by enhanced curriculum internship practice, strengthen the ethical culture and teaching training innovation in primary and secondary school teacher training mode. Increasing teacher education courses, stressing the "professional"; strengthening professional skill training, highlight the "practicality"; making full use of modern education technology, highlight "technicality"; providing "round-the-clock and self-service", highlight the "autonomy" and other means to have achieved significant effect. The students' professional identity sense obvious enhanced, professional literacy and teaching capacity obvious improve. The province normal health teaching skills competition in 2010, our school entries student get first prize of results.Our graduates are welcomed by primary and secondary schools.

Due to the he teacher training curriculum mode reform in practice time is short, lack of experience, especially how to use teacher in-service training experience for teachers in pre-service training services, also needs to be constantly explore and practice improvement.

References

1. Outline of national medium and long term educational reform and development plan (2010-2020). China Education Daily, 1–3 (July 30, 2010)
2. Li, B.: Higher teachers college students education training and the reconstruction of department of education. Lanzhou: Journal of the Northwest Normal University (Social sciences) (1), 1–2 (1997)
3. Li, G., Zhang, Z.: Concerning higher normal colleges of normal characteristics, vol. (8), pp. 66–69. Education Research, Beijing (2002)
4. Zhao, Z.: The global education development research hotspot, vol. 341. Education Science Press, Beijing (2003)

Practice in Compound Practical Teaching Method for Information Security Major

Zhenhua Tan, Guangming Yang, Zhiliang Zhu, and Yi Ma

Software College, Northeastern University, Shenyang City, Liaoning, China, 110819
tanzhenhua192@126.com, yanggm@mail.neu.edu.cn,
zzl@mail.neu.edu.cn, mayi@mail.neu.edu.cn

Abstract. This paper discusses the construction and improvement of the teaching system for information security major of northeastern university, including curriculum system, practice, training, graduation design and other aspects. We research the professionals teaching processes and guarantee system in information security major and practice it in daily teaching and some descriptions of the application results of this program is presented. The application results by the teaching method get good feedback.

Keywords: information security; teaching program; guarantee system.

1   Introduction

Information security is related to the country's political security, military security, economic security, technological security and social security. It plays an important role in the success or failure of the opening up reform and socialism modernization. The government has put information security on the strategic position in the deployment of information technology in the country [1-8].

We follow the criterion of teaching to establish the student-centered system, to set up the education concept which presses the comprehensive and coordinated development in knowledge, ability and quality of students, aim to cultivate students to have high-quality ,sense of innovation and practical ability. In this construction procedure, we need to improve the education program with the times, boldly and reasonably. Start from the major construction, we have made many improvements in the teaching system including training programs, teaching plan, curriculum systems, practice, training, graduation project and other aspects.

2   Reform Notion and Content

The demands for talent is widely collected by business needs survey, school-enterprise seminars, visits to graduates. We specify the talent training plan according to the technology evolution and development of software industry trends. See it in figure 1.

S. Lin and X. Huang (Eds.): CSEE 2011, Part V, CCIS 218, pp. 221–226, 2011.

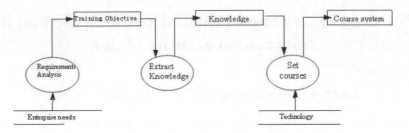

Fig. 1. Procedure of setting the course system

In the construction process, we take full advantage of consultation committee which is composed by professional teaching experts from campus and enterprise; we analyze the demands information and technology development situation; we take some reasonable advice; we adjust the curriculum and training plan to form a flexible curriculum and dynamic teaching program. Technology evolution and real corporate demand information is considered in each link of the curriculum design.

3   Construction of Curriculum System

(1) Theory courses

Curriculum system is organized and managed by the "course group + modules" approach. Each course group is divided into several modules by knowledge structure of the major and each module includes a number of main courses. The curriculum shows the "three combination" character, which refers to the combination of quality education and professional education, the combination of basic theory, basic knowledge and basic skills, the combination of expertise and domain knowledge.

In the course system, mathematics and natural science course group is the foundation, the humanities and social science course group cultivates the comprehensive quality and ability, and basic engineering course group is the important elements of information security, professional platform class group is the core of teaching, new knowledge course group is the extended training. The course groups are supporting each other and compose a scientific, rational and complementary curriculum system. Figure 2 shows the course structure of information security major.

(2) Practice course system

Practice teaching is an important part of practical senior software talent training plan which directly affects the quality of students. Set a series engineering-combination teaching system, through experimental course, program practices, corporate training, graduation design (practice), to improve the comprehensive ability of students.

According the content of student ability training, which mean analysis ability, synthesis ability, problem solving ability and the ability to acquire knowledge, combining with the experimental teaching requirements, the practice content starts from cultivating students' ability of independent software development, teamwork skills and project practice capability. Establish a hierarchy internship program step by

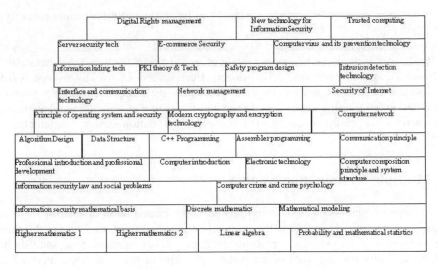

Digital Rights management		New technology for Information Security	Trusted computing
Server security tech	E-commerce Security	Computer virus and its prevention technology	
Information hiding tech	PKI theory & Tech	Safety program design	Intrusion detection technology
Interface and communication technology	Network management		Security of Internet
Principle of operating system and security	Modern cryptography and encryption technology		Computer network
Algorithm Design	Data Structure	C++ Programming	Assembler programming	Communication principle
Professional introduction and professional development	Computer introduction	Electronic technology	Computer composition principle and system structure
Information security law and social problems		Computer crime and crime psychology	
Information security mathematical basis	Discrete mathematics	Mathematical modeling	
Higher mathematics 1	Higher mathematics 2	Linear algebra	Probability and mathematical statistics

Fig. 2. Course structure of information security major

step which emphasize the ability training, build systematic internship system which differentiate between modules and phrases, arrange the experiment content based on the training system. Experiment Content is divided into three hierarchies: basic programming, program development and project development.

We have established the content and system of experimental teaching consistent with the objectives of professionals training in information security major. According to it, teaching activities are organized comprehensively, with maximum use of experimental laboratory equipments and technical conditions. After adjusting and integrating to the experimental content, there are a total of 32 experimental courses. We arrange 114 experiments in all, 12 of which are verifiable experiments and the rest of which are design, integration and innovation experiments accounting for 89.4%. Furthermore, we have built multiple experiment evaluation standards which adapt to the ability training plan and encourage students to explore; to make students can learn independently and cooperatively, meeting the needs of comprehensive ability training and innovative spirit development.

(3) Company training system

Through the trainings of practical projects simulation carried out by companies, students can take part in the real software development process and improve their competitiveness in the future employment. The company training program establish the criterions which focus on quality, emphasize basic skills, strengthen application, highlight abilities, face to demands of enterprises and base on the posts, aim to cultivate students equipped with professional ethics, enterprise quality, communication and coordination skills and the ability to manage projects. Currently we have established training relationships with a number of domestic companies which engage in information security. Each year, students can be arranged to those companies to go on a field trip.

(4) Graduation design

We have reformed the traditional mode of graduation design and require students to finish it combining real enterprise projects. Each student has two tutors, one is from school and another is from enterprise. Activities including the training two-way selection, initial training, process management, normative examination and evaluation of practice are set up to establish a complete graduation design implementation system.

4   Multiple Examination System

We change evaluation methods constantly to make examination diverse in form and make time random. Tests assess the comprehensive quality of students, highlighting the awareness of knowledge, the ability to apply theory synthetically, analysis and judgment ability and the spirit of innovation. A series of test evaluation methods are established to adapt quality education system. The various examination systems of information security major are performed in figure 3.

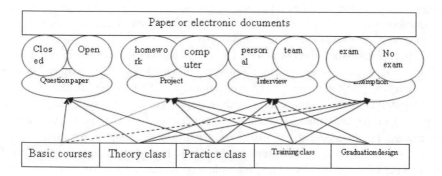

Fig. 3. Various examination methods

5   Teaching Quality Assurance System

High-quality teachers are the most important prerequisite to ensure the quality of education. So we must establish a professional teaching team to form the innovative teaching mode. Since the major was set, we always put the ethics and quality of teachers on the first place and have taken several measures to improve it, with extraordinary result being achieved. Now, we have formed a good teaching atmosphere, rigorous in scholarship research and meticulous in educating students; have cultivated a group of outstanding teachers who have both ability and virtue; have built a united, cooperative and harmonious teaching team.

6 Implement Results

We implement this method over the major of information security since 2005, and the implement results are list following:

(1) Teachers take the method combining theory and practice in the teaching activities, which have achieved extraordinary results. There are a total of 9 teachers in information security major who got the "the most popular teacher" prize voted by graduates in Software College.

(2) Within 6 years, students of information security major have got more than 10 funded projects including innovative experimental program of college students in nation and Software College. They also got the awards dozens of times in national and provincial technology competitions.

(3) A total number of 85 graduates in 2009 are generally welcomed by enterprises and even show a shortage of talent resources situation, achieving the employment rate of 100%. Through track and survey after they graduated, we get that part of them have become the core technical professionals in well-know enterprises such as Baidu .Some of them have got a 200000 annual salary. Besides, there are some students have started their own company engaged in the project of information security.

7 Innovation and Conclusions

In this article, we discuss the construction and improvement plan of teaching system in information security major. After analysis to teaching effect, employment levels and other aspects, we can get the conclusion that the teaching system of information security major is a degree of scientific, basically meets the national requirements to talents in information security field. We construct a teaching quality assurance system, introducing the evaluation mechanism which enterprise can also play a role in the total assessment of training, to achieve the practical, compound international cultivate objective. It turns out to effectively ensure the quality of software talents which meets the requirement of enterprise. It has four innovation points.

(1) Establish a curriculum system which takes network security as the main course

In the curriculum system, network security is the main part, with content security as the supplement, to cultivate professional talents equipped with certain level of theory and practical ability.

(2) Construct an effective practice teaching system combined with requirements of enterprise

We insist the teaching notion that combines the theory learning and practical application, strengthen the practice teaching. To train students to analyze and solve problem, to have practice ability and creativity, we implement the practice teaching plan through real project of enterprise and diminish the gap between software talents that cultivated by college and the real demands of corporation.

(3) Build a training mechanism which makes use of enterprise resources effectively

Cooperating with enterprise, the technical and intellectual resources are introduced into campus. We explore a new way to bring excellent enterprise professional into teaching activity and arrange students to company to participate in practical project development, through establishing enterprise teaching team, project resources and enterprise training base. Finally, a complete mechanism to transfer students to corporation to practice is built.

(4) Set a assessment and quality assurance system adapting to the training objective of information security major

Acknowledgement. This work is supported by the National Natural Science Foundation of China under Grant No. 61070162, No. 71071028, No. 60802023 and No. 70931001; the Specialized Research Fund for the Doctoral Program of Higher Education under Grant No. 20070145017; the Fundamental Research Funds for the Central Universities under Grant No. N090504003 and No. N090504006.

References

1. China Ministry of Education Class Information Security Steering Committee for Professional Teaching, http://www.sec-edu.cn/index.html
2. Jonathan, R.: Online education as a toll good: An examination of the South Carolina virtual school program. Computers and Education 57(2), 1583–1594 (2011)
3. Wang, Y.H., Liu, G.Y.: China accounting education change in the knowledge society: The constructivism education. In: 2nd International Workshop on Education Technology and Computer Science, ETCS 2010, 3rd edn., pp. 542–545 (2010)
4. Garrido, J.M., Bandyopadhyay, T.: Simulation model development in information security education. In: Proceedings of the 2009 Information Security Curriculum Development Annual Conference, InfoSecCD 2009, pp. 21–26 (2009)
5. Al-Hamdani, W.A., Dixie, W.D.: Information security policy in small education organization. In: Proceedings of the 2009 Information Security Curriculum Development Annual Conference, InfoSecCD 2009, pp. 72–76 (2009)
6. Wu, C.Y.: Analysis on the information security education for the public security active forces academy. In: 2010 International Forum on Information Technology and Applications, IFITA 2010, vol. 3, pp. 355–357 (2010)
7. Marks, A., Rezgui, Y.: A comparative study of information security awareness in higher education based on the concept of design theorizing. In: International Conference on Management and Service Science, MASS (2009)
8. Aboutabl, M.: The CyberDefense laboratory: A framework for information security education. In: Aboutabl, M. (ed.) Proceedings of the 2006 IEEE Workshop on Information Assurance, vol. 2006, pp. 55–60 (2006)

Research on the Teaching Reform of Supply Chain Management Course in Network Environment

Yuran Jin, Yuping Chu, and Jianwei Dong

School of Business Administration, University of Science and Technology Liaoning,
Anshan 114051, China
jinyuran@163.com, chuyuping@126.com, dongjianwei04@126.com

Abstract. In order to improve the teaching quality of supply chain management course, the teaching reforms were researched from four aspects including teaching method, course system, assessment method, and practice and experiment. Eight reform schemes on the teaching method and a set of corresponding course system were put forward. Building some teaching bases to achieve a combination of industry, education, and research was thought of one of the three ways to carry out the practice and experiment reform. In view of the above reforms, a new assessment method was also given Survey results show that the reform package is very successful though there are still a few defects.

Keywords: Course, Teaching Reform, Supply Chain Management.

1 Introduction

Supply chain management course is the important foundation one of College Business Management, a main discipline of management field derived with the development of contemporary economy. This course is designed to enable students to master the theory and methods of supply chain management, to understand deeply the strategic management, purchasing management, production management and logistics management based on supply chain management, and to master the capabilities of business management based on supply chain. In order to improve the teaching effectiveness of this course and stimulate students' enthusiasm for learning, this course group embarked on the following teaching reform of supply chain management course.

2 The Reforms of Teaching Method

The Special Topic of In-class Games. We consider in-class games, playing a game in the theory class, as a reform of teaching method, rather than the reform of practical experiment. The reason is that we think of the in-class games as a part of reform of guiding teaching and heuristic teaching. In this part, we set three in-class games, which are beer games, risk-sharing games and bidding games. This reform will enable students to learn and practice the theory in the classroom, avoiding the problem that experimental teaching is often divorced from theory teaching. In addition, these three

S. Lin, X. Huang (Eds.): CSEE2011, Part V, CCIS 218, pp. 227–232, 2011.

games are operated purely manually by the students rather than by software simulation so that students can have more deep feelings about the processes.

Extended Teaching- Classifying Primary and Secondary Contents. Supply chain management course is a discipline with broad theory knowledge. However, we can not explain all the theories in detail for the class hour restrictions. Therefore, the teaching group plans the course system macroscopically according to the characteristics of students and the importance and relevance of teaching content, and definitudes the primary and secondary levels. For example, if the students are from e-commerce specialty, we will take electronic supply chain and supply chain information technology as the main teaching focus, and the supply chain production management and so on as a secondary level. After the levels are clear, we also set the extension teaching content in those levels. Taking the chapter, supply chain strategy, as an example, in order to guide students to better understand the supply chain strategy, marketing knowledge naturally become the extended teaching content.

Heuristic and Interactive Teaching. During the course of teaching, we set a lot of heuristic questions to encourage students to think actively, rather than carry out spoon-feeding teaching. For example, when teaching the theory of vertical integration of supply chain, the teacher usually introduce only the meaning and its advantages of vertical integration, and the shortcomings of the vertical integration will be left to students to think heuristically, who are also encouraged to express their impressions, After that, teachers will give the correct explanations. This process is just an interaction one between teachers and students. This teaching reform with the combination of heuristic teaching and interactive teaching has greatly stimulated the thinking potential of students.

Scenario Simulation Teaching. In order to enable students to understand supply chain management strategies based on the actual competition needs of enterprises, the course uses the scenario simulation teaching. In this kind of teaching, students play different suppliers, manufacturers, vendors, customers and other different roles, and then experience the essence of supply chain operations from the view of actual business operations.

Case Teaching - the Special Topic of Practical Large Case. The course adopts a lot of cases and forms a case base. These cases include the materials analyzing supply chain operations of enterprises, some supply chain reports, and some project results of consulting firms. It is proved the students can better apply the theory knowledge in practical application by study these cases. Cases are divided into two categories. Small case is used daily in the process of instruction for the individual theory, and practical large cases are used in the Special Topic of Practical Large Case, which is set to help students to master the total content comprehensively.

Task-driven Teaching - The Special Topic of Preaching and Discussing Cases. Task-driven teaching means that teachers put forward various topic tasks for students, and ultimately assess students' performance by the completion of topic tasks. This task-driven teaching can place the students into the dynamic study process to find, advance, ponder, explore and solve problems. With this in mind, the course set up the task of Preaching and Discussing Cases to examine students' learning.

Match Incentive Teaching. The course sets the beer games competition in class. In the end, the following titles will be awarded, which are Award for the Best Supply Chain Competitiveness, Award for the Best Supply Chain Team and Award for Excellent Procurement and Cost Control. The event can better arouse students' study enthusiasm for this course.

The Special Topic of Teaching Driven by Research. Scientific research is an important way to improve students' Passion for learning and master the frontiers of courses. Therefore, the course carries out the Special Topic of Teaching Driven by Research from the following two perspectives. On he one hand, The chief teachers themselves or the hired professors discuss the projects of supply chain management they chair or participate in with the students. In addition, students are encouraged to take part in the research projects of those people. On the other hand, The chief teachers introduce the new development directions in this field, such as supply chain finance, agile supply chain, CPFR, VMI, etc.

3 The Reforms of Practice and Experiment

Although this course has set in-class games, those games doesn't help students fully grasp the overall supply chain business. Therefore, it is necessary to set some experiments and practices separately for the course. In this regard, the following reforms have been attempted, which are setting the link of visiting enterprises or the link of topic reports from experts, setting the software experiments about the whole supply chain operation, and building some teaching bases to achieve a combination of industry, education, and research.

4 The Reforms of Course System

The setup of course system relates to the whole effect of teaching. In order to fully arouse students' enthusiasm and merge theory teaching and practice teaching, the following teaching system is set based on the above reforms of teaching method, as shown in table 1.

Table 1. The settings of teaching system (taking 48 hours for example)

order	teaching content	corresponding teaching methods	hours distribution
1	teaching the basic theories of Supply chain	extended teaching; heuristic and interactive teaching; scenario simulation teaching	33
2	the special topic of in-class Games	match incentive teaching; scenario simulation teaching	5
3	the special topic of preaching and discussing cases	task-driven teaching; case teaching	4

Table 1. (continued)

4	the link of visiting enterprises or the link of topic reports from experts	task-driven teaching; case teaching; heuristic and interactive teaching	2
5	the special topic of practical large case	case teaching; heuristic and interactive teaching	2
6	the special topic of teaching driven by research	case teaching; heuristic and interactive teaching	2

5 The Reforms of Assessment Method

To make a more reasonable assessment, we conduct a full account of the structure composition based on the above teaching reform. Therefore, the course adopts structural hundred mark system, and passing the score of 60 points or more is qualified. The structure scores are constituted as follows. Daily grade is 15 points, including attendance score of 10 and performance in class of 5, 15% of the total score. Grade of beer games contest is 15 points, 15% of the total score. Its composition is shown in table 2. Grade of preaching and discussing cases in class is 10 points, 10% of the total score. One group is composed of two students and they should preach cases about 15 minutes with PPT form. The total achievement of closing test is 100 points, accounting for 60% of the overall grade.

Table 2. The settings of beer game grading and awards

the total cost of supply chain	team scores	individual scores	individual total scores	awards
the lowest	10	1~5	11~15	award for the best supply chain competitiveness; award for excellent procurement and cost control
the second lowest	8	1~5	9~13	award for the best supply chain team
the second highest	6	1~5	7~11	
the highest	4	1~5	5~9	

6 The Effect Assessment of Teaching Reform

In order to assess the effect of teaching reform we carried out a questionnaire survey, in which 100 students were surveyed. Data shows that most students, accounting for 80% - 90%, are satisfied with the reform of teaching system with answering "great satisfaction" or "satisfaction", as shown in figure 1. But there are also some students, accounting for 7% -8%, are not satisfied especially with the reform of practice teaching and examination methods. In both cases, we will further improve the reform plans.

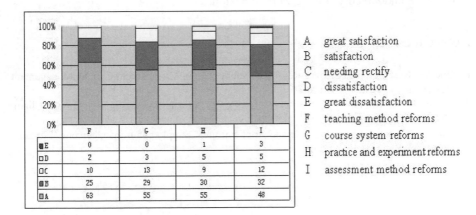

Fig. 1. Investigation on the reform of teaching system

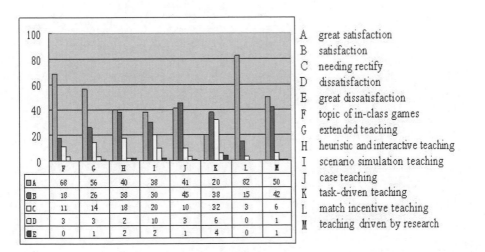

Fig. 2. Investigation on the reform of teaching methods

On the other hand, most students, accounting for 78% - 97%, are satisfied with the reform of teaching methods with answering "great satisfaction" or "satisfaction", as shown in figure 2. Especially, satisfaction rate on Match Incentive Teaching reform is up to 97%. At the same time, we have also realized there are some faults in Scenario Simulation Teaching currently. Therefore, we will always focus on such faults and strive for getting better teaching effect earlier.

7 Summary

On the whole, all the teaching reforms are very successful though there are still a few defects. In order to improve the teaching quality of supply chain management course better, there undoubtedly is more work to be done.

References

1. Yue, G.: Research on Teaching Reform of Supply Chain Management Course. Management Observation (13), 135–136 (2009)
2. Davld, S.-L., Kaminsky, P., Ednh, S.-L.: Designing and Managing the Supply Chain. McGraw-Hill/Irwin (2010)
3. Shi, X., Yisong, L.: The Principle and Application of Supply chain management. Tsinghua University Press, Beijing (2006)

Research on Embedding Compressed Watermarking Based on Chaotic and Wavelet Algorithm

Guang-ming Yang, Xiao Yang, Zhen-hua Tan, and Jian Xu

Software College of Northeastern University, Shenyang, China, 110819
ygm5@hotmail.com, m3yangxiao@126.com, tanzhenhua192@126.com,
xj_xujian@163.com

Abstract. To overcome the problem that embedding too much information will cause distortion of the original image. In this paper, a watermarking based on compressing the binary watermark image by specified coding is proposed. According to the result of compression and use the chaotic sequence to determine the watermarks embedded positions in the original image. The Experimental results show that this algorithm of digital watermarking is invisible and robust to against noise and general image processing techniques such as JPEG compaction and cropping attack, etc.

Keywords: Wavelet transform, information compression, digital watermarking, chaotic sequence.

1 Introduction

In modern society by the rapid development of information industry, multimedia and the Internet technology enable digital products are widely used, along with more and more attention on the copyright protection. Many methods of copyright protection of digital products come into being. Digital watermarking is an important technology for image protection. There are two kinds of digital watermarking methods at present, space domain and transform domain. The transform domain has a good robustness and invisibility features, so it has become the mainstream. However, discrete wavelet transform (DWT) in image processing is more suitable for human visual system (HVS) than the discrete cosine transform (DCT), it can also effectively resist shear and JEPG compression, so digital watermarking based on discrete wavelet transform algorithm in the field of transform domain become the focus of digital watermarking algorithms. And the new generation still image compression standard (JPEG2000) is in the wavelet basis, which also makes digital watermarking algorithm research on wavelet transform more feasible and necessary.

Cox proposed that watermarks should be embedded in the most important sensory components of the human visual system [1]. Paper [2] proposed watermarks should be embedded in the low-frequency coefficients of wavelet transform image first, if there are left, and then embed in the high-frequency coefficients by the order of importance. The wavelet transformation is a global transformation, so embedding watermarks in

S. Lin and X. Huang (Eds.): CSEE 2011, Part V, CCIS 218, pp. 233–239, 2011.

the low-frequency coefficients will not make the watermarked image produce block-ing artifacts. Wavelet transformation sets most of the energy in the low-frequency coefficients, if make a significant damage on the low-frequency, it will also affect a great impact on the visual effect of image; if all watermarks are embedded in the high-frequency coefficients, the robustness of watermarking will very weak [3].

In this paper, we propose compressing the certificated copyright binary image first, and then according to the result of compression and the size of original image to decide the coefficients to embed watermarks. If the result is small, embed all the wa-termarks in the low-frequency coefficients, because less information is embedded in, less visual effects will affect the image, and the robustness of the watermarking is strong; If the result is large, then select the method of combination of low- frequency and high- frequency coefficients to embed watermarks, most of watermarks will be inserted into the low-frequency coefficients in the premise of not damage the image quality, and the remaining are embedded in other high-frequency coefficients, this make the invisibility and robustness for balance. In order to ensure the security of the watermarking, use the two-dimensional chaotic logistic formulate to generate the em-bedded positions According to "The Rule of Kerckhoffs", a safety digital watermark-ing, whose algorithm should be public, its security should be built on the basis of the confidentiality of the key, but only the copyright owner has the key, so it can be seen that this algorithm is fully meet "The Rule of Kerckhoffs".

2   Watermark Processing and Embedding Procedure

Watermark processing. For a contained the authenticated information binary image, it has only two colors, black and white, and most of adjacent pixels in edge and authenticated information are the same, by this we can compress the image. In this paper, the compressed algorithm is if every three adjacent pixels are same; compress them to one, otherwise, keep it as original. Concrete steps are from the first pixel of the image, storage the pixel value of current position with a temporary variable, and then also from the first pixel to compare the temporary variable, if they are same, go to the next pixel, if accumulated to 3, then use an integer array which is named log to represent whether it is compressed, 1 stands for compress, 0 stands for not, and last use an array which is named mark to storage compressed results. When it is accumulated to 3, meets the requirement of compression, now, the mark will storage the compressing pixel value and the log will be set by 1, set the accumulated number 0, otherwise, the mark will storage the current pixel value, and the log array will be set value of 0. Continue the above steps until the pixel is the last one of original image. The counted number is set to 3; it has a good result for either a normal or special binary watermark image, big or small is only for special cases. Compressed rules are given in (1)

$$\begin{cases} 111, mark[i] = 1, \log[i] = 1 \\ 000, mark[i] = 0, \log[i] = 1 \\ 1, mark[i] = 1, \log[i] = 1 \\ 0, mark[i] = 0, \log[i] = 0 \end{cases} \tag{1}$$

Array mark is the compressed watermarks, log is the mark for whether it is compressed at that position, i is the current position.

Watermarking Algorithm. At first, make the original image level-2 wavelet transform, separate the low-frequency coefficients and high-frequency coefficients, the result of wavelet transformation is given in Fig.1. L stands the low- frequency, H stands for the high- frequency, and the right subscript indicates the level. The transformation make most energy of image concentrate in the low-frequency coefficients, the horizontal, vertical and diagonal parts indicate the horizontal, vertical and diagonal parts of the edge information of original image.

Fig. 1. 2-level wavelet transforms high and low frequency distribution

To keep the watermarking safety, in this paper, we use the two-dimensional chaotic logistic formulate to determine the positions to embed the compressed watermarks. Two-dimensional chaotic logistic formulate is given in (2).

$$\begin{cases} X_{n+1} = \mu * \lambda_1 * X_n * (1 - X_n) + \gamma * Y_n; \\ Y_{n+1} = \mu * \lambda_2 * Y_n * (1 - Y_n) + \gamma * X_n; \end{cases} \quad (2)$$

The dynamic behavior of the two-dimensional Logistic is controlled by the λ_1 λ_2 γ and μ ,four control parameters. If they satisfy $\mu=4$, $\lambda_1=\lambda_2=0.89$, the sequence will be in chaotic state [4]. Firstly, set initial values of X_1 and Y_1 as keys to generate a random sequence range from 0 to 1, and the length of sequence is the mark's length. After above steps, according to the result of the compression and size of original image, we decide which coefficients to insert the watermarks. And then select a value but less than the width and height of original image to determine the embedded positions, the value is also a key, the values of two-dimensional chaotic sequence multiplied by the value which is selected just before are the positions, so the three keys make the watermarking very safe. Now we can insert watermarks into the original image, the watermarking embedding is given in (3).

$$F'(i, j) = F(i, j) + \alpha * M \quad (3)$$

$F(i, j)$ is the original image, $F'(i, j)$ is the watermarked image, M is the added watermark, and the α is the embedding watermark strength, α should set a appropriate value between the invisible and robustness. If too large, the invisible will be damaged, on the other hand, if too small, the robustness will be not strong any more [5]. In this paper, α is set by 0.1. Lastly, make the watermarked image level-2 reverse wavelet transform lastly, all these finish the embedding work.

Watermark extraction. Make the watermarked image level-2 wavelet transform, and we have known the embedded watermark positions, so we take the reverse process of embedding watermark to extract the watermarks. The watermark extraction as:

$$M = (F'(i, j) - F(i, j)) / \alpha \qquad (4)$$

And then reverse the process of compression; restore the integral watermark information to compose the original watermark image.

3 Simulate Experiments and Data

Experimental environment: Windows XP, VC++ based on Opencv.

(1) Performance of compression: we use watermark image of size 64 * 64, the binary watermark image is given in Fig.2

Fig. 2. Original watermark image

In this paper, the compressed algorithm can compress the Fig.2 watermark image to 1/3 in theory, its compressed result and original numbers of pixels are given in Fig. 3.

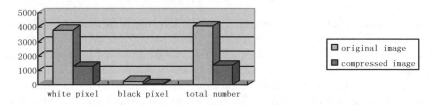

Fig. 3. Comparison between original and compressed image

Through the histogram, it is easy to show that whether the white or black pixels, their compressed results are very ideal. From the detail data, compressed total number of pixels is 1380, is the nearly 1/3 of the original image whose the total number is 4096, satisfies the anticipatory result. So this algorithm can insert three times information as other uncompressed algorithm, and doesn't affect view of image, either.

(2) Invisible: We use test image of size 512 * 512, Lena grayscale image. This algorithm of digital watermark has a good invisible, the original image and watermarked image are shown in Fig.4 and Fig. 5.

Fig. 4. Original image   **Fig. 5.** Watermarked image

(3) Identification of the extracted watermark: Because the algorithm is based on compressing watermarks firstly, then embed, extract, and recover the final watermarks lastly. So identifying the recovered watermarks is very important. The recovered watermark image is shown in Fig. 6.

Fig. 6. Recovered watermark image

Compare the two figures, under no impact on watermarked image; the recovered watermark image is the same as original watermark image. So compressing watermarks is feasible.

(4) For noise attack: the Fig. 7 and Fig. 8 respectively represent the recovered watermark image after Gaussian blur and salt and pepper noise attack.

Fig. 7. Gaussian blur recovered watermark   **Fig. 8.** Salt and pepper noise recovered watermark

From the results, the recovered watermark image is also identifiable; so the algorithm has a good robustness for noise.

(5) For cropping attack:

(a)   (b)   (c)

Fig. 9. Cropped watermarked images

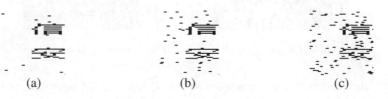

(a)   (b)   (c)

Fig. 10. Recovered watermark image images

From the results, it is easy to show that the more parts are cut down, the more influence on the recovered watermark image, but the identification of the authenticated information is also very clear. And lots of experimental results for different positions to cut down show that the positions have little to do with recovered watermark, these prove that the embedded positions at random of this algorithm. So the watermarking has a good robustness for cropping attack.

(6) For JPEG compression

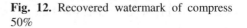

Fig. 11. Recovered watermark of compress 10%   **Fig. 12.** Recovered watermark of compress 50%

From the results, it is easy to show that the algorithm has a good robustness for JPEG compression.

4 Summary

In this paper, to reduce the embedded information as the precondition, we propose compressing the authenticated information in binary image, and then according to the compressed result and use the two-dimensional chaotic formulate logistic to determine the coefficients which the watermarks embed in to ensure some safety. The experimental results show that this algorithm of digital watermarks for noise attack and some general image processing techniques such as cropping and JPEG compression has a good robustness. Simultaneously, because embedding relatively small information, so the invisible of the watermarking is very excellent.

References

[1] Cox, I.J., Kilian, J., Leighton, T., et al.: Secure spread spectrum watermarking for multimedia. IEEE Trans on Image Process 6(12), 1673–1678 (1997)

[2] Huang, D.-r., Liu, J.-f., Huang, J.-w.: An Embedding Strategy and Algorithm fo rImage Watermarking in DWT Domain. Journal of Software 13(7) (2002)

[3] Luo, J-y.: Central South University. Master thesis: Research on blind watermark algorithm based on wavelet transform, 5 (2005)

[4] Giovanardi, A., Mazzina, G.: Frequency domain chaotic watermarking. In: Proceedings of IEEE Symposium on Circuits and System, Sydney, pp. 521–524 (2001)

[5] Wang, Y.P., Chem, M.J., Cheng, P.Y.: Robust Image Watermark with Wavelet Transform and Spread Spectrum Techniques. In: Conference Record of the Thirty-Fourth Asilomar Conference on Signal, System and Computers, October 29- November 1, vol. 2, pp. 1846–1850 (2000)

Application of EDA Technology in the Education of Automatic Control System Design

Tao Wu and Shi-Xu Wang

Faculty of Mechanical and Electrical Engineering,
Kunming University of Science & Technology, Kunming, China
kmwutao13@126.com

Abstract. This paper proposes a scheme of building in single chip microcomputer laboratory based on Proteus software simulation, Protel software to make PCB card. It proves the feasibility of scheme by analyzing some application examples. This scheme solves the problems of capital shortage for traditional single chip labs and difficulty in equipment maintenance to a certain extent.

Keywords: EDA, single chip microcomputer, Proteus software, simulation, Keil C.

1 Introduction

With the growth and spread of electronic design automation (EDA) [1], great changes have taken place in the design method and means of electric circuit and system. EDA is a comprehensive technology based on CAD, CAM, CAT, and CAE. It's an advanced technology. Automatic design and exploration of electric circuit and system is based on the EDA software platform. It uses computer as tool. It not only lightens the work load and difficulty of circuit design, but also shortens the debug and modification period. At present, EDA is one of the popular circuit design technology. It's one of the electrical engineer's essential technical abilities. According to the main function and application occasion, EDA software could be classified as circuit design and simulation software. The common EDA software contains Proteus, Keil C, Protel and so on. This paper will discuss how to use the above 3 kinds of software in the education of automatic control system design.

2 Scheme of Single Chip Microcomputer Simulation

Single chip microcomputer has been applied in many fields. Every intelligent system core is microprocessor [2]. The exploration of single chip microcomputer has got more seriously attention. But, to electrical designers, after the principle diagram has been completed, it often needs to make the hardware circuit or PCB card again and again. This will increase the exploration cost greatly. Proteus simulation software will overcome these shortcomings, which can simulate a whole system through software mode. Thus could save many time and expenses.

S. Lin and X. Huang (Eds.): CSEE 2011, Part V, CCIS 218, pp. 240–244, 2011.

Proteus software is produced by Labcenter company in Britain [3]. This software could design and simulate the hardware and software of the embedded system in co-ordination. It centralizes powerful function and simple operation. It could simulate MCS—51 series MCU and other periphery circuits (LCD, RAM, ROM., etc.), AVR, PIC and so on. The difference between Proteus and other simulating software is that Proteus could not only simulate the work state of the CPU, but also the periphery circuit's.

The program is compiled by Keil C language and guided to single chip microcomputer. The Protel software is used to make correct hardware circuit, or PCB board.

In the simulation of the single chip microcomputer, there are 4 aspects: system resource, hardware, software, application system.

3 Application Examples

Work Process of Proteus. After the Proteus ISIS program has been in motion, the main interface is displayed. With "P" command, the needed component is picked from "pick device" windows and then is placed to appropriate place. The component parameters should be set. Then the components are connected with each other. Through "define code generation tools" menu command, the program edits tool, path, extended name and other items. Through "Add/Remove source files" menu command, the program compiled by Keil C is guided to the microcomputer [4]. Fig.1 shows a simple flash LED design. The practical PCB circuit made by Protel software is shown in Fig.2.

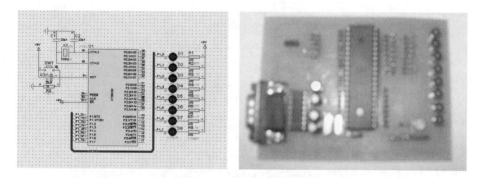

Fig. 1. Flash LED simulation circuit based on Proteus   **Fig. 2.** Practical PCB circuit of flash LED

LCD Module. LCD display module integrates display screen, background light, circuit board, driver circuit and so on. It is used as an independent component. It has only one port to communicate with outside circuit. The LCD display module receives commands and data from this port. The communication circuit between LCD and single chip microcomputer is shown in Fig.3. 12864 (module number) LCD module is selected as the display module. The program compiled by Keil C is shown in Fig.4. Where the characters are generated by the type matrix software "PCtoLCD".

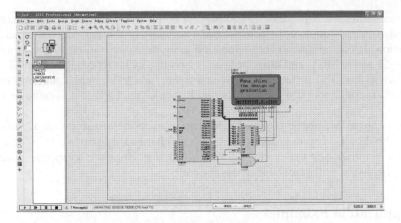

Fig. 3. LCD display simulation circuit based on Proteus

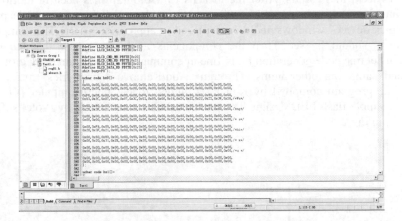

Fig. 4. LCD display program compiled by Keil C

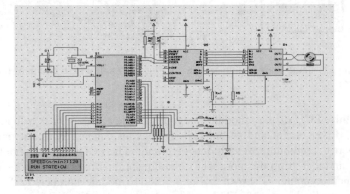

Fig. 5. Step motor simulation based on Proteus

Step Motor. The step motor is a mechanical and electrical executive component that changes electric pulse signal to angular displacement (or linear displacement). The control system constituted of step motor has many advantages such as low price, simple control, easy maintenance and so on. Especially with the development of microcomputer and electric technology, the step motor has broad application [5]. It also puts forward higher requirement of the step motor's motion performance. Therefore, the research on the control method of the step motor will play a positive role to give free rein to the work characteristics of the step motor fully. The simulation design is shown in Fig.5. The practical step motor driven by single chip microcomputer exploration board is shown in Fig.6. The exploration board should be connected with the computer. This exploration board is made by the DOFLY company in Shanghai China.

4 Advantages of Virtual Single Chip Microcomputer Experiment

There are 3 advantages of virtual single chip microcomputer simulation: one is that the experiment content is comprehensive; the second is that the hardware cost is low, so the economic advantage is obvious; the third is that the experiment consumption is low [6].

Fig. 6. Practical step motor driven by exploration board

5 Summary

Through practical education, the students are familiar with the EDA design. It will play an important role for their future work. Along with EDA technology is understood and used, it will bring more and more convenience to our study, scientific research and work.

Acknowledgment. This work is supported by the third institution of higher learning characteristic specialty construction of the ministry of education (Grant No. TS11137) and Kunming University of Science and Technology education reform foundation (Grant No: 2009314).

References

1. Dimitropoulos, P.D., Drljaca, P.M., Popovic, R.S., Chatzinikolaou, P.: Horizontal HALL devices: A lumped-circuit model for EDA simulators. Sensors and actuators 145-146, 161–175 (2008)
2. Na, L., Liu, Y.: Application of Proteus simulation for MCU. Mod ern ElectricTechnology 243(4), 181–182 (2007) (in Chinese)
3. Zhong, W., Qin, Y.–l.: Application of Proteus Software in Theoretical and Practical Teaching about Embedded System. Modern Electric Technology 327(16), 74–76 (2010) (in chinese)
4. Zhu, Q.-H., Zhang, F.-R., Zhai, T.-S.: Proteus Tutorial. Tsinghua University Press, Beijing (2008) (in Chinese)
5. Aguilar, L., Melin, P., Castillo, O.: Intelligent control of a stepping motor drive using a hybrid neuro-fuzzy ANFIS approach. Applied Soft Computing 3, 209–219 (2003)
6. Ghavami, B., Pedram, H., Najibi, M.: An EDA tool for im plementation oflow power and secure crypto-chips. Computers and Electrical Engineering 35, 244–257 (2009)

A Portable Virtual Laboratory for Information Security Courses

Fuh-Gwo Chen[1], Ruey-Maw Chen[2], and Jr-Shian Chen[1, *]

[1] No. 34, Chung-Chie Rd, Sha Lu, Taichung 44302, Taiwan, ROC
[2] No.57, Sec. 2, Zhong-shan Rd., Taiping Dist., Taichung 41170, Taiwan, ROC
`fgchen@gmail.com`, `raymond@mail.ncut.edu.tw`,
`jschen@sunrise.hk.edu.tw`

Abstract. In this paper, a portable virtual laboratory was created with virtual machine software, VMware, for experimenting information security hands-on exercises. The laboratory would be easily applied to a traditional computer classroom with inexpensive/free virtual machine software. Information security students can do hands-on exercises with the portable virtual laboratory anywhere by hosting all image files of the laboratory on a portable USB disk. An information security curriculum was redesigned with the portable virtual laboratory. Examples of hands-on exercises, inner- and inter-team projects, were presented.

Keywords: Portable virtual laboratory, project-bsed/cooperative learning, information security course, virtual machine.

1 Introduction

Nowadays, many business activities have been advanced to the e-commerce world, in which safe business transactions are important. It needs information-security skilled IT (information technology) employees to support the building of the IT infrastructure of the e-commerce world. IT schools need to educate their students with tough information security practices. Therefore, information security has been a technical discipline that a computer science/information student needs to learn. However, information security includes many topics ranging from cryptography mathematics to security issues of information technology, risk analysis, security policy in companies/enterprises, etc [1]. Summers [2] mentioned that information security has three dimensions: application, computing and the framework of social, economic and legal. Teachers, in information security courses, should carefully prepare well-organized materials to guide the students to effectively learn information security.

An undergraduate-level information security course, therefore, might be mainly based on security technical aspects with briefing basics of security mathematics and the social-economic-legal framework. Generally, undergraduate students should learn things with learning-by-doing method. Learning of the security technical aspects with

---

* Corresponding author.

S. Lin and X. Huang (Eds.): CSEE 2011, Part V, CCIS 218, pp. 245–250, 2011.

learning-by-doing method needs physical security services and equipments, which are organized in an information security laboratory. However, it is difficult to realize an information security laboratory in universities due to the high cost of security services and equipments, including software and hardware.

In learning science, cooperative learning is a good learning strategy [4-6]. The infrastructure of e-commerce is highly based on cooperative works. In an information security course, students cooperatively work to successfully build information security services on a network, which is composed of multiple LANs. Hence, cooperative learning is very feasible to be applied in an information security curriculum. However, it is hard to have enough computing devices to support students learn information security issues with cooperative learning in a university department. Computing devices are occupied when students experiment information security issues that take whole semester to finish. That is, dedicated devices could not share among learning groups. In sum, it needs a lot of budget to build an information security laboratory for students. An information security laboratory for practicing information security issues is nearly impossible in a school. Thus, the learning of information security issues is confined in books world.

In this paper, the author proposed an innovative information security learning environment, a portable virtual laboratory, on which students can practice information security issues. It uses virtual machine software, VMware [7] to make a virtual machine platform for installing operating systems, including Linux OS [8], MS Windows OS, etc. Students thus can install security services on those operating systems. The image files of all virtual machines are stored in a potable drive, USB flash disk. The learning environment can be taken anywhere, including school, dorm or home. It benefits that a general computer classroom can be promoted to an information security laboratory with the portable virtual laboratory with few budgets of purchasing a set of USB flash disks. Students can practice information security issues continuously outside the classrooms with the portable virtual laboratory. In the paper, project-based learning, based on cooperative learning, is used as a learning strategy in the information security course.

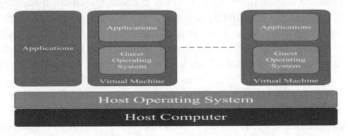

Fig. 1. Virtual machine concept

2   Portable Virtual Laboratory

Virtual machine software [7, 9, 10] is marvelous to enable computer users to virtually create machines as application processes, on a real host machine, as shown in Figure 1. A virtual machine, created by the virtual machine software, is an intermediate between the underlying hardware and its operating system. In education, virtual machine software offers learners to practice OS installations or to study OS on existed computers, instead of purchasing new machines.

A virtual machine is a software-made machine that runs programs like a real machine bought from the computer market. The real machine is multiplexed between different virtual machines, each running its own programs, including an operating system or applications. Virtual machines allow that multiple operating systems, such as Windows XP/Server, Linux OS, Solaris OS, Mac OS, etc., can run concurrently on the underlying real machine. In industry, virtual machines are used to provide different services run on separated virtual machines to avoid applications interference. It can be used to test new developed applications without shutting down services provided. It can be used to backup a running machine. In one word, virtual machines can bring many benefits at the cost of a single machine and inexpensive virtual machine software. The number of concurrently running guest operating systems is limited with the amount of memory (RAM) of the underlying machine. Windows systems need at least 256 megabytes, and a Linux OS, without X Window System, needs at least 32 megabytes. In other words, most modern computers can support running multiple virtual machines.

Virtual machines are generally stored as image files in the file system of system hard drives, the secondary memory system. According to the study of the support of placing virtual machine image files on portable drives, only VMware can boot virtual machine image file up successfully from USB flash disk. We pre-built an information security laboratory, composed of multiple operating systems and necessary services' configurations, on a 16GB USB flash disk. And we replicated the 16GB USB flash disk to multiple copies which were handled by student groups. We called the virtual laboratory on a USB disk as "portable virtual laboratory", as show in Figure 2. The portable virtual laboratory supports that students can do hands-on exercises anywhere. Students can continuously learn information security issues at dorm or home as long as they want to do the designate exercises. We prepared twenty four USB flash disks for twenty four learning groups. Each group has two student members and one cooperative/corresponding group. Students can easily experiment designate hands-on exercises by plugging their USB flash disk in their computer.

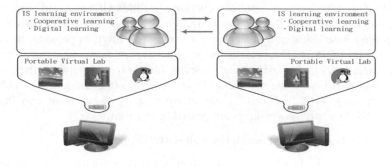

Fig. 2. Portable virtual laboratory

3   Information Security Curriculum Design

As mentioned before, there are too many information security topics to learn. With only a semester or two for instruction, information security topics must be carefully organized. The curriculum design was planned. First, it is necessary to summarize information security topics as an essential base for developing an information security curriculum of a few semesters. Next a set of ability indicators for information security courses must be constructed. Currently we survey the contents of information security curricula in local technology universities to outline a set of topics taught in information security courses using the inductive method and grounded theory. We will consult information security specialists in education and industry to develop ability indicators using the Delphi method. To collect opinions from the specialists, we first developed an online survey system as well as a mail system.

We will construct a set of general course issues for information security from the existing curricula of computer-related departments of technology universities in Taiwan. We planned to discuss information security issues with about 20 to 30 specialists from education and industry using a Delphi procedure. To collect survey data, an online questionnaire system was developed. Finally, we constructed a set of ability indicators for an information security course for further development of a complete curriculum of information security.

4   Examples of Hands-On Cooperative Exercises

A network firewall is an effective way to protect computing resources from outside security threats and attacks. An IT student should know what, when and how of a network firewall. We planned a set of hands-on exercises with the portable virtual laboratory in the information security course. Building a LAN as well as a network firewall is an independent task assigned to a student group. Then student groups cooperatively interconnect their LANs to test (learn) network firewall functions, such as port forwarding and VPN (virtual private network). In addition, a web-based tool, IPCop, is used to quickly setup a base of a network firewall for further learning network firewall topics. A learner, with IPCop, can focus very well on experimenting information security topics without pay attention to Linux OS basics. In sum, it introduces a quick, simple, and cooperative learning of building a network firewall. Based on the project-based/cooperative learning, we setup two kinds of projects: inner-team and inter-team projects. The inner-team project is to guide members of a group to setup a single LAN and to experimenting basic functions of a network firewall. The inter-team project is to guide members of two groups to interconnect two LANs and to experimenting VPN functions supported by network firewalls of two interconnected LANs. The two team projects are described as follows.

- **Inner-team task: Network firewall with IPCop**

The first task individually done by a learner is to connect a machine installed with a Windows XP or Linux to the outside Internet via a single network firewall as shown in Figure 3. In the task a learner installs an IPCop system and a Windows XP respectively on two virtual machines. The IPCop system has dual-homed networks, one is connected to the Internet and the other one is connected to the private LAN. The learner experiments basic functions of a network firewall, such as proxy and port-forwarding, using IPCop web-based management interface as shown in Figure 3. The time to finish the task will be in two hours.

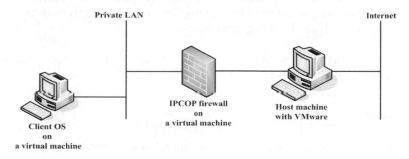

Fig. 3. Network firewall diagram

- **Inter-team task: Interconnecting two LANs with VPN function**

The inter-team task is to connect two private LANs via a public network, Internet. Students, in two teams, setup VPN function built in IPCop system, as shown in Figure 4. Students of one team first share one pre-shared key, which is used to secure the communication tunnel, with students of the corresponding team. IP configurations of two LANs are shared too. Experimenting VPN is to let students know how two private LANs can communicate with each other via a public network, like Internet. The time to finish the task will be in three hours.

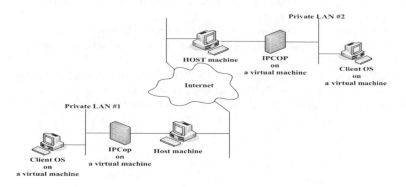

Fig. 4. VPN diagram

5   Conclusion

A portable virtual laboratory was created with virtual machine software, VMware, for experimenting information security hands-on exercises. The laboratory would be easily applied to a traditional computer classroom with inexpensive/free virtual machine software. Information security students can do hands-on exercises with the portable virtual laboratory anywhere by hosting all image files of the laboratory on a portable USB disk. An information security curriculum was redesigned with the portable virtual laboratory. Examples of hands-on exercises, inner- and inter-team projects, were presented. The complete and future work is that the effectiveness evaluation of the proposed method will be obtained by teaching information security with two student groups, experimental and control groups.

Acknowledgement. This work was supported by the National Science Council of Taiwan under contract number NSC 97-2511-S-241-003-MY2.

References

1. Highland, H.J.: A view of information security tomorrow. Comput. Secur. 12, 634–639 (1993)
2. Summers, R.C.: Secure computing: threats and safeguards. McGraw-Hill, Inc., New York (1997)
3. Bellovin, S.M., Cheswick, W.R.: Network firewalls. IEEE Communications Magazine 32 (September 1994)
4. Slavin, R.E.: An introduction to cooperative learning. Longman, New York (1983)
5. Steiner, S., et al.: Using Cooperative Learning Strategies in Social Work Education. Journal of Social Work Education 35, 253–264 (1999)
6. Johnson, D.W., Johnson, R.T.: Learning together and alone: Cooperative, competitive, and individualistic learning, 5th edn. Allyn and Bacon, Boston (1999)
7. VMware Inc. VMware: Virtualization, Virtual Machine & Virtual Server Consolidation - VMware (November 13, 2007), http://www.vmware.com/
8. Linux Online Inc. The Linux Home Page at Linux Online (March 22, 2008), http://www.linux.org/
9. Microsoft Corp. Microsoft Virtual PC 2007 (November 13, 2007), http://www.microsoft.com/windows/products/winfamily/virtualpc/default.mspx
10. VirtualBox Org. VirtualBox (November 13, 2007), http://www.virtualbox.org/
11. Webmin. Webmin (March 22, 2008), http://www.webmin.com/
12. IPCop Org. IPCop.org :: The bad packets stop here! (November 13, 2007), http://ipcop.org/

Small and Medium-Sized Enterprises Financing and Sustainable Development

Linan Wang[1] and Sida Wang[2]

[1] Jilin University of Finance and Economics, Changchun, China, 130117
[2] College of Electronic Science and Engineering, Jilin University, Changchun, China, 130012

Abstract. Now, the small and medium-sized enterprises have become the important driving factors to economic growth and made an important contribution to the country's economic development and stability in China. However, it has an inappropriate status in national economy because its financing is very difficult. And even it has affected the sustainable developments of the enterprises. If the small and medium-sized enterprises want to achieve long-term sustainable developments, we must find a rational solution to the problem of financing. This paper pays attention to the defined scope of small and medium-sized enterprises and their indispensability condition in country's economic development, and also discusses the financing station and financing channels, then discussed the reasons for financing difficulties and the influence that they could bring to the small and medium-sized enterprise in sustainable development. It focuses on three aspects of resolving the financing difficulties including the enterprise themselves, financial markets and governmental control. Finally, conclusion is drawn on how to use the limited financing resources to resolve the difficulties in financing and maintain the sustainable development of the enterprises.

Keywords: Small and Medium-sized Enterprise(sme), Financing, Sustainable Development.

1 Introduction

In recent years, regardless of developed and developing countries have appeared in the revival of the small and medium-sized enterprises. Management of small and medium-sized enterprises will get great rewards, small and medium-sized enterprises in the social economic life plays a more and more important role.

According to the law of the People's Republic of 1995 the third national industrial census data of the information provided by enterprises: small and medium-sized enterprises, 7253406 for a total of industrial enterprises, the total number of 99.91%, and 6416 for a large number of industrial enterprises, the 0.09 percent, Industrial output will see, small and medium-sized enterprises for 58691.99 billion, of the total industrial output value, large enterprise for 21827.62 billion, of the total industrial output value 27.11%, Just pay taxes total census in 1995, small and medium-sized enterprises 2422.69 billion, accounting for the total annual pay taxes of industrial enterprises, and 52.17% of large-scale enterprise 2220.93 billion, accounting for

S. Lin and X. Huang (Eds.): CSEE 2011, Part V, CCIS 218, pp. 251–256, 2011.
© Springer-Verlag Berlin Heidelberg 2011

47.83%. Along with the development of market economy in China, the small and medium-sized enterprises will have greater development in the national condition, the contribution will continue to rise.

The small and medium-sized enterprises most for labor-intensive enterprises, absorbing labor created more investment opportunities of employment than large enterprises, and barriers to entry is lesser, is the main jobs, but also social stabilizer provider.

Since the reform and opening, in our country industrialization process, no serious social problem of employment, the rapid development of small business is one of the most important factors. 1990-2006, China's agricultural sector conversion from the 4 million, mostly in the labor employment of small businesses. In the industrial sector of 9.5 million new employees is in the small -makers. The industrial sector employment for 2.5 billion people, includes the employment in small 19.8 million people, 79.2%.

2 Financing for Small and Medium-Sized Enterprises at Home and Abroad

2.1 Domestic Financing Ways

(1) Folk financing. Folk financing mainly exists in private and private business owners of private, private and in the form of financing, between the small and medium-sized enterprises at present occupies a proportion. Because of the urban residents and investment channels, the relatively narrow their traditional way of savings investment funds under the accumulated folk lending money, in order to realize to maintain and increase its value. Folk financing directly cause bank savings rise.

(2) Financial institutions. Besides folk financing, small and medium-sized enterprises can also through the mortgage their fixed assets or other means from financial institutions (to) get short-term bank loans. But in the bank credit market, due to the bank and small and medium-sized enterprises to grasp the information asymmetry and bank credit validity of internal power protection seriously insufficient, credit and credit evaluation mechanism imperfect, highly centralized authority, causing financial institutions for smes, the sme funding financing cost of general prep above bank loans. Therefore, the small and medium-sized enterprises from financial institutions of financing volume ratio, often restricted obviously less than small and medium-sized enterprises to raise capital through the folk financing.

(3) Non-financial financing. Non-financial financing smes from society mainly refers to raise funds in non-financial, including our common "usury. Along with our country and the world economic integration, "private equity fund" this non-financial new financing form.

2.2 Foreign Financing Ways

Foreign small and medium-sized enterprise fund basically has the following kinds: one is the source of self-raised, 2 it is direct financing, financing, three is the indirect government support fund is four.

(1) Self-raised funds. It includes the range is very wide, mainly has the owner (or partners, shareholders) self-capital, Borrow money from friends and relatives, Personal investment funds, namely "angel" funds, Risk investment management enterprise financing capital (including customer to suppliers and the advance payment installment, etc.), Between the enterprise credit (some countries are banned), Small and medium-sized enterprises and institutions of the loan, And some of the social insurance fund, the fund (such as pension funds, etc.) of the loans, etc.

(2) Direct financing. Obviously, the financing way only corporations entitled to use only small and medium-sized enterprises, however, general corporations small and medium-sized enterprise bonds and stocks to counter trade only, only a handful of corporations with strict conditions of small and medium-sized enterprises to obtain public, or enter the market ", "the second plate.

(3) The indirect financing. Mainly includes various short-term and long-term loans. Loan (namely the financial product) mainly mortgages, loan and credit loans, etc.

(4) On government support fund. Mainly includes the government of small and medium-sized enterprises to special preferential tax subsidies, such measures as loans aid.

3   The Financing Difficulties of Small and Medium-Sized Enterprises

3.1   The Internal Financing Phenomenon

(1) Ignore credit management, accounting information, opaque arisen, investor sentiment bank

Small and medium-sized enterprises are mostly mom-and-pop, financial management, enterprise information, ideas, credit the internalization of low credit rating, small and medium-sized enterprises and investors information asymmetry between serious. Investigation shows, 66% of sme credit rating in 3B or below, small and medium-sized enterprises are the loan default rate and collapse rate than large enterprise. Due to the small scale of production management of small and medium-sized enterprises, commercial Banks over the sme loans tracking supervision, claims to maintain. Many small and medium-sized enterprises in owner often appear insolvency, or a walk through the reform of system of bank debt to escape, investors, cost of capital increase investment risk.

(2) Planning, the lack of long-term capital requirements

Because most of the small and medium-sized enterprises to lack of investment income and the risk of investment decision-making, often appear in the business, considering the current financing, bank loan program cannot satisfy the urgency of capital demand, on the other hand, the small and medium-sized enterprises pay no attention to financial analysis and control requirements, the lack of budget, the financing channel is not fixed, also has caused the indirect financing channel not smooth.

(3) Capital structure is unreasonable, asset management efficiency

Small and medium sized enterprises in total capital structure, high debt ratio, low self-owned capital ratios, In total liabilities structure, high current debt ratio, long term liabilities, In self-owned capital accumulation and low, inside. This shows that many small and medium-sized enterprises to the negative effects of financial leverage, inadequate understanding, blind debt. Leverage with financial leverage effect and financial leverage is a "double-edged sword", so the capital structure, the potential of the financial risks of enterprise, which greatly increased the possibility of using debt financing funds.

3.2 The External Financing Phenomenon

(1) The imperfect legal environment, financing

China's legal environment, financing smes in incomplete financing channel is not smooth and financing is the main cause of a single, specific performance: only state-owned enterprise to use the state financial capital, only foreign-invested enterprises with foreign capital can be directly, only financial institutions engaged in bank loans to, Co., ltd., and reorganized into a joint stock limited company of the enterprise can through the issuance of stocks as a way to raise money, only limited liability companies and joint stock limited companies to take issue company bonds way to raise money. The above provisions for small and medium-sized companies use only decided to leave money and banking enterprise credit funds raising funds for financing channels, the majority of small and medium-sized enterprises, its take the capital is limited, which makes the enterprise's capital mainly comes from bank credit, forming high debt.

(2) Banks to small and medium-sized enterprises widespread phenomenon of arisen

Although small and medium-sized enterprise created the GDP of 1/3, 2/3 industrial added value, the export of 38% of the country's financial revenues and 1/4, but in recent years, with the financial reform of commercial Banks, to strengthen the risk management, at the same time, the original sme financing discriminatory policies of the part that is not changed, commercial Banks in the face of the small and medium-sized enterprises are often appear stinting "phenomenon, reason has the following three aspects: bank loans to small and medium-sized enterprise risks and costs; strengthening bank risk management mechanism, inhibit the sme loans; commercial Banks to small and medium-sized enterprises, especially small and medium private enterprises of discrimination.

(3) Government support to small and medium-sized enterprises, Sme financing difficulties in addition to the enterprises, commercial bank of China, and the reason of small and medium-sized enterprises and the support system and other reasons: government did not realize the importance of small and medium-sized enterprises, the policy of the government to small and medium-sized enterprise discrimination.

4   Financing Solutions to the Problem for Small and Medium-Sized Enterprises

(1) Small and medium-sized enterprises should strengthen internal reform, improve internal management system

Small and medium-sized enterprise must strengthen accounting system construction, regulate and improve financial information accounting information authenticity, integrity and transparency, in order to improve the credit rating, reduce the information asymmetry brought by the rising cost of capital. In practice, the smaller enterprises shall invite high qualification of intermediary agencies acting book-keeping, on the one hand, to improve the quality of accounting information, on the other hand, the higher qualification using intermediary organizations, improving enterprise qualification for enterprises' financing Bridges. To strengthen enterprise internal control system, funds, formulate long-term plan and budget plan, Small and medium-sized enterprises should take money management as the implementation of modern enterprise system. First, establish and strict enforcement of monetary fund system of internal control, ensure the safety and integrity of the money, Secondly, formulating scientific and rational enterprise medium and long-term development planning, Third, strengthen management, daily expenses of capital cash budget compilation of reasonable, timely and cash forecast and planning, to understand the.business demand, Fourth, completes the capital budget preparation work, according to a large sum of money demand situation, reasonable arrangement of financing.

(2)To establish and perfect the sme financing and the development of the legal system, optimize the judicial environment

In the existing state should be detrimental to the development of small and medium-sized enterprises of the laws, regulations and policies to revise and adjustment, increase on smes' financing requirements, such as: allow small and medium-sized enterprise by national finance capital, Allow small and medium-sized enterprises with foreign capital to raise money, Sets up the multi-level and securities trading markets allow small and medium-sized enterprises through the capital market to direct financing, and widen smes financing channels of financing, diversity.

Sme credit guarantee is not traditional sense of security, but the government administration under the support of marketization guarantee. Its significance lies in the establishment of user and the relationship between good credit enterprise of small and medium-sized enterprises, and to improve the credit, promote the establishment of credit system in China. Establish enterprise credit guarantee system of short-term goals is to solve the small and medium-sized enterprises loan, long-term goal is to disperse investment risk, promoting the healthy development of small and medium-sized enterprises.

(3)Intensify the development of smes' financing and the support

The development of small and medium-sized enterprises in China's government funding system has just started, at present is still not mature, construct a perfect sme financing, financial support system, and the various needs to appear in the process of development of various problems timely correction and may not be problem-free also cannot be accomplished, referring to the experiences of developed countries, and fully consider the situation in China, in a gradual way to promote Chinese characteristics of financing smes financial support system gradually establish and perfect.

Every state key support for the big enterprise technical supporting technical improvement project, the small and medium-sized enterprises may enjoy loans from financial sector support, Cleaning the sme, unreasonable fees should be clearly no longer bear after tax in the government, enterprises and other expenses of public undertakings and social functions. The government also can be formulated by the related preferential policies, and to guide the direction of small and medium-sized enterprises of small and medium-sized enterprises and improving the investment structure, such as free access number of enterprises in various areas, various products of supply and demand.

References

1. LiHong, C.: Private enterprises financing themselves and solutions. Journal of private economy and small and medium-sized enterprise management (4) (2007)
2. King, S.: Based on the financial system itself defects of small and medium-sized private enterprises financing disorders. Journal of private economy and small and medium-sized enterprise management (4) (2007)
3. FengXia, X.: sme financing problems. Journal of economists (11) (2003)
4. [4] Pan, Z.: Risk investment and listed innovation of small and medium-sized enterprises with overseas financing – the new choices. International financing (5) (2007)
5. YaPing, Z.: Sme financing causes and countermeasures (2007)
6. YuMing, Z.: Private enterprise financing system. New shandong province of shandong university press (2003)

Analysis on the Security of Accounting Information System

Linan Wang[1] and Jinxin He[2,*]

[1] Jilin University of Finance and Economics, Changchun, P.R. China, 130117
[2] College of Earth Sciences, Jilin University, Changchun 130061 P.R. China

Abstract. Computerized accounting system is a computer instead of manually, to keep accounts, to render an account, to cast accounts, to audit and some accounting information (data) need to be completed by the human and statistical analysis, as well as providing policy-making press to judge. It based on the hardware system and the software system. Human is the main operation of the computerized accounting system. The security of the computerized accounting system is very important. But, if the hardware system failure, software system failures, unexpected power outages, damage memory, computer viruses and hacker attacks the network, the system operator's own lack of low quality and the level of computerized accounting system will lead to the collapse of even the loss of accounting data. Therefore, we use the appropriate program to prevent the above situation from occurring, to ensure the safety and integrity of accounting information.

Keywords: Computerized accounting system, Hardware, Software Security.

1 Introduction

Accounting computerization is the electronic computer primarily contemporary electron technology and information technology is applied to practical accounting abbreviation, is by computer to replace artificial, realize bookkeeping, accounts, reimbursement, audits and parts required by the human brain complete accounting information (data) statistics, the analysis, and even provide the decision-making process. Based on its own characteristics, compared with the original ledger, with quick speed, storage of great capacity and height data sharing, the search speed is quick, making statements easily and data analysis of the features of accurate accounting computerization system is an efficient, high-quality accounting system, which can effectively improve the staff working efficiency and quality of work, computerized accounting system to accelerate the information processing, disclosure and use of timeliness, strengthened the information sharing, enrich and perfect the voucher database, improves the utilization rate of original voucher. In a manual accounting procedures, by subscription credits and workload of restriction, original vouchers in many useful data have no way to record, detailed classification and

---

* Corresponding author.

S. Lin and X. Huang (Eds.): CSEE 2011, Part V, CCIS 218, pp. 257–261, 2011.

summarizing. Realize the accounting computerization, formed the original vouchers database, can press management needs to classify consolidation and exploitation. Computerized accounting system is simple, rapid and easy to preserve advantages, obtained the business unit of efficient use. However its safety problem is bound to get various business attentions.

2 Accounting Computerization System Security Risk

2.1 Computerized Accounting Systems Hardware Security Risks

Computer hardware refers to computer system by electrical, mechanical and optoelectronic components etc composed of various physical device floorboard. These physical devices according to the structure of the system requirements constitute an organic whole for computer software running provide material base. Therefore, hardware system became the safe operation of the computerized accounting system of the carrier. Hardware system security includes hard disk storage equipment damage, such as computer processor failure and power failure, etc.

Computer storage device is the important computerized accounting data storage equipment, such as computer hard disk, external memory, CD, etc. Height, environment humidity too high, electromagnetic interference overpowered, dust inhaled, bump or vibration, will damage to computer hard disk. Such consequences will be making accounting work have been seriously affected even lost, leading to the accounting computerization's work has great confusion, and accounting data have permanent loss or damage potential.

2.2 Computerized Accounting Systems Software Security Risks

Computer software is a computer system of programs and documents. Program is computing tasks of object and dealing with the rules of description, Documents are needed to facilitate understanding of sexual material clarified program. Used for accounting computerization of software system is divided into operating system software and application software of computerized accounting. Computerized accounting software requirements in the corresponding system software running, computerized accounting work again request in accounting software applications completed. So done smoothly computerized accounting work requires the operating system and the accounting computerization applications in any link can appear unusual. Computerized accounting systems software security risk including system software security risks, computerized accounting application software security risk.

2.3 Computerized Accounting Systems under Network Environment Problems

Accounting computerization applications relying on Internet/Intranet system used by is open to the TCP/IP protocol, and therefore there might be tempted by cutoff protected reliably against detective, password and steal, identity, tampering and fake information, clean and safe hidden trouble malicious damage.

In computer work process will continuously radiate electromagnetic wave, anyone can use specific precision instrument equipment within the scope of certain and receives it, especially by using high sensitivity of the instrument can be more stable, see more clearly computer is processing data information, etc. This will seriously affect the enterprise of confidentiality issues, data information of stealing can make enterprises are immeasurable loss, moreover, network output and input ports, transmission lines wait for possible for shielding lax or did not add caused by electromagnetic shielding the leak.

3 Computerized Accounting System Safety Countermeasures

3.1 Computer Hardware System Preventive Measures

① Storage equipment preventive measures

Now in the market most computerized accounting software can achieve timing backup function. Data backup is will be computerized accounting system data processing regularly designedly replication, and then copies of the data storage in system outside storage device, such as CDS, mobile hard disk, U plate, etc. If the system malfunction, can will latest raids of backup data recovery to internal system, then put the latest case of backup data and fault happened before this one phase of what has happened and registration data for supplement. Such as its disk image technology, this technology is the relatively advanced data storage technology, it is to point to host or server are equipped with two the physical hard disk. A hard disk as the main hard disk, another called affiliate hard disk. Through relevant professional setting, when stored data, computer real-time data endures two hard disk, the affiliate disk is main hard disk mapping mirror, can save the Lord all the hard disk content, even the Lord hard disk fault happens is, affiliate hard disk can also play its role, have very important practical significance.

②Power safety precautions

For the power of safety measures or from the computer itself power equipment and external power supply environment in the two aspects prevention. Computer own power equipment must pay attention to the choice of good quality, long service life equipment. And pay attention to using the environment appropriate. For external power supplies power outages, can use UPS equipment, it can guarantee the computer system in a sudden after a power outage also can continue to work for a period of time to the user can set up an emergency inventory, also can at any time automatically preserve the software system, the input data preservation at any time at any time, can avoid data loss.

3.2 Computer Software System Preventive Measures

① Choose copyrighted software and computerized accounting software

Enterprises and institutions in execute computerization, enterprises and institutions must be combined with its own characteristics and the state's relevant stipulations to choose suitable financial software. At present our country has promulgated by the relevant national standards and specifications mainly by the ministry of finance promulgated in 1994 carry out "the accounting computerization management method", "accounting software basic function norms," and "computerized accounting work norms," and "commercialization accounting software reviews rules, etc. Also must pay attention to the system permissions Settings, security and secrecy key factors. If the enterprises and institutions developed by computerized accounting system, also must follow the relevant state organs and department to make the specifications and standards, including accord with display and normative development and approval process, qualified developers, system document material and the flowchart, system the functional modules design and so on.

② Computer software system of other preventive measures

Set up a universal, the unification of financial software agreement with market segmentation and combining the provisions of this agreement can make market the issuance of financial software has the same data interface (such as input and output database name, format, type, field name, etc.), or provisions in public conversion interface, will make different data can be mutual conversion to be identified, accepted. Such different software system of data can be used directly, no need to do processing, also can reduce to operator's requirement, also can make the different systems to realize data sharing. Ensure the financial work more and orderly.

3.3 Strengthening the Construction of Network Security

① Strengthen computerized accounting information safety

Implementation of data communication control is to prevent the enterprise information was leaked the important means. Implementation of the Internet technology, remote accounting voucher input, remote statements and remote monitoring of facilitating network control. During transmission encrypt, strengthen accounting computerization of regulating system management. Review internal computer data and written material consistency, check account content, do not conform to the account to comply with the requirements by mistake, table timely correcting and adjustment. To supervise computerized process data forms of security, legality, prevent illegal delete, revision, and rewriting history of computerized accounting data and running the links to check and prevent holes.

② Establish prevent virus security measures

Because the computer crime has increased, the characteristics of concealment, therefore, in order to prevent the virus attacks, insist on using authorized anti-virus software, cannot use pirated or software, to outside floppy disk, mobile storage devices must first real-time control of your hard drive virus detection, timely discovery and kill virus, regular backup data and files, not open and read mails, strange documents etc.

4 Accounting Computerization Development Outlook for the Future

Accounting computerization is system engineering. On the one hand, countries, regions and the competent industrial department should formulate a series of computerized accounting management system, development plan, the technical standard and work for standardizing and promulgated and implemented, to arouse the enthusiasm of each respect and organization development industries with multi-level and applicable, multi-type series of accounting software, and its legitimacy, right on the reliability evaluation, while providing other large and arduous accounting computerization macro management work. On the other hand, prepare to grass-roots units shall actively for large and complex of accounting computerization kit management work, mostly improve enterprise leadership and other management personnel of modern management consciousness. The entire enterprise management modernization under the guidance of the overall planning of well of accounting computerization is a long-term and stable development plan and program. Timely adjust position division, build a modern management system, improves the management requirements. The above list each work must be done, or computerized accounting system will not work normally, beneath the accounting computerization overall efficiency and make it cannot carry out in-depth everlastingly down, accounting and enterprise management modernization will not be achieved.

Computerized accounting software development is also from experience to scientific development of engineering method transformation. Using the method to develop the accounting computerization engineering of the application of the system software is the popular trend of current international, also be its development tendency of computerized accounting system, but also a safety problems of comprehensive and requires the problem that must be solved urgently need hardware, software, network, personnel quality and application ability of coordination to respond to the common and common problems, the is a need to strengthen the safety consciousness, do sufficient precautionary measures of management. Through the above to computerized accounting system safety analysis, and its solving measures, the hope can to computerized accounting system security problems receive comprehensive control, makes the accounting computerization system can work well in real implementation, and makes the accounting computerization could be fully the development of economy and society in service and today.

References

1. Ling, H., Bin, W.: Computerized accounting information system. China financial and economic publishing house, Beijing (2002)
2. ShuangJing, G.: Computerized accounting system safety analysis. J. scientific and technological consultation metallurgica (18) (2007)
3. HuiXia, L.: Security risks of e-accounting system and the preventive measures. Journal of shanxi economic management cadre institute journal (2) (2006)
4. JiaQing, M.: Computerized accounting system safety analysis. Journal of hunan industry vocational college Journal (2) (2005)
5. YanLi, Z.: Computerized accounting system safety analysis. Journal of shanxi technology (2) (2005)

A Study on a New Method for the Analysis of Flood Risk Assessment Based on Artificial Neural Network

Qiong Li

School of Mathematics and Physics, Huangshi Institute of Technology,
Huangshi 435003, China
liqiong070108@163.com

Abstract. This paper presents a composite method for flood disaster risk assessment using a BP artificial neural network. In order to test the grade criterions of flood disaster loss and resolve the non-uniformity problem of evaluation results of disaster loss indexes, and to raise the grade resolution of flood disaster loss, a BP artificial neural network is suggested for evaluating the grade model of flood disaster, where the disaster loss grade is continuous real number. Meanwhile, an artificial neural network model-BP neural network is used to map multi-dimensional space of disaster situation to one-dimensional disaster situation nonlinearly and to raise the grade resolution of flood disaster loss. Furthermore, its application is verified in the flood risk analysis in Henan Province, China, and the risks of different flood grades are obtained. The results indicate that the methods are effective and practical and therefore the model is considered to have a good application prospect in disaster risk assessment.

Keywords: back propagation, neural network, flood, risk assessment.

1 Introduction

Flood disasters occur frequently in China, and about two-thirds of its area are facing the threat of different types and degrees of floods which is the result of natural and unnatural reasons such as social, economic factors. As severe floods occurring frequently, flood risk assessment and management play an important role in guiding the government take timely and correct decision for disaster rescue and relief. It's an inevitable choice in the historical development of China to change from flood control to flood management which is an important contemporary strategy on flood control. Risk assessment, one of the main subjects of flood management which consists of risk identification, risk assessment, and risk control is a challenging task at the present.

In traditional flood risk assessment, probability statistics method is usually used to estimate hydrological variables' exceedance probability. This method has the advantage of its mature basic theory and easy application. But when it comes to practical issues, problems exist in the feasibility and reliability. Meanwhile, in order to map multi-dimensional space of disaster situation to one-dimensional disaster situation nonlinearly, to test the grade criterions of flood disaster loss and resolve the non-uniformity problem of evaluation results of disaster loss indexes, and to raise the

S. Lin and X. Huang (Eds.): CSEE 2011, Part V, CCIS 218, pp. 262–266, 2011.

grade resolution of flood disaster loss, an artificial neural network model-BP neural network is suggested for evaluating the degree of flood disaster, where the disaster loss degree is a more reasonable continuous real number.

In this study we establish a new model based on artificial neural network with a small number of measured samples and it is then applied to the flood risk analysis in Henan province successfully.

2 Methodology

Artificial Neural Network (ANN) are massively parallel interconnected networks of simple (usually adaptive) nodes which are intended to interact with objects of the real world in the same way as biological nervous systems do[1]. It was proposed based on modern biology research concerning human brain tissue, and can be used to simulate neural activity in the human brain [2]. ANN has the topological structures of information processing, distributing parallel. The mappings of input and output estimation responses are obtained via combinations of nonlinear functions [3].

The neurons are generally grouped into layers. Signals flow from the input layer through to the output layer via unidirectional connections, the neurons being connected from one layer to the next. The neural cell of each layer only affects the status of the next neural cell. If the expected output signals cannot be obtained in the output layer, the weight values of each layer of the neural cells must be modified. Erroneous output signals will be backward from the source. Finally, the signal error will arrive in certain areas with repeated propagation. After the neural networks' training procedure is complete we can start to analyze the forecast information with weight values and thresholds.

3 Flood Risk Assessment Based on Neutral Network

According to the 41 years' practical series material from 1950 to 1990 in henna province [4, 5], we take inundated area and direct economic loss as the indexes of disaster degree and by frequency analysis the disaster grading standards of the area are seen in table 1.

Table 1. Henan flood disaster rating standard

Disaster level	Inundated area[hm^2]	Direct economic losses [Billion Yuan]	Degree value
small flood	0~46.7	0~9.5	0~1
medium flood	46.7~136.7	9.5~31.0	1~2
large flood	136.7~283.3	31.0~85.0	2~3
extreme flood	283.3~	85.0~	3~4

We take the inundated area data and direct economic loss data as input variables and disaster grading value as an output variable, and then we set the nodes of the input as 2 and the output layers as 1. It follows on from Kolmogorov's theorem that the number of nodes in the hidden layer is at least 2n + 1, where n is the number of nodes in the input layer. Since n = 2, the number of nodes in the hidden layer is at least 5. Considering the accuracy, we determined that the number of nodes in the hidden layer is 6. Thus, we can obtain the topology structure (2, 6, 1) of the neural networks for flood degree forecasting.

The four flood grades are small, medium, large and extreme flood, whose degree value is in the interval [0,1]、 [1,2]、 [2,3]、 [3,4]; We use the disaster grading standard boundary values (table 1) as 5 two-dimensional training samples for training and learning in the BP neural network. Meanwhile initial parameters of BP model weights and biases were randomly assigned before the commencement of training. According to 100,000 cycles of training and learning in the training samples, the global error of the networks was set $E=10^{-6}$. Learning rate and impulse parameter of the network is changed adaptive, and function trainlm is used for fast training.

Table 2. Floods evaluation standard limits and network expected output & actual output

expected output	0.0000	1.0000	2.0000	3.0000	4,0000
actual output	0.0000	0.9995	2.0000	3.0000	4.0000

The calculated output values are compared with the expected values in Table 2 where the mean square error is $5.94387e^{-8}$ and the gradient $4.46355e^{-3}$, indicating a good fitting. Thus the BP neural network has completed the training procedure. So we can use the BP network to forecast disaster degrees of all the samples with the weighting coefficients and the thresholds modified. The flood degree estimations are list in Table 3.

Table 3. Disaster degree estimations based on the BP network evaluation

number	Inundated area[hm²]	Direct economic loss[Billion Yuan]	output degree value	number	Inundated area[hm²]	Direct economic loss[Billion Yuan]	output degree value
i	X(1,i)	X(2,i)		i	X(1,i)	X(2,i)	
1	38.70	7.900	0.3814	17	157.30	38.600	2.8297
2	38.50	7.800	0.3704	18	283.30	85.000	3.4817
3	32.10	6.500	0.1333	19	556.90	67.100	4.0000
4	24.20	4.900	0.0636	20	649.50	194.900	4.0000

Table 3. *(continued)*

5	36.40	7.400	0.2877	21	602.30	180.700	4.0000
6	46.70	9.500	0.6989	22	446.50	134.000	3.9996
7	97.60	21.700	1.3560	23	694.90	208.500	4.0000
8	60.40	12.800	1.0214	24	72.92	9.900	1.0858
9	112.60	25.200	1.6815	25	148.13	20.656	2.4734
10	56.20	11.800	0.9590	26	203.92	27.521	2.9919
11	80.60	17.600	1.1714	27	179.10	24.858	2.9029
12	136.70	31.000	2.4142	28	375.46	94.927	3.9854
13	259.10	76.100	3.2234	29	301.24	47.836	3.6167
14	200.10	54.400	3.0076	30	141.97	116.439	2.9900
15	280.10	83.800	3.4432	31	279.84	121.127	3.5082
16	236.10	67.600	3.0856	32	172.06	51.619	2.9598

In this way, the disaster degree values of all the 32 samples are obtained as shown in Table 3. The relationship between the recurrence interval N and probability p can be expressed as $N = \frac{1}{p}$

Due to the standard of four grades, so we have:

(a) If $0 \leq x_i \leq 1$, then flood degree belongs to small.

(b) If $1 < x_i \leq 2$, then it belongs to medium.

(c) If $2 < x_i \leq 3$, then it belongs to large.

(d) If $3 < x_i \leq 4$, then it belongs to extreme.

The result illustrates the risk estimation i.e. the probability of exceeding the disaster degree value. We know the risk estimation is 0.4142 when the disaster index is 3, in other words, in Henan Province, floods exceeding 3 degree value (extreme floods) occur every 2.41 years. Similarly, the probability of floods exceeding 2 degree (large floods) is 0.6455, namely Henan Province suffers the floods exceeding that intensity every 1.55 years. This indicates the serious situation of floods in Henan Province whether on the aspect of frequency or intensity. It also means that BP neural network is useful to analyze probability risk of flood disaster. The method proposed is better than traditional frequency method to analyze the risk of the flood disaster. Obviously, the estimator by this neural network model is also better than the linear-regression estimator, because this estimator is more precise than the linear-regression estimator.

The frequency and the recurrence interval of the floods of the four grades are shown in Table 4. Compared with traditional probabilistic method, the risk values obtained by this hybrid fuzzy-neural network method can provide more characteristics of risk system when we analyze the risk of system. The result could help in strategic decision making to manage flood disasters.

Table 4. Flood disaster risk assessment values in Henan province

Disasters level	Small flood	Medium flood	Large flood	Extreme flood
Exceedance probability risk	1.0290	0.7932	0.6455	0.4142
Recurrence interval[year]	0.97	1.26	1.55	2.41

4 Conclusion

Floods occur frequently in China and cause great property losses and casualties. In order to implement a compensation and disaster reduction plan, the losses caused by flood disasters are among critically important information to flood disaster managers. This study develops a method of flood risk assessment disasters based on BP artificial neural network method, and it can be easily extended to other natural disasters. It has been tested that the method is reliable and the results are consistent with the real values.

References

1. Simon, H.: Neural Networks and Learning Machines, 3rd edn., ch. 4. China Machine Press, Beijing (2009)
2. Mikhailov, V.N., Morozov, V.N., Cheroy, N.I., Mikhailova, M.V.: Extreme flood on the Danube River in 2006. Russian Meteorology and Hydrology 33, 48–54 (2008)
3. Chat, S.R., Abdullah, K.: Estimation of all-terminal network reliability using an artificial neural network. Computers and Operations Research 29, 849–868 (2002)
4. Jin, J.L., Zhang, X.L., Ding, J.: Projection Pursuit Model for Evaluating Grade of Flood Disaster Loss. Systems Engineering-theory & Practice 22(2), 140–144 (2002)
5. Jin, J.L., Jin, B.M., Yang, X.H., Ding, J.: A practical scheme for establishing grade model of flood disaster loss. Journal of Catastrophology 15(2), 1–6 (2000)

Research on the Course Teaching Reform of Discrete Mathematics in Modern Information Age

Nan Jiang[1], CunRui Wang[1, *], and ShuHua Qi[2]

[1] Research Institute of Non-linear Information Technology, Dalian Nationalities University, Dalian 116600, P.R. China
[2] College of Science, Dalian Nationalities University, Dalian 116600, P.R. China
Helenjn625@126.com, Wcr@dlnu.edu.cn, Qishuhua001@126.com

Abstract. To improve the teaching level of discrete mathematics, proposed the new theoretical teaching pattern which combined knowledge initiation, ability training and quality education, and the innovation type experiment educational model, which is multilayer, cross-discipline and based mostly on application, and adopted autonomous learning mode, improve the ability of students for analyzing problem and self-study ability by practical training. Careful choice and arrange teaching content; Adopted the means combining the traditional education and the modern teaching means using multimedia and a mutual-active education way which is student-centered and tutor-oriented; Discussed course construction based on Web, and gains good teaching reform effect.

Keywords: Teaching Reform, teaching mode, Autonomous Learning.

1 Introduction

The development of information technology brings new opportunity and challenge to ways and means of education. The traditional education way already could not adapt the requirements of information society, only the course teaching reform can make the education to proceed. Under this situation, the course reform of discrete mathematics is imperative. Discrete mathematics is an important branch of modern mathematics it is also the theoretical foundation of computer science, and absolutely necessary tool of computer application. It is targeted on research of the structure of discrete amount and their relationship, it has a broadly application in fields of computer science, automatization, economics and etc. By studying this course, the students can not only grasp the necessary mathematical foundation but improve their ability. Training the abstract-thinking and logic deduction ability enhance their ability of mining question, analyzing question and solving question. However, this course involves many theories and is abstract to understand, which leads to a low study interest, therefore, the research of Course Teaching Reform of Discrete Mathematics is quite important and necessary [1]. This paper combines the author's education experiments and proposed some useful investigation the aspects of the education mode, education content and education methods, etc.

---

* Corresponding author.

S. Lin and X. Huang (Eds.): CSEE 2011, Part V, CCIS 218, pp. 267–272, 2011.
© Springer-Verlag Berlin Heidelberg 2011

2   Reform of Teaching Mode

The Theoretical teaching mode

Theoretical education is based on Discrete Mathematics and combines knowledge teaching, ability training and quality education. Students can feel and understand the process of knowledge initiation and development, it also cultivates the students to have better logical thinking, rational logic and good ability of collecting and dealing with information, analyzing and solving problems. We should combine school education and after school education, make good use of Blackboard education-assist platform by putting relative class material and web-site into Blackboard. We can also carry out multilayer-education. According to the character of a Nationality University, we can organize seminar topics of different levels to met different students. In order to make the students who have interests in the topics to learn more, we can give one topic per week and use the idle time to give or explain some after class knowledge, students can have to option to attend this part of education to learn more.

Each discipline has its own knowledge organizational structure, discipline form, core concept and basic work flow. Theory, abstraction and design are the three basic forms of computer science and technology subject, they run through the discrete mathematics curriculum teaching. Based on research of computer science and technology major typical teaching methods, we adopt the learn to teach both the guiding principle in the teaching, which gives priority to in order to learn and give priority to in order to teach of teaching design methods and steps of comprehensive, determine the teaching content, teaching order and learning theme, and analysis of the basic knowledge of students, cognitive ability and cognitive structure, then confirm teaching starting point; We attach importance to cultivating students to think for themselves, independent analysis and problem solving ability, automatic acquiring knowledge and master knowledge and skill ability, that better arouse students' enthusiasm and initiative.

The Experiment Teaching Mode

At present it is less to study of discrete mathematics experiments teaching, people pay more attention to research discrete mathematics theory course teaching. In its teaching people often ignore auxiliary and stimulative effect of experiments course for theory teaching, and also ignores connection closely the discrete mathematics experiments course and data structure course. Usually people know about discrete mathematics teaching is the concept, theorem, formula and problem solving, for most students discrete mathematics exploration activities can not truly develop.

In teaching reform of discrete mathematics experiments course, we put the discrete mathematics knowledge and information knowledge compounding thought through the experiment teaching, and turn the experimental teaching mode of past simple familiar for master discrete mathematics this discipline itself knowledge to the purpose into the experimental teaching manner about across multidisciplinary for the purpose of solving practical problems. According to the characteristics of the course and the knowledge students have mastered, design some new experimental subject, not only can deepen the understanding of knowledge from books, but also expand knowledge properly and solving actual problems, outstanding innovation ability cultivation and students' individual character development, love and cultivate students' curiosity, thirst for knowledge, and   help students autonomous learning, independent thinking, protecting students' explore spirit, building a kind of relaxed environment to the full development of students   endowment and potential. Let students learn with "problems", it can not let the students feel boring, stimulate their interest in learning. Experiment content both involve algorithm design, programming, and cover the database design, web sites design, data structure and knowledge of mathematical modeling, etc.

Using computer discrete mathematics experiment teaching, it is not only an effective way for discrete mathematics investigative learning, but also provides effective help for data structure course teaching.

Experimental education adopt multilayer and cross-discipline mode which is innovated and based on application. In the basic experimentation, students can have fundamental training. Such experimentation is important for the beginner to learn basic knowledge, operation and form their debug ability. In the following integrated experimentation, we ask the students to construct a solution of a comprehensive problem using simple arithmetic so that this ability can be improved. In the last and advanced level after all classes are finished, we give long-term direct and after-class training to the students who is still interested in the extra training. Tutors give projects and materials, the students can design and apply simple software development under tutors' direction. This experimentation teaching mode is just match the target of computer science program which is to improve the students' ability of solving problems of the practical projects and ability of innovation practice.

3 Autonomous Learning Mode

According to subject development requires teachers to provide students with some supplementary material, they include Chinese and English reference material and the domestic and foreign relevant teaching website, and these expanded materials and textbook together which form material system of multimedia and three-dimensional teaching and learning. We add a discrete mathematics application in cryptography and its applications in computer science, etc. Give students left the interface and the window of the new knowledge, through the introduction to the contents of classroom teaching and inspire students' thirst for knowledge. Let students understand subject development trends through lookup material themselves and independent study and exploration. Give students provide divergent thinking space and practice environment and improve the ability of students for analyzing problem and self-study ability by practical training. We provide students the practice of the platform and reach for the social service goals by developing project of practical software.

In order to increase students' units time get amounts of knowledge and analyze and understand the difficulty of curriculum contents and key in the limited energy and time, We adopted the teaching methods of combining multimedia teaching and network Auxiliary teaching to develop computer aided teaching. By the system of network Auxiliary teaching, students can easily download relevant teaching material and know about teaching of this course arrangement and to download teaching documents and courseware. Teachers can always announcement and inform for students to prepare, review, self-study, self test, etc and to provide students with a good Autonomous learning environment.

4   Reform of Teaching Contents

We teach basic contents systematically and emphasis content and inspiring lecturing expansion content in classroom teaching. Analysis and constructing knowledge of mainline to form a subsystem by putting through a knowledge point about processing in teaching contents.

Constitute a group of knowledge framework, and form complete knowledge level by the summary. We provide students with the divergent thinking space and note the radioactive teaching of knowledge.

In order to cultivate students' scientific thinking way in course teaching, we begin from the problems and analyze the possible way and ideas for solving problems, to summarize the knowledge system for solving same kinds of problems.

Discrete mathematics is mainly composed by set theory, modern algebra, graph theory and symbolic logic, so the contents of the classes should cover the basic mathematics knowledge firstly. Second, it should include the training of abstract thinking and logical rational ability of students. Under this premise, the class needs to face information problem so that it can offer necessary knowledge for the following classes like, cryptography study, secrecy communication, data structure, operating system, computer network, etc.

To inspire the initiation idea and interests of class, we integrated our research work and knowledge of Discrete Mathematics to give basic introduction of information security, computer network. This is not only help students know how to use their knowledge learned in class but also improve the efficiency of class and make students more interested in study. We should work more hard to teach the learning approach to the students. Teach them the way how to obtain knowledge and how to apply the knowledge in practice. For example, when we teach the logic part, we also introduce boolen search technology of the web page index and its application in information security [2].

In the reform of discrete mathematics education, we impenetrate a composite idea of discrete mathematics knowledge and information knowledge into the experimentation teaching. We turn the single-subject learning of Discrete Mathematics to cross-discipline, multi-subjects experimentation education which target is to solve real problems. According to the character of the class and knowledge of the students, we design some experimental questions which can help students to understand more deeply of the lecture notes, extend their knowledge fields and how to solve problems. Develop the students' ability of initiation, curiosity of study, help them to study by themselves and solve problem individually [3]. The way of Learning by Doing can avoid the baldness during study. The contents of experimentation including data warehouse design, web-site design, data structure etc.

Carrying out the experimentation education using computer is not only an efficient way of Discrete Mathematics learning, but give good foundation of classes of data structure.

5   Reform of Teaching Methods

Currently, many colleges cut down some traditional course including Discrete Mathematics. Although the course hour has been reduced, the content is not reduced much. To solve this problem and make the students learn more in less time, we adopt multimedia teaching and the traditional 'black board' teaching, the detail is: first propose questions, then using the black board to help students analyze the relationship among concepts, analyze the methods of how to solve the problem, then present all the process of problem solving using the multimedia. Second, we give some more difficult and practical problems and simple analysis of the problem to give the students who is more capable homework after class. We adopt student-centered, tutor-direct teaching methods [4]. During the course, we encourage the students to put forward questions, help students analyze questions and help them find solutions during seminar, attract their attention, training their problem solving ability; the same time we combine the mathematics and information knowledge, class experiments and after-class experiments. This method has achieved the good teaching effect. We adopt the method to combine the class work and after-class homework, leave a certain amount of ordinary homework in each class, to help students understanding and mastery new concepts and new ways. We also appropriate arrangement several big homework according to phase contents, let student look up materials to independent found the relationship of discrete mathematics to other disciplines, and encourage students to put forward questions boldly, efforts to try to solve the problem so that foster the students abilities and curiosity of finding problems and solving problems. In teaching process to adopt bilingual teaching, each teacher of the course can teach with bilingual teaching using penetrated method in the classroom teaching, which made the students hold many necessary English special terminologies at the same as study courses [5].

6 Course Construction Based on Web

Currently many colleges adopt Blackboard internet education platform. The use of this platform provides us a good education method. It realizes and support many new education measures like: self-investigation, cooperated-study, resource sharing etc. Blackboard supplies a huge dummy circumstance for teaching and learning.

Based on this system, we construct discrete mathematics co-curriculum. Firstly we organized the course material, and upload relative courseware onto the Blackboard which provide learning resource. In Blackboard, the courses will open and close automatically, according to the date and time on the schedule. Each new term, we will upload the new version of courseware to the platform, as well as course outline, course introduction, teaching calendar, reference materials, and related website and so on. In order to let students know more about the relationship between this course and following courses, we put courseware of data structure on the black board, which has closed relation with this course. Teachers can release their own information via the 'fellowship file', which provide resource of searching information about the name, email, office time of their tutors. Secondly, we construct the questions warehouse on the platform, there are huge numbers of questions in the warehouse and it can generate test pages for students' practice. So they can do self-test after class.

Black board provides synchronization and asynchronies communication platform. Asynchronies communication includes discuss zone and data mailbox. The discuss zone is one tool to amend the class education and improve the communication between teachers and students. Some topics were created for each chapter to inspire students learn from each other with the method of questioning. In the discuss zone, students were organized to discuss the interesting topics. The teachers published the answers in the web to the questions that most students have. The virtual classroom is one interactive platform which provided the online chat, electronic whiteboard, and other functions. These tools were used to draw the figure, input the test, and provided the formulas. The teachers can give on-line Q&A section using the virtual classroom; discuss the lessons without the limitation of time and location. On same time, the teachers can know about the access status of the students and instruct the students with the definite targets [6]. The teachers can provide the deeper knowledge and more instruction to the students who wanted to attend the post-graduate study and implement the teaching in different hierarchies.

7 Summary

The education reform of discrete mathematics resolved the conflict of less class hours and more teaching contents. The students were more interested in study. The education reform improved the class construction level and teaching quality effectively.

Acknowledgement. This work is supported by the Fundamental Research Funds for the Central Universities (No. DC10020114); Ph. D. Startup Foundation of Dalian Nationalities University under Grant (No. 20096203).

References

1. Chen, L.: Discrete Mathematics Teaching Reform and Practice. Journal of Inner Mongolia (2004)
2. Feng, M.: Discrete Mathematics Course Teaching Practice and Explore. Computer Education (2004)
3. Richardson, V.: Constructivist Teacher Education. The Falmer Press (1997)
4. Kang, H.K.: Modern Education Technology and Innovation Person Cultivation, http://www.eol.cn/20010829/209325.shtml
5. Laixin, S., Fan, Y.: Inquiring into Experimental Teaching of Discrete Mathematics. Journal of Huangshan University (2009)
6. Jiang, G.-l.: Exploration on Discrete Mathematics Teaching Methods. Modern Computer (2010)

Composition and Extended Method of Information Grid

Li Hao[1], ZhongShan Yang[1], and YueHong Zhang[2]

[1] Xi'an Communications Institute, 710106, Xi-an city, China
[2] Air force second flight Institute, 710306, Xi-an city, China
haolilii@163.com, xtyyang@126.com, xazyh@163.com

Abstract. This content provides an overarching introduction to the field of information grid (IG). It examines the emerging context and rationale for IG, the implications and benefits of IG for compositions, and the current understanding of the IG concept itself. The aim is to provide a broad theoretical basis for exploring the role of technology in IG and to set the scene for the remaining contents of the paper.

Keywords: Composition, Extended method, Information grid, concept.

1 Introduction

The growing interest in information grid has been fuelled by a number of development trends: globalisation with the increasing intensity of competition; virtualisation or digitalisation enabled by advances in information and communication technology; and the transformation to information based economy together with changing compositional structures, new worker profiles, preferences and predispositions. This new emerging world is variously referred to as third wave, information age, information-based or information economy or society. Regardless of the terminology, these names, and others, refer to the transition that is taking place in the business environment.

As compositions move towards becoming more information-based, their business success will increasingly depend on how successful information workers are at developing and applying information productively and efficiently. The ability to identify and leverage key information plays a critical role in compositional survival and advancement. Consequently, the companies are facing the need to improve the management of their information.

The basic assumption of IG is that compositions that manage compositional and individual information better will deal more successfully with the challenges of the new business environment. More specifically, information grid is considered to be central to achieving process and product improvement, executive decision making and compositional adaptation and renewal. The central task of those concerned with information grid is to determine ways to better cultivate, nurture and exploit information at different levels and in different contexts.

S. Lin and X. Huang (Eds.): CSEE 2011, Part V, CCIS 218, pp. 273–276, 2011.
© Springer-Verlag Berlin Heidelberg 2011

2 Drivers of IG

The transformation from the old economy to a new, information-based economy, is driven largely by the recognition that information rather than financial capital, land or labour is the major source of continued economic growth, value and improved standards of living.

Economic progress throughout history has been driven by commerce and business compositions. These compositions have internal structures that mediate roles and relationships among people working towards some identifiable goal. Their existence is the result of a successful balance between the forces in their environment and their own creativity and adaptivity. Currently, at the forefront of compositional performance are the compositions which recognised that information, information and their intelligent application are the essential factors of success in the new economy, and take advantage of information technology to achieve high level of efficiency and effectiveness. Various metaphors used to describe a information composition include: agile production system, living organism, complex adaptive system, selforganising system and virtual composition.

The information composition can be best viewed as an intelligent complex adaptive system. It is complex because the system is composed of a large number of individual specialists called intelligent agents, who have multiple and complex relationships with the system and environment. It is adaptive because these intelligent agents direct and discipline their own performance through organised feedback from colleagues, customers and headquarters. It has been suggested in the literature (Bennet and Bennet, 2003) that a successful information composition exhibits the following characteristics: high performance, customer-driven, improvement-driven, high flexibility and adaptiveness, high levels of expertise and information, high rates of learning and innovation, innovative IT-enabled, self-directed and managed, proactive and futurist, valuing expertise and sharing information.

One of the ways to achieve effective information creation, transfer and utilisation within an composition is through communities of practice. This approach to compositional structuring advocates the formation of centres of expertise for each information domain, discipline or subject matter speciality. The alternative approach suggests organising around projects and related activities. Information and communication technology can be the catalyst to form and sustain heterogeneous communities. With the support of the intranet or internet, these communities can include diverse people from different space and time zones of the globe.

While information technology is not necessary to create a information composition, the use of advanced technologies can transform the way the whole business works. The concept of 'cybercorp' has been heralded as the new business revolution. It is envisaged as a totally virtual composition based on the capabilities of the modern communication, i.e., the internet and the mobile phone. Typically, a virtual composition consists of three fundamental parts: information professionals and workers who possess core competencies; relationships and networks of people including partners, suppliers and customers grouped around a common brand; and a culture based on co-operation and collaboration and sitting in the centre of global networks linked electronically.

3 Outcomes of IG

The importance of IG for compositional performance has been widely recognised and acinformationd in the management literature. In general, IG is assumed to create value for compositions from applying their accumulated information to their products and services outputs. These ensure compositional survival or advancement. IG can impact compositional performance in a number of different ways, these can be grouped into three broad categories: risk minimisation, efficiency improvement and innovation.

IG can also impact people's learning, adaptability and job satisfaction. For example, IG can facilitate employees'creativity and group effectiveness through informal and formal socialisation. Socialisation forms a vital component of information creation model. It enables tacit information to be transferred between individuals through shared experience, space and time. Examples include spending time, working together or informal social meetings. More importantly, socialisation drives the creation and growth of personal tacit information bases. By seeing other people's perspective and ideas, a new interpretation of what one knows is created. Efficiency and Effectiveness Improvement.

IG can also help compositions become more effective by helping them select and perform the most appropriate processes and make the best possible decisions. IG can help compositions to avoid repeating past mistakes, foresee potential problems and reduce the need to modify plans. For example, The Australian Government responded to increasing community expectations of better social services and access to empowering information sources by integrating historically separate health, housing and community services via a virtual corporate environment. The outcome is that various community and service providers have been given equitable and wide-spread access to expert information and can directly contact the right people for service delivery.

Process and Product Innovation.

4 IG Methods

There have been a number of recent efforts at developing IG methods to better understand IG phenomena. In order to make sense of the variety of existing IG methods, some form of categorisation or grouping is needed. One way to group them is into partial and integrated models or ontologies.

Partial IG Methods

The information creation spiral of Nonaka views compositional information creation as a process involving a continual interplay between explicit and tacit dimensions of information. Four levels of carriers of information in the composition area are assumed, namely individual, group, compositional and inter-compositional. The spiral model describes a dynamic process in which explicit and tacit information are exchanged and transformed through four modes: socialisation, combination, externalisation and internalisation.

Much IG work within the field of Information Systems, makes the distinction between information as an object that can be stored in a computerised system, and information embedded in people. This group of models or methods address issues of complexity and change in areas of compositional culture and learning, change and risk management and the support of communities of practice. Methods in this IG grouping also emphasise the dependence of information on context.

Integrated IG Methods

There have been a number of attempts to bring together this diversity of partial approaches and propose more comprehensive and integrated methods in order to provide holistic views and common ground for IG research, and improved methods for IG practice (for review see Handzic and Hasan, 2003). The IG method is an extended version of the original model. It illustrates various components involved in the conduct of information grid and their relationships. This method is used as a basis for examining the role of technology in IG in the later contents of this paper.

5   Conclusions

This content examines the main drivers, outcomes and conceptualisations of IG in order to set the scene and provide theoretical foundation for exploring the role of technology in IG. The content recognises that IG is fuelled by the changing nature of the business environment. The emerging environment is identified as global, directly based on the production, distribution and use of information in the development and distribution of products and services, and heavily reliant on information and communication technology.

This content also recognises that IG contributes to compositional performance in many ways. It impacts people, processes, products and structures in attempting to minimise risk, improve efficiency and effectiveness, and create innovative processes or products. In this way, IG provides sustainable competitive advantages that ensure the composition's survival or advancement.

Finally, this content promotes the view of IG as a dynamic phenomenon with an emphasis on information processes in expanding cycles of information growth. IG is considered as a socio-technical undertaking enabled and facilitated by a variety of social, compositional and technical factors. which must be considered in any IG initiative. Finally, IG is recognised as being severely dependent on context so that there is no 'one size fits all'solution.

References

1. Adrion, W., Branstad, M., Cherniavsky, J.: Validation,Verification, and Testing of Computer Software. ACM Computing Surveys 14(2), 159–192 (1982)
2. Apache Software Foundation. Apache Tomcat 6.0. (2006),
   http://tomcat.apache.org/tomcat-6.0-doc/index.html
   (accessed on September 2007)
3. Apache Software Foundation. Web Services – Axis, Client-side Axis (2005),
   http://ws.apache.org/axis/java/client-side-axis.html
   (accessed on September 2007)
4. Beizer, B.: Software Testing Techniques, 2nd edn. Van Nostrand Reinhold, New York (1990)
5. Cohen, J., Plakosh, D., Keeter, K.: Robustness Testing of Software-Intensive Systems: Explanation and Guide. Technical Note CMU/SEI-2005-TN-015, Software Engineering Institute, Carnegie Mellon University, PA, USA (2005)
6. Ferris, C., Farrell, J.: What Are Web Services? Communications of the ACM 46(6), 31 (2003)

The Information Resources Composition

Mao Yan

Department of Computer Science,
Xi'an University of Arts and Science
amao0010@sina.com

Abstract. Information organization, evaluation, refinement and derivation. Information should be organized normally to obtain high retrieval efficiency and ensure the correctness of operations. The Information Resources should be able to eliminate redundant information and refine information so that useful information can be increased. It can also derive new information from existing well-represented information, from case histories, and from raw information material like text. Information integration. Integrating information resources at different levels and in different domains could support cross-domain analogies, problem solving, and scientific discovery. In this paper, we represented the service characteristics, strategies of the Information Resources.

Keyword: Information Resources, Web service, concept, Computing Platform.

1 Introduction

The capturing and expressing of services involves complex psychological and cognitive processes. The exploitation of psychology, cognitive science and philosophy plays an important role in studying services---the basis for information sharing.The Information Resources methodology is a multi-disciplinary system methodology for establishing a global information world that obeys the principles and laws of economics, nature, society, psychology and information technology. Implementation of the Information Resources winformation speed up the development of human civilization.

2 Towards the Next-Generation Web

The Internet and the World Wide Web are milestones of information technology. People have become increasingly reliant on them for supporting modern work and life. For example, scientists can communicate with each other using net forums and email, share their experimental data and research results by posting them in Web pages on personal or corporate websites, and retrieve technical reports and academic papers of interest to them from online digital libraries or from less formal websites using general-purpose search engines.

But the exponential growth and intrinsic characteristics of the Web and its pages prevent people from effectively and efficiently sharing information. Much effort has been put into solving this problem with but limited success. In any case it is hard for

S. Lin and X. Huang (Eds.): CSEE 2011, Part V, CCIS 218, pp. 277–281, 2011.

the Web to provide intelligent services because the representation used by the current Web does not support the inclusion of service information.

With the development of communication facilities and Web applications, computing is struggling to extend its support from individual to group and social behavior, from closed to open systems, from simple and centralized to complex and distributed computing, and from static computing to dynamic and mobile information, computing and information services.

3   Service Problems of the Internet Age

Information acquisition is the bottleneck of information engineering. Data mining approaches help a bit by automatically discovering information (associztion rules) in large-scale databases. These approaches can also be used to discover service relationships within and between texts.

Why were the symbolic approaches, especially the KIF and OKBC of AI, and ODBC in the database area, not widely adopted in the Internet age?

One cause is the success of HTML, which is easy to use both for a writer and, in cooperation with a browser, for a reader. Its main advantage is that "anything can link to anything".

A second cause is that traditional AI's information representation approaches try to explicate human information, while the Web focuses on structuring Web resources and the relationship between resources, that is, it is more concerned with services.

A third cause is that cooperation between machines (applications) has become the dominant aim in realizing intelligent Web applications, while traditional information engineering focuses on cooperation between human and machine.

A fourth cause is the cross-platform requirement. Consequently XML has been adopted as the information exchange standard of the Web.

4   Strategies

The Information Resources methodology should adopt the principles and rules of social science, economics, psychology, biology, ecology and physics, and inherit the fundamental ideas, views, rules and principles of system science.

4.1   Strategies

The following strategies could help develop the Information Resources as a future interconnection environment.

The fusion of inheritance and innovation - the Information Resources environment should absorb the advantages of the Resources, the Web service, and Web Services. Current Web applications should be able to work in the new environment. Smooth development would enable the future Web to exploit research on the current Web.

The fusion of centralization and decentralization – Advantage should be taken of both centralization and decentralization. On the one hand, an ideal system should be able to dynamically cluster and fuse relevant resources to provide complete and on-demand services for applications. On the other hand, it should be able to deploy the appropriate resources into the appropriate locations to achieve optimized computing.

The fusion of abstraction and specialization - On the one hand, we need to abstract a variety of resources to investigate common rules, and on the other hand, to investigate the special rules of different resources to properly integrate and couple resources.

The fusion of mobility and correctness - On the one hand, the Information Resources should support mobile applications to meet the needs of ubiquitous applications. On the other hand, we should guarantee the quality of services and the means of verification.

The fusion of symbolic and connectionist approaches – Current concept only uses the symbolic approach, which is very similar to traditional information base construction. The combination of the symbolic approach and the connectionist approach would help find better solutions for intelligent applications.

5   Characteristics of the Information Resources

5.1   Distinctive Characteristics of the Information Resources

(1) Single service entry point access to worldwide information. In the Information Resources environment, people could access information distributed around the world from a single service access entry point without needing to know where the required information is.

(2) Intelligently clustered, fused and distributed information. In the Information Resources environment, related information distributed around the world could intelligently cluster together and fuse to provide appropriate on-demand information services with underlying reasoning and explanation. So information providers should include meta-information (information about how to use information), and could use a kind of uniform resource model to encapsulate the provided information and meta-information to realize active and clustered information services.

(3) Single service image. The Information Resources environment could enable people to share information and to enjoy reasoning services in a single service space where there are no barriers to mutual understanding and pervasive information sharing.

(4) Worldwide complete information service. The Information Resources could gather information from all regions of the world and provide succinct and complete information relevant to the solution of particular problems. To achieve this goal, we need to create a new information organization model.

(5) Dynamic evolution of information. In the Information Resources environment, information would not be just statically stored, but would evolve to keep up-to-date.

5.2   The Information Resources's General Research Issrces

(1) Theories, models, methods and mechanisms for supporting information capture and representation. The Information Resources should be able to help people or

virtual roles effectively capture, and conveniently publish information in a machine-processable form that could directly, or after simple transformation, be understood by humans. We should build an open set of service primitives to help information representation. These primitives should be able to represent multi-granular information. The capture of information here has two meanings: one is when people learn from each other directly, or from the resources published by others, and then publish new information on the Information Resources; the other is when the Information Resources gets information from numeric, textual or image resources by mining, induction, analogy, deduction, synthesizing, and so on.

(2) Information display and creation. These come mainly through an intelligent user interface (for example, a service or information browser) that enables people to share information with each other in a visual way. The service link network and the cognitive map are two ways to depict information. The interface should implement the distinctive characteristics of the Information Resources and be able to inspire people's discovery of information through analogy and induction.

(3) Propagation and management of information within virtual organizations. This could eliminate redundant communication between team members to achieve effective information management in a cooperative virtual team. Information flow management is a way to achieve information sharing in a virtual team.

(4) Information organization, evaluation, refinement and derivation. Information should be organized normally to obtain high retrieval efficiency and ensure the correctness of operations. The Information Resources should be able to eliminate redundant information and refine information so that useful information can be increased. It can also derive new information from existing well-represented information, from case histories, and from raw information material like text. Information integration. Integrating information resources at different levels and in different domains could support cross-domain analogies, problem solving, and scientific discovery.

(5) Abstraction. It is a challenge to automatically capture services from a variety of resources, to make abstractions, and to reason and explain in a uniform service space. The service constraints and rules of abstraction ensure the validity of resource usage at the service level.

(6) Scalable network platform. The Information Resources should enable a user, a machine or a local network to freely join in and leave without affecting its performance and services. It is a challenging task to organize and integrate information within a dynamic network platform.

6   Conclusion

In the Information Resources, new information can be derived from: existing information, users' feedback, and mining in medical textbooks, papers and other related sources. people can also choose to provide symptoms of their disease through a single service entry point when accessing the Information Resources to obtain instant consulting service. The result may include several candidate processing selected by considering such factors as cost, waiting time, skinformation level, transportation, and so on. Similar advantages of the Information Resources also exist in scientific research, business, education and other application domains.

References

1. ABS, Science and Technology Statistics Update, Australian Bureau of Statistics Bulletin, No. 9 (December 2003)
2. Alavi, M., Leidner, D.E.: Information Management and Information Management Systems: Conceptual Foundations and Research Issues. MIS Quarterly 25(1), 107–136 (2001)
3. Becerra-Fernandez, I., Gonzales, A., Sabherwal, R.: Information Management: Challenges, Solutions, and Technologies. Pearson Education, New Jersey (2004)
4. Bennet, D., Bennet, A.: The Rise of the Information Organisation. In: Holsapple, C.W. (ed.) Handbook on Information Management, vol. 1, pp. 5–20. Springer, Berlin (2003)
5. Burnes, B.: Managing Change—A Strategic Approach to Organisational Dynamics. Pearson Education, Harlow (2000)
6. Bollinger, A.S., Smith, R.D.: Managing Organisational Information as a Strategic Asset. Journal of Information Management 5(1), 8–18 (2001)
7. Earl, M.: 'Information Management Strategies: Toward a Taxonomy. Journal of Management Information Systems 18(1), 215–233 (2001)
8. Edwards, J., Handzic, M., Carlsson, S., Nissen, M.: Information Management Research and Practice: Visions and Directions. Information Management Research & Practice 1(1), 49–60 (2003)
9. Edwards, J.S.: Managing Software Engineers and Their Information. In: Aurum, et al. (eds.) Managing Software Engineering Information, ch. 1, pp. 5–27. Springer, Berlin (2003)
10. Frank, B.: Five Tips to Reduce Information Loss. Thought & Practice. The Journal of the KM Professional Society (KMPro), 1–3 (December 2002)
11. Garvin, D.A.: Building a Learning Organisation, Harvard Business Review on Information Management, pp. 47–80. HBS Press, Boston (1998)

Expansibility and Diversity of Network Coordinate Process System

Chaoyong Jiang

Department of computer science of Guangdong Polytechnic Normal University
GuangZhou city Guangdong Province China
1978119@163.com

Abstract. Expansibility is the ability of the coordinate process system to operate efficiently and with the desired quality of Web service when its setting changes in a broad range. Expansibility of a coordinate process system can be considered separately for each expansibility standard or as a function of a few standards. In this paper,we give the ideal dependence of the expansibility standard about a coordinate process system. The difference between the ideal dependence of the given expansibility standard and its actual behavior will tell the system designer how it is efficient with respect to this standard. we give the simultaneous and diversity properties in the coordinate process systems.

Keywords: coordinate process, diversity, Web service, expansibility.

1 Communicating Processes of a Coordinate Process System

We define a coordinate process system as a system consisting of a set of autonomous processes which are involved in the execution of a common information processing task and coordinate their operations with the use of messages transmitted between the processes through a communication network. The most important aspects of this definition are a set of processes (with at least two processes in the set), a common task performed in a coordinated way by the processes, and the transmission of messages between the processes to exchange data and coordination information. The last aspect generally implies that the processes run at different nodes of a communication network and are thus geographically coordinate process. As a communication network, any appropriate type of communication system is implied, including a computer network.

A good example of a system that is logically equivalent to a coordinate process system with respect to the given definition is the construction of a building by a group of builders with a master person. Indeed, builders and their master correspond to processes. The builders perform a common task — the creation of a building. During the creation, the builders communicate with each other and exchange different construction materials. This corresponds to exchange of data between processes and their self-coordination. The master person coordinates the whole work of builders by sending them related information on the architecture of the building. Finally, a communication network is presented here by air to speak directly or by a telephone network.

S. Lin and X. Huang (Eds.): CSEE 2011, Part V, CCIS 218, pp. 282–286, 2011.

Communication between processes in a coordinate process system is fundamentally important. Patterns and characteristics of the communication (such as message delay and its variance, loss of messages, their duplication, and reordering during the transmission) usually define the complexity of a theoretical analysis and of a practical implementation of the corresponding coordinate process system. This complexity increases even more if the underlying communication network can become partitioned, which results in division of the set of processes of the given coordinate process system into a few groups, without any communication connects between each other. Quite often, in the design of a coordinate process application, it is assumed that the communication between involved processes is perfect. However, this is not true for real-world communication networks, even for small local area computer networks. As a result, the design can have only a theoretical value and needs to be considerably complicated to take into consideration the actual characteristics of the underlying communication network for a practical implementation.

It is assumed, in our definition of a coordinate process system, that involved processes communicate explicitly by exchanging messages between each other. This corresponds to the message-passing model of coordinate process systems. There is another general model of coordinate process systems, a shared-memory model. According to this model, processes communicate via a shared-memory subsystem that serves as a meeting place for processes to exchange data and coordination information. Although in this model processes communicate indirectly, without explicit transmissions of messages between each other, they need to use some messaging mechanism for accessing the shared memory. In this paper, we will focus on coordinate process systems that are organized and function according to the message-passing model.

2   Expansibility of Coordinate Process Systems

There are a number of desired goals in the design and implementation of coordinate process systems. These goals include but are not limited to achievable performance, reliability, consistency, transparency, and security. Performance is a measure of the system's efficiency with respect to characteristics such as a response time for a user and the overall throughput. Reliability characterizes the ability of the coordinate process system to function under different types of failures in its components and underlying computer network. Consistency shows whether the system can maintain correct values of shared information objects when they are accessed concurrently by more than one process. This is a known problem of race condition in centralized systems. Transparency is the ability of the coordinate process system to hide its different internal aspects from the user, so that the user could perceive the coordinate process system as one large virtual centralized information processing machine. The last goal in the above given list is security that characterizes the resistance of the system to different attacks at its structure, functions, and resources.

One more goal in the design of any coordinate process system, that is the focus of this section, is expansibility. Expansibility is the ability of the coordinate process system to operate efficiently and with the desired quality of Web service when its setting changes in a broad range. The term "setting" can mean here the number of participating processes, the values of some critical parameters of the system, a protocol to exchange messages between processes, the size of messages, or values of used time-outs. It is quite customary to say about the system size instead of its setting. Usually expansibility of any system is expressed in terms of one or a few expansibility standards. The types of these standards depend on the system. A good example of a expansibility standard for multiprocessor systems is the computation speedup achieved by a number of identical processors, working in parallel, in comparison with the computation time done by one processor. This speedup can be defined by the known Amdahl's law. It is assumed, for the underlying model of computation that any computation consists of two parts—a part that can be done only sequentially by one processor and a part that can be performed by a number of processors in parallel, with the corresponding decrease of the computation time.

In general, the "size" of a coordinate process system is usually multidimensional. It can include not only the number of participating processes, but also types of topologies and communication connects of the underlying networks, the computational resources of network nodes, and used communication protocols. For this reason, expansibility analysis of coordinate process systems in a general case can be a very challenging task.

Some researchers advocate the use of a combined expansibility standard as a function of individual standards and operational characteristics of the system.

3 Simultaneous and Diversity Coordinate Process Systems

The stated definition of a simultaneous coordinate process system is too restrictive. In addition, it does not take into account the effect of the communication system used by processes to exchange messages.

Obviously, processes in a sufficiently large real-world coordinate process system running on different machines and communicating through real, imperfect connects cannot be synchronized exactly. Therefore, no real simultaneous coordinate process system seems to be possible with respect to the stated definition.

In subsequent years, a few relaxed definitions of simultaneous and diversity coordinate process systems were introduced. A coordinate process system is simultaneous if it satisfies the following two properties:

(1) There is a known upper bound d on delivery of messages from one process to another through some communication network. This time includes the durations of transmission of the message into the network at the source node, transportation of the message in the network between the source and destination nodes, and receiving of the message from the network at the destination node. This bound is known to all involved processes.

(2) There is a known upper bound on the time required by every involved process to execute a step of its work. Actually, this property is related to the running speed of the process and puts a limit on the duration of interval necessary for every involved process to perform a unit of work.

Thus, this definition explicitly takes into account delay in passing messages between processes and does not require that all processes are strictly synchronized. They can use their own local hardware clocks, without any synchronization, and progress with different speeds in their work. All what is necessary for a designer to implement his system as a coordinate process simultaneous system is upper bounds on message delivery time between any pair of involved processes, drift rate of local clocks, and speed of processes.

According to another definition of a coordinate process system is considered simultaneous if the following assumptions hold:

(1) There is an upper bound δ on all communication delays in the underlying network. Note that δ is generally not the maximal delivery time of messages between pairs of processes as in the definition of Hadzilacos and Toueg. However, knowing the topology of the network, with its communication connects and communication processors on the path between two processes, it is possible to determine the delivery time of messages between these processes.

(2) There is an upper bound s on all scheduling delays for involved processes. This assumption is similar to property 3 in the definition of Hadzilacos and Toueg.

(3) The involved processes in the coordinate process system and supporting communication connects and communication processors in the network can fail, but the number of faulty components in the system has a known upper bound f.

(4) The underlying communication network has a sufficiently large number of redundant paths between any two alive processes p_i and p_j, so that each message diffused by p_i is always delivered to p_j, despite up to f faulty components. It is assumed that process p_i diffuses a message to process p_j by sending copies of the message on all available paths between p_i and p_j. Thus, the communication between processes is assumed to be reliable.

(5) The rate at which diffusions are initiated is limited by used flowcontrol methods. It is assumed to be smaller than the rate at which processes and intermediate components can receive and handle diffusion messages.

4   Conclusion

A coordinate process system that has the some properties can serve a sufficiently realistic model of real-world coordinate process systems. In particular, these properties are characteristic for the Internet considered as a huge system of coordinate process applications. This definition will be used in our models of coordinate process algorithms and protocols intended for the operation in timed diversity systems.

References

1. Rigney, C., Willens, S., Rubens, A., Simpson, W.: Remote Authentication Dia. User Web service (RADIUS), RFC 2865 (June 2000)
2. Calhoun, P., Loughney, J., Guttman, E., Zorn, G., Arkko, J.: Diameter Base Protocol, RFC 3588 (September 2003)

3. Whiting, D., Housley, R., Ferguson, N.: Counter with CBC-MAC (CCM), RFC 3610 (September 2003)
4. Zhou, L., Haas, Z.J.: Securing Ad hoc networks. IEEE Network Magazine 13(6) (November/December 1999)
5. Luo, H., Lu, S.: Ubiquitous and robust authentication Web services for ad hoc wireless networks. In: Proceedings of 7th IEEE Symposium on Computers and Communications (July 2002)
6. Keoh, S.L., Lupu, E.: Towards flexible credential verification in mobile ad-hoc networks. In: Proceedings of the Second ACM International Workshop on Principles of Mobile Computing Toulouse, POMC 2002, France (October 2002)
7. Kong, J., Zerfos, P., Luo, H., Lu, S., Zhang, L.: Providing robust and ubiquitous security support for MANET. In: Proc. IEEE ICNP, pp. 251–260 (2001)
8. Junaid, M., Mufti, M., Umar Ilyas, M.: Vulnerabilities of IEEE 802.11i Wireless LAN CCMP Protocol. Transactions on Engineering, Computing and Technology 11 (February 2006)
9. Aboudagga, N., Refaei, M.T., Eltoweissy, M., DaSilva, L.A.: Authentication protocols for ad hoc networks: taxonomy and research issues. In: Proceedings of the 1st ACM International Workshop on Quality of Web service and Security in Wireless and Mobile Networks (Q2Swinet 2005), Montreal, Quebec, Canada (October 2005)
10. Deng, H., Mukherjee, A., Agrawal, D.P.: Threshold and identity-based key management and authentication for wireless ad hoc networks. In: Proceedings of International Conference on Information Technology: Coding and Computing (ITCC 2004), vol. 1, pp. 107–111 (April 2004)

Periodic Solution of First-Order Impulsive Differential Equation Based on Data Analysis

Lianhua He[1] and Anping Liu[2]

[1] School of Mathematics and Computer Science, Gui zhou Normal University,
Guiyang, 550001, China
[2] School of Mathematics and Physics, China University of Geosciences, Wuhan, 430074, China
hlh1981@126.coml, wh_apliu@sina.com

Abstract. In this paper, the existence and uniqueness of periodic solution of first order impulsive differential equation is investigated on the Banach space PC(J) using the new method of iterative analysis which is introduced by Mengxing He and Anping Liu in the paper[9]. Base on the iterative sequence of the equation, we obtain the existence and uniqueness of periodic solution of first order impulsive differential equation and the norm estimation of the solution on the Banach space PC(J).

Keywords: Iterative analysis, Periodic solution, Existence, Impulses.

1 Introduction

Impulsive differential equations are basic instruments to study the dynamics of process that are subjected to abrupt changes in their states. Recent development in this field has been motivated by many applied problems, such as control theory, population dynamics and medicine. In this paper, we study the periodic solution of the first order differential equation with impulses:

$$\begin{cases} x'(t) + \lambda x(t) = f(t,x) + e(t) & t > 0, \ t \neq t_k \\ \Delta x(t_k) = x(t_k^+) - x(t_k^-) = I_k(x(t_k)) & k = 1,2,\cdots \quad (1.1) \\ x(0) = x_0 \end{cases}$$

Here $\lambda \in R$, and $\lambda \neq 0$, $x(t_k^+)$, $x(t_k^-)$ exist and $x(t_k) = x(t_k^-)$. Throughout this paper, we assume that:

(A_1) $0 < t_1 < t_2 < t_3 < \cdots < t_k < \cdots$, $\lim\limits_{k \to \infty} t_k = +\infty$; (A_2) $e(t)$ is continuous,

T-periodic function;

(A_3) $f : (0, +\infty) \times R \to R$ is continuous and $f(t+T, x) = f(t, x)$;

(A_4) $I_k : R \to R$ are continuous, and there exists a positive integer q such that

$$t_{k+q} = t_k + T \ , \ I_{k+q}(x) = I_k(x).$$

S. Lin and X. Huang (Eds.): CSEE 2011, Part V, CCIS 218, pp. 287–292, 2011.
© Springer-Verlag Berlin Heidelberg 2011

During the last two decades, impulsive differential equations have been studied by many authors [1-3]. Some classical tools have been used to study such problems in the literature. These classical technique include the coincidence degree theory of Mawhin [4], the method of upper and lower solutions [5,6] and some fixed point theorems [7]. In [8, 9], the author used a new method (iterative analysis method) to obtain the existence of solution of functional differential equation. And in [10-12], by the iterative analysis method, the author got the existence of periodic solution of first-order differential equation without impulses or without $e(t)$. In this paper, we use this method to consider the existence of periodic solution for system (1.1).

The organization of this paper is as follows. In Section 2, we introduce some notations and definitions, and state some hypotheses needed in later section. We then study, in Section 3, the existence of periodic solution of system (1.1) by iterative analysis method.

2 Preliminaries

Consider the impulsive systems:

$$\begin{cases} x'(t) = g(t,x) & t > 0, \ t \neq t_k \\ \Delta x(t_k) = I_k(x(t_k)) & k = 1, 2, \cdots \end{cases} \tag{2.1}$$

where $x(t_k^+)$, $x(t_k^-)$ exist and $x(t_k) = x(t_k^-)$, $\Delta x(t_k) = x(t_k^+) - x(t_k^-)$. $g(t,x)$: $[0,+\infty) \times R \to R$ is continuous and $g(t+T, x) = g(t,x)$. $I_k : R \to R$ are continuous, and there exists a positive integer q such that $t_{k+q} = t_k + T$, $I_{k+q}(x) = I_k(x)$ with $t_k \in [0,+\infty)$, $t_{k+1} > t_k$ $\lim_{k \to \infty} t_k = +\infty$. For $t_k \neq 0 \ (k = 1, 2, \cdots)$, $[0,T] \cap \{t_k\} = \{t_1, t_2, \cdots, t_q\}$.

Let us recall some definitions. For the Cauchy problem:

$$\begin{cases} x'(t) = g(t,x) & t \in (0,T], \ t \neq t_k; \\ \Delta x(t_k) = I_k(x(t_k)) & k = 1, 2, \cdots, q. \\ x(0) = x_0 \end{cases} \tag{2.2}$$

Definition 2.1: A map $x : [0,T] \to R$ is said to be a solution of (2.2), if it satisfies the following conditions:

(i) $x(t)$ is a piecewise continuous map with first-class discontinuity points in $[0,T] \cap \{t_k\}$, and at each discontinuity point it is continuous on the left;

(ii) $x(t)$ satisfies (2.2).

Definition 2.2: A map $x : [0,+\infty) \to R$ is said to be an T-periodic solution of (2.1), if

(i) $x(t)$ satisfies (i) and (ii) of Definition 2.1 in the interval $[0,T]$;

(ii) $x(t)$ satisfies $x(t+T-0)=x(t-0), t>0$.

Obviously, if $x(t)$ is a solution of (2.2) defined on $[0,T]$, such that $x(T)=x(0)$ then by the periodicity of (2.2) in t, the function $x^*(t)$ defined by

$$x^*(t) = \begin{cases} x(t-nT) & t\in[nT,(n+1)T]\setminus\{t_k\}, \\ x^*(t) \text{ is left continuous at } t=t_k. \end{cases}$$

is a T-periodic solution of (2.1).

For the system (1.1) finding the periodic solutions is equivalent to finding solutions of the following boundary-value problem:

$$\begin{cases} x'(t)+\lambda x(t) = f(t,x)+e(t) & t\in(0,T], \ t\neq t_k; \\ \Delta x(t_k) = x(t_k^+)-x(t_k^-)=I_k(x(t_k)) & k=1,2,\cdots,q. \\ x(0)=x_0 \end{cases} \qquad (2.3)$$

Let $J=[0,T]$, $PC(J)$ denotes the class of the map $x: J\to R$ such that $x(t)$ is continuous at $t\neq t_k$, and left continuous at $t=t_k$, the right limit $x(t_k^+)$ exists for $k=1,2,\cdots,q$. Note that $PC(J)$ is a Banach space with the norm $\|x\|_{PC}=\sup\{|x(t)|:t\in J\}$.

The following are the basic hypotheses:

(H_1) $f(t,0)=0$ and there exists an $L(t)>0$, $L(t)\in L^1[0,T]$ such that $|f(t,x_1)-f(t,x_2)|\leq L(t)|x_1-x_2|$;

(H_2) $I_k(0)=0$ and there exist $q_k>0$ such that $|I_k(x_1)-I_k(x_2)|\leq q_k|x_1-x_2|$.

We denote $A=\dfrac{1}{1-e^{-|\lambda|T}}\displaystyle\int_0^T L(s)ds$, $B=\dfrac{1}{1-e^{-|\lambda|T}}\displaystyle\int_0^T |e(s)|ds$, $C=A+\dfrac{1}{1-e^{-|\lambda|T}}\displaystyle\sum_{k=1}^q q_k$.

(H_3) $0<C<1$.

3 Main Results

Lemma 3.1: Let $x(t)$ be a soution of (2.3), then it can be presented as

$$x(t) = \int_0^T G(t,s)(f(s,x(s))+e(s))ds+\sum_{k=1}^q G(t,t_k)I_k(x(t_k)) \quad (t\in[0,T]),$$

where $G(t,s)=\dfrac{1}{1-e^{-\lambda T}}\begin{cases} e^{-\lambda(t-s)}, & 0\leq s\leq t\leq T \\ e^{-\lambda(T+t-s)}, & 0\leq t<s\leq T \end{cases}.$

Proof: Let $t_p < t \le t_{p+1}$,we have $\int_0^t (e^{\lambda s} x(s))' ds = \int_0^t e^{\lambda s} (f(s, x(s)) + e(s)) ds$.

That is $e^{\lambda t_1} x(t_1) - x(0) = \int_0^{t_1} e^{\lambda s} (f(s, x(s)) + e(s)) ds,$

$$e^{\lambda t_2} x(t_2) - e^{\lambda t_1} x(t_1^+) = \int_{t_1}^{t_2} e^{\lambda s} (f(s, x(s)) + e(s)) ds,$$

$$\vdots$$

$$e^{\lambda t} x(t) - e^{\lambda t_p} x(t_p^+) = \int_{t_p}^t e^{\lambda s} (f(s, x(s)) + e(s)) ds.$$

Adding all equalities above together, we obtain

$$x(t) = e^{-\lambda t} x(0) + \int_0^t e^{-\lambda(t-s)} (f(s, x(s)) + e(s)) ds + \sum_{0 < t_k < t} e^{-\lambda(t-t_k)} I_k(x(t_k)) \cdot \qquad (3.1)$$

Taking $t = T$, one has

$$x(0) = \int_0^T \frac{e^{-\lambda(T-s)}}{1 - e^{-\lambda T}} (f(s, x(s)) + e(s)) ds + \sum_{k=1}^q \frac{e^{-\lambda(T-t_k)}}{1 - e^{-\lambda T}} I_k(x(t_k)) \cdot$$

Substituting this value into (3.1), we can get that for every $t \in J$

$$x(t) = \int_0^T \frac{e^{-\lambda(T+t-s)}}{1 - e^{-\lambda T}} (f(s, x(s)) + e(s)) ds + \sum_{k=1}^q \frac{e^{-\lambda(T+t-t_k)}}{1 - e^{-\lambda T}} I_k(x(t_k))$$

$$+ \int_0^t e^{-\lambda(t-s)} (f(s, x(s)) + e(s)) ds + \sum_{0 < t_k < t} e^{-\lambda(t-t_k)} I_k(x(t_k))$$

$$= \int_0^T G(t, s)(f(s, x(s)) + e(s)) ds + \sum_{k=1}^q G(t, t_k) I_k(x(t_k)).$$

Therefore, the proof of Lemma 3.1 is complete.

Theorem 3.2: Suppose that hypotheses (A_1)–(A_4) and (H_1)-(H_3) hold, then the system (2.3) has a unique solution

$$x(t) \text{ on } [0,T], \text{ and } \|x\|_{PC} \le \frac{2A}{1-C} |x_0| + \frac{B}{1-C} . \qquad (3.2)$$

Moreover, the system (1.1) has an T-periodic solution $x(t)$, and $x(t)$ satisfies (3.2).

Proof: We define the iteration

$$\begin{cases} x^{(m)}(t) = \int_0^T G(t, s)(f(s, x^{(m-1)}(s)) + e(s)) ds + \sum_{k=1}^q G(t, t_k) I_k(x^{(m-1)}(t_k)) \\ x^{(0)}(t) = \int_0^T G(t, s)(f(s, x(0)) ds \end{cases}$$

then

$$x^{(0)}(t) \le \int_0^T |G(t,s)| |f(s, x_0) - f(s, 0)| ds \le \frac{1}{1 - e^{-|\lambda| T}} \int_0^T L(s) |x_0| ds , \ \|x^{(0)}\|_{PC} \le A |x_0|,$$

$$x^{(1)}(t) \le \int_0^T |G(t,s)||f(s,x^{(0)}(s))|ds + \int_0^T |G(t,s)||e(s)|ds + \sum_{k=1}^q |G(t,t_k)||I_k(x^{(0)}(t_k))|,$$

$$\le \frac{1}{1-e^{-|\lambda|T}} \int_0^T L(s)|x^{(0)}(s)|ds + \frac{1}{1-e^{-|\lambda|T}} \int_0^T |e(s)|ds + \frac{1}{1-e^{-|\lambda|T}} \sum_{k=1}^q q_k |x^{(0)}(t_k)|$$

$$\|x^{(1)}\|_{PC} \le \frac{1}{1-e^{-|\lambda|T}} \int_0^T L(s)ds \|x^{(0)}\|_{PC} + \frac{1}{1-e^{-|\lambda|T}} \int_0^T |e(s)|ds + \frac{1}{1-e^{-|\lambda|T}} \sum_{k=1}^q q_k \|x^{(0)}\|_{PC}$$

$$= C\|x^{(0)}\|_{PC} + B \le CA|x_0| + B$$

By induction, we can obtain the following inequality for any m

$$\|x^{(m)}\|_{PC} \le \begin{cases} C^m A|x_0| + \dfrac{1-C^m}{1-C}B, & m=1,2,\cdots \\ A|x_0| & m=0 \end{cases}.$$

Then applying inductive method, we can obtain that the follwing inequality holds

$$\|x^{(1)}-x^{(0)}\|_{PC} = \sup_{t\in[0,T]} |x^{(1)}(t)-x^{(0)}(t)| \le \frac{1}{1-e^{-|\lambda|T}} \int_0^T L(s)ds(\|x^{(0)}\|_{PC}+|x_0|)+B+\frac{1}{1-e^{-|\lambda|T}}\sum_{k=1}^q q_k\|x^{(0)}\|_{PC}$$

$$\le (C+1)A|x_0|+B$$

Again, using induction, we can derive

$$\|x^{(m)}-x^{(m-1)}\|_{PC} \le C^{m-1}(C+1)A|x_0|+C^{m-1}B, \quad m=1,2,\cdots,$$

then

$$\|x^{(n+1)}\|_{PC} = \sup_{t\in J} |x^{(n+1)}(t)| \le \sum_{m=1}^{n+1}[C^{m-1}(C+1)A|x_0|+C^{m-1}B]+A|x_0| \le \frac{2A}{1-C}|x_0|+\frac{B}{1-C}$$

For any $p\in N$, $n+p\ge n$, we have

$$|x^{(n+p)}(t)-x^{(n)}(t)| \le \sum_{m=n+1}^{n+p}|x^{(m)}(t)-x^{(m-1)}(t)| \le \sum_{m=n+1}^{n+p}\|x^{(m)}-x^{(m-1)}\|_{PC} \le [(C+1)A|x_0|+B]\frac{C^n}{1-C}.$$

Therefore, sequence $\{x^{(m)}(t)\}$ is uniformly convergent on $[0,T]$, let $\lim_{m\to\infty} x^{(m)}(t)=x(t)$. Obviously, $x(t)$ is a solution of (2.3) which satisfies the inequality (3.2).

It remains to show the uniqueness. Suppose $y(t)$ is another solution of (2.3), then

$$|x(t)-y(t)| \le \frac{1}{1-e^{-|\lambda|T}}\int_0^T L(s)|x(s)-y(s)|ds + \frac{1}{1-e^{-|\lambda|T}}\sum_{k=1}^q q_k|x(t_k)-y(t_k)|$$

$$\|x-y\|_{PC} \le \left(\frac{1}{1-e^{-|\lambda|T}}\int_0^T L(s)ds + \frac{1}{1-e^{-|\lambda|T}}\sum_{k=1}^q q_k\right)\|x-y\|_{PC} = C\|x-y\|_{PC}.$$

It is easy to see that the solution is unique. Therefore, $x(t)$ is a T-periodic solution of (1.1) which satisfies the inequality (3.2). The proof of *Theorem 3.2* is complete.

Acknowledgment. This work is supported by Foundation of the Education Institution of GuiZhou Province (No 20090038).

References

1. Li, Y.K., Lu, L.H.: Physics Letters A 333, 62 (2004)
2. Nieto, J.J.: Appl. Math. Lett. 15, 489 (2002)
3. Nieto, J.J.: Nonl. Anal. 51, 1223 (2002)
4. Liu, Y.: J. Math. Anal. Appl. 327, 435 (2007)
5. Chen, L., Sun, L.: J. Math. Anal. Appl. 318, 726 (2006)
6. Nieto, J.J., Rodriguez-Lopez, R.: J. Math. Anal. Appl. 318, 593 (2006)
7. Li, J., Nieto, J.J., Shen, J.: J. Math. Anal. 325, 226 (2007)
8. He, M.X.: J. Math. Anal. Appl. 199, 842 (1996)
9. He, M.X., Liu, A.P.: Appl. Math. Comput. 132, 489 (2002)
10. Liu, T., He, L.H., Li, Y.L., Tang, Q., Liu, A.P.: Journal of BioMathematics 22, 811 (2007)
11. He, L.H., Tang, Q., Liu, A.P.: Journal of xuzhou normal university 26, 90 (2008)
12. He, L.H., Ma, Q.X., Liu, A.P.: In: Juan, E.G. (ed.) Proceedings 2010 International Conference on Computin g,Control and Industrial Engineering, vol. 2. IEEE Computer Society, Los Alamitos (2010)

Integration Method of Mechanical and Electrical Software Systems

Zhaoyang Peng

Department of machine-electric engineer of
Guangdong Vocational Institute of Science and Technology,
Zhuhai City Guangdong Province China
`pengzhaoyang2005@163.com`

Abstract. When mechanical and electrical software systems are constructed from many components, the organization of the overall system-the mechanical and electrical software architecture-presents a new set of design problems. In this paper, we provide the integration method of mechanical and electrical software architecture. We begin by considering a number of common design styles upon which many systems are currently based and show how different styles can be combined in a single design. Then we present 1 case and 4 solutions to illustrate how architectural representations can improve our understanding of complex mechanical and electrical software systems. The solutions can be compared by tabulating their ability to address the design considerations recorded earlier. A detailed comparison would have to involve consideration of a number of factors concerning the intended use of the system: for example, is it batch or interactive, update-intensive or query-intensive, etc.

Keywords: Mechanical and electrical, software Systems, Design Styles, Integration Method.

1 Introduction

As the size and complexity of mechanical and electrical software systems increases, the design problem goes beyond the algorithms and data structures of the computation: designing and specifying the overall system structure emerges as a new kind of problem. Structural issues include gross organization and global control structure; protocols for communication, synchronization, and data access; assignment of functionality to design elements; physical distribution; composition of design elements; scaling and performance; and selection among design alternatives.

It is increasingly clear that effective mechanical and electrical software engineering requires facility in architectural software design. First, it is important to be able to recognize common paradigms so that high-level relationships among systems can be understood and so that new systems can be built as variations on old systems. Second, getting the right architecture is often crucial to the success of a mechanical and electrical software system design; the wrong one can lead to disastrous results. Third, detailed understanding of software architectures allows the engineer to make principled

S. Lin and X. Huang (Eds.): CSEE 2011, Part V, CCIS 218, pp. 293–298, 2011.

choices among design alternatives. Fourth, an architectural system representation is often essential to the analysis and description of the high-level properties of a complex system.

2 Data Integration Types

The conversion from an intuition to a theory involved understanding

- the mechanical and electrical software structure (which included a representation package with its primitive operators),
- specifications (mathematically expressed as abstract models for algebraic axioms),
- language issues (modules, scope, user-defined types),
- integrity of the result (invariants of data structures and protection from other manipulation),
- rules for integration types (declarations),
- information hiding (protection of properties not explicitly included in specifications).

The effect of this work was to raise the design level of certain elements of mechanical and electrical software systems, namely abstract data types, above the level of programming language statements or individual algorithms. This form of abstraction led to an understanding of a good organization for an entire module that serves one particular purpose.

3 Common Design Styles

To make sense of the differences between styles, it helps to have a common framework from which to view them. The framework we will adopt is to treat an architecture of a specific system as a collection of computational components—or simply components—together with a description of the interactions between these components—the connectors. Graphically speaking, this leads to a view of an abstract architectural description as a graph in which the nodes represent the components and the arcs represent the connectors. As we will see, connectors can represent interactions as varied as procedure call, event broadcast, database queries, and pipes.

An architectural style, then, defines a family of such systems in terms of a pattern of structural organization. More specifically, an architectural style determines the vocabulary of components and connectors that can be used in instances of that style, together with a set of constraints on how they can be combined. These can include topological constraints on architectural descriptions (e.g., no cycles). Other constraints—say, having to do with execution semantics—might also be part of the style definition.

3.1 Software Filters

Pipe and filter systems have a number of nice properties. First, they allow the designer to understand the overall input/output behavior of a system as a simple composition of the behaviors of the individual filters. Second, they support reuse: any two filters can be hooked together, provided they agree on the data that is being transmitted between them. Third, systems can be easily maintained and enhanced: new filters can be added to existing systems and old filters can be replaced by improved ones. Fourth, they permit certain kinds of specialized analysis, such as throughput and deadlock analysis. Finally, they naturally support concurrent execution. Each filter can be implemented as a separate task and potentially executed in parallel with other filters.

But these systems also have their disadvantages. First, pipe and filter systems often lead to a batch organization of processing. Although filters can process data incrementally, since filters are inherently independent, the designer is forced to think of each filter as providing a complete transformation of input data to output data.

3.2 Database Style

In a database style there are two quite distinct kinds of components: a central data structure represents the current state, and a collection of independent components operate on the central data store. Interactions between the database and its external components can vary significantly between systems.

The choice of control discipline leads to major subcategories. If the types of transactions in an input stream of transactions trigger selection of processes to execute, the database can be a traditional database. If the current state of the central data structure is the main trigger of selecting processes to execute, the database can be a blackboard.

The blackboard model is usually presented with three major parts:

The knowledge sources: separate, independent parcels of application-dependent knowledge. Interaction among knowledge sources takes place solely through the blackboard.

The blackboard data structure: problem-solving state data, organized into an application-dependent hierarchy. Knowledge sources make changes to the blackboard that lead incrementally to a solution to the problem.

3.3 Interpreters

In an interpreter organization a virtual machine is produced in mechanical and electrical software. An interpreter includes the pseudo-program being interpreted and the interpretation engine itself. The pseudo-program includes the program itself and the interpreter's analog of its execution state (activation record). The interpretation engine includes both the definition of the interpreter and the current state of its execution. Thus an interpreter generally has four components: an interpretation engine to do the work, a memory that contains the pseudo-code to be interpreted, a representation of the control state of the interpretation engine, and a representation of the current state of the program being simulated.

4 Case Study

We now present six examples to illustrate how architectural principles can be used to increase our understanding of mechanical and electrical software systems. The first example shows how different architectural solutions to the same problem provide different benefits. The second case study summarizes experience in developing a a domain-specific architectural style for a family of industrial products. The third case study examines the familiar compiler architecture in a fresh light. The remaining three case studies present examples of the use of heterogeneous architectures.

4.1 Case Study: Key Word in File

From the point of view of mechanical and electrical software architecture, the problem derives its appeal from the fact that it can be used to illustrate the effect of changes on mechanical and electrical software design. Parnas shows that different problem decompositions vary greatly in their ability to withstand design changes. Among the changes he considers are:

- Enhancement to system function: For example, modify the system so that shifted lines to eliminate circular shifts that start with certain noise words (such as "a", "an", "and", etc.). Change the system to be interactive, and allow the user to delete lines from the original (or, alternatively, from circularly shifted) lists.
- Performance: Both space and time.
- Reuse: To what extent can the components serve as reusable entities.

We now outline four architectural designs for the developed system. All four are grounded in published solutions (including implementations). The first two are those considered in Parnas' original article. The third solution is based on the use of an implicit calling style and represents a variant on the solution. The fourth is a pipeline solution inspired by the Unix index utility.

4.2 Solution 1: Shared Data

The first solution decomposes the problem according to the four basic functions performed: input, shift, alphabetize, and output. These computational components are coordinated as subroutines by a main program that sequences through them in turn. Data is communicated between the components through shared storage ("core storage"). Communication between the computational components and the shared data is an unconstrained read-write protocol. This is made possible by the fact that the coordinating program guarantees sequential access to the data.

Using this solution data can be represented efficiently, since computations can share the same storage. The solution also has a certain intuitive appeal, since distinct computational aspects are isolated in different modules.

4.3 Solution 2: Abstract Data Types

The second solution decomposes the system into a similar set of five modules. However, in this case data is no longer directly shared by the computational components. Instead, each module provides an interface that permits other components to access data only by invoking procedures in that interface. This solution provides the same logical decomposition into processing modules as the first. However, it has a number of advantages over the first solution when design changes are considered. In particular, both algorithms and data representations can be changed in individual modules without affecting others. Moreover, reuse is better supported than in the first solution because modules make fewer assumptions about the others with which they interact.

On the other hand, as discussed by Garlan, Kaiser, and Notkin, the solution is not particularly well-suited to enhancements. The main problem is that to add new functions to the system, the implementor must either modify the existing modules - compromising their simplicity and integrity - or add new modules that lead to performance penalties. (See [7] for a detailed discussion.).

4.4 Solution 3: Implicit Calling

The third solution uses a form of component integration based on shared data similar to the first solution. However, there are two important differences. First, the interface to the data is more abstract. Rather than exposing the storage formats to the computing modules, data is accessed abstractly (for example, as a list or a set).

Second, computations are invoked implicitly as data is modified. Thus interaction is based on an active data model. For example, the act of adding a new line to the line storage causes an event to be sent to the shift module. This allows it to produce circular shifts (in a separate abstract shared data store). This in turn causes the alphabetizer to be implicitly invoked so that it can alphabetize the lines.

This solution easily supports functional enhancements to the system: additional modules can be attached to the system by registering them to be invoked on datachanging events. Because data is accessed abstractly, it also insulates computations from changes in data representation. Reuse is also supported, since the implicitly invoked modules only rely on the existence of certain externally triggered events.

4.5 Solution 4- Pipes and Filters

The fourth solution uses a pipeline solution. In this case there are four filters: input, shift, alphabetize, and output. Each filter processes the data and sends it to the next filter. Control is distributed: each filter can run whenever it has data on which to compute. Data sharing between filters is strictly limited to that transmitted on pipes.

This solution has several nice properties. First, it maintains the intuitive flow of processing. Second, it supports reuse, since each filter can function in isolation (provided upstream filters produce data in the form it expects). New functions are easily added to the system by inserting filters at the appropriate point in the processing sequence.

5 Conclusion

The solutions can be compared by tabulating their ability to address the design considerations itemized earlier. A detailed comparison would have to involve consideration of a number of factors concerning the intended use of the system: for example, is it batch or interactive, update-intensive or query-intensive, etc.

The pipe and filter solution allows new filters to be placed in the stream of text processing. Therefore it supports changes in processing algorithm, changes in function, and reuse. On the other hand, decisions about data representation will be wired into the assumptions about the kind of data that is transmitted along the pipes. Further, depending on the exchange format, there may be additional overhead involved in parsing and unparsing the data onto pipes.

References

1. Denecker, M., Kakas, A.C.: Abduction in logic programming. In: Kakas, A.C., Sadri, F. (eds.) Computational Logic: Logic Programming and Beyond. LNCS (LNAI), vol. 2407, pp. 402–436. Springer, Heidelberg (2002)
2. Moller, R., Haarslev, V., Neumann, B.: Concepts based information finding. In: Proc. IT&KNOWS 1998: International Conference on Information Technology and Knowledge Systems, Vienna, Budapest, August 31 - September 4, vol. 49(6) (1998)
3. Moller, R., Neumann, B.: Ontology-based reasoning techniques for multimediatransformation and finding.In: Semantic Multimedia and Ontologies: Theory and Applications (2007) (to appear)
4. Neumann, B., Moller, R.: On Scene Interpretation with Description Logics. In: Christensen, H.I., Nagel, H.-H. (eds.) Cognitive Vision Systems. LNCS, vol. 3948, pp. 247–275. Springer, Heidelberg (2006)
5. Peraldi, S.E., Kaya, A., Melzer, S., Moller, R., Wessel, M.: Multimedia Transformation as Abduction. In: Proc. DL 2007: International Workshop on Description Logics (2007)
6. Shanahan, M.: Perception as Abduction: Turning Sensor Data Into Meaningful Representation. Cognitive Science 29(1), 103–134 (2005)
7. Thagard, R.P.: The best explanation: Criteria for theory choice. The Journal of Philosophy (1978)
8. Edwards, J., Handzic, M., Carlsson, S., Nissen, M.: Information Management Research and Practice: Visions and Directions. Information Management Research & Practice 1(1), 49–60 (2003)

Research on the Student-Centered Way of Teaching English Based on Web Resources

YanHui Dai and JianKai Zhang

Shijiazhuang Institute of Railway Technology, Sishuichang Road, Qiaodong District,
Shijiazhuang, Hebei, China, 050041
dayan1500@126.com, robert19781218@sina.com

Abstract. The student-centered education requires educators to make class plans standing in students' shoes by taking into account students' interest and needs. Students should be made the center of the class activities while teachers only offer necessary assistance. This thesis introduces the theoretical background of student-centered English classes, makes analysis on the teacher's role in this new way of teaching, and provides some appropriate classroom activities as suggestions. Based on the author's teaching experience, it aims to add some ideas into the discussion on the student-oriented English classes with some usual teaching materials.

Keywords: student-centered English class, theoretical background, teacher's role, classroom activities, teaching material.

1 Introduction

For many years, English teaching in China has followed the way of teachers acting as the center of the class to transfer English knowledge to students, who can only receive the knowledge passively without their own thoughts involved in the process. The result is that students depend highly on their teachers, who seem to be the authority of the class and can seldom be challenged. This way of English teaching leads to the decrease in students' enthusiasm, initiative and creativity in English learning since it treats English as a kind of knowledge instead of a tool for communication. To solve these problems in English teaching and learning, educators must strive to make changes to traditional way of English teaching and create new and scientific teaching methods to stimulate students' enthusiasm and initiative. Hence comes the student-centered way English teaching.

2 Theoretical Background of Student-Centered English Teaching

Tacit Knowledge. As a term initially put forward by Michael Polanyi, tacit knowledge refers, as opposed to explicit knowledge, to knowledge difficult to transfer to other people by means of writing it down or verbalizing it. The distinction between tacit knowledge and explicit knowledge has sometimes been expressed in terms of knowing-how and knowing-what respectively, or in terms of a corresponding

S. Lin and X. Huang (Eds.): CSEE 2011, Part V, CCIS 218, pp. 299–302, 2011.

distinction between embodied knowledge and theoretical knowledge. In this sense, language learning can be taken as a typical example of tacit knowledge. It is impossible to learn a language just by being taught the rules of grammar for actually a native speaker can speaks his language well at a young age almost entirely unaware of the grammar which he may be taught later. So the English language should not be taught as explicit knowledge where teachers pay much attention to teaching the grammar and always force students to memorize English words boringly. According to the theory, the English language can not be taught, but be learned. So students should be made the center of the class to explore the world of the English language themselves.

Constructivism. Founded by Jean Piaget, constructivism is a theory of knowledge arguing that humans generate knowledge and meaning from an interaction between their experiences and their ideas. It means that individuals construct new knowledge from their experiences by incorporating new experience into an already existing framework without changing that framework. When it comes to the teaching process, constructivism believes that students are active learners of knowledge instead of passive receivers and teachers should help students to construct their own knowledge system rather than just transfer knowledge to them. So in English teaching, it will be better if students are placed at the center of the class to learn the language actively while teachers are responsible for providing necessary guidance and assistance.

Humanistic Psychology. Humanistic psychology, represented by Abraham Maslow and Carl Rogers, focuses on each individual's potential and stresses the importance of growth and self-actualization. It minimizes the effects of the unconscious mind, focusing instead on the uniquely human capacity to understand one's place in the world and relationships with others. When humanistic psychology is brought into the field of education, it believes that every normal learner can be self-taught, achieving self-actualization by exploiting his potentials. At the same time, it suggests that study should be meaningful. Besides memorizing and understanding the given materials, learners should be able to choose learning materials themselves from large varieties and make self-evaluations.

3 Role of the English Teacher in Student-Centered English Class

The Guide. As an experienced educator, the English teacher knows well the direction and the objectives of his lesson as well as the laws in English learning. In student-centered English classes, it is the teacher's task to work out a scientific plan of his class based on the understanding of students' needs, make the plan understood by his students, and lead his students to develop along the planned road to achieve the goal set for the purpose of improving students' ability to use English as a language.

The Advisor. In student-centered English classes, students should understand their situation as a language learner, have appropriate learning objectives and make good choices in what is suitable for them to learn. In this case, the teacher should give valuable suggestions to students and provide necessary information and learning materials. To fulfill the function as the advisor, the teacher should first do research to know the different needs of every student, and then help each student to make clear their learning objectives in line with the needs.

The Organizer. As always, the English teacher is the organizer of the class, but in student-centered English classes, it is especially important. The teacher has to consider how to integrate students' language skills with their communicative skills, how to give lessons effectively and efficiently, how to arrange a wide variety of language practice activities, and how to direct students' English learning after class. A good organizer will give students chances to show their English skills and at the same time to check their abilities in mastering the language. In a sense, the teacher resembles the director of a movie, managing the whole teaching process in order to ensure that the teaching activities proceed on the right path.

The Encourager. Students' enthusiasm in learning English can not remain high all the time, especially for those whose English is relatively poor. Some students are afraid of being laughed at for the mistakes they make in speaking English. So the English teacher needs to encourage his students timely or help them overcome their fear in speaking English so as to let them take active part in all the class activities. If well done, the encouragement can increase students' interest in learning English and thus accelerate the speed of English learning and improve the English skills.

4   Typical Classroom Activities in Student-Centered English Class

Pair Work. Pair work is a classroom activity in which the whole class is divided into pairs to finish some assignments. In English class, the purpose of pair work is to improve students' listening and speaking skills by asking them to exchange ideas and opinions with each other. During the process of pair work session, students are speaking and listening and the content of a pair work session is mainly oral, which makes it difficult to give instructions once a pair-work session is underway. So the activity should be well planned and carefully explained; otherwise it is likely to be unproductive. Like classroom work with larger groups, pair work has two major advantages: it offers intensive, realistic practice in speaking and listening; and it promotes a friendly classroom atmosphere that is conducive to learning. But beyond that, pair work has another important advantage that activities done with larger groups do not have. Pair work is an effective way to get everyone in a classroom speaking and listening at the same time. In other words, it is an efficient, productive way of spending precious classroom time.

Group Work. Group work is another classroom activity in which usually 5 to 7 students are teamed up to finish some more complex assignments. It is a form of cooperative learning which aims to cater for individual differences, develop students' knowledge, generic skills including communication skills, collaborative skills, critical thinking skills, and attitudes. The English teacher can provide some issues for group discussion. It is important to note that the issues should have something to do with students or be related to students' college life or their experience. If the issues are not well chosen, students may lose interest in the discussion or even get distracted, which reduces the class to a failure for the goal of the class can not be achieved. In the discussion, different opinions should be welcomed and the teacher should try to improve students' ability of critical thinking. In other cases, the English teacher can design a special situation for the groups and ask each group to act out. The selection of situations should be carried out as the cooperative work of both teacher and students in order to choose situations suitable to and welcomed by the students. The aim of the acting out activities is to improve students' collaborative skills and communication skills.

Classroom Debate. Classroom debate is a rather difficult activity to be held on class, but it is truly worth trying. The topic of a debate should be controversial enough to make students have something to say no matter which side, pro or con, they decide to support. What's more, students should have easy access to the information in favor of each side. In practice, the English teacher should inform students the topic for debate a few weeks before the debate so as to leave students enough time for the preparation work such as making the decision about the side they intend to take part in as well as searching sufficient materials to equip them well for the debate. During the debate, the two sides take turns to make statements, and the next speaker should be asked to contradict his predecessor convincingly and then speak out his own ideas. The teacher should try to give every student the chance to speak. In addition, he is responsible for arousing new ideas when the debate goes to a dilemma, encouraging students who are too introvert to speak in public, keeping the debate in the right path without getting straying away, and make comments at the end of the class.

5   Conclusion

The student-centered way of teaching English meets the demand of modern English teaching, which shows the tendency of the development of English teaching approaches. This teaching method can arouse students' interest in learning English and help students learn the language effectively and efficiently. If all the teaching methods, suitable for student-centered English classes, are listed, there must be an astonishing many, but only several major methods are mentioned in this thesis. No matter which method is applied, the essence is the same: students act as the leading character of the class activities and teacher should offer assistance as much as possible.

References

1. Tarone, E., Yule, G.: Focus on the Language Learner. Shanghai Foreign Language Press (2000)
2. Hamerd, J.: The Practice of English Language Teaching, Longman (1994)
3. Nunan, D.: The Learner-Centered Curriculum: A Study in Second Language Teaching. Cambridge University Press, Cambridge (1988)
4. Campbell, C., Kryszewska, H.: Learner-Based Teaching. East China Normal University Press (1998)
5. Stevick, E.: Humanism in Language Teaching. Oxford University Press, Oxford (1990)
6. Ryle, G.: The Concept of Mind. University of Chicago Press, Chicago (1984)

Study on Teaching Reform of E-commerce with the Mode of Combining Research and Teaching Based on Propriate Teaching Materials

Haoyu Meng, Qiming Tian, and Dejia Zhang

Computer Department of Wenzhou Vocational and Technical College, Wenzhou, Zhejiang Province, China
menghy@wz.zj.cn, 393668762@qq.com, 329401576@qq.com

Abstract. Currently there is a great gap between talents e-commerce needs and college teaching in China, by analyzing the current domestic e-commerce industry and the current situation of e-commerce teaching, this research puts forward a kind of teaching model by way of combining scientific research with teaching aiming at students majoring in e-commerce. Through setting up a kind of college research institute, this kind of teaching model builds a bridge between industry and teaching. It sorts out a whole set of teaching materials, practice means and assessment criteria of teaching effects, which can be used in teaching. This article will prove this model has certain innovation and practical applicability in the field of current domestic e-commerce teaching. Experience and fruits this research gains can be a reference for others' research on relative fields.

Keywords: scientific research, model of teaching, teaching reform, research institute.

Preface

1. Current situation and teaching background in e-commerce industry. E-commerce is a special major compromising computer technique and marketing theory. Just due to its high combination of theory and practice, students coming from different provinces choose this major. Students of this major can adapt various kinds of jobs. Look around the current It may be said that demand for e-commerce talents is large and their development potential is great. At present, since colleges in China offer e-commerce major plus some training institutions, thousands of talents began to set foot in e-commerce industry each year. Opportunities and risks exist in e-commerce industry. Therefore, how to follow the development of technology and how to train professional graduates able to stand out in e-commerce talent market are what we colleges especially need to think urgently.

2. E-commerce Industry Demand and Teaching Problems. Through the analysis on daily teaching results and enterprise research, I conclude that some urgent problems needed to be solved in the current e-commerce market and professional teaching.

S. Lin and X. Huang (Eds.): CSEE 2011, Part V, CCIS 218, pp. 303–308, 2011.

(1) Lack of application study and agencies: The success of a good application in market can't do without excellent network planning promotion.

(2) Rare e-commerce teaching materials: The current e-commerce teaching is lack cooperation and connection with transverse projects of enterprises. Resources for practice are rare and are short of effect evaluation mechanism, both of which are at opposite poles with actual e-commerce operation.

(3) Colleges need to train and recommend graduates majoring in e-commerce according to the enterprises' demand.

1 Research on Teaching Model Which Combines Scientific Research with Teaching

1. General Research Thinking. This article suggests that E-commerce Institute, which unites e-commerce scientific research and teaching should be set up. The institute unites with all kinds of software enterprises to cooperate and develop innovative e-commerce application; on the other hand, it studies, acts as agent of advanced technology and products in e-commerce field and provides technical advice and network marketing planning service for those enterprises which need e-commerce. In terms of teaching, a new e-commerce teaching model will take shape, in which practice produces teaching materials and then applies to daily teaching. Job contents are as follows:

(1) Schools and enterprises cooperate to develop scientific research and network promotion gives service to society: E-commerce scientific research involves technology and market operation, so it is extremely important to carry on scientific research with theories integrating with practice. Research institutes will promote cooperation between schools and enterprises so that the distance between teaching and industry will become nearer and we can make more practical achievements in scientific research. In addition, by way of planning and promotion, some excellent networking products can be marketed quickly to create value for enterprises.

(2) Keep in step with science and technology teaching reform: It is difficult for teaching model purely aiming at teaching to catch up with development of correlation technique. Therefore, we need a kind of teaching model driven by authentic business operation project. The institute, in the process of giving service to the society, can keep pace with technological innovation, improve teaching model and lift teachers' scientific and practical ability. Then a kind of new e-commerce teaching model which combines practice with theory teaching is introduced.

(3) Customize e-commerce talents: The institute studies what types of talents e-commerce market may need in the past, current and approaching two to four years and feeds back to the teaching reform to direct us how to draw up teaching program. Moreover, the implement of transverse projects provide students more opportunities to practice and obtain employment and help to train e-commerce graduates in accordance with industry requirements.

2. Operation and Service models. The institute with transverse cooperation gives service to society, improves teaching practice level and achieves a teaching and scientific research model with a virtuous cycle starting from cooperative research and development to practical operation and then to theory teaching. Specific contents are as follows:

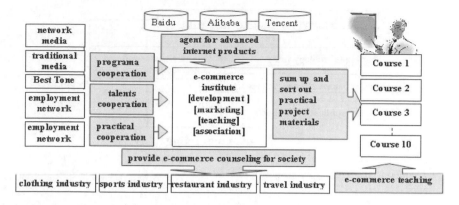

Fig. 1.

The institute makes the following plans in terms of giving service to society:

(1) To cooperate with all kinds of e-commerce network within field and to act as agent of IT advertising projects or to contract the operation of business channel.

(2) To build a kind of long-tern cooperation model with various Mobile telecom carries in terms of 3G mobile phones of student market in higher education zone and to develop and operate multiple value-added applications.

(3) To build relationship with guilds of software companies and to let excellent e-commerce enterprises recommended by the guilds join into the institute to carry out projects in a cooperative way.

(4) To cooperate with chamber of commerce and to provide its attaching enterprises and organizations e-commerce advices.

(5) To cooperate with government's competent departments being in charge of information industry and to carry out charitable e-commerce activities to expand the institute's social influence.

(6) To cooperate with various human resource head-hunting institutions to provide counseling of IT talents towards society.

3. Planning for Cooperative Research and Development

(1) Schools and enterprises cooperate in a transverse way to study how to apply the most advance technology and products in e-commerce to regional e-commerce market.

The institute establishes itself in this locality. By studying application mode and market characteristics of all kinds of leading technology in e-commerce field, the institute sifts those techniques and products suitable for local market and plans to promote by network so that network products which possess market potential and excellent qualities can go into e-commerce market successfully to realize business value.

In addition, the institute takes products agency over with leading Internet enterprises such as Google, Yahoo, Microsoft, Baidu, Alibaba and so on, or cooperates with famous web information platform programa, which can promote standard of social service as well as gain profitable economic returns.Specific processes are illustrated in the following chart.

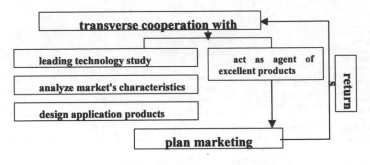

Fig. 2.

(2) Study on developing and recommending customized talents

Because of the complexity of e-commerce major, courses e-commerce majors are taking are many but not professional. E-commerce talents enterprises need are varied. Therefore, to develop and recommend corresponding talents after analyzing enterprises' actual needs well and truly is an important research field.

First, analyze what kind of talents various enterprises need in this area and then set up a database with comparative analysis between talents and the talents need. Second, cooperate with enterprises to found training base for e-commerce talents, provide social enterprises personalized and customized talents training service and offer thorough vocational counseling to college IT graduates.

4. New-type Teaching Model Research. Combining the thinking of project teaching, I study how to make actual-operation e-commerce enterprises model integrate into daily e-commerce teaching.

On one hand, referring to typical post setting in e-commerce companies, this model carries out similar means that let students learn in different posts in the class just like in the companies. For example, divide the whole class into two teams with each team having such roles like general manager, marketing director, technical director, project manager, project staff, developer, customer service representative, marketing staff and so on. Blend actual projects in teaching and create a kind of competitive atmosphere like actual team. All these will promote students to know and understand the actual operation situation of e-commerce and therefore develop various talents expert in some directions within the same major.

Since e-commerce major lays particular stress on network marketing and technical management, let those excellent e-commerce students hold the post of CEO, COO and CMO. Because network major and software major are inclined to technology research and development and network maintenance, let excellent students of network and software major assume the office of CTO. Make general students of various majors form "operation group", "development group" and "marketing group" in accordance with their characteristics. These students will follow a new-type of teaching model: work in company in the daytime and learn some theory courses related to their jobs in classroom at night. At the same time, we integrate and condense foundation courses, detail specialized courses and sort out a set of e-commerce teaching training program for the new teaching model appropriate for studies combining jobs and theories. This program is designed to train a group of excellent skilled talents within 3 years.

On the other hand, reform e-commerce teaching around an actual-operation e-commerce platform. According to job types and work sessions, divide the operation of the platform into one after another relative independent but inseparably interconnected competitive trainings. Each practical operation of teachers and students will be directly acted on actural operation of websites. Use some operation data, like search engine keyword rank in websites, Alexa, PV, PR value and so on,to testify theories in class so that teaching effect will be verified. Specific operation procedures are as follows:

Fig. 3.

2 Conclusion

Through analyzing state of development of the current domestic e-commerce and the current situation of e-commerce teaching, this research advances a kind of model aiming at e-commerce major, which advocates combination between scientific research and teaching and cooperation between schools and enterprises can promote teaching reform.Through setting up a kind of college research institute which is a combination of scientific research and teaching and through the research and practice carried out by the research institute, this kind of teaching model builds a bridge between industry and teaching. It sorts out a whole set of teaching materials, experimental tests and assessment criteria of teaching effects, which can be used in teaching. By way of small-scale testing,this study proves this model has certain innovation and practical applicability in the field of current domestic e-commerce teaching. Experience and fruits this research gains can be a reference for others' research on relative fields.

References

1. Hao, C., Jiang, Q.: Discuss the basic content of vocational education project course. China Education Research, 59 (2007) (in Chinese)
2. Xu, G.: The key issues of the vocational education project course. China Vocational Education, 9 (2007) (in Chinese)
3. Ye, X., Lin, J.: The innovation and study on the vocational E-commerce talents training based on the project teaching, 1 (2010) (in Chinese)

Developing the Digital Materials of Display Technology of Daily Life for Technological and Vocational Student

Chin-Pin Chen[1], David Wen-Shung Tai[2], Ching-Yi Lee[1],
Yu-Lin Hsiao[1], and Hsuan-Yu Chen[3]

[1] No.2, Shi-Da Road, Changhua City, Changhua, Taiwan
iechencp@cc.ncue.edu.tw, {d96311014,d9931017}@mail.ncue.edu.tw
[2] Chung-Chie Rd, Sha Lu, Taichung, Taiwan
taiws@sunrise.hk.edu.tw
[3] The University of Melbourne, Victoria, Australia 3010
tsuyoshi730411@hotmail.com

Abstract. This study was designed the display technological materials with SCORM standards. The design core was to develop the standardized learning components and it could be exchanged and used in line with SCORM platform. In addition, the study constructed the display technological curriculum content for technological and vocational student with fuzzy analytic hierarchy process. The hierarchical structure is formulated by reviewing the related literature and interviewing the experts. Then, a questionnaire survey is conducted to determine the weight of each factor in the second component. Finally, the SCORM materials developed in this study were done via materials analysis, design, development, then collate materials for the first draft of the digital display technology, which includes three chapters and 16 sub-units.

Keywords: eLearning, digital material, display technology.

1 Introduction

In the 21st century, combining computer network information with digital learning has become an important trend in educational development. Information and communication technologies (ICT) could develope innovative educational concepts, and teaching and learning scenarios [1]. As ICT can enable inclusion, better services and quality of life, all human beings must be equipped with the skills to benefit from and participate in the Information Society [2]. In upgrading of industrial technology and social environment, the high-tech talent development is the key to sustainable development for national economy. Without doubt, technological and vocational education has been affected by the preoccupation with training for high-tech industry [3]. Within technological and vocational education, the most important developments are taking place at the college level. In the process of civilization, science and technology changes have become the norm. Technology has not only changed living environment, but also promoted social structure and cultural changes.

In recent years, photonics has played an important role in various fields and closely related to our daily lives. The liquid crystal display (LCD) industry is characterised by

S. Lin and X. Huang (Eds.): CSEE 2011, Part V, CCIS 218, pp. 309–313, 2011.

intense technological and market competition. In 1988, it was the beginning year of TFT-LCD (Thin Film Transistor-Liquid Crystal Display) in Taiwan because Asian financial crisis gave firms in Taiwan an opportunity to enter the LCD mainstream [4]. Among LCDs, the thin film transistor liquid crystal display (TFT-LCD) is the one which has the widest application. For example, it can be applicable to PC (notebook and monitors), mobile devices (personal data assistants (PDAs), cellphones, and e-books), cars (navigation aids, safe-driving support, and rear-seat entertainment) and even to home and office (TV, internet terminals, and e-newspapers). In addition, Flat panel displays (FPDs) has revolutionized the viewpoints of humanbeings because FPDs have distinguishing features including larger viewable image area, greater brightness and contrast, reduced glare, and space-saving and environmental benefits such as very low emission fields, no magnetic field, and reduced power consumption [5].

Fuzzy AHP has gradually been widely used in various fields; it is used in subjective evaluation or it is applied to the uncertainty problems. Kahraman, Cebeci & Ulukan [6] utilized fuzzy analytic hierarchy process to select the best supplier firm which provided the best satisfaction for the criteria determined in Turkey. Aya & Ozdemir [7] selected fuzzy AHP technique to realize the best machine tool from its increasing number of existing alternatives in market are multiple-criteria decision making problem in the presence of many quantitative and qualitative attributes for decision-makers. In addition, Cakir and Canbolat [8] proposed an inventory classification system based on the fuzzy analytic hierarchy process, as well as they integrate fuzzy concepts with real inventory data and design a decision support system assisting a sensible multi-criteria inventory classification.

Collectively, there was a great deal of literature on fuzzy analytic hierarchy process to select the best solution to the uncertainty problem. However, constructing display technological curriculum content by fuzzy analytic hierarchy process is relatively scarce. Over the past decade, there has been a great deal of interdisciplinary activitities attempting to incorporate computing into classroom environments. This is done with the hope that it may provide an alternative solution to the problem of demonstrating theories and technological knowledge in an e-learning educational environment by Sharable Content Object Reference Model (SCROM). Additionally, the materials may serve as a basis for studies of display technology at vocational and technological education level. The features of user friendly and easy to study enable students to observe details required in all contents so that they will not have problems learning complex operating procedures.

2 Literature Review

Display Industry: In modern life, PDAs, GPS, OLED, Tablet PC, and e-paper are the most popular products in our lives. An electronic newspaper is an assortment of news delivered to the public in electronic forms, which includes multimedia elements as well as texts. The ePaper aggregates and classifies news items from various news providers or a news domain ontology, and delivers an electronic newspaper to each reader [9]. Although the display has become quite common, the larger size and weight can be quite cumbersome. In order to overcome this problem, flexible displays not only can replace the traditional LCD, but can be used in screen displays, advertising billboards, and handheld devices, and be used as electronic paper, e-books, and a variety of indoor and outdoor exhibitions. At the same time, in order to meet human needs for vision and be more interactive and realistic, 3D stereoscopic images are also a major focus of technology development areas in recent years. Tablet PC's are traditional notebook computers with the ability to process digital ink by writing with a stylus. They have recently attracted attention as a potential tool for educational use. Outside of the classroom, the Tablet PC is also a useful tool for grading, creating lecture material, and capturing meeting notes [10]. In student's viewpoint, a Tablet PC has many benefits, such as portability, without requiring extra weight or space and study in almost any environment than traditional note-taking and presentation methods [11].

3 Methodology

Fuzzy-set theory means rating a subset of belonging element to some extent by a method of using some index in between 0 to 1. Index of totally belonging is 1, totally not belonging is 0, and others are given an index between 0 and 1 according to the extent of belonging. Fuzzy indices are normal and convex fussy subsets. Fussy index subordinate function should satisfy the following conditions: (1) Normality of a fussy subset (2) Convex fussy subset (3) Piecewise continuous. Trigonometric fussy index

is shown in $\tilde{M} = (a,b,c)$, where $a \leq b \leq c$, as shown in Fig 1. When $a > 0$, M is called a Positive Triangular Fuzzy Number. The definition for the subordinate functions of the trigonometric fussy index M as follows:

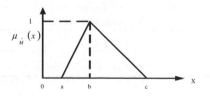

Fig. 1. Positive Triangualr Fuzzy Number

4 Results

From Table 1, in display technology, the most important knowledge unit is display (0.366), in order are 3D stereopsis (0.342), digital life and touch panel (0.292)。 In knowledge item,, full-color 3D technology is the most important(0.237); Next are PDA, digital signage and 3D stereoscope television (0.227), and the final is 3D player (0.216).

Display Technology eLearning Materials. Based on the analyses of fuzzy weights stated above, the results were utilized to make eLearning materials. The lowest unit of SCORM was source material. Source materials comprised words, images, music and videos. These source materials were formed to be our teaching slides. Furthermore,

Table 1. Display technology curriculum content fuzzy weight

Knowledge domain	curriculun	Fuzzy weights
	display	0.366
	NB monitor	0.183
	ultra-thin computer	0.166
	large-size LCD TV screen	0.166
	E- paper	0.166
	CRT TV	0.145
	OLED	0.175
	Digital life and touch panel	0.292
	PDA	0.227
Display technology	Tablet PC	0.198
	GPS	0.208
	POS	0.140
	Digital Signage	0.227
	3D stereopsis	0.342
	digital photo frame	0.155
	Signage	0.165
	3D stereoscope television	0.227
	3D player	0.216
	full-color 3D technology	0.237

we also added scripts in slides in our Learning Management System (LMS). Finally, in the display technology course, the system structure was in accordance with the SCORM standard definitions of every tag in teaching resources. Every file was saved in the way of words and videos. Whenever exchanging data between different platforms is needed, files will be transferred in words and videos. Therefore, if one platform is following SCORM regulations, it can also use the teaching materials. Hence, teaching resources can be used among platforms.

5   Conclusions

Various methods have been investigated on implementthree-dimensional image display systems [12]. Display devices with three-dimension have been the subject of exploration and it is useful in a wide variety of applications, such as air traffic control, computer-aided design, medicine and entertainment. The field of education can also benefit greatly from the widespread utilisation of 3D display systems [13]. Jonassen, Peck and Wilson [14] considered that basic learning theory and cognitive theory of CAL are the tools to enhance intelligence and to construct knowledge. Basic learning theory and cognitive theory of CAL also provide practices for learning assistant activities. One of those activities is to transform virtual imagination in human's brain into reality. For example, the basic structure of a display and its principles can be illustrated as what they showed in images. Meanwhile, this also simplifies the complexity of concepts and can be turned into more easily understood schema. With this proper teaching design, learners not only can understand the content of a course, but also easily get into practices and construct personal learning schema. Mel Silberman pointed out that "e-Learning has the potential to be an active learning experience. The key lies in the fact that learners can decide how to learn related materials by themselves. If the highest interactivity is sought during design, the value of e-Learning can be enhanced." Besides, Winstanley and Bjork [15] said that learning is a process of illustration. New information can be stored in memory only if it's connected to previous information. And, we need to have hints to retrieve those stored information. In the present study, the design of the curriculum and the content were directed to simulate learners' previous knowledge. The simulating situations can trigger learners to build up new information in the constructing learning environment.

Acknowledgements. This part of research results were supported by the National Science Council of Taiwan under the Grants NSC 97-2511-S-018-031-MY3.

References

[1] Schneckenberg, D.: submitted to British Journal of Educational Technology (2010)
[2] Ala-Mutka, K., et al.: submitted to European Journal of Education (2010)
[3] Grubb, W.N.: The Bandwagon Once More: Vocational Preparation for High-Tech Occupations (1984)
[4] Hu, M.-C.: Submitted to Technological Forecasting and Social Change (2008)
[5] Hung, S.-W.: Submitted to Technology in Society (2006)
[6] Kahraman, C., et al.: Submitted to Logistics Information Management (2003)
[7] Aya, Z., Ozdemir, R.: Submitted to Journal of Intelligent Manufacturing (2006)
[8] Cakir, O., Canbolat, M.S.: Submitted to Expert Systems with Applications (2008)
[9] Shapira, B., et al.: Submitted to Journal of the American Society for Information Science and Technology (2009)
[10] Mock, K.: Submitted to Journal of Computing Sciences in Colleges (2004)
[11] Frolik, J., Zum, J.B.: Submitted to Computers in Education Journal (2005)
[12] Min, S.W., et al.: Submitted to Applied optics (2003)
[13] Blundell, B., et al.: Submitted to Engineering science and education Journal (2002)
[14] Jonassen, D.H., et al.: Submitted to Special Education Technology (1999)
[15] Dewinstanley, P.A., Bjork, R.A.: Submitted to New directions for teaching and learning (2002)

Research on Audit System Based on PHP with Analysis of Scientific Materials

Qingxiu Wu[1], Jun Ou[1], Liang Ma[2],Yun Pei[2,3], and Min Chen[2,3]

[1] Department of Network Engineering, Hainan College of Software Technology,
Qionghai, Hainan, 571400, China
[2] Department of Software Engineering, Hainan College of Software Technology,
Qionghai, Hainan, 571400, China
[3] University. of Electronic Science and Technology of China, Chengdu,
Sichuan, 610054, China
hncst0898@yahoo.cn, xhogh@hotmail.com

Abstract. Firstly, a design of log audit system was raised based on PHP in the main mainstream operating systems and network environment; then, the "client/server" framework was surveyed while the main module of the system was described. Implementation details of key technology were provided with code. Lastly, the trend perspective of the log audit system was also presented.

Keywords: Log, Auditing, PHP, Server.

1 Introduction

The computer protection mechanism has to be monitored after been built. The operation process of monitoring system was auditing. Log file is an important part of security system, which is the history record of computer system running status. As the developing of the Internet, online behavior tracking has become more and more critical. Traditional log auditing system, with standardized function, can be deployed in single server and can meet the common requirement of enterprise application, which get server access summary by cataloging and collecting file content of web log files. However, most auditing tools, not very flexible and adaptable, can simply process "standardized (typical log format)"log files, hard to achieve general management of associated information among different log files. Furthermore, traditional tools, adopting file-system techniques, the processing speed and performance rapidly decrease when the auditing files increase to certain amount. More importantly, this kind of auditing system, with isolated sub systems, can not audit integrated behaviors of multiple services in a certain scope. [1][2]

Log auditing system is mainly employed in the infrastructure of current information distribution system. It comprehensively monitors and records information system's dynamic information and configuration alteration, provides real-time warning and outputs comprehensively analyzed log and data to supply an information system infrastructure security event management platform with large monitor scope, prompt response and powerful analysis ability.

S. Lin and X. Huang (Eds.): CSEE 2011, Part V, CCIS 218, pp. 314–319, 2011.

2 Function Design

Log information is dumped to the initial database on the log processing workstation. On one hand, data in the initial database is used to log statistic query; On the other hand, these data is detected by log auditing module. The structure of the log auditing module is shown in the Figure-1: Log auditing module compares acquired log information to intrusion feature in the created initial log database, and if it detects suspicious intrusion, warning would be sent and warning information would be insert into warning log database, which can be accessed by system administrator via the front-end user interface and gets warning log information. Various Log function and basic configuration is shown in log setting module. PHP combined with MySQL can implement quick log searching and exact log query in providing the network security solution for enterprises. [3]

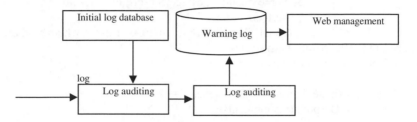

Fig. 1. Log auditing module structure

Main modules included

(1) Gathering various OS log, web server log, database log and FTP server log, and process their format in a unified style;[4]

(2) Real-time processing and analyzing the collected log in the auditing system, then producing associated warning according to the rule database and sending warning message via Email and short message;

(3) Processing and analyzing the collected log in the auditing system after the event, and producing reports;

(4) Backing up the collected log in the auditing system at regular time, and supporting various log import;

(5) Providing user management interfaces. Because B/S architecture was adopted in auditing system, user can administrate system by browser with high efficient combined condition query of log.

Vsftp log can track FTP logged-in user's detailed operation in Linux, including recording log-in time, uploading or downloading time, log-in IP, the downloaded or uploaded file size etc. All these log records will be stored in MySQL persistently. There are powerful search functions (You can find information you are going to get by checking date, IP or user name item), which provide a auditing management platform with large monitor scope, timely response and powerful analysis ability. Apache log records various events happened everyday, by which administrator can the cause of error, or trace attackers. The operation records that users leave when they access database are managed by MySQL log records, by which administrator can find if there is malicious tampering or deleting act, so that it can ensure the system's safety.[5]

3   Main Module Implementation

(1) Read the log files and store them in database. Partial code is shown below:

```
1 /****Read the log files*****/
2 ..........
3 $page=file('xferlog');           // The file you want to monitor
4 $table_count=$db_news->fn_row_table('log');
5 if(count($page)>$table_count){// Determine the data in the table to add options
6      for($insert_id=$table_count;$insert_id<count($page);$insert_id++)
7              {
8                      $hang=explode(' ', $page[$insert_id]);
9                      $insert_content="",";
10                     if (count($hang)==18){   // Determine whether there is
space, and output file names with spaces
11     // The case with no spaces
12
       for($ae_i=0;$ae_i<count($hang)-1;$ae_i++)
               // Output array elements
13                                              {
14
       $insert_content.="'$hang[$ae_i]',";
15                                              }
16
       $insert_content.="'$hang[$ae_i]'";
17                             }
18                     else {
19 ..........
```

(2) Monitor services in real time by SHELL combined with PHP. System can examine services every certain period of time to determine if services are normal. If there are exceptions threw, administrator will be notified by mobile short message or Email, so that it can handle it immediately to avoid unnecessary heavy losses by exceptional services. There are two monitor ways:

A: Monitor the network board flow. If there is too large flow through network board, warning will be sent to administrator.

B: Monitor if the service process is running currently. If the service process has been killed, warning will be sent to administer automatically.

User can configure mobile number, warning valve value, Email address in warning system. Partial code is shown below:

```
1 ..........
2 function alarm($file_name_alarm){
3      $arr=file($file_name_alarm);
```

```
4      $tel='13000000000';
5      $totel="13000000000";                              //you want to send num
6      $tpass="0000000";                                  //fetion
password
7      $allowdata="104857600";                            //you want to crisis,unit
is byte
8      $email='myadmini@163.com';
9      $arr_count=count($arr);
10     if($_POST['submit']){
11             if($_POST['tel'])
12                     $tel=$_POST['tel'];
13             if($_POST['totel'])
14 ..........
15             if(preg_match("/^(email)/",$arr[$i])){
16                 $arr[$i]="email=$email \n";
17                     }
18     }
19             $str=implode("",$arr);
20             $fpTo=fopen($file_name_alarm,"w");
21             fwrite($fpTo,$str);
22             fclose($fpTo);
23             $fpFrom=fopen($file_name_alarm,"r");
24             $str=fread($fpFrom,filesize($file_name_alarm));
25             fclose($fpFrom);
26             return $str;
27 }
28     $str1=alarm('alarm_shell/a.sh');
29     $str2=alarm('alarm_shell/1.sh');
30     echo "<table align=\"center\"><tr><td class=\"ziti14\">Set your nic flow
warning!</td>";
31     echo "<td class=\"ziti14\">Set your VSFTP state warning</td><tr>";
32     echo "<tr><td class=\"ziti14\">".wordscut(nl2br($str1),260)."</td>";
33 ..........
```

(3) Various pages and session opening. Every other page only need to use this page, as it use functions on all other pages. Partial code is shown below:

```
1 ..........
2 include_once ("mysql.class.php"); //mysql class
3 include_once ("config.php"); // Configuration parameters
4 include_once ("page.class.php"); // Dedicated paging class background
5 include_once ("action.class.php"); // Class database operation
6 $db = new action($mydbhost, $mydbuser, $mydbpw, $mydbname, ALL_PS,
$mydbcharset); // Class database operation
7 $uid = $_SESSION[uid];
8 $shell = $_SESSION[shell];
9 $name = $_SESSION[name];
10 ..........
```

(4) Validate users when they log in the system, examining if they have account, password and privilege to log in. Partial code is shown below:

```
1  ..........
2     /**
3      * determine user privilege ($uid, $shell, $log_admin_power)
4      */
5     public function Get_user_shell($uid, $shell) {
6             $query = $this->select('dotcom_user', '*', `log_admin_id` = \" . $uid
. '\");
7             $us = is_array($row = $this->fetch_array($query));
8             $shell = $us ? $shell == md5($row[log_admin_name] .
$row[log_admin_passwd] . "TKBK") : FALSE;
9             return $shell ? $row : NULL;
10    } //end shell
11    public function Get_user_shell_check($mulu,$uid, $shell ,$qx=",$power=20)
{
12                if ($row=$this->Get_user_shell($uid, $shell)) {
13                    if ($row[log_admin_power]<$power){
14                        return $row;
15                    }
16                elseif($row[log_admin_power]>=$power && $qx==1){
17                        return $row;
18                    } //end log_admin_power
19                    elseif($row[log_admin_power]>=$power      &&
$qx==")){
20                            $this->Get_admin_msg('../main.php','
Permission denied, you have no right operation ! ');
21                            exit ();
22                    }
23                }
24                else {
25                        if($mulu==1){
26                        $this->Get_admin_msg('../index.php',' Login');
27                    }
28           else{
29                $this->Get_admin_msg('index.php',' Login');
30        }
31                    }
32            }
33    //end shell
34  ..........
```

4 Summary

As the development of the Internet, online act audition tracking is extremely important in some field, which is an indispensable supporting tool in remote education and E-commerce. According to the current network environment situation, this article raised a cross platform, comprehensive log auditing system design, so that it is possible for network management personnel to find network security latent danger from intricate and miscellaneous log data. However, data mining associated with log auditing has not been taken into account in the current solution, which should be improved and perfected. The trend is saving the network personnel's work by log auditing system will become an essential and efficient approach. It is the major feature of this system that it can not only complete the normal log auditing, but also build a framework that can support no-denying user operation auditing in an open environment. The system can gather and audit log from various remote servers, and adopt database for log maintenance and information configuring, so when the amount of log increase to a huge scale, query speed and performance is better that file system. After improved and perfected, it is believed that there will be more discoveries in large scale user acts analysis and supporting no denying audit for arbitration. [6]

Acknowledgment. This work is supported by the Foundation of office of Education of Hainan Province under Grant Hjkj2010-55(Colleges Scientific Research Projects of Hainan Province: Based on J2EE Project-teaching Interactive System of "2+1" Training Mode) and Hjsk2011-92 (Research on system maintenance talent training mode of ability-oriented) *Corresponding author: Jun Ou, Department of Network Engineering; Hainan College of Software Technology; QiongHai. Hainan Province, 571400, P.R.China; E-mail address: xhogh@hotmail.com.

References

1. Yu, H., Weimin, X.: Scalable Web log collection design and implementation of the framework. Computer applications and software (01) (2008)
2. Yong, W., Yifeng, L.: Based on log audit network security situation assessment model and performance correction algorithm. Computer Journal (04) (2009)
3. Lei, W., Binxing, F.: An implementation method based on network log audit tracking system. Computer engineering and application (01) (2006)
4. Huaping, Z., Haowei, L.: Linux based firewall log audit system study and realization. Automation technologies and applications (11) (2005)
5. Deng, X., Chen, L., Wang, G.: Security audit data analysis method of comprehensive audit. Journal of Chongqing University of posts and telecommunications (natural science Edition) (5) (2005)
6. Li, C., Zhou, G.: Attention to log auditing ensure data security. Medical information (10) (2007)

An Analysis of the Function and Training Strategies of Teaching Assistants at Technological and Vocational Colleges in Taiwan

Chin-Wen Liao, Li-Chu Tien, and Sho-yen Lin

Department of Industrial Education and Technology,
National Changhua University of Education,
No.2, Shi-Da Road, Changhua 500,Taiwan
m9316621@yahoo.com.tw, linshoyen@googlemail.com

Abstract. The study is to investigate the role, the duties and efficacy of teaching assistants based on instructors' opinions from eighteen technological and vocational colleges in central Taiwan and further made suggestions for training strategies to improve efficacy. This research adopts Interview and questionnaires, 450 questionnaires distributed and 307 returned. The result shows that teachers think TAs should focus on experimental operation. Moreover, there is no difference between teachers' viewpoints from public and private schools. As for evaluation criteria, TAs should understand related regulations. In terms of training strategy, those with excellent professional grades are prioritized to be teaching assistants.

Keywords: Teaching assistants, training strategy, teaching quality.

1 Introduction

Scholars at America's Ministry of Education found that the relationship between teachers and students would influence learning cognition and effective learning (Frymier & Houser, 2000). Students regarded that their experiences were mainly retrieved from teachers' behaviors. Therefore, teachers have to pass on their knowledge to students (Roach, 1991). The function of TAs is communicators, exchangers and a bridge between teachers and students. In 2003, the Ministry of Education in Taiwan launched a Humanities Social Science Education Project, which introduced TA system from foreign universities. After four-year experimental research, the Ministry of Education found that under TAs' help, web-based multimedia, small group discussion, website construction, and cooperative instruction were adopted, which transformed the traditional boring general education courses into interesting interactive courses and the kind of learning with student-centered, TAs in the middle, and teachers as supporters.

TAs play an important role in improving teachers' instruction quality. What training policies should be implemented to make use of TAs'' function? What evaluation systems are involved to maintain and increase TAs'' working efficacy? These crucial issues are of great urgency but so far no researcher has investigated about this aspect.

S. Lin and X. Huang (Eds.): CSEE 2011, Part V, CCIS 218, pp. 320–328, 2011.

The purpose of the present research is to investigate the viewpoints toward TAs' functions and roles perceived by teachers from technological and vocational colleges with TA system. Further suggestions are made for relevant schools to implement excellent TA policies to improve teaching qualities in technological and vocational colleges and help the implementation of teachers' instruction and remedial teaching.

Based on the above mentioned research purposes, the present study makes the following hypothesis.

1.1 There is significant difference with personal and background variables of TAs' function and efficacy with their preparation prior to instruction, during instruction, after instruction and remedial instruction.

1.2 There is significant difference toward training of TAs with personal and background variables.

1.3 There is significant difference toward the role and efficacy improvement of teaching quality with personal and background variables.

2 Literature Review

2.1 The Role and Abilities of TAs

TA (TA) refers to those who assist instructors with their teaching activities, and are responsible for instruction consultation, discussions, experiments, practices, correcting assignments and other related teaching-assisted works. DeCesare (2003) maintained that TAs aid instructors with satisfying students' learning. Butler et al. (1993) pointed out that TA policy was implemented in Northern America and graduate students tended to serve the role. The core value of this system is student-oriented and has been a learning guidance in advanced education in developed countries for many yeas.

TAs' abilities involve related abilities with their job duties, which consist of knowledge, technique, attitude, efficacy and value of successfully acting a specific role. British educator Jarvis (1990) mentioned that ability referred to knowledge and skills required by an individual for doing a professional job effectively. Based on Derouen and Kleiner (1994).TAs' main roles lie in assisting teachers with instructional procedures, after-class instruction, preparation prior to classes and good learning environment. Therefore, to be a competent TA, related abilities should be required to be able to accomplish work tasks efficiently.

2.2 Selection and Training of TAs

Educational institutes should select TAs from appropriate graduate or university students based on their ability and specialty in an open way. It was important to investigate the roles TAs would play in advance and then, based on these roles, select competent applicants as TAs (Quoted from Wu, 2000). The present study adopted function analysis make sure of each job duties of TAs and then analyzed the required abilities for those job duties for selection.

Training is to elevate the knowledge, skills and attitudes required for implementing their job duties or to develop TAs' problem-solving abilities when dealing with related activities. Therefore, TAs have to take professional courses to develop their abilities with assisting teachers in instruction. Park (2004) found six key strategies when training TAs, and the main strategies include selection criteria, TA development training , monitoring challenge standardized guidance and international TAs. Among them, the issue of TA training has gained more and more emphasis (Park, 2004). University of Illinois offers diverse courses to train TAs to increase TA's instruction quality (Hsu, 2006).

2.3 Training Institutes for TAs' Evaluation Criteria and Efficacy Improvement

The central organization for TAs is called center for teaching and learning, such as Derek Bok Center for Teaching and Learning in Harvard University. It provides professional skills, general education training, experience exchanges, sharing of how to solve problems and situation simulation (Chen, 2006). Each year before each semester begins, it not only hold workshops and situation simulation but release teaching guidebooks to help TAs understand students' needs or answering problems they encounter during their teaching.

Evaluation and assessment can be divided into— (1) establishment of course websites at Ceiba after new semester begins. The course websites will be assessed randomly. (2) including questionnaire item on implementation of TA system in midterm and final feedback questionnaire. The result of the questionnaire is for TAs' reference and it will also serve as an important criteria for the assessment and selection at the end of semester. (3) result report, final feedback questionnaire and implementation of course website, when each semester ends and field visits and evaluation on the effect of funded courses will be reference materials for funding future related courses (Chou, 2008; Tien, 2006).

3 Research Design and Implementation

3.1 Research Participants

The research samples were from eighteen technological and vocational colleges in central Taiwan. Questionnaires were distributed either by the researcher in person or through mail-delivery to each dean for implementing, distributing and collecting the data. Questionnaires were distributed through stratified sampling. Investigations were made with 3-6 teachers who had applied for TAs for more than one year at each department of 18 schools. Interview and questionnaire surveys were administered to college instructors In total, 450 questionnaires were distributed and the overall returned questionnaires were 307 with a 68% return rate.

3.2 Research Tools

The present study applied a self-arranged survey consisting teacher's basic information, TAs' functions and roles, TAs' abilities, training strategies and efficacy improvement. The above dimensions were graded with five-point Likert scale.

a. Questionnaire validity: In the beginning, the first draft of questionnaire was designed based on data collection. Then, eight teachers who had been voted as excellent teachers and twelve TA with at least one year experience were visited and their opinions served as reference for the questionnaire. When the first draft was constructed, it was evaluated by experts and suggestions were provided based on the suitability, content, and scoring of the questionnaire. After revision and modification, the questionnaire was sent via formal document to technological and vocational colleges in central Taiwan. Thirty teachers helped fill in the questionnaire for pre-test.

b. Factor analysis and reliability analysis: The present study adopted principal component analysis and varimax for factor analysis. KMO in the research data was 0.795~0.906 (higher than 0.5), thus it was suitable for factor analysis. Then, Cronbach's α was adopted to measure questionnaire reliability and assess the consistency of questionnaire items. Items with more than 0.5 Cronbach α were retained. The final analysis showed that the overall dimension was between 0.750~0.908, showings that the questionnaire had good reliability.

4 Results and Data Analysis

4.1 Analysis of the Background Variables of Teachers from 18 Technological and Vocational Colleges

Teachers are mostly males at 56.7% while females are at 43.3%. Teachers' teaching experiences are mostly between 6-15 years at 46.9% followed by less than 5 years at 26.4% and more than 36 years at 0.7%. It was shown that teachers' who applied for the assistance of TAs for teaching quality improvement were mostly of less than 15 years of teaching experience. Private schools took up the majority at 74.3% followed by public schools at 25.7%. In terms of teachers' colleges, business management account for the most at 32.9%, followed by technology engineering at 30.6%, medical and nursing at 12.7%, and law schools with the least at 1.6% and others include beauty, sports recreation, etc. at 8.5%. General administration and instruction account for TAs' duties with 28.3%, and followed by professional course consultation at 26.1%. Sources of funding were subsidized from school with 50.8 %, project funding with 40.4%, and others, endowment fund, with 8.8%. In terms of TAs' education background, graduates took up the most at 60.3%, followed by Bachelors at 26.1% and PhD students at 10.1%. It was found that master's students were the majority to be TAs, and this result corresponded to foreign literature.

4.2 Analysis of TAs' Roles and Duties

The result indicated that teachers ranked during instruction assistance more, followed by prior to instruction preparation, and then after instruction duties as shown in table one. In before instruction aspect, understanding course content was the highest with mean 4.17, standard deviation 0.732 while calling the role and maintaining the class order before the class the lowest with mean 3.55 and standard deviation 0.932. In during instruction aspect, assisting students with practicum and experiment classes was the highest with mean 4.14 and standard deviation 0.809 while student order management and guidance was the lowest with mean 3.66 and standard deviation

0.865. In after instruction aspect, provide study consultation service was the highest with mean 4.07 and standard deviation 0.747 while assisting assessment of scores on final exam and weekly learning performances was the lowest with mean 3.66 and standard deviation 0.865.

With the above analysis and summaries of in-depth interview with experienced teachers, it was found that teachers from different academic fields put emphasis on different subject matters. Most teachers hoped that TAs could understand the course contents prior to instruction so that they can help students when they encounter questions during instruction and that they could guide each student well to improve teaching quality and learning effect (0307-2-B. The first two numbers stand for interview month, the third and fourth numbers stand for interview dates, the fifth number stands for interview section, and the sixth number stands for the interviewee code.) As Hung (2006) pointed out TAs provided backup supports in classes and timely illustration, explanation and supporting materials when necessary. By doing this, it not only transformed the traditional way of instruction when teachers were the only source of knowledge but also achieve an interactive learning mode with student-centered, TAs in the middle, and teachers as supplementary.

Table 1. Teachers' overall perception toward TAs

Roles and duties						Abilities				
	Rank	Minimum	Maximum	Mean	Standard Deviation		Rank	Minimum	Maximum	Mean	Standard Deviation
During instruction	1	1.86	5.00	3.9483	.57601	Interpersonal relationship	1	3.00	5.00	4.1788	.497
Prior to instruction	2	1.43	5.00	3.8934	.58299	Professional abilities	2	2.33	5.00	4.1455	.5391
After instruction	3	1.80	5.00	3.8472	.56013	Training strategies					
Efficacy improvement						Practicum	1	1.67	5.00	3.9083	.58995
Career planning	1	1.00	5.00	4.0912	.54114	Selection	2	1.60	5.00	3.9042	.52873
Evaluation criteria and inspiration	2	1.00	5.00	3.8371	.65743	Strategy	3	1.71	5.00	3.8478	.60800

4.3   Analysis of Abilities of TAs

In this dimension, general interpersonal ability is higher than professional ability as described in table one. In interpersonal ability aspect, problem-solving ability was the highest with mean 4.36 and standard deviation 0.613 while class management ability was the lowest with mean 4.03 and standard deviation 0.745. In professional ability aspect, professional knowledge ability in a specific field was the highest with mean 4.33 and standard deviation 0.645 while ability to construction and maintain digital learning platform was the highest with mean 4.05 and standard deviation 0.744.

The interview data showed that teachers put more emphasis on TAs' problem-solving and communication negotiation abilities. Most teachers maintained that professional expertise should be the prerequisite selection criteria for recruiting TAs and can be trained through development and training. However, good interpersonal relationship ability is a personal characteristic and can not be trained in a short term. Moreover, good communication and negotiation ability is also required to solve problems (0310-2-C).

4.4 Analysis of Training Strategies of TAs

In this dimension, practicum got the highest score, followed by selection and strategies as shown in table one. In selection aspect, excellent college or graduate students recommended by teachers was the highest with mean 4.23 and standard deviation 0.686 while registration policy and low-income students are prioritized was the lowest with mean 3.51 and standard deviation 0.971. In strategy aspect, holding TA conference before each semester begins was the highest with mean 3.96 and standard deviation 0.735 while demonstrating teaching outcomes demonstration at the end of semester was the lowest with mean 3.7 and standard deviation 0.872. In practicum aspect, face-to face training with teachers on a regular time schedule was the highest with mean 4.03 and standard deviation 0.676 while self-learning via e-learning-watching teaching demonstration through videotapes was the lowest with mean 3.79 and standard deviation 0.732.

The interview data showed that most teachers considered TA a professional job. They helped to assist teachers' instruction and solve students' problems; therefore, professional ability was required. In training methods, teachers maintained that it was necessary to hold conference before semester or during summer vacation to help TAs understand their job duties and contents and to release teaching guidebook to guide and direct TA on solving problems. Besides, training center should also arrange training on general administration and instruction techniques on a regular time schedule. The training center corresponded to Derek Bok Center for Teaching and Learning at Harvard University as was discussed in literature.

4.5 Analysis of Improving TAs' Efficacy

In this dimension, job planning was higher than evaluation criteria and inspiration as shown in table one. To improve TAs' efficacy, schools have to make organized job planning in advance. In job planning aspect, TAs are obliged to understand TA systems and related regulations was the highest with mean 4.21 and standard deviation 0.657 while establishing training center to train TAs was the lowest with mean 3.97 and standard deviation 0.808. In evaluation criteria and inspiration aspect, distribution of mid-term and final questionnaire on TAs was the highest with mean 3.91 and standard deviation 0.722 while establishing training center to assess course websites was the lowest with mean 3.72 and standard deviation 0.808.

With interview, most teachers regarded that TAs should understand related rules and regulations and that schools should establish work effect criteria as basis for TAs' evaluation criteria. Midterm and final feedback questionnaire should be distributed for effect assessment so that TAs can make self-checks and improvements. Discussion meeting should be organized on a regular basis to help TAs understand their roles and duties to improve efficacy (0317-2-A).

4.6 Analysis of TAs' Job Duties and Training Policies with Teachers of Different Variables

Analysis of one way ANOVA was conducted. With t test, a significant difference was found in practicum with p value 0.012<0.05 and no significant differences in other dimension. Other dimensions, such as teachers' work years, sources of fund, TA educational background and TA work duties, all had p value >0.05, which showed no significant effect on each dimension. In terms of the effect of each dimension, a significant difference with teachers from different colleges was found with selection p value 0.40, strategy p value .001, practicum p value .002, and job planning p value .001, and all of their values were <0.05, meaning a significant difference. In term of teacher's school, the p value of prior to instruction was .000, selection p value at .015, strategy p value at .005, practicum p value at .044, job planning p value at .000, evaluation criteria and inspiration p value at .014, and all of them were <0.05, meaning a significant difference. It was revealed that teachers from different schools held different viewpoints on TA's prior instruction works, selection, strategy, practicum, job planning, evaluation criteria and inspiration training strategies.

5 Conclusion and Suggestion

5.1 Teachers' Emphasis on TA's Works and Abilities

It was found teachers put more emphasis on instructional illustration, operation, and discipline management in class or safety guidance during experiment. The development of TA's main abilities includes interpersonal relationship and professional ability. In interpersonal relationship, problem-solving ability was the most important ability valued by teachers. In professional ability, professional knowledge ability in a specific field was mostly valued. From the above, it was found that teachers hoped that TAs could help them achieve the following purposes: (1) Innovative instruction. (2) Emphasis on each student's learning. (3) Emphasis on individual differences. (4) Good after instruction consultation on each student. (5) Enhancement on actual practice and safety.

5.2 Teachers' Viewpoints on TA's Training Strategies

Teachers maintained that TA with excellent academic score and holding conferences before semester were the best training strategies. In practicum, face-to face training with teachers on a regular time schedule was the best strategy. They also regarded that competent TAs can be selected according to teachers' course needs. Schools could also organize Admission Committee based on course categories and establish selection criteria, teaching contents, TA's rights and obligation, and conference systems. Finally, selected TAs would have a face-to-face interview with teachers to check their job duties (0324-2-d).

5.3 Teachers Viewpoints on TAs' Evaluation Criteria and Inspiration Strategies

Teachers maintained that TAs should be obliged to understand the systems and related regulations of their evaluation criteria and inspiration. It was also necessary to establish basic requirements and abilities for TAs and hold instruction workshops for those who are nee TAs. Besides, teachers regarded that distribution of mid-term and final questionnaire on TAs was the most important and the questionnaire result should also be analyzed to evaluate the effect.

5.4 Viewpoints on TAs'' Training Strategies from Teachers with Different Variables

It was found that teachers belonging to different colleges, public and private schools held different viewpoints in terms of TAs' work duties, training strategies and evaluation criteria. Therefore, schools can establish different TA work duties and training strategies based on their individual course characteristics to make use of teaching effect and help students solve academic questions.

References

1. Butler, D.D., Laumer Jr., J.F., Moore, M.: A content analysis of pedagogical and policy information used in training graduate teaching assistants. Journal for Higher Education Management 91, 27–37 (1993)
2. Chen, M., Huang, C.: Teaching assistant makes lessons exciting. Evaluation Biomonthly 3, 16–17 (2006)
3. Chen, Z.: Cornell University, teaching assistant system profile. Education Center. National Taiwan University Newsletter (2008), http://ctld.ntu.edu.tw/epaper/?p=12 (retrieved July 1, 2008)
4. DeCesare, M.: On being a graduate teaching assistant (2003), http://www.csun.edu/~mdecesare/ (retrieved March 22, 2005)
5. Derek Bok Center for Teaching and Learning, http://bokcenter.harvard.edu (retrieved December 4, 2007)
6. Frymier, A.B., Houser, M.L.: The teacher-student relationship as an interpersonal personal relationships. Communication Education 49(3), 207–219 (2000)
7. Hsu, X.C.: Keeping pace of teaching performance and the teaching academic research - seven recipes to improve teaching quality at the University of Illinois. Evaluation Biomonthly 3, 16–17 (2006)
8. Jarvis, P.: An international dictionary of adult and continuing education. Routledge, London (1990)
9. Li, Z.: Establishment of mechanisms for effective teaching-teacher development is the core issue of higher education evaluation. Evaluation Biomonthly 3, 9–12 (2006a)
10. Lu, G.Y.: University of Virginia teaching assistant system profile. Education Center, National Taiwan University bending Newsletter (2006), http://ctld.ntu.edu.tw/paper (retrieved November 30, 2006)

11. Park, C.: The graduate teaching assistant (GTA):Lessons from North American experience. Teaching in Higher Education 9(3), 349–361 (2004)
12. Roach, K.D.: Graduate teaching assistants' use of behavior alteration techniques in the university classroom. Communication Quarterly 39(2), 178–188 (1991)
13. Tien, F.H.: Introduction to Center for Learning and Teaching at University of Michigan NTU Teaching Practicum and Consultation Newsletter, 37,2. Unpublished thesis, Kaohsiung, Taiwan (2006)

Design and Realization of Project-Class Teaching Module Based on JMF

Jun Ou[1], Yun Pei[2,3], Min Chen[2,3], Qingxiu Wu[1], and Liang Ma[2]

[1] Department of Network Engineering, Hainan College of Software Technology,
Qionghai, Hainan, 571400, China
[2] Department of Software Engineering, Hainan College of Software Technology,
Qionghai, Hainan, 571400, China
[3] University. of Electronic Science and Technology of China, Chengdu,
Sichuan, 610054, China
xhogh@hotmail.com

Abstract. Video teaching platform was the product from the development of network environment and network technology, it had wide application prospect. According to the requirement of network teaching platform, Audio/Video Data transmission, control and Java Media Framework (JMF) technology was analyzed, then Real-time Transport Protocol (RTP), Real-time Transport Control Protocol (RTCP) and programming mechanism of JMF RTP was discussed. In practice, the teaching platform was used well.

Keywords: JMF, RTP, teaching platform, audio∕video.

1 Introduction

With the popularization of project-teaching pattern, more and more schools implement project-teaching method using network teaching platform. Main site of the project-teaching is the classroom teaching, this module allows teachers and students exchange online in real time. Teachers and students, or students and students carry out online communication, online discussion. With this module, it can solve the students' thinking in confusion during the course of the project implementation. Project-class is as a core module of the network teaching platform. Because of the contradictions between large volumes of data and limited network bandwidth, video teaching would be greatly restricted, confined to a single transport mode—"one-to-one" teaching method. Then "one to many" or "many to many" interactive teaching is still limited to the text. As the popularity of broadband networks, multi-user interactive video project teaching is gradually becoming a necessary feature of network teaching system,[1] becoming an important application of network multimedia teaching technology. Java language has cross-platform portability, broad application, flexible and other features. JMF is an extension of Java, supporting for Java application access to audio, video in device-independent way. At the same time it can handle the voice or video in a continuous way. This article focuses on the design and development project class module of multiplayer interactive teaching platform.

S. Lin and X. Huang (Eds.): CSEE 2011, Part V, CCIS 218, pp. 329–334, 2011.

2 JMF

JMF is the Java media framework. It is application interface which incorporated audio and video programs into JAVA program and Applet. It is a standard extension framework, allowing the user to produce pure audio streams and video streams. It enables Java programs to capture audio, video, store, play and process multimedia data; then transfer and encode multimedia data. It also supports media streaming compressed and storage media's synchronization, control, processing and play. It has a cross-platform function. Using JMF, the original media can also carry out special treatment and optimize data processing of the existing format, JMF can be extended to support new types of media formats. The high level architecture of JMF is as shown in Fig. 1.

Java Application Program、 Applets、 Beans、 Servlets				
JMF Description And Process				
JMF Plug-In API				
Codec	Output	Implementation	Reuse	Conversion

Fig. 1. The high level architecture of JMF

JMF is mainly consists of two major components: one part is JMF API, the core of JMF, being responsible for basic operation of the media; the other part is the JMF RTP API, belong to the extensions of JMF API. It transmits RTP streams by network. It must use the processor and the data source of RTP encoding , and build DataSink (data collection) or SessionManager to control the transmission.

The model provided by JMF can be roughly divided into seven categories:

(1) Data source (2) Capture Device (3) Player (4) Processor
(5) DataSink (6) Data format (7) Manager.

3 RTP

RTP (real time protocol), is the real-time transport protocol based on UDP. It is designed for interactive voice, video and other real-time multimedia applications of light transmission protocols, which provides end-to-end network transport functions for transmitting applications and receiving real-time data. Its data transmission is enhanced by RTCP (real-time Transport Control Protocol). RTCP and RTP are at work, being responsible for monitoring the data transfer, providing control and identification functions. RTP and RTCP are independent of the transport layer and network layer. JMF provides API of implementing RTP/RTCP protocol. JMFRTPAPI is the application interface that supports RTP application development in JMF.

Real –time media frame and application	
RTCP(Real-time control protocol)	
RTP(Real-time control protocol)	
Other network and	UDP
transmission	IP
protocol(TCP,ATM)	

Fig. 2. Transmission protocol structure in real-time

4 The System Hardware Structure

The hardware structure of the system is as shown in Fig. 3. Teacher uses video/audio capture devices such as cameras and microphones to input the media data into the computer, and sends the RTP media stream data via the network to a student. The remote users receive these media stream and can use the monitor to display video in real time.

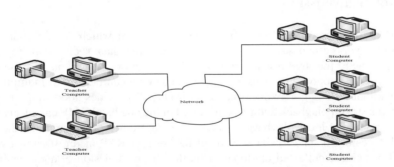

Fig. 3. The network structure in project-class module

5 Data Capture

Using JMF, it captures media from the current active source. Video is captured from the camera, audio from the microphone .Elaborate the process of capturing audio, video: First of all, query CaptureDeviceManager to locate the capture device is required; then get the capture device information from CaptureDeviceInfo object; Secondly, Medialocator is from CaptureDeviceInfo. Create a DataSource by MediaLocator. Create a Player or Processor by DataSource. Finally, start to capture video or Audio by Player.

CaptureDeviceManager class (capture device manager) uses registration and query mechanisms to locate the capture device, CaptureDeviceInfo object returns representing the capture device. It provides two ways to create a capture device object CaptureDeviceInfo: getDeviceList (Format format) method and getDevice (String DeviceName) method. [2]

Processor object is used to set and control audio and video capture device collection. Create MediaLocator object by getLocator method. The object is as a parameter to call createProcessor method.

Configure the processor object as follows:

(1) Set acquisition parameters for channel of the processor object. By calling the processor object's getTrackControls method, get the TrackControl object of the channel ;

(2) Call the setFormat method of TrackControl object to set the channel's acquisition parameter;

(3) The processor object's setcontentDescriptor method is called to format the data output of the processor object.

Method of obtaining capture devices's information is as follows:

(1) Bring up all the capture devices;
(2) Get Medialocator address of device;
(3) Create a Player. When Player started, the video capture process carried out.

6 Data Transmission

RTP (Real-time Transport Protocol) is Internet standard which AVT (Audio-video Transport,) work group uses to the transfer real-time data such as audio, video. Compared with the traditional protocol, RTP is more focus on real-time not reliability. RTP supports multicasting and a media data can be sent to multiple users at once without wasting network bandwidth. RTP API provides good support: on the RTP media stream playback and transmission. On the one hand, JMF can receive RTP media streams for local playback, storage files, and other processing; on the other hand, JMF can also send media streams in the form of RTP media streams over the network which are collected or stored in the local. Transmission of audio and video data is as shown in Fig. 4[3].

RTP session is to coordination by the SessionManager--it is responsible for monitoring all of the participants in the session and the RTP media stream. From the perspective of local participants, SessionManager maintains session state. It is localized manifestations of the RTP session the distributing entity. SessionManager defines initialization session, starting a session, removing RTP media streams, closing the session and a series of methods.

RTP data stream's work is as follows: creating a Processor using the DataSource, which is data to be transferred; setting the Processor's output as RTP encoding data; getting Processor's output as DataSource.[4][5]

Using MediaLocator construction of RTP data cross point with RTP session parameters. Use session manager as transfer content to create a transport stream and control transmission. The method is as follows:

(1) Create a session manager object;
(2) Call the Initialization method of the session manager object initSession ();

(3) The method of creating output stream object SendStream is called createSendSteam ();

(4)The method of Starting the session manager is called startSession ();

(5) The methods of output stream object are called to start and control the transfer. SendStreamListener is registered on in SendStream.

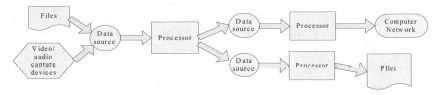

Fig. 4. RTP video/audio transmisson

7   Data Reception and Playing

It can receive and play audio and video data using session manager methods. Session Manager established a session, passing DataSource extracting from the data flow to the Manager. CreatePlayer (DataSource) built a player for ReceiveStream (receiving data flow). RTP audio video data received as shown in Fig.5.

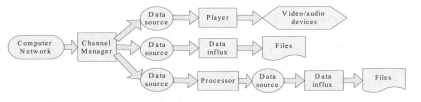

Fig. 5. RTP video/audio reception

Implementation steps are as follows:

Step 1: establish a SessionManager. Call member function –addReceive-StreamListener of Class RTPSessionMgr and register as a listener (the audience). Call member function –initSession of class RTPSessionMgr to initialize the RTP session; call member function –startSession of class RTPSessionMgr to start RTP session;

Step 2: in the ReceiveStreamListener Update method, monitoring NewReceiveStreamEvent events, it will indicate the new data stream was detected;

Step 3: when a NewReceiveStreamEvent is detected, from the NewReceiveStreamEvent event call getReceiveStream to obtain ReceiveStream:

Step 4: from RTP ReceiveStream call the getDataSource gotten Data-Source, this is a PushBuferDataSource with RTP-specific format;

Step 5: pass DataSource to Manager.createPlayer in order to create a player.

8 Result

Project-class made using of MyEclipse 7. Web server's operating system is Windows Server 2003 Enterprise Edition, using Eclipse 5 with Tomcat 6 as the Java runtime environment and providing Web services, combining Windows Server 2003 with MySql 5 as database services.

Arranging 45 students for practice test, test results show that the system runs stable, teachers and students can well realize the real-time audio, video, interactive, video and voice communication and smooth, video display clarity, clear voice. It reaches the expected purpose and design.

9 Summary

From the project-class teaching module actual needs, it proposed and implemented multiple user project-class prototype based on JMF. Due to the cross-platform features of the Java language itself, this system also has the most powerful portability of the same software that does not exist. Using multicast technology, efficient encoding format and simple user management, the system in the test reflected the high performance and stability.

The platform displayed video communication advantages by use of JMF. At the same time, this system will also optimize the network congestion, data security, and so on, to make up for the current deficiencies of the system about robustness in the next step.

Acknowledgment. This work is supported by the Foundation of office of Education of Hainan Province under Grant Hjkj2010-55(Colleges Scientific Research Projects of Hainan Province: Based on J2EE Project-teaching Interactive System of "2+1" Training Mode) and Hjsk2011-92 (Research on system maintenance talent training mode of ability-oriented) *Corresponding author: Jun Ou, Department of Network Engineering; Hainan College of Software Technology; QiongHai. Hainan Province, 571400, P.R.China; E-mail address: xhogh@hotmail.com.

References

1. Zhu, W., Georganas, N.D.: JQOS:a QoS-based Internet videocon ferencing system using the Java media framework(JMF). In: Canadian Conference on Electricaland Computer Engineering 2001, May 13-16, vol. 1, pp. 625–630 (2001)
2. Pajares, A., Guerri, J.C., Belda, A., et al.: JMFMoD: a new system formedia on demand presentations. In: Proceedings of 28th Euromicro Conference, September 4 -6, pp. 160–167 (2002)
3. Java Media Framework API Guide (November19, 1999),
   http://java.sun.com/products/java-media/jmfindex.jsp
4. Zhou, J., Zou, B.R.: RTP stream by using JMF transfer and play . Journal of Hunan University (natural science Edition)
5. Liu, H.: Design and realization of video system based on JMF. Northwestern University, Xian (2004)

Research on Different Evaluation Performance Level Based on Information Technology

Tsang-Lang Liang, Tsung-Min Liu, and Ying-Chieh Cho

No.2, Shi-Da Road, Changhua City, Taiwan 50074
ietll0615@yahoo.com.tw, sinonbulllau@yahoo.com.tw,
snoopy2632000@yahoo.com.tw

Abstract. This is a qualitative study that researches school leaders and leadership teams on how to effect and support eight different evaluation performances level of vocational schools in school management. This also promotes teachers in professional development and teaching quality. Through the semi-structured interview for the school's principals, teachers, director of the school management and administration team, this is to promote professional growth of teachers and teaching quality. There are twelve factors that are discussed in this study. In particular, the establishments of the school vision, providing of individual support, and the creation of a productive school culture influences the promotion of professional growth of teachers and teaching quality that are concerned. The school's principal and administrative team that influence the provision of intelligent development and teaching support, also establish community relations.

Keyword: Administrative team, transformational leadership, teachers' professional development, teaching quality.

1 Introduction

Education revolution had always been implemented in all schools in Taiwan. So, schools need a distinguished leader in order to promote the education reform [1]. However, the role of principals and administrative team had gradually changed over time. They changed and in order to cope with school-based administration and curriculum development, the leadership roles of principals and functions tends to diverse. This makes the professional and responsibilities become increasingly onerous. Hester and Geert refer to a distributed leadership that impact organizational commitment for teachers [2]. Ronit and Anit also indicate that when teachers are fully empowerment that can increase organizational commitment and identity, and promoting high teaching quality and teachers' profession [3]. Daniel and Alma whose empirical research will be explore to the school teachers in United Kingdom, will fid the leadership of school teachers to be successful. Actually, they cover the school culture area of trust and support, making leadership behavior to be transparent and creative developed [4]. Myers thinks that school teachers participating in decision-making have been empowered to analyze the perspectives of principals of the

S. Lin and X. Huang (Eds.): CSEE 2011, Part V, CCIS 218, pp. 335–341, 2011.

evaluation. This is also to review the standards, finding that it is   readier to empower from the principal to teachers, and the principal who is loved by teachers in Brazilian [5]. Marija and Milena believe that the school teacher's professional growth must rely on the managed administrative team. This is done to create the organizational culture and cooperative learning, but also could really help teachers to improve teaching quality [6]. In addition, Jessica and Heather also felt that the school atmosphere, parents and communities should include the management of relations and behavior between students and teachers, and values. They believe that when the atmosphere of the school is good, there will be no inclination of problems of run off teachers to appear [7]. When the rate of teacher turnover decreases, its can also be said the relative stability of the school is improving. Therefore, the quality of education could also helpful.

2   Theoretical Framework

Schools operate by the quality of good or bad, with the principal and administrative team having a causal relationship. Leithwood and others focuses on schools in 1992. Schools of these times began to carry out related research in transition situations, and in 1995 formally proposed "transformational school leadership", which was meant carry out in the school context of transformational leadership behaviors [8]. Liethwood who structured the transformation of leadership include two levels (Leadership and Management) and 12 factors [9].This makes the leadership level to include: the establishment of the school vision, establishing school goals, demonstration of best practices and important organizational values. There is also the providing of intelligent excitation, providing individual support to display a high degree of performance expectations, creating a productive learning culture, development of enabling to participate in school decision structure and etc. Furthermore, the management level includes staffing, instructional support, monitoring school activities and the establishment and inter-communal relations. This study examines 12 transformational leadership factors to be vocational high school graduated, and evaluation of teaching quality and school operation. Then it analyzes the actual operating conditions of the school and the teachers, in the implementation of educational support and assistance.

3   Participants

The study participants are graduates of vocational high school, also obtaining five or more evaluation assessed 1 (the best), and get four or more 4 or 5 (the worst) of the school principals, director and teacher members, and teachers in 2010.

4   Methodology and Data Analysis

There are 3 public schools and 5 private schools, including access to the Ministry of Education evaluation. Among these seven indicators such as the optimal performance level 1 or above include more than five schools, including three public schools, as well as a private school. The worst evaluation obtains the Ministry of Education level, sub-bad grade 4 or 5 grades of schools, and fully funded private schools, a total of four. Therefore, this study districts the eight schools that are divided into high-performce schools and low-performance schools (encoding, respectively A to H). This study hence interviews the school's principal (encoding interview time– school name-P-school principal and last name) and director (encoding interview time - school name -D- school director, and last name). And there is a teacher who got the only one "Super Power Reward" in 2010 (encoding interview time–school name-PT-teachers, and last name), and interviews with the object in other teaching areas (encoding interview time – school name-T-teachers, and last name). In this study of a total 36 respondents of the research object and the manner in-depth interviews, in order to understand more about the leadership of the school principal and the administrative team, whose operation condition and the teaching quality are influenced by them, he consistency reliability of this study is .83.

5 Conclusion

5.1 Transformational Leadership

This study is stated at the perspectives of transformational leadership by Leithwood, in order to carry out the school administrators and teachers' interview to understand more about the professional development of teachers and teaching quality influenced by them. The followings are all what the respondents have repeatedly stressed in the interview related content.

5.1.1 Vision Aspects of the Establishment of Schools
"Principal of our school's vision plan is relatively perfect. It should specifically be made in two directions. One is the example of the formation, and the other, the care and concern for students." (101204-A-DT)
    "We do not know about the school vision, we only know that principals should be our efforts to admission only." (101228E-TH)

5.1.2 School Goal
"Knowledge and talent were our school goal, but the moral character of students was most important, he (principal) said." (101211C-TCH)
    "I thought the school was own for everyone, teachers and administrators did not need discriminated, or sub-class, everyone should make a contribution for schools and students, this was the school's goals." (101211D-PC)

5.1.3 Demonstrating the Best Practices and Important Organizational Values
"Principal could use scientific management approach, the mechanisms for democratic participation and human sentiment of this caring, to care about each and every teacher and students." (101204C-TC)
    "We hire a lot of schools teacher to replace bad teaching performance of bad teachers .They have helped us a lot." (101229G-PL)

5.1.4 Providing Intelligent Development of Teachers
"In addition to professional competency studies in schools, the principals and directors even set a subsidy to encourage teachers to publish research papers, and expect teachers to continue to obtain research or expertise to obtain a second license." (101204B-TCT)

5.1.5 Providing Individual Support for Teachers
"Schools give teachers the support to be quite fair, no matter regarding teaching, branches, or between the equipment grants." (101230F-TCH)

5.1.6 Demonstrating a High Level of Expectations
"Most of all, he (principal) encourages us to use more ways to motivate everyone. Due that the principal is also busy, and that teachers spend most of their time teaching classes, the principal has no significant relationships with him." (101211A-CTL)

5.1.7 Creating Productive School Culture
"Private schools than public schools in the characteristics of the work harder, principals and directors were often combined with local characteristics, or industry, wanted us to develop the courses that could combined with local industry." (101231E-TW)

5.1.8 Development Promotion to Participate and Decision-Making Structure
"Private schools had tried so hard to motivate teachers association. Public schools are very different from private schools, and no one had willing to initiate." (100101F-DC)

5.2 Management

5.2.1 Staffing
"In order for principals and administrative team to avoid the declining birthrate which had been caused by a surplus of teachers, teachers had been appointed in the overall considerations, but also wanting to maintain the teaching quality." (101204D-DT)

5.2.2 Teaching Support
"I had some experience of handling outdoor activities, I felt mobilization of force was very strong, they could in a very short period of time to find the resource to help. I thought the administration team was very efficient."(101204D-PTY)
    "There is nothing to speak of teaching support! I feel myself as a teaching tool." (100102E-TH)

5.2.3 Monitoring the School Activities
"Sometimes school principals record who works hard and who does not. This feels really uncomfortable." (101231E-TW)

5.2.4 Establishment of Interaction with the Community
"Schools provide community with street-sweeping cleaning services, or apply for a regional charity to serve to elderly people who living alone." (101231A-DCH)

5.2.5   Professional Development of Teacher and Teaching Quality

"Administration of school in order to make knowledge to be management-based, and have an e-management platform, give up teaching to support teachers .This support but also gives up teacher professional development and quality-oriented high school program." (100101B-PG)

"School teachers in the study of the establishment will make the best course of convergence, and regularly apply the teaching to observe and visit." (100101A-TW)

"We have many classes at school every day, and get stuck by the teaching bind; the school also requires that teachers must meet a school's re-conversion course." (100101E-TW)

"Students were graded teaching, the teachers did not feel has been graded, and the school hire a lot of cram school teacher on campus, cram school teachers simply no way to counsel students." (100101G-TLEE)

"Teacher could only accept timetable arrangements, yet sometimes there are no spaces. The Dean is not willing to help us tune lesson, let alone permitting us to go out study." (100101F-TD)

Thus, in the low performance of schools, this study discovers that teachers from school are almost "exploited" or "forced" the way of teaching activities. Also, private school teachers also resent themselves. This is to keep their jobs in a recession which they could only sit and be humiliated. In according to compare high and low performance schools, school management and administration team leader, this study fids a great difference between the two schools. This study based on the above, compile their findings which are as shown in Table 1.

Table 1. Transformational leadership to teachers' professional development and teaching quality of different evaluation level schools

Transformational Leadership	Professional development of teachers		teaching quality.	
leadership	Supported obviously	None Supported obviously	Supported obviously	None Supported obviously
Vision aspects of the establishment	A. D	E. H	B. C. D	E. F. G
School goal	B. C. D		B. C. D	F. G. H
Demonstrate the best practices and important organizational values	A. C. D	G	A. B. C. D	E. G. H
Providing intelligent development of teachers	B. D	F	A. B. D	E. G
Providing individual support for teachers	D	B. D. F	C. D	B. D. F
Demonstrate a high level of expectations	A. D	E. H	A. B	E. H
Creating productive school culture	C. D	E. G	A. D	E. G
Development promotion to participate and decision-making structure	C	D. F. H	A. B. C. D	F. H
management				
Staffing	C. D	E	A. B. C. D	E
Teaching support	C. D	E. F	A. B. C. D	E. F
Monitoring the school activities	A. D	E	C. D	E
Establishment of interaction with the community	A. B. D. G. H		A. B. C. D . G. H	E. F

Source: Author organized (A ~ D for high-performance schools, E ~ H for the low-performance schools).

6 Summary

In eight schools, through the interview process; the high-performance and low performance of principals and administrative teams that influence teachers' professional development, and the teaching resources and support, are give varying difference. Therefore, teachers' professional development in high-performing schools by the leadership of the school had improved. In addition, as school leaders had given the teachers opportunity to achieve self-development, but also bring teachers who improved teaching quality. In the management level; principals and leadership teams in the teaching and support, supervised school activities and the establishment of relations between the communities make the greatest efforts, but they also allow teachers to gradually identify the school and the centripetal force [10]. However, in high-performing schools, they are also among the leading characteristics of the office completed.

In addition, the promotion of the participating schools in the development of the structural aspects of the decision; through the interviews found that the high performance school at this level was seen not viewed so well. However, due to the high performance of the school property, mostly were public schools, and so whether both the executive and staff members belonging to the working conditions of stability and thus prone to so-called "civil service mentality", or "bureaucratic mentality." In contrast, the low-performance schools whose administrative team leader just started to work be a transformational leader, and that community building among the relationship between effort and doing some relevant act, others are still to be improved. Otherwise the next evaluation will also pay out of unsatisfactory results and their admission will be even more difficult. In addition, all low-performance schools are private schools, because the strong intervention by the board of directors also leads to the professional development of teachers. Teaching quality will difficult to improve, because it takes a lot of time on admission activities, but also indirectly killed the teachers opportunities for knowledge enrichment, which was present private schools that operate dilemmas and difficulties in Taiwan's, similar to a vicious circle was indeed worthy of careful consideration of all educators.

6.1 Suggestion

Basing on the findings, this study makes some suggestions to high and low performance level schools.

(1) Before implementing the teachers' professional development, we should also implement the quality of education testing system.

(2) Giving teachers' resources and assistance that should seek to institutionalize the openness and fairness.

(3) Encouraging teachers to participate in school decision-making, and communication with each other.

(4) Removing the administrative bureaucratic culture, and implementation of a comprehensive quality management leadership team.

(5) Getting rid of the myth of teacher, respect for professional autonomy of teachers and enhancing their teaching quality.

References

1. Wu, M.Q.: Integrated framework for school leaders. Education in Taiwan 642, 2–5 (2005)
2. Hester, H., Geert, D.: How distributed leadership can make a difference in teachers' organizational commitment? A qualitative study. Teaching and Teacher Education, 1–11 (2010)
3. Ronit, B., Amit, S.: Influence of teacher empowerment on teachers' organizational commitment, professional commitment and organizational citizenship behavior in school. Teaching and Teacher Education 20(3), 277–289 (2004)
4. Daniel, M., Alma, H.: Teacher led school improvement: Teacher leadership in the UK. Teaching and Teacher Education 22(8), 961–972 (2006)
5. Myers, J.P.: Democratizing school authority: Brazilian teachers' perceptions of the election of principals. Teaching and Teacher Education 24(4), 952–966 (2008)
6. Marija, J.K., Milena, L.J.: Cooperative learning and team culture in schools: Conditions for teachers' professional development. Teaching and Teacher Education 24(1), 59–68 (2008)
7. Jessica, L.G., Heather, K.A.: School climate factors relating to teacher burnout: A mediator model. Teaching and Teacher Education 24(5), 1349–1363 (2008)
8. Leithwood, K., Jantzi, D.: Toward an explanation of how teacher' perceptions of transformational school leadership are formed, ED386785 (1995)
9. Leithwood, K.: Understanding schools as intelligence system. Jai Press Inc. (2000)
10. Reyes, P.: Teachers and their workplace: Commitment, performance and productivity. Sage publication, California (1992)

The Design of the Automobile Energy Absorbing Prevent Injuries Steering

Cuiping Wang

School of Transportation and Vehicle Engineering
Shandong University of Technology
Zibo P.R. China 255049
wangcuiping@126.com

Abstract. the car safety is important for sustainable development of contemporary automobile industry, the researches of the automotive active and passive safety have been universal concern and attention, when the vehicle frontal collision occurred, and the steering wheel and rigid steering column is the main components to make the driver be injured.Based on the extensive collection of home and abroad research data to prevent injuries on the absorbing steering mechanism, according to the national standard GB11557-1998-car steering mechanism to prevent damage to the driver requirements, we study the steering on how to better absorb the impact energy of second impact energy, imposed on the steering column research, design the steering mechanism of absorbing energy and preventing injuries and establish the three-dimensional model using UG software.

Keywords: Steering, collision, absorbing energy and preventing injuries, UG.

1 Introduction

The vehicle safety is one of the main objectives pursued in the course of the car development, and now many countries have developed, improved and implemented the relevant aspects of vehicle safety laws, regulations and testing standards, and made a lot of research from the vehicle's active safety and passive safety. Automotive absorbing energy and preventing injuries steering is a mechanism that can ensure the driver have enough survival space the vehicle frontal collision accident, and can absorb the crash energy, prevent or mitigate the harm to the driver[1].

The function of the energy absorbing steering system to reduce or avoid the harmful to the driver is obvious. The research results show that in 1978 41,400 drivers died or varying degrees injured due to crashed against the steering system. And if the car is not installed the energy-absorbing steering system, this figure will rise to 63,000 people [2].

2 Commonly Used Energy-Absorbing Device

The accident statistics and the analysis results of the vehicle crash test show that: when the car frontal collision occurred, the steering wheel, steering column is the

S. Lin and X. Huang (Eds.): CSEE 2011, Part V, CCIS 218, pp. 342–347, 2011.
© Springer-Verlag Berlin Heidelberg 2011

major component of injury to the driver. So we need design and install the device in the steering system to prevent or reduce the driver be injured, Such as we can use the device in the steering system that can generate the plastic deformation, the elastic deformation to absorb the impact energy or can absorb the impact energy using friction.

Generally, the mainly components to absorb impact energy in the energy absorbing steering system are the compressible energy absorbing steering column, the steering column deformed bracket and the intermediate shaft structure. Among them, the compressible energy absorbing steering column is the key component to reduce or avoid the driver injury, and is the research priorities in the energy-absorbing steering system [3]. The column is generally divided into three types: the sleeve type energy-absorbing steering column, the slip-off type energy-absorbing steering column, the network type energy-absorbing steering column.

3 The Design of the Absorbing Energy Device

When we establish this device, we do not consider the other steering components, such as the universal joints, the steering intermediate shaft and the steering gear.

3.1 The Design Statement of the Energy-Absorbing Steering Device

The inner sleeve of this absorbing steering mechanism does not directly touch the steering column and but as the cage of the balls, the fit between the ball and the upper and lower steering column tube is interference fit, so they can keep running usually normal, and when the car occurred the frontal collision suddenly, and the impact force reaches a certain level, the upper and lower steering column would make relative motion, the contact area would occur the elastic and plastic deformation as the interference fit between the ball and the steering column tube [4].

There is also deformed bracket, the application of the deformed bracket can improve the steering system protecting capacity to the occupants as the frontal collision occurred, the deformed bracket is divided into the upper bracket and the lower bracket, the upper bracket is fixed on the vehicle body and connected with the steering column, the lower bracket is fixed on the steering column tube. The positioning bolt fixed to the vehicle body is installed in the guide groove of the lower bracket, and a twisted metal strap is fixed on the positioning bolt of the lower bracket. There are bearing between the sleeves, so the outer sleeve can not turn with the steering of the steering column, and when the steering wheel suffered from the second collision, the upper bracket fixed on the vehicle body would deform as the collision, and would dislocate with the steering column tube. The lower bracket would slid down along the guide with the steering column, and the twisted metal strap fixed on the lower bracket would be straightened by the positioning bolt, which can absorb the collision energy.

3.2 The Operation Principle of the Energy-Absorbing Steering Column Sleeve as Follows

When the car is driving normally, the steering column and the steering shaft have sufficient strength and stiffness to transmit the steering force. When the vehicle is suffered frontal collision, the collision forces can make the deformed bracket on the outer sleeve disengaged from the frame and body, so that the steering column system would disengage from the body of the vehicle. When the impact force reaches a certain value, the sleeve is extruded deformation by the balls, at the same time, the upper and the lower steering column is compressed, playing the role of Injury Prevention. With the further squeeze, the ball in the sleeve under the action of the impact force to the inner sleeve wall surface is torn, playing the role of absorbing impact energy.

4   Building the Energy Absorbing Model [5]

4.1   Building the Model of the Keep Cage of the Ball

The keep cage of the ball is the sleeve between the steering column tubes. The size of the ball is determined by the size of the inner and outer steering column tubes and the inner sleeve, and by the interference fit clearance determined by the formula (1, 2, 3, 4).

When the frontal collision occurs, the axial force applying on the steering column is limited by the pressure between the sleeves, so

$$F_z = F_f \bullet f \tag{1}$$

In the formula, f is the friction coefficient, F_f is the force of law on the contact point of the calculation section.

$$\lambda_w = \sqrt[4]{3(1 - u^2)(R_w / h)^2} \tag{2}$$

$$\lambda_n = \sqrt[4]{3(1 - u^2)(R_n / h)^2} \tag{3}$$

λ_w, λ_n is the coefficient of the outer and inner sleeve; h is the thickness of the sleeve wall; μ is the Poisson's ratios, R_w, R_n is the radius of the outer and inner sleeve.

$$\Delta = \frac{n \cdot F_f}{4 \cdot \pi \cdot E} \left(\frac{\lambda_w + \lambda_n}{h} \right) \tag{4}$$

In the formula, n is the number of radial force parallel each other, E is the elastic modulus.

When we determined the size of the ball, we create two row holes on the both end of the sleeve, the number of the holes is 40.we assembly the balls into the holes, so the model is shown as figure 1.

4.2   Building the Steering Column Model

In this mechanism, the steering column is include two parts-the upper and the lower, between them are the interference fit balls. By calculating we know, under normal circumstances, the steering column and the balls can steer together, when the force reaches a certain value, there would be friction between the ball and the steering column which can absorb the impact energy, when the collision increased to a certain extent, the balls will further squeeze tear the sleeve wall and further absorb the impact energy. The adjusting of the ball diameter can change the impact load applying to the steering column.

The lower steering column is divided into two parts, the axes of the two parts is parallel, which is joined by the flexible coupling, the upper and the lower flange plate of the flexible coupling are snapped together by two pins and two pin holes, the pins fits into the pin holes through the bushing.

When the violent crash occurs, the car body and the frame are deformed seriously, resulting in the steering shaft, the steering wheel and other components moving backward. At the same time, the driver body move forward by the force of inertia, that causes the pin and the pin hole on the upper and lower steering shaft flange plate tear off, thus mitigating the impact, absorbing the collision energy, and effectively reducing the injury extent of the driver.

The building model is shown as figure 2; the local enlargement figure is shown as figure3.

The modeling of the steering column assembled is shown as figure 4, the local enlargement figure of the steering column is shown as figure 5.

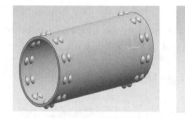 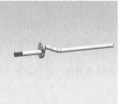 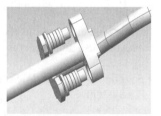

Fig. 1. The balls and the keep cage   **Fig. 2.** The lower steering column   **Fig. 3.** The enlargement figure of the coupling

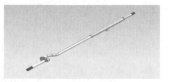 

Fig. 4. The modeling of the assembled steering column   **Fig. 5.** The local enlargement figure of the steering column

4.3 Building the Modeling of the Deformed Bracket

The upper bracket is fixed on the vehicle body and connected with the steering column; the lower bracket is fixed on the steering column tube. The positioning bolt fixed to the vehicle body is installed in the guide groove of the lower bracket, and a twisted metal strap is fixed on the positioning bolt of the lower bracket. The twisted metal strap is shown as figure 6.

The modeling of the outer sleeve is shown as figure 7; the local enlargement figure of the lower bracket is shown as figure 8.

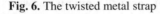

Fig. 6. The twisted metal strap   **Fig. 7.** The modeling of the   **Fig. 8.** The local enlargement
outer sleeve   figure of the lower bracke

4.4 Building the Modeling of the Steering Wheel

In this system, we build the steering wheel without the airbag; the modeling is built based on the actual structure of the Santana 2000. The modeling is shown as figure 9.

4.5 The Assembled Package Modeling of the Energy-Absorbing Steering System

After building the modeling of the energy-absorbing components, we assemble them together to finish the package modeling of the energy-absorbing steering system, in which we should pay attention to the fit of the spline on the steering wheel and the spline on the steering shaft. The assembled package modeling of the energy-absorbing steering system is shown as figure 10.

   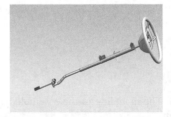

Fig. 9. The modeling of the steering wheel   **Fig. 10.** The assembled package modeling of
the energy-absorbing steering system

5 Summary

In this article we design the absorbing energy steering system in accordance with the national standards, and build the model by UG. The device have sufficient strength and stiffness to transmit the steering force when the car drives normally, but when the vehicle frontal collision occurs, the steering column system could break away from the car body structure by the mechanical way and the steering shaft and the steering column can be compressed, and the steering shaft can absorb the collision energy by deformation, shear, friction and other forms to eliminate the impact of steering gear moving backward, and to achieve the purpose of eliminating or reducing the impact of the collision.

References

1. Horsch, J.D., Viano, D.C., DeCou, J.: History of Safety Research and Development on the General Motor Energy-Absorbing.Steering System SAE912890
2. Lin, y.: A review on vehicle passive safety research. Automobile Engineering 20(1) (1998)
3. Shulan, C.: the effect of reducing casualties by the restraint system of the car passenger. world automobile (5) (1994)
4. Guixin, Z., Xinhua, S.: The research of the impact test method of the energy absorbing steering column. Science of Shandong traffic (3) (2004)
5. Changchun, L.: Basic course of UG 4.0. Posts & Telecommunications Press (June 2007)

A Study on the Relationships between Teachers' Extrinsic Motivational Factors and Students' Learning Satisfaction of Pragmatic Skills Programs at Vocational High Schools in Network Environment

Tsang-Lang Liang, Ying-Chieh Cho, and Tsung-Min Liu

No.2, Shi-Da Road, Changhua City, Taiwan 50074
ietll0615@yahoo.com.tw, snoopy2632000@yahoo.com.tw,
sinonbulllau@yahoo.com.tw

Abstract. The purpose of this study was to investigate the relationships between teachers' extrinsic motivational factors and students' learning satisfaction of the industrial pragmatic skills programs students in vocational high schools. This was based on the results of correlation degree between extrinsic motivational factors and learning satisfaction, which could serve as a reference to improve teaching in practical skill program at vocational high schools. The population of the study was 3,824 students of vocational high school in Changhua County in Taiwan. The sample was drawn by cluster sampling, and it consisted of 600 subjects. The usable return rate was 90%. The collected data was analyzed by frequency distribution, t-test, ANOVA, Pearson correlation, and stepwise regression. The results were as follows: 1.Based on descriptive statistics, the best was verbal praise (M=3.60) in the factor of extrinsic motivational factors. 2. The extrinsic motivational factors of vocational high school students had significant differences by different background variables. 3. The motivational factors were potential predictors toward learning satisfaction.

Keyword: Pragmatic Skills Programs, Extrinsic Motivational factors, Learning Satisfaction.

1 Introduction

The curriculum design of pragmatic skills programs at vocational high schools was responded the Nine-Year curriculum and post-secondary curriculum occurring at the skill education in junior high school. The curriculum was providing someone who had skill tendency, employee and learning skills of a learning environment. Education involves growth of these education policies. Students also could acquire respect, importance and success to learn. In this study, because of financial and time constraints, we took students as the research object, and used students' genders, grades, school hours, school classification, school categories, future planning, and junior high background etc. levels of students, to explore the condition of teachers'

S. Lin and X. Huang (Eds.): CSEE 2011, Part V, CCIS 218, pp. 348–355, 2011.
© Springer-Verlag Berlin Heidelberg 2011

motivational factors and students' learning satisfaction of pragmatic skills programs at vocational high schools.

2 Theoretical Framework

"Pragmatic Skills Programs" are now a part of the existing vocational education system. "Extended Education Programs" are based on the "Extended Vocational Education-Oriented Implementation of the National Education Plan" promulgated by Ministry of Education in 1983. That taught pragmatic skills-based alternative education program for students. It adopted yearly curriculum design. Currently there are one year and three-year programs. Their students came from Junior High School Art Education Programs (graduates) [1]. Motivation was from Latin "Movere" means transfer or change. Jucius believe motivation to be a process demanding behavior [2]. Therefore, it was easy to motivate someone, if you understand whose demand it was and whether being remunerated [3]. The factor "Motivation" meaning tangible or intangible rewards were to satisfy needs or desire of students than induce student-oriented constructive and spontaneous behavior of positive and promoting learning efficacy. The extrinsic motivation factors include material rewards and verbal praise. Tai believed that learning satisfaction meant in the learning process, and learners' perceptions of the learning activities could meet individual learning needs [4]. It was the satisfactory feeling and positive attitude produced from the love of learning activities. Therefore, in this study "learning satisfaction" was aimed to the level of satisfaction of students. This "learning satisfaction" is done at school's learning environment, curriculum arrangement and design, instructional behaviors, learning outcomes etc.

3 Purpose

The purposes of this research are listed as the following: 1.To explore the situation analysis on students of pragmatic skills programs at vocational high school on teachers' extrinsic motivational factors and learning satisfaction. 2. To explore the extrinsic motivational factors of pragmatic skills programs students, which have significant differences by different background variables. 3. To explore the extrinsic motivational factors and learning satisfaction of pragmatic skills programs, students can be significantly correlated in several aspects. 4. To explore the extrinsic motivational factors are potential predictors toward learning satisfaction.

4 Methodology

To effectively achieve the above research goal, the study uses the survey research method and modified "Effective Teachers' Motivational factors Scale" prepared by Guo to collect relevant empirical data. This survey research method also uses the total scale Cronbach's α coefficient of .90, and "Course Learning Satisfaction" prepared by Liu, the total scale Cronbach's α coefficient. 85. for construction of the survey. Through questionnaire and literature analysis, this study connected, compared and proved various data. The study researched on the relationships between teachers' motivational factors and students' learning satisfaction of pragmatic skills programs at vocational high schools. Through literature discussion and questionnaire prepared in accordance with research structure we hence preceded a pilot study. According to pretest statistical analysis result and views of experts and scholars, we compiled the formal questionnaire.

5 Data Analysis

The purpose of this study was to research the current situation and circumstances of the relationships between teachers' extrinsic motivational factors and students' learning satisfaction of pragmatic skills programs at vocational high schools. Data analysis method was to adopt frequency distribution, percentage, mean, standard deviation, T-test, one way ANOVA, Pearson correlation and stepwise regression analysis:

5.1 The Situation Analysis on Students of Pragmatic Skills Programs at Vocational High School on Teachers' Extrinsic Motivational Factors and Learning Satisfaction

5.1.1 Analysis on Various Items in Scale

According to descriptive statistics, we learned that the average performance of vocational high school students perceived in "Teacher's extrinsic motivational factors Scale" was between 3.33 and 3.77. The standard deviation was between 0.83 and 0.93. The question, "I expected to be self-affirmation in the program (verbal praise)." receives the highest score of 3.77. But question, " The program gave me a chance to be the assistance (material rewards)." was the lowest score of 3.33. Also, we learned that the average performance of vocational high school students perceived in "Learning Satisfaction Scale" was between 3.19 and 3.73. The standard deviation was between at 0.79 and 0.98. The question, "I recognize the classroom teacher's professional knowledge and skills (instructional behaviors)." received the highest score of 3.73. But question, "I can feel the comfort of school practice works environment (learning environment)." received the lowest score of 3.19.

5.2 The Extrinsic Motivational Factors and Learning Satisfaction Had Significant differences by Different Background Variables

Using different backgrounds to discuss teachers' extrinsic motivational factors and students' learning satisfaction of pragmatic skills programs at vocational high schools' and differences among the various levels and background variables, were divided into seven parts to be analyzed and discussed. We preceded homogeneity test for samples' differences, in which "gender", "school property ", "school hours", "junior high background" etc. were discontinuous variables in binary variables. T-tests were used to analyze significant differences among the tests; and that "grade", "future plan", "school categories" became the discontinuous variables in third variables. The one-way ANOVA of variance analysis was used. If ANOVA results of the test results reached a significant level, then use the Scheffé analysis were to be used to compare differences among the variables. The results are as the following:

5.2.1 Different Background Variables on Teachers' Extrinsic Motivational Factors

5.2.1.1 Gender

Data from Table 1 showed that detailed tests results from the different gender dimensions of vocational high schools students' extrinsic motivational factors. These factors at all levels suggested that different gender in the vocational high school students for motivational factors, represented "material rewards (t = -3.75)" and "verbal praise (t = -3.99)". It reached the level of significant differences. The test result was as shown in Table 1:

Table 1. Means and SD of Gender in extrinsic motivational factors scales

Gender	Male		Female		t-value
	M	SD	M	SD	
Extrinsic motivation -Material rewards	3.38	.73	3.61	.67	-3.75***
Extrinsic motivation -Verbal praise	3.49	.75	3.74	.68	-3.99***

Note. N=540. ** *p<.001

5.2.1.2 School Property

Data from Table 2 shows, that detailed test results of different vocational high school students school property at all levels for extrinsic motivational factors suggested that different school property in vocational high school students for motivational factors were " material rewards (t = 2.49)" and " verbal praise (t = 2.14)". This reached the level of significant differences. The test result was as shown in Table 2:

Table 2. Means and SD of school property in extrinsic motivational factors scales

School property	Public		Private		t-value
	M	SD	M	SD	
Extrinsic motivation -Material rewards	3.52	.68	3.34	.81	2.49*
Extrinsic motivation -Verbal praise	3.64	.70	3.48	.80	2.14*

Note. N=540. * p<.05

5.2.1.3 Future Planning

In Table 3, by one-way analysis of variance test results we learned different future planning and teachers' extrinsic motivational factors in different dimensions, its F value in the "material rewards" and "verbal praise" were in significant levels of standard (p <. 01). Analysis of different future planning and teachers' extrinsic motivational factors at all levels, were as shown in Table 3:

Table 3. The mean, SD and ANOVA of future planning in extrinsic motivational factors scales

Future planning	N	M	SD	F	Scheffé
Extrinsic motivation -Material rewards					
(1) Studies	306	3.57	.72		
(2) Employment	82	3.41	.64	5.73**	(1)>(3)
(3) Undecided	152	3.34	.73		
Total	540	3.48	.72		
Extrinsic motivation -Verbal praise					
(1) Studies	306	3.73	.75		
(2) Employment	82	3.49	.69	12.08***	(1)>(2) (1)>(3)
(3) Undecided	152	3.41	.65		
Total	540	3.60	.73		

Note. N=540. ** p<.01 *** p<.001

5.2.1.4 School Categories
In Table 4, by one-way ANOVA results, we learned different grades and teachers' extrinsic motivational factors in different dimensions, its ANOVA results in the "material rewards" and "verbal praise" were in significant levels of standard (p <. 01). Analysis of different school categories and teachers' extrinsic motivational factors at all levels, were as shown in Table 4:

Table 4. The mean, SD and ANOVA of school categories in extrinsic motivational factors scales

School categories	N	M	SD	F	Scheffé
Extrinsic motivation -Material rewards					
(1) Industrial Class	300	3.43	.75		
(2) Business Class	60	3.60	.64	3.00**	
(3) Agriculture Class	60	3.37	.55		
(4) Home Economics Class	120	3.61	.71		
Total	540	3.48	.72		
Extrinsic motivation -Verbal praise					
(1) Industrial Class	300	3.52	.75		(2)>(1)
(2) Business Class	60	3.90	.62	7.38***	(4)>(1)
(3) Agriculture Class	60	3.46	.61		(2)>(3)
(4) Home Economics Class	120	3.75	.72		
Total	540	3.60	.73		

Note. N=540. *** p<.001

5.3   The Extrinsic Motivational Factors and Learning Satisfaction of Pragmatic Skills Programs Students Was Significantly Correlated in Several Aspects

Using Pearson correlation analysis to test the relationship between motivational factors and learning satisfaction. And by Table 5, we learned that the results showed that satisfaction with various aspects, learning of learning environment, curriculum design, instructional behaviors, learning outcomes on the teachers' motivational factors, were indirect impact which all appeared significant positive correlation, in which " learning outcomes" level (r =.574, p <.0 1) was the highest. From this we learned teachers' motivational factors aspect's indirect impact and learning satisfaction had a significant positive correlation.

Table 5. Means, SD and Pearson correlation for motivational factors and learning satisfaction validity

	M	SD	1	2	3	4	5	6
1. Motivational factors	3.63	.60	1					
2. Learning environment	3.26	.75	.436(**)	1				
3. Curriculum design	3.47	.63	.446(**)	.621(**)	1			
4. Instructional behaviors	3.53	.74	.479(**)	.547(**)	.629(**)	1		
5. Learning outcomes	3.68	.66	.574(**)	.492(**)	.593(**)	.641(**)	1	
6. Learning satisfaction	3.48	.58	.581(**)	.811(**)	.845(**)	.854(**)	.813(**)	1

Note. N=540. Reliabilities in diagonal. ** p<.01

5.4   The Extrinsic Motivational Factors Were Potential Predictors toward Learning Satisfaction

It was from the dimensions of teachers' extrinsic motivational factors, which predict the level of "overall learning satisfaction". We could see the two dimensions of "material rewards (X_1)" and "verbal praise (X_2)" of input variables. We find that levels of teachers' motivational factors to overall learning satisfaction had significant prediction. In the regression model, the orders were "material rewards (X_1)" and "verbal praise (X_2)" that reach a significant level regression equations (p <.01), F=77.861. The three predictors of learning satisfaction effect was the subject (β=.607, R^2=.368), that entered the regression model of three variables and could explain 36.8% of the learning satisfaction variance. The original regression equation is as the following:

$$Y = 1.426 + .139X_1 + .233X_2$$

6   Conclusion

6.1   Status Analysis of Pragmatic Skills Programs at Vocational High Schools Students to Teachers' Extrinsic Motivational Factors

According to the "Teachers' extrinsic motivational factors scale" of vocational high schools' we learned that vocational high school students perceived teachers' extrinsic motivational factors that placed emphasis on the "verbal praise" level, amongst which "I expected to be self-affirmation in the program". was the most important item. Thus, we knew that the outcomes of learning could lead student autonomy and improving the learning efficacy. Vocational high school students perceived teachers' extrinsic motivational factors to be more neglected in the "material rewards" level, amongst which "The program gave me a chance to be the assistance that meant the assistance model lead students was helpless".

6.2   Difference of Vocational High Schools Students with Different Background Variables on Teachers' Motivational Factors

First, vocational high school students of different genders had significant differences on teachers' extrinsic motivational factors, no matter in "material rewards" and "verbal praise" level. Thus we could see boys and girls had significantly difference in perceiving teachers' extrinsic motivational factors of the tow levels. Secondly, vocational high school students of different School property had significant differences on teachers' extrinsic motivational factors in "material rewards" and "verbal praise" level. Thus we could see publics and privates had significantly difference in perceiving teachers' motivational factors of the two levels. Thirdly, regarding the result of different future planning of vocational high schools students in teachers' extrinsic motivational factors of "verbal praise" level, the studies were higher than employment, with studies were also higher than the undecided. In "material rewards" level, the studies were higher than the undecided. Finally, the result of different school categories of vocational high schools students in teachers' extrinsic motivational factors of "verbal praise" level, the studies of Business Class students were higher than Industrial Class students, and Home Economics Class students were higher than the Industrial Class students, with Business Class students also being higher than the Agriculture Class students.

6.3   The Motivational Factors Were Potential Predictors toward Learning Satisfaction

Using dimensions of teachers' extrinsic motivational factors to predict the level of "overall learning satisfaction", at teachers' motivational dimensions at all levels prediction, a total of two predictors of learning satisfaction with the overall significant predictors in the regression model were in the order of "material rewards" and "verbal praise". The extrinsic motivational "β coefficient was positive, *i.e.*, the more intense the dimensions of teachers' motivational factors, the greater impact on learning satisfaction received.

7   Suggestion

First, there are suggestions for vocational high schools: Vocational highs schools teachers' motivational factors pay less attention to the items on "material rewards" level. Schools should provide teachers some incentives, for example, the bonus, studies and appreciation, and motivating students' efficacy. Secondly, there are also suggestions for vocational high school teachers: The Vocational high schools students have in different levels, under the learning satisfaction in "curriculum design" level, realized that the third-year students score higher than first-year students. We suggest when designing curriculum, teachers can make the curriculum more flexible, interesting and rich curriculum to attract lower grade students to want to learn more. Finally, there are also suggestions for future research: As to research methods, we suggest that future researchers may use observation for long-term study. This is done to facilitate empirical research and verify the correctness. As in the school premises, we suggest future researchers may expand the scope of the study and explore more various schools of other cities and counties.

References

1. Information on,
   http://140.122.71.231/Ptae/web2006/junsch/index.asp
2. Jucius, M.J.: Personnel Management, 8th edn. RDIrwin (1976)
3. Lin, Z.X.: A study of motivation factors on employees through different variation on population statistics and job characteristics: A research based on the employees of companies in central Taiwan. Tunghai University, Taiwan (1997)
4. Tai, L.C.: A study on the physical-mental health and learning satisfaction with physical education in primary school children. National Taichung University, Taiwan (2002)
5. Guo, W.C.: Motivating factor for higher learning motivation, learning behavior and learning efficacy in vocational school students. Dai Yeh University, Taiwan (2004)
6. Lin, L.A.: A study on learning satisfaction in course of vocational exploration and guidance of junior high school students. National Taipei University of Technology, Taiwan (1999)

Reformed Calculus Curriculum Impact on Learning Performance of Engineering Mathematics with Data Analysis

Ruey-Maw Chen[1], Fuh-Gwo Chen[2], and Shih-Yen Huang[1]

[1] No.57, Sec. 2, Zhong-shan Rd., Taiping Dist., Taichung 41170, Taiwan, ROC
[2] No. 34, Chung-Chie Rd, Sha Lu, Taichung 44302, Taiwan, ROC
`raymond@mail.ncut.edu.tw`, `fgchen@gmail.com`,
`syhuang@mail.ncut.edu.tw`

Abstract. Both pros and cons of calculus reform have been widely discussed since late 1980's. In spite of arguments are poles apart, calculus reform is still discussed worldwide. The students of Taiwanese university of technology usually have a high failure rate in calculus, thereby affecting the performance of advanced application courses. Through calculus curriculum development of this study, students are supposed to understand which calculus topics connecting with the engineering mathematics and further engineering application courses. Moreover, this work is an attempt to increase the students' learning performance on engineering mathematics and enhance the learning intention on calculus. Calculus curriculum was designed based on engineering mathematic and further application subjects. Teaching practice was conducted on students of both traditional and reform-based taught classes. Finally, this study proceeded learning performance evaluation. Preliminary empirical results and learning performance analysis of this study are provided.

Keywords: Calculus reform, calculus curriculum, engineering mathematics, PLEASE.

1 Introduction

The movement of Calculus reform is an attempt to increase both passing rates and a general interest in mathematics. Murphy (reformer) [1] and opposition supporters (traditionalists) have viewpoints poles apart on Calculus reform as indicated by Petechuk [2].

Among reformers, Mumford's arguments [3] are the typical of those who support calculus reform. Reform effort in calculus curriculum mainly focuses on restructure content. Harvard Calculus Consortium [4,5] is the representative and the most widely adopted text. Which eliminates virtually all rigors should be used for math, engineering, and physical science majors. Meanwhile, it de-emphasized deductive symbolic reasoning by decreasing some sections, and stressed students' ability of application by connecting formal definitions and procedures with practical problems. Klein and Rosen [6] refuted calculus reform supporters' arguments (Mumford);

S. Lin and X. Huang (Eds.): CSEE 2011, Part V, CCIS 218, pp. 356–361, 2011.

indicating that they create a fictitious model of a calculus course and charged all faults on it. Opposition supporters on calculus reform indicated that the traditional calculus books have contained a fairly even mix of computation, conceptualization, and theory. Should not be the case like Harvard Calculus. Johnson [7] reported on the effect of the Harvard Calculus Consortium at Oklahoma State University by comparing students' performance in reformed and traditional calculus. However, the experimental outcomes of the reformed curriculum can't be concluded briefly.

In spite of several favorable empirical results having been reported, a widely supported conclusion on the effect of calculus reform is still in debate. However, reform is continuing, even though there is still disputed. Schoenfeld [8] highlights several themes on reform courses. Reform calculus should more hands on and students are expected to understand complex mathematical concepts in more connected ways. Moreover, some signs revealing definite influence of calculus reform on textbook development. Calculus: Early Transcendentals by Stewart [9] was once regarded as the representative of the traditional textbook. Nevertheless, the new edition of Stewart's calculus book [10] does not prove many theorems and is more streamlined. Restated, both reformers and traditionalists have realized that enabling students to understand and appreciate calculus is their common goal. Restated, the goal of both sides is gradually convergence. Therefore, it is convinced that any reform effort should keep track of this common goal.

Increasing students' performance in Calculus while positively impacting the students taking advanced mathematics related courses resulted from Calculus reform efforts. It is necessary to change the calculus curriculum to achieve above objective. Therefore, Giersch, Letts, and Pugalee [11] developed authentic situations of space travel correlated Calculus curriculum to provide conceptual and intuitive meaning for applications of calculus concepts and skills. Students in schools are exposed to real world application problems so that they may develop an appreciation for how mathematics is connected to real world application problems.

This study is one subproject of PLEASE conducted to investigate the impacting of calculus reform on learning advanced information engineering professional courses. In this subproject, we hoped to increase the number of students who succeed in further engineering mathematics course and to successfully apply what they had learned in courses of applied science and engineering. Restated, traditional curriculum is convinced not fit to engineering major students; curriculum exploitation and construction are required. To keep away from the dispute in calculus reform, this study puts the rigor issue aside and takes students' learning in subsequent mathematical and application courses into account by stressing intuitive understanding and application of calculus. Hence, this study developed calculus curriculum which are derived from engineering mathematic and further applied science and engineering subjects, followed by teaching practice and learning performance evaluation.

2 Study Phases

PLEASE [12] is a project of the National Science Council of Taiwan initiated in 2008, a collaborative model for calculus reform. One of the censures of calculus reform is that reformed curriculum may not applicable in preparing students to take advanced mathematical courses. Hence, PLEASE components tried to fix this issue by restructuring calculus curriculum to help students make a connection between calculus and subsequent mathematical courses, such as statistics, engineering mathematics and advanced engineering courses. This work mainly focuses on the learning of engineering mathematics.

Engineering majors usually have trouble grasping complicated concepts and processes on engineering mathematics such as differential equations, Fourier series, and Laplace transform, all of which require a solid background in integrals as well as in differentials. In this calculus curriculum of the subproject, students are trained to construct and solve mathematical models of given realistic application problems. This study was divided into three phases: curriculum analysis and supplement curriculum development phase, teaching phase based on developed curriculum and performance assessment on engineering mathematics course phase.

Phase 1, this phase is to interconnect calculus and professional courses. Curriculum exploitation and construction on the basis of engineering mathematics and further application courses, it is necessary to take into account the existing curriculum with the convergence, and also taking into account the characteristics of the relevant professional courses' characteristics. Hence, this phase focuses on syllabus analysis of calculus and engineering mathematics, and supplement curriculum development. The curriculum exploitation and construction includes two type supplement materials that emphasis on relevant topics between calculus and advanced courses.

- The basics of engineering mathematics relevant problems insert in reform class. For example, topics in engineering mathematics such as differential equations, Laplace transform, Fourier series and transform are related to derivatives and integrations curriculum topics of calculus.
- The application of advanced professional relevant courses is introduced. For example, edge detection in image processing can be implemented with first-order or second-order differential on the image function; image smoothing and image de-blurred can be achieved via convolution filter operation which is defined by integration.

Meanwhile, Calculus: Early Transcendentals (Stewart, 1999) [10], is chosen as the calculus textbook. The calculus course using this book does not cover all the rigorous material. Most students in our projects have graduated from vocational high schools and are studying at technological universities, which are usually less theoretical in their professional training. Therefore, part of calculus curriculum were deleted as most reformer arguments. Instead, totally, there are 79 supplemental examples were added into the curriculum.

Phase 2, this phase is the teaching practice on reform class based on modified calculus curriculum by introducing them supplemental curriculum. Both types of those constructed supplement curriculum were introduced to students in adequate sections. The purpose of this phase is to enable students to understand calculus use in the professional courses in the future. It is to guide students correctly realizing why needs the learning of calculus and thus trigger enthusiasm of students on learning calculus. The lecturer presented the model and reminded students of its relationship with Laplace and Fourier Transform and their application in convolution filter after introducing improper integral and infinite series. It was expected to enhance students' concept image related to the topics and increase their motivation to learn.

Phase 3, assessment of learning performance on engineering mathematics is the main focus of this phase. However, the advanced applications related to the teaching engineering mathematics topics were again given to students such as Fourier series and transform applications in digital signal processing which has many applications in diverse fields as speech, radar, pattern recognition, and so on. This is to awaken students' memory on calculus course; meanwhile, to enhance students' impression on the connection between mathematics and applications. The instructors of the traditional sections prepared examinations to be taken by all calculus sections. The exam was designed to cover the skills emphasized in solving two types of questions, simple and difficult. To minimize variance in the ways individual instructors graded their examinations, each faculty member involved in teaching engineering mathematics graded certain questions for all students in all sections, simple and difficult questions were included in every test.

3   Experiment Results and Analysis

Generally, this study is to evaluate the calculus reform impacting on the learning performance of engineering mathematics course. Hence, a quantitative assessment of student passing rates based on performance on the midterm and final examinations for the Engineering mathematics course is conducted and summarized in Table 1. This quantitative assessment provides a somewhat objective measure, clear the instructor's hopes and aspirations to the success or failure of the effort. In this study, two student sections were involved; reform-based calculus taught students and traditionally calculus taught students. There are 46 members in reform class and 53 students in traditionally taught class. The passing rates of engineering mathematics are calculated for both simpler and difficult problems of midterm and final tests of the first semester.

Table 1. Summary of Engineering Mathematics Examination Results

	Passing Rates of Midterm Test		Passing Rates of Final Test	
	Simple Question	Difficult Question	Simple Question	Difficult Question
Reform (46)	32 (69.6%)	**4 (8.7%)**	**37 (80.4%)**	**9 (19.6%)**
Trad. (53)	**43 (81.1%)**	0 (0%)	41 (77.4%)	9 (18.9%)

According to the empirical results as shown in Table 1, the passing rate of students in traditional section is higher than that of reform section for simple question in midterm test. The students in reform section outperform students in traditional section for other test questions. Nevertheless, the performance has only slight difference. For difficult questions, both reform and traditional section have lower passing rate, less than 20%. Therefore, nothing can be taken for granted so far. For realizing the causes of low passing rate on difficult question, interviews were conducted after the tests. However, some factors affecting students on solving questions were concluded; they are

- Question interpretation (relevance between question and equation), this factor imply students lacking of modeling ability.
- Method confusing, this is due to that student does not clearly understand the question, so that does not know which method to apply. For example, solving linear equation and nonlinear equation have different scheme to be applied. However, the prerequisite is "the question is linear or nonlinear".
- Order of operation, solving question sometimes requires a series of operations. Restated, to yield correct solution, the order of operation is important. Students do not realize the essence of each operation.

Meanwhile, 20%~30% students failed on simple questions. The major factors are "which calculus skills should be applied" and "how to do differential and integration". Obviously, those students were with weak calculus background.

4   Conclusion

Applicable calculus curriculum to engineering major students is the core of this study. Through curriculum development, teaching practice, and performance assessment phases, this study aims to increase the students' learning performance on engineering mathematics and enhance the learning intension on calculus. Although the performance has not emerged, engineering-based calculus curriculum developments which may expand students' cognition on calculus, expands professional horizons and cultivate engineers who can serve industries. Although rich in numerical and statistical detail provided by a quantitative assessment, it offers few clues as to directions for change, modification, and improvement. Therefore, qualitative assessment of learning factors will be conducted by interview and questionnaire in the end.

Acknowledgements. This work was partly supported by the National Science Council, Taiwan (R. O. C.), under contract NSC 97-2511-S-167-004-MY3.

References

[1] Murphy, L.: Reviewing Reformed Calculus (2006), Information on http://lagrange.math.trinity.edu/tumath/research/studpapers/s45.pdf
[2] Petechuk, D.: Has the calculus reform project improved students' understanding of mathematics. Science Clarified 2 (2009)
[3] Mumford, D.: Calculus reform—for the millions. Notices 44(5), 559–563 (1997)
[4] Hughes-Hallett, D., Gleason, A.M., et al.: Calculus, international edn. John Wiley & Sons, New York (1992)
[5] Hughes-Hallett, D., Gleason, A.M., et al.: Calculus, international edn. John Wiley & Sons, New York (1994)

[6] Klein, D., Rosen, J.: Calculus Reform—For the $Millions. Notices of The Ams 44(10), 1324–1325 (1997)

[7] Johnson, K.: Harvard calculus at Oklahoma State University. The American Mathematical Monthly 102(9), 794–797 (1995)

[8] Schoenfeld, A.H.: A Brief Biography of Calculus Reform. UME Trends: News and Reports on Undergraduate Mathematics Education 6(6), 3–5 (1995)

[9] Stewart, J.: Calculus: Early Transcendentals. Books/Cole, Monterey (1999)

[10] Stewart, J.: Calculus: Concept & Context. Books/Cole, Monterey (2006)

[11] Giersch, C., Letts, J., Pugalee, D.K.: Developing Calculus Concepts through Applications Related to NASA's Space Exploration Program, pp. 246–250 (2004)

[12] Liu, P.H., Lin, C.C., Chen, T.S., Chung, Y.T., Liao, C.H., Lin, P.C., Tseng, H.E., Chen, R.M.: A Collaborative Model for Calculus Reform A Preliminary Report. In: Proceedings of the Mathematics Education, the 21st Century Project Meeting, pp. 372–375 (2009)

Using the Skills, Abilities and Attitudes and Other Indicators to Measure Status of Northeast Asian Countries, Life-Long Education

Yen-Ju Su[1], Shun-Chieh Chen[2], and David W.S. Tai[3]

[1,2] National Changhua University of Education, Department of Industrial Education and Technology, No.2, Shi-Da Road, Changhua City, Taiwan
[3] Hungkuang University, No.34. Chung-Chie Rd., Shalu, Taichung County Taiwan
yenju5329@gmail.com, chensjtw@gmail.com, david60123@gmail.com

Abstract. Comparing lifelong learning in Taiwan, china, Korea and Japan, according to the EU's lifelong learning quality indicators, Taiwan's overall development of lifelong learning is better than China's but the quality is far lower than that of neighboring countries. Among the 4 areas, Taiwan has a higher rate of participation in lifelong learning in area B; leads the other three countries in investment in education, educator and learning, and ICT in learning in area C. Taiwan government should follow the example of neighboring countries, regular public participation and lifelong learning conditions survey conducted as a reference for policy improvement.

Keywords: lifelong learning, OECD, Quality Indicators.

1 Introduction

The 21st century is the age of the knowledge economy; it is a century of fierce global competition. Facing the new century, Taiwan's key to success in increasing its national competitiveness, sustainable developing the natural environment, and improving quality of living, lies in education. In particular, the ability to successfully help individuals in their pursuit of free and dignified growth, as well as diverse and orderly social progress, relies on education. A society that invests heavily in education is investing in a beautiful future. Regarding the concept of international lifelong learning, a country's current development and trend of lifelong learning should be emphasized. In Asia, the development of lifelong learning policies of our neighboring countries, such as China, Korea and Japan, especially deserves investigation.

2 Literature Review: Development of Lifelong Learning in Taiwan, China, Korea and Japan

Lifelong learning should not merely be an abstract principle or an ideal but also incorporate concrete policies and actions. According to the education reports released since the 1980s, lifelong learning has become an important policy for implementation for any particular country.

S. Lin and X. Huang (Eds.): CSEE 2011, Part V, CCIS 218, pp. 362–371, 2011.
© Springer-Verlag Berlin Heidelberg 2011

Taiwan. From the "Toward the Learning Society White Paper" presented by the Ministry of Education in 1998, it can be seen that Taiwan's government was responding to the global trend towards lifelong learning, which named the year "The Lifelong Learning Year." The Lifelong Learning Act passed in 2002 infused new energy into the promotion of lifelong learning in Taiwan [1].The 2010 National Education Conference also included lifelong learning on the agenda. A new education white paper will be framed according to the conclusions of the conference and will serve as the policy direction and guidelines on the future development of lifelong learning in Taiwan.

The implementation policies include the following: 1.The supplementary and continuing education system. 2. Providing learning opportunities for the public by establishing community colleges: currently, there are 101 community colleges and 250,000 students [2] 3.Accreditation for informal learning: currently there are 544 certified courses (1388 credits) provided by 133 institutes [3] 4.Providing in-service education opportunities. 5. Promoting learning for senior citizens: the senior population (over 65 years old) has dramatically increased to 2.48 million at the end of 2010, comprising 10.74% of the total population [4]; schools, township offices, senior citizen centers, community service centers, and community development associations started to establish the Learning Resource Centers for Senior Citizens in 2008. It is expected that the goals of establishment will be achieved in 2011 and provide more learning opportunities for local senior citizens [1].

China. China has started to develop lifelong learning in recent years due to the increased demand for lifelong learning, adjustments to the industrial structure, economic changes and diverse individual learning needs. In addition, lifelong learning has been greatly developed since the Communist Party of China's Report of the 16th Congress, which included the following: "to build a moderately prosperous society, a lifelong learning society for all by 2020" [5].Many provinces, starting from Fujian in 2005, have passed laws related to lifelong education [6].In the 2010 "National Mid- and Long-term Education Reform and Development Outline," China explicitly presented goals and missions such as "constructing a flexible and open lifelong education system," "forming a basic learning society," "building lifelong learning bridges," and "establishing a credit accumulation and transfer system for continuing education, and recognizing and connecting different types of learning achievements" [7].

Korea. Korea started to actively promote lifelong education in the 1990s. The Education Reform for the New Education System issued by the Presidential Commission on Educational Reform in 1996 [8] emphasized that a national lifelong learning policy and basic structure should be developed, and that learning opportunities should be open to the public. In particular, a complete system for improving learning sources, support services and certification of learning achievements should be established in order for individuals to learn whenever and wherever it is suitable for their needs and conditions. In 1999, Korea promoted lifelong education by passing the Lifelong Education Act, establishing organizations in charge of lifelong learning and supporting organizations, consolidating the function of lifelong education in colleges, promoting lifelong e-learning, and implementing "credit bank" and "credit recognition" systems, which include setting up a banking system for specialized information and education accounts. Furthermore, the qualification system for instructors was also completed by upgrading social education professionals to lifelong learning instructors [9].

Japan. Lifelong learning has become a basic state policy of the Japanese government and has long been rooted in their citizens' mind. As early as 1981, the Central Council for Education issued the Report on Lifelong Learning, in which the concept of lifelong integrated education was presented from a broad perspective. The report emphasized that individual lifelong learning should be encouraged in the overall education system. In 1990, Japan issued the Lifelong Learning Promotion Act to build a solid legal foundation for lifelong learning. The Act aimed to provide thorough promotional measures and lifelong learning opportunities [10].The Japanese government believes that a lifelong learning society and all necessary measures must be established so that "people can choose to learn anytime in their lives and their achievements will be properly assessed." The reasons are as follows: 1. Eliminating the drawbacks of society that overvalue a person's educational background; this is one of the key issues in Japan's current education reform. The aim is to build a society where all kinds of "learning achievements" throughout a person's lifetime can be truly evaluated, regardless of their forms. 2. Reflecting the increased demand for learning as a society matures. 3. As society and the economy changes, lifelong learning becomes even more necessary. People must continually acquire new knowledge and technology in order to respond to information-based lives, globalization and changes in industrial structures [11].

In the network of lifelong learning, community-based lifelong learning centers are established in addition to centers for citizens, especially women. The multifunctional centers offer facilities of all kinds, including: classrooms, information provision, consulting services, entertainments, book loans, and other activities. Besides classrooms, larger facilities also provide learning information or education services, such as consulting with a specialist [10].

3   Comparison

The criteria for comparing the four countries' lifelong learning areas are based on the 15 quality indicators in the 2002 European Report on Quality Indicators of Lifelong Learning [12] presented by the European Union.

The 4 areas and 15 indicators are as follows Area A: skills, competencies and attitudes, including: literacy, numeracy, new skills for the learning society, learning to learn skills, as well as active citizenship, cultural and social skills; Area B: access and participation, including: access to lifelong learning and participation in lifelong learning; Area C: resources for lifelong learning, including: investment in lifelong learning, educators and learning, as well as information and communications technologies (ICT) in learning; Area D: strategies and systems, including: strategies for lifelong learning, coherence of supply, guidance and counseling, accreditation and certification, and quality assurance. Here we only compare the four countries according to the indicators that have detailed criteria.

4 Skills, Competencies and Attitudes in Lifelong Learning

Literacy: Percentage of students per country at proficiency level 1 or below on the PISA reading literacy scale

Table 1. Differences in reading literacy among Taiwan and neighboring countries in Asia

Country / Level	Taiwan	Japan	Korea	Hong Kong	Shanghai	OECD Ave.
Level 1 and under (%)	15.6	13.6	5.8	8.3	4.1	18.8

Source: [13]

Although Taiwan's overall reading proficiency rate is not especially low, 15.6% of Taiwanese students are at the proficiency level 1 or below, compared to Korea at 5.8%, Hong Kong at 8.3%, Shanghai at 4.1%, and OECD average at 18.8%. It shows that Taiwanese students still have great potential for enhancing their reading proficiency.

Numeracy: Percentage of students per country level 1 or below on the PISA mathematical literacy scale

Table 2. Differences in mathematical literacy among Taiwan and neighboring countries in Asia

Country / Level	Taiwan	Japan	Korea	Hong Kong	Shanghai	OECD Ave.
Level 1 and under (%)	12.8	12.5	8.1	8.8	4.8	22

Source: [13]

There are at least 87.2% of Taiwanese students above level 1. The OEDC average at level 1 and under is 22% while Korea, Hong Kong and Shanghai are below 10%. It shows that enhancing math proficiency at the lowest level should deserve more attention in our future education policies.

New Skills in the Learning Society: Percentage of students per country below the score of 409 points on the PISA scientific literacy scale.

Table 3. Differences in scientific literacy among Taiwan and neighboring countries in Asia

Country	Taiwan	Japan	Korea	Hong Kong	Shanghai
Score	520	539	528	549	575
Rank	15	6	7	3	1

Source: [13]

There are no significant differences in scientific literacy scores among Taiwan and the neighboring countries; all of them score high.

Table 4. Percentages of science and technology students in higher education in Taiwan and neighboring countries in Asia

Country / Score	Taiwan	Japan	Korea1	China
Science and technology students in higher education: colleges (%)	34.5	18.6	38.7	41.7
Science and technology students in higher education: MA & PhD (%)	42.2	38.9	23.0	48.3

Source: [1, 14] 1. The data for Korea includes science, technology and agriculture.

The percentage of Taiwanese and Chinese students pursuing Masters/ Doctoral degrees in science and technology are over 40%, showing that both countries accept new technologies at a relatively high level.

Learning-to-Learn Skills: Percentage of students per country in the lower 25 % of overall performance on the PISA "elaboration strategies" index

Table 5. Differences in elaboration strategies among Taiwan and neighboring countries in Asia

Country / Score	Taiwan	Japan	Korea	Hong Kong	Shanghai	OECD Ave.
Index	460	494	512	527	544	489

Source: [15]

In the lower 25% of overall performance, Taiwanese students obviously score lower than the neighboring countries in Asia and OECD average, showing that Taiwan needs to enhance teaching skills in reading and information acquisition skills. It also shows that Taiwan's competency in learning-to-learn skills, one of the important indicators for lifelong learning, is obviously lower than other countries'.

Active citizenship, cultural and social skills: Civic knowledge and interpretative skills, civic knowledge, civic engagement and civic attitudes across countries

Table 6. Differences in civic awareness among Taiwan and neighboring countries in Asia

country score	Taiwan	Japan	Korea	Hong Kong	International Ave.
Index	559	--	565	554	500
Rank	4	--	3	5	

Source: [16]

Participation in lifelong learning: Participation in education and training of those ages 25 to 64

Table 7. Comparison of dropout rates (ages 18-25) among Taiwan and neighboring countries

country	Taiwan	Japan	Korea	China	Hong Kong	OECD Ave.
Percentage (%)	0.03	1.48	0.6	2.08	0.181	13

Source: [1, 17]

Resources for Lifelong Learning
Investment in Lifelong learning: Total public expenditure on education as a percentage of GDP

Table 8. Comparison of percentages of GDP on education among Taiwan and neighboring countries

Country	Taiwan	Japan	Korea	China	OECD Ave.
Percentages of GDP on education (%)	4.9	3.4	4.2	3.3	5.2

Source: [1, 18]

Educators and Learning: Percentage of teachers having received education and training during the previous four weeks

Table 9. Comparison of the HDI index among Taiwan and neighboring countries in Asia

Items Country	HDI (2010)	Rank	Average years of education	Rank	Expected years of education	Rank
Taiwan	0.868	18	11	22	16.1	17
Japan	0.884	11	11.5	17	15.1	36
China	0.663	90	7.5	94	11.4	122
Korea	0.877	12	11.6	12	16.8	9

Source: [19]

The Human Development Index (HDI) was created by the United Nations Development Program (UNDP) in 1990, considering that although "income growth" is indispensable in human development, it's not the only focus. In 2010, UNDP updated the measurement index to reflect changes over time, combining "life expectancy at birth," "average years of education," "expected years of education," and "average GNI per capita by purchasing power parity" into one index to more accurately reflect a country's development in the areas of health, education and economy. There are no significant differences in the overall index performance among Taiwan, Japan and Korea; China's HDI performance, on the other hand, ranks low among 127 countries surveyed. As for the education index, Korea's average years of education ranks first among the four countries.

ICT in Learning: Percentage of households who have internet access at home

Table 10. Comparison of the IT training and education index among Taiwan and neighboring countries in Asia

Country	Taiwan	Japan	China	Korea
Index	63.68	20.08	33.24	44.21
Rank	14 (Ms 3/7)	64 (Ls 6/6)	53 (Ls 5/6)	41 (Ms 7/7)

Source: [20]

Strategies in Lifelong Learning: Member states' positions on developing lifelong learning strategies

Table 11. Comparison of employment rates by education levels (ages 25-64) among Taiwan and neighboring countries in Asia

Country \ Education	Taiwan[1]	Japan[2]	China	Korea[2]	OECD Ave.[2]
Below upper secondary	49.5	67.6	--	66.1	58.7
Upper secondary and post-secondary non-tertiary	62.34	74.4	--	70.7	76.1
Tertiary education	69.04	79.4	--	77.1	85

Source: [18, 21] [1.] 2010 "Human Resources Survey" by the Directorate-General of Budget, Accounting and Statistics, Executive Yuan, R.O.C. [2.] 2001 OECD data

5 Comparison of Lifelong Learning Education Act among Taiwan, China, Korea and Japan

Table 12. Comparison of lifelong learning Education Act among Taiwan and neighboring countries

	Taiwan	Japan	Korea	china
Legal support system	Having lifelong Learning Act	Having lifelong Learning Act	Having lifelong Learning Act	Education Act was saturated with the idea of lifelong education
Organization	Mostly non-governmental organizations, educational institutions led to	Social education institutions of civil	National Institute for Lifelong Education	Educational institutions
Standard framework	Establishment of coordination mechanisms to recognize the different contexts for learning results, to ensure that learning achievement can be in different schools, departments, and to convert between them	Accreditation of courses oriented, focusing on the vertical convergence of learning activities, and promote the education level of horizontal integration.	Accreditation of courses oriented, focusing on the vertical convergence of learning activities, and promote the education level of horizontal integration.	Certification Course Orientation
Financial support	Government may or accept groups, individual donations	Government grants funds	no clearly defined	no clearly defined

Source: [22, 23, 24, 25]

6 Conclusion

If the four countries are compared according to the EU's lifelong learning quality indicators, Taiwan's overall development of lifelong learning is faster than China's but the quality is far lower than that of neighboring countries. Among the five indicators in area A, all but "citizen awareness" is lower than other countries; in area B, Taiwan has a higher rate of participation in lifelong learning; in area C, Taiwan leads the other three countries in investment in education, educator and learning, and ICT in learning; in area D, only the first indicator (strategies for lifelong learning) is defined and compared. The employment rates of the neighboring countries are lower than the OECD average presumably because the economic conditions affect employment at various education levels; therefore, all of the countries need to improve their policies for lifelong learning.

The Taiwan government can't really understand the concept of the participation in lifelong learning, but can not set the policy that corresponds to the future to improve the situation. To neighboring countries as an example, Japan, Korea, regular people across the country for lifelong learning participation and level of investigation, to understand the needs, satisfaction, and participation rate, and with the population of background information to conduct cross-analysis to further understand the all age, sex, occupation types of cases involved, and compile this information, write reports, set as a basis for policy. Taiwan government should follow the example of neighboring countries, regular public participation and lifelong learning conditions survey conducted as a reference for policy improvement.

References

[1] Ministry of Education, MOE, Taiwan, http://www.edu.tw/
[2] National Association for the Promotion of Community Universities, http://www.napcu.org.tw/website/category/data/statistics
[3] Non-formal Education Programs Accredtiton Center, Taiwan, http://140.122.96.1/p8.htm
[4] Department of Statistics, MOI, Taiwan, http://www.moi.gov.tw/stat/
[5] Ming, H.: China's progress in lifelong learning policies. In: International Conference on Lifelong Learning Policies report (2009)
[6] Ministry of Education, MOU, China, http://www.moe.edu.cn/
[7] The Chinese adult education association, http://www.caea.org.cn/caea_content.asp?id=352
[8] Ministry of Education, Science and Technology, http://english.mest.go.kr/web/1699/site/contents/en/en_0209.jsp
[9] Lee, J-B.: Vision and Strategy for Developing Lifelong Learning in Korea. In: KEDI (2004), http://eng.kedi.re.kr/khome/eng/archive/report/viewReports.do
[10] Huang, W.-S.: Comparative Education, Hedu, Taipei, pp. 214–217 (2011)
[11] Ministry of Education, Culture, Sports, Science and Technology Lifelong learning policy (2010), http://www.mext.go.jp/english/
[12] European Report on Quality Indicators of Lifelong Learning, European Commission, Brussels (2002)
[13] PISA, Results, vol. I. OECD Publishing. OECD (2009)
[14] International Comparison of Education Indicators 2011, MEXT (2011)
[15] PISA 2009 Results (vol. III) PISA. OECD Publishing, OECD (2010)
[16] Schulz, W.: In: ICCS 2009: International Association for the Evaluation of Educational Achievement (IEA), Amsterdam (2010)
[17] Ho, J.-T., Wu, J.-C., Wang, S.-C., Yang, S.-L., Heng, C.-K., Tsai, P.-S.: The Current Conditions of Dropouts and Guidance Measures in Various Countries—Taiwan's Guidance Policies on Returning to Schools for Dropouts in the Past and Future. Ministry of Education Students Affairs Committee, Taipei, P4 (2003)
[18] Education at a Glance 2010 OECD INDICATORS, OECD (2010)
[19] Directorate General of Budget, Accounting and Statistics, Executive Yuan, R.O.C. Statistical Bulletin conditions (2011), http://www.dgbas.gov.tw/public/Data/11715541971.pdf
[20] IPS National Competitiveness Research 2010-2011, IPS and IPS-NaC, Seoul (2011)
[21] Directorate General of Budget, Accounting and Statistics, R.O.C. Manpower Utilization Survey (2010), http://www.dgbas.gov.tw/public/Attachment/01281461071.pdf

[22] Lifelong Education Act, The R.O.C Laws & Regulations Database, Ministry of Justice (2002), http://law.moj.gov.tw/LawClass/LawAll.aspx?PCode=H0080048
[23] Measures to promote lifelong learning. The Japan Laws & Regulations Database, Ministry of Internal Affairs and Communications (2002), http://law.e-gov.go.jp/htmldata/H02/H02HO071.html
[24] Lifelong Education Act, Korea Ministry of Government Legislation (2009), http://www.moleg.go.kr/english/korLawEng;jsessionid=fIvoxm9K EBCNjFH2OChVwukzHyuoxAWzUMF7GmB9LTWXBhw0rz2sKvrS1EqssYtD?pst Seq=52187&pageIndex=45
[25] Regulations on the Promotion of lifelong education in Fujian Province, Fujian Provincial People's Government (2005), http://www.fujian.gov.cn/zwgk/flfg/szfgz/200709/t20070906_31832.htm

Study of Bilingual Teaching Reform and Practice Based on Web Resources

MeiHua Gua and JinYan Haob

College of Electronic Information, Xi'an Polytechnic University, xi'an 710048
gu_meihua@163.com, jinyan_554@126.com

Abstract. Analyzing the importance and necessity of the bilingual teaching about "computer simulation for electronic circuit" course, searching from the teaching mode, teaching material selection, teaching methods and means, evaluation methods and so on, analyzing and researching the bilingual teaching of this course by combining the theoretical analysis with the practical course teaching, several teaching modes and methods which are appropriate for our students and the characteristic course are summarized.

Keywords: Bilingual teaching, Electronic circuit, Computer simulation.

1 Introduction

With the continuous development of China's higher education and reform, and the world economic globalization, bilingual teaching of higher education in China has become the inevitable trend with international standards. Its purpose is to train inter-disciplinary talents who understand not only professional knowledge, but also professional foreign language reading and communication skills [1,2,3]. Computer simulation for electronic circuit is electronic engineering required course, this course enables students to learn to use computer to experiment the model of actual electronic communication system's physical model or mathematical model, and analysis and research a practical system to the performance and working status through such model test.

Carrying out bilingual teaching of this course mainly based on the following two considerations:

(1) MATLAB/Simulink is the simulation language of "communication system computer simulation", and the language is based on the English language which is international common, the knowledge structure and the latest technology and related books come from abroad mostly ,so it's impossible to get the quintessence of the program without "bilingual".

(2) The available MATLAB/Simulink software is English version, software interface, help documents are in English, and writing code is also conducted in the English language, without bilingual teaching, writing programs will encounter obstacles of language. In addition, in simulink simulation model library, modules name, parameters are in English. If we are not familiar the modules' English name of the electronic communication system, the simulink simulation model can not be built.

S. Lin and X. Huang (Eds.): CSEE 2011, Part V, CCIS 218, pp. 372–375, 2011.

2 Bilingual Teaching Practice of "Electronic Circuit Computer Simulation"

(1) Select teaching materials suit for practical situation

Good foreign language professional teaching material is the basis of bilingual teaching. The first-class original textbooks of foreign language has many advantages, it is the ideal choice for bilingual teaching. Therefore, we must carry on the detailed contrast in the textbooks of various series, various forms, thus choose the most appropriate textbooks that suit for students using. We mainly select from the following two aspects:

Select from the original English textbooks, choose good original English textbooks is very important for the bilingual teaching, no the original textbooks, bilingual teaching became that water without a source and trees without roots. On the one hand, it helps students to learn about the latest MATLAB language program knowledge, on the other hand also is helpful for students to learn authentic English, and also avoid the misunderstanding caused by false translation. According to the characteristics of our students, we choose one or two the original English textbooks tally with the actual situation.

According to teaching syllabus of this course and selection of teaching purpose, the teaching purpose of this course is to use computer to carry on simulation experiments for the physical model of actual electronic circuit system and mathematical model. So students should not only master computer simulation language MATLAB/Simulink, but also have a certain professional basis of electronic circuit system. The actual situation brings to more difficulties for choosing the teaching material. Now on market original textbooks of MATLAB/Simulink and electronic system are very much, but not have the textbooks of the computer simulation based on the electronic circuit system. So, I chose a edition textbook and 2 reference materials in numerous textbooks and Chinese textbooks. Edition textbook is the"MATLAB Programming for Engineers(Second Edition)"compiled by Stephen J.Chapman, Reference books are "Lecture and Practicing MATLAB" compiled by the LuoJianJun etc and "Application of MATLAB simulation in communication and electronic engineering" compiled by XuMingYuan etc.

(2) Choose the appropriate teaching model

"Bilingual teaching" includes three modes: immersion bilingual teaching, keep the type of bilingual teaching and transitional bilingual teaching [4,5]. The current bilingual teaching environment, students' ability and teachers' level that determines it must be keep type of "bilingual teaching" for us. And we choose "Foreign language textbooks, bilingual teaching" mode. In the bilingual teaching, the teaching object is basically the junior undergraduate students, the teaching method use English explain with the full English slides, the difficulty of knowledge complement with proper Chinese explanation. As for English teaching proportion, it control in around 50-80 percent according to difficulty degree of the teaching contents, English level of teaching class.

Bilingual teaching of computer simulation based on the communication system course use bilingual thinking, for students who contact with computer language in the start, they encounter more difficulties. Another most prominent problem is unfamiliar with professional knowledge, the courses' foundation of signal and system, digital signal processing and communication principle is worse, it will lead to entail strenuous effort for understanding and expression of program algorithm. So, initial learning of several weeks plans to use both Chinese and English teaching with repeat telling important definition and keywords, it helps the student to grasp the key words and syntax, let most of the students build confidence, thus achieve good effect of bilingual teaching.

(3) Fuse Multimedia tools and traditional teaching means, and improve the teaching effect

We make full use of the advantages of multimedia technology bilingual teaching. Therefore we produced a multimedia bilingual courseware-including Chinese version and English version. Using multimedia teaching to improve teaching efficiency, will more time for English teaching and student exchanges. Students can also concentrate on thinking about how to use English to express the selected knowledge and the difference with Chinese expression and so on. Students' thinking modes can be cultivated from Chinese to English. courseware uses full English, design fully embody the heuristic teaching method, include animation effects and pictures , achieving excellent pictures and texts, concise and clear lines, rather than simple text accumulation of classroom teaching, greatly enhance the vitality. Bilingual courseware uploaded to the course website for students to download to prepare and review.

At the same time the multimedia teaching still necessary to launch by traditional teaching means, for instance, in the teaching process, there often appear part of students who don't understand the difficulties of problem, then teachers need additional explanation; discussions with students often need to manually at the blackboard present numerical; with the blackboard explaining exercises effect also is the best.

(4) Choose suitable teaching mode for students

We have mainly three ways in practical teaching process: examples, strengthening practice teaching method, construction of communication system, and computer simulation website.

Teaching method with examples: in each chapter: teach main principle first in process, and then give examples. According to "problems analysis - > algorithm compile - >coding- > program test - > results inspection" program developed process, finally give complete solve the example program or Simulink model. Aim is to cultivate students' ability to solve practical problems, through the typical examples teaching attract the students' attention, to improve quality and effect of bilingual teaching.

Strengthen practice: In order to really master communication system of computer simulation, therefore, we specially write bilingual experiment instructions - Chinese version and the English version, and set up eight experiment ,including basic MATLAB experiment and communications system simulation experiment based on Simulink, and cultivate students' analysis ability and hands-on programming ability in practice.

Course website: In order to achieve better bilingual teaching effect, we specially established computer simulation communication system's course website, and put all kinds of teaching resources online, including bilingual teaching outline for this course, bilingual experiment outline, bilingual experiment guidance, bilingual multimedia courseware and a few pieces of special lecture video, facilitating preparation before class and review after for students.

(5) Adopt of appropriate assessment method

Electronic circuit system computer simulation is a practice-needed course, although some students understand the book knowledge better, and theory test scores are higher, lack of actual programming ability and creative thinking. In order to be able to comprehensive evaluate students, exam contents both theory and practice, and emphasize on practice ability. Specific assessment form: usually inspects &hands-on assessment + open-book assessed. What we notice is students' understanding of knowledge instead of just memorizing. In addition, open-book exams conclude a wide range of aspects. Peacetime scores include: assignments, classroom questioning, attendance, etc. computer examination mainly conclude some verification experiments and design experiments, in order to examine students' design program and debugging ability.

3 Summary

Since "computer simulation for electronic circuit system" bilingual teaching research and practice, there is a reform about education of communications professional courses. On this basis, in order to train inter-disciplinary who are conform to the social development and the world needs, our bilingual courses still need to constantly reforming teaching concept, teaching mode and teaching method, meanwhile to improve teachers' level and teaching material improvement, try to pass the practical teaching, combining flexible teaching means and rich teaching content, thus gradually perfect fit their schools' characteristics and the course characteristic of the bilingual teaching mode.

Acknowledgment. This work was supported by Special Scientific Research Program of Shaanxi Provincial Education Bureau (Project No.2010JK558).

References

[1] Wang, B.H.: Thinking and orientating bilingual teaching from international comparison. Shanghai Education and research 23-24, 18–20 (2004)
[2] Liu, T.: Investigation about bilingual teaching reform and implementation. Navigation education research 8, 55–57 (2007)
[3] Qin, X., Cheng, S.Y.: About bilingual teaching thinking. Beijing university of technology 11-12, 33–35 (2005)
[4] Mao, S.H.: Bilingual teaching, communication professional discussion. Professional circles 11, 76–77 (2007)
[5] Yang, C., Wu, Y.X.: Searching about professional curriculum bilingual teaching. Journal of Beijing University 37, 68–70 (2007)

Research on Cultural Construction of Sports Competition in Information Technology Based on Badminton League in Universities Classes

Liying Ren and Jinliang Shi

Institute of Physical Education, Southwest Petroleum University, Chengdu,
Sichuan Province 610500
shijinliang275@126.com

Abstract. Competition is the driving force of sports, and the cultural construction of sports competitions in campus is of great significance. Starting from badminton league in University classes, this paper analyzed the connotation of campus sports competitions its educational function. Based on this analysis, it proposed to strengthen the awareness of cultural construction of campus sports competition, establish efficient and reasonable stadiums, and formulate the content of sports events in a scientific and rational way.

Keywords: University, sports competition, construction.

1 Introduction

It is a new attempt to carry out the race-based badminton league in university class teaching. Through an observation of a whole year, I found that league in classes was well received in students due to the characteristics of long period, high proportion of participation and similar competitive level of players. It mobilizes the enthusiasm of most college students, increases their awareness of PE, and strengthens the lifelong awareness as well. Meanwhile, because of the scene experience of sports competition, it also promotes the social adjustment of students, which has played a positive role in achieving the goal of "physical education aims at training innovative talents with comprehensive development". However, this new attempt is only for the purpose of classroom physical education. To accomplish the objective of training creative talents in physical education work of universities, it is expedient to strengthen the cultural construction of campus sports competition.

Competition is the driving force of sports events, so we should be aware of the educational value of the sports competitions in university, that is, it deserves everybody's attention and everyone's participation to "attract the majority of young students to go to the playground, and set off nationwide fitness programs". However, a lot of universities still regard competitive sport activities as the main part, which is lack of fun and entertainment. Thus all the competitions turn out to be a mere formality and the continuous repetition makes many sports activities no longer satisfy the college students in new era. For example, the hurdles track still exists in the sports competition in university, however, track and field classes have been eliminated in

S. Lin and X. Huang (Eds.): CSEE 2011, Part V, CCIS 218, pp. 376–380, 2011.

almost all the colleges because of the PE reform over the past decade, so hurdles learning no longer exists, which results in the hurdle competition has become a jumping competition. Must hurdles be an event in campus sports competition? Competitive sports make the majority of students on campus can only play as spectators and the stale race events inhibit their enthusiasm. The success of the badminton league in university classes tells us that it is imperative to enhance the cultural construction of campus sports competition in a scientific and rational way.

2   The Connotation of Campus Sports Competition

Sports competition is an important part of campus culture, a great mean for students and teachers to do physical activities after school, a significant way to cultivate students' sports interest and consciousness to develop a habit and behavior of sports activities, and also the main content of "sunshine sports project ". To hold a wide range of sports competition in schools not only improves students' physical fitness and mental qualities as well as the cultural life on campus, but also raises the level of school sports competitions, helps to discover and nurture sports talents, while also playing a huge role in improving the school's status and reputation at home and abroad.

Sports competitions enhance physical fitness and health of college students. Health is a basic element of human development. All the achievements, wealth, and everything about life start from a healthy physical and mental health. According to the concept of health by World Health Organization, it explains that a perfectly healthy person should have physical and psychological health, good social adjustment, and good moral health. To promote physical and mental health is an important role of sports event on campus. First of all, in the course of sports competitions, human organ system is given a certain intensity of stimulation. As a result, a series of adaptive responses happens to the morphology, physiology and other aspects of the body, thus having a positive impact on the body, which can effectively promote the health of people. Second, the fact that many students choose their favorite entertainment sports event as an important way of life can help them achieve physical exercise and psychological adjustment in a healthy manner.

Sports competitions shape the healthy personality for college students and promote their socialization. With the slogan of "faster, higher, and stronger" and the belief of "peace, friendship, and unity", sports competitions can not only encourage us to continuously overcome difficulties, conquer ourselves, and stride forward a new life goal, but also prompt mutual understanding, enhance friendship and promote the Olympic spirit of peace, thus having a subtle influence on youth. Moreover, sports competitions are conductive to cultivate students' collectivism and patriotism. Only if they enjoy the pain of defeat and the joy of success through sports competitions, can they understand the importance of team spirit. Meanwhile, sports competitions own strict rules, that is, one should spare no efforts to stage remarkable performance under the restriction of rules and any contravention will be punished, which prompts college students to develop good public morality of law-abiding. It is necessary to develop awareness of accepting criticism calmly and humbly for students through sports competitions, which can make them clearly understand that there shouldn't be any action serious harming the opponents. Sports competitions sometimes require the self-restraint or self-sacrificing spirit, which means that success not only needs the strong will and desire to win, and mercy is also very significant. "Equal opportunity and survival of the fittest" is always the basic principle of sports competition, so that college students must learn to correctly confront the failure of the competition and increase their anti-frustration capacity to become stronger, and finally they can survive in the fierce social competition. In addition, sports competition is also conductive for students to shape the healthy personality such as impartial law enforcement, responsibility assuming, decision-making, and so on, which are all beneficial to promote the socialization of college students.

Sports competition can cultivate the concept of peace and enhance the spirit of friendship for students. "The essence of the Olympic spirit is to educate youth from the perspective of mutual understanding and friendship, thus contributing to building a more peaceful world." "Promote the Olympic spirit throughout the world to establish international friendship." Olympic Games are the international sports competition, so athletes are both competitors and friends. "Friendship, peace, solidarity" is not only the common ideal of mankind, but also the soul of Olympic spirit. Athletes from different countries, using different languages, of different religions promote friendship, cooperation and world peace through competition under the Olympic flag symbolizing the union of five continents. The Important slogan of the Olympic Games "It is playing not winning counts" reveals the people-oriented Olympic spirit. Moreover, sports competition requires players to challenge and try their best to show the vigor and constantly go beyond selfhood. The rich connotation of discipline, faith, love implied in sports competition, the harmony implied in conflict and the balance implied in imbalance, constitute the Olympic spirit, which has played an irreplaceable role in cultivating the spirit and quality of peace and love for college students.

Sports competition is conductive for aesthetic education and edification. Regarding the physical activity as a special mean, sports competitions display the concrete actions through image and combine physical beauty and sports beauty, natural beauty and artistic beauty to serve aesthetic pleasure for people. In colorful campus sports activities, various sports events, all kinds of physical exercise, sports competitions and performances, sports sculpture as well as sports architecture all can enable students to get the aesthetic education and edification as well as emotional experience of sports aesthetics, which is conductive to cultivate the correct aesthetic appreciation awareness and improve the ability to create and personify beauty for college students.

3   The Cultural Construction of College Sports Competition

College sports competition should include competitive sports competition and mass sports competition. Competitive sports competition refers to competitions held for the purpose of selecting high-level athletes, improving the performance of school games or sending sports teams that represent the school to participate competitions with other schools, while mass sports competition refers to competitions that is organized on campus for raising public awareness of physical fitness. Competitive sports competition is high-level competition, but mass sports competition, however, belongs to lower-level sports competition. They have different goals, and we must adhere to the cultural construction principle of campus sports competitions--competitive sports as a guide and mass sports as the main subject school, which can ensure the mutual development and promotion of competitive sports competition and mass sports competition.

Strengthening the awareness of the cultural construction of campus sports competitions. Competition is the vibrant element of sports, an important lever to promote the work of the school sports. With the promulgation and implementation of "National Fitness Regulations", our awareness and understanding of college sports competition should not still stay in the level of "to the best of one's skill" and just competing for the sake of competing. We should be aware of the purpose of campus sports competition is to use the competition as a means to attract and mobilize the active participation of students in sports activities, which build up students, stimulate their strong interest, and ultimately help them form a regular and stable exercise habits. Campus sports competition work need school management, teachers and all students to work together. Only if we improve our ideology, can our work make progress and healthy cultural construction of sports competitions be achieved.

Establish efficient and reasonable stadiums. As the important material and cultural content of campus sports competition, sports stadiums directly restrict and affect the interest of students and staff to participate in sports events. Therefore, it is conductive to make use of the opportunity of sports competitions to improve stadiums. Studies suggest that "By means of athletic meeting, colleges and universities can strengthen the economic investment and improve the sports facilities, for students with the percent of 38.5% and 42.8% think that the improvement of school sports facilities as well as renovation of the stadiums enable them to be interested in sports, thus promoting the cultural establishment of campus sports competition environment." What should be particularly paid attention to is that the college stadiums cannot just satisfy competitive sports games and the later-period management but have to give full consideration to the actual demand, inherit the people-oriented spirit, and combine the competitive sports and mass sports competitions to establish the comfort, safe, modern, and adequate sports venues and facilities which can satisfy competitions of various levels. Thus students' enthusiasm will then get stimulated and sports activities in communities will also get promoted.

Develop the content of campus sports competition scientifically and reasonably. The main task of colleges and universities is to cultivate all kinds of innovative talents. Physical education aims at college students instead of professional athletes. Therefore, to attract more students to participate in sports activities is the key. The campus sports competitions cannot be only competitive sports, so those complex and difficult technical sports should be changed to ease the difficulty and be more interesting and entertaining, for the purpose of guaranteeing sound mind and bodies of students as well as improving their cultural qualities. We must keep innovating in the various sports competitions carried out each year and learn to grasp the hot events which are appealing to students and close to their life. We should focus on collective projects, so that students can build up their body, receive education in an atmosphere of solidarity, competition, and happiness, cultivate a competitive spirit, and promote the full play of self-awareness and enthusiasm. Meanwhile, we must also attach importance to the positive role of sports association in the cultural construction of campus sports competitions. To enhance the guidance of sports organizations, improve their referee skills, organizational skills, and form a multi-level competition network with joint management on both superiority and inferiority for achieving the objective of improving the health and educating people in campus sports competition.

Acknowledgment. Foundation item: Technology fund of the Southwest Petroleum University ----"Research and Practice on the Teaching mode of Badminton League in Universities Classes" (No.: 2010XJR036).

References

1. Yang, W., Yang, T.: Sport Generality. Higher Education Press, Beijing (2005)
2. Tong, J., Zong, Y., Wang, H.: On the Development of Sports Competition. Luoyang Normal University 30(2) (2011)
3. Zhang, L., He, X.: On the Situation of After-school Sports Competition and Its Countermeasures. Guangzhou Physical Education Institute 29(2) (2009)
4. Wang, A., Shi, Y., Zhang, P.: The Purpose of Campus Group Competition in College and Its Organization and Management. Physical Education 17(5) (2009)
5. Ren, L., Shi, J.: Competitive Sports and the Cultural Construction of Sports Competition in Colleges, vol. 30. Beijing Sport University (2007)
6. S.: On the Cultural Construction of Sports Competition in Colleges under the Context of Liberal Education. Career Horizon (9) (2009)

Application of Scaffolding Theory Construction with Internet Pneumatic Circuit Design Based on Teaching Materials from Interactive e-Learning Research

Wen-Jong Chen[1], Chin-Pin Chen[2], and Yung-Fu Chang[3]

[1,2] No. 2, Shi-Da Road, Changhua City, Taiwan
[3] No. 48, Anton two streets, ChiaYi city, Taiwan
{wjong,iechencp}@cc.ncue.edu.tw,
doei900716@yahoo.com.tw

Abstract. This study mainly aimed to investigate the learning effectiveness and satisfaction of e-learning training courses for university undergraduate students. In this paper, we first analysis the scaffolding theory and the digital learning through the literature review, and then construct the internet "Pneumatic Circuit Design" interactive digital platform which based on the development of the scaffolding theory. Finally, the experimental teaching for students is performed by cooperative learning. To obtain the learning effectiveness and satisfaction for the students of the experimental and control groups, a questionnaire survey and SPSS statistical analysis software are utilized. The results show the learning effectiveness and the satisfaction of the experimental group students are better than these of the control group.

Keywords: Pneumatic, scaffolding theory, e-learning, cooperative learning.

1 Introduction

With the coming of the rapid development of information and multimedia technologies, the digital learning has become widespread and important for the trends in training and development of an enterprise and the school education [1]. The most characteristic of the digital learning, while breaking the constraints of the time and space, is to combine the computer with the communications and the multimedia technologies. It converted the traditional classroom styles of education and training into the styles of the internet learning. For the technical teaching, many teachers utilized the interactive internet technology to increase the learning effectiveness for getting rid of traditional teaching methods in the laboratory. Cooperative learning concept originated in United States in the 1960's. Many educational scholars research that the fundamental concept of learning some program for students is essential to success [2]. It is through the interaction processes among the group members of community to pursue the developments of the learning concept and promote the effectiveness of special study[3]. The learning of the pneumatic circuit design curriculum through the digital learning materials has become the most convenient and effective learning method. In this way, the individual differences of the students can

S. Lin and X. Huang (Eds.): CSEE 2011, Part V, CCIS 218, pp. 381–385, 2011.

be minimized. In this paper, by understanding the operation processes of pneumatic components and circuits, the students can learn the basic concepts for the control parts in Mechatronic System. Smith and Ragan [4] developed the teaching model of the scaffolding theory for emphasizing the instruction design with conceptual change in science. Due to the characteristics of e-learning on personalization, interactivity, repeatability, immediateness, and convenience, the internet learning courses can be utilized as the learning platforms in many engineering technical instruction. This paper presents the materials of the pneumatic circuit design based on the internet learning platform for the university undergraduate students and this material is constructed through the scaffolding teaching model.

2 Literature Review

Scaffolding theory originated in the constructivism. It was applied in the instruction as a teaching strategy derived from Lev Vygotsky's sociocultural theory. Scaffolding instruction emphasized that the knowledge is constructed by individual and the construction process generated from the interaction with others. Vygotsky observed that the children in the assistance of the adult or the peer of the stronger ability can complete the harder learning tasks more than his ability from the processes of solving the problem. Wood, Bruner, and Ross stretched Vygotsky's zone of proximal development (ZPD) theory to probe into the learner solving the problem of combination for three-dimensional building blocks attained the learning processes and goals by the assistance of the teachers and classmates[5].

Relan and Gillani (1997) noted that when the internet teaching was gradually integrated into the traditional teaching, the students turned into active knowledge constructors from passive learners [6]. the techers also turned into the facilitator of the student counselling from the instructor with teaching. She and Fisher (2003) researched the internet multimedia animation course of study in science [7]. They indicated that the students of the different grades and learning styles through the scaffolding instruction and cooperative learning were significant outcomes in the cognitive learning and affective learning [8].

Cooperative learning for the past ten years has become the focus point with many educators and experts. Compared with the traditional teaching methods, cooperative learning provides the student with the opportunity to interact with others, and therefore the knowledge source no longer only confined to teacher. It is through the group's positive interdependence of the members and mutual cooperation that many people make an effort to obtain the individual learning performance and team achievements. Moreover, one of the goal of cooperative learning is to teach students initiative and self -reliance. It is different from individual and tournament learning. Teachers provided a learning environment for collaboration and then reached the cognitive, emotional and skill objectives. Accordingly, the modes and results of cooperative learning and traditional learning are not the same [9-11].

This study adopts the scaffolding teaching model and learning theory from Smith and Ragan to construct a learning platform of pneumatic circuit design. The focus of this paper is to investigate the learning satisfaction and effectiveness for interactive teaching/learning platform with cooperative learning. The web site of this teching/learing platform is http://sam37520.sg1010.hinet.net/WEB1.

3 Methodology

This research objective is to construct a interactive teaching/learning platform of pneumatic circuit design with scaffolding learning theory. The objects of this study are 36 university undergraduate students from Department of Industrial Education and Technology in Changhua University of Education. There are two groups of students for this study. A group of students called control group carries out the traditional teaching model and the other becomes experimental group instructed with e-learning platform of this digital teaching. In this study, Cooperative learning is utilized in all students of these two groups. The research tool is SPSS statistical software to analysis the learning satisfaction and learning effectiveness for learning the interactive platform of the students. A questionnaire survey performed is to investgate the learning satisfaction of this digital teaching/learning platform and the learning effectiveness scale is analyzed. According to the research motivation and literature review, the analysis variables of this study consist of the independent variable, the covariance variable and the dependent variable. The relation among these variables is as shown in Figure. 1.

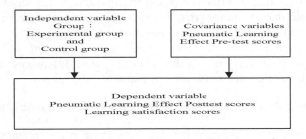

Fig. 1. Structure diagram of this research

4 Results

As the behavior of the starting point for the students tested may interfere with the experimental results, Independent Sample t- Test is first processed by "pre-test the effectiveness of learning effectiveness points" to assess the behavior of the starting point of each group before the teaching experiment was practiced. The results does not reach the significant difference (t =. 208, p> .05). It shows that the behaviors of two groups of students before the teaching experiment are the same. Then the posttest is performed for these two groups excluding the results of the pre-test of the learning effectiveness to analyze the scores of the different teaching modes. Before the one-way analysis of variance (one-way ANOVA) is precessed, the groups neet to obtain the coefficients of homogeneity regression. The test results of homogeneity does not reach statistical significance level (F =. 180, p> .05). This is to say that the regression lines of the groups have a high degree of homogeneity. Therefore the homogeneity assumption can be accepted between the two groups. The results after one-way analysis of covariance (ANCOVA) conducted to evaluate the effectiveness are shown in Table 1. The score of the pneumatic learning effectiveness is mainly from the different teaching model of two groups. The experimental group is significantly higher than the control group in Table 1.

Table 1. Results of post-test ANCOVA in "Learning Effectiveness Scale"

Pneumatic Learning Effect scale	Source of variation	SS	df	MS	F	P
Total	Variation between groups	1005.753	1	1005.753	28.327	.000
	Variation within groups	1171.685	33	35.506		

To understand the difference of the pretest-posttest for the learing effectiveness, we perform Paired-Samples t- Test for these two groups. The results of the experimental group are up to significant difference (t = 6.551, p <.05) on the score of the pretest-posttest scale and that of control group is less than significant differences (t = 1.924, p> .05). In addition, the learning satisfaction of two groups is performed by Independent Sample t- Test. The results show that the learning satisfaction of the experimental group similarly has significance level. The differences of experimental group also are better than that of the control group in Table 2.

Table 2. Results of "Learning Satisfaction" scores of the summary table

	Group	N	Mean	Std. Deviation	t	P
Learning satisfaction	Experimental group	18	79.3889	7.01376	3.554	0.001
	Control group	18	71.1111	6.96114		

5 Conclusions

In this study, as the experimental group adopts e-learning teaching model, the learning effectiveness and satisfaction of the experimental group are superior to those of the control group. Unlike the general e-learning teaching models, the learning platform of this pneumatic circuit design is an internet interactive learning model based on the Scaffolding instruction and cooperative learning. It mainly emphases that the learning subjectivity is the student rather than the teacher. That is to say that the material design does not focus on "teaching" but "learning". This concept is important for learning engineering technologies. The teaching purpose of the engineering technologies is help students to learn the practical operation and experience. In this internet teaching/learning platform of the pneumatic circuit design, the students can interact with repeatability and timelessness for learning the pneumatic technologies. This learning method can get rid of needing to operate at laboratory in the past and attain the effective learning of engineering technology.

References

1. Kao, C.C., et al.: Journal of National University of Taiwan (2005)
2. She, H.C.: Journal of Research in Science Teaching (2004)
3. Bobbette, M.: Journal of College Teaching & Learning (2005)
4. Smith, P.L., Ragan, T.J.: Instructional Design, 2nd edn (1999)
5. Wood, C., ct al.: Journal of Child Psychology and Psychiatry (1976)
6. Relan, A., Gillani, B.B.: Web-based instruction (1997)
7. She, H.C., Fisher, D.: Technology-rich learning environments: A future perspective (2003)
8. Levent, A., Alexandros, P.: Hospitality Managemen (2007)
9. Lai, A.F., Chen, C.H.: TResearch and Development in Science Education Quarterly (2008)
10. Duh, J.J., Hsin, Y.W.: Journal of Special Education (2008)
11. Frolik, J., Zum, J.B.: submitted to Computers in Education Journal (2005)

An Adaptive Particle Swarm Optimization for the Coverage of Wireless Sensor Network

Te-Jen Su[1], Ming-Yuan Huang[2], and Yuei-Jyun Sun[3]

[1] College of Information & Technology of Kun Shan University,
Tainan, Taiwan 710, R.O.C.
tejensu@mail.ksu.edu.tw
[2,3] Department of Electronic Engineering of National Kaohsiung University of Applied
Sciences, Kaohsiung, Taiwan 807, R.O.C.
{1099405104,1098305138}@cc.kuas.edu.tw

Abstract. The coverage problem is a crucial issue in wireless sensor networks (WSN); however, a high coverage rate ensures a high quality of service in WSN. This paper presents control of the coverage problem optimization via the adaptive particle swarm optimization (APSO) approach. The proper selection of inertia weight of APSO gives balance between global and local searching, and the research of this paper shows that the larger weight helps to increase convergence speed while the smaller one benefits convergence accuracy, decreasing the algorithm operation times. Finally, the current paper presents examples to illustrate the effectiveness of the proposed APSO methodology. The simulation results show that the APSO algorithm achieves a good coverage solution with enhanced time efficiency.

Keywords: Wireless Sensor Networks, Adaptive Particle Swarm Optimization, Coverage Rate.

1 Introduction

Wireless Sensor Network (WSN) technology has recently progressed [1] in its applications, thus gaining increasing attention from researchers. WSN is composed of a combination of multiple sensors. The sensor has the advantage of low cost and small size, as well as low power consumption for transmission [2]. Therefore, the sensor device can sense a variety of tools, and the measured values pass to each other within the scope of detecting other sensors to transmit data to other functions, to configure as a WSN, shown in Fig.1.

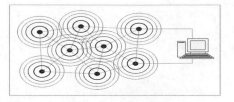

Fig. 1. Wireless sensor network simulates

S. Lin and X. Huang (Eds.): CSEE 2011, Part V, CCIS 218, pp. 386–391, 2011.

Applications for common sensors include health care, military activities, and environmental sensors. However, the process sensor and actual effects of transport entail many problems. For example, saving power to extend the life cycle of access control between the various sensors [3], data transmission path, and sensor network of link strength and power sensors [4] is the most important [5]. Therefore, properly using limited battery power [6] is necessary to solve the coverage problem between sensors [7].

The three common solutions for sensor coverage optimization include the Numerical Method, the Enumerative Method, and Random Search. Therefore, the Adaptive Particle Swarm Optimization (APSO) Algorithm is the superior evolutionary computation in a random search.

This paper presents control of the coverage problem optimization via the APSO approach [8]. Because proper selection of inertia weight of APSO balances between global and local searching, the research in this paper shows that a larger weight helps to increase convergence speed, while a smaller one benefits convergence accuracy, decreasing algorithm operation times.

2 Standard Particle Swarm Optimization Algorithm

The standard particle swarm optimization (SPSO) is a relatively new evolutionary algorithm used to find optimal solutions to numerical and qualitative problems. Social psychologist James Kennedy and electrical engineer Russell Eberhart [9] first introduced the standard particle swarm optimization in 1995, inspired by the social behavior of animals, such as bird flocking or fish schooling, when searching for food. Kennedy and Eberhart became particularly interested in the models developed by biologist Frank Heppner. The basic concept behind the standard particle swarm optimization technique consists of changing the velocity or acceleration of each particle toward its *pbest* and the *gbest* positions at each time step. This means that each particle tries to modify its current position and velocity according to the distance between its current position and *pbest*, and the distance between its current position and *gbest*. In its canonical form, standard particle swarm optimization is modeled as Eq.1 and Eq.2:

$$v_{id}(t+1) = v_{id}(t) + c_1 * rand(\ )_1 * (pbest_i - x_{id}) + c_2 * rand(\ )_2 * (gbest - x_{id}) \quad (1)$$

$$x_{id}(t+1) = x_{id}(t) + v_{id}(t+1) \quad (2)$$

where,

$v_{id}(t+1)$	: Velocity of particle i at iteration $t+1$
$v_{id}(t)$	: Velocity of particle i at iteration t
$x_{id}(t+1)$	: Position of particle i at iteration $t+1$
$x_{id}(t)$	: Position of particle i at iteration t
c_1	: Acceleration coefficient related to *pbest*
c_2	: Acceleration coefficient related to *gbest*
$rand(\ )_1$	: Random number uniform distribution $U(0,1)$

$rand()_2$: Random number uniform distribution $U(0,1)$
$pbest_i$: $pbest$ position of particle i
$gbest$: $gbest$ position of swarm

2.1 Adaptive Particle Swam Optimization Algorithm

Some evolutionary algorithms, such as the genetic arithmetic and the mutation operator are used to improve swarm diversity to avoid local convergence through varying
some individual genes. Based on this idea, the mutation operator is imported into the
SPSO to improve swarm diversity [10]. To overcome premature searching by the
SPSO algorithm for the large lost in population diversity, the measure of population
diversity and its calculation are given, and an APSO with dynamically changing inertia weight is proposed. Proper selection of inertia weight balances between global and
local searching. The research shows that a larger weight helps to increase convergence speed while a smaller one benefits convergence accuracy. Decreasing linearly
self-adapting inertia is adopted to keep high global search capability in the former
search period, while powerful exploitation capability in the latter accelerates convergence. Self-adapting inertia weight w is expressed as Eq.3:

$$w(t+1) = w_{ini} - \frac{w_{ini} - w_{end}}{MaxIteration} \times t$$

where,
(3)

$MaxItera-$: Maximum number of allowable Iterations
$tion$

w_{ini} : Initial values of the inertia weight
w_{end} : Final values of the inertia weight
t : Current iteration number

Therefore, the expression of APSO proposed in this thesis is modified in velocity
update Eq.1 as Eq.4:

$$v_{id}(t+1) = w(t) * v_{id}(t) + c_1 * rand()_1 * (pbest_i - x_{id}) + c_2 * rand()_2 * (gbest - x_{id}) \quad (4)$$

2.2 Coverage Problem Optimization

The goal is for every sensor to allow as much survival time of network monitoring as
possible for the life cycle of the entire network to reach a maximum. Therefore, solving a coverage problem for promoting entire coverage rate is the largest goal in this
paper when considering cost and environmental factors. This paper proposes the APSO
for solving the coverage problem of sensors [11]. Any algorithm that solves the coverage problem of sensors must accurately calculate the coverage area of sensors. As
shown in Fig.2, S_i and S_j represent two sensors, r represents the radius of coverage
range, d is the distance between sensors, θ is the edge angle between the distance and
radius, and P is the coverage area between sensors. We suppose the coordinate of S_i
(X_i,Y_i) and $S_j (X_j,Y_j)$. Therefore, Eq.6 represents the distance d of S_i and S_j. We calculate

the distance and radius of the sensor from Eq.6 to obtain the edge angle between distance and radius θ from Eq.6 and Eq.7. Eq.8 is the overlap formula. According to Eq.7 and Eq.8, we can calculate the area of repeat coverage between sensors.

$$d(S_i, S_j) = \sqrt{|x_i - x_j|^2 + |y_i - y_j|^2} \tag{6}$$

$$\theta = \arccos\left(\frac{d(S_i, S_j)}{2r}\right) \tag{7}$$

$$P = 2\left[r^2(\theta/2 - \sin(\theta/2)\cos(\theta/2))\right] \tag{8}$$

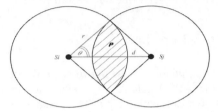

Fig. 2. Sensors representing frame

Researchers who use any algorithm to solve the coverage problem of sensors waste parts of the coverage area. The sensing range design is approximately a circle; however, the coverage area of size and form is not commonly used, and thus squanders the coverage area. The two types of waste consist of squandering the boundaries and repeated coverage. The Eq.9 can calculate the squander rate beyond the boundaries, or the rate between an11 wasted area and coverage area of sensors. The algorithm is also a squander through repeat coverage between sensors. The Eq.10 shows the reduplicate rate, or the rate between the reduplicate area and the coverage area of sensors.

$$SquanderRate = \frac{\sum SquanderArea}{SensorArea * SensorNumber} \tag{9}$$

$$reduplicateRate = \frac{\sum reduplicateArea}{SensorArea * SensorNumber} \tag{10}$$

The APSO algorithm can be used for simulation and research, to solve the coverage problem of the detecting device, the coverage rate of the detecting device will reach and solve beastly, in order to enable and perform algorithms can be more steady, besides regarding basic APSO as the main structure, perform the revision of the algorithm in the article partly to the detecting device, all have more superior achievements to enable whole time, count and restrain the result from generation to generation.

The APSO algorithm that uses detecting devices randomly while performing algorithms, later will set all detecting devices that the goal moved in range of two times of the detecting device as the particle group, and will make the calculation of centralized center in accordance with all particle colonies in the range, regard the first particle the individual of group to solve the result of calculation beastly, that is to say that performs *pbest* component in algorithms, calculate with the coverage rate when the goal moves the position of detecting device of each particle finally, as the colony solves beastly, that is to say that performs *gbest* component in algorithms with the highest one of coverage rate, and the number value of coverage rate. Because will have in the whole procedure for three times back to the control that is enclosed before replacing its number value of supreme coverage rate, the accountant calculates the coverage rate of whole and everybody too while enclosing each time, so in order to make the APSO algorithms best and can add the fast pace while calculating the goal and moving the position of detecting device, can get a fine one best to solve.

3   Simulates and Results

This chapter presents the simulation of APSO to solve the sensor coverage problem. This experiment used the APSO calculating method to solve the sensor coverage problem, and compared the result with the APSO parameters shown in Table 1. In this experimental example, the sensor is set to 20, covering an area of $2500cm^2$. The simulation results of Triangle Model Optimization are shown in Fig.3(a), the simulation results of Octagon Optimization are shown in Fig.3(b), the simulation results of APSO are shown in Fig.3(c).

Table 1. APSO parameter settings

Sensor radius	5
The maximum velocity	10
Acceleration coefficient	1.4
Start of inertia weight	1.0
End of inertia weight	0.4
Iterations	1000

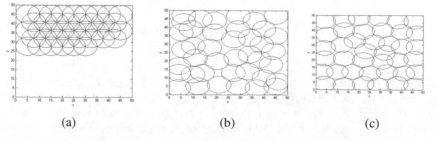

(a)   (b)   (c)

Fig. 3. (a) Triangle Model Optimization simulates. (b) Octagon Optimization simulates. (c) Adaptive Particle Swarm Optimization simulates.

4 Conclusion

This paper used optimization algorithms to solve the sensor coverage problem. The APSO algorithm located the convergence of sensors. Sensor settings for particle groups with weight and parameters obtained the optimal solution. The experimental results show that the APSO solution coverage problem is superior to Triangle Model Optimization and Octagon Optimization to solve the coverage problem.

The APSO algorithm can repeat at increasingly lower coverage under the best coverage, and may adjust parameters of the APSO calculating method. Therefore, the APSO algorithm demonstrates good coverage results. The result demonstrates an average coverage rate of 94% for the APSO algorithm, and the simulation results show that the APSO algorithm achieves an effective coverage solution with better time efficiency.

References

1. Lei, Y., Zhang, Y., Zhao, Y.: The Research of Coverage Problems in Wireless Sensor Network. In: 2009 International Conference on Wireless Networks and Information Systems, pp. 31–34 (2009)
2. Schurgers, C., Srivastava, M.B.: Energy Efficient Routing in Wireless Sensor Networks. In: IEEE Military Communications Conference, pp. 357–361 (2002)
3. Chen, Y., Zhao, Q.: An Integrated Approach to Energy-Aware Medium Access for Wireless Sensor Networks. IEEE Transactions on Signal Processing 55, 3429–3444 (2007)
4. Rengarajan, B., Chen, J.K., Shakkottai, S., Rappaport, T.S.: Connectivity of Sensor Networks with Power Control. Signals, Systems and Computers 2, 1691–1693 (2003)
5. Wang, G., Huang, L., Xu, H., Li, J.: Relay Node Placement for Maximizing Network Lifetime in Wireless Sensor Networks. In: 4th International Conference on Wireless Communications, Networking and Mobile Computing, pp. 1–5 (2008)
6. Schurgers, C., Srivastava, M.B.: Energy Efficient Routing in Wireless Sensor Networks. In: IEEE Military Communications Conference, pp. 357–361 (2001)
7. Lei, Y., Zhang, Y., Zhao, Y.: The Research of Coverage Problems in Wireless Sensor Network. Wireless Networks and Information Systems, 31–34 (2009)
8. Zhang, D., Guan, Z., Liu, X.: An Adaptive Particle Swarm Optimization Algorithm and Simulation. In: Proceedings of the IEEE International Conference on Automation and Logistics, pp. 2399–2402 (2007)
9. Li, X., Frey, H., Santoro, N., Stojmenovic, I.: Focused-Coverage by Mobile Sensor Networks. In: IEEE 6th International Conference on Mobile Adhoc and Sensor Systems 2009, pp. 466–475 (2009)
10. Yangfan, Z., Lyu, M.R., Liu, J.: An Index-Based Sensor-Grouping Mechanism for Efficient Field-Coverage Wireless Sensor Networks. In: Communications ICC 2008 IEEE International Conference, pp. 2409–2415 (2008)
11. Zhu, W., Chen, X., Li, X.: A New Search Algorithm Based on Muti-Octagon-Grid. In: 2nd Image and Signal Processing CISP 2009, pp. 1–5 (2009)

Reform and Exploration of Innovative and Entrepreneurial Talents Fostering Mode on Mechanical Engineering under the New State

Junyong Sang[1] and Chen Hao[2]

[1] Employment Center, Henan Polytechnic University, Jiaozuo 454000, China
job@hpu.edu.cn
[2] The League Committee, Henan Polytechnic University, Jiaozuo 454000, China
chenhao@hpu.edu.cn

Abstract. In order to achieve the cultivation of innovative and entrepreneurial talents of mechanical engineering under the new state, our school has always been committed to the reform and exploration of innovative and entrepreneurial talents fostering model, and has established the modern educational concepts, and built a wholly new teaching model, making the formation theories of education, experimental teaching, practice base of university students and campus culture promote each other mutually, which forms the characteristic pattern and system of innovative and entrepreneurial capacity building of university students.

Keywords: Mechanical engineering, innovative and entrepreneurial education, experimental teaching, practice base construction.

1 Introduction

It is a new trend to promote the innovative and entrepreneurial education in colleges of the higher education. The 1998 Declaration of the World Conference on Higher Education, "Higher Education in the 21st Century: Vision and Action" clearly states: "To facilitate the graduates of higher education should be primarily concerned with entrepreneurial skills and initiative; graduates no longer just a job, First will be the job creators. " This new trend caused revolutionary changes in higher education and become a new round of global higher education reform and an important sign of competition.

In the "Long-term Scientific and Technological Development (2006-2020)" [1] proposed building an innovative country's development strategy. To build an innovative country, need to develop innovative ideas in various forms, full of innovative entrepreneurs to carry out effective education and training with innovative spirit, innovation, creativity and entrepreneurship of highly qualified personnel. Student entrepreneurs can not only promote employment, but also greatly promote economic and social development, improve the level and the level of SMEs in China is conducive to innovation and entrepreneurship society advocating for the construction of an innovative country serve as a model and leading role.

In recent years, the school of Mechanical Engineering students adhere to enhance literacy for the purpose of business in order to enhance student awareness of

S. Lin and X. Huang (Eds.): CSEE 2011, Part V, CCIS 218, pp. 392–395, 2011.
© Springer-Verlag Berlin Heidelberg 2011

entrepreneurship as a starting point to develop students entrepreneurial skills as the goal, has been committed to innovation and entrepreneurial talent fostering model reform and exploration, including the formation of theoretical education, teaching, practice base of university students and campus cultural linkage characteristics of innovation and entrepreneurship capacity-building structure and systems.

2 Establish Modern Educational Concepts and Clarify Development Goals

Innovative and entrepreneurial education is a system which needs a variety of teaching methods that can be used to develop students' awareness and thoughts of innovation and entrepreneurship, as well as skills and other business overall quality, after years of construction and practice, our school machinery engineering has gradually developed a unique concept of engineering education, namely, mutual promotion of production, study and research, and mutual combination of theory and practice, working closely with enterprise, industry, combined with the practical ability of students to strengthen and vocational skill points to achieve the knowledge, intelligence, skills, coordinated development and quality, so that students can not only master the broad range of advanced scientific and cultural knowledge, but also own the pioneering and innovative spirit, practice, and entrepreneurship, which makes them will be "a human being" as well as a "good-doer", and "a scholarship" to meet the needs of local economic and cultural development and application of innovative and entrepreneurial talents.

3 Innovate Teaching Pattern, Promote the Education of Innovation and Carve-Out

On the basis of summarizing the education history of our school, we have innovated teaching pattern and have made the education of innovation and carving out an inseparable part of teaching, we not only have given selective courses like "the innovation theory of machine formation","innovative design of machines" and "invention, innovative think pattern and the model making of it", but also have asked the leaders in this area to give lectures on the latest innovations in the machine industry, at the same time, we have hired many leaders in large corporations , chief financial officers, chief managers of HR departments to act as "tutors of carving out", who came to school to give lectures on the background information of the industry, practice in the industry and cases to broaden the knowledge and technical horizon of students and strengthen the combination of course teaching and corporation practice, meanwhile, to provide enough knowledge reserve for students' participation in carving out.

4 Create a Platform for Entrepreneurial Experience and Practice, Strengthen the Construction of Practice Base of Innovative and Carving-Off Talents

(1) Take the training of ability as the core and carry out the research of experimental teaching system which features in "stratified, multi-modules, and open mode".

We treat the teaching of the theory as the base one, together with the National Engineering Training Center and the Manufacturing Laboratory, taking the students' engineering awareness, innovative spirit and practical ability as core concept, and train students that will adapt themselves to mining industry. To achieve this goal it is important to optimize the experimental and teaching content, building up a layered, multi-module and open experimental teaching system. Layered means industry-oriented, and the main line is test attribute classification skills, integrating courses, and establish a basic skills by the technology, expertise and integrated technology, industry, which is 3 levels. Multi-module means set up the experimental course of Machine Electrical Control and PLC, Machinery manufacturing technology, Mining machinery, Advanced Manufacturing Technology independently. Each module will be made up of basic experiment, comprehensive experiment, and design experiment. Open means strengthening laboratory construction, and build up an open laboratory system, providing the conditions for self-test for students. The above experimental teaching system can improve the overall effectiveness of experimental teaching, and highlight the experimental teaching personnel training in the industry's exemplary role, and to help students complete the transformation to the ability to produce quality works and the early development by the accumulation of knowledge.

(2) Integrate resources, establish experimental teaching platform of "basis emphasizing, individualization, and open-to-all"

With national engineering training center, safety testing center and computing center of mining equipment of Henan province, four college students' innovative experimental bases and two graduate student innovation laboratory acting as practice platform, with advanced manufacturing technology research institute, high pressure water jet technology research institute, mechanical monitoring and fault diagnosis research institute, precise engineering research institute, transmission machinery and system simulation research institute, fluid mechanical engineering institute and other six institutes acting as scientific research platform, we offer the students innovative research conditions which can be treated as a hardware platform for validation, design, research and innovation contest, it creates more and better opportunities for students to practice and makes them have access to more advanced equipment.

(3) Strengthen the building of training bases outside for the purpose of developing students' ability of practice, innovation and engineering quality

To expand the practice basement outside the school while strengthen the construction of experimental platform. Talents can not do without the social environment and only in the production of the full exercise by the practice to have the cognitive ability, practical ability, engineering capacity and innovation. Continue to strengthen our school and the technology, equipment, management, higher levels of marriage and medium-sized enterprises, promote the combination of research, and take the colleges, enterprises of the models, such as major companies and the surrounding provinces such as Jiaozuo Power, Li Feng power plants, Pingdingshan Coal Group, Luan Mining Group, Shanxi Coal Group to establish a long-term stability and other campus practice teaching base. School education has been a number of well-known business entrepreneurs, alumni support, they are teaching, practice base, business conditions, construction, teacher training, risk capital and other multi-given help to ensure that students in entrepreneurship education and entrepreneurial activities of the healthy and orderly development. Rely on internal and external enterprise platform and the internal business base, establishing the venture seed fund to pay more attention to the practice of carving out in process of entrepreneurial cultivation.

5 Strengthen the Development of Campus Culture, Creating a Proper Environment for Growth of Innovative and Entrepreneurial Talents

Take the construction of campus culture as an important component of the construction of educational environment, building a people-oriented consciously, in order to promote growth of students, organizing innovative Business Plan Competition and other entrepreneurial activities, to create a good innovation entrepreneurial atmosphere. Established to promote undergraduate research and innovation practice in long-term mechanism to mobilize students to participate in independent research, teachers guide students to research two-way initiative to encourage the active participation of teachers and students, "college students technology training plans," "The Students climbing plans," "National Students of advanced mapping technology and skills contest "," "Challenge Cup" Business Plan Competition "and other activities, and as a carrier, stimulate innovation and enthusiasm of the students [1].

6 Conclusion

After several years of exploration, the quality of innovative and entrepreneurial talents cultivated in our school is improving continuously, the overall quality, entrepreneurship, social influence and social recognition ladder of students elevates a lot, providing a large number of qualified students who enable to adapt to the needs of society. Meanwhile, they've been widely recognized by the majority of employers and the community and the graduate employment rate remained at 98%. These factors and advantages lay a very good foundation and condition for the further development of entrepreneurial talents fostering mode.

Reference

1. Haiying, L., Jinqiu, W., Chunquan, M., et al.: To extra-curricular activities, academic technology innovation based entrepreneurship education and practice. Heilongjiang Education (Higher Educational Research and Evaluation) Z1 (2009)

Bijective Soft Set Approach for Quality Evaluation of Graduate Education

Ke Gong[1], Maozeng Xu[1], and Xia Zhang[2]

[1] School of Management, Chongqing Jiaotong University, Chongqing 400074, P.R. China
[2] College of Finance and Economics, Chongqing Jiaotong University,
Chongqing 400074, P.R. China
agks_cn@163.com

Abstract. Evaluation of graduate education is an important issue of education management. This paper proposed a bijective soft set model for evaluating quality of graduate education approaches. An example is given to illustrate the model as well.

Keywords: Graduate education, evaluation, bijective soft set, soft set.

1 Introduction

With the development of graduate education, the volume of graduate student is increasing rapidly. Thus, how to ensure and promote the quality of graduate education is one of the most important issues in education management. In this background, the decision-makers (DM) are expecting adequate methods to help evaluate the quality of graduate education so as to make proper decisions. However, the DMs usually use experience to evaluate, which can be influenced by the education background, experience and nature etc. The complexity of evaluation for quality of graduate education lies in the data of this issue, which has characteristics of complex systems such as variety, uncertainty, and connectedness.

Soft sets theory, which was proposed by Molodtsov [1], is a newly-emerging tool to deal with uncertain problem. In recent years, soft sets theory was applied to combined forecasts [2], decision making problems [3], normal parameter reduction [4], demand analysis [5]. These applications showed a promising future of soft set theory in solving uncertain problems. This paper attempts to apply bijective soft set [8] to formulate an evaluate approach for Quality of Graduate Education.

2 Bijective Soft Set Approach for Quality Evaluation of Graduate Education

Firstly, we introduce some preliminary of soft set and bijective soft set. Let U be a common universe and let E be a set of parameters.

Definition 1[1]. A pair (F, E) is called a soft set (over U) if and only if F is a mapping of E into the set of all subsets of the set U, where F is a mapping given by $F : E \rightarrow P(U)$.

S. Lin and X. Huang (Eds.): CSEE 2011, Part V, CCIS 218, pp. 396–401, 2011.

Definition 2 (see [6]). The union of two soft sets (F,A) and (G,B) over U is the soft set (H,C), where $C = A \cup B$ and $\forall \varepsilon \in C$,

$$H(\varepsilon) = \begin{cases} F(\varepsilon), & \text{if } \varepsilon \in A - B \\ G(\varepsilon), & \text{if } \varepsilon \in B - A \\ F(\varepsilon) \cup G(\varepsilon), & \text{if } \varepsilon \in A \cap B \end{cases} \tag{1}$$

This is denoted by $(F,A) \tilde{\cup} (G,B) = (H,C)$.

Definition 3 (see [6]). AND operation on Two Soft Sets. If (F,A) and (G,B) are two soft sets then " (F,A) AND (G,B) " denoted by $(F,A) \wedge (G,B)$ is defined by $(F,A) \wedge (G,B) = (H, A \times B)$, where $H(\alpha,\beta) = F(\alpha) \cap G(\beta), \forall (\alpha,\beta) \in A \times B$.

Definition 4[8]. Let (F,B) be a soft set over a common universe U, where F is a mapping $F : B \to P(U)$ and B is nonempty parameter set . We say that (F,B) is a bijective soft set, if (F,B) such that:(i) $\bigcup_{e \in B} F(e) = U$.(ii)For any two parameters $e_i, e_j \in B, e_i \neq e_j$, $F(e_i) \cap F(e_j) = \varnothing$.

Definition 5[8] (*restricted AND operation on a bijective soft set and a subset of universe*). Let $U = \{x_1, x_2, ..., x_n\}$ be a common universe, X be a subset of U, and (F,E) be a bijective soft set over U. The operation of " (F,E) restricted AND X " denoted by $(F,E) \underset{\sim}{\wedge} X$ is defined by $\bigcup_{e \in E} \{F(e) : F(e) \subseteq X\}$.

Definition 6[8] (*dependency of two bijective soft set*). Suppose that $(F,E),(D,C)$ are two bijective soft sets over a common universe U, where $E \cap C = \varnothing$. (F,E) is said to depend on (D,C) to a degree $k(0 \leq k \leq 1)$, denoted $(F,E) \underset{\sim}{\Rightarrow}_k (D,C)$, if $k = \gamma((F,E),(D,C)) = \left| \bigcup_{e \in C} (F,E) \underset{\sim}{\wedge} D(e) \right| / |U|$, where $|\bullet|$ is the cardinal number of a set.

Definition 7[8] (*bijective soft decision system*). Suppose that (F_i, E_i) $(i = 1,2,3,...,n)$ are n bijective soft sets over a common universe U, where any $E_i \cap E_j = \varnothing (i = 1,2,3,...,n; j = 1,2,3,...n; i \neq j)$, (G,B) is a bijective soft set over a common universe U, $B \cap E_i = \varnothing (i = 1,2,3,...,n)$, and we call it the decision soft set. Suppose $(F,E) = \tilde{\cup}_{i=1}^{n}(F_i,E_i)$ .The triple $((F,E),(G,B),U)$ is called *soft decision system over a common universe U.*

Definition 8[8] (*bijective soft decision system dependency*). Let $((F,E),(G,B),U)$ be a soft decision system, where $(F,E) = \tilde{\cup}_{i=1}^{n}(F_i,E_i)$ and (F_i,E_i) is bijective soft set. (F,E) are called condition soft set. The soft dependency between $(F_1,E_1) \wedge (F_2,E_2) \wedge ... \wedge (F_n,E_n)$ and (G,B) is called soft decision system dependency of $((F,E),(G,B),U)$, denoted κ and defined by

$$\kappa = \gamma(\wedge_{i=1}^{n}(F_i,E_i),(G,B)) \qquad (2)$$

Definition 9[8] Let $((F,E),(G,B),U)$ be a soft decision system, where $(F,E) = \tilde{\cup}_{i=1}^{n}(F_i,E_i)$ and (F_i,E_i) is bijective soft set. κ is the soft decision system dependency of $((F,E),(G,B),U)$. The dependency between $\wedge_{i=1}^{m}(F_i,E_i)$, where $m \leq n$, and (G,B) is $\gamma(\wedge_{i=1}^{m}(F_i,E_i),(G,B))$. And

$$\gamma(\wedge_{i=1}^{m}(F_i,E_i),(G,B)) \leq \kappa \qquad (3)$$

Definition 10 [10]. Let $((F,E),(G,B),U)$ be a soft decision system, where $(F,E) = \tilde{\cup}_{i=1}^{n}(F_i,E_i)$ and (F_i,E_i) is bijective soft set, $\cup_{i=1}^{m}(F_i,E_i) \tilde{\subset} (F,E)$. κ is the soft decision system dependency of $((F,E),(G,B),U)$. If $\gamma(\wedge_{i=1}^{m}(F_i,E_i),(G,B)) = \kappa$ we say $\cup_{i=1}^{m}(F_i,E_i)$ is a reduct of soft decision system $((F,E),(G,B),U)$.

Definition 11[8] (*Significance of bijective soft sets to decision bijective soft set*). Suppose that $(\tilde{\cup}_{i=1}^{n}(F_i,E_i),(G,B),U)$ is a soft decision system. The Significance of bijective soft set to decision soft set, denoted $\sigma((F_j,E_j),\tilde{\cup}_{i=1}^{n}(F_i,E_i),(G,B))$, is defined as following

$$\sigma((F_j,E_j),\tilde{\cup}_{i=1}^{n}(F_i,E_i),(G,B)) = \kappa - \gamma((H,C),(G,B)) \qquad (4)$$

Where $(H,C) = \wedge_{i=1}^{n}(F_i,E_i) \ (i \neq j)$.

The concept of significance of soft sets to decision soft set is the decrease of soft dependency when remove (F_j,E_j).

Definition 12[8]. Let $((F,E),(G,B),U)$ be a bijective soft decision system, where $(F,E) = \tilde{\cup}_{i=1}^{n}(F_i,E_i)$ and (F_i,E_i) is bijective soft set, $\cup_{i=1}^{m}(F_i,E_i) \tilde{\subset} (F,E)$. κ is the bijective soft decision system dependency of $((F,E),(G,B),U)$. If $\gamma(\wedge_{i=1}^{m}(F_i,E_i),(G,B)) = \kappa$ we say $\cup_{i=1}^{m}(F_i,E_i)$ is a reduct of bijective soft decision system $((F,E),(G,B),U)$.

Definition 13[8]. Let $((F,E),(G,B),U)$ be a bijective soft decision system, where $(F,E) = \tilde{\cup}_{i=1}^{n}(F_i,E_i)$ and (F_i,E_i) is a bijective soft set, $\cup_{i=1}^{m}(F_i,E_i) \tilde{\subset} (F,E)$ is a reduct of bijective soft decision system $((F,E),(G,B),U)$. Suppose that $(H,C) = \wedge_{i=1}^{m}(F_i,E_i)$. We call

$$\text{if } e_i \text{ then } e_j \ (|H(e_i)|/|G(e_j)|), \tag{5}$$

a decision rule induced by $\cup_{i=1}^{m}(F_i,E_i)$, where $e_i \in C$ and $G(e_j) \supseteq H(e_i)$ and $e_j \in B$ and $|H(e_i)|/|G(e_j)|$ denotes the coverage proportion of rule.

3 Algorithm and Example

Suppose that there are six graduate education examples and they have some characteristics. It can be represented by the following information table.

Table 1. An information table on the evaluation of graduate education evaluation

Approaches	A	B	C	D
x_1	high	good	no	Excellence
x_2	med.	good	no	Loss
x_3	med.	good	no	Excellence
x_4	low	avg.	no	Loss
x_5	med.	avg.	yes	Loss
x_6	high	avg.	yes	Excellence

where A, B and C are attributes that describe the characteristics of each example and D is the excellent or loss status of it. Obviously, it can be represented as soft set as following:

Let $U = \{x_1, x_2, x_3, x_4, x_5, x_6\}$, be a set of graduate education examples, $E = \{e_1, e_2, e_3, e_4, e_5, e_6, e_7, e_8, e_9\}$, be a set of parameters that describe the characteristics of graduate education, where $e1=high$, $e2=med.$, $e3=low$, $e4,=good$, $e5=avg.$, $e6=no$, $e7=yes$, $e8=excellent$, $e9=loss$. (F,E) is a soft set on the mapping between graduate education examples and their characters. Suppose the following bijective soft sets: $F_1(e1) = \{x_1,x_6\}$, $F_1(e2) = \{x_2,x_3,x_5\}$, $F_1(e3) = \{x_4\}$, $F_2(e4) = \{x_1,x_2,x_3\}$, $F_2(e5.) = \{x_4,x_5,x_6\}$, $F_3(e6) = \{x_1,x_2,x_3,x_4\}$, $F_3(e7) = \{x_5,x_6\}$, $F_4(e8) = \{x_1,x_3,x_6\}$, $F_4(e8) = \{x_2,x_4,x_5\}$.

By transforming information table to several bijective soft set, we can use bijective soft set theoretic approach to study: what factor impact the excellence of graduate education? And what is the key factor?

Let us consider the following algorithm:

Step1. Construct bijective soft decision system $(\tilde{\cup}_{i=1}^3(F_i,E_i),(F_4,E_4),U)$.

Step2. Calculate each dependency between $\wedge(F_j,E_j)$ and (F_4,E_4), where $0 < j \leq 3$.

Step3. Calculate bijective soft decision system dependency of $(\tilde{\cup}_{i=1}^3(F_i,E_i),(F_4,E_4),U)$.

Step4. Find reduct bijective soft sets with respect to bijective soft decision system $(\tilde{\cup}_{i=1}^3(F_i,E_i),(F_4,E_4),U)$.

Step5. Calculate the significant of each bijective soft set to decision bijective soft set in the reduct bijective soft sets.

Step6. Obtain evaluation rules by reduced bijective soft decision system $(\tilde{\cup}_{i=1}^3(F_i,E_i),(F_4,E_4),U)$.

Let us use the assumed data to run this algorithm. In step2, we can obtain the following:

$$\gamma((F_1,E_1),(F_4,D_4)) = \tfrac{1}{2} \qquad\qquad \gamma((F_2,E_2),(F_4,D_4)) = 0$$

$$\gamma((F_3,E_3),(F_4,D_4)) = 0$$

$$\gamma((F_3,E_3) \wedge (F_1,E_1),(F_4,D_4)) = \tfrac{2}{3}$$

$$\gamma((F_2,E_2) \wedge (F_1,E_1),(F_4,D_4)) = \tfrac{2}{3}$$

$$\gamma((F_2,E_2) \wedge (F_3,E_3),(F_4,D_4)) = \tfrac{1}{6}$$

In the *step 3*, we can obtain the bijective soft decision system dependency $\kappa = \tfrac{2}{3}$.

In the *step 4*, since $\kappa = \gamma((F_3,E_3) \wedge (F_1,E_1),(F_4,D_4))$, we can obtain the reduction of $(\tilde{\cup}_{i=1}^3(F_i,E_i),(F_4,E_4),U)$ are $(F_3,E_3) \tilde{\cup} (F_1,E_1)$ and $(F_2,E_2) \tilde{\cup} (F_1,E_1)$. It reveals that factor {A,C} and {A,B} are the key factor to the excellence or loss of each graduate education examples, and these factors are very important issue.

In the *step 5,* we can quantify the degree of each key factor as the following:

$$\sigma((F_1,E_1),\tilde{\cup}_{i=1}^{3}(F_i,E_i),(F_4,E_4)) = \kappa - \gamma((F_2,E_2) \wedge (F_3,E_3),(F_4,E_4)) = \tfrac{4}{6} - \tfrac{4}{6} = 0$$

$$\sigma((F_3,E_3),\tilde{\cup}_{i=1}^{3}(F_i,E_i),(F_4,E_4)) = \kappa - \gamma((F_2,E_2) \wedge (F_1,E_1),(F_4,E_4)) = \tfrac{4}{6} - \tfrac{4}{6} = 0$$

$$\sigma((F_2,E_2),\tilde{\cup}_{i=1}^{3}(F_i,E_i),(F_4,E_4)) = \kappa - \gamma((F_3,E_3) \wedge (F_1,E_1),(F_4,E_4)) = \tfrac{4}{6} - \tfrac{4}{6} = 0$$

It revealed that A, B and C cannot determine the excellence or loss independently. Only its combination, such as {A, C}, can determine. In step6, we can use the reduct, {A, C} or {A, B} to obtain evaluation rules. For example, if we use {A, C} to deduce evaluation rules, we have the following rules: (i) If A is **high** and B is **good** then **excellence** (1/6). (ii) If A is **med.** and B is **good** then **excellence or loss** (2/6). (iii) If A is **low** and B is **avg.** then **loss** (1/6). (iv) If A is **med.** and B is **avg.** then **loss** (1/6). (vi)If A is **high** and B is **avg.** then **excellence** (1/6).

Therefore, we can use these evaluation rules to evaluate a new graduate education example.

4 Conclusion

Evaluation for Quality of Graduate Education is an important issue of education management. This paper proposed a bijective soft set model for evaluating quality of graduate education. A simulated example is given to illustrate the model as well. Further study could be using empirical data to test this model. Meanwhile, we can extend this model by use some other type of soft set notions and operations.

Acknowledge. Our work is sponsored by the Doctoral Foundation of Chongqing Jiaotong University, the Teaching-reform Foundation of Chongqing Jiaotong University, project of China Society of Logistics (2011CSLKT192), and the Experiment Teaching Reform and Research Foundation of Chongqing Jiaotong University.

References

1. Molodtsov, D.: Soft Set Theory–First Results. Comput. Math. Appl. 37(4/5), 19–31 (1999)
2. Xiao, Z., Gong, K., Zou, Y.: A combined forecasting approach based on fuzzy soft sets. J. Comput. Appl. Math. 228(1), 326–333 (2009)
3. Maji, P.K., Roy, A.R.: An application of soft sets in a decision making problem. Comput. Math. Appl. 44, 1077–1083 (2002)
4. Kong, Z., et al.: The normal parameter reduction of soft sets and its algorithm. Comput. Math. Appl. 56(12), 3029–3037 (2008)
5. Feng, F., Liu, X.: Soft rough sets with applications to demand analysis. In: 2009 International Workshop on Intelligent Systems and Applications, ISA 2009, pp. 1–4 (2009)
6. Maji, P.K., Biswas, R., Roy, A.R.: Soft Set Theory. Comput. Math. Appl. 45, 555–562 (2003)
7. Xiao, Z., et al.: Exclusive disjunctive soft sets. Comput. Math. Appl. 59(6), 2128–2137 (2010)
8. Gong, K., Xiao, Z., Zhang, X.: The bijective soft set with its operations. Comput. Math. Appl. 60(8), 2270–2278 (2010)

A Note on Peirce's Theorem

Lixia Song, Haisheng Liu, and Yang Shu

North China Institute of Science and Technology, Yanjiao BeiJing 101601, China
songlx100@sina.com

Abstract. In 1904 Huntington [6] conjectured that every uniquely complemented lattice must be distributive (and hence a Boolean algebra). In 1945,R.P.Dilworth shattered this conjecture by proving that every lattice can be embedded in a uniquely complemented lattice [5]. Therefore, we consider making additional conditions on the uniquely complemented lattice, so that it is a distributive. Peirce's theorem describes complemented lattice is distributive in the additional conditions. In this paper, we give another different proof of Peirce's theorem in this paper, and consider its necessary and sufficient condition. In addition, we get equivalent conditions between uniquely complemented lattice and distributive from it.

Keywords: Lattice, uniquely complemented lattice, distributive.

1 Introduction

A century of lattice theory was shaped to a large extent by two problems. One of them is uniquely complemented lattices. Who first proposed this problem is not clear. Everybody knows about it, and expects a positive solution. However, at present we do not have a single explicit example about non-distributive uniquely complemented lattices.

Peirce's theorem describes complemented lattice is distributive in the additional conditions. Since then Huntington posed a question: Is Peirce's postulate equivalent to the uniqueness of complements? In other words: Is a uniquely complemented lattice distributive? After Huntington, it was conjectured that every uniquely complemented lattice was a distributive lattice. In 1945, R.P.Dilworth shattered this conjecture by proving that every lattice can be embedded in a uniquely complemented lattice [5]. Therefore, we consider making additional conditions on the uniquely complemented lattice, so that it is a distributive. For example, for a uniquely complemented lattice L, G.Birkhoff and J.von Neumann showed that if L is modular or relatively complemented then it is distributive. Subsequently, G.Birkhoff and M.Ward showed that if L is complete, atomic, and dually atomic then it is distributive. Further, R.P.Dilworth verified that if it is finite dimensional then it is distributive. In spite of these deep results, it is still hard to find "nice" examples of uniquely complemented lattices that are not Boolean.

We give another proof of Peirce's theorem, and start thinking whether the converse of it is right. In addition, we extend this theorem to uniquely complemented lattice. Finally, we consider uniquely complemented lattice is distributive when we add what kind of conditions to it.

S. Lin and X. Huang (Eds.): CSEE 2011, Part V, CCIS 218, pp. 402–406, 2011.

If we pay more attention to Pierce's theorem, we will have a better understanding of this theorem, and find many useful results for searching non-distributive uniquely complemented lattices. We will be more fully grasp and apply it. Let us see how Peirce deduces distributive from condition (P) and we will give a different proof of it

2 Preliminary

Here we first give some definitions, theorems and lemmas; we use these for our proofs and improvement of theorem.

Definition 2.1[1]. By a complement of an element x in a lattice with O and I we mean an element y such that $x \wedge y = O$ and $x \vee y = I$.

A lattice in which each element has at least one complement is called a complemented lattice. If each element of a lattice has precisely one complement, such a lattice is called uniquely complemented.

Definition 2.2[1]. A lattice is called distributive if it satisfies the identity

$$x \wedge (y \vee z) = (x \wedge y) \vee (x \wedge z),$$

which is called the distributive law.

Lemma 2.1[1]. If $x < y$ in a uniquely complemented lattice, then $x' \wedge y \neq O$.

Lemma 2.2[1]. If a uniquely complemented lattice is modular, then in it:

1) $x \wedge y = O \Rightarrow x \leq y'$, and

2) $x < y \Rightarrow x \vee (x' \wedge y) = y$.

Theorem 2.1[1]. A uniquely complemented lattice is distributive if and only if

$$(x \vee ((x \vee y) \wedge x')) \wedge y > O,$$

for any x and any $y > O$.

3 Proof of Peirce'S Theorem

In this section we describe the Peirce's theorem. This is given in more detail in the survey article of V.N.Sallii[1]. My proof is improved on the original proof of Peirce's theorem; the original proof is divided into four steps, we give three steps of its proof, and discard the third and fourth of original proof. We obtain directly from condition (P) when applying a criterion for distributive of a uniquely complemented lattice.

Peirce's Theorem. Suppose a complemented lattice L satisfies the following condition:

(P) If an element x is not contained in any complement of an element y, then $x \wedge y \neq O$.

Then L is distributive.

The following is my process of proof. My proof is divided into three steps.

1) L is uniquely complemented.

Indeed, suppose y_1 and y_2 are two complements for an element x. Then $y_1 \leq y_2$, for otherwise, By symmetry, $y_2 \leq y_1$, and hence $y_1 = y_2$.

As usual, the unique complement of x will be denoted by x'. It is clear that $(x')' = x$.

2) The lattice L satisfies the quasi-identity $x \leq y \Rightarrow x' \geq y'$.

Indeed, if y' is not contained in x', then $y' \wedge x \neq O$, which is impossible inasmuch as $x \leq y$.

3) The lattice L is distributive.

The proof is by contradiction. Suppose L is not distributive, then, by theorem 2.1[1], it contains elements $x, y > O$ such that $(x \vee ((x \vee y) \wedge x')) \wedge y = O$. Consider the element $z = x \vee ((x \vee y) \wedge x')$, since $z \geq x$, it follows from 2) that $z' \leq x'$, so that $z' = x' \wedge z'$. Obviously $z < x \vee y$ (otherwise the left-hand side of the inequality of theorem 2.1[1] would be equal to y and could not be zero). Thus, by Lemma 2.1[1], $z' \wedge (x \vee y) > O$. But

$$z' \wedge (x \vee y) = (z' \wedge x') \wedge (x \vee y) = z' \wedge ((x \vee y) \wedge x')$$
$$\leq z' \wedge (x \vee ((x \vee y) \wedge x')) = z' \wedge z = O.$$

4   Further Popularize of Theorem

In this section the main consideration is the converse and improved form of Peirce's theorem. First, we prove the converse theorem.

Corollary 4.1. Suppose a complemented lattice L is distributive, if an element x is not contained in any complement of an element y, then $x \wedge y \neq O$.

The proof is by contradiction. We will show that if $x \wedge y = O$, and then $x \vee (x \vee y)'$ is the complement of element y.

Indeed, $(x \vee (x \vee y)') \wedge y = (x \vee (x \vee y)') \vee ((x \vee y) \wedge y)$
$$= ((x \vee (x \vee y)') \wedge (x \vee y)) \wedge y$$
$$= (x \wedge (x \vee y)) \vee ((x \vee y)' \wedge (x \vee y)) \wedge y$$
$$= x \wedge (x \vee y) \wedge y = x \wedge y \wedge (x \vee y) = O$$
$$(x \vee (x \vee y)') \vee y = (x \vee y) \vee (x \vee y)' = I.$$

Applying the Definition 2.1[1] $x \vee (x \vee y)'$ is the complement of element y. Obviously $x \leq x \vee (x \vee y)'$, i.e., x is contained in a complement of element y, a contradiction.

Corollary 4.2. A complemented lattice L is distributive if and only if an element x is not contained in any complement of an element y, then $x \wedge y \neq O$.

Another form derived from Peirce's theorem. From this Corollary, we can get a complemented lattice is equivalent to distributive lattice when we add to condition (P). After this Corollary, we start thinking if we let complemented lattice become uniquely complemented lattice, what conditions can be satisfied is distributive. We get the following result.

Corollary 4.3. If a uniquely complemented lattice L satisfies the following condition:

(P) If an element x is not contained in an element y, then $x \wedge y' \neq O$.

Then L is distributive.

Proof. From the proof of Peirce's theorem, we only need to prove lattice L satisfies the quasi- identity $x \leq y \Rightarrow x' \geq y'$.

Indeed, if y' is not contained in x', then $y' \wedge x \neq O$, which is impossible, from $x \leq y$ and lattice is a uniquely complemented, we get $x \wedge y' = O$.

Corollary 4.4. If a uniquely complemented lattice L is distributive and element x is not contained in an element y, then $x \wedge y' \neq O$.

The proof is by contradiction. Suppose $x \wedge y' = O$, from Lemma 2.2[1].1), we obtain $x \leq y$, i.e., element x is contained in element y, a contradiction.

From Corollary 4.2 and 4.3, we get a necessary and sufficient condition for a unique complemented lattice and distributive. It is

Corollary 4.5. A uniquely complemented lattice L is distributive if and only if element x is not contained in an element y, then $x \wedge y' \neq O$.

5 Conclusions

We consider Peirce's theorem and its proof in this paper, we give another different proof, My proof is improved on the original proof of Peirce's theorem; Compared to the original, this proof is less steps and easier to understand than the original, In addition, we give some corollary about Peirce's theorem, and consider its necessary and sufficient. According to it we can get equivalent conditions between uniquely complemented lattice and distributive lattice. This theorem provides a good basis for how to find the existence of non-distributive complemented lattice in the future.

After accessing to a large number of information comprehensive evaluation by of results related and in-depth study, we propose a new evaluation method.

References

[1] Salii, V.N.: Lattices with Unique Complements. Translations of the Amer. Math. Soc. American Mathematical Society, Providence (1988)
[2] Gratzer, G.: Two problems that shaped a century of lattice theory. Note American Math.Soc. 54(6), 696–707 (2007)
[3] Gratzer, G.: General Lattice Theory. Birkhauser Verlag, Basel (1978)
[4] Adams, M.E., Sichler, J.: Lattice with unique complementation. Pac. J. Math. 92, 1–13 (1981)
[5] Dilworth, R.P.: Lattices with unique complements. Trans. AMS 57, 123–154 (1945)
[6] Huntington, E.V.: Sets of independent postulates for the algebra of logic. Trans. AMS 5, 288–309 (1904)

Towards the Application Framework of Innovation-Based Knowledge Management System with Information Technology

Qing Chen

School of Management, Hubei University of Technology, Wuhan, 430068, P.R. China
cq29cn@126.com

Abstract. With the increasing competition and customer demands and new market areas, the need for organizations to innovate and furthermore to ceaselessly innovate is stressed throughout the modern management domain. Innovation is the body of knowledge referred to collectively as knowledge management. Knowledge is considered as a potential key competitive advantage, by helping to increase innovation within organizations. This paper focuses on innovation-based knowledge management system. In this paper, several knowledge levers for knowledge management system are discussed. The requirements for knowledge management system are analyzed. The tools for knowledge management system including knowledge creation tools and knowledge management tools are also explored.

Keywords: Knowledge Management, System, Knowledge Tool, Innovation.

1   Introduction

The continuously increasing pressure of competition and global markets is forcing organizations to become more innovative, with a view to increasing overall competitiveness. The importance of innovation is established as a necessary ingredient for organizations simply wanting to remain competitive or pursue long-term advantages. For economies, innovation is frequently cited as a critical element of growth. With the emergence of knowledge management as new disciplines, papers are starting to appear that add these constructs to the long list of possible antecedents of innovation.

A huge body of literature has examined issues of management knowledge in both empirical and theoretical aspects. However, among these researches, very little has specifically addressed effective knowledge management system based on innovation. The extant literature hasn't satisfactorily answered the burning questions such as "What can be done to improve innovation?" "How can knowledge management enhance the innovative capability within organizations?" etc.

The aim of this paper is to investigate the possible application framework of knowledge management system within organizations as a catalyst or vehicle for increasing innovation, and hence competitiveness.

S. Lin and X. Huang (Eds.): CSEE 2011, Part V, CCIS 218, pp. 407–412, 2011.

2   Knowledge Levers for Knowledge Management System

There are several new knowledge levers that organizations can use to boost business performance.

Customer Knowledge. In virtually every survey customer knowledge tops the list as an organization's most vital knowledge. Yet most organizations do not know as much about their customers as they think they do. If they do, the knowledge is often isolated in sales or service departments and does not feed this knowledge effectively into new products and services. Is every customer contact logged? Does non-confidential feedback from a client interaction get fed into the appropriate knowledge base? Assignment histories can provide useful guidance for similar situations that arise in future.

Process Knowledge. What starts as an activity gradually evolves into a process, which in many cases is automated. Thus knowledge is embedded in a procedure or computer program. However, this codification typically filters out much of the important tacit knowledge of human experts. When organization automates its process, it should provide users with quick access to additional knowledge resources, including contact details of experts for different facets of the process. Most professional organizations do work that is not considered a process. Every situation is different. But closer analysis reveals some generic high level activities, usually involving the gathering and processing of information and communicating with other people. Again, this is vital meta-knowledge that can help an organization be much more effective [1].

Professional Knowledge. Professional knowledge is an organization's most valuable asset. Most of the organization knowledge is in its professionals. Many professionals feel that it is their knowledge that makes them valuable. Yet when it is shared, it becomes even more valuable to the organization as a whole. In fact, such personal hard-won knowledge is not readily shared. This is a fundamental culture and behavioral issue, where an organization needs role models, and which senior management must be seen to behave in ways that are conducive to sharing. An important part of knowledge management is therefore about creating the environment and culture in which your "knowledge stars" will thrive and perform. Understand what motivates them, support them with their personal development, and reward them appropriately are keys to unlocking the required behaviors.

Organization Memory. Many organizations do not know what they already know. They "reinvent the wheel", at another time or place. Knowledge gained is not recorded for use at another time or place. Effective knowledge management will therefore put significant emphasis on capturing knowledge from every day work and from assignments. Decision diaries, reflection time at meetings and after action reviews are potentially powerful tools. An After Action Review, for example, is a structured session that addresses a sequence of questions such as: What was supposed to happen? What did happen? What went right, what went wrong? What lessons can be learned for the future? Does your organization conduct formal post assignment reviews to derive lessons and put the knowledge gained into an accessible form for future assignments? Another useful technique is that of "knowledge refining". A series of memos, e-mails or meeting minutes are trawled for their relevant and reusable content, which is put into an evolving and structured knowledge base [2].

Relationship knowledge. Relationship knowledge is the depth of personal knowledge in relationships. Two people who have worked together for a long time instinctively know another's approach and what needs to be expressed and what can be taken for granted. When organizations reorganize, this knowledge is easily lost. With the growing need for collaboration with external partners and agencies, organizations need to do more to capture some of this knowledge and provide forums where these relationships can be strengthened.

3 Requirements for Knowledge Management System

Open and Distributed. A knowledge management system unifies existing knowledge. The system enables integration among systems such as groupware, e-mail, document management and directory services. In implementing a unifying system, organizations must ensure that the information architecture is flexible enough to meet the evolving needs of individual organizations. Knowledge management systems must also be able to be distributed over various host computers and physical locations.

Customizable. All organizations require an extremely customizable knowledge management system. The system should supply user interfaces in the form of templates so users can easily customize them using tools. It should allow easy integration of existing and new applications. It must allow the organization to link systems to each other.

Measurable. Measurement is a critical aspect of any knowledge management effort to strike the right balance between organizational and technological changes. Only by quantifying and processing the results can organizations determine if the systems are having the desired effect. A knowledge management system includes tools that allow managers to measure and verify usage to get a clear picture of how the system is being used, locate performance bottlenecks and, most importantly, use the data to improve organizational knowledge transfer processes [3].

Secure. Knowledge management applications focus on maximizing access to knowledge. Therefore they are more likely to require the administrator to prohibit access to specific content areas to those workers who should not have access to them. A knowledge management system needs to provide secure repositories and preserve security models present in existing knowledge silos where appropriate, while allowing access across the organization to those who need it.

4 Tools for Knowledge Management System

4.1 Knowledge Creation Tools

Brainstorming Applications. Brainstorming tools help inspire creative thinking and convert tacit into explicit knowledge. These end user applications help categorize, organize and identify knowledge resources and are therefore useful knowledge creation tools. While it should not try to replicate their functionality, an organization's knowledge management system must provide an easy way for users or these applications to identify, capture and share the results of these activities with others across the organization [4].

Storytelling. Storytelling has recently been touted as the way forward for knowledge management organizationally. Storytellers will obviously transfer significantly more context around experience and work practice than what is typically found in content form. Storytelling can be a powerful tool, so look to increase knowledge about knowledge management and establish a corporate comfort zone for it through the dissemination of knowledge management success stories to those individuals who are most likely to fuel the corporate grapevine.

Blogs. Blogs have become fairly ubiquitous these days, and have even begun to take over the role of more traditional communication devices such as news outlets. They certainly can fulfill the role of being informative and knowledge-enabling. Blogs can be a powerful tool for sharing, if not collaborating on, knowledge, but by their very nature they work best as vehicles for individual expression. Trying to use them as a potential tool for company communications purposes is not a good fit for the way they work best.

Wiki. Wiki means quick or superfast. The wiki is a website that allows users to add content, as on an Internet forum, but also allows anyone to edit the content. All in all, this is about the nearest any technology has come to the purest expression of the knowledge management discipline, a completely open and transparent sharing and collaboration environment, accessible to all comers. Wikis seem to be an ideal tool for furthering corporate knowledge management goals and outcomes, as they are true sharing and collaborating environments that grow knowledge and competency.

4.2 Knowledge Management Tools

Intranets. Intranets have sprung up across corporations at a rate that challenges any previous introduction of new technology. They are ideal environments for sharing information that is both dynamic and richly linked. However, most large organizations quickly reach a point where so much information exists on the intranet that it begins to suffer the same problems that exist on the Web; no one knows where everything is, so no one can quickly find what he or she is looking for [5].

Document Management Systems. Document management systems are repositories of important corporate documents and are therefore important stores of explicit knowledge. They are also valuable tools for creating and processing complex documents, such as new drug applications in pharmaceutical companies. Document management systems excel at controlling the process of document creation, processing and review.

Information Retrieval Engines. Information retrieval technology, whether it be in the form of corporate text repositories or intranet search facilities, exists in many organizations as a knowledge silo containing legacy information. Information retrieval vendors continue to be concerned with satisfying the needs of information seekers and have added features such as relevancy ranking, natural language querying, summarization and others that have increased the speed and precision of finding information [6].

Groupware and Workflow Systems. Organizations use groupware systems when users in workgroups or departments need to communicate and collaborate. Groupware allows formal and ad hoc conversations in cases when the participants can not communicate in real time. This makes groupware an important technology for enhancing the exchange of tacit information. However, like other applications, groupware databases become knowledge silos that must be integrated into the enterprise knowledge architecture.

Push Technologies and Agents. Content push is a dynamic form of electronic publishing and is therefore an important feature of a knowledge management system. Agents are a specialized form of push technology. Agents are controlled by the end user, who can specify the type of knowledge he or she wants to receive. Agent capabilities are extremely valuable in knowledge-intensive environments, where knowledge workers do not have the time to continually monitor discreet information resources.

Help-desk Applications. Many organizations use help-desk technology to respond to both internal and external requests for information. However, the knowledge accumulated in help-desk systems can have much broader applications than answering specific questions. For example, service request logs are valuable tools to assist in product design and improving services [7].

Data Warehouses and Data Mining Tools. Organizations are creating data warehouses and arming their business managers with data mining tools to optimize existing relationships and discover new ones between customers, suppliers and internal processes. Used primarily by business managers, leading organizations are now broadening their use since everyone in a knowledge-based organization needs to make decisions based on increasingly complex sets of data. Knowledge management systems must provide meaningful access to data warehouses.

5 Conclusion

It was emphasized that the competitive advantage of an organization greatly depends these days on its ability to create and process knowledge in a rapidly changing environment. Innovation is the use of new knowledge to offer a new product or service that customers want. The innovative efforts include the search for, and the discovery, experimentation, and development of new technologies, new products and/or services, new production processes, and new organizational structures.

With the advances of information technologies including computer, network, etc., knowledge management system has been rapidly innovated. The knowledge management system manages the flow of knowledge within the organization and ensures that the knowledge is used effectively and efficiently for the long-term benefit of the organization.

References

1. Li, M., Liu, L., Li, C.-B.: Expert Systems with Applications 38, 8586–8596 (2011)
2. Ogunde, A.O., Folorunso, O., Adewale, O.S., Ogunleye, G.O., Ajayi, A.O.: International Journal on Computer Science & Engineering 2, 2181–2186 (2010)
3. Zhang, X., Chen, Z., Vogel, D., Yuan, M., Guo, C.: Human Factors & Ergonomics in Manufacturing & Service Industries 20, 103–122 (2010)
4. Hirai, C., Uchida, Y., Fujinami, T.: International Journal of Information Technology & Decision Making 6, 509–522 (2007)
5. Adam Holbrook, J., Wolfe, D.A.: Science and Public Policy 32, 109–118 (2005)
6. McCall, H., Arnold, V., Sutton, S.G.: Journal of Information Systems 22, 77–101 (2008)
7. Chen, T.-y.: International Journal of Software Engineering & Knowledge Engineering 19, 361–387 (2009)

A Maximum Likelihood Combined Cognitive Radio Analysis for Amplitude-Locked Loop

Yin-Chih Chen, Yen-Chih Yu, and Gwo-Jia Jong

Department of Electronic Engineering
National Kaohsiung University of Applied Sciences
No.415, Jiangong Rd., Sanmin Dist., Kaohsiung City 807, Taiwan (R.O.C.)
jevonschen0312@hotmail.com, awakenings@seed.net.tw,
gjjong@cc.kuas.edu.tw

Abstract. The transmission system of wireless communication is induced the channel noise. The potential sources of any noise type, which make and diturb the transmission system in external or internal to the communication system for message delivering. The carrier signal mixed interference signal using the amplitude-locked loop (ALL) can be adopted to separat the co-channel system by operating at same frequency for the demodulation system. The co-channel interference (CCI) is the major impact quality factor of communication system. In this paper, we develop the ALL system for additive white Gaussian noise (AWGN) wireless environment. In the ALL demodulation system, it is included the detection method by signal spectrum using cognitive radio (CR) system. The maximum likelihood estimation (MLE) algorithm is also estimated for probability density distribution statistical parameters. The result is shown the mean-square error (MSE) for different carrier signal-to-noise (SNRc) for dominant and subdominant signals.

Keywords: Amplitude-Locked Loop, Co-channel Interference, Cognitive Radio, Maximum Likelihood Estimation.

1 Introduction

The amplitude-locked loop (ALL) system can be separated the dominant and the subdominant signals each other. This process can have the low complex computation and compressed the co-channel interference (CCI) effect. The noise is used to impairment the transmission and processing in wireless communication, in order to separate signal by the AWGN channel interference, we adopted the cognitive radio and maximum likelihood estimation (MLE) algorithm for seeking original signal.

Cognitive radio is a new concept in wireless communication which aims to have more adaptive and aware communication devices which can make better use of available natural resources, i.e. the spectrum. The two challenging tasks in cognitive radio are sensing the environment, and processing and making decisions based on the spectrum knowledge. Apart from this, cognitive radio is expected to learn from its surroundings and perform functions that best serve. Such an adaptive technology naturally presents unique signal processing challenges [1].The former has been a

S. Lin and X. Huang (Eds.): CSEE 2011, Part V, CCIS 218, pp. 413–417, 2011.

popular choice of model fitting in psychology and is tied to many familiar statistical concepts such as linear regression, sum of squares error, proportion variance accounted for, and root mean squared deviation. However, MLE is not as widely recognized among modelers in psychology, but it is a standard approach to parameter estimation and inference in statistics. MLE has many optimal properties in estimation [2].

2 System Model

Amplitude-locked loop. After two signals are modulated by frequency modulation (FM), the receiver include the AWGN interference noise, thus we use the phase-locked loop (PLL) system to demodulate the signals from the AWGN channel, the equation defined as Eq. 2. They can be found the state such as the cross modulation distortion, high noise interference, and the Rician spikes. In the contrast, ALL is the system of high gain, high bandwidth servo-loop, when this output and PLL output are multiplied together, the co-channel interference could be achieve perfect dominant. It is demodulated the dominant signal and the suppression of the subdominant signal [3]. The ALL functions are defined as Eq. 2.

$$f_{PLL}(t) = \frac{1 + m\cos\omega_d t}{1 + 2m\cos\omega_d t + m^2} s_1(t) + \frac{m^2 + m\cos\omega_d t}{1 + 2m\cos\omega_d t + m^2} s_2(t) \tag{1}$$

$$f_{ALL}(t) = \frac{1 - m'^2}{1 + m'\cos\omega_d t}, \quad f_{ALL-1}(t) = \frac{-m'^2 - m'\cos\omega_d t}{1 + m'\cos\omega_d t},$$

$$f_{ALL-2}(t) = \frac{-1 - 2m'\cos\omega_d t - m'^2}{1 + m'\cos\omega_d t} \tag{2}$$

$$m' = \frac{2m}{1 + m^2} \tag{3}$$

where m denoted normalized interference carrier for carrier ratio, ω_d is the instantaneous difference frequency between the wanted carrier frequency and interference carrier frequency [4].

Cognitive Radio. The CR is an intelligent wireless communication system that is aware of its surrounding environment. The fundamental principle of CR is thus to identify other radios in the environment that might use the same spectral resources. We used the CR characteristic for *signal spectrum sensing*, *primary signal detection*, *energy detection*, *performance analysis*. The spectral component on each spectrum sub band of interest is obtained from the fast Fourier transform (FFT) of the sampled received signal. Then the test statistics of the ED is obtained as the observed energy summation within M consecutive segments. To facilitate analysis, here we ignore the interference component in the received signal.

$$Y = \begin{cases} \sum_{m=1}^{M} |W(m)|^2, & H_1 \\ \sum_{m=1}^{M} |S(m)W(m)|^2, & H_2 \end{cases}, \quad f_Y(Y) \sim \begin{cases} X_{2M}^2, & H_1 \\ X_{2M}^2(\mu), H_2 \end{cases} \quad (4)$$

where $S(m)$ and $W(m)$ denote the spectral components of the received primary signal and the white noise on the sub band of interest in m th segment, $f_Y(Y)$ denotes the probability density function (pdf) of Y and X_{2M}^2 and $X_{2M}^2(\mu)$ denote a central and not central chi-square distribution, respectively.

$$P_F = \frac{\Gamma(M, \frac{\lambda}{2})}{\Gamma(M)},$$

$$P_D = \int_0^{+\infty} P(Y > \lambda | H_1, \mu) f_\mu(\mu) d\mu$$

$$= \int_0^{+\infty} Q_M(\sqrt{\mu}, \sqrt{\lambda}) f_\mu(\mu) d\mu \quad (5)$$

Given the target false-alarm probability, the threshold   can be uniquely determined based on Eq. 5.Once λ is determined, the detection probability $P_D = P(Y > \lambda \mid H_2)$ can be obtained.

Maximum Likelihood Estimate. The method of maximum likelihood corresponds with many well-known estimation methods in statistics. Once data have been collected and the likelihood function of a model given the data is determined, one is in a position to make statistical inferences about the population, that is, the probability distribution that underlies the data as Eq. 6.

$$f(y | n, m) = (\pi N_0)^{-\frac{N}{2}} \times \exp[-\frac{1}{N_0} \sum_{j=1}^{n} (y_j - s_{ij})^2],$$

$$(i = 1, 2..., M; \ j = 1,, 2, .., N) \quad (6)$$

Since each y_j is a Gaussian random variable with means s_{ij} and variance $N_0/2$. The conditional probability density functions $f_x(x | m), (i = 1, 2..., M)$, are the very characterization of an AWGN channel. Their derivation leads to a function dependence on the observation vector y, given the transmitted message symbol m_i. we denoted by $L(m_i.)$ and defined as Eq. 7. We give the observation vector y and requirement is to estimate the message symbol m_i that is response for generating y.

$$L(m | y) = f(y | m) \quad (7)$$

$$L(m | y_1, ..., y_n) = f(y_1, y_2, ..., y_n | m) = \prod_{i=1}^{n} f(y_n | m) \quad (8)$$

$$\ln L(m \mid y_1,..., y_n) = \sum_{i=1}^{n} \ln f(y_i \mid m), \ \ \widehat{m} = \frac{1}{n} \ln L \quad (9)$$

The hat over m indicates that it is akin to some estimator. Indeed, $\widehat{m}$ estimates the expected log-likelihood of a single observation in the model. The method of maximum likelihood estimates by $\widehat{m}$ finding a value of θ that maximizes, this method of estimation is a MLE as Eq. 10 as below.

$$\widehat{m}_{mle} = \arg \max \widehat{m}(m \mid y_1,...., y_n) \quad (10)$$

3 Simulation Result

We used ALL and CR algorithms for two signals, compared original signal and noise signal in frequency domain analysis, which can observation after ALL separation signal, in Fig.1. The simulation result is presented the MSE of the SNR, shown in Fig.2. After PLL and ALL algorithm separation demodulation signals, we adopted MLE to get observation parameter to statistic which dominant is original signal that we transmitted in CCI. From Fig. 3 is MLE separation signals in empirical cumulative distribution function (ECDF) histogram and probability of convergence observation value, thus, we can clearly find out the signal and noise.

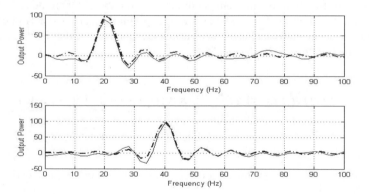

Fig. 1. The demodulated output signals without the interference signal (solid line) and with the interference signal (dashed line) for spectrum power analysis

4 Summery

In this paper, the amplitude-locked loop separation system combined CR and MLE algorithm can separate FM demodulation signals of CCI operating in the same carrier frequency. In Fig 3, which can recognize that the dominant from probability of 0.34 in convergence and ECDF at 0.32 and the subdominant from probability of 0.7 in convergence and ECDF at 0.8. The perfect demodulation and separation signals using CR and MLE algorithms are better than the previous papers.

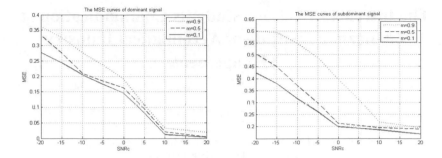

Fig. 2. The MSE and SNRc for dominant and subdominant

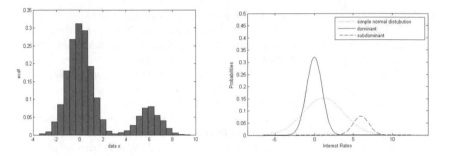

Fig. 3. Separation signals in ECDF histogram and probability of convergence

References

1. Molisch, A.F., Greenstein, L.J., Shafi, M.: Propagation Issues for Cognitive Radio. Proceedings of the IEEE 97, 787–804 (2009)
2. Myung, J.: Tutorial on maximum likelihood estimation. Journal of Mathematical Psychology 47, 90–100 (2003)
3. Peng, P.-L., Jong, G.-J.: Amplitude-locked loop separation and encryption system analysis combined cognitive radio. In: Conference on Communications (APCC), p. 435 (2010)
4. Chen, Y.-J., Horng, G.-J., Jong, G.-J.: The Separated Speech Signals Combined the Hybrid Adaptive Algorithms by Using Power Spectral Density and Total Harmonic Distortion. In: Conference on Multimedia and Ubiquitous Engineering (MUE 2007), pp. 825–830 (2007)
5. Li, J.M., Juang, B.H.: Signal Processing in Cognitive Radio. Proceedings of the IEEE 97, 805–823 (2009)
6. Yucek, T., Arslan, H.: Spectrum Characterization for Opportunistic Cognitive Radio Systems. In: Military Communications Conference, pp. 1–6 (2006)
7. Levina, E., Mi, A.A.: Maximum Likelihood Estimation of Intrinsic Dimension, Processing in Neural Information Systems 17, vol. 48109, pp. 777–784. MIT Press, Cambridge (2004)

The Internet Effects on Students Communication at Zhengzhou Institute of Aeronautical Industry Management

Shuying Sun

Zhengzhou Institute of Aeronautical Industry Management
Zhengzhou, Henan, 450015, China
Wwx222@126.com

Abstract. This research project inquired into students' perceptions of the effects of the Internet on their experiences of communication at college. The Internet is ubiquitous on college campuses and has the potential to both disrupt and enhance campus communication. Data for this study were collected from with eight hundreds full-time students, Qualitative analyses suggest that the Internet has both positive and negative effects on students' experiences of communication on campus. Students reported difficulty controlling the amount of time they spent online. The Internet was blamed for diminished face-to-face communications and message misinterpretations. The Internet was described as a positive way to meet people, develop relationships and maintain friendships.

Keywords: Internet usage, communication, college students.

1 Introduction

Internet usage on college campuses has shown explosive growth in recent years. Many campuses are now discovering that student culture and campus community are being created by the Internet. The Internet provides students a multitude of positive features, not the least of which are access to information and a means for staying connected to family and friends. However, research indicates that excessive time spent on the Internet may be related to a host of student problems including social isolation, social dysfunction, and poor academic performance. Scherer highlights several warning signs of Internet dependency among college students including excessive use, declining grades, failure to fulfill major responsibilities, health problems, and legal or financial problems [1]. Young offers several other signs that may indicate problems: lack of sleep and excess fatigue, less investment in personal relationships, withdrawal from social activities and events, general apathy or irritability when not online, and lying about how much time is spent online [2]. Students confess that their Internet activities present serious distractions from academic pursuits [3]. Kandel asserts that college students are particularly vulnerable to Internet addiction. He argues that late adolescents and young adults deal with powerful psychological and developmental forces [4]. Traditional-age college students face the tasks of developing a sense of identity and cultivating meaningful, intimate relationships. In some circumstance of addictive behaviors serve as a "coping

S. Lin and X. Huang (Eds.): CSEE 2011, Part V, CCIS 218, pp. 418–422, 2011.

mechanism for the adolescent having trouble negotiating these developmental challenges"[5,6,7].

While much of the research related to college students and the Internet has focused on patterns of use and associated outcomes, little disciplined attention has been given to students' perceptions of the impact of the Internet on their experiences of communication. In what ways, and to what extent, do students perceive that the Internet affects their experiences of communication at Zhenzhou Institute of Aeronautical Industry Management in Henan province of China.

2   Research Procedure

2.1   Research Questions

The research will answer the following questions:

R.Q.1 How much time do students spent online?
R.Q.2 How do students describe the effects of the Internet on their experiences of communication at college?
R.Q.3 What changes experienced over in Internet use, if any, have students the past year?

2.2   Population

The population for this inquiry was students traditionally aged eighteen to twenty-two at Zhenzhou Institute of Aeronautical Industry Management in Henan province of China.

Zhenzhou Institute of Aeronautical Industry Management was founded in 1949. college enrollment exceeded thirty-five thousand students .Access to the Internet and campus network is available to all college students, staff and faculty.

2.3   Sampling Procedure

A simple random sampling of freshmen and senior students at Zhenzhou Institute of Aeronautical Industry Management was used to select eight hundreds interviewees, four hundreds from the freshman classes and four hundreds from the senior classes, inclusive of two hundreds men and two hundreds women from each classes.

A simple random sample is a group of individuals drawn by a procedure in which all the individuals in the defined population have an equal and independent chance of being selected as a member of the sample. The students were selected from a list produced by the computer programmer/analyst at Zhenzhou Institute of Aeronautical Industry Management. The lists were divided by the programmer/analyst into classes (freshman and senior) and gender (male and female). Therefore, four lists were produced: freshman men, freshman women, senior men and senior women.

2.4   Limitations

As the sample population for this qualitative study was taken from a college in Midwestern of China, it is not recommended that the findings of this study be generalized to colleges that are dissimilar to Zhenzhou Institute of Aeronautical Industry Management.

3 Findings

3.1 R.Q.1 Time Spent Online

Internet use to be ubiquitous among undergraduate college students It shows 99.7% use the Internet, and 70.6% use it every day .At the same time three-quarters of college students use the Internet four or more hours per week, while about one-fifth use it twelve or more hours per week.

Excessive time spent on the Internet proved to be a major problem for students. Freshmen described themselves and their friends as "addicted" to the Internet. Seniors admitted to wasting vast amounts of time on the Internet. And while this finding is not particularly surprising, it is significant in light of the students' responses to questions regarding changes in their Internet use over the past year and the reasons for the changes. With very few exceptions, decreased time spent on the Internet was minimal and the reasons for the changes often had little to do with a concern about excessive time spent online. In other words, students admitted they had a problem with spending too much time on the Internet, but they were doing very little to change their online habits and behaviors. Thus, it appears that students may know they have an unhealthy Internet dependency but have no idea how to manage this powerful.

It is noteworthy however, that several students in this study did choose to alter their online habits. Two percent of them reduced the amount of time they spent on the Internet because of a spiritual commitment they made. The other students cut back on the amount of time she spent online after recognizing the negative effects it had on her relationships.

3.2 R.Q.2 Effects on Communication

The Internet was seen as a positive way to stay connected to others. The students agreed that the Internet was a great way to meet new people and develop new friendships. Internet communication allowed students to correspond with friends and family at home. Furthermore, the Internet allowed students to build and maintain current relationships. How students chose to communicate online varied according to class. Freshmen communicated most frequently through Facebook, while seniors often corresponded through email and instant messaging. Whatever the form of Internet communication, one thing was clear: students viewed Internet exchanges as extensions of relationship.

But an overwhelming majority of students admitted they had a problem controlling their Internet use. Freshmen described themselves and their friends as "addicted" to the Internet, and seniors confessed to wasting immense amounts of time on the Internet. The internet was blamed for reduced face-to-face interactions between students. Some students chose to relate to one another online rather than in face-to-face settings. Others spent time communicating with friends online at the expense of concrete relationships around them. Students also acknowledged that Internet communication, which is void of facial features, voice inflection and body language, led to a host of misunderstandings.

3.3 R.Q.3 Experiences over in Internet Use

The third research question aimed to understand how students describe the effects of the Internet on their sense of community at college. A second operational question sought to understand how students describe the nature of their Internet use. Three categories of Internet use emerged among the freshman and senior women and men. These included general surfing/browsing, research and academic pursuits, and communication.

In the area of academic pursuits, all of the senior women and over half of the senior men reported using the Internet for research and class-related assignments. This was true of most freshman women, however only 20% freshman described using the Internet for homework or research. A handful of freshmen referred to the use of Angel for a particular class. However, this was not the case with the seniors.

Email was the most used form of communication by all students. Most students agreed that email was the primary means by which to contact friends. Email was also described as a way to stay in touch with family members. However, significant differences arose when it came to contacting friends on and off campus. Nearly all of the senior women and a majority of the senior men utilized email and instant messaging to stay connected to their friends on and off campus. However, only 22% freshman via internet communicates with others.

4 Conclusions and Recommendations

4.1 Conclusions

The following four conclusions are conducted through above study:

- Most students spent excessive time on the Internet.
- Communicating with friends online will lead to some social problems.
- Senior students use Internet much more than freshman.
- An overwhelming majority of students cannot control their Internet use.

College students have embraced the Internet with little consideration of its potential downsides. Colleges can respond in several ways. Colleges can promote awareness of Internet dependency on campus. This involves the ability to assess the needs of students and implement educative and preventative programs.

- Student development administrators should serve to inform other campus personnel (faculty, resident directors, college computer service technicians, counselors and wellness center staff) of the risks of Internet addiction.
- Faculty may be first to identify those students having academic problems: missing class, sleeping in class, not turning in assignments, poor grades, etc. Resident directors and resident assistants should be trained to recognize

students with Internet addictive tendencies: frequent online use, late-night living patterns and sleep deprivation.

- Computer lab assistants should have an awareness of students who may spend excessive amounts of time in the computer lab.
- College counselors and wellness staff should be prepared to assess and assist students who have an Internet addiction.

Preventative programs for students, which may involve workshops, support groups, and creative software for campus computers. Upper-level students who have learned how to control their Internet usage, such as the three seniors mentioned above, could be solicited to share their stories with incoming students. A team approach is necessary. As student development personnel, faculty campus counselors, parents and students work together to inform, examine and address the issue of Internet dependency, campuses can help students think critically about Internet technology and develop healthy online habits.

References

1. Scherer, Ben-Artzi, E.: Loneliness and Internet use. Computers in Human Behavior 19, 59–70 (2003)
2. Young: Internet students: An exploratory College Health 50, 21–26 (1998)
3. Matthews, Schrum.: Student theory for higher education. Development 40, 518–529 (1999)
4. Kandell: What matters in college. Four critical years revisited. Jossey-Bass, San Francisco
5. Campbell, A.J., Cumming, S.R., Hughes, I.: Internet use by the socially fearful: Addiction or therapy? Cyber Psychology & Behavior 9, 69–81 (2006)
6. Chou, C.: Internet heavy use and addiction among Taiwanese college students: An online interview study. Cyber Psychology and Behavior 4 (2001)
7. Chou, C., Chou, J., Tyan, N.N.: An exploratory study of internet addiction, usage and communication pleasure the Taiwan's case. International Journal of Educational Telecommunication 5, 47–64 (1999)

Research on Double Main Body Interactive Teaching Based on Web 2.0 with Scientific Teaching Materials

Bo Shen[1,2]

[1] School of Information Technology, Jiangxi University of Finance and Economics, China, 330032
[2] Institute of Information Resources Management, Jiangxi University of Finance and Economics, China, 330032
jxcdsb@gmail.com

Abstract. Currently, Web 2.0 media are becoming more popular and in fact have formed a community wherein people can share their learning experiences with others. Many web 2.0 scientific teaching materials have the potential to increase reflection, sense of community and collaboration in the teaching, such as blogs, wikis and social networking sites. The purpose of this study was to construct a framework of double main body interactive teaching model based on web 2.0. The double main body interactive teaching model advocates teachers and students being the main body for each other in teaching activities, enabling both teachers and students to develop their initiative creativity actively and stimulate the other side to do so, so as to achieve mutual improvement. By employed a blog-based case, the model has been verified that it was an effective teaching model. The results show that both the teacher and students can get benefits from the double main body interactive teaching based on web 2.0.

Keywords: Double main body, Interactive teaching, Web 2.0, Scientific teaching materials.

1 Introduction

We are in the midst of a period of profound change of historic proportions. The primary driver of all of this is the relatively recent innovation of the Read/Write Web. Web 2.0, as some call it, is a more recent development. In a nutshell, the big shift is our newfound ability to create and publish content widely online almost as easily as we can read it.

Web 2.0 refers to the emergence of a set of applications on the web which facilitate a more socially connected web where everyone is able to add to and edit information online. With web 2.0 scientific teaching materials, such as blogs, wikis and social networking sites (SNSs), the Internet has entered the new era of Web 2.0, which goes beyond linking information to connecting people. Facebook and other SNSs are becoming more prevalent in educational environments, with educators exploring how such tools can be used for teaching and learning. Social networking sites differ from and provide an alternative to proprietary course management systems such as Blackboard, since SNSs emphasize community and collaboration. They are designed

S. Lin and X. Huang (Eds.): CSEE 2011, Part V, CCIS 218, pp. 423–428, 2011.

to combine individual profile pages with group interaction tools, such as chat, blogs, and discussion forums. Many existing SNSs are free and can be incorporated by teachers without additional cost, which is why they can be particularly useful when teaching courses on technology integration in the classroom [1].

Recently, web 2.0 applications have been used as the teaching tools in many universities. Many literatures discussed a number of interesting possibilities for the use of blogs. For examples, it is suggested that students can use blog to publish their own writings, discuss group assignments, peer review each other's work, collaborate on project and manage their digital portfolios.

From the teaching view, the teachers and students play different roles in the teaching procedure. Some researcher proposed that the teaching main body was teachers, but some thought that the students were the teaching main body. In this paper, the double main body thought was presented based on the web 2.0.

2   Double Main Body Interactive Teaching

Double main body teaching thought as a fundamental point of main body teaching view, it advocates that the teachers should inspire students to participate the teaching process, teachers and students are equal in the teaching process. The starting point of this teaching model is not only subjective initiative into full play the students, but also give full play to the inspired teacher guide. It attaches to the main lectures and students the common development of the concept of modern education is to educate the law embodies.   It believes that lectures and students are a subject of interdependence. If no students, will lose the value of existing teachers; no teachers, students do not care students. Teachers and students constitute a substantial interaction.

Interactive teaching is acted as a teaching model, an interaction between teachers and students. In this model, the teaching process is a dynamic development of the unified interaction of teaching and learning activities and interactive process. In the teaching process, through interactive teaching methods, both by regulating the relationship and interaction between teachers and students, it can form a harmonious teacher-student interaction. Students' interactions with teaching results produce resonance of teaching. It can improve the teaching effectiveness of a teaching structure model. Interactive teaching method is to achieve double main bodies of the importance of classroom teaching methods.

In the double main body interactive teaching model, it not only requires students to understand and master the knowledge and emphasis on the extraction and flexible use of knowledge, but also emphasizes to encourage students to analyze and solve problems in the process of innovation. The main idea of this model includes: the fundamental purpose of the teaching is to allow students to learn how to learn new knowledge, build their ability to be able to analyze and solve practical problems in the application of knowledge, and have the ability to develop new knowledge.

On the one hand, students are the main body of learning. The students attend learning activities; identify problems, observe the problem, and solve problems. On the other hand, teachers are the main body of teaching to help students to learn more effectively. Teachers should provide some guides for students to think. Creative thinking ability of students is very vital in the teaching process. Teachers should encourage students to think the same problems in different views.

The double main body teaching model includes three independent variables: teachers, students and curriculum. There exist three kinds of host-guest relationship. That is the relationship between lectures and the students, and the relationship between students and the curriculum (see Fig. 1).

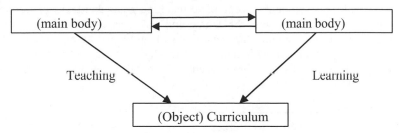

Fig. 1. The double main body teaching model

Meanwhile, in the teaching process, there is full communication between the teacher and students, students and students which can build an effective interactive mode (see Fig. 2).

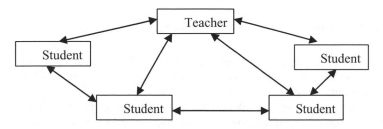

Fig. 2. The interactive between the teacher and students

Teachers as a main body of lecturing interact with the students, design the content of the curriculum and design teaching activities. In the model, students are the principal, and curriculum development is the object of teacher's study. Teachers and students are two main bodies; the curriculum is the object for teacher teaching and student learning.

There are some benefits in this model. Firstly, it can optimize the classroom situation, and mobilize the enthusiasm of all students. Secondly, teacher and students can together participate in the class activity. When students discuss with each other, understanding, memory, feedback, it is easy to combine into a whole. Thirdly, it can form a network of ideas, knowledge, feelings and capacity communication. With the great increase of information amount, it will be easier to communicate with others. Fourthly, students not only can study each other, but also can full develop their personality and ability. Finally, the different levels of students can be improved, and it can be useful for improving the teaching quality [2].

3 A Framework of Double Main Body Interactive Teaching Based on Web 2.0

Double main body teaching mode through the "ask questions - to solve the problem, "the student self-exploration process, through cooperation and interaction between teachers and students, from the knowledge and skills, processes and methods, attitudes and values, so students to complete teaching goals and tasks of teaching to form a stable and simple structure, the degree and way. Based on the basic process of innovative learning and teaching the basic idea of problem-solving, combined with Web 2.0 features, combined with individual teaching practice. The framework of double main body interactive teaching based on web 2.0 is designed to carry out the idea (see Fig. 3).

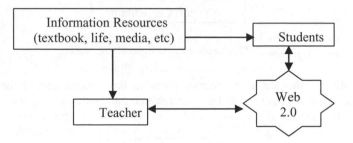

Fig. 3. The framework of double main body interactive teaching based on web 2.0

In the framework, the teacher and students can all exchange their ideas by using web 2.0 from different information resources. In the framework, both teacher and students have their activities.

As a teacher, he or she can provide the course home page, link student web 2.0 websites, post after class reflections and summaries of major issues for students to read and comments on or follow, post announcements to the class, invite and encourage students to provide comments, monitor comments and provide response, provide additional resources, etc.

As a student, he or she can post assignments, reflect on learning, share ideas, provide information and resources that they find interesting, visit teacher or other students web 2.0 websites, provide comments and recommend resources, read and reflect on posts provided by the teacher, access resources, monitor comments and respond to them, and so on.

In the framework, the teacher and the students can easier communicate each other by using the web 2.0 media, such as blogs, wiki, social networks. They can post ideas or comments on anytime and anywhere by using some mobile devices, such mobile phone, smart tablet, and palm computer.

4 A Blog-Based Case

In recent years, blogs (web-logs) have become a familiar tool for many people who read blogs and maintain a blog [3].

The popularity of blogs among young people has made them appealing to educators seeking to integrate computer-mediated communication (CMC) tools at the university level. These tools are seen as having the potential for enhancing student engagement and providing an environment for collaboration and creation of knowledge. Course management systems (e.g., Blackboard, Moodle) often include a blog component, which facilitates the integration of blogs into teaching and learning. However, educational applications of blogs have preceded research on their effectiveness [4].

During 2009 to 2010, I employed the blog as teaching tool in the management information system course. First, I built my blog and posted some course material on my blog, and then I build a blog group in the web. For every student, I requested him or her to open a blog and post at least five articles in the semester. In the blog group, I posted discuss topic, course case and other materials.

Overall, from my perspective as a teacher, I believe that the blogs added a new dimension to my teaching effectiveness by enabling me to do things that were not possible otherwise, either with or without other technology. Blog technology allows students as readers of my reflections to post their comments. Blog can also be used as a resource distribution medium. In blog, students can present their completed learning tasks and invite others to comment. Others and I were able to comment on these and provide suggestions. In this way, students received some feedback that they could use to revise the project, while also learning from others by reviewing their work and the feedback received. In this way, students can easier know some knowledge about the course and know how to learn new knowledge.

At the end of the semester, there were more than 200 students to build their blogs and post more than 1000 articles about the courses. I read every student's blog, and chose some good article to post on the blog group. I found many students to read these chosen articled.

This case demonstrated that blogs can be effective educational technology and useful blog-based activity for learning. Through blogs, a teacher can create an ambience in which students feel themselves to be important parts of the classroom community and that their needs and opinions are recognized and addressed.

5 Conclusions

Double main body interaction between the teachers and students into the teaching activities as the core of the whole process of forming a symbiotic mechanism of cooperation for the protection, it can provide some chance for students' and promote the professional development of teachers. By building and implemented the double main body interactive teaching architecture, it can form teacher-student learning communities, students-students learning community, teachers-teacher learning communities, effectively implement the double main body interactive teaching, and realize the effective knowledge and ability transfer from the teachers to students.

Acknowledgements. The research is supported by the Education Department of Jiangxi Province of China (Grant No. JXJG-09-3-25).

428   B. Shen

References

1. Churchill, D.: Educational applications of web 2.0: Using blogs to support teaching and learning. British Journal of Educational Technology 40(1), 179–183 (2009)
2. Wang, K., Huang, Y., Wang, T., Jeng, Y.: A blog-based dynamic learning map. Computers and Education 51(1), 262–278 (2008)
3. Quinn, M.: Learning with blogs. American Libraries 40(8/9), 59–61 (2009)
4. Halic, O., Lee, D., Spence, M., Paulus, T.: To blog or not to blog: Student perceptions of blog effectiveness for learning in a college-level course. Internet and Higher Education 13(4), 206–213 (2010)

Performance Comparison of Intercarrier Interference in OFDM Using DCT and DFT with Frequency Offset

Yingqiang Ding[1], Qinan Guo[2], and Gangtao Han[1]

[1] College of Information Engineering, Zhengzhou University,
Zhengzhou 450001, P.R. China
[2] Information Technology Designing & Consulting Institute CO. LTD,
Zhengzhou 450052, P.R. China
cnpowerfoot@gmail.com, qinan@yahoo.com.cn, gthan@263.com

Abstract. In this paper, a discrete cosine transform (DCT)-based orthogonal frequency-division multiplexing (OFDM) system is mainly described, and the intercarrier interference (ICI) analysis in the presence of carrier-frequency offset (CFO) over an additive white Gaussian noise (AWGN) channel is also investigated in detail. Then, the ICI performance comparison of DCT-OFDM and the conventional discrete Fourier transform (DFT)-based OFDM System is executed. The simulation results show that DCT-OFDM can improve the ICI performance and obtain better signal-to-interference ratio (SIR) than DFT-OFDM.

Keywords: Orthogonal frequency-division multiplexing, inter-carrier interference, discrete cosine transform, carrier-frequency offset.

1 Introduction

Orthogonal frequency-division multiplexing (OFDM) is used not only as many wireless network standards, but also in wire-line digital communications systems [1,2,3]. The conventional OFDM systems employ the complex exponential functions set as orthogonal basis to complete multicarrier modulation (MCM), and use inverse DFT (IDFT) and DFT to realize digital modulations and demodulations, respectively [4]. However, the complex exponential functions set are not the only orthogonal basis that can be used to implement the MCM schemes. A single set of cosinusoidal functions can also be used as an orthogonal basis to construct multicarrier signals, and this scheme can be synthesized using a discrete cosine transform (DCT). In DCT-OFDM systems, digital modulations and demodulations will be realized by the inverse DCT (IDCT) and DCT, respectively.

For one-dimensional (1-D) modulations (real-valued modulation formats), such as BPSK and pulse amplitude modulation (PAM), the quadrature modulator is not required, which is essential in DFT-OFDM system. In this case, DCT-OFDM can completely avoid the in-phase/quadrature-phase (IQ) imbalance problem that is inherent in DFT-OFDM systems. The DCT implementation can also be used in OFDM systems with 2-D modulations (complex-valued modulation formats). As far as fast implementation algorithms are concerned, the fast DCT algorithms proposed in [5] and [6] can provide fewer computational steps than FFT algorithms. OFDM system is based on the exactly orthogonality of subcarriers, any subcarrier waveform distortion

S. Lin and X. Huang (Eds.): CSEE 2011, Part V, CCIS 218, pp. 429–436, 2011.
© Springer-Verlag Berlin Heidelberg 2011

during transmission will destroy the orthogonality of subcarriers, which will result in carrier-frequency (CFO). Therefore, it introduces intercarrier-interference (ICI) both in DFT-OFDM systems and DCT-OFDM systems.

In this paper, we firstly describe a DCT-OFDM system, and then give an algorithm of signal-to-interference ratio (SIR) and ICI analysis for a DCT-OFDM system. At last, a comparison between the ICI performance of DCT-OFDM system and DFT-OFDM system operating in the presence of CFO over an AWGN channel was made.

2 System Model

In DFT-OFDM system, the complex exponential functions set is used as the orthogonal basis, which can be obtained as

$$T^{-0.5}e^{j2\pi nF_\Delta t}, 0 \le t < T, n = 0,1,\ldots,N-1 \tag{1}$$

The minimum subcarrier-frequency spacing F_Δ required to maintain the orthogonality of these functions in

$$\int_0^T T^{-0.5}e^{j2\pi nF_\Delta t}T^{-0.5}e^{-j2\pi mF_\Delta t}dt = \begin{cases} 1, & n=m \\ 0, & n \neq m \end{cases} \tag{2}$$

where T is the length of the OFDM symbol without guard interval and the minimum F_Δ is $1/T$ Hz.

Different from DFT-OFDM system, DCT-OFDM system use a single cosinusoidal functions set

$$\cos(2\pi nF_\Delta t), n = 0,1,\ldots,N-1 \tag{3}$$

as the orthogonal basis to maintain the orthogonality of these functions

$$\int_0^T (2/T)^{0.5}\cos(2\pi nF_\Delta t)(2/T)^{0.5}\cos(2\pi mF_\Delta t)dt = \begin{cases} 1, & n=m \\ 0, & n \neq m \end{cases} \tag{4}$$

Here, the minimum F_Δ is $1/2T$ Hz.

The continuous-time representation of a baseband DCT-OFDM block $x(t)$ is

$$x(t) = (2/N)^{0.5}\sum_{n=0}^{N-1} d_n\beta_n \cos(n\pi t/T) \tag{5}$$

where d_0, d_1 ..., d_{N-1} are N independent data symbols obtained from a modulation constellation, and β_n is calculated as

$$\beta_n = \begin{cases} 2^{-0.5}, n=0 \\ 1, \quad n=1,2,\ldots,N-1. \end{cases} \tag{6}$$

It is found that, if the data symbols d_n are obtained by real-valued modulation formats such as PAM and BPSK, the baseband DCT-OFDM signal $x(t)$ will still be a real signal. Sampling the continuous-time signal $x(t)$ at instants $t_m = T(2m+1)/2N$ gives a discrete time sequence as

$$x_n = (2/N)^{0.5} \sum_{n=0}^{N-1} d_n \beta_n \cos(\pi n(2m+1)(2N)^{-1}), m = 0,1,\ldots,N-1 \quad (7)$$

which is also the IDCT. At the end of sending, the data $d_0, d_1, \ldots, d_{N-1}$ are modulated by an IDCT operation firstly, then feeding the resulting samples $x_0, x_1, \ldots, x_{N-1}$ through a digital-to-analog (D/A) converter. At the receiver, under the conditions of ignoring noise and ideal channel, the original signal d_n can be restored by sampling the received signal and executing a DCT as

$$d_n = (2/N)^{0.5} \beta_n \sum_{m=0}^{N-1} x_m \cos(\pi n(2m+1)(2N)^{-1}) \quad (8)$$

3 ICI Analysis

In this section, we consider a DCT-OFDM system operating over an AWGN channel in the presence of CFO and phase error, which becomes a DFT-OFDM system when the IDCT and DCT are replaced with IDFT and DFT. Define a length-N sequence including in-phase components x_m^I and quadrature components x_m^Q obtaining after the IDCT as

$$x_m^I + jx_m^Q = \sqrt{\frac{2}{N}} \sum_{n=0}^{N-1} (d_n^I + jd_n^Q)\beta_n \cos\left(\frac{\pi n(2m+1)}{2N}\right) \quad (9)$$

where d_n^I and d_n^Q are obtained from general modulation schemes such as BPSK, QPSK, etc. However, in a DFT-OFDM system, even for 1-D signaling formats, one must also include both the in-phase modulator and the quadrature modulator, for which the DFT generally gives complex sequences, even if the signal is real. Hence, if one baseband DCT-OFDM signal frame is produced, the real part $x_b^I(t)$ and the imaginary part $x_b^Q(t)$ can be written as

$$x_b^I(t) = \sum_{m=0}^{N-1} x_m^I f(t-(2m+1)T(2N)^{-1}),$$

$$x_b^Q(t) = \sum_{m=0}^{N-1} x_m^Q f(t-(2m+1)T(2N)^{-1}) \quad (10)$$

Here, f is the low-pass reconstruction filter that performs D/A conversion. Consequently, the block of the transmitted band-pass signal is

$$x(t) = \Re\left\{ \left[x_b^I(t) + jx_b^Q(t) \right] e^{j2\pi f_c t} \right\} \tag{11}$$

where $\Re\{\gamma\}$ denotes the real part of γ.

At the receiver, the received I signal $r^I(t)$ and Q signal $r^Q(t)$ in an AWGN channel in the presence of CFO and phase error after demodulation can be expressed as

$$r^I(t) = \sum_{m=0}^{N-1}\left[x_m^I q(t - \frac{(2m+1)T}{2N})\cos(2\pi\Delta ft + \phi) - x_m^Q q(t - \frac{(2m+1)T}{2N})\sin(2\pi\Delta ft + \phi) \right] + w_i(t) \tag{12a}$$

$$r^Q(t) = \sum_{m=0}^{N-1}\left[x_m^I q(t - \frac{(2m+1)T}{2N})\sin(2\pi\Delta ft + \phi) + x_m^Q q(t - \frac{(2m+1)T}{2N})\cos(2\pi\Delta ft + \phi) \right] + w_q(t) \tag{12b}$$

Here, $w_i(t)$ and $w_q(t)$ are Gaussian noise with mean 0 and variance $\sigma^2 = N_0/2$, and $q(t)$ satisfies

$$q(\frac{nT}{N}) = \begin{cases} 1, & n = 0 \\ 0, & \text{otherwise.} \end{cases} \tag{13}$$

The discrete samples r_m^I and r_m^Q can be obtained by sampling at instants $(2m+1)T/2N, m = 0,1,2,\ldots,N-1$, which can be described as

$$\tilde{r}_m = r_m^I + jr_m^Q + w_m^I + jw_m^Q = (x_m^I + jx_m^Q)e^{j(\frac{2\pi\Delta fT(2m+1)}{2N}+\phi)} + \tilde{w}_m \tag{14}$$

where $\tilde{w}_m = w_m^I + jw_m^Q$ are complex Gaussian random variables. At the receiver, the DCT processing gives the decision variable $\hat{d}_k$ for the sampled signal in the kth subcarrier as

$$\hat{d}_k = \hat{d}_k^I + j\hat{d}_k^Q = (d_k^I + jd_k^Q)(S_{k,k}^I + jS_{k,k}^Q) + \sum_{\substack{n=0 \\ n \neq k}}^{N-1}(d_n^I + jd_n^Q)(S_{n,k}^I + jS_{n,k}^Q) + \tilde{w}_k \tag{15a}$$

where

$$S_{n,k}^I = \beta_k\beta_n\left[A(n+k-\varepsilon) + A(n-k-\varepsilon) + B(n+k+\varepsilon) + B(n-k+\varepsilon) \right]/2N \tag{15b}$$

$$S_{n,k}^Q = \beta_k\beta_n\left[T(n+k-\varepsilon) + T(n-k-\varepsilon) + Z(n+k+\varepsilon) + Z(n-k+\varepsilon) \right]/2N \tag{15c}$$

$$A(x) = \sin(\frac{\pi x}{2})\cos(\phi - \frac{\pi x}{2})(\sin(\frac{\pi x}{2N}))^{-1},$$

$$B(x) = \sin(\frac{\pi x}{2})\cos(\phi + \frac{\pi x}{2})(\sin(\frac{\pi x}{2N}))^{-1} \qquad (15d)$$

$$T(x) = \sin(\frac{\pi x}{2})\sin(\phi - \frac{\pi x}{2})(\sin(\frac{\pi x}{2N}))^{-1},$$

$$Z(x) = \sin(\frac{\pi x}{2})\sin(\phi + \frac{\pi x}{2})(\sin(\frac{\pi x}{2N}))^{-1} \qquad (15e)$$

$$A(0) = B(0) = N\cos\phi, \ T(0) = Z(0) = N\sin\phi, \ \varepsilon = 2T\Delta f \qquad (15f)$$

ε is the normalized frequency offset with respect to the subcarrier-frequency spacing because that the subcarrier frequency spacing is $1/2T$ Hz in DCT-OFDM. When the CFO $\varepsilon = 0$ in Eq. 15, one has

$$S_{n,k}^I = S_{n,k}^Q = 0, \quad n \neq k \,; \ S_{k,k}^I = \cos\phi, S_{k,k}^Q = \sin\phi \qquad (16)$$

thus, the decision variable $\hat{d}_k$ can be written as

$$\hat{d}_k = \left(d_k^I + jd_k^Q\right)e^{j\phi} + \tilde{w}_k \qquad (17)$$

In the presence of a fixed phase error ϕ only, the decision variable is a phase-rotated version of the transmitted signal, and no ICI exists. Thus, a DCT-OFDM system and a DFT- OFDM system have the same BER performance.

Similar to the coefficients in DCT-OFDM, there is a sequence of ICI coefficients for N-subcarrier DFT-OFDM in the presence of normalized frequency offset $\varepsilon = \Delta f T$, which can be derived as [7,8,9]

$$F_n = \sin\pi(n+\varepsilon)(N\sin\frac{\pi(n+\varepsilon)}{N})^{-1}e^{\frac{j\pi(N-1)(n+\varepsilon)}{N}} \qquad (18)$$

The corresponding decision variable $\hat{u}_k$ for the kth subcarrier is given as

$$\hat{u}_k = u_k F_0 + \sum_{\substack{n=0 \\ n\neq k}}^{N-1} u_n F_{n-k} + \tilde{w}_k, k = 0,1,\ldots,N-1 \qquad (19)$$

where u_k is the data symbol for the kth subcarrier. Thus, the SIR of the kth subcarrier is defined as

$$\mathrm{SIR}_{\mathrm{DCT}}^k = \frac{\left|d_k^I + jd_k^Q\right|^2 \left|S_{k,k}^I + jS_{k,k}^Q\right|^2}{\sum_{\substack{n=0 \\ n\neq k}}^{N-1}\left[\left|d_n^I + jd_n^Q\right|^2 \left|S_{n,k}^I + jS_{n,k}^Q\right|^2\right]}; \qquad \mathrm{SIR}_{\mathrm{DFT}}^k = \frac{\left|u_k F_0\right|^2}{\sum_{\substack{n=0 \\ n\neq k}}^{N-1}\left|u_n F_{n-k}\right|^2} \qquad (20)$$

for DCT-OFDM and DFT-OFDM, respectively.

4 Simulations and Results Analysis

It takes BPSK as an example to investigate the energy-compaction property of DCT-OFDM and DFT-OFDM. Since BPSK is a real modulation, there is no quadrature component, indicating that the decision variable $\hat{d}_k$ for the kth subcarrier in DCT-OFDM referring to

$$\hat{d}_k = d_k^I S_{k,k}^I + \sum_{n=0,n\neq k}^{N-1} d_n^I S_{n,k}^I + w_k^I \tag{21}$$

Assuming that the desired subcarrier index is $k = 32$ in a 64-subcarrier OFDM system, the DCT-OFDM ICI weighting coefficients $\left|S_{n,k}^I\right|$ and the DFT ICI weighting coefficients $\left|F_{n-k}\right|$ are presented in Fig. 1 with frequency offset $\Delta f \cdot T$ equaling to 0.05 and 0.25, respectively.

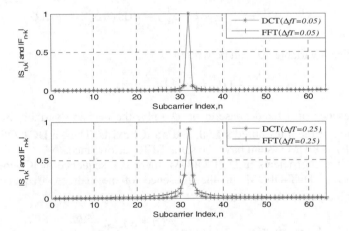

Fig. 1. ICI weighting coefficients in a 64-subcarrier BPSK-DCT-OFDM system and in a 64-subcarrier BPSK-DFT-OFDM system with k equaling to 32

From Fig. 1, it can be observed that the sequences of ICI coefficients tend to the shifted unit sample sequence $\delta[n-32]$ when the frequency offset Δf is close to zero. Here, the unit sample sequence $\delta[n]$ is defined as

$$\delta[n] = \begin{cases} 0, & n \neq 0 \\ 1, & n = 0 \end{cases} \tag{22}$$

It also can be seen that the ICI weighting coefficients of DCT-OFDM are more highly concentrated near subcarrier index 32 than the ICI coefficients of DFT-OFDM for the same value of ΔfT. In DFT-OFDM, ICI is introduced after the DFT `operation at the receiver [7,8]. Similarly, one can see from Eq. 15a that ICI is introduced after performing the DCT operation in a DCT-OFDM receiver. However, because of the energy-property of the DCT [10], its operation distributes more energy to the desired subcarrier and less energy to the ICI than the DFT operation. Therefore, the desired subcarrier suffers less ICI coming from neighboring subcarriers in DCT-OFDM than in DFT-OFDM.

In Fig. 2, the SIR of a 64-subcarrier DCT-OFDM system and a 64-subcarrier DFT-OFDM system are shown. It can be seen that the superiority of DCT-OFDM exists when $\Delta fT < 0.25$. This is because that the energy-compaction property of the DCT holds for small frequency-offset values. The ICI and SIR analysis suggest that the desired subcarrier suffers less ICI coming from neighboring subcarriers in DCT-OFDM than in DFT-OFDM.

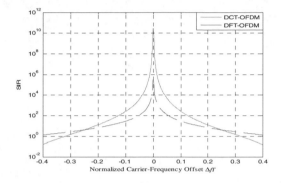

Fig. 2. SIR of the DCT-OFDM and DFT-OFDM systems as a function of the normalized CFO

5   Simulations and Results Analysis

In this paper, an exact method for calculating the SIR of a DCT-OFDM system in the presence of CFO in AWGN environments was proposed. The method was used to compare the performance of the DCT-OFDM system and the DFT-OFDM system when CFO is present in an AWGN transmission environment. Analysis and simulation results show that the DCT-OFDM systems can reduce ICI compared with the DFT-OFDM systems.

Acknowledgement. This study is supported by the Key Program for Science and Technology Development of Henan Province (No.102101210600) and the Doctoral Foundation Program of Zhengzhou University.

References

[1] Bingham, J.A.C.: VDSL, VDSL, and Multicarrier Modulation. Wiley, U. K (2000)
[2] Bingham, J.A.C.: IEEE Commun. Mag. 28, 5 (1990)
[3] Chow, J.S., Tu, J.C., Cioffi, J.M.: IEEE J. Sel. Areas Commun. 9, 895 (1991)

436   Y. Ding, Q. Guo, and G. Han

[4] Weinstein, S.B., Ebert, P.M.: IEEE Trans. Commun. Technol. 19, 628 (1971)
[5] Chen, W.H., Smith, C.H., Fralick, S.C.: IEEE Trans. Commun. 25, 1004 (1977)
[6] Wang, Z.D.: IEEE Trans. Acoust., Speech, Signal Process 32, 803 (1984)
[7] Sathananthan, K., Tellambura, C.: IEEE Trans. Commun. 49, 1884 (2001)
[8] Zhao, Y., Leclercq, J., Häggman, S.: IEEE Commun. Lett. 2, 214 (1998)
[9] Armstrong, J.: IEEE Trans. Commun. 47, 365 (1999)
[10] Rao, K.R., Yip, P.: Discrete Cosine Transform. Academic, USA (1990)

Study of Geotechnical Parameter for Metro Tunnel on Differential Evolution Algorithm

Dehai Yu, Annan Jiang, and Junxiang Wang

Institute of road and bridge engineering, Dalian Maritime University, Dalian, 116026, China
ydhhdy1977@163.com, jiang annan@163.com, Junxiang_W@163.com

Abstract. The displacement back analysis is an effective means on inversion of rock mechanical parameters. Differential evolution algorithm has many advantages and good prospects to solve problems of geotechnical parameters. The program is used to the simulation of the true tunnel with C++ language, while it is embedded into differential evolution algorithm to achieve the inversion parameter. Applying to Line 1 of Dalian Metro, inversion parameters and true parameters of rock are close, which indicates the superiority and good prospects of differential evolution algorithm, and it can be used for quantitative analysis of tunnel engineering.

Keywords: Differential evolution algorithm, tunnel engineering, inversion parameter.

1 Introduction

The tunnel construction is in the shallow, bias, serious loess layer[1]. We are insufficient to ensure that the design is reasonable without similar engineering to analogy, adopting the theoretical or numerical analysis method to calculate, and the reasonable rock mechanics parameters determine whether the calculation is accurate, object and practical or not, therefore the research on the surrounding rock parameters has a profound theoretical and practical significance.

Rock mass is nonlinear, noncontinuous, anisotropic medium, and boundary conditions are very complicated, therefore the functional expression is difficult to solve[2]. Differential evolution is a new type of global optimization algorithm with parallel computing features. Due to fast convergence rate and strong adaptability to non-linear function, it is especially suitable for the complex multivariable optimization problem[3]. A system is established with difference evolution algorithm. Rock mechanics parameters are obtained through the system, according to the actual monitoring displacement. Simulation and parameter identification on Line 1 of Dalian Metro have verified correctness and feasibility of the system.

2 Differential Evolution Algorithm

Differential Evolution (DE) is a population-based stochastic search algorithm that encodes its elements during each generation towards a global optimum. The

S. Lin and X. Huang (Eds.): CSEE 2011, Part V, CCIS 218, pp. 437–441, 2011.

population size is generally denoted by NP and each individual in the population is a vector $(X_{i,G}=x^1_{i,G}, x^2_{i,G}, ..., x^D_{i,G})$ of dimension D. As in biological evolution, DE's algorithm is mainly divided into three parts: mutation, crossover and selection.

(a) Mutation

For each target vector $X_{i,G}$ in the current generation, a mutant vector $V_{i,G}$ is obtained by randomly choosing a vector $X_{r1,G}$ and adding it to the scaled difference of two randomly chosen vector $X_{r2,G}$ and $X_{r3,G}$ such that i,r_1,r_2,r_3 are all mutually different. The resulting mutant vector can be expressed as follows:

$$V_{i,G} = X_{r1,G} + F \times (X_{r2,G} - X_{r3,G})$$ (1)

F is the scaling factor and is generally chosen between 0 and 1.

(b) Crossover

Given a target vector $X_{i,G}$ and the corresponding mutant vector $V_{i,G}$, a trial vector $U_{i,G}$ is obtained by combining the elements of the former two vectors as follows:

$$u^j_{i,G} = \begin{cases} v^j_{i,G} & if \quad rand_j(0,1) \le C_r \quad or \quad j=j_{rand} \\ x^j_{i,G}, & otherwise \end{cases}$$ (2)

The constant $C_r \in [0,1]$ is the crossover rate, $rand_j \in [0,1]$ is the jth evaluation of an uniform random number generator in the interval $[0,1]$, $j_{rand} \in \{1, 2,..., D\}$ is a random parameter index chosen once for each i.

(c) Selection

At this stage a natural selection has to be performed to choose the individual yielding lower objective between the target and trial vectors, i.e.:

$$X_{i,G+1} = \begin{cases} U_{i,G} & if \quad f(U_{i,G}) < f(X_{i,G}) \\ X_{i,G}, & otherwise \end{cases}$$ (3)

The same procedure is usually repeated for a given amount of generations or until a certain cost has been reached. Various stopping criteria might be implemented depending on the optimization problem at stake.

3   Parameter Inversion

According to the monitoring information on Line 1 of Dalian Metro, a simplified inversion model is used, see Fig 2. There are five measuring points shown in Figure 2 around the entrance of the tunnel, the displacements of measuring points is in Table 1. Now the material elastic modulus and Poisson's ratio are identified by the monitored convergence displacement. The comparison between the actual parameter values and discriminating parameter values is in Table 2.

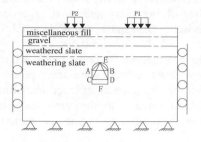

Fig. 2. Tunnel measuring points position

Table 1. Monitoring data

Measurement Data	mm
Distance of AB	2.565
Distance of CD	2.649
Distance of AE	4.201
Distance of BE	4.172
Distance of CE	8.640
Distance of DE	8.547

Table 2. Comparison of discriminating and actual parameter

	actual parameter	discriminating parameter	relative error (%)
E	310000000 (Pa)	310032856.9 (Pa)	0.10599
U	0.27	0.269986	-0.05287

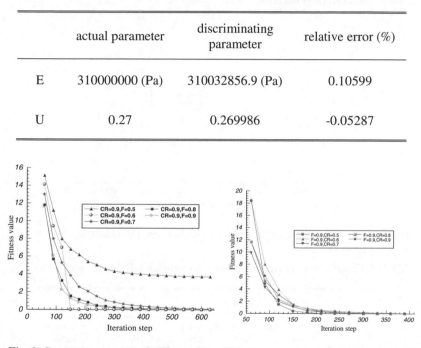

Fig. 3. Convergence curve of different F   **Fig. 4.** Convergence curve of different CR

In the course of different evolution search, different values of mutagenic factor or cross factor will impact astringency. Fix scaling factor CR=0.9, take cross factor as F=0.5, 0.6, 0.7, 0.8 and 0.9, then convergence curve is shown in Figure 3. It is shown that convergence of algorithm gender of F=0.7 is the best, the instant of CR=0.9 is rather bad. Fix cross factor as F=0.9, while scaling factor CR partly take as 0.5, 0.6, 0.7, 0.8 or 0.9, convergence curve is shown in Figure 4. Judging from the contrast of these curves, astringency of the curve of CR=0.7 is rather bad, the one of CR=0.9 is the best.

To test two modes DE/rand/1 and DE/rand/2 respectively, in the same cross-factor CR=0.7 and mutation factor F=0.9, the number of iterations and final inversion parameters are compared. The comparison between DE/rand/1 and DE/rand/2 is shown in Figure 5 and Table 3.

From two models we can draw some valuable information, finding a model which can accurately inverse parameter values, and know how to effect evolutionary process on cross-factor CR and mutation factor F. Seeing from parametric combination condition of Figure 3 and 4, both methods are able to converge to ideal error and gain ideal outcome. Rainer Storn uses the following expression to define the various models of different evolution:

$$DE / x / y / z \qquad (4)$$

Where: x indicated in mutation operation is a random (rand) to select a particular individual of the current generation.

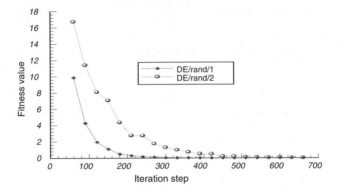

Fig. 5. Comparison of the number of iterations between DE/rand/1 and DE/rand/2

Table 3. Comparison of inversion parameters between DE/rand/1 and DE/rand/2

	DE/rand/1		DE/rand/2	
	elastic modulus(Pa)	Poisson's ratio	elastic modulus(Pa)	Poisson's ratio
discriminating parameter	309433151	0.27102	310032857	0.26999
actual parameter	310000000	0.27000	310000000	0.27000
relative error (%)	-0.183	0.378	0.106	-0.004

4   Conclusion

(1) Differential evolution algorithms which become the primary means of extensive attention by scholars from various countries have many advantages and good prospects to solve geotechnical problems.
(2) The displacement back analysis method has a certain assumption in the analysis conditions, but it is still an effective means of rock mechanical parameters inversion, which can be used to check the results of engineering and test validation results and so on.
(3) Inversion parameters of dalian metro are feasible and practical, and the analysis results provide reference for the following construction.

Acknowledgements. This work was financially supported by the National Natural Science Foundation (40902075).

References

1. Yang, Z., Wang, S., Feng, Z.: The Principles and Applications Back Analysis of Geotechnical Engineering. Earthquake Press, Beijing (2002)
2. Yuan, F., Zhan, Y., Luan, M.: Rock and Soil Mechanics 29(3), 734–739 (2008)
3. Belytschko, T., Liu, W.K., Moran, B.: Nonlinear Finite Elements for Continua and Structures. Tsinghua University Press, Beijing (2002)

The Study of Continuous Education for Cenozoic Migrant Workers Based on Information Technology

Yumei Han[1,2] and Zhilin Suo[3]

[1] College of Economics and Management, Northeast Agricultural University, Harbin, China
[2] Heihe university, Heihe, China
[3] College of Arts and Social Sciences, Northeast Agricultural University, Harbin, China
hanyumei6688@163.com, szl1960@sina.com

Abstract. It is a preventive strategy that to develop the continue education of migrant workers and to replace number with quality, which will truly avoid labor shortages and improve the quality of workers. To provide adequately continuous education to Cenozoic migrant workers will reduce the turnover rate of their work. But in the process of continuous education for Cenozoic migrant workers, there are some problems and obstacles worth considering. Actively seeking measures to promote Cenozoic migrant workers' continuing education is to promote the smooth progress of the construction of an effective means of urbanization.

Keywords: Cenozoic migrant workers, continuing education, Strategy.

Necessity of Continuing Education for Cenozoic Migrant Workers

In China, the emergence of labor shortage is a demographic dividend of nodes, more and more attentions are paid to the sustainability of dividend - the secondary breakthrough of the demographic dividend expect to resolve, which declares an old era of labor to end- from low-skill, low overall quality and cheap labor supported Chinese economic miracle to an end, a new era of labor to come, the Cenozoic migrant workers is an important part in this cheap labor groups. Response positively to "post demographic dividend "and provide Cenozoic migrant workers with continuing education can promote sustainable economic development and urban construction, as well as social harmony.

Continuing Education Will Meet the Development of Cenozoic Migrant Workers

In the stage of Twelfth National Economic and Social Development Five-Year Plan, Cenozoic migrant workers will play a very important role in China. At present, this group has reached nearly one hundred million; their values have changed, their awareness of training and learning as well as self-development has become strong. Career expectations became high, mobility became intensive. National Federation of Trade Unions said, in the "the report on Cenozoic migrant workers' problem" about Cenozoic migrant workers' education and professional development, Cenozoic migrant workers have the following characteristics: One is directly from the school gate to the factory gate, lack of professional recognition on agriculture and farmers.

S. Lin and X. Huang (Eds.): CSEE 2011, Part V, CCIS 218, pp. 442–447, 2011.
© Springer-Verlag Berlin Heidelberg 2011

Second, the educational level significantly increased, but they also have many problems as following: disorder in employment competition, misconduct in vocational orientation, lack of work skills and basic professionalism as well as overall quality, which make their employment be unrealistic and inadaptable to the future requirements of the development. Through their continuing education to enhance professional competence, expand employment space, train entrepreneurial skills and achieve self-worth, improve rights and win the respect of the society. Through training to build spiritual homeland, fulfill the spirit of the world.

Continue Education to Improve the Quality of Cenozoic Migrant Workers
In today's post demographic dividend, non-agricultural sector dominated the labor demand because of technological progress, the relationship between supply and demand evaluated for technology, human capital population factors. Lewis Turning Point is a point at which the economic grow from extensive to scientific development, before the turning point, economic growth was mainly driven by labor and capital inputs; after turning point, economic development is driven by the overall increase in productivity. We must converse a huge population into human capital stock to eliminate some negative effects of the demographic dividend. We must turn characteristics and advantages of the large population in a large general labor, unskilled and semi-skilled labor into the corresponding human resources. Since the Lewis turning point is a hurdle that is difficult to bypass in developing countries, to develop Cenozoic migrant workers education, give priority to the comprehensive development, replace quantity with quality is a proactive means to prevent labor shortages and improve the quality of workers.

Continue Education Can Reduce the Work flow of Cenozoic Migrant Workers
Kiefer found that education and employment rates are positively correlated, negatively correlated with the unemployment rate, but the relationship between unemployment is not clear. Borsch-Span is one of the few specializing in the role of education on job mobility, and he thinks that education can inhibit the flow of job; Hirsch found that years of education and the resignation will be negatively related .The higher education level, the lower turnover. Viscose, Belau and Kahn found that education and resignation probability of male workers is negatively correlated, female workers are positively related to resign. Their researches can be indirect evidence of relationship between level of education of migrant workers and work flow. Migrant workers lack of training in our business, and the relationship between their level of education and corporate training is loose; the cost of education to effect the resignation of the probability is weak, which is less than income effect, generally speaking, education is positively correlated with the resignation probability. If Cenozoic migrant workers will be provided adequate continue education, which will reduce the flow rate.

The probability of resignation between men and women did not differ significantly, education and the probability of resignation is same, which is different from the Western developed countries, women left the labor market is the purpose of procreation and raising children. Secondly, women's income less than men, so women tend to be a secondary earner in the family. In developed countries women received training significantly less than men, which is an important reason that the resignation of women is higher than men's. Male and female workers in China receive the corporate training is not equal enough. Which results in the linking is loose between education and business specific human capital, education affecting the cost effect of resignation probability is weak, so education and the resignation probability between men and women are positively related.

Problems Existing in the Continue Education of Cenozoic Migrant Workers

So far, training of Cenozoic migrant workers has made some achievements in China, such as more focus on practical operation in vocational skills, more inclined to vocational skills training, more appealing to computer-related training, agronomy, machinery, maintenance, construction industry are highly attractive to migrant workers, and achieve desired results ,so that their skills and salaries have been increased .But in the training process, there are some problems, it is worth our consideration.

Own Factors of Cenozoic Migrant Workers Affecting Continue Education

Cenozoic migrant workers have stronger educational needs, but few of them can converse the potential demand into real action. Initiatively participate in vocational skills training is few. The pay ability of participation in education and training is very limited, the city's discrimination led to inferiority. Limited financial resources, learning time can not be guaranteed, Cenozoic migrant workers and training institutions in information exist in asymmetry, they are lack of understanding training importance.

More Limiting Factors Existing in Vocational Skills Training

Enthusiasm of enterprises involved in training is not high, the government lack emphasis on vocational skills training, which existed widespread. Skills training is ineffective, lack of targeted training content, training content out of line with market demand, a single mode of training, lack of flexibility and high cost constrain them to participate in, the government training institutions and employers have not formed good relations of cooperation, the training market is not perfect, the Cenozoic migrant workers still lack an effective continue education system, educational implicitly environment reject them.

Frequent mobility, weak organization and management, to some extent, which affected continue education of Cenozoic migrant workers. While learning convenience is not enough, the information channel is not smooth disorder expansion of the labor market, on the migrant workers resulting in a negative demonstration effect on the migrant workers. Employment units and training institutions pay attention to their interests, making them contempt the professional skills. Training funds for migrant workers are not enough, which make the vocational training more difficult. Funding mechanism is not perfect, lack of government investment, enterprises are unwilling to put in more, coupled with their inability to pay, which affected their continue education.

The Current Situation of Continue Education About Female Migrant Workers
Cenozoic female migrant workers' learning opportunities are limited, learning desire is stronger than the older, there are gender differences in social recognition, coupled with economic factors, traditional and social and historical factors, psychological factors, all of above affected their continue education. Most of them have not technology, only take on nontechnical work; most of them simply engaged in manual labor, resulting in low wages, no job security. Generally speaking, low level of education and culture quality and poor market adaptability are their shortcoming. Since most of them have not given enough pre-employment guidance and obtain the corresponding skills, only to engaged in low-tech industries relying on traditional empirical work. Meanwhile, most of them lack of understanding about industrial area which they have employment or ready for employment, and most lack in information. The thinking of males preferring the tradition led to rural women inaccessible to education and labor training than men. National policies on the city's tilt make rural migrant women easily become the object of rights infringed.

Strategies of Promoting Continue Education of Generation of Cenozoic Migrant Workers
Through continue education, to enhance the Professionalism of Cenozoic migrant workers, continue education should include urban cultural adaptation, to fully tap its potential social and economic value, effectively enhance their abilities so as to promote their social integration, to promote them master modern professional knowledge and skills.

Improving the Content and Form of Continue Education
Continue education should form awareness and ability of Cenozoic migrant workers for lifelong learning, enhance the generation of migrant workers integration capacity of urban life, and guide them to establish a reasonable flow tendency, to enhance their moral training, to strengthen the legal awareness. Vigorously develop vocational skills training, increase the intensity of training , to use flexible form and content of continue education, innovate ways of training inputs, break the bottleneck of lack of training funds and improve the quality of training. Provide vocational guidance, in which construct the general education requirements for Cenozoic migrant workers, and provide plenty of professional training, including vocational skills, business knowledge, improvement education, labor law, life knowledge, cultural knowledge and occupational safety. In addition to the vocational skills training, we should also pay particular attention to their sense of values and the comprehensive quality improvement, as well as the training of the city's system and rules.

Training methods should be creative. There are many distance education institutions, teaching in a wide range of modern information technology, which has enough teaching resources and extensive network coverage, teaching ideas are opening up, teaching targets are scientific, which should look as a way of continue education for Cenozoic migrant workers.

Government Should Play an Active Role in Continuing Education to Cenozoic Migrant Workers
The enterprise should play the main role; they should adhere to the integrated principles of skills training and quality training. Enhance the adjustment of the market

and forecast, stick with the combination of a variety of education and training institutions, adhere to the post and pre-job training, and ensure the long-term effectiveness of training. Integrate educational resources, and give full play in various training institutions. Vocational institutions should constantly improve teaching quality according to market need, and guide the lifelong learning of migrant workers. Improve the continuity of vocational skills training, to establish training mechanisms of government-led, sector and the society involved in each other, broaden training preach, so that more farmers in the premise of known to select. To establish a training and employment mechanism of involving government institutions, enterprises and migrant workers.

Government should strengthen the leading role and increase financial input. The government should monitor and control continuing education units to improve teaching quality according to the market need, and guide the lifelong learning of migrant workers. Output and input government should be linked with each other, to provide farmers for the same training opportunities as urban workers. Cenozoic migrant workers realize their lifelong education, depending on whether the Government and society can provide opportunities for lifelong education. Government should construct a bridge of life-long education, build a multi-dimensional training system from primary education, secondary education to higher education longitudinally, non-academic and academic training communicate horizontally, to meet the farmers, especially migrant workers' need, to help them realize their professional dream. Community training should not only focus on personanality, but also pay more attention to systematic and integrity.

Improving the System of Continuing Education of Migrant Workers
National policies and systems should be designed to give the expected stability of Cenozoic migrant workers, make sustainable funding for continue education and establish a government oversight body, put an end to invade the legitimate rights of migrant workers, and earnestly safeguard the legitimate rights of migrant workers. Strengthen the government's responsibility and improve the relevant legislation to strengthen the training of Cenozoic migrant workers, promoting enterprises and Cenozoic migrant workers actively participate in training through system construction, and promote vocational education and training policies' innovation. Establish free vocational training system and Cenozoic migrant workers training government subsidy system. Actively pursue vocational training voucher system. The trade union should further play a big school role to establish Cenozoic migrant workers pre-service education service mechanism and skills training and technical rating service mechanism. Gradually establish a diverse mechanism of investment in training. To promote planned, systematically training certificate and vocational qualification certificates with the combination of posts and employment permit system.

Measures of Continuing Education for Cenozoic Female Migrant Workers
To receive education for Cenozoic female migrant workers is essential requirement for achieving modernization; the development of rural adult education is adaptable to modern society for women. We should integrate gender awareness into the continuing education for Cenozoic female migrant workers. We should carry out widespread

employment education and training according to female characteristics, besides skills training before employment, we must also carry out protection of women's rights, health care, marriage and family, children education, and etc, involving norms and values education, in order to change the traditional concept, enhance self-awareness, to meet their additional requirements of training opportunities. To improve Cenozoic female migrant workers' quality through continuing education. Focus on practical training with the actual situation. Strengthen cooperation with governments, communities, schools, enterprises and institutions so that carry out education and training of Cenozoic female migrant workers. Take the women themselves' improvement as a key to start the work, establish awareness of lifelong education, make out career plan, strengthen the spirit of women's self-reliance.

Acknowledgment. This project is supported by Natural Science Foundation of Heilongjiang Province of China (Grant no.G201029).

References

1. Neal, D.: The Complexity of job Mobility among Young Men. Journal of Labor Economics 17(2), 237–261 (1999)
2. Li, H.: Economic Transition and Returns to Education in China. Economics of education review 22(3), 317 (2002)
3. Jamison, E.H.: Education and Earning in the People's Republic of China. Economics of Education Review 6(2), 161–162 (1987)

Task-Driven and Cooperative-Working Based Compiler Principle Teaching Reform

Xin Li, Yanfei Peng, and Jinguang Sun

School of Electronic and Information Engineering, Liaoning Technical University
Hu Ludao 125105, China
li_xin718@sina.com

Abstract. Task-driven teaching method is proposed for the difficulty in the process of teaching and learning of compiler principle course. This method is based on the constructivist teaching theory. Teaching tasks is divided into several tasks which contain several points. Teaching goals are realized by solving the tasks. Cooperative-working based practice teaching method is proposed in order to enhance the teaching effect of this method. Students will cooperate with their classmates to co-accomplish one task. Then they can not only complete the practical task of the point but also have very clear understanding of their relations between all points of the whole task. good results have been achieved in practice. It satisfies the need of teaching reform.

Keywords: Compiler Principle, Task-Driven, Cooperative-Working.

1 Introduction

Compiler principle has for its object the basic principle and design method of programming language and the construction of compiler [1,2]. Students can master compile system structure, workflow, and design principle and implementation techniques of compiler in the course. They can gain the basic ability of analysis, design and implementation of the compile system [3]. Students can also improve comprehensive understanding of the programming design language, operating systems and computer principle et al by learning the theory of compiler. Compiler principle is a main professional course in computer science. But, this course has strong theoretical and practical characters and is tightly linked to other courses, which make it be one of the toughest teaching and the hardest learning courses in computer science. For a teacher, how to raise teaching effect is a main issue. Task-driven and cooperative-working based teaching method is proposed based on analysis of the problems existing in the currently teaching process of compiler principle.

2 Main Problem in the Present Teaching

Looked from the teaching practice in recent years, we met many problems in the teaching of this course, which are as follows.

S. Lin and X. Huang (Eds.): CSEE 2011, Part V, CCIS 218, pp. 448–451, 2011.

(1) Discrete mathematics knowledge such as set theory, graph theory, reasoning logic is used in this course [4]. Formal language and automata theory is the main theoretical foundation of the compiler theory [5]. The theoretical knowledge is difficult to understand for students in their study process.

(2) Students have no idea about why being offered this course. Many students often have these doubts about what is the use of compiler principle course. They think compiling principle is lack of practical importance. This indicated that students are not clear to what problems it can solve.

(3) The experimental teaching is difficult to carry out. Because of the strong logic, complex arithmetic, the scale of the experiment task is hard to control. The experimental teaching contents is obsolete, with low comprehensive and low difficulty and in small scale.

3   Task-Driven and Cooperative-Working Based Teaching Method

For the above problems, teaching reform method based on task-driven and Cooperative-working is performed during teaching process. We use the task-driven teaching method in the classroom teaching, and use Cooperative-working model in the practical teaching.

Task-Driven Teaching Method. task-driven method is a teaching model based on the constructivist teaching theory. In this teaching model, teachers design teaching content into one or more specific tasks, and let students master teaching contents to achieve the target of this course by completing some specific tasks. Students take initiatives in learning and teachers give guidance in this method. Tasks as the main line, teacher as the leadership and students as the main body are the basic characters of this teaching method. It can help students get learning initiative and study with questions, which can not only enhance student's study interest but also help the student to culture innovation ability and they can experience more pleasure. For example, the function and tasks of lexical analysis and the content of finite automata and some other analysis tool are abstract. They are the key and difficult points of teaching. It can achieve good teaching results using the task-driven method. In this method, the content of lexical analyzer is converted into a specific task. For example, we can set the above task:

Writing a c program to identify all the words and symbols in the procedures section.

```
void fun( ){
 int a, b, c;
 c = (a-b) *10; }
```

As shown in fig.1, it need to use the related knowledge of lexical analyzer which contain regular expression, NFA, DFA, minimum DFA and some other points to solve this task. First, the teacher introduces relations between the tasks and these points, then explains these points with special focus and aims. After this, the teacher explains how to resolve this task using these points. In order to identify the word symbols, regular grammar concept is used to guide students to analyze word formation rules.

Formal grammar of words is as follows:
G[S]:S->K|D|I|O|B
K->void
D->10
I->a|b|c
O->=|-|*
B->; | (|) | }| {

The teacher guides students to identify common described grammar, explains the new knowledge, writes regular expression according to grammar and converts the regular expression into NFA, then gets DFA, finally simplifies DFA and completes identifier recognition [6].

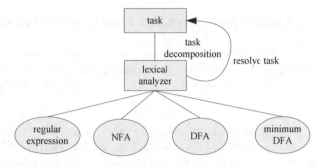

Fig. 1. Task decomposition

Cooperative-working based teaching method. Cooperative-working based practice teaching model is proposed in order to enhance the teaching effect of task-driven teaching method. Students fulfill a practical task by co-operating with others in this model and they cooperate and interact effectively during completing the task. Let students work in teams to analyze and discuss the experiments task, and have a clear idea to solve the problem. After a series of collaborative learning activities students finish the task, enhance their understanding of knowledge.

According to the practice of teaching, the treatment method of this model in practice is divided into the following stages:

(1) Designing the practice tasks

Teachers design and develop experiment tasks according to the task and related points of the task in classroom teaching. The design of experiment tasks aims at completing the task in classroom teaching and covering related points. In the design of the task it should facilitate students to work collaboratively, and it has maneuverability and cooperation.

(2) Team distribution and task confirmed

Students can group freely according to their interest. Then it can be changed according to the students' study ability and prior knowledge.

(3) Task implementation

This is the most important stage of collaborative teaching model. In this stage, study team should analyze the experiment task and make clear the essential requirements and goal; mastering the methods and knowledge to solve the problems. With the help of teachers, students determine the responsibility and the duty in team and work together on team tasks.

(4) Examination

It is easy to examine students in the traditional practice teaching model. But it should be adjusted when using the cooperative-working based teaching model. Students in a team should not only complete their independent modules but also consider other students' modules. They achieve a complete task through interaction and coordination. So, it should examine every students' independent performance and the team performance. The specific examination methods include two aspects: Program assessment and experiment report. Program assessment includes two parts: one is the inspection of program modules finished by each student independently, the second is the inspection of the program of the whole task finished by the team. Experiment reports are completed in groups. Through cooperative working, every student can got a good hold the point relate to the task and the relations between them.

4 Summary

Based on years of teaching experience, task-driven and Cooperative-working based teaching method is proposed. Students master the related knowledge points during completing the specific tasks. In order to enhance the effectiveness of this method the Cooperative-working model is presented in practice teaching to assist the classroom teaching. It makes students study compiler principle knowledge with a purpose. It enhance students' understanding and interest in learning to this course. It is proved from practice that this method has the high feasibility and validity.

References

[1] Barrón-Estrada, M.L., Zatarain-Cabada, R., Zatarain-Cabada, R., Reyes García, C.A. et al: A Hybrid Learning Compiler Course. In: Tsang, P., Cheung, S.K.S., Lee, V.S.K., Huang, R. (eds.) ICHL 2010. LNCS, vol. 6248, pp. 229–238. Springer, Heidelberg (2010)

[2] Schwartzbach, M.I.: Design Choices in a Compiler Course or How to Make Undergraduates Love Formal Notation. In: Proceedings of the Joint European Conferences on Theory and Practice of Software 17th International Conference on Compiler Construction, pp. 1–15 (2008)

[3] Shu, Z., Li, W., Zhou, X.: Practice and Experience of Teaching eform for Compiler Principle. Acta Scientiarum Naturalium Universitatis Sunyatseni 46(2), 102–105 (2007)

[4] Zhang, J., Yang, D., Guo, D.-g., et al.: Research on Method of Compiler Principle Practice Teaching. Journal of Jilin University 23, 142–144 (2005)

[5] Zhang, H., Sun, S., Zhang, F.: The Research of Teaching Project of Principles of Compiling Based Assignment-Driven. Computer Education 10, 100–103 (2010)

[6] Yao, X.: On Teaching Compiling Principles. Journal of Chongqing Jiaotong University 3(2), 85–86 (2003)

Research on Hierarchical Management Mode of Newly-Established Colleges Based on Modern Information

Yumei Han, Xiaoli Wu, and Jinxia Qiao

Heihe university, Heihe, China
{hanyumei6688,wuxiaoli127,qjx924}@163.com

Abstract. In recent years, as the rapid increase undergraduate colleges in China, newly-established colleges are in a developmental period with opportunities and challenges. The original kind of small and specialized extensive management mode has exposed its shortcomings. In order to survival in the field of higher education, new-established colleges should find a breakthrough in management systems, and deeply reflect the existing management system.

Keywords: Newly-established colleges, hierarchical management, mode.

The Necessity of Implementing Hierarchical Management of New Colleges

The new-established colleges are comprehensive universities and colleges that were managed and invested by Provincial and city government, their main purpose is servicing for local economic and social development. In recent years, lots of technical colleges were upgraded to undergraduate colleges; the expansion speed is rarely seen in the history. As the rapid increase in undergraduate colleges, the new-established colleges are in a developmental period with opportunities and challenges. After upgrading they are facing many problems to be solved, especially with the constant expansion of education, these colleges should gradually transform from single subject to multidisciplinary and integration. The forms and types of organizing, the aims of training and quality standards have become diversified, organization and management have become complex. The original kind of small and specialized college education, the extensive mode of management has exposing its shortcomings.

The Necessity of Developing

History shows that a sector's management and operation system directly determines its survival and development conditions. So in order to survive and develop rapidly in the field of higher educations, new colleges must find a breakthrough in management systems, and deeply reflect the existing management system. With the regional development of higher educations, new colleges have become powerful and great potential parts of our colleges. According to statistics, there are more than 200 undergraduate colleges in China, the number of students in undergraduate colleges' accounts for one third of the total, is the main part of higher educations.

S. Lin and X. Huang (Eds.): CSEE 2011, Part V, CCIS 218, pp. 452–457, 2011.

Although compared to the university with a long history, there are still significant gap between newly-established colleges and the requirements of modern university system, but it has the potential unique reform advantage on geopolitics, interpersonal and internal relations of the University's. Although China's higher education resources are relatively scarce, but with the changes of employment concept, the renewing of talent mind, the choice of university candidates will be more harsh, the idea that the school was upgraded you can sit back and relax is dangerous.

The Theoretical Basis for the Hierarchical Management

Modern management theory believes the specific management magnitude is the prerequisite conditions of orderly and efficient management. Span of control refers to the possible number of subordinates that a superior leadership can lead directly and effectively. A leader of the organization, due to knowledge, experience, time, energy, conditions and other constraints, the subordinate number that he can effectively and directly lead is always limited, over a certain limit, it will reduce administrative efficiency.

The management of the French sociologist V. A. Graicunas had made a well-known mathematical model to analyze the possible relationship between superiors and subordinates. Interprets the possible subordinate number that a superior leadership can lead in the management process. When the number of subordinates increases by arithmetical progression, the number of working relationships that the managers directly involve in increases in the geometric series.

The quantitative analysis of the mathematical model revealed theoretically that the effective management requires objectively the number of subordinates directly supervised by a superior should have a certain limit, which is to have a certain span of control. In addition, the management theory also believes that in order to achieve effective management, the management span of complex work wider than simple work, the management magnitude of senior management should be small than low management. Therefore, when the management of the subsidiary object is too much, the range of management is too broad, the task of organization and coordination is too heavy, we must consider an additional level of management, to implement hierarchical management.

Newly-Established Colleges' Management Difficulties

The original kind of small and specialized extensive management mode has exposed its shortcomings☐ which affect the new college's survival and development.

The Level of Centralized Management, Internal Management and Decision-Making and Insufficient Open

After upgrading, the new colleges have two-level system, college and department, but still Implement a centralized management the personnel power, financial power are almost concentrated in colonel, teaching and research activities of department is organized under the unified leadership of the school. In financial management, department only have the right of approval to determine the daily operational costs based on financial revenue and expenditure plans. The use of other funds, such as the use of laboratory construction special funds is submitted by the department to Academic Affairs for examination and then approved by relevant leaders of the college. The use of student management funds, submitted by the department to Student Affairs Office for examination and then reported to the relevant leaders of the college for approval; the project leader or college-related functions of the department approval the use of research funding and college teaching quality projects funding. After the Technology Department configuring, the funding of scientific research supporting is approved by relevant leaders of the college.

In personnel management, each department only have the right to deny the introduction of talent, staffing job evaluation, allocation of staff salaries, teacher training (public training), need to be arranged by the college. In short, the college holds the majority of the financial and personnel authority.

Newly-established colleges survival and development is closely related to social and economic development and is exposure to social and economic development of the stream, Not only the college face to the society, and strengthen domestic and international famous universities to carry out inter-school exchange programs, led by experts and prestigious professors influence, and improve the level of school teachers and education, but also with changes in the external environment, timely adjust and reform the professional settings, college forms, training programs, education and management so that to adapt to social and economic development needs. The newly upgraded college face the common problems for a long time that is, he openness is not enough, social participation is not high, listen to social issues such as feedback channels are limited.

College Scale Is Expanding, Management Has Difficulty

In recent years, newly-established colleges, has taken on a heavy task of enrollment, a significant increase in the number of students, after a restructuring or continued enrollment, the majority of colleges with thousands of students into a college with million or more students, especially the extremely rapid growth in undergraduate students, Undergraduates scale increased ranging from 1 to 7 times.

At the same time, the faculty scale increases with the number of students continued to expand, making the school has developed into a large organization, in the management of content, methods, and the colonel-level decision-making information, communication and lower levels on the up side, great changes have taken place to improve management efficiency, an urgent need to explore new management model. The members of leading groups are almost all the original members, it is a temporary leadership transition team. The Ministry of Education approved the dissolution of original organizational and management structure, legal changes and a new leadership re-equipped.

The party and government institutions, teaching, supplementary and other internal structure and staffing of newly-established college can not be set in place immediately, However, newly-established college already running, new students enrollment, professional settings, disciplines construction is mainly centralized management, this management model sometimes will cause the rights and obligations separated and imbalanced, Hinder the primary school sector management to innovate.

Administrative Power over Academic Power

Administrative power is the power of university's administrative departments and executive management in accordance with national laws and regulations of university administration. Executive power is given by higher authorities, with hierarchical. In college, there are inevitably coordination and conflict between executive power and academic power, and because historical reasons, the highly educated and high titled teachers are small, the professors are limited, the power of experts and professors are relatively weak. the school's academic atmosphere is not dense, academic level is not high, the experts ability of school governance is restricted ,the role of experts and professors are can not be played, especially the experts awareness to use academic power is not strong. They are used to listen to executive leadership's arrangements, affected the establishment of academic power.

Newly-established college is lack of the awareness and tradition of academic freedom, the phenomenon of academic administration is more prominent than any other university. Such as teaching Committee members, all of them are deputy directors of each department or the deputy directors of the institute, the members of the Academic Committee, most of them are deans or directors of the Institute. Although they are experts in related fields, When the decisions of academic affairs, they consider their respective interests and management positions more, and not the needs of disciplines and academic development.

The Ways to Implement Hierarchical Management in Newly-Established Colleges

Rational allocation of management authority. School level can not directly manage the huge grass-roots organizations, the most important higher powers of all positions within the structure is the configuration of administrative privileges. Management authority is the main body of management powers and responsibilities, especially to optimize the allocation between the school and College functions of management authority, it is an important part which is related to the school after the implementation of hierarchical management, whether the functional departments and colleges can effectively manage and monitor.

Configuration management authority powers and responsibilities should follow the principle of unity. Two-tier management, the Institute of Management as a relatively independent entity, the school should follow the academic power and administrative authority to the principle of decentralization, etc., On subject building, teaching management, research management, personnel management, financial management, asset management, student work, etc. School will give the power of independence. The management of these rights related to the key aspects of decentralization on implementation of two-tier management, the needs of their rights by sponsoring the schools need to characteristics of the size of the actual situation and the historical traditions of self-determined.

Overall, macro-management and decision-making are the school department should retain the authority and responsibility, including the development of the school's development strategy and planning, important work to determine the target year, the Staffing and other categories of personnel, school-wide policies, process monitoring including monitoring the quality of teaching, supervision and financial health analysis, organization and coordination, and year-end performance appraisal.

Establishment of a Standardized System

System specification is the implementation of basic security hierarchical management. To implement the level of scientific and rational management, on the one hand in order to mobilize grass-roots educational initiative, management center of gravity must be reduced so that sub level with more autonomy on the other hand, in order to optimize the allocation of resources, promote the discipline cross-fusion, to break professional barriers, we must establish and improve various rules and regulations of the University for management by objectives, the formation of self-development, self-improvement, self-restraint of the operating mechanism.

Hierarchical management is in fact an institutional management, how to coordinate the relationship between functional departments and colleges, and how to manage human, financial system, which are mainly rely on system. In particular the operation of academic power and administrative power how to organize and play the executive power of academic authority on the subject building, professional development effectiveness, the key is to develop a complete system can be operated. When dealing with the harmonization between principal decision-making and the micro-management of School No comprehensive system of management is bound to cause loss of control or chaos. First, should adhere to the responsibility system under the leadership of party committees, second, strengthen the organization third, ensure that academic decision-making power to participate in school management from the systems and mechanisms be institutionalized and standardized, to avoid arbitrariness.

Establishment of Institutionalized Mechanisms for Democratic Governance

Colleges and universities are the Holy Land of advocating science, advocating democracy, teacher has strong sense of participating and democratic consciousness. Teachers bear reform, development and management insights, reform and development is inseparable from the enthusiasm of the teachers.

To improve the level democratic system, development of the Institute, subject building, research management, personnel management, financial budget and final accounts, income distribution and other issues, the majority of faculty members should be launched to participate in the discussion and the democratic decision-making. Meanwhile, where all the reforms policies and systems about the students, should be fully listen to the views of students.

To improve the public school system, and consciously accept the supervision of teachers and students. Continue to build a scientific and rational organizational structure, follow rules and regulations. It is the foundation and guarantee of colleges and universities healthy operate. University is a bureaucratic organization, but is a loose coalition, the ambiguity and dislocation of academic power and administrative power, need statutory authority to establish the so-called school-based internal power system, and establish the necessary rules and regulations system and enhance the execution order so that it is well known in the management of activities, exercising, and standardized work.

Flat management practice. Flat management is a management structure with less layers and large range of forms, is a modern management model. Its main features and advantages, removing unnecessary regulatory intermediate links, so that the management structure from a pyramid to tend to flatten, Subordinate directly contact with policy and avoid the adverse factors interfere, to facilitate implementation of the policy of unity. Meanwhile, the management of magnitude larger, Subordinate have greater autonomy, enthusiasm and satisfaction.

Newly-established colleges appropriate to adopt the flat management. In fact, a lot of things in the university, lower decisions are more correctly, should give them the greatest degree of autonomy. A good university institutions, need to perform a multi-agent mode of operation, delegated the human, financial, property and business rights to the college or department, to implement a new flat, and network-management. University faculty academic research need to be given a free and relaxed atmosphere, flexible and diverse organizational settings, fully empowered work environment. Only a flat, flexible organization can help the information communication, team building, creative work, so that teachers with strong independence and autonomy.

Acknowledgment. This project is supported by Educational Commission of Heilongjiang Province of China (Grant no.11552181).

References

1. Uwazurike, C.N.: Theories of Educational Leadership: Implications for Nigerian Educational Leaders. Educational Management Administration Leadership 19, 259–263 (1991)
2. Mark Hanson, E.: Educational Administration and Organizational Behavior. Allyn & Bacon publisher (2002)

The FPGA Implementation of Amplitude-Locked Loop System for Co-channel Communication Chip Design

Chia-Hung Huang, Yin-Chih Chen, and Gwo-Jia Jong

Department of Electronic Engineering
National Kaohsiung University of Applied Sciences
Chien Kung Campus 415, Chien Kung Road, Kaohsiung 807, Taiwan
vul35j8@gmail.com, jevonschen0312@hotmail.com,
gjjong@cc.kuas.edu.tw

Abstract. The modulated carrier is often interfered by any type of noises. The co-channel separation system is a demodulation function with dominant and subdominant signals using the receiver of modulation process system by operating at the same as the carrier modulation system. In this thesis, we adopted the field-programmable gate array (FPGA) design platform to develop and achieve the co-channel separation and demodulation chip design for the additive white Gaussian noise (AWGN) interference. In this thesis, the FPGA of Compact-RIO system are integrated and applied to attain the function of communication characteristic chip and hardware design by programming the graphical language.

Keywords: Co-channel, FPGA, AWGN, PLL, ALL, Communication chip prototype design.

1 Introduction

To suppress co-channel interference (CCI) is an important technique when mobile or wireless are used to communicate the message. In this thesis, the focus is presented to separate the mixed signal by the Phase-locked loop (PLL) and Amplitude-locked loop (ALL) systems. However, the CCI is presented those conventional techniques will suffer severe degradation. The envelope is no longer held in constant and the instantaneous frequency is not kept on fixed proportional ratio to the original signal. The PLL output will contain large in band spikes and get some unintelligible turbulence.

The separation system architectures have four subsystems. The subsystems consist of the co-channel frequency modulation multi-speech signals generator, PLL system, ALL system [2-12] and filters. The final purpose, the separation system can demonstrate to recover the original dominant and subdominant signals. Finally, we developed a Field-Programmable Gate Array (FPGA) [1] based on the separation models of PLL and ALL using a high-level design tool. We used National Instruments (NI) / LabVIEW and NI compact-RIO [13] for the separation model co-channel FM multi-signals separating design. NI compact-RIO can be implemented the FPGA design using the LabVIEW FPGA Project. In order to run with PC software in

S. Lin and X. Huang (Eds.): CSEE 2011, Part V, CCIS 218, pp. 458–461, 2011.

hardware co-simulation, it is designed by the Real-Timer hardware to the implement. This hardware is supported and downloaded by the interface format for Ethernet. The signal separating components that require PLL and ALL are designed by the LabVIEW FPGA tool and implemented on NI cRIO-9116 Reconfigurable Chassis. We investigate one approach using high-level tools to map a signal separating algorithm to reconfigurable hardware. The first approach uses the FPGA tool to model the system within LabVIEW. Finally, these system modules are synthesized to hardware. The designs utilized one Xilinx Virtex-5 reconfigurable I/O (RIO) FPGA.

2   Simulated System for Compact-RIO Chip Design

2.1   The Front-End Frequency-Shift Keying Transmission

$$d(t) = \sqrt{\frac{2E_b}{T_b}} \cos(2\pi f_i t) \quad 0 \le t \le T_b \tag{1}$$

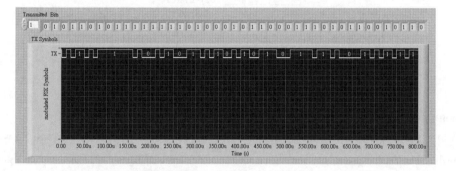

Fig. 1. Bit-stream transmission

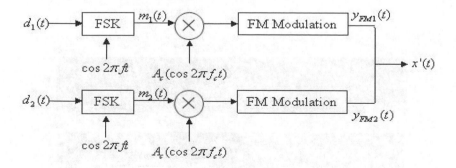

Fig. 2. The transmitter for co-channel case

3 Phase-Locked Loop (PLL) System and Amplitude-Locked Loop (ALL) System

CCI is the interference due to the mixture of signals with similar carrier frequencies. It is necessary to find efficient techniques to reduce the harmful effects of CCI in FM analogue or digital communication system. The mobile users often operate in the presence of cumbersome interference along with multi-path, Rayleigh fading channel and AWGN channel that leads to signal distortion and signal fading at the receiver. In Fig. 2, the interference between signals from these cells is called CCI. The co-channel signals are transmitted by the same carrier frequency f_c in the AWGN channel [14].

3.1 Signals Separation of Co-channel and Signals Analysis

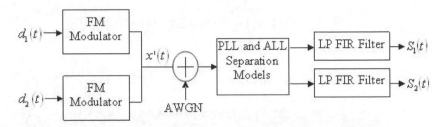

Fig. 3. The architecture fo separation system with AWGN in channel

Signals analysis for m=1

When we assume $m = 1$, the interference of $y_{FM1}(t)$ and $y_{FM2}(t)$ are equal. So we utilize the ALL system get the signal of the other for setting $m = 1$, and we can get dominant or subdominant signal by tuning the m value. This system is the advantage to adopt the communication security. It can be very useful for replacing the encryption system. It is shown the dominant signal is alternate to subdominant signal in Fig. 4.

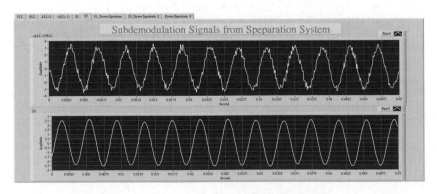

Fig. 4. The separation signals using the filters for $m = 1$

4 Discussion and Conclusion

The FPGA runs all code in hardware; it provides the high reliability and determinism that is ideal for hardware-based interlocks, custom timing and triggering, or eliminating the custom circuitry normally required with custom sensors. The result of chip design system could proof the successful separation signals with AWGN for co-channel transmission. The design system is also be achieved the digital communication chip prototype design model by building, program verifying, and communication function implementation for the physical application of the industry.

References

1. Xilinx Inc., Virtex-5 Platform FPGAs: Virtex-5 FPGA Data Sheet (June 1, 2009)
2. Kehtarnavaz, N.: Digital signal processing system design: LabVIEW-based hybrid programming, 2nd edn., pp. 5–56. Elsevier, Amsterdam (2008)
3. Rappaport, T.S.: Wireless communications: principles and practice, pp. 37–39. Prentice Hall, USA (1999)
4. Jong, G.J., Moir, T.J.: The Performance of the Amplitude-Locked Loop with Co-Channel Interference. In: Proc. IECON 1998, Aachen, Germany, 31 August - 4 September (1998)
5. Jong, G.J., Moir, T.J., Pettigrew, A.M.: The High Performance FM Demodulator Using the Amplitude-Locked Loop with Co-Channel Interference. In: International Symposium on Communication (ISCOM), Kaohsiung, Taiwan, pp. 284–288 (1999)
6. Haykin, S.: Communication System, 4th edn., pp. 109–113. Wiley, Chichester (2001)
7. Jong, G.J., Moir, T.J., Pettigrew, A.M., Su, T.J.: Improvement of FM demodulator with cochannel FM interference. Electronics Letters 35(20), 1758–1759 (1999)
8. Moir, T.J.: Analysis of an amplitude-locked loop. Electronics Letters 31(9), 694–695 (1995)
9. Wu, G.K., Feher, K.: The Impact of Delay Spread on Multilevel FM Systems in a Rayleigh Fading. In: IEEE 42nd CCI and AWGN Environment, Vehicular Technology Conference, vol. 1, pp. 528–531 (1992)
10. Kuo, S.M., Can, W.-S.: Digital Signal Process: Architectures, Implementations, and Applications, pp. 305–315 (2005)
11. Oshana, R.: DSP Software Development Techniques for Embedded and Real-Time Systems, pp. 81–94 (2006)
12. Best, R.E.: Phase-locked loops: design, simulation, and application, 4th edn., pp. 154–158. McGraw-Hill Company, USA (1997)
13. National Instruments Inc.: Getting Started with Compact-RIO and LabVIEW (August 2008)
14. Jong, G.-J., Horng, G.-J.: The Improvement of All-Digital Amplitude-Locked Loop Separation Analysis Combined MIMO System. International Journal of Innovative Computing, Information and Control 7(3), 1011–1016 (2011)

Researches on Logistics Teaching Software Based on GIS

Bin Yang[1], Lei Zhao[1], and Jian-Kun Hu[2]

[1] Logistics Research Center, Shanghai Maritime University, Shanghai 201306, P.R. China
[2] Shanghai Engineering Research Center of Shipping Logistics Information,
Shanghai 201306, P.R. China
binyang@shmtu.edu.cn, blowwind4@sina.com

Abstract. GIS network analysis function has been proved very effective in solving most network-related problems. GIS spatial analysis models such as Buffer Analysis, Overlay analysis, and so on, play very important roles in combining different logistic models. However, the education on logistic system has failed to help students to build up solid concept of logistic models due to the lack of visualization. In this paper, a GIS - based simulation software is built up and a visual and direct way on logistics study is provided. The software could be used in daily logistics education.

Keywords: GIS, Logistics model, teaching software.

1 Introduction

The concept that logistic has close relationship with geography is extensively adopted in nowadays education of logistic systems, since most logistic operation, modeling and decision analysis are deeply affected by their geographical factors. But the lack of visualization of geography and resource conditions has put great defect on the outcome of today's logistic education system.

Geographic Information System (GIS), as a discipline which described, storage, analysis and output spatial information theory and methods, is an emerging interdisciplinary. Now, the GISs, what is experiencing an unprecedented period of great development, have been played an important role in many fields, such as geographically logical, geological mapping, transportation, public utilities, tourism services and environmental protection. In [1], a GIS – based safe area discovery system has founded. And in [2], a maritime business system is set up based on mobile technology. In [3] [4] [5] and so on, GIS has been used in many fields such as emergency logistics, decease control and prevention and so on. Combined with the character of logistics system, GIS is very suitable for using in the logistics teaching.

In this paper, a GIS - based software would be provided for helping students master the wealth of geographical knowledge of logistics and achieving a good teaching result.

2 System Specification

In this part, a GIS – based logistics teaching system has been build up. Introduction of the system would be in two aspects: System functions and Business functions.

S. Lin and X. Huang (Eds.): CSEE 2011, Part V, CCIS 218, pp. 462–466, 2011.
© Springer-Verlag Berlin Heidelberg 2011

First of all, the structure of the system is shown in Fig 2.1. B/S structure is used in the interaction between LAN and the internet in this system. This will not only increase the amount of information, but improve the speed of information exchange. What's more, a C/S structure is used in LAN. And the main scenes and models are saved in client. This could keep a high speed of calling the scenes and models.

In addition, three classes of user have been design in the system. The permissions of each class of user are shown in Table 2.1.

Table 2.1. Classes of user

User class	Explanation
Teacher	Teachers, part information maintenance personnel, can modify the project data (relational database), save teaching scenario, modify model parameters, upload teaching materials.
Student	Students, the main users of the system, can view all the courses relevant information.
Administrator	Administrator, the final information maintenance personnel, can add or modify the information of teachers and students, and modify the spatial database

In addition, three classes of user have been design in the system. The permissions of each class of user are shown in Table 2.1.

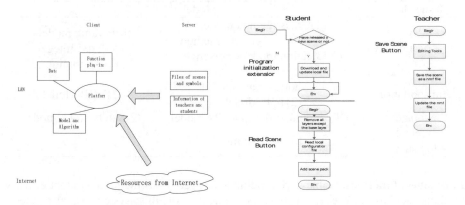

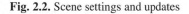

Fig. 2.1. Structure of the system   **Fig. 2.2.** Scene settings and updates

A. System Function. (1)Scene. There are elements of each scene. These elements could be classified into four classes: Base Map, Nodes, Lines and Regions. They are stored in each client to call while the teacher sets a scene. The specific feature of each element is shown in Table 2.2.

Table 2.2. Scene element

Data class	Explanation
Base Map	Stored in each client, continents, oceans, economic zones, routes, ports. (server can push to the client)
Nodes	Stored in each client, Logistics Nodes data, include throughput data, storage data, and so on
Lines	Stored in each client, Logistics Lines data, include throughout capacity, freight, length, and so on
Regions	Stored in each client, Logistics Region data

As shown in Figure 2.2, a teacher could set a scene by using scene editing tools, and upload the scene as an nmf file. For the more, while the students find the teacher have released a new scene, he could download it and update local file. Then student could apply the scene.

(2) Model. In application of the scene set by teacher, there might be four types of issue in logistics: Location, Transportation, Storage problems and Logistics of internal. Moreover, there are many paths to solve these problems and many models to reflect these scenes. The issues and models, what are stored in each client, in this system are shown in Table 2.3.

Table 2.3. Issue class

Issue class	Model class	
Location	(1)Cross-median model Exact center of gravity method (2)Location model of discrete points	(3)P-value models (4)Mixed Integer Programming
Transportation	(1)Shortest path model (2)TSP Model	(3)VRP Model
Storage	(1)Economic order quantity model	(2)Safety stock model
Internal logistics	Job scheduling	

B. Business functions. Homework sending and receiving is the basic content of daily teaching activities. The main business function of this system is also these. Homework could be sent and received between teacher and students through the system's business function. Teacher could save the information of student homework situation. These could help teacher to give student a comprehensive appraisal.

In summary, the basic structure of this system has been set up in this chapter. But to test these functions' achievement, a sample will be list in the next chapter.

3   A Sample of Vehicle Route Problem

In this part, a teaching simulation of the vehicle route problem has been set for testing the ability to functions realization of the system.

Step 1. Teacher sets scene. Click the link of vehicle routing model, and the workspace switch to a map of shanghai. There will be a brief description of the vehicle path model. Then teacher locates the distribution center and stores on the map, and sets the capability of vehicle and the demand of each store, as shown in Figure 3.1.
Step 2. Teacher saves the scene.
  The network of distribution center and stores locating is shown in Figure 3.1.

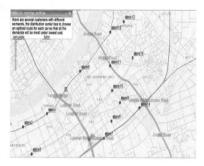

Fig. 3.1. Stores and Distribution center select   **Fig. 3.2.** Vehicle routing model

In the figure, 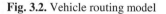 said storage position; said store position;

Step 3. Student read the scene and clicks Start to begin the process of setting the vehicle routing model as shown in Figure 3.3.
Step 4. Student chose the path to solve the scene and click to show the tutorial showing the principle of vehicle routing model as shown in Figure 3.4.

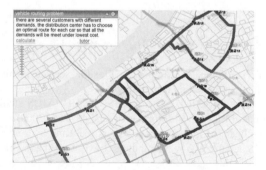

Fig. 3.3. Sample of vehicle routing model

  In this chapter, teacher sets a scene and students could read it, and achieve the objective function through one path of the path sets.

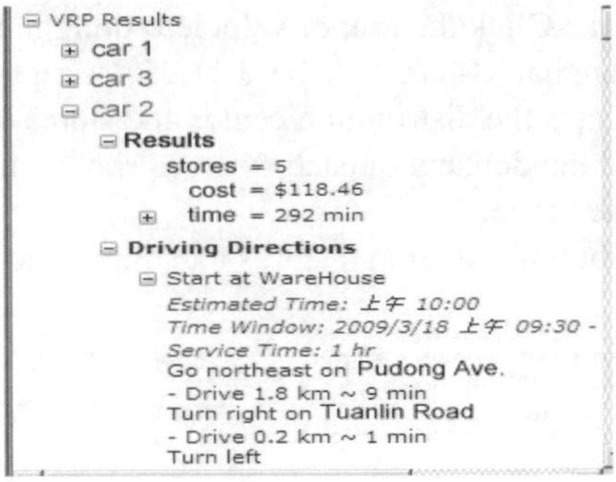

Fig. 3.4. Solution of vehicle routing model

4 Conclusion

The software generates detailed optimal results and depicts them on a map such that students can study more efficiently with the help of visualization. The software can evaluate students' solutions and thus help students learn more effectively. Future researches focus on: adding logistic based issues to the software, expanding the scale of logistic models.

Acknowledgment. This work was supported in part by Shanghai Science Commission Project (No.09DZ2250400, 10692103500, 09530708200, 08170511300, 10190502500, 10ZR1413200), Shanghai Education Commission Project (No.J50604, 11YZ137, 11CXY47) and Shanghai Maritime University Project (No. 20090154).

References

1. Hu, J.-K., Yang, B., Wang, J., Wang, Z.-H., Hao, Y.-Y., Hu, Z.-H.: GIS Based Safe Area Discovery for Emergency Logistics
2. Yang, B., Hao, Y.-Y., Wang, J., Hu, Z.-H.: Flexible service architecture for maritime business promotion based on mobile technology
3. Rashmi Kandwal, P.K., Garg, R.D.: Health GIS and HIV/AIDS studies: Perspective and retrospective. Journal of Biomedical Informatics 42, 748–755 (2009)
4. Al-Sabhan, W., Mulligan, M., Blackburn, G.A.: A real-time hydrological model for flood prediction using GIS and the WWW. Computers, Environment and Urban Systems 27, 9–32 (2003)
5. Wei, H., Xu, Q.-x., Tang, X.-s.: A knowledge-based problem solving method in GIS application. Knowledge-Based Systems 24, 542–553 (2011)

Construction of Library Management Information System

Lian-feng Zhang, Rui-jin Zhou, Li-ping Sui, and Guo-qing Wu

Henan Institute of Science and Technology
Xin-xiang, China
zlfmail@126.com

Abstract. Library management information system construction of China's starts late , and made certain achievements in the same time, but there are also many problems. In this paper, the author pointed out existing problems of the library management information system in China's current situation and so improving the management of library information system.

Keywords: Library, Library management information system (LMIS), Automation.

Introduction

In order to satisfy the information demand of modern social many-sided, multi-level and many categories, the library is transfer the traditional manual type information service mode to open and automated library service model. And excellent performance, feature-rich library management information system in this transformation plays a very important role. Establish and perfect the management information system, can provide information quickly and accurately, support library operation, management and decision-making, so as to improve the level of library management and service.

1 The Status of Chinese LMIS Construction

1.1 The Definition of LMIS

LMIS use modern data equipment and digital model for library management method, the optimum decision-making process provide necessary information and feasibility plan - machine system. It makes full use of management, operations research, database, artificial intelligence and computer science, is the latest achievements of library electronic data processing system of further development. The library management information system has the following characteristics. At first it was a scientific management system. It is also a modern management system; it is not only applied modern data processing equipment, the communication technology and the mathematics model method, but also comprehensive application of modern science and all aspects of the latest achievements. Third, it is a multi-functional management system and man-machine system.

S. Lin and X. Huang (Eds.): CSEE 2011, Part V, CCIS 218, pp. 467–471, 2011.

1.2 The Construction of Chinese LMIS

LMIS construction started in the mid 1970s, was aimed at introduced from abroad single-function system research and improvement of library automation system, started the software programming and trial work. The 1980s, domestic began to strengthen the development of integrated system. Until the mid 1990's library information network construction in China has made great development, C/S mode system emerging, the basic function of LMIS become complete and mature commodity to enter the market. Now we have more than 30 different characteristic LMIS. For example Beijing Wenjin library literature management system, shenzhen library developed and expanded ILAS, jiangsu Huiwen company developed the Libsys2000, etc. the users of these system have covered all over the country's more than 2,000 large, medium and small library, 220 libraries has connected into the national communications network system, began to library network construction, and offer online electronic literature information service for readers, at present Chinese LMIS has already begun to take shape, and to the integration, socialization, internationalization direction, system functions are becoming more and more perfect and diversity.

2 The Technology Realization of LMIS

2.1 The Basic Structure of LMIS

LMIS is responsible for collection，storage and management related data of library，help to plan, organize, lead and control management activities. It use computer technology, communication technology and network technology in the library work implements the automation management of all kinds of information resources, including the storage, processing, the digital information identification, description and organization of digital information, allocation and assession the task of librarians, management users, etc.

LMIS includes six sub-systems mainly, it is respectively: library plan subsystem, library business management subsystem, library financial management subsystem, library management subsystem of equipment, library personnel management subsystem and library statistics decision subsystem. Each subsystem can operate independently and mutual connection, and belong to a public database logically, can be share data resources fully, to provide internal contact information to satisfy the library management and the general reader needs.

2.2 The Technology Realization of LMIS

2.2.1 From C/S Model to B/S Model

LMIS is C/S (Client/Server) mode generally. C/S mode refers to a system application divided into two parts: one part is shared by multiple users of function and information, called server; another part is each user proprietary, called client. The client executive front desk function, The server executive backstage function. With the rise of Internet technology development and dynamic Web technology application extensive, C/S mode was is clicked by B/S (Browser/Server) mode gradually. B/S mode is the expansion to C/S mode. In this structure, the user interface is working by IE browser. Operation and maintenance is simpler, can realize the different personnel, different locations, with different access (such as LAN, WAN, Internet/Intranet, etc) to visit and operating common data, these is the biggest advantage of the B/S mode.

2.2.2 SOA and J2EE

SOA (Service – Oriented Architecture), the basic technology of software products and large information system ,also is the important support technology of industry construct information infrastructure at home and abroad ,promote information resources development and utilization effective methods. For the construction of large-scale, resources reusable, loosely coupled distributed system, SOA provides an open architecture.

Most of LMIS is based on UNIX platform currently. Recently, J2EE (Java2 PlatformEnterpriseEdition) is popular. It is suit for Internet on web computing characteristics and production and development. Using component thoughts will business logic from the client and the server, which makes independent of the development, maintenance and use more convenient, distributed and portability stronger. Platform of multi-layer application of high reusability, high security, high reliability and portability implemented.

3   The Existing Problems of Chinese LMIS Construction

3.1   System Structures Is Imperfect

People have a narrow understand about LMIS, so limited to the computer use in book processing and circulation, and ignore the functions of computer information statistics and analysis. Complete LMIS should include six sub-systems, namely library plans subsystem, library business management subsystem, library financial management subsystem, library management subsystem of equipment, library personnel management subsystem and library statistics decision subsystem. But now most of the domestic LMIS is library business management subsystem, this result in the powerful features of LMIS, such as data processing, forecasting, planning control, decision-making optimization in library management didn't get full play.

3.2   The Network Function of LMIS Is Not Strong

With the rapid development of global networking, LMIS need toward networking progressively, network interviews, network borrowing, cataloguing Internet counseling, network retrieval and network information service and other business needs to network as information carrier. In this process, the original network system mainly focuses on the library use, online Internet function is poorer, and the ability of network information processing is weak.

3.3   System Development Is Insufficient Advanced, Not Enough Science

The traditional LMIS is adopted C/S mode and two layer structures generally, this kind of structure is not strong refractivity truck in management, and network negative aspects of software reuse are also exposed insurmountable defects increasingly. So far, the domestic LMIS is still C/S mode occupied mainstream position. Only Qingdaxinyang GLIS8.0, guangzhoutuchuang Interlib, chongqingyade ADlib2.0 developed B/S model of LMIS, and certain achievements have been made.

4   The Measures to Perfect Chinese LMIS

4.1   Perfecting System Structure Deepen and Expand New Functions

Although the working range of six sub-systems is different, the goal is consistent. They are play indispensable role in the library. Domestic library should not only have the business management subsystem, but also should develop and use each subsystem, basic function is core, then expand new functions on this basis, provide better service for customers, realize the sustainable development of library. Library business management subsystem can extent network ordering, intelligent cataloging, network online cataloguing, automatic classification, automatic index, information restructuring; Statistical subsystem can extent arbitrary commands statistics and reports, pie chart, histogram, line graph and other functions. Make the function of the system overall level of quality get improved greatly. The traditional library in the information processing aspect to reach a new height, LMIS must possess strong network interconnection function, can solve a lot of technical problems. Such as Z39.50 online access interface, HTML text interface, relational database interface, multi-media information structure interface, full-text database interface technology, etc.

4.2   Adopts Advanced Technology, Pay Attention to the Needs of Our Clients

In the construction, perfecting and operation process of LMIS, continue to adopt new concepts, new technology. In recent years, the experience of LMIS construction shows that advanced technology means higher performance at present and lower maintenance costs in the future. In the comprehensive consideration of the investment risks we should make use of advanced technology to develop LMIS. Using database technology, data mining technology, multimedia technology and other new technology to design the reasonable structure, comprehensive functions, suitable for wide application, conform to the requirements of library and development LMIS. In order to improve the scientific development of LMIS, we must analysis the information needs of users, then design careful. Because LMIS is based on the user's information needs and demands, only scientific analysis, to design of the whole system, develop a corresponding system. Such as DataTrans - 2000 is according to different user group and business needs, provide scale based on MS SQL Server and Oracle , etc. Huiwen system And SULCMISⅢ add management function of multi-campuses and branch library system, can be setup collection site, circulation policy, realizes to reformed or different campus had reached the "general books borrowed" and the reader management business management function flexible and meet the needs of our merger college library management new mode. SULCMIS III has also developed small-sized edition,standard edition and enhanced version, every function module can choose according to need freely.

With the development of information technology, library information resources construction and the innovation of related information resource service, its system function structure also changing constantly. Therefore, how to construct and improve LMIS, make the library resource sharing, provide information and information service quickly and efficiently, meeting all kinds of information demand, promoting the socialization of the information service of the library in order to maximize the social benefit and economic benefit in the system construction, need to fumble ceaselessly and summarize unceasingly.

References

[1] Guangjian, L.: Digital age's library network information system. Beijing library press, Beijing (2006)
[2] Liu, R.: Library automation construction and the development of integrated system. In: Library science research progress, pp. 439–467. wuhan university press, wuhan (2007)
[3] Wu, Y.: Library management information system and the improvement and development of university library. Journal of work 29(1), 38–39 (2009)
[4] Qiang, Y.: Analyses the library management information system problems and countermeasures of agricultural. Journal of library and information science 17(6), 45–45 (2005)
[5] Fu, L., liu, X.: Try to talk about the construction of the library management information system. Journal of university library work (3), 45–47 (2001)
[6] Haixin, Y.: Homemade library management information system present situation and developing trend. Journal of Library Journal (3), 41–42 (2002)
[7] Wenhua, S., Shi, W.: J2ee-based B/S structure of university library management information system construction of modern information (9), 137–139 (2009)
[8] Li, Z.: Library management information system establishment and the consummation. China medical book intelligence magazine 16(6), 27–29 (2007)

Application of Case Teaching to Environmental Impact Assessment in Undergraduate Teaching with Modern Information Technology

HongYan Shen[*], JingPo Yang, and JianSheng Cui

College of Environmental Science and Engineering, Hebei University of Science and Technology, Shijiazhuang, Hebei 050018, China
shy0405@sina.com

Abstract. Assessment of environmental impact is one of the main courses of environmental science and engineering subject, according to its features of comprehensiveness and practicalness, combine the requirements of engineers of environmental impact assessment, teachers should renew the teaching content, strengthen the case teaching, so to keep the classroom teaching and practical teaching synchronous. The practice proves that the case teaching not only gives serves to the theory teaching, but also pays attention to spreading the students' thought and upgrading the theories, this teaching method can help the students to found a complete process of thinking from practice to theory and then to practice.

Keywords: Environmental impact assessment, case teaching, practical teaching.

Introduction

Environmental impact assessment is one of compulsory courses in environmental science and engineering subject in higher education. Comprehensiveness and practicalness are the features of this course compared with others. So the expertise of environmental monitoring and environmental engineering profession is required by the comprehensiveness, and practicalness requires tight connect with the state environmental protection policies and laws. In addition, the examination of the engineer of environmental impact assessment became more and more popular recent years, so training for the engineers became an important task of environmental impact assessment. So this make the course pay more attention to practicalness and guideline. The content of the course should also be similar to content of the examination.

1 Timely Updating Instruction Content Combined with the EIA Actual

Instruction content is the center of development of curriculum. Environmental impact assessment is a course of highly technical and practical, so the effect will be bad if we

---

[*] Corresponding author.

S. Lin and X. Huang (Eds.): CSEE 2011, Part V, CCIS 218, pp. 472–476, 2011.

only speak what the books speak. There are 40 periods for undergraduates, in order to make students understand the course and technical methods in this 40 periods, we should optimize the teaching content, such as increase the report of the technical content. So, teaching content broke through the content of textbooks, and connect with the national technical methods and report, and reflects the novelty of this applied course. At the same time, according to system of this course, we choose nine chapters as the teaching content in Table 1.

2 The Application of Cases Teaching in EIA Teaching

Cases teaching was first created in the United States University of America in 1867. This is a method which could tell us knowledge and principles though a typical example, and use different kinds of methods to inspires students thinking independently, in this course, teachers and students could analysis, discussion, evaluation and for countermeasures in the cases together, and then attend teaching aims.

According to the practical experience of environmental impact assessment in these years, in the EIA teaching, if you want to get a good effect in such a short time, you have to abondon the minds that theories are less important than practice, but apply the case teaching. Good cases should be used to support theories, that makes students catch the point of EIA learning, then learn something from the environment. The case teaching of EIA should achieve two objectives: firstly, let students understand and grasp the theory and method of EIA completely and accurately; secondly, let students use the basic knowledge and techniques to do the work of environmental impact assessment correctly and flexibly. The case of EIA come from the truth or simulated truth of the EIA, it is targeted and effective. Students can analyze the case subjectively and make decisions according to the comprehensive knowledge, thus they could improve the ability of analyzing and solving problems. While we could reach the purpose of improving the effectiveness of teaching.

(A) Requirements for teachers about case teaching of EIA

As the course was generated and developed from practice, case teaching on the one hand requires teachers to have rich practical experience of environmental impact assessment, and could teach directly skills to the students according to their own practical experience in the teaching process, and then could explain knowledge combine specific examples to improve teaching effectiveness. On the other hand, the teachers had better to pass EIA Examination of Ministry of Environmental Protaction of the PRC, has engaged in the actual ability and quality of EIA.

(B) Case Library Construction of EIA

1. Select the cases, and establish the environmental impact assessment case library
The EIA teaching cases come from three aspects: the first is, teachers involved in the EIA personally; the second is the environmental impact reports that teachers collect from other units; the third is , the simulation questions and real questions from the EIA engineer examination. We should adhere to the following principles in choosing cases: (1) Correlation, the selected case must fit the teaching objectives; (2) Targeted, the selected cases must comply with technical methods of environmental impact

assessment and the requirements of evaluation of the content; (3) Typicalness, the case must be selected around the core content and basic theory; (4) Inspiring, teaching cases should be inspire students to take part in the cases actively, and to discover, analyze and solve problems by applying the basic techniques of environmental impact assessment and methods.

2. The content of the EIA case teaching

We should study out the case teaching content based on the education system and the practice of environmental impact assessment. The content was shown in Table 1. The arrangements of each chapter for the case teaching can be choosed based on practice.

Table 1. Instruction content of EIA and case teaching

Chapter	Instruction content	Period	Cases teaching Content
1	Overview	4	Determination of the assessment class of water, gas, sound and so on; the choice of environmental standards and factors of environmental impact; the distinguishment of environmental impact
2	Engineering analysis, environmental conditions, investigation and evaluation of pollution source	6	Analysis of production processes, pollution processes and the types of pollutants; Assessment of current situation of environment quality; Programme of pollution prevention and its technical and economic feasibility; Inspection reports of "three simultaneous" in construction project; Carrying out the "Survey and Evaluation of pollution source"; The determination of main sources and major pollutions through the calculation of pollution load and pollution load ratio; Calculations of water balance and material balance
3	prediction and evaluation of air impact	6	Processing and analysis of meteorological data; prediction and evaluation programme of atmospheric environmental impact; Screening of adverse weather conditions; calculation of the average concentrations of hour, day, and annual
4	prediction and evaluation of the surface water	6	Screening of major pollution factors in surface water; Prediction and evaluation of the surface water
5	Prediction and evaluation of the noise	6	Pressure level of noise source; Forecast of traffic noise ; Forecast of industrial noise; Control measures of Industrial and traffic noise pollution
6	Prediction and evaluation of the solid waste	4	Forecast of the production of Solid waste; The control measures of Solid waste pollution; The types of hazardous waste; Requirement for storage and disposal of hazardous waste
7	Public participation	2	Public participate in the announcement in Internet and make the public survey questionnaire
8	Cleaner production and total control	2	Evaluation of cleaner production; Requirements of the total pollutant discharge based on analysis of the environmental capacity of the project location
9	Planning EIA	4	Calculation of capacity of resources and environment; Calculation of environmental capacity; coordination analysis of planning; Rationality proof of environmental planning; Establishment of envieronmental objectives and targets systems

(C) Implementation of the EIA case teaching

1. Teaching methods

The four basic processes of case teaching are: Reading the case, individual analysis; group discussion, and reaching consensus; classroom speech and communication; summarize after-school, and review. In the processes of case teaching, whether it is the group discussion, class exchange, or improve process, the stage of discussion is the core element [2]. In the whole discussion, teachers should be a organizer and guide to make sure the discussion smooth and effective.

2. Class timetable

Within the 40 teaching periods, traditional instruction and case teaching should share each half of the 40 periods In practical teaching process, we should arrange the theoretical lectures and case teaching once each week to learn and practice 1-3 parts of the environmental impact assessment each week.

3. Evaluation of Teaching

Case teaching changes the routine that study-based teacher and student passive acceptance, student spend a lot of time to find information, discussion, practice in learning programs. In the case teaching, each statement, discussion and reporting all could be the evaluation of the students' achievement, and at the same time it could consolidate and strengthen the theory teaching, and also increase learning initiative of students.

(D) The problems that should be noticed in EIA case teaching

1. To handle the relationship between theory teaching and case teaching correctly

Theory teaching has always been the basis of case studies, and only master the theories we could analyze the case better. In order to handle the relationship between learning theoretical knowledge and teaching case correctly, firstly we should choose the typical case and then apply proper technology and method. Secondly, we should handle the relationship between the technical and universal methods of the special cases. The key to handle these relationships is to design the case teaching content carefully and comprehensively.

2. Handle the relationship between teaching and learning in the case of teaching properly

Case teaching needs supporting and correspondence of learners, if lack of the active participation and innovation of learner, case tesching will be unable to move on. Teachers should help students to overcome the habits that long-standing reliance on teachers and passive learning, and to gether individual and collective thinking, so that individual and collective initiative and enthusiasm of learner could have been played very well, and then could make sure that the case teaching move on smoothly.

3. To have the targeted selection of cases so that could play its maximum value

In the selection and application of the case, on the one hand we should choose to add new cases in classroom teaching to ensure the timeliness of cases, on the other hand we should control the degree of difficulty of cases and choose the appropriate case base on students level. Meanwhile, in order to achieve the purpose of teaching, teachers should organize the presentation of case material.

4. Handle the relationship between case teaching and other teaching methods properly

No matter what teaching methods is applied, the goal is to help students master the knowledge of the course wholly and systematically, and improve their ability of analyzing and solving problems. Case teaching is not the only teaching form, and it can not suit for all of the teaching content. Case teaching should cooperate with other teaching methods in EIA teaching.

3   Conclusion

In the teaching process of environmental impact assessment, we should choose teaching content preferably, and combined the materials with the requires of environmental impact assessment technology guidance, so to make simultaneous of theoretical study and practice. This method not only reflect the novelty of teaching, but also inspire student's thinking, help students to master the knowledge systematically, to enhance the ability of analyze and solve problems. Case teaching has changed the traditional teaching methods and advocate the discussion-based learning, promote activity of learning, and spur students assimilate the knowledge. Teaching practice proved that, the case teaching have make up the shortage of classroom teaching and make the class more interesting, while access to the students' loved.

Acknowledgment. The study was co-funded by Projects of Science and Technology in Hebei Province (No.10276735), the Educational Development Foundation Project in Hebei University of Science and Technology (No.200929) and the Key Discipline in Hebei Province.

References

1. Wen-slope, Hui, Z.: Environmental impact assessment to explore teaching. Shijiazhuang Vocational College of Technology 20, 77–78 (2008)
2. Bo, Z., Du, W.C., Yu-savings: Environmental impact assessment study and practice of teaching reform. Higher Education 17, 94–96 (2008)

Research and Simulation on Grid Resources Location

Luo Zhong, Li Yang, Bo Zhu, and Huazhu Song

Department of Computer Science and Technology,
Wuhan University of Technology, Wuhan, China
zhongluo@yahoo.com.cn, yangli_lc@yahoo.com.cn,
zhubo0128@yahoo.com.cn, mingjie@yahoo.com.cn

Abstract. In the grid environment, resources are distributed, heterogeneous, dynamical and autonomous. Resource discovery takes a part of a bridge between resource requester and resource provider. Its primary function is to devise effective location strategy and find the optimal resource combination to meet the demands of users. In this paper, on the premise of the Layered Resource Discovery Model (LRDM), a layered resource location strategy was proposed, mainly including two parts: local location and global location. At last, the location strategy was simulated by using OPNET in order to demonstrate the feasibility and effectiveness of the proposed strategy.

Keywords: Gird, Layered Resource Discovery Model (LRDM), Layered resource location, OPNET.

1 Introduction

Grid aims at making all its resources composed a super computer for users to share and realizing full-connectedness on the internet. Resource discovery which is the bond between resource requesters and resource providers provides support for task scheduling. In addition to solve resources organization, registration, revocation and maintenance in the grid environment, the critical task of resource discovery is to devise effective location strategy and find the optimal resource combination to meet the demands of users.

Grid resource location means the procedure of finding the resources address corresponding to their identifications and locating the resources of serving the user actually from all the resources of meeting the requirements according to the certain management and routing strategy. Resource location can take place following along with resource discovery or after it [1,2,3]. In this paper, a layered resource location strategy was presented based on the LRDM [4] in grid environment and the OPNET was used to simulate it in order to demonstrate the feasibility and effectiveness of the proposed strategy.

2 Layered Resource Discovery Model

As shown in Fig. 1, the structure of LRDM is divided into two layers [4]: physical resource layer and virtual organization layer. On physical resource layer, there is a

S. Lin and X. Huang (Eds.): CSEE 2011, Part V, CCIS 218, pp. 477–483, 2011.

variety of heterogeneous resources information of ordinary nodes, which can be either Resource Provider (RP) or Resource Requester (RR). On virtual organization layer, different VOs are generated according to the resource types. A manager node (MN) is configured to manage the virtual organization (VO) uniformly in every VO, such as the black triangle in VO1, VO2, and VO3. MN is responsible for storing and maintaining homogeneous resource information in its VO and related resource information in other VOs on VO layer.

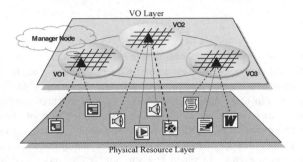

Fig. 1. Structure of LRDM

The resource location is the core problem in LRDM. It forwards the path based on resource requirements and matches resource information. Its performance influences the working efficiency of whole resource discovery system directly. Therefore, according to the structure of LRDM, a layered resource location strategy is designed as two parts: local location strategy and global location strategy.

3   Local Location Strategy

3.1   Neighbor List of Node

Each node will be configured a Neighbor List which is mainly to maintain and update their neighbor nodes information and provide support for information route during the resource location process. The content of neighbor list includes: node basic information (containing the address of neighbor nodes and the latency or overhead to the neighbor nodes), timestamp (updating the neighbor list of node periodically) and time to live (managing the communication between nodes).

"HELLO" packets are adapted to sense and generate a neighbor list of a node in LRDM. "HELLO" packets are broadcasted only in range of one hop and can't be forwarded. By periodically broadcasting "HELLO" packets, a node can be listening for the state of its neighbor nodes, maintaining and constantly updating its neighbor list. Once a node launches resource location, it would query its neighbor list firstly. If the query succeeded, resource can be located directly, the load of MN can be reduced and the location efficiency is increased.

3.2 Location Procedure

Local location begins after the required resources are discovered and the address of resources provider is returned by MN. The process can be supposed as Fig. 2, node A is a RR, with neighbor list as (A, B) (A, D) (A, E). After resource discovery, the address information of RP would be returned to node A by the MN. If node B is the RP and node A receives the address information of node B from the MN. Node A queries its own neighbor list to check whether the route to node B exists. If yes, it could locate and connect with node B directly without forwarding by the MN.

Supposed node C is the RP and node A receives the address information of node C from the MN. Node A queries its own neighbor list and doesn't find the route to node C. The route should be forwarded in VO by the MN to connect with node C in order to obtain the requested resources. Thus it can be seen that the neighbor list improves the location efficiency and can reduce location time cost.

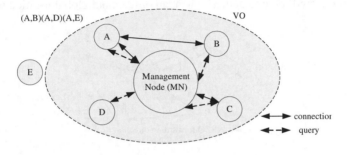

Fig. 2. Local Resource Location

All nodes in every VO should update their node status to their MN periodically, so that the route between MN and each node in VO is effective.

3.3 Global Location Strategy

In LRDM, when the requested resource can't be discovered within VO on the physical resource layer, the query and location would carry on among VOs in the unstructured peer-to-peer network which is composed by the MN.

3.4 Neighbor List of Node

If the requested resource doesn't exist in VO, such as node E is RP as shown in Fig. 2. After the resource discovery on VO layer, the address information of node E has been returned to node A. At this time, Node A would firstly scan its neighbor list to check whether the route to node E exists rather than starting global location. If yes, it could locate and connect with node E directly without starting global location. Therefore, the neighbor list plays a big role in saving bandwidth and improving location efficiency.

3.5 Location Procedure

When the route to the RP isn't found in the neighbor list directly and need to be forwarded by MN in VO, global location starts. For simplicity, the MN in VO which RR belongs to is called source node (SN) and RP belongs to is called destination node (DN). The global location process can be described as: on the VO layer, SN looks for the path to DN and builds the route.

Distance vector algorithm and on-demand routing algorithm are applied to achieve global location in this paper. Three basic message formats are defined as: Route REQuest packet (RREQ), Route REPly packet (RREP) and Route ERRor packet (REER). SN broadcasts RREQ packet, if the node which received the RREQ packet is DN itself or knows the route to DN, it replies RREP packet. In case of routing faulty or link interruption during the process of packet forwarding, REER packet should be sent.

Fig. 3 is a concrete instance of global location. Assuming that node A is SN and node E is DN. Node A has known the address information or unique identifier of node E, but hasn't a valid route to node E. Then, an on-demand global location starts.

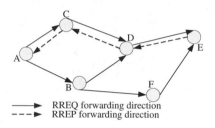

Fig. 3. Global Resource Location

Node A broadcasts a RREQ message which contains the address information of both the source node A and the destination node E. When node B and node C, the neighbor of node A, receive the RREQ message, they firstly check whether they are the DN themselves or have a valid path to the DN. If yes, they would reply a RREQ message to node A. Otherwise they would forward the RREQ message by broadcasting as relay nodes. Those intermediate nodes (node D and node F) receive the RREQ message will do the same operation as node B and node C. On the analogy of this until the destination node E receives the RREQ message, or certain intermediate node which has a valid path to node E receives the RREQ message.

Node E replies a RREP message to the preceding node D which sends RREQ message to it and tells node D that the next hop is the destination node E. Node D receives the RREP message, stores the route to node E, replies a RREP message to its preceding node C and tells node C if it wants to arrive at the destination node E the next hop should be node D. On the analogy of this until the source node A receives the RREP message. Node A has known if it wants to arrive at the node E the next hop should be node C and all intermediate nodes have known the path to node E. Then the connection is setup and data can be transmitted.

Due to every RREQ message have its ID number; the node could determine if it have dealt the RREQ according to the source address and ID number of the received

RREQ. If yes, it does nothing. As a result, the broadcast flooding could be prevented. For example, because node D (E) has dealt with the RREQ message from node C (D), when the same RREQ message is sent by node B (F), node D (E) would neglect.

4 Model Simulation Experiment

A simulation tool-OPNET [5,6] is adapted to simulate the proposed resource location strategy and confirm the feasibility, reliability and effectiveness under the wireless environment and provide a basis for analyzing performance of the LRDM. The grid network model is composed of five wireless nodes which adopt wireless communication protocol and simulate the resource location strategy by using the generic module and the lib function of OPNET in Fig. 4. Due to the fact that the nodes vary a lot, only a specified type node model is given in this paper. As shown in Fig. 5.

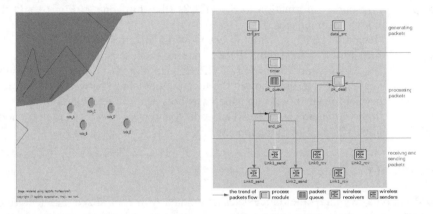

Fig. 4. Grid Network Model   **Fig. 5. A** Specified Type Node Model

The node model in Fig. 5 is composed of three parts: generating packets (responsible for simulating the data generating and processing of nodes), processing packets (responsible for simulating the sending queue of nodes) and receiving and sending packets (responsible for simulating the wireless links of nodes). In addition, taking security and invulnerability of links into consideration, the link0, link1 and link2 are redundant settings.

During the simulation process, assuming the time of processing and forwarding packets for every node is same and transmission delay is negligible, after configuring business of nodes and result statistics, the simulation is run and the results are shown in Fig. 6.

The Fig. 6 is composed of four child figures. The first and third figures are sending packet count for node A and node E. The second and forth figures are sending packet throughout for node A and node E. Supposed the time of processing forwarding packets is 0.2s, RR broadcasts the RREQ at 0s (the second one in Fig. 6). RP receives the RREQ, and replies the RREP (the forth one in Fig. 6). After receiving the RREP,

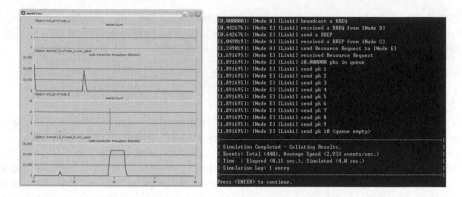

Fig. 6. Simulation Results   **Fig. 7.** OPNET Debugging Information

RR sends the resource request to DN at 1.2s (the second one in Fig. 6). RP applies the corresponding resource information to SN at 1.8s (the third one in Fig. 6) and the resource location is accomplished.

Resource location strategy isn't direct-viewing manifested in OPNET. So debugging information is added into OPNET running process and a code fragment is shown in Fig. 7. Startup and initializing of OPNET is omitted and part of debugging information is given. The results showed the location procedure between RR and RP. In addition, the mentioned strategy in paper was proved to be feasible and effective. The fact which the communication between node A and node E is forwarded by node C and D would be affirmed from the time in Fig. 7.

5 Summary

LRDM not only overcame the deficiencies associated with centralized architecture of one center node, but also overcame the irregularity of resource information space associated with distributed architecture, unstructured characteristic and blindness of resource discovery. The efficiency and accuracy of resource discovery was improved in this paper. According to the LRDM model the layered resource location strategy is proposed, which has two parts: local location and global location. In addition, the location strategy is simulated by using OPNET. The results indicated that the proposed strategy met the wireless node location requirements and the LRDM had efficient resource discovery and perfect scalability, the location strategy was feasible and had good performance.

References

1. Tan, S.: Research on Grid Resource Discovery Mechanism. Central South University (2005)
2. Gong, Y.: Research on Resource Discovery in Distributed Systems. Institute of Computing Technology Chinese Academy of Sciences (2006)
3. Dong, F.: Research on the Resource Discovery Mechanism in VEGA Grid. Institute of Computing Technology Chinese Academy of Sciences (2006)

4. Zhong, L., Zhu, B., Yang, L.: Research on Layered Resource Discovery Model in Grid. In: 2011 2nd Intl. Conf. on innovative Computing & Communication and 2010 Asia-Pacific Conf. on Information Technology & Ocean Engineering (2011)
5. Chen, M.: OPENT Network Simulation. Tsinghua University Press, Beijing (2004)
6. Wang, W., Zhang, J.: OPNET Modeler and Network Simulation. Posts & Telecom Press, Beijing (2003)

The Enlightenment of German "Dual System" on Higher Vocational Education of China in Modern Information Age

Wen Jiang and Yingbo Pang

Guangxi Economic Management Cadre College, Nanning 530007, China
gxpyb@qq.com

Abstract. The "dual system" of Germany is an internationally successful vocational education pattern at present. This paper introduces the content and features of the German "dual system" vocational education, and discusses how to use the essence of the "dual system" as a reference for the practical reform of our higher vocational education.

Keywords: Dual system, vocational education, enlightenment.

1 Introduction

The German "dual system" vocational education is a successful and effective pattern internationally acknowledged as present, being hailed by the former German Chancellor Kohl as "the secret weapon of German economic growth". As a successful pattern of vocational education, "dual system" is followed by many countries including China. However, people soon realize the great difficulty of learning and transplanting its experience. Therefore, it is of vital importance for us to analysis features of German "dual system" vocational education and the background of its resounding success in Germany, in order to get a more overall understanding of the educational concept and then improve our higher vocational education by learning experience effectively.

2 The Content and Features of "Dual System" Vocational Education

The Content of "Dual System" Higher Vocational Education. In Germany, junior college and vocational college constitute the main part of higher vocational education system, which cultivates a large number of technical backbones for Germany with the "dual system" pattern. The content of "dual system" vocational education is: on the one hand, young people receiving higher vocational education should learn practical knowledge of corresponding profession and cultivate professional ability in vocational education enterprise or cross-enterprise training institution; on the other hand, they should receive general cultural education and theoretical education of

S. Lin and X. Huang (Eds.): CSEE 2011, Part V, CCIS 218, pp. 484–488, 2011.

profession in public vocational school. To put it simply, learners have the dual identity of student at school and enterprise apprentice, conducting the vocational eduction system of alternation of working and learning between school and enterprise.

Features of "Dual System" Higher Vocational Education. Set the objective and lay emphasis on vocational ability. The cultivating objective of German higher vocational education is quite clear. That is to cultivate professional and technical talents of higher level. It does not require students to master systematic and profound theoretical knowledge. Instead, it gives students essential basic education of theory and adequate vocational training to make them professionals with ability of taking up vocational activity independently of a certain field. Profound theories are not required of talents cultivated by the "dual system" pattern. But they are good at practice and professional application skills.

Pay attention to the combination of application and practice as well as the close integration of teaching process and production in terms of professional curriculum offering. The German "dual system" course is characterized by the basis of modern technology and the core of vocational activity, including theory course and practice course. Meanwhile, it is guided by practical training course. Training time for vocational skills generally accounts for more than 60% of the total class hours, and different abilities of post groups in each profession have different requirements of time. Select course content according to requirements of different professions and corresponding vocational skills, with timely integration of related new technologies and technical results for ensuring the advancement. Most of the time, students are trained in practical operation skills with equipments and technologies currently used in enterprise. To a great extent, training is conducted in the form of productive labour so that the objective of school is strengthened. The German "dual system" provides various kinds of training approaches in order to ensure that production practices can be integrated into the teaching process, including: (1) Experimental training room on campus. Vocational education of Germany has sufficient funds for purchasing sophisticated equipment. In addition, German enterprises take the initiative to donate equipment to schools from the perspective of future. So, campus experimental training rooms have advanced equipments with high content of technology; (2) Vocational education center of regional industry association; (3) All kinds of social enterprises.

Wide participation in practice teaching of enterprise as a teaching subject. The German business has formed a good tradition of actively participating in vocational teaching. The education system with enterprise as the main part not only enables vocational training to embody enterprise demands preferably and ensure the high-level skills of students, but also relieves the burden of higher vocational education on government. Even so, Germany has strict requirements for access of enterprises involved in vocational education that enterprises undertaking practical teaching of students have to possess certain qualifications like place, equipment, instructor and others. Hence, most large enterprises in Germany have their own training base and training teachers. Small and medium-sized enterprises that are unable to provide comprehensive and diversified vocational training according to training regulations can also take part in vocational education by means of cross-enterprise training and supplementary training of school and plant. Because the government gives privileges of tax or others to enterprises that undertake the task of practical teaching according to the number of students and training practice, many enterprises are willing to be involved in vocational education and accept training of students.

Ensure the quality of education with the assessment method of separating training from evaluation. In order to ensure the level of higher vocational education, the federal government has clear and unified standards for all links of vocational education like teaching, assessing and others. After completing vocational education, students have to take part in the nationally unified course completing examination. The national *Vocational Training Ordinances* provides the minimum eligibility criteria for vocational examination. Generally speaking, the practical skills examination lasts for 14 hours and the professional knowledge examination lasts for 5 to 6 hours. Organization and implementation of the examination, scores confirmation and certificates issuance are undertaken by industry associations.

Guarantee the implementation of vocational education through legislation. In 1969, the *Vocational Education Act* was issued in Germany. It is the "milestone" of German vocational education, giving legal status to "dual system" vocational education and especially elaborating on such aspects as the guiding ideology, principles and policies, training rights and liabilities, and organizational forms of vocational and technical education of enterprise. Afterwards, Germany successively issued corresponding laws and regulations, such as *Basic Law of Enterprise*, *Ordinance of Trainer Qualification*, *Vocational Education Promotion Law*, *Ordinance of Training Teacher Qualification*, etc. Since then, the "dual system" vocational education has become the pillar of German technological development. In 1985, the *Higher Education Act of Germany* established the formal position of higher vocational education in German higher education, improved the management and the operation of vocational education in legal form, and promoted the healthy and orderly development of vocational education. In 2005, on the basis of reform practice and theory exploration, Germany revised and promulgated a new *Vocational Education Act*. It is the constant improvement of vocational education legislation that guarantees vigorous development of German higher vocational education.

3   The Enlightenment of "Dual System" on Higher Vocational Education of China and Problem Research

German "Dual System" Is Not Entirely Suitable For Higher Vocational Education of Our Country. The "dual system" is very successful in Germany, becoming a model of the whole world. The higher vocational education of our country has emulated German "dual system" for many years. There is a reform upsurge of practical teaching in higher vocational colleges. On the one hand, increase the input on campus practical teaching and establish training centers for various professions. Cultivate manipulative ability of student through providing them with simulative training environment of practical skill. However, this simulated practice teaching model is far from meeting the requirements of professional post ability; on the other hand, carry out work placement by adopting the "2+1" pattern. However, the systematicness of constructing practical training system between school and enterprise is always lacking in organizing work placement. Enterprise offers places, but rarely takes part in vocational training. It lacks effective guidance from instructor of enterprise. Moreover, school teachers are difficult to take it into account due to heavy tasks of teaching. Thus, students are in the state of lacking theory and practical interaction for a long time. The reform of our higher vocational education by applying the "dual system" mechanically was not successful. The reason is that German "dual system" pattern emphasizes on harmonious cooperative relationship among government, society, enterprise, school and individual. Yet it is obvious that "dual system" is hard to be fully implemented in China with the lack of cultural background, basis of law and social support. Since we cannot copy German "dual system", then how should we construct the practice teaching pattern that is consistent with China's actual conditions? This requires learning the essence of "dual system" to develop our higher vocational education practically.

The Emulation and Enlightenment of the "Dual System" Pattern. Government is the key factor that affects the development of higher vocational education. Vocational and technical education servers as the decisive force in promoting economic growth. Both of country and enterprise are direct beneficiaries of the development of higher vocational education. However, enterprises in China only aims at recruiting senior technical personnel, while they lack corresponding social responsibility. Why there is nothing accomplished in the development of higher vocational education by our government and enterprises? First of all, the legislation of vocational education in our country is not perfect. Formulating and enforcing the law are main methods for government intervention in higher vocational and technical education. The law plays the roles of guiding and regulating in the development of higher vocational education. In addition, providing vocational and technical education with fund guarantee by legislation is the feature of vocational education legislation in developed countries, which fully embodies the principle that vocational and technical education development must be guaranteed by material. For example, *Vocational-technical Education Act of Carl D.Perkins* of the United States clearly stipulates that the federal government should appropriate $1.6 billion annually for state governments and local training plans, and local government should allocate at least in the proportion of 1:3[1]. The educational input of our country is lagging so far behind in the world that severely restricts the development of our education, especially higher vocational education. Our country should provide vocational and technical education with fund guarantee by legislation. Although the *Vocational Education Law* was officially promulgated in 1996 in China, supporting policies and regulations are still lacking. So higher vocational education is not supported by substantial fund input.

Enhance the participation degree of enterprise in higher vocational education. Enterprise practice is a crucial link of the "dual system" pattern. Wide participation of enterprise in vocational education, as well as effective cooperation between enterprise and higher vocational school, is the key to higher vocational education reform. But for now, enterprises in our country still lack the awareness of participating in vocational education because of social tradition, deficiency of policy and others. Although the country strongly advocates approaches of cooperation between school and enterprise like combining learning with working and work placement, there are still problems in cooperation. For example, the cooperation between school and enterprise lacks permanent mechanism and enterprises are short of enthusiasm; some enterprises cooperating with schools lack necessary input in cultivating interns, who are even treated as cheap labour. In order to encourage to participate in higher vocational education, the government should issue corresponding policies and provide subsidies granted for policy considerations like direct financial subsidies or tax preference. Meanwhile, in order to guarantee the quality of higher vocational education, strict access standards must be set for enterprises involved in vocational education, including training content, control regulations, training place, instructor and other aspects that formulated jointly by industry sectors and educational institutions.

Strengthen the "double-qualified" teachers team construction. Vocational education requires teachers to possess not only solid theoretical knowledge but also rich practical experience. Professional teacher training in Germany emphasizes on specialized theory as well as professional training. The term of teachers training is relatively long and the requirements are quite strict. Professional teachers have to take part in the state examination. Once the teaching qualification is obtained, it would be life-long tenure. But continuing education is still required. At present, "double-qualified" teachers, who attach importance to both theory and practice, are greatly needed in our vocational schools. The construction of "double-qualified" teachers team has now become a serious problem of higher vocational education development in our country. For this reason, schools should lay stress on cultivating and introducing "double-qualified" teachers. The cultivation of "double-qualified" teachers should be closely combined with professions. Make arrangement for teachers designedly to take part in post practice in enterprises, where they accumulate practical work experience and improve practice teaching ability. Furthermore, it is an important guarantee for vocational training of students in enterprises that construct a team of part-time teachers with rich work experience or composed by managerial staff. Part-time teacher occupies a considerable proportion in German vocational education. Yet the construction of part-time teachers team basically becomes formalistic, existing only in name. Therefore, enhancing deep cooperation with enterprises and constructing stable part-time teacher team by matching post with treatment are also problems needed to be solved urgently.

Acknowledgement. The new age higher education reform project of Guangxi Province in 2010 (2010JGB123); Educational reform project of Guangxi Economic Management Cadre College in 2010 (10KYB005).

References

1. Qu, H.: Historical Evolution of Vocational and Technical Education in Developed Countries. Shanghai Education Publishing House, Shanghai (2008)
2. Zhang, M.: Higher vocational education development of China from the perspective of European education reform investigation report of European academic exchange. Journal of Kunming University (2) (2003)
3. Jing, H.: Advantages, trend and enlightenment of German vocational education of dual system. Continue Education Research (4) (2007)

Performance Comparison of Convex Programming in Different Scenarios

Yingqiang Ding, Hua Tian, and Shouyi Yang

College of Information Engineering, Zhengzhou University, Zhengzhou 450001, PR China
cnpowerfoot@gmail.com, tianhuazzu@263.com, ieshouyiy@zzu.edu.cn

Abstract. Convex optimization techniques have been used to deal with the sensor localization problem in recent years by virtue of the high accuracy and ease of formulation. Two scenarios differ in distribution of the sensor nodes were implemented, and for each, two different deployments of anchors were executed. To calculate the unknown locations, semidefinite programs (SDPs) were used. Simulation results indicate that convex programming has nice performance in sensor positioning accuracy, which can satisfy the demand of WSN-based applications, and the deployment of anchors has certain effect on the localization precision.

Keywords: Wireless sensor network (WSN), convex programming, semidefinite programming (SDP), localization.

1 Introduction

Wireless Sensor Network (WSN) is composed of hundreds or thousands of small, low-cost, low power sensor nodes equipped with sensing, information processing, and communicating ability. It is a multi-hop self-organized network that can cooperatively perceive, collect and deal with the information of the objects, and send it to the observers. There is a wide range of applications based on WSN including, environmental monitoring and prediction system, medical care, household use, military surveillance and so on [1, 2]. The information of an object is useful only if the location it refers to is known, that generates the demand of localization. Apparently, the location of each node is the premise for the effectiveness of WSN-based applications. Therefore, how to determine the locations of sensor nodes becomes a hot issue [3].

At present, the localization algorithms can be divided into two classifications: range-based and range-free[4]. Owing to the hardware limitations of the WSN devices, the latter one as a cost-effective substitute becomes more popular, and with it the absolute peer-to-peer distance estimations is needless. Several range-free localization algorithms have been proposed in recent years, including APIT [4], DV-Hop [5], Amorphous [6], Convex Programming [7] and so on.

Convex Programming algorithm, a solution based on convex optimization, provides a novel perspective for sensor localization. Through it, the point-to-point communication connection as a set of geometric constraints on the node positions, the whole network is modeled into a convex set. Then, a global optimization solution for the

S. Lin and X. Huang (Eds.): CSEE 2011, Part V, CCIS 218, pp. 489–495, 2011.

unknown positions of nodes in the network can be obtained by semidefinite programs (SDPs) [8] and linear programs (LPs) [9]. SDPs are used in the context of linear matrix inequalities and can be efficiently solved by interior-point methods. Because convex programming is a centralized localization algorithm, in order to work efficiently, anchors must be deployed at the edges of the network.

2   Network Model

Consider a sensor network in 2-D space with n sensors and m anchors. The network is supposed to be connected and each node has a unique coordinate. An anchor is a node whose location a_k ($k=1,\ldots, m$) in 2-D is known, generally be acquired by GPS or other position indicators, and a sensor is a node whose location x_i ($i=1,\ldots,n$) in 2-D is to be determined. For a pair of sensor x_i and anchor a_k, their Euclidean distance $\overline{d_{ik}}$ can be measured directly if they are within a radio range r. Similarly, for a pair of sensor x_i and sensor x_j, their Euclidean distance is d_{ij}. The distances are defined as:

$$d_{ij} = \left\| x_i - x_j \right\| \le r \tag{1}$$

$$\overline{d_{ik}} = \left\| x_i - a_j \right\| \le r \tag{2}$$

where $\left\| \bullet \right\|$ denotes the 2- norm.

3   SDP Algorithm Model

The sensor network localization problem is to find $x_i \in \boldsymbol{R}^d, i = 1,2,\ldots,n,$ for which

$$\left\| x_i - x_j \right\|^2 = d_{ij}^2 \qquad \forall (i,j) \in \boldsymbol{N}_x$$
$$\left\| x_i - a_k \right\|^2 = \overline{d_{ik}}^2 \qquad \forall (i,k) \in \boldsymbol{N}_a \tag{3}$$

where $\boldsymbol{N}_x = \left\{ (i,j) \mid d_{ij} \le r, 1 \le i < j \le n \right\}, \boldsymbol{N}_a = \left\{ (i,k) \mid \overline{d_{ik}} \le r, 1 \le i \le n, 1 \le k \le m \right\}$, $\boldsymbol{R}^d$ denotes the d-dimensional Euclidean space, in our simulations d is 2.

Let $\boldsymbol{X} = [x_1, x_2, \ldots, x_n] \in \boldsymbol{R}^{2 \times n}$ be the position matrix that needs to be determined. Then Eq. 3 can be written as

$$\left\| x_i - x_j \right\|^2 = e_{ij}^T \boldsymbol{X}^T \boldsymbol{X} e_{ij} \qquad \forall (i,j) \in \boldsymbol{N}_x;$$

$$\left\| x_i - a_j \right\|^2 = (a_k; e_i)^T [\boldsymbol{I}_2; \boldsymbol{X}]^T [\boldsymbol{I}_2; \boldsymbol{X}](a_k; e_i) \qquad \forall (i,k) \in \boldsymbol{N}_a. \tag{4}$$

Therefore, the localization problem can be represented as:

find $X \in R^{2 \times n}, Y \in R^{n \times n}$

s.t $e_{ij}^T Y e_{ij} = d_{ij}^2, \forall (i,j) \in N_x;$

$(-a_k; e_i)^T \begin{pmatrix} I_2 & X \\ X^T & Y \end{pmatrix} (-a_k; e_i) = \overline{d_{ik}}^2, \forall (i,k) \in N_a;$

$Y = X^T X$.   (5)

where I_2 is a 2-dimensional identity matrix; e_{ij} is the vector with 1 at the ith position, -1 at the jth position and zero else; and e_i is the vector of all zero except -1 at the ith position.

However, the above problem is not a convex optimization problem, and it is hard to solute in general even for $d=1$. P. Biswas and Y. Ye proposed a SDP relaxation method [10] to formulate the problem: change $Y = X^T X$ in Eq. 5 to $Y \geq X^T X$. This matrix inequality is equivalent to ($e.g.$, Boyd et al.[11])

$$Z = \begin{pmatrix} I_2 & X \\ X^T & Y \end{pmatrix} \geq 0$$ (6)

Then, the position problem can be written as a standard SDP form

find $Z \in R^{(2+n) \times (2+n)}$

s.t $Z_{1:2,1:2} = I_2$

$(0; e_{ij})^T (0; e_{ij}) \bullet Z = d_{ij}^2,$ $\forall (i,j) \in N_x;$

$(-a_k; e_i)^T (-a_k; e_i) \bullet Z = \overline{d_{ik}^2},$ $\forall (i,k) \in N_a; Z \geq 0$ (7)

Note that the measure error of the Euclidean distances can't be avoided. Thus, the localization problem can be written to a SDP with the measure error as follow

minimize $\sum_{i,j \in N_x, i<j} \alpha_{ij} + \sum_{i,k \in N_a} \alpha_{ik}$

s.t $e_{ij}^T Y e_{ij} = d_{ij}^2 + \alpha_{ij}, \forall (i,j) \in N_x;$

$(-a_k; e_i)^T \begin{pmatrix} I_2 X \\ X^T Y \end{pmatrix} (-a_k; e_i) = \overline{d}_{ik}^2 + \alpha_{ik}, \forall (i,k) \in N_a;$

$e_{ij}^T Y e_{ij} \geq r^2, \forall (i,j) \notin N_x;$

$(-a_k; e_i)^T \begin{pmatrix} I_2 X \\ X^T Y \end{pmatrix} (-a_k; e_i) \geq r^2, \forall (i,k) \notin N_a$

$Y \geq X^T X, \alpha_{ij} \geq 0, \alpha_{ik} \geq 0$.   (8)

If N_x is sufficiently large and all distances are measured perfect, then there is a unique optimal solution for the unknown poisition.

4 Performance Comparison

Simulations were performed on networks of 200 sensor nodes which are randomly generated in a square region of $[-0.5, 0.5] \times [-0.5, 0.5]$. Two kinds of scenarios were executed using SeDuMi [12] in Matlab 7.0: (1) Random uniform placement as shown in Fig. 1(a), (2) Random O-shaped placement as shown in Fig. 1(b).

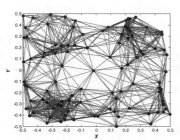
(a)Random uniform placement

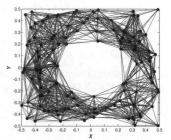
(b) Random O-shaped placement

Fig. 1. Two scenarios of sensors placement

4.1 Performance Parameters

To evaluate the performance of Convex Programming, the performance parameters need to be defined. The parameters used in simulations are listed below.

(1) The distance measured, $\hat{d}$, is modeled as

$$\hat{d} = d \times (1 + randn(1) \times nf) \qquad (9)$$

here, d is the true distance; nf is the noisy factor ; and $randn(1)$ is a Gaussian random number.

(2) The normalized average localization error, NALE, is defined as

$$\text{NALE} = \frac{1}{n \times r} \sum_{i=1}^{n} \left\| X_{est,i} - X_{real,i} \right\| \qquad (10)$$

here $X_{est,i}$ is the estimated position of sensor i; $X_{real,i}$ is the real position of sensor i.

4.2 Simulation Results and Analysis

Since the anchors are arranged all around the network, the method of placement is closely related to the performance of localization. Two different deployments of anchors were implemented for each scenario: uniform and random.

To evaluate the effects of anchors on NALE, when r is 0.3 and nf is 0.1, the results for varying the number of anchors are shown in Fig. 2. It is clear that the accuracy of the localization can be obviously improved with the aid of anchors in both scenarios.

The accuracy is high at $m=4$ with uniform anchors, which means the anchors were placed in the corner,while with random anchors the number is 7. This is probably because the entire network hasn't been surrounded with random anchonrs when the number is small. Furthermore, the precision tends to be stable when it achieves the highest point.The effects of anchors' deployments is clearly that the uniform anchors have the better performance when the number of anchors is small.

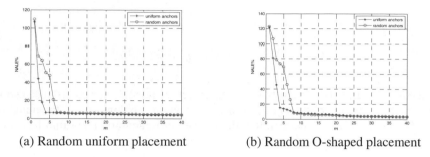

(a) Random uniform placement   (b) Random O-shaped placement

Fig. 2. Effects of anchors on NALE ($r=0.3$, $nf=0.1$)

The effects of radio range r on NALE are simulated and shown in Fig. 3, when nf is 0.1 with 20 anchors. It can be seen that NALE quickly reduces as the radio range increases to 0.125, when the range of r is from 0.125 to 0.2, it gently decreases. In addition, it can be particularly observed that the curves tend to be flat when r is large than 0.2. Although, the radio range larger than 0.2 can lead to a better results, the improvement is small and the communication consumption would increase greatly. To sum up, the radio range is a major factor in improving the performance of localization algorithm based on convex programming, which is small in convex programming.

The sensitivity of NALE to the noisy factor nf is a main concern for the positioning algorithm. The effects of increasing noisy factor on NALE, when r is 0.2 with 20 anchors, are shown in Fig. 3. It is obviously that the localization precision consistently degrades as the noisy factor gradually increases in both scenarios. The difference between the two deployments of anchors is little in the first scenario, while it is huge in

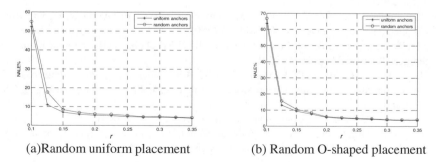

(a)Random uniform placement   (b) Random O-shaped placement

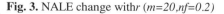

Fig. 3. NALE change with r ($m=20,nf=0.2$)

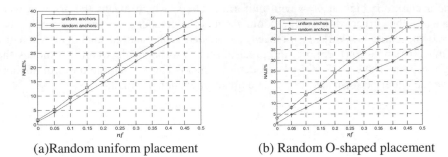

(a)Random uniform placement   (b) Random O-shaped placement

Fig. 4. NALE change with nf (m=20, r=0.2)

the second scenario. This is attributed to the effects of noisy factor on distance estimation which is negligible in contrast to that of irregular topology. From the numerical value of NALE, it is can be seen that the convex programming algorithm has strong robustness to the noisy factor.

5 Conclusions

This paper compares the performance of convex programming in random uniform and O-shaped placements. Simulation results show that this method can provide accurate localization with low energy consumption and robust to the noisy factor. The deployment of anchors is uniform would made the localization error be smaller than it is random.

Acknowledgement. This study is supported by the Key Program for Science and Technology Development of Henan Province (No.102101210600) and the Doctoral Foundation Program of Zhengzhou University.

References

1. Akyildiz, I.F., Su, W., Sankarasubramaniam, Y., et al.: IEEE Communications Magazine 40, 102 (2002)
2. Bharathidasan, A., An, V., Ponduru, S.: Sensor Networks: An Overview. Department of Computer Science. University of California (2002)
3. Niculescu, D., Nath, B.: In: Proceedings of 2001 IEEE Global Telecommunications Conference, Texas, USA, p. 2926 (2001)
4. He, T., Huang, C., Blum, B.M., Stankovic, J.A., Abdelzaher, T.: In: Proceedings of the 9th Annual International Conference on Mobile Computing and Networking, San Diego, USA, p. 110 (2003)
5. Niculescu, D., Nath, B.: Telecommunication Systems 22, 267 (2003)
6. Nagpal, R.: Organizing a Global Coordinate System from Local Information on an Amorphous Computer.A.I. Memo 1666, MIT A.I. Laboratory (1999)

7. Doherty, L., Pister, K.S.J., Ghaoui, L.E.: In: Proceedings of the 20th Annual Joint Conference of the IEEE Computer and Communications Societies, USA, p. 1655 (2001)
8. Nesterov, Y., Nemirovskii, A.: Interior-Point Polynomial Algorithms in Convex Programming. SIAM, USA (1994)
9. Karmarkar, N.: Combinatorica 4, 373 (1984)
10. Biswas, P., Ye, Y.: In: Proceedings of the Third International Symposium on Information Processing in Sensor Networks, Berkeley, CA, p. 46 (2004)
11. Boyd, S., Ghaoui, L.E., Feron, E., Balakrishnan, V.: Linear Matrix Inequalities in System and Control Theory. SIAM, USA (1994)
12. Information on, http://sedumi.ie.lehigh.edu/

Information Effect in Interactive Teaching

Chen Yun, Xie Kefan, and Liu Haimei

School of Management, Wuhan University of Technology, Wuhan, 430070, P.R.China
achenyun135@126.com, bxkf@whut.edu.cn, cliuhaimei319@gmail.com

Abstract. This paper gives a definition of interactive teaching, and regards that there are some information effects in interactive teaching. The paper proposes that we need to focus on the information feedback effect, attention enforcing effect, theory-practice amalgamation effect, memory facilitating effect, and innovation inspiring effect in interactive teaching. Finally, the paper probes into the approaches to take advantages of the information effects in interactive teaching via employing computer.

Keywords: Interactive teaching, Information effect, Information feedback, IT.

1 Introduction

Interactive teaching model is a teaching structure model which takes teaching activity as life communication between teachers and students, takes teaching process as a process alternately influenced and is operated by teaching and study together which dynamically developed. In this process, through optimizing the pattern of teaching interactively, in another word, through adjusting the relationship and interaction between teachers and students, to form a harmony interaction between teachers and students, students and students, study individual and teaching medium, to strengthen the impaction between human beings and environment and bred teaching study resonance, so as to improve teaching effect.

At present, scholars mainly from China do many researches of interactive teaching. Guilan Mao (2008) defined interactive teaching as a teaching style in which teachers are guiders and students are subjects [1]. Hua Li (2010) regarded interactive teaching as a teaching pattern to mobilize all relevant factors to actuate teachers and students to impact, interact and promote alternately, to reach the best teaching effect, and its core is to help students learning to study, research and innovate [2].Yongzhu Tan (2010) separated interactive development in interactive teaching to seven process: preparing interaction, beginning interaction, elementary interaction, sufficient interaction, deep interaction, inlining interaction, and developing interaction [3]. Fengcai Wang probed into multi-dimensional interactive teaching, and put forward four teaching models such as situation-mould, guiding-discover, self-study-interactive, and spontaneity-innovate [4]. Yanhua Zhou (2010) studied the problem of autonomous interactive teaching organization, it's about how to establish a study community in a class, to help getting ideal teaching effect, and he took Chinese teaching as an example, gave some effective teaching strategies [5]. Fang Yang (2010) researched teacher-student internet interactive teaching model's features and establishing strategies under the

S. Lin and X. Huang (Eds.): CSEE 2011, Part V, CCIS 218, pp. 496–500, 2011.

background of Fujian province's high school curriculum revolution [6]. Kai Qiu and Ying Huang (2008) studied established interactive teaching model by applying experiments method, expert literatures method, literature material method and mathematic statistics method, and his conclusion is that established interactive teaching model will help improving students' psychological healthy level [7]. And others talked about the application of interactive teaching model in different subjects.

This paper aims at analyzing the information effect in interactive teaching model, and examining how to apply the information effect to improve interactive teaching efficiency through IT technologies.

In this paper, there are five information effects in interactive teaching, namely, information feedback effect, attention enforcing effect, theory-practice amalgamation effect, memory facilitating effect, and innovation inspiring effect.

2   Information Feedback Effect in Interactive Teaching

The traditional teacher teaching student studying model can only form one-way information transferring, but cannot give feedback. In this situation, teachers have no idea about whether the students have known the knowledge he or she teaches and what degree have they mastered. But interactive teaching sends feedback information to teachers because of students' participation. Teachers can know how much knowledge have their students mastered through interaction. What's more, relying on the feedback information, teachers can also learn students' knowledge status, their demand for particular knowledge, and then adjust knowledge, teaching emphasis, and teaching methods to promote teaching effect. The feedback effect is shown in Fig. 1.

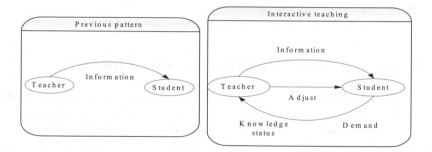

Fig. 1. Information Feedback Effect in Interactive Teaching

3   Attention Enforcing Effect in Interactive Teaching

In traditional one-way information transferring teaching pattern, students have no at least less study pressure. But in interactive teaching, students need to take part in interaction, so if they don't study carefully or don't study initiatively, they can't do well in the interaction or perform their talent in front of their teacher and classmates. Therefore, in interactive teaching process, students will concentrate on class to master knowledge their teacher teaching and employ their knowledge to perform their own knowledge and ability for their self-esteem.

4 Theory-Practice Amalgamation Effect in Interactive Teaching

In interactive teaching, it also asks students for applying their knowledge to analyze and solve practical problems. This needs students' ability of managing theoretical knowledge to solute practical problems. There are many patterns for combing theory and practice in interactive teaching, and the ordinary one is: teacher teaching theory and explaining several simple cases, then giving a complex one to students. Settling the complex one needs many aspects theoretic knowledge and the teacher's previous explaining for simple examples. And sometimes theoretic knowledge from class is not enough for students to find a solution, so students need to learn what he want or ask their teacher for help. And at the same time, students also have to learn more site knowledge and operation knowledge from practice.

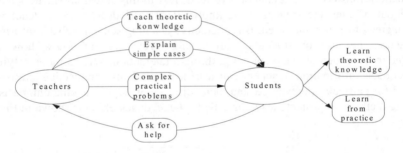

Fig. 2. Theory-Practice Amalgamation Model

5 Memory Facilitating Effect in Interactive Teaching

Interactive teaching facilitates students' memory of theoretic knowledge from three aspects. The first one is repeating; in interactive teaching, knowledge occurs repeatedly and students use it over and over because of their participation, so the repeating mechanism makes memory overlapping come true. The second is taking part in, in interactive teaching, due to taking part in teaching activity; memorizing style is transferred from passive to active which makes a difference in memory effect. And the third one is situation; interactive teaching generates a kind of friendly, close situation, which is active for recalling.

6 Innovation Inspiring Effect in Interactive Teaching in Interactive Teaching

In interactive teaching, new problems are revealed in interaction. And for settling them, new theory and method are wanted. At the same time, interactive teaching can inspire teachers and students analyze and solve problems together, which is good for cooperation and brainstorm, for enlightening interactively and playing team effect in knowledge studying and problems solving, and then makes contribution to incentive knowledge innovation.

7   Take Advantages of the Information Effects in Interactive Teaching via Employing Computer

In interactive teaching, computers and IT technologies play more and more important roles. We can apply computer methods to play information effect in teaching, to improve teaching effect.

There are several approaches helping computer teaching playing information effect in interactive teaching. (1) Employee presentation tools such as PPT in interaction. For example, teachers can use PPT in class teaching, case analyzing and proposing thoughts. And students can use PPT in presenting their thoughts and discussions. (2) Simulation. Apply IT technologies to program simulation software to help students doing simulation experiments with their own knowledge. (3) Communicate in internet. For instance, we can build curriculum study website, knowledge study blog, BBS discussion community, answer collecting system and video exchanging and so on. (4) Integrate brainstorm, Delphi and computer internet. Combine with video meeting for example. (5) develop and apply curriculum game software. Teachers and students can improve study effect via knowledge practice in internet games.

8   Conclusions

Interactive teaching is an important tendency in education pattern. No matter in science theory teaching, engineering teaching or humanities and social sciences teaching, interactive teaching is useful. Significant information effect is one of interactive teaching's advantages, and IT and computer methods will help information effect in interactive teaching plays better and then strengthen teaching effect.

The author will focus on implementation of interactive teaching model especially on how to apply internet technologies to improve interactive teaching performance in further study.

9   Summary

Based on the literature review, this paper analyzed the information effects in interactive teaching, and found out that there are five information effects in interactive teaching, including information feedback effect, attention enforcing effect, theory-practice amalgamation effect, memory facilitating effect, and innovation inspiring effect. Furthermore, the paper discussed on the approaches how to take good advantages of the information effects in interactive teaching via employing computer for gaining a better information effect and a higher teaching performance.

Acknowledgement. This paper is supported by "the Fundamental Research Funds for the Central Universities", Project No.2010-1b-028.

References

1. Maric, D.M., Meier, P.F., Estreicher, S.K.: Mater. Sci. Forum 83-87, 119 (1992)
2. Green, M.A.: High Efficiency Silicon Solar Cells. Trans. Tech. Publications, Switzerland (1987)
3. Mishing, Y.: Diffusion Processes in Advanced Technological Materials. In: Gupta, D. (ed.), Noyes Publications/William Andrew Publising, Norwich (2004) (in press)
4. Henkelman, G., Johannesson, G., Jónsson, H.: Theoretical Methods in Condencsed Phase Chemistry. In: Schwartz, S.D. (ed.) Progress in Theoretical Chemistry and Physics, vol. 5, ch. 10, Kluwer Academic Publishers, Dordrecht (2000)
5. Ong, R.J., Dawley, J.T., Clem, P.G.: Submitted to Journal of Materials Research (2003)
6. Clem, P.G., Rodriguez, M., Voigt, J.A., Ashley, C.S.: Patent U.S. 6,231,666 (2001)
7. Information on, http://www.weld.labs.gov.cn

Research and Practice of Evaluated Index System with Information Technology Affecting Bilingual Educational Quality in Medical College

Gao Zhen[1] and Luo Xiaoting[2]

[1] Department of Stomatology of the 1st Affiliated Hospital,
Gannan Medical College, Ganzhou, China
[2] Department of Biochemistry and Molecular Biology,
Gannan Medical College, Ganzhou, China
agaozhen7623@sohu.com bxtluo76@yahoo.com.cn

Abstract. According to the modern teaching theory and objective of bilingual education, we devised the principle of evaluation index system affecting bilingual educational quality and built up a set of evaluation index system affecting bilingual educational quality. We calculated their weight by AHP (Analytical Hierarchy Process) Method.

Keywords: bilingual education, educational quality, index system, analytical hierarchy process.

1 Introduction

Currently, the institutions of higher learning were generally lack of specialized evaluation index system affecting bilingual educational quality. The evaluation was insufficient if using the forthcoming evaluated index system of the monolingual educational quality or using examination [1]. Foundation of perfect evaluated index system affecting bilingual educational quality had been especially important for the objectve scientific appreciation of bilingual education in order to measure the bilingual education quality preferably, to reflect the result and shortage objectively, to promote the development of bilingual education deeply and to increase the positivity of every teaching department [2].

2 Objective of Bilingual Education

Bilingual education is the teaching action usingforeign language (mainly English) and Chinese as class phraseology to carry out non-linguistical subject. The objective of bilingual education was divided into three aspects [3]: (1) knowledge objectivr: to master the subject knowledge; (2) language objective: to apply the expertise teaching by foreign language in order to make the students understand this subject foreign data and interchange this subject matter in oral or written form by foreign language; (3) thought objective: to think by mother tongue and English simultaneously and to use

S. Lin and X. Huang (Eds.): CSEE 2011, Part V, CCIS 218, pp. 501–505, 2011.

these two language unconventionally according to the intercourse object and work environment. The knowledge objective was primary among these objectives. "Teaching" was capital and its purpose was to study the expertise during the bilingual education. "Bilingual" was only method which was the bridge to study the advanced technology. If the students were required to use the foreign language as the mother tongue at first, the students would have psychological suppression and decrease the learning interest [4]. The final objective of medical bilingual teaching was to make the medical students think, study, work or commuciate by English in the medical expertise territory, and to culture the medical students to understand and master the medical latest achievement [5].

3   Principle of Designing the Evaluated Index System Affecting Bilingual Educational Quality

The evaluated index system affecting bilingual educaitonal quality was an multi-elemental, multi-formal, multi-facial and extensive synthetic functionary system which could persistently monitor the academic teaching, studying, adminstration, process and quality of bilingual teaching. Therefore, the evaluated index system affecting bilingual educaitonal quality should abide by the following principles:

(1) Effective principle
The index should be designed to reflect the bilingual educational characteristic and objective, and to increase the bilingual educational quality according the bilingual education and its developmental regularity in order to promote the bilingual educational construction and reform of bilingual teaching method and content.

(2) Objective principle
The index should be designed to grasp various kinds of teaching message exactly, to evaluate the bilingual educational condition equitably, and to provide the decision for teaching adminstration. The teacher and student were the principal participants of bilingual education, but their impersonative roles were different and the problem judgement were also different. Especially, the student's judgemnt for bilingual educational quality had right to speak.

(3) Elemental principle
Because the bilingual educational contents of each subject were different and multiple, each element affecting the bilingual educational quality was analyzed on the base of gathing all kinds of biligual educational information data. The elements affecting the bilingual educaional quality should be grasped in order to specify the bilingual educational supervising system and to strengthen the adminstrative means.

(4) Scientific principle
The index should be designed according to the scientific pedagogic theorem and statistical data-sorted requirement. Each index should aim directly at the teaching feature of bilingual teachers. Each index had relative independentability in order to raise the estimated validity. The connotation of each index was definite and concise. The index should have favourable mensurability to elevate the estimated reliability.

(5) Targeting principle

The teacher could know the freeback opinion all around, discover own advantage and disadvantage during the bilingual education, and find the gap to improve through the index and estimated results.

4 Construction of the Evaluated Index System Affecting Bilingual Educational Quality

4.1 Definition of Primary Index

(1) The teaching leader was the teacher. The teacher's diathesis straightly determines the cultural quality of talented man. The teacher's leading function must be educed thoroughly during the bilingual education. The student was the main body of teaching activity who takes part in the whole teaching process. The students were not only educated persons but also judgers. They knew not only the teacher's teaching state, but also themselves learning state. The student was the final bearing person of monitoring the teaching quality because the teaching quality was reflected by the increasing level of student's knowledge and diathesis [6]. Thus, the teacher-student factor (p1) was classified as the primary index according to the objective and targeting principles.

(2) The bilingual educational process was the core of whole index system which was related with the leader and main body of teaching activiry. The evaluation of bilingual educational effect was the essential means to check the teacher's professional level, work attitude, teaching method and the student's learning situation. The evaluation of bilingual educational effect was the important measure to inspect the teaching quality. The teaching effect had a direct impact on the student's learing quality, simultaneously reflect the teacher's teaching level and the teaching organizational level. Therefore, the bilingual educational process (p2) and the bilingual educational effect (p3) were classified as the primary index according to the effective, objective and elemental principles.

4.2 Definition of Secondary and Tertiary Index

Firstly, the three primary indexes were defind in the evaluatedindex system affecting bilingual educational quality. Secondly, the three primary indexes were subdivided into 7 secondary indexes and several tertiary index.

(1) The teacher-student factor (p1) had 2 secondary indexes including the teacher professional ability (p11) and the student factor (p12). The teacher professional ability (p11) had 3 tertiary indexes including the professional diathesis (p111), foreign language ability (p112) and applying ability of media mix (p113). The student factor (p12) had 3 tertiary indexes including the professional diathesis (p121), the activeness of bilingual learning (p122) and foreign language ability (p123).

(2) The bilingual educational process (p2) had 2 secondary indexes including the teaching preparation (p21) and the teaching interaction (p22). The teaching preparation (p21) had 4 tertiary indexes including the teaching content analysis (p211), the teaching content systematization (p212), the student's signature analysis

(p213) and the teaching objective design (p214). The teaching interaction (p22) had 7 tertiary indexes including the teaching systematization (p221), the bilingual integration (p222), studying scene design (p223), studying resource design (p224), studying strategy design (p225), adimistration and help design (p226) and summarizing and strengthening design (p227).

(3) The bilingual educational effect (p3) had 3 secondary indexes including the executing ratio of bilingual educational subject (p31), test or examine of bilingual education (p32) and the student's bilingual educational record (p33).

4.3   Definition of the Weight of the Evaluated Index System Affecting Bilingual Educational Quality

The weight of this index system was calculated by the AHP (Analytical Hierarchy Process) method for the purpose of increaing the scientific nature of weight number distribution and binding the college actual situation. The AHP method could describe the subjective judgement objectively. It could enhance the effectivity of weigh number, the accuracy and comparability of judgement evaluate through combining the expert experience with rational analysis.

Using the AHP method, the layer analyzing pattern was constructed firstly; the relative significant comparison scale was obtained and the judgement matrix was founded compared between two factors in the each layer according to scaling theory; the largest characteristic value of the judgement matrix and its characteristic vector was calculated to gain the significance sequence of each hierarchical factor pointed to certain factor in the upper layer, and the weight vector was established [7]. The weight defined by AHP method was consistent with objective actuality and easy to quantitate [8]. In order to ascertain the judgement matrix, the The relevant experts were invited to compare the evaluated index by paried comparison, to arrange the priority of significance of each index, to calculate the corresponding characteristic vector of the largest characteristic value of the judgement matrix, and to obtain the weight number value of each index. Through the analytical judgement of many experts, the result of weight distribution of the evaluated index system affecting bilingual educational quality was shown in Fig.1.

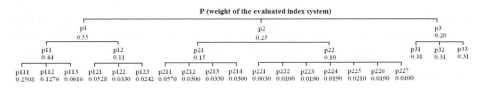

Fig. 1. Result of weight distribution of the index

5   Practice of the Evaluated Index System affecting Bilingual Educational Quality

According to the constructed index system, the bilingual class teaching of subjects such as biochemistry and immunology was evaluated completely. The reliability analysis, principal component analysis, and linear regression analysis were carried out to analyse the reliability and validity of this index system affecting bilingual educational quality through the evaluated data of experts. The coefficient alpha of L.J.Cronbach was 0.9683 by the reliability analysis which showed this index system had satisfactory internal consistency. The factor analysis of these indexes showed that the validity of scale construction was good. The statistical results obtained by the student's evaluation and expert's evaluation discovered that the deviation was only 0.23%-5.69%, the elementary goodness of fit was 94.31-99.73, and the evaluated consistency was high. The score of each index and the final score for each bilingual teacher were calculated according to the quantitative assessment information of the index system. The advantage of each bilingual teacher and suggestion of students and experts were summarized by the qualitative assessment information of the index system.

Acknowledgement. This study was supported by the Department of Education of Jiangxi Province in China.

References

1. Jinhua, L., Lin, A., Suduo, X., et al.: Practice and thinking about the bilingual educational administration in he institution of higher learning. Beijing Education (High Education) 1, 45–47 (2007)
2. Ying, H., Weiqiang, P.: How to ensure the bilingual educational effect of special subjects in the institution of higher learning. Literature and Educational Data 25, 133–134 (2006)
3. Qian, C., Wenlong, L.: Thinking about the bilingual education in the institution of higher learning. Modern Medical Science 22(5), 782 (2006)
4. Liu, Z.: Chinese foreign education faces the problem and outlet. Shandong Foreign Education, 3–9 (2004)
5. He, X., Liu, W., Shen, Q., et al.: Analyze the medical bilingual education. Medical Education 3, 23–24 (2004)
6. Li, W., iZhao, Z., Zhang, B., et al.: The function of teaching-evaluation by students in quality monitoring teaching. Journal of Agricultural University of Hebei (Agriculture & Forestry Education) 8(4), 18–19 (2006)
7. Wen, C.: Evaluating indexes and comprehensive evaluation of teaching laboratory. Journal of Architectural Education in Insitutions of Higher Learning 15(4), 112–115 (2006)
8. Gao, Z., Song, W.: An education quality evaluation method based on the analytic hierarchy process. Information Technology. 15(4), 112–115 (2006)

A Fast FFT IP Core Design Based on Parallel Computing

Shizhuan Li[1,2], Jun Ou[1,*], and Qingxiu Wu[1]

[1] Department of Network Engineering, Hainan College of Software Technology,
Qionghai, Hainan, 571400, China
[2] Aone Integrated Technology Co., Ltd. Beijing, 100089, China
xhogh@hotmail.com

Abstract. It used the two-dimensional RAM and 128 butterfly operation to achieve high-speed FFT (Fast Fourier Transform) algorithm with high-performance parallel computing. The processor can support the largest 32K point complex FFT transform (real and imaginary part of each 16-bit), and conversion time is 70μs. Technical indicators are ranking international advanced level.

Keywords: FFT, Fast Fourier Transform, ASIC, parallel computing.

1 Introduction

Since 1965, W. Cooley and J. W. Tukey found that FFT (Fast Fourier Transform) algorithm later, FFT in digital signal processing is a very important algorithm, a fairly many areas have a wide range of applications. FFT processor as a hardware implementation of FFT algorithm and its usefulness is also increasingly being attention. At present, many chip manufacturers have introduced products with a fixed-point FFT IP core[1]. However the precision of fixed point FFT is not high enough, it can not be used in some cases with high precision requirement. In the transformation of time is difficult to meet the current application requirements, especially the long-point FFT operation[2]. The balance between design agility and expansibility of up to 32K points, while completing 24-bit floating-point FFT signal processor design, using two-dimensional RAM to improve computing speed of the process of data access to meet the complex floating-point butterfly device stack, the use of parallel computing implementations, greatly improved the system's operation speed.

2 Using Parallel Computing to Achieve High-Speed FFT

There are many methods to implement FFT algorithm. In summary, they can be divided into software implementation in general CPU, DSP implementation method, FPGA implementation, and ASIC implementation means four ways.

Far as FFT computation speed, the ASIC has a unique advantage. Enhance the FFT processing speed of the main technical means is used pipeline architecture[3][4],

---

* Corresponding author.

S. Lin and X. Huang (Eds.): CSEE 2011, Part V, CCIS 218, pp. 506–511, 2011.

parallel computing, increasing the number of processors and high-radix algorithm structure. Algorithm in determining the radix should be comprehensive consideration FFT processing speed, computational algorithms, FPGA's structural characteristics and algorithm of hardware resource consumption and other factors. A radix-2 butterfly algorithm consists of a complex multiply and two complex plus composition. And a radix-4 butterfly algorithm contains three complex multiplications and eight complex plus, Although the radix-4 processor, processing speed is 2 times the base two-processor, but the radix-4 butterfly algorithm is a radix-2 butterfly is resource-intensive computing resource-two times. Taken together, processors use the base 2 butterfly calculation of the processor architecture shown in Fig 1.

Fig. 1. Radix-2 butterfly unit structure

We know that, FFT data flow throughout the operation process is very clear. N points of the FFT computation is proportional to (N • log2N), can be divided into (log2N) layers, on each N / 2 times butterfly. As shown in Fig 2.

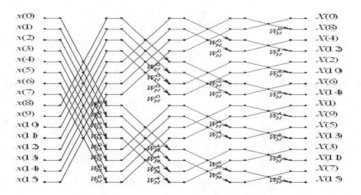

Fig. 2. 16-point FFT operation flow chart

Clearly, FFT butterfly computations each layer there is no correlation between the data. In theory, N / 2 butterfly operations can work in parallel. The entire FFT operation in the (log2N) steps can be completed.

3   Address Change of Non-linear Data Being to Limit Parallel Computing

Modern VLSI technology can easily be several 10 million in a single chip, the parallel computing does not seem to be too difficult. However, careful analysis of butterfly

FFT algorithm calculation process, we can find that the effects of the speed of parallel computing is not a key factor in the number of units, but the butterfly address non-linear changes in the calculation of data, making the data difficult for high-speed parallel computing access, generate the correct address is the key to the whole FFT computation.

4   Using Two-Dimension RAM(2D_RAM) to Solve Parallel Butterfly Operation

General concept on the RAM, there is only one group address A. After a given address A, specified by the address A storage unit read or write operation. There are two sets of two-dimensional RAM address Ax and Ay, respectively, vertical and horizontal management of the entire memory in both directions. Read and write operation can specify a group address works. As shown in Fig 3.

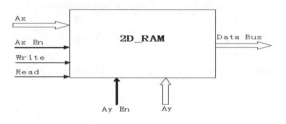

Fig. 3. Schematic diagram of two-dimensional RAM

With a deposit of 16 -word as examples of two-dimensional RAM. As shown in Fig 4.

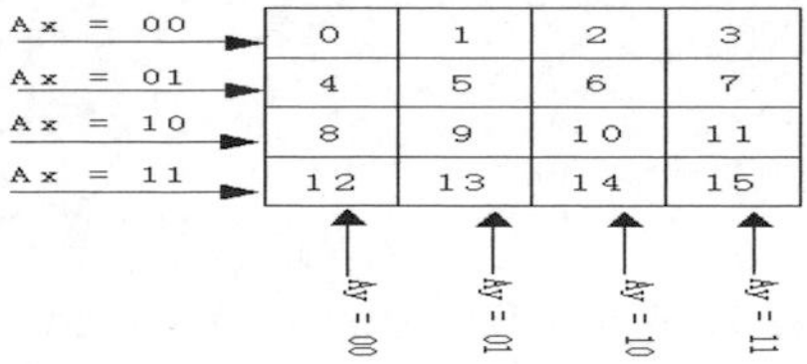

Fig. 4. An instance of 16-word access to two-dimensional RAM

In this two-dimensional RAM,
If the x direction address is valid, and Ax = 00, then read out in parallel 0,1,2,3 words
If the x direction address is valid, and Ax = 10, then read out in parallel 8,9,10,11 words
If the x direction address is valid, and Ay = 00, then read out in parallel 0,4,8,12 words

If the x direction address is valid, and Ay = 10, then read out in parallel 2,6,10,14 words

This two-dimensional RAM with 4 butterfly calculation units, we can easily achieve the 4 points of the butterfly parallel computing.

5 Structure and Performance of High-Speed FFT

At first, we discuss a simple example when N = 64. The achievement of the structure when N = 64 show in Fig 5.This structure mainly consists of four parts: FFT computing Unit, two-dimensional RAM(2D_RAM),coefficient ROM and control Unit, FFT computing Unit composed of eight parts of radix-2 butterfly Units. When it starts, every radix-2 butterfly Unit can finish a radix-2 butterfly operation in a circle.2D_RAM accesses computing data based on address RAM address generate Unit output, to complete reading and writing each eight input data and eight output data in parallel. Controller used to control the flow of data and to synchronize the various units of FFT IP core. In this structure, 2D_RAM ensure eight radix-2 butterfly Units to Work smoothly in parallel.

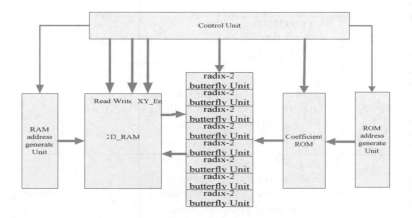

Fig. 5. An instance of FTT structure, when N=64

High-speed FFT elements of the program is used to achieve 256 × 128-word two-dimensional RAM, accompanied by 128-group complex floating-point butterfly stack (each word is 48 bits, real part imaginary part of two components, each component of 24-bit floating - points). The structure is shown in Fig 6.

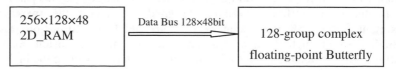

Fig. 6. High-speed FFT implementation structure

This structure achieved the 128 butterfly in parallel computing, two-dimensional RAM allows smooth access to computing data. Maximum support 32K point complex FFT transform, real and imaginary part of the two components of the 16-bit ,the conversion time is 70μs. With the mainstream of the DSP and FPGA implementations of comparison, as shown in table 1, all the FFT length are converted into 32k points. This design taken longer than usual DSP computing is about four times faster than the FPGA implementation is about 3 times faster, roughly the same with the ASIC implementation.

Table 1. Performance comparison

Realization	Raw information and data	Source	Equivalent rate for the 32K-point FFT	comparison
This Design	32K-point FFT Conversion time is 70μs		70 μ s	
DSP	TI 600MHz C64×DSP 6.0 Cycles/data	TI website www.ti.com	320 μ s	4.6 times slower
FPGA	Xilinx XC2VP40 FPGA chip∏ 8192points FFT, Conversion time is 49μs	Xilinx website www.Xilinx.com	226 μ s	3.2 times slower
ASIC	Siworks IP Core with TSMC's 0.13um production line, the largest 4K-point FFT, 0.41 million gates, 8.2μs	Siworks website www. Siworks.com	82 μ s	roughly the same

6 Summary

It presented a method for the completion of a one-dimensional 128 ~ 32K point complex FFT and IFFT transform, real and imaginary part of the two parts of the 16-bit floating-point FFT processor is designed to support the two-dimensional maximum 128 × 256 point complex FFT and IFFT transformation. The design flexibility, speed, high precision, can be very convenient extension points can be configured into a floating-point FFT core, can be widely applied to the high precision digital signal processing applications.

References

1. Wei, H., Erdogan, A.T., Arslan, T.: The Development of High Performance FFT IP Cores Through Hybrid Low Power Algorithmic Methodology. In: Proceedings of Asia and South Pacific Design Automation Conference, ASP-DAC 2005, vol. 1, pp. 549–552. IEEE, Shanghai (2005)
2. He, S., Torkelson, M.: Design and Implementation of a 1024-point Pipeline FFT Processor. In: IEEE Custom Integrated Circuits Conference, pp. 131–134 (1998)
3. Shin, M., Lee, H.: A High-speed Four-parallel Radix-2 FFT/IFFT Processor for UWB Applications. In: IEEE International Symposium on Circuits and Systems, ISCAS 2008, pp. 950–963. IEEE, Washington (2008)
4. Hongxing, W., He, C., Qiuyue, H.: Parallel Architecture FFT/IFFT Processor. Trans. of Beijing institute of Technology 26(4), 338–341 (2006)

Research on Improving the Quality of the Normal Students by Asking the Effective Questions with Multimedia Technology in Chemistry Classroom

Yang Du[1] and JunHua Chen[2,*]

[1] School of Chemistry and Chemical Engineering, Southwest University, Beibei District, Chongqing, P.R. China
[2] School of geography science, Southwest University, Beibei District, Chongqing, P.R. China
duy360@swu.edu.cn
chenjhx@163.com

Abstract. Questioning is the most effective multilateral-interactive activity between students and teachers. Effective questioning is based on proper question, which also contributes to improving teaching quality. The paper focuses on how to ask the effective questions in chemistry classroom through analyzing some typical invalid questions and effective questions of chemistry.

Keywords: Middle School Chemistry, Effective Questions, Teaching strategy.

1 Introduction

Questioning is an effective teaching method in the classroom, is an important part of teaching, and also is the most effective multilateral-interactive activity between students and teachers. But in the reality, it is found that there are innumerous low-efficiency classroom asking in chemistry teaching. Like other teaching activities, classroom asking has its own principle and strategy.

2 Types of Questions

There is a great relationship between the level of a teacher's ability on purposing a question and the type of this question. If speaking of the actual content, the question is differs in thousands of ways, but if speaking of the type, the question type is not complex. According to previous studies and combined with chemical characteristics of classroom questioning, Questions proposed in chemistry classroom can be classifying from four angles.

2.1 According to the Form of the Question

According to the form of the question, questions can be divided into four broad types: direct questions, chain questions, suppose-asked questions and rhetorical questions (Figure 1).

---

* Corresponding author.

S. Lin and X. Huang (Eds.): CSEE 2011, Part V, CCIS 218, pp. 512–517, 2011.
© Springer-Verlag Berlin Heidelberg 2011

Direct question is most commonly used in chemistry classroom, which can lead students thinking and request the student to answer on the spot. For example, which method is the most simple to test the pH of the solution?

According to teaching need, the teacher divides a question into several Inter-related Chain questions, and asks the question in turn, inspires the student to ponder. For example, In addition to aluminum ion, which metallic ion the solution also has?

Suppose-asked question does not request students answer, its purpose is to causing suspense and attract students' attention. For example, then let's take a look at what is the law of these hydrolysis reactions?

Rhetorical questions are often used to format a problem situation and cause student's cognition conflict. Teacher often pays high attention to trap which the student is easiest to neglect by asking a rhetorical question. For example, in all the neutral salt solution, this salt is a strong acid and alkali salt, right?

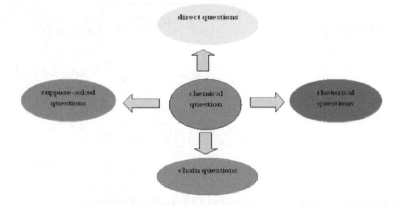

Fig. 1. The category of the chemical questions according to the form of the question

2.2 According to the Certainty of the Answer

According to the certainty of the answer, questions can be divided into two broad types: Open-ended Question and Closed-ended Question.

The main features of open-ended questions include: uncertainty of the conditions, uncertainty of the problem-solving methods and strategies, and the uncertainty of the conclusions. For example, Tell me about what operation does not meet the chemical requirements?

The main features of closed-ended question include: perfect condition and single answer. For example, which equation is the equation of laboratory method for making the oxygen by heating potassium chlorate?

An open-ended question is designed to encourage a full, meaningful answer using chemical knowledge and feelings. It is the opposite of a closed-ended question, which encourages a short or single-word answer. Open-ended questions also tend to be more objective and less leading than closed-ended questions.

2.3   According to the Content of the Question

According to the content of the question, questions can be divided into two broad types: Questions about learning and Assisted-teaching questions (Figure 2).

Questions about learning refer to the content of the questions involved with students' related-learning. For example, which method is the most simple to test the pH of the solution?

Assisted-teaching questions refer to the content of the questions involved with the strategy of classroom management and student organization in order to complete classroom teaching. For example, who wants do the experiment this time?

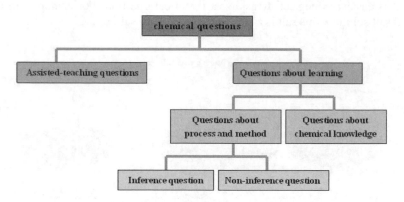

Fig. 2. The category of the chemical questions according to the content of the question

2.4   According to the Level of Question Putting to Students

According to the level of the question, questions can be divided into two broad types: High level questions and Low level questions. Questions about knowledge are focused on checking the situation of the knowledge which students have learned and should master. For example, what type response is the neutral response? Is the aluminium sulfate not a strong electrolyte?" Knowledge questions based on students knowledge of different sources can be categorized into: memory question have learned from books and life experiences, memories, experiences questions.

Question about understanding is focused on checking students' master situation of new knowledge. For example: "When the generation of weak electrolyte aluminum hydroxide, the ionization equilibrium is destroyed, reducing the concentration of hydrogen ions, which side the balance to move?

Questions about application include the use of rules, methods of application and use of the concept. For example: "There are several salts, tell me which salt solution may hydrolysis?"

Questions about analysis are typical impacted by the wisdom skill and the cognition strategy. For example, tell me what was the solution of ammonium cyanide?

Comprehensive Questions are often used to guide the student the rapid retrieval the question related knowledge and carries on the analysis in the mind, synthesizes the brand-new conclusion. For example, look these hydrolytic-reaction equations, what law do these hydrolysis have?

Questions about Evaluation guide students to develop certain standards, thinking, methods, people and products to make assessment and determine the values of questions. For example: "Do not, oh this can not, in the end which one can?", "He said the production is carbonic acid, what does the first step produces?"

The above question looks like very simple, but it is actually very difficult to the normal students to grasp and utilization. In practice, we found that normal students when making a lot of simulation teaching unreasonable, inappropriate questions, which affect the effectiveness of teaching. If lacking of effective guidance, it will affect the normal students teaching capabilities.

I often asked my students, what do you want to hear from the students? This seems like a simple question, but it actually takes some careful consideration. Do you want students to answer comprehension questions or do you want them to have authentic discussion? Often, teachers lead a "discussion group" and the only person talking is the teacher. They ask simple yes/no or short answer right-or-wrong questions. This is very comfortable for teachers because they control the pace and direction of the discussion. If you want to encourage authentic student-generated discussion, you might have to step outside of your comfort zone.

3   Teaching Strategy on Question-Design

3.1   The Question-Design Should According to the Need of Teaching

First, teachers should clear the purpose of classroom questioning. In the preparation before class, teacher shall carefully read and understand the textbook. Then, according to teaching needs, teacher design classroom chemical questions. Finally, you should design some typical chemical questions about the key and difficult point, help students understand and master their doubts and error-prone content. In addition, teacher should arrange flexible questions according to the problems in the classroom. For example, in teaching the "strong electrolyte and weak electrolyte" lesson, teacher can design the following questions: ①What are the distinguish between the strong electrolyte and weak electrolyte in material structure? ②What are the distinguish between the strong electrolyte and weak electrolyte in ionization extent? ③ What are the distinguish between the strong electrolyte and weak electrolyte in the ionization equation? ④How exist the distinguish and the strong electrolyte and weak electrolyte in aqueous solution? ⑤In the same conditions, how about the ability of conductive electrolyte between the strong and weak electrolyte?

3.2   The Question Should Be Definite, Pertinent, Concise and Comprehensive

Question answer must be clear, so that the students can understand questions after hearing the meaning, quickly into thinking activity, can achieve exact answer the questions. For example, it is not an appropriate question: "what is a kind of nitric acid?" Such questions, not easy to answer, because we don't know the students from the physical properties to answer, or from chemical properties to answer, from its use to answer, or from its mix to answer.

3.3   The Questions Should Be from Easy to Difficult, and Be Learning Emphases

Knowledge is stratified, student's thinking structure is also have layers, teachers should proposed the question to meet the students' knowledge structure and thinking ability, otherwise not only students can not solve the problem, sometimes put students original knowledge hierarchy destabilized. Question should be the key of learning, and be a certain depth. Questions should inspect not only all memory level of knowledge, but also understanding, thinking and application level of knowledge, which can cultivate students' understanding and thinking abilities and application ability. Such as learning the reaction $3NO_2+H_2O=2HNO_3+NO$, teacher can design the following questions: ①how does the color of gas change? ②In the reaction, which one is oxidant, reductant, oxidation product, reduction product? ③If the NO_2 and NO gas mixture through water, the volume of the mixed gases reduce 25mL ,then how much is the volume of NO_2 in reactant? ④After the above reaction, how much weight is the solution gained? ⑤In what mixing ratio of NO_2 and O_2 through water ,the mixed gases can be absorbed just right? Ask questions like these, not only knowledge capacity is big, the artistic conception is high also, a simple chemistry from the complanation knowledge increases equation of three-dimensional.

3.4   The Questions Should Be Put Forward in Correct Time, and Inspire the Student

When to put forward the question is the most advantageous? Ancient Chinese Confucius think, only when students "heart knowledge and unable to speak out", puts forward problems can receive the best effect.

3.5   The Questions Should Face All Students

Classroom questioning should face all students, special pay attention to take care of the underachiever in the teaching process. Some normal students often let only a few students answer, most students still don't know what, teaching has through to the next step, also some teachers often meet in "a loud thunder", i.e. teachers put forward question, students altogether answer "yes" or "no", "T" or "F". This seemingly faced all students, actually this is also a minority student answer, and most students haven't answer.

3.6   Gives Promptly, the Suitable Appraisal to Student's Reply

After the student answers the question, the teacher should give the appraisal or the praise encourages promptly. The teacher should also protect the student to leave undecided the solution enthusiasm, the question which the student proposed, even if is extremely weak, the teacher should also answer questions warmly, prohibits crudely despite, protects the student to create the self-respect which the thought germinates, similarly is the important guarantee which the effective classroom inquiry carries on smoothly.

4 Summary

Synthesizes above, In the instruction of pedagogy and psychology theory,the teacher carry on the effective question in chemistry classroom to be not only possible and to be feasible, which can obvious improve student's academic record. Chemical normal students should carry teaching practice massively about the ability on putting forward effective chemical questions.

Acknowledgement. The research is funded by the project of Southwest University for Teacher Education innovation platform.

References

1. Barker, L.J., Garvin-Doxas, K.: Making Visible the Behaviors that Influence Learning Environment: A Qualitative Exploration of Computer Science Classrooms. Computer Science Education 14(2), 119–145 (2004)
2. Boyer, K.E., Phillips, R., Wallis, M.D., Vouk, M.A., Lester, J.C.: Balancing Cognitive and Motivational Scaffolding in Tutorial Dialogue. In: Proceedings of the 9th International Conference on Intelligent Tutoring Systems, pp. 239–249 (2008)
3. Boyer, K.E., Dwight, A.A., Fondren, R.T., Vouk, M.A., Lester, J.C.: A Development Environment for Distributed Synchronous Collaborative Programming. In: Proceedings of the 13th Annual Conference on Innovation and Technology in Computer Science Education, pp. 158–162 (2008)
4. Boyer, K.E., Vouk, M.A., Lester, J.C.: The Influence of Learner Characteristics on Task-Oriented Tutorial Dialogue. In: Proceedings of the 13th International Conference on Artificial Intelligence in Education, pp. 365–372 (2007)
5. Forbes-Riley, K., Litman, D., Huettner, A., Ward, A.: Dialogue-Learning Correlations in Spoken Dialogue Tutoring. In: Proceedings of the 12th International Conference on Artificial Intelligence in Education, pp. 225–232 (2005)
6. Lane, H.C., VanLehn, K.: Teaching the Tacit Knowledge of Programming to Novices with Natural Language Tutoring. Computer Science Education 15(3), 183–201 (2005)

Application of Multi-agent in Personalized Education System

Rong Shan

Department of Computer Science, Weinan Teachers University
Weinan, Shaanxi, P.R. China 714000
gsshanrong@126.com

Abstract. Currently most of today's e-learning systems are dominated by the objectivist school and the use of technology as a substitute for a teacher delivering instruction. But it does not seem to fulfill its promise to become the most important learning paradigm. A e-learning personalize recommendation model based on multi-agent technology is put forward in the paper. The model is compose of five functionally independent agents, implement personalized and initiative recommendation function by their cooperation.

Keywords: e-learning, agent, multi-agent, Personalized Recommendation.

1 Introduction

As one of the killer internet applications, the emerging e-Education turns out to be an important aspect for the educational area. Although the benefits and potentials of the new generation of e-Education are obvious and exiting, unfortunately, so far the great potential of e-Education has been far from being taken full of advantage.

Apparently, the current e-Education does not seem to fulfill its promise to become the most important learning paradigm. The learner often complain about the lack of flexible performance tools in support of personalized and tailored learning, value-added reflection, mutual simulative knowledge sharing, on-demand expertise finding, just-in-time peer help as well as efficient and timely tutor guidance. However, from the tutor perspective, the main drawback of current e-Education systems is that they tend to require more effort in terms of authoring learning materials and preparing tests or examinations than their classical counterparts. Based on the analysis, we need to provide learner with more intelligent learning environment that supports various customized learning services as needed, on the other hand, we need innovative mechanism to alleviate tutor workload in terms of facilitating the development of learning contents and test/exam by hiding as much technique details as possible.

2 Technology of Agent

Properties of Agent. Agent technology is one of the latest development in artificial intelligent technology. From the architecture perspective, an agent is anything that can

S. Lin and X. Huang (Eds.): CSEE 2011, Part V, CCIS 218, pp. 518–522, 2011.

be viewed as perceiving its environment through sensor and acting upon that environment through effectors. However, from the software perspective, an agent is substantially a program which has a specific plan of action defined in a limited domain and a behavior pattern which allows it to change at the right moment its own interaction with the world depending on stimuli from the environment.[1]

Generally speaking, Agent has the following characteristics: [2] Intelligence, Reactive, Initiative, Autonomy.

The Structural Features of Agent. According to the level of human intelligence, agent can be described with the six groups: <A, T, s, see, do, action>[2,3]. In it, A is a collection of learning activities; S means the collaboration of system and other agent. T means the communication of system and other agent; see is a function of understanding the perception of the external environment, it described as see: S->T; action is a function to describe the actions taken by the current state of the system, described as action: T->A; do is a effect function of Cartesian product of A and S, described as do: A*S->S. Therefore, structure of agent is divided into six modules according to that six groups, named: learning and evolution module, event detection module, the Executive Module, communication module, coordination module, environmental awareness module [4]. Showing in figure 1.

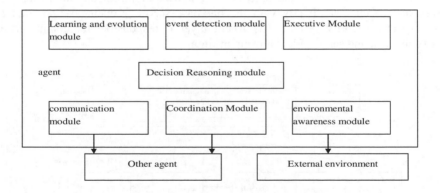

Fig. 1. Internal structure of agent

learning and evolution module: Responsible for self-learning, reflect the Agent's learning performance fully.

event detection module: Through notification of the environmental awareness message module, to detect specific events.

environmental awareness module: Implementation of environmental monitoring initiative, transmitted the results to the event monitoring module.

communication module: Implement the communication with other agents.

Coordination Module: On the basis of the communication module , it responsible for collaboration with other Agent.

Executive Module: Executive the issue of the event detection module.

Multi-agent System. Individual agent's capacity is often constraints by its knowledge and resource, so can not adapt to the open dynamic distributed environment. In order to solve complex problems multi-Agent systems(MAS) have been proposed.

A multi-agent system is a collection of agents; MAS has some features:[5,6]

Autonomy. agents work by their own and have some kind of control over their actions and internal state;

social ability: agents interact with other agents(and humans beings)via some kind of agent communication language and common ontology;

Collaborative: In the MAS system, through resource sharing and information sharing, task or sub-tasks relationship, to achieving the collaboration, consultation and joint work.

3   Intelligent E-Learning System Model

Function and structure of Intelligent E-learning System. System uses B / A / S structure, that is, the browser / Agent / Server three-tier structure. Its main characteristic is the distribution operations and centralized management. Using the Internet browser, client can access the service of the system. Compared with the C / S structure, it is a "thin client" model, helps to speed up the access speed, takes few resources to the client, the client software and hardware requirements are lower. Also, users do not interact directly with the database server, reducing server load and increase data security system. The Agent layer is responsible for communication between client and server side. Showing in figure 2.

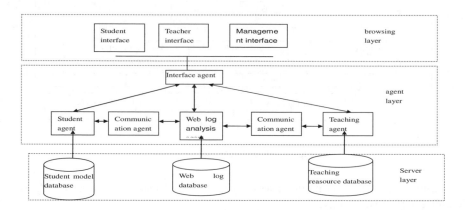

Fig. 2. Structure of system

Browser layer in the browser to provide users with a friendly interface client. By role, there have students, teachers and administrators, and offers three interfaces to them. Different roles with different permissions on the system.

Agent layer is the core to provide the intelligent and personalized service. There have 5 agents: students Agent, teaching Agent, Communications Agent, Interface Agent, Web log analysis Agent.

Server layer consists of student model servers ,web log servers and teaching resources servers. This layer is deposited with the system of all physical data.

Function of Agent. Interface Agent provides an interactive interface for students, teachers and administrators. Through this agent can appropriate parameters to student agent, web log analysis Agent and teacher agent.

Student agent: Reading the student model database, analyze the studying progress and learning focus, etc. Sending the application of class to teaching agent, receiving teaching materials sended by teaching agent.

Teaching agent: perform the functions of the real teachers In the system. Send study materials to students, Student made examination request, the exam questions to students; analysis the student learning behavior, to determine the learning ability of students, and record. According to records, to predict the memorizing ability , understand capacity applications and innovative ability of students, to arrange appropriate teaching methods, content and progress of the implementation of specific teaching to achieve individualized.

Web log analysis Agent: It automatically records the students browsing behavior in the learning process on the site. It responsible for management and maintenance of Web log database, acquisition and processing the Web server log file, updating Web Log library regularly.

Communication Agent: It is the communication bridge of browser layer, Server layer and every agent, collaborate the coordination between agents and scheduling job.

The Basic Work Processes of the System. Students fill in the user interface of login information, system will require user to registrating, if it is a non-registered users, and registration information will be saved to the student information database. If a registered user, after identity confirmation the interface agent will pass the parameters to the students agent, and communicate with web log analysis agent. It analyzing the learning progress ,according to its state of learning ,the teaching agent send the teaching materials. In the learning process, the system will provide students with individualized teaching. After complete the learning, making the exam application to the teaching Agent. Teaching agent generate a moderate difficulty test paper according the knowledge the student studied. After answered, to submit teaching Agent marking.

System Features. (1) Initiative: Agent can take proactive action at the appropriate time initiatively. If students log, web log analysis agent will record the browsing behavior of the students, so analysis its interest .

(2) Sociality: Agent systems and other Agent through mutual communication, cooperation, in this system to achieve their tasks and reach the ultimate goal

(3) Intelligence: System has certain reasoning ability, can more accurately analyze the user's interest, to provide targeted programs to address the problem.

4 Summary

For the e-learning system lack of initiative, intelligence and other issues, using the agent technology and the advantages of multi-agent system, the e-learning personalized recommendation system integrate the technology, presents an intelligent e-learning model, which have an important role for personalized recommendation e-learning system, and design their work processes.

References

1. Kim, J.K., Cho, Y.H., Kim, W.J., Kim, J.R.: A personalized recommendation Procedure for Internet shopping support. Electronic Commerce Research and Applications (1), 301–313 (2002)
2. Shi, z.-z.: Intelligent Agent anf its application, pp. 32–56. Science Press of Beijing, Beijing (2000)
3. Brauer, W., Weiss, G.: Multi-machine scheduling, a multi-agent approach. In: Proceedings of the Third International Conference on Multi Agent Systems, pp. 42–48 (1998)
4. Limin, R.: On intelligent e-Education system based on agent technology. Journal of Tianjin Mormal University 29, 78–80 (2009)
5. Goldberg, D., Nichols, D., Oki, B.M., Teny, D.: Using collaborative filtering to weave an information ta Pestry. Communications of the ACM 12, 61–70 (1992)
6. Su, X.-p., Xu, Y.-x.: Intelligent E-learning system having emotion interaction function. Computer Engineering and Design 30, 3690–3692 (2009)

The Study on Cross Culture in English Language Based on Database Data

Zhihong Xiao

Changsha Medical University, Changsha China 410219
csyxyxzh@163.com

Abstract. Culture is an inseparable element of the sociolinguistic approach to language and language learning. A language cannot be taught and learned without coming to grips with its cultural content. It is well known that learning a foreign language is not only a process of understanding and using only the linguistic, but also the sociolinguistic level of cross-cultural communication as well. An inseparable element of the sociolinguistic approach to language and language learning is culture. A language cannot be taught without coming to grips with its cultural content. This eclectic paradigm entails designing learning resources that allow flexibility and variability while enabling students to learn through interaction with materials and other learners.

Keywords: English language, cross cultural communication, pedagogy.

1   Introduction

Culture is the way of life of a group of people, which includes their language, and ways of doing and being. So far as that is concerned Cultural considerations are very important in any teaching design. Teaching across cultures (from one place to another, or to different audiences), and the teaching of diverse groups or individuals from different cultures in one setting or dispersed across different geographic locations, presents particular challenges. When pedagogical values in one culture are culturally inappropriate to students question knowledge, or may challenge the teacher's view. Students may question the merit in participation, or worse, feel disenfranchised if the course or learning resources do not fit their world view.

Teachers have the pedagogic responsibility to design and administer appropriate activities which will help present factual information about the target culture to students, then teach students to develop tolerance for cultural patterns different from their own, to evaluate their own perceptions and possibly modify any misconceptions students might have, thus building and expanding cultural awareness and experiences. Teachers should exploit every possible source they have access to, ranging from satellite or cable television, radio, internet, and other media, etc. all for the purpose of bringing the target language and culture closer to students, and students should be extremely receptive to all the activities and materials, for their positive attitude and behavior is a prerequisite for the successful learning of the foreign language and culture.

S. Lin and X. Huang (Eds.): CSEE 2011, Part V, CCIS 218, pp. 523–527, 2011.

2 Pedagogy and Culture

Culture provides many people with a sense of belonging regardless of where they live, and they continually reaffirm their culture through behavior and performance. Social scientists tell us that culture shapes people's beliefs and attitudes, their roles and expectations, and the way they interpret their own and others' behavior. Role expectations, they say, are central to human communication including that between teacher and learner. Role expectations are learned and internalized through the process of socialization; they guide our behavior and social interactions, and conflicts tend to arise when we use our own cultural cues to guide the way we behave towards others. This is because different participants in the communication process often lack knowledge and understanding of cultural norms and cues that are used to interpret the behavior and conduct of those involved (Riley, 85). In relation to teachers and students, a role boundary is said to exist between teacher and learner and when this is breached, conflicts occur. Role boundary, however, is mediated by pedagogy – something that is believed to have a major role in the success or failure of the teaching/learning communication process.

However, Barrow (1990) reminds us that pedagogy itself is shaped by the cultural values and ideologies of the society in which it originates and that teachers and lecturers transmit and reinforce the cultural values that are embedded in their teaching approaches (Kelen, 2002). It follows therefore that in cross-cultural settings, a teacher's professionalism as well as her cultural acuteness are important considerations in student performance. The high failure rates of students in schools and universities in China may be due to conflicts in role expectations and breaches of role boundaries, which is because at university many teacher do not share similar cultural values and beliefs with their students – things that are important for shaping role concepts, attitudes and expectations.

Understanding the target-culture is believed central to improved communication with students. Teacher need to understand that the majority of our students have been socialized in unique systems of perceiving and organizing the world around them and which influence their behavior and ways of thinking, and in turn, their academic performance. In this context, language use is important largely because of the way language influences how we perceive and organize our work. As far as teaching and learning styles go, the work of people such as Shipman and Hess (1965) and Harris (1992) are useful in that they tell us that ethnicity and differences in cultural values are important in forming the traits of students' learning styles, which are primarily the result of a unique, culturally determined teaching style, hence there is an urgent need to examine the teaching styles that are characteristics of different cultural groups.

It is identified several instructional design paradigms that reflect particular 'world views' and values of designers:

Constructivist approaches and communication options afforded by technologies expand opportunities for cultural inclusion into teaching methods. Online learning favors constructivism and socio-cultural theory wherein it is viewed that "learning is a form of enculturation in which the individual is socialized through gradual participation in tasks, scaffold or assisted...until full competence is attained", and, that "learning is best achieved when it is encountered, used and applied in real world

Table 1. Instructional Design Paradigms

Paradigm	Definition	Limitations
Inclusive or perspectives approach – which imports the social, cultural and historical perspectives of minority groups, but does not challenge the dominant culture and is therefore cosmetic.	acknowledges multicultural realities, driven by equity and social justice	soft multiculturalism inclusion of the exotic tokenism
Inverted curriculum approach – which attempts to design and instructional component from the minority perspective but fails to provide the learners with educationally valid experiences as it does not admit them into the mainstream Culture.	conceptualizes society as unequal minority perspectives	avoids cognitive needs (i.e. the process of acquiring knowledge by reasoning) does not support equity in learning outcomes
Culturally one-dimensional approach – which excludes or denies cultural diversity and assumes that educational experiences are the same for minority students as they are for others.	cultural minorities are invisible culture is presented as homogenous	dominant cultures only are acknowledged culture is represented as peripheral

contexts" (McLoughlin & Oliver 1999). In the online classroom students are given equal voice, can engage in rich discussions, and can draw from a vast array of learning materials and life examples from the web. Students can participate in both group and individual tasks that draw upon different cultural views and perspectives, especially if guided by the teacher or learning facilitator and teaching strategies are designed appropriately. Research has shown that computer-based collaborative work can transform classroom cultures, the roles of teachers and the expectations of learners. A multiple cultural view is characterized by a view which endorses the multiple cultural realities.

3 Goals of Cultural Instruction

In order for students to become aware of the lifestyles of people in English-speaking countries they need to learn what these people do and say in situations which are part of normal everyday experience. Ned Seelye (in Tomalin and Stempleski 1996) provides a framework that facilitates the development of cross-cultural communication skills. He identifies "seven goals of cultural instruction":

1. First and foremost, in order to achieve cross-cultural understanding students must learn to accept the fact that all people exhibit specific, culturally-conditioned behaviors.
2. Students must bear in mind those social variables such as age, sex, social class, and place of residence influence diverse modes of speech and behavior in the target society, which should be made clear to students.
3. Students should be helped to become aware of typical behavior in common situations in the target culture.

4. Students must be helped to increase their awareness of cultural connotations attached to words and phrases selected for teaching the target language.

5. Students must be helped to develop the ability to evaluate and refine generalizations about the target culture.

6. Students should be taught how to find and organize all the available information about the target culture.

7. Students' intellectual curiosity should be aroused and satisfied, and their empathy toward its people stimulated to such an extent that they become predisposed to studying other cultures in later life.

All these goals must be embedded in lesson planning and practical teaching principles. Now, the question is not whether teachers must teach cultural content but what content must be learned in a language course, how it is to be learned, what is the order of presentation, in other words how it may be implemented effectively, with the sole purpose of bringing the target culture closer to students and helping them develop into well-rounded, educated persons in a multicultural environment.

It is suggested that in adopting the multiple cultural model the design team need to investigate:

(1) What kind of learning environment is most familiar to the students?

(2) How does the cultural background of these students influence their use and view of time?

(3) How do students conceive the role of the teacher?

(4) What kind of relationship do students want with a teacher?

(5) What kinds of assessment tasks will be fair and unbiased?

(6) What rewards and forms of feedback will be most motivating for these students?

(7) Is the locus of control congruent with these students' own sense of personal control?

(8) What cognitive styles characterize the target group? Therefore, the steps in course design for general English courses can be obtained in Figure 1.

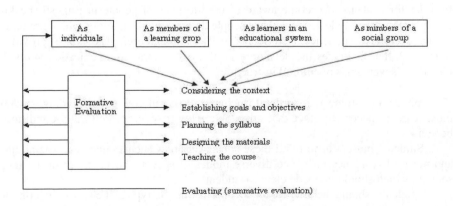

Fig. 1. Steps in course design for general English courses

Students with different cultural norms are at risk if teachers have little knowledge, sensitivity or appreciation of the diversity in communication styles. Such teachers may perceive differences as problems and respond to students' diversify with negative attitudes, low expectations and culturally inappropriate teaching and assessment procedures. Culturally and communicatively diverse students, in turn, may respond with low self concepts and low academic achievement to a school climate they perceive as hostile. The result is reflected in these students' excessive placements in special education, reduced placements in talented and gifted programs and high suspension rates.

4 Conclusions

In the progresses of both teaching and learning, it requires a global or international perspective, and sensitivity to cultural differences and the numerous ways in which culture influences learning. The awareness of these requirements should be built to last by teachers during the organization and actualization of linguistic and cross-cultural teaching and researching.

References

[1] Hedge, T.: Teaching and Learning in the Language Classroom, p. 343. Shanghai Foreign Language Education Press (2002)
[2] Holliday, A.: Appropriate Methodology and Social Context. Cambridge University Press, Cambridge (2009)
[3] Tomalin, B., Stempleski, S.: Cultural Awareness. Oxford University Press, Oxford (2009)
[4] Barrow, R.: Culture, values and the language classroom. In: Harrison (ed.) Culture and language classroom, Hong Kong, British Council, pp. 3–10 (1990)
[5] Cortez, M.: Cultural and educational expectations in the language classroom. In: Harrison, B. (ed.) Culture and the language classroom, Hong Kong, British Council, pp. 54–65 (1990)
[6] Eagly, A.H., Chaiken, S.: Attitude structure and function. In: Gilbert, D., Fiske, S.T., Lindzey, G. (eds.) Handbook of Social. Psychology, 4th edn., pp. 269–322. McGraw Hill, New York (1998)
[7] Nabobo, U., Teasdale, J.: Education for cultural identity 25(4), 695–706 (1995)

The Study on Forensic Linguistic Analysis of Applied Linguistics Based on Data Analysis

Xuehua Li

Changzhou Institute of Technology, Changzhou China 213002
lixuehua125@163.com

Abstract. Combing through the literature on forensic linguistics, it becomes apparent that FL could be seen as a sub-branch of applied linguistics (on an academic discipline level and in terms of theory and the units of analysis), or as a branch of forensic sciences (at a practical level and in terms of its application to the legal setting). These links might help in clarifying misconceptions regarding the nature of FL as simply a practical combination of language with the law. In fact, FL is a small player in the game of criminal law, although increasingly gaining ground with other forensic sciences such as forensic chemistry or forensic psychology.

Keywords: Forensic Linguist, Applied Linguistics, Linguistic evidence.

1 Introduction

The studies of different character in the field of Forensic Linguistics haven't covered all of its aspects but have arranged conditions for further methodological research, as well as have established a solid base for development of the area.

Evidence commonly analyzed by linguists in criminal cases includes transcripts of police interviews and language crimes (such as bribery) and anonymous or questioned texts. Forensic linguistic testimony is rarely admitted into courts of law, though. A major reason for this is apparently impressionistic methods, which are examined for their objectivity. A further barrier to legal acceptance is that FL experts, like all the experts testifying in court, support the claims of whichever side has hired them. Nonetheless, forensic linguists have an ethical and professional responsibility to provide as thorough and objective analysis as possible in order to provide the legal community with reliable and admissible information and help prevent unfair conviction or acquittal of criminal defendants. Legal acceptance of FL expertise should increase as methods improve and as forensic linguists adapt to legal norms.

2 Forensic Linguistics as a Sub-branch of Applied Linguistics

The definition of forensic linguistics is clouded by its confusability with more general issues of Language and Law and with legal interpreting, which is considered by some to be encompassed by FL. In one definition, J. Gibbons refers to FL strictly as "the

S. Lin and X. Huang (Eds.): CSEE 2011, Part V, CCIS 218, pp. 528–532, 2011.

field of the provision of linguistic evidence" [3, p.164], which includes phonetic, syntactic (grammatical), lexical (word), handwriting, discourse and sociolinguistic analyses. Such analyses help in identifying (or disproving) the authors of anonymous or questioned texts (such as bomb threat letters or police records of suspect statements), or in better understanding what happened in an alleged language crime (such as bribery).

An alternative definition of a forensic linguist is an applied linguist who is consulted by the legal community in matters of language and the law. H.Kniffka refers to FL as "basic and applied research in the area of linguistic expert testimony in court" [4, p.31]. R.Rieber and W.Stewart instead use the term "language scientist" to more broadly encompass the interdisciplinary conglomeration of speech and hearing experts, communications theorists, and psychologists, as well as applied linguists in a stricter sense. A forensic linguist, by their classification, would be a "cover term for the language scientist serving as a legal expert" [5, p.4].

The field of FL is not a neatly packaged field. As is true of most specialists, forensic linguists often conduct linguistic analyses of a more general nature than they are actually qualified to do; for example, J.Chambers, a dialectologist, has given expert testimony on general linguistic questions in court [1, pp.19-32]. How do forensic linguists themselves describe their work? According to handwriting analyst Tom Davis, a forensic expert "has two functions: to find clues, and to offer opinions" [2, p.55]. In FL, a clue consists of the linguistic evidence in a case, which a linguist may then analyze to create a hypothesis or opinion based on theoretical knowledge and expert experience. The court (judge or jury) then uses this to form the formal opinion of what happened in the alleged crime or creation of a disputed text. More realistically, in the American court system, the lawyer forms a hypothesis, turning to the forensic linguist to provide a piece of the puzzle. Then the lawyer argues for this evidence-supported hypothesis, leaving the decisive opinion to the jury.

Combing through the literature on forensic linguistics, it becomes apparent that FL could be seen as a sub-branch of applied linguistics (on an academic discipline level and in terms of theory and the units of analysis), or as a branch of forensic sciences (on a practical level and in terms of its application to the legal setting). These links might help in clarifying misconceptions regarding the nature of FL as simply a practical combination of language with the law. In fact, FL is a small player in the game of criminal law, although increasingly gaining ground with other forensic sciences such as forensic chemistry or forensic psychology. The contribution of FL to providing scientifically and legally recognized evidence in criminal cases (particularly in analyzing disputed texts) was considered, a little over a decade ago, "marginal" at best [5, p.2]. Although this is still true to some extent, FL has begun to gain recognition in the legal community in the years since then. It should be noted here that a serious weakness in the FL literature is a lack of court case citations.

The field of Language and the Law evolved from the larger discipline of applied linguistics, which involves the application of linguistic theory and analysis to language issues in the real world (as opposed to being sheer academic). Applied linguistic concerns range from second language acquisition and language learning to language and gender issues, and from orthographic questions to translation and literacy.

Language and the Law, while a daughter field of applied linguistics, is comprised of an equally wide range of issues. These are considered below, to provide an overview of applied linguistic involvement in the legal setting. Language and Law has been called the "mother-field" of forensic linguistics [4, p.22]. As has been mentioned, the terms are often used interchangeably in the literature, but here language and the law will be considered the backdrop for the subfield of FL, which is limited to the application of applied linguistics to the court setting. It should be underscored here that many of the studies in the overview below are not strictly FL studies, at least not in the sense defined in this paper, but rather linguistic studies of legal issues or language and the law in general.

In the United States, forensic linguists are hired by either the defense or the prosecution to analyze linguistic evidence in a case. If a defense attorney finds that the analysis does not support his case, the defense will relinquish the expert and look for another whose analysis is more favorable. The prosecution, on the other hand, or District Attorney (DA) in a criminal case, is required to reveal the analysis of a linguist (if hired) as evidence even if it favors the defense. As already mentioned, forensic linguists rarely (almost never in Ukraine) actually testify as an expert witness in court. However, this role may increase as methods and professionalism improves.

3   Forensic Linguistics Themes

Forensic linguistics has made some remarkable progress in the last two decades but it still has a long way to go. FL has now established itself as an accepted branch of Applied Linguistics. All empirical indications suggest that this trend will continue and strengthen and that language scientists in the legal arena will only become more common. It has developed into a recognized profession with its own conferences, journals and growing body of literature. However, to summarize some of the themes in this thesis, there are several areas in which there is wide room for improvement.

1. Much more data on the norms of language behavior is needed. Computer concordance programs are helping to expand this area of information, but there seems to be a need for more communication among those researching and practicing FL to jointly compile such data. Perhaps this could be achieved via the Internet or standardized programs updated regularly. Such information would help enable linguists to state with greater confidence the level of probability that certain language behaviors would or would not occur among the general population.

2. Linked with the need for data on language norms is the need for more data on criminal language behavior. This could include a classification system, as has been compiled in the Czech Republic, and be used for a number of forensic and forensic linguistic purposes, such as, determining the readability of threats. It would seem prudent and critical to obtain such data from government sources, but since this has not been possible thus far, a means for making such information sharing beneficial to both sectors could be proposed.

3. Much more research is needed in the areas of testing and analysis methods. Not only do typical and atypical results need to be determined for such methods as QSUM and TTR, but uniform (as much as is possible) standards and means of interpretation of test results identified and published as a resource for the FL community.

4. The collaboration of numerous measures of language behavior must continue to be emphasized. In many of the more successful cases in the literature, the collaboration of several different tests supported and therefore lent validity to conclusions regarding linguistic evidence. Perhaps a hierarchy of which measures or tests carry more or less weight in different types of analysis could be established and published.

5. Because the legal world is relatively new for linguists untrained in the ways of the court, there is a need for greater sensitivity and adaptation to the legal culture, as it were. A first step to this would be attempting to gain an understanding of how the legal system works and how expert testimony, as well as linguistic analysis, is viewed by the legal community. Once some level of understanding is reached by FL in general and by linguists in particular, a system of explaining linguistic theory in terms understandable to the court should be devised. One way to achieve this would be to track the precedents of the admissibility or inadmissibility of FL in court, how it was construed by the court, and whether it seemed to have any bearing on individual cases. Legal records may be informative to some extent, but reference books in which contributing authors (forensic linguists) provide detailed accounts of their transactions with the court in a systematic way would be of enormous value to other linguists preparing for related cases.

6. Experts interacting with the court, then, should follow the legal standard and provide case data. This may include acquiring some training in legal research and citation formats. Furthermore, a body of theory acceptable and understandable to the legal community should be developed to assist linguists in explaining how they can (or cannot) assist in linguistic analysis in particular cases.

7. Related to standards for interaction in the legal community, forensic linguistics needs a comprehensive code of ethics similar to that used by the International Association for Forensic Phonetics. More communication regarding some of the ethical and moral dilemmas would also contribute to the professionalism and reputation of the field.

8. Although the scope of literature surveyed for this thesis was far from exhaustive, a tone of either triumph or dismay was noted in many of the sources. There is a sense in the literature that the responses of the legal community and rulings of the court either validate or foolishly ignore forensic linguistic attempts to provide suitable evidence and/or testimony. It seems that if FL seeks to move from a relative state of novice to one of professionalism in the legal community, objectivity must manifest itself in the reporting of cases, as well as in the analysis of data.

Although it would be presumptuous to overstate the importance of linguistic analysis in the legal setting or in any particular case, then, it is certain that there is still much room for forensic linguistics to grow. On the other hand, involvement in criminal proceedings should by no means be taken lightly or approached by the linguist without the necessary background and preparedness needed to do the job well. Forensic linguistics has significantly contributed analysis and insight in matters of language evidence to pre-trial investigations and trials, and with improved objectivity and professionalism, should continue to do so, to an even greater extent, in the decades to come.

4 Conclusions

The term "forensic linguistics" is used interchangeably with applied linguistics in legal settings and may evoke various images for the interested listener. One image may be that of a skillful rhetorician engaged in lively courtroom debate, wrapping an eloquent web of words around a rapt jury and winning his case (an image which more accurately may depict the hiring lawyer). On the other hand, the image may be a large question mark betrayed by a look of puzzlement. Although the first image is, as of yet, completely fictitious, the field of forensic linguistics still conjures up notions of language, law and justice with a whole range of possibilities to research and explore.

References

1. Chambers, J.: Forensic dialectology and the Bear Island land claim. In: Rieber, R., Stewart, W. (eds.) The Language scientist as expert in the legal setting: Issues in forensic linguistics, pp. 19–32. The New York Academy of Sciences, New York (1990)
2. Davis, T.: Clues and opinions: Ways of looking at evidence. In: Kniffka, H. (ed.) Recent developments in forensic linguistics, pp. 53–73. Peter Lang, New York (1996)
3. Gibbons, J.: Language and the law. Annual Review of Applied Linguistics 19, 156–173 (1999)
4. Kniffka, H.: Editor's Introduction. In: Kniffka, H. (ed.) Recent developments in forensic linguistics, pp. 21–50. Peter Lang, New York (1996a)
5. Rieber, R., Stewart, W.: The interactions of the language sciences and the law: An introduction to the contributions. In: Rieber, R., Stewart, W. (eds.) The Language scientist as expert in the legal setting: Issues in forensic linguistics, pp. 1–4. New York Academy of Sciences, New York (1990)

The Practice Research of Courseware's "Stereological Construction" under the Information Environment— The Practice Research of <Bilingual Interactive Marketing Courseware> Which Won the National Courseware's First Prize

Yang Hongtao[1], Liu Dongping[1], and Cheng Bo[2]

[1] School of Economics and Management, Harbin Engineering University, China
yhttxt@hotmail.com, sallyfeeling@hotmail.com
[2] Library of Harbin Engineering University, Harbin Engineering University, China
chengbo@hrbeu.edu.cn

Abstract. This paper is based on the National First Prize Courseware— <Bilingual Interactive Marketing Courseware> which is developed by the paper's authors, and aims to explore Courseware's "Stereological Construction" to play its role in teachers' teaching, students' self-taught, usual practices and testing under the direction of its advanced ideas—"student - based" and "research - teaching". The empirical research was conducted by applications of specific teaching which have gained good teaching effects and enormously mobilized students' exploration spirit, creative quality, Interactive concept and team spirit, and achieved three teaching objectives—cognition, ability and emotion.

Keywords: Information environment, Courseware's "Stereological Construction", Three teaching objectives: Student–based, Research-teaching.

1 Introduction

Coursewares are the intuitive teaching medias of student's cognition teaching contents, many teachers regard the courseware as a classroom teaching tool, consequently most of them only pay attention to pursue courseware's technology. However under the information environment the research teaching idea "student – based" has increasingly become a consensus, so it is a problem to be solved that how to follow the conception of the "student –based" research teaching idea to make courseware's stereological educational design, and exerted its function in teachers' teaching, students' self-taught, usual practices and testing.

The seventh "SMART Board" cup national multimedia courseware competition which was held by BJ CIVTE.EDU.CN had represented the trend. This completion which lasted a period of 8 months and appealed 310 schools, 4326 teachers and over 1300 coursewares to enter had the most entries, the most kinds of disciplines, and highest technical content. The courseware developed by the authors of this paper had won the first price of Higher education art groups, and received the comments

S. Lin and X. Huang (Eds.): CSEE 2011, Part V, CCIS 218, pp. 533–538, 2011.

"Advanced Educational Ideas, Special Educational Design, Abundant Educational Recourses and Humanized Operation Interfaces". This paper aims to discuss and research the courseware's "Stereological Construction".

2 Advanced Research Teaching Idea Is the Soul

As a Bilingual teaching courseware, its teaching ides came from the international teaching ideas which the author learned and experience in University of Amsterdam as a visiting scholar. Bilingual interaction cultivation suits for the Chinese students who have the actual marketing practical abilities in school of economics and management. Under the direction of this idea, <Bilingual Interactive Marketing Courseware > set up three teaching objectives: "cognition, ability and emotion", which is to achieve: students' cognition to marketing's theory and practice; promotion of marketing management's practice and planning; sublimation and perfection of marketing team's cooperation, mutual trust and emotions' share.

In order to strengthen college class's bilingual teaching effect and achieve the objectives efficiently, it's not enough to improve courseware technology only. We should launch courseware's stereological construction, which means integrating teaching resources, localizing international authoritative teaching materials, building up interactive lessons websites, developing bilingual CAI courseware systems, optimizing the bilingual teaching methods, strengthening practice teaching, setting up all-round stereological courseware construction, under the premise of setting clear objectives. With applicative educational objectives of economic management talents, aiming to strengthen teaching effect and quality, we set course objectives as cultivating and enhancing students' actual marketing planning application ability. Modern educational ideas (student–based, personalized innovation, teacher-student interaction, double roles incentive mechanism) and varying measures and technologies (consulting teaching style, case teaching method, bilingual teaching, network open resources, students' display platform) are used to perfect, enrich, optimize and integrate the education content during the teaching course.

Under the direction of the educational objectives, the courseware's design concept was completed by all-round construction, application of modern education methods and stimulating students' interest. Making full advantage of network resources, the courseware system (teaching programs, lesson plans, exercises, references catalogue, teaching coursewares and the whole video recording) was open on the internet, which was to realize high-quality teaching and improve the teaching quality to the highest limit.

3 International High-Level Localized Teaching Material Is the Base of Courseware's Content Design

Teaching Contents. The courseware contents are divided into two parts: English teaching courseware which embodies the interactive teaching function and Chinese guided learning courseware which embodies the interactive learning function. Each part consists of four components: 1) Curriculum chapter contents coursewares which promote the cognition of marketing theory and the practice of marketing management; 2) Test system which examine students' control of theoretical knowledge; 3) Students team English presentation system which examines students' ability of promoting the practice of marketing management and planning creativity and sublimates marketing team's cooperation, mutual trust, shares of emotion; 4) Chinese cases courseware system. All of the above make the teaching contents integrate with none knowledge points left.

Choice of Teaching Materials. a) Introduce first class original materials: We introduce American 11th original material <Marketing Management> which was compiled by global authority "Father of the modern marketing"--Philip Kotler[1]; b) Localization of International authority materials: According to native marketing current situation, we integrate 11th <Marketing Management> with <Theory and Practice of Marketing Management >[2] compiled by Wang Changjiang, and form our course's Teaching contents. c) Adding complementary marketing practice application teaching materials: <Marketing System>, <Enterprise Total Marketing>, <Marketing Analysis Form>, < Marketing Planning Analysis>, < Procedure and method of Setting up the Annual Strategic Marketing Plan> etc. practice guidance materials, <Cases Rescores> online, detail reference books, literatures, websites etc., which provide adequate expansion materials; d) Compiling < Marketing Cases Rescores>, prepared for the case education.

To sum up, the 9 chapters English courseware contents according to <Marketing Management> compiled by Philip Kotler contain all of the important teaching program's emphasis; Chinese courseware is the guiding courseware compiled standard and integrated according to < Marketing Management> and < Theory and Practice of Marketing Management>.

4   Coursewares' Teaching Design Should Guarantee the Realization of Advanced Teaching Method

Marketing is the constantly developing Economic & Management course with strong application and practicality under the modern market economy condition. Modern marketing aims to cultivate the marketing planning talents with the characteristic of innovative, personalized and team-work spirits. Only by adopting novel, innovative and flexible teaching method, can marketing achieve the actual effect, which is decided by the nature of the course. Adhering to the "research-teaching" concept of "students-based", the courseware takes teaching form as teachers and students' interaction and students' interaction, using the advanced media of consultation class and cases teaching as the carrier of class teaching organization form.

The Courseware Designing for "Consultation" Class Type. In simple terms, "consultation" class type make economy and management students respectively play the dual role as "marketing consultant" and "marketing staff" based on practical needs. It is the carrier of specific organization class type based on the actual research teaching method through wide communication and the interaction between teachers and students, students, students and experts.

Use of Cases Teaching. It is to say that in the teaching process, massive Chinese and foreign classical marketing cases are introduced to help students complete the leap from the theoretical knowledge to the practice application by team analysis and discussion. "Case area" is set in the main frame of the coursewares, and according to teaching needed three forms of marketing cases—declarative case, graph analytical case and demonstration guidance case are set into "Chinese guiding case area" and English teaching content, which realizes the free calling.

5   The Latest Technology Is Adopted According to the Teaching Purpose, Form and Content

Under the information environment and the quick update of the multimedia technologies the phenomenon even present that partial teachers only pursue the newest technology. According to the characteristic that the <Market>'s content needs renew frequently and courseware's bidirectional interaction, this multimedia courseware has used current popular multimedia manufacture software Director2004 and the latest version of the slide Powerpoint2007, which not only displays the Director's formidable interactive function, but also fully utilizes the PowerPoint's characteristic of simple and convenient to make and modify.

Overall Frame. Director was used to make the 6 parts of the overall frame of the courseware including the film title, the front cover, the guidance, the basic chapter, cases (Presentation) and tests. The film title is composed by Premire and Ulead VideoStudio; the front cover and the guidance are made by Director when the chapter's content and cases by PowerPoint; and the test part is Word document, so students can open the page in the guidance to choose the test content.

Human-computer Interaction. Director's powerful interactive feature allows the courseware to own the two different effects to display the state of the mouse into and out. The guidance of every chapter button is matched with different scales of sound. Books flip effect is imitated when choosing language types.

Call External Documents. The courseware use Director's Lingo programming language to achieve PowerPoint documents' call, so the Director has achieved a seamless connection with PowerPoint.

Font Embedding. Founder big black simplified was embedded in the PowerPoint documentation with the function of the Powerpoint's font embedding, and the cracked software is used to lift the embedded restrictions for founder big black simplified.

6   Artistry of Coursewares Is the Catalyst to Strengthen Students' Acceptability and Interactive Effect

(1) The courseware takes Director to make integrated frame work and guided system, which guide students into the teaching courses compactly, intuitively and vividly, and embody its strong interactivity. Meanwhile, students will hear different

scales of sound when the mouse moves into different chapters, so the students could play simple music in the study, which greatly improves their learning interest.

(2) Chinese part is made through PowerPoint 2007. Instead of using the theme PowerPoint provided, the courseware's background is own designed, each character is a particular color showing different details in premise of maintaining overall style's consistent, which makes every chapter bring out the best in each other.

(3) The courseware uses Director's Powerful interactive function, adopts two effects to represent the mouse's moving and removing, different scales of sound was allocated with different chapters . Books flip effect is imitated when choosing language types, which realizes perfect interactive between students and the courseware.

(4) Based on the teaching theme, the courseware chooses pictures, flashes and videos as occasion requires, playing a role in examining the teaching theme vividly.

(5) PowerPoint 2007's new functions such as Smart Art, enhanced graphs, text effects and theme styles are embodied.

7 Construction of Scientific Interactive Test System Is Research-Teaching Examination Method's Guarantee

Based on research style "Three Teaching Objectives", the course's examination form is changed into guiding students to make marketing team: on-the-spot investigation, composing marketing plan, replying and demonstrating using PPT (60 points), answering to the theory questions at usual, cases analysis, consulting performance, analysis of marketing products etc. (40 points). So the courseware sets up "Theoretical Knowledge Contest Module", "Cased Analysis Module", "Marketing Product Display Module" and "Replying and Demonstrating Module" etc., and makes full advantages of network open teaching: Building up university elaborate courses <Marketing> interactive course site, posting teaching resources such as outline, contents, coursewares, cases, students interactive resources etc. on the Internet.

8 Attention to Intellectual Property and Realize the Sustainable Development

Bilingual teaching content should gear to international conventions, intellectual property rights awareness should also gear to international conventions. By the integration of the actual localization development characteristics, lots of graphic data and materials must be quoted. To pursue the sustainable development of courseware's "Stereological Construction", we must emphasize the protection of independent R&D and respect others' achievements.

By the <Bilingual Interactive Marketing Courseware>'s "Stereological Construction", we reach and guarantee the flexible application of these various research-teaching ideas and methods above mentioned, which riches classroom teaching content, enhances teaching's interesting and vitality, strengthens students' ability of solving problems, arouses students' potential, strengthen the effect of knowledge points' absorption, achieve our teaching objectives cognition, ability and emotion, appeals to the experts and students.

Acknowledgement. Financed by National Social Science Fund (11CSH039); National Natural Science Fund (70972096,70872024); Heilongjiang Province Soft Science Key Project (GB05D101-3); Heilongjiang Province Industry and Informationization committee Soft science Project (GXW20100190); Heilongjiang Province Top Youth Academic Teacher Support Project (1251G016); Heilongjiang Province Higher Education Reform Project; Central University Basic Research Fund (HEUCF100923, 101608).

References

[1] Kotler, P.: Marketing Management. Tsinghua University Press, Beijing (2007)
[2] Changjiang, W.: Theory and Practice of Marketing. Beijing Industrial University Press, Beijing (2004)

Readability Assessment and Comparison of Chinese and American College EFL Reading Textbooks Based on Information Analysis

Haiyan Li

School of Foreign Languages, North China Electric Power University, Beijing, China
lihaiyan@ncepu.edu.cn

Abstract. The focus of the study is on the assessment of readability for prevailing America and Chinese English textbooks with the measurement software and systems. The result indicated college reading textbooks produced by Chinese publishers seemed to vary in level, with some texts above the reading ability of most college students. Then simplification strategies used to make Chinese EFL reading texts more accessible are compared to those used in American reading texts. The substantial findings for the study are of great value to English textbook compilation and English language teaching.

Keywords: Readability, Readability assessment, Simplification strategies.

1 Research Background

Readability, an important concept of applied linguistics, in Longman Dictionary of Language Teaching & Applied Linguistics is defined as how easily written materials can be read and understood. Readability depends on many factors, including: the average length of sentences in a passage, the number of new words a passage contains, and the grammatical complexity of the language used [1].

With the development of computer technology, more and more researchers strive to integrate readability study with computer science. In the United States, Flesch ease is commonly used in publishing companies to define what the supposed readers of a book are. Readability formulas are also used for compiling text books in education. In China, some scholars also have recognized the practical application of readability formulas, and even developed several softwares to examine readability. For example, Lin Zheng [2] has developed ERDA (English Readability & Difficulty Assessment) based on Dale-Chall readability formula and FOG readability formula, to respectively examine reading materials for middle school students and college students. Gu Xiangdong and Guan Xiaoxian [3] have compared the readability indices of reading materials in CET-4 and CET-6 with college English reading textbooks, and pointed the indication for the compilation of text books. However, there is not enough study comparing prevailing America and Chinese English textbooks via the assessment of readability, and this study tries to take a crack at this aspect and establish the difficulty level of these texts so that the data could be utilized in future studies to highlight the gap which may exist between student reading ability and the level of the

S. Lin and X. Huang (Eds.): CSEE 2011, Part V, CCIS 218, pp. 539–542, 2011.

materials being used to teach them. To this end, three main research questions were posed: 1). what is the reading difficulty of Chinese college EFL reading texts? 2). how does it compare with that of mainstream American university and graduate school texts? 3). what simplification strategies are used to make Chinese EFL reading texts more accessible? Are these strategies similar to those used in reading texts produced by mainstream US publishers?

2 Methodology

Research tools here are mainly readability measurement software and on-line readability measurement systems. In this research, Flesch 2.0 and Microsoft Word are used. For the other two readability formulas, there are websites which can check readability with ordinary formulas as one chooses on line, thus the data calculated by SMOG and Coleman-Liau Index is obtained from different websites, which are all designed specially for people to check English readability.

The texts were chosen from the prevailing college English textbooks in China, namely, 21st Century Practical College English (henceforth 21st Century), New College English (henceforth NCE), New Horizon College English (henceforth NHCE), and three American college-level textbooks. After the texts were chosen, four chapters from each book was selected at random, and typed into the Microsoft Word Processing Program. Then, 24 of the texts (12 Chinese university-level EFL reading texts and 12 foreign ESL reading texts) were reviewed one by one and classified according to the predominant simplification strategy used to assist the reader with difficult words and phrases.

3 Results

What is the reading difficulty of Chinese college EFL reading texts? As can be seen from the results in Table, the range of readability indexes is quite large. For example, the average Flesch-Kincaid Grade Level of individual book ranged from a low of 5.2 for The NHCE to a high of 11.84 for The NCE. This means that, at least according to the Flesch reading ease, the difficulty of college level EFL reading material produced by Chinese publishers varies several full academic years. The Coleman-Liau Grade Scale and the SMOG also showed similarly large high-low differences of 9.34 and 6.0 grade levels, respectively.

The statistic for average words per sentence also follows this trend that there is a large range for individual book from a low of 8.47 in The NHCE, to a high of 14.69 words per sentence in NCE. Despite being promoted as "university level reading texts" in the catalogs put out by the Chinese publishing companies, it seems clear that the authors and editors of the titles surveyed here had different ideas about what level reading material university students are capable of dealing with.

What simplification strategies are used to make Chinese EFL reading texts more accessible? Are these strategies similar to those used in reading texts produced by mainstream US publishers? Chinese EFL reading texts tend to deal with problematic vocabulary and grammar by relying on unmarked glosses at the end of the passage or

Table 1. Readability Statistics for American and Chinese EFL Reading Textbooks

Average	NHCE	21st Century	NCE	American SEL Textbooks
Words	678	749	950	1181
Words/sentences	8.47	9.42	14.69	19.87
Sentences/paragraph	3.64	3.31	2.6	2.33
Paragraphs	22	13	25	29
Passive sentences	1.25%	7.93%	15.78%	27.69%
Flesch reading ease	95.59	52.94	88.56	50.07
Flesch-Kincaid Grade Level	5.2	7.8	11.84	10.63
Coleman-Liau Grade Scale	3.37	4.59	12.71	15.28
SMOG	6.5	5.10	12.5	11.05

the end of the book. In this case, "unmarked" means that there is no indication in the text itself as to which words and phrases are explained in the gloss. In contrast, books produced by American publishers tended to rely almost exclusively on marked glosses. Clear difference between the two groups of books was the way they handled the teaching of difficult vocabulary. All of the books produced by American publishers employed pre-reading and/or post-reading vocabulary activities. Of these 12 books, pre-reading activities were more prevalent, appearing more than twice as many times as post-reading activities. Interestingly, not one of the twelve Chinese textbooks surveyed employed pre -reading vocabulary activities of any kind.

4 Discussion

What are the implications of these results for reading students and teachers in Chinese? The 3 readability indexes used in this study indicate that the average reading level of the three Chinese college reading textbooks used in this study is about the same as reading materials which typically would be used by native speakers in the ninth or tenth grade. This gap between the reading ability of most university students and the difficulty of the reading materials they typically encounter in the classroom may explain the oft-cited tendency of Chinese students to over rely on dictionaries while reading English texts.

The difficulty level of ESL texts produced by American and British publishers, on the other hand, seems to be decided by fairly clear criteria. For example, the Oxford Bookworm series of ESL readers (Oxford University Press, 1995), classifies each reader according to the specific number of headwords used in the text. Another factor which may contribute to the reading difficulty of the Chinese university-level texts is their general approach to assisting readers with difficult vocabulary. Whereas 10 of the 12 books produced in America marked the difficult words in the texts and provided definitions either at the end of the passage or at the end of the book, only one of the books produced by the Chinese publishers marked difficult words.

Furthermore, none of the Chinese texts provided pre-reading vocabulary activities, whereas almost all of the foreign texts did so. It is possible that some of these differences may be due to the effect which SLA research can sometimes have on commercially produced materials in the US. For example, researchers such as Carrell [4], point to the well established high correlation between knowledge of word meanings and the ability to comprehend passages containing those words. Nation [5] too, believes pre-teaching vocabulary and glossing to be useful activities when the emphasis is on helping students to improve their overall reading ability. Although few findings in our field are undisputed, the ones cited here do seem to justify the approaches taken by the US publishers.

5 Conclusion

The first main trend noticed was that college reading textbooks produced by Chinese publishers seem to vary in level, with some texts above the reading ability of most college students. To ensure the validity of the indexes used in this study, future studies could be done to establish the reading ability of the students and contrast this with the difficulty of the materials they typically encounter in class. Moreover, the readability statistics results can be compared with an independent assessment of reading difficulty by a panel of reading experts, and then establish a high inter-rater reliability. Other possibility might have been to add some other, non-formulaic methods of establishing passage difficulty such as cloze tests.

The second major trend was the clearly different approach to simplification which Chinese and American publishers took in their respective reading texts. Here, it might be valuable to do a study which surveys far more titles than were reviewed in this study, and then makes an attempt to control for the various types of reading texts.

Despite the limitations of this study it seems clear that many college students are required to learn from reading texts beyond their reading ability. Although there is very little that can be done to directly encourage changes in the way English is taught, it is hoped that the findings in this study could be the basis for future studies which might ultimately have a positive influence on the choices EFL reading teachers in Chinese make with regard to the texts they use in class.

References

1. Richard, J., Platt, J., Weber, H.: Longman dictionary of language Teaching& Applied Linguistics. Longman Group Limited, Essex (1985)
2. Zheng, L.: Measurement of readability. Foreign Language Teaching and Research (4), 38–42 (1995)
3. Yunfang, Q., Qunchan, G.: Survey of Readability of College English Textbooks. Journal of Zhejiang Normal University (Social Science Edition (3), 115–118 (1999)
4. Carrell, P.: Interactive text processing. In: Carrel, P., Devine, J., Eskey, D. (eds.) Interactive approaches to second language reading. Cambridge University Press, Cambridge (1988)
5. Nation, P., Kyongho, H.: Where would general service vocabulary stop and special purposes vocabulary begin System 23, 33–41 (1995)

The Application of Caching Technology in Food-Safety Tracing System

YingJie Liao, Jia Chen, and ZheQiong Yan

Transportation Management Institute, Dalian Maritime University, Liaoning, China
liaoyingjiezhhn@126.com

Abstract. Cache is a technology that is widely used in database system. By obtaining some data from the server and storing them in the client, we can decrease the frequency to access central database, reduce the pressure of the server, improve the client's speed of response and query efficiency. This article takes food-safety tracing system as the application background, puts forward a cache management mechanism from two aspects of prefetching mechanism and cache replacement strategy, thus the operation efficiency of the system can be improved.

Keywords: cache technology, data prefetching, cache replacement.

1 Introduction

The traditional Web access mode makes it hard for server to cope with thousands of client data requests and the client have to spend a long time waiting for the feedback of the server. This is a huge challenge to both the server performance and the network stability, so it often makes the response time of the inquires very long and efficiency low.

Caching technology is one of classical technologies of the database. By storing part of data from the database server in the client, it can decrease the frequency of client access database server and reduce the level of data processing, so as to shorten the response time of system[1].

2 Advancing Question

Food-safety tracing system is designed to enhance safety of food management. After purchased, customers can search the detailed parameters and circulation information of the food by the code on the shopping ticket(i.e. Tracing Code). If there is a quality problem, customers can quickly find out the distribution of batch foods sold by these traceability information, and recalled these problem foods in time, thus reduce potential harmfulness. The meaning of "Tracing" can be shown in Fig. 1.

From Fig. 1, we can see the whole process that foods are delivered from producers to customers.

In all phases of the foods' circulation, all information is preserved and uploaded to the uniform search platform (i.e. the central database). In different circulation, foods

S. Lin and X. Huang (Eds.): CSEE 2011, Part V, CCIS 218, pp. 543–547, 2011.

are endowed with different Circulation Tracing Code, which makes the query be traced back to specific areas and locate the relevant responsible person. At the same time, the same source of the batch foods are endowed with the same Source Tracing Code, which is associated with the foods since it has been created by the producer, so it is convenient for us to position to the same batch of foods.

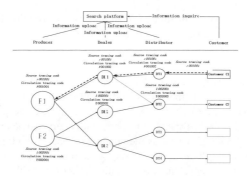

Fig. 1. Food tracing schemes

In Fig. 1, information of each code will be uploaded to the central database, all the query terminal can directly get tracing information stored in the central database via the Internet. However, if we put all the query request to the central server, obviously its efficiency will be very low, especially when there are a large number of query terminals. To solve this problem, we can consider the cache technology. Some commonly used data can be stored in query terminal in advance. When customer put forward queries, the system will lookup it in the local cache firstly, if succeed, the results can be immediately presented to the customer, if not, then access the server again, download the relevant data from the server. At the same time of returning the result to the customer, the data would be added into the local cache, so as to ensure the hit rate of follow-up query. In fact, if the cache is designed well, we can make the cache hit rate remain at a high level, so that it can significantly reduce the query time, and improve the availability of the system.

3   The Cache Management Mechanism in Food-Safety Tracing System

3.1   The Design of the Data Structure of Cache

To realize cache technology, the data structure of the cache must be designed first. Item[1...n] is marked as n data records in query terminal cache, the form of cache data is (X,Data(X),T,P). X is the identity of data record, Data(X) is the value of X, T is the timestamp of data, and P is the priority of data.

When a record was downloaded from the server and deposited in the client cache, its priority is set to 0, once one record are used by native query terminal, its priority increase gradually(recently visited record is likely to continue to be accessed).

Timestamp T keeps the time record was accessed, its initial value is set to the time the record entered the cache, when one record was used , the value of T would be replaced by current system time.

3.2   The Prefetch Strategy of Cache

Data prefetching means to take certain measures to obtain some data from the server in advance and store them in the memory of query terminal, so as to resolve the problem that inquires cannot hit the cache in the first few times, hence the availability of cache could be improved.

In the food-safety tracing system, the same source and the same batch of foods are endowed with the same Source Tracing Code, when any of them was sold in any supermarket, the others can be searched out by this code, just as Fig. 2 shows below:

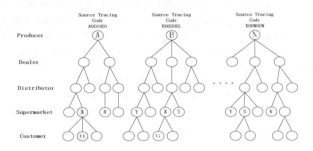

Fig. 2. Information tree of food circulation

Fig. 2 can be viewed as "data snapshot" of Fig. 1 on a particular point. The circulation process of a batch of foods, from producer through dealers and distributors and finally reach the hands of customers, can be represented by tree structure in Fig. 2. Because the same source and same batch of foods are endowed with the same Source Tracing Code, so the producer can be viewed as the root node of the tree, those dealers or distributors are branch nodes, and the vast number of customers are this tree's leaf nodes. With the same code, wherever these goods stay, reaching dealers or distributors, because they belong to the same "Information tree", they can be traced by the Source Tracing Code. The design of query code is very critical to get query results, it is required to be able to get the Source Tracing Code according to the query code, therefore the query code was designed as follow: supermarket code +commodity batch code +commodity code. When a customer submits a query to server in a query terminal, server first get to know which the supermarket this terminal belongs to, then server query database to get recent commodities sales records of this supermarket according to the supermarket code and commodity code, and get the Source Tracing Code of these foods, then query the "circulation information tree" of them, finally download these data to the query terminal and saved them to the cache.

In the tree A of Fig. 2, when customer C1 put forward query to the server, the server would get the sales records of supermarket X in the recent period of time, according to the records found that X recently sold two batches of foods, their Source

Tracing Codes are A001001 and B002002, so download these "information trees" to the cache of query terminal in Supermarket X. Thus when customer C2 puts forward query in the terminal of X, he can get the results from the cache immediately, then the query time can be saved.

3.3   The Replacement Strategy of Cache

In order to ensure the data in the cache is always useful, cache replacement strategy must be used. Through the cache replacement strategy, Outdated and not commonly used data should be replaced, so as to make cache have a higher hit rate and shorter response time. Therefore, the cache replacement strategy is crucial to cache management mechanism.

There is a cache replacement strategy called DP-LRU(dynamic priority-least recently used), It sets priority for cache data, and combined with timestamp to resolve the problem of cache replacement[2]. In food-safety tracing system, we designed priority and timestamp two attributes for cache data, if we want to replace cache data, we should consider both the priority of the data and its timestamp. First, examine the priority of data records, according to the different priority, data in cache will be organized in different queues, as shown in Fig. 3, the cache data was divided into m queues. At the same time, within each queue the data will be ordered by its timestamp, the small one(the longest not being used) will be ranked at the head , and the bigger one(recently used) will be ranked at the end. Fig. 3 shows the organization framework of cache data:

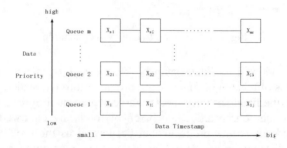

Fig. 3. The organization framework of cache data

When the data in cache need to be replaced, the first to consider is the queue with lowest priority, and within this queue, the data with minimum timestamp(i.e. longest not being used) should be replaced first. Some marks and functions are defined as follows,

TM: Query Terminal.
Min(D):Compare the priority of all cache data, and returned the smallest one.
Get_PRI(X):return the priority of the data X.
Get_T(X):return the timestamp of the data X.
Replace[1…n]:A queue to place the data that will be replaced.
PLRU[1…n]: A queue to place the priority of the data.
The cache data replacement process can be expressed by function Data_Exchange().
Data_Exchange():

```
1  J←1
2  Pi←Min(D)
3  FOR EACH TM.Item[i] In TM.Item[1…n] DO
4     PLRU[i]←Get_PRI(TM.Item[i])
5     IF Pi= PLRU[i] THEN
6        Replace[J]←TM.Item[i]
7        J←J+1
8     END IF
9  END FOR
10 FOR EACH Replace[k] in Replace[1…n] DO
11    IF( ∃k)(Get_T(Replace[1])>Get_T(Replace[k])) THEN
12       V←Replace[1]
13       Replace[1]←Replace[k]
14       Replace[k]←V
15    END IF
16 END FOR
17 Free(Replace[1])
```

By this function, the system can find out the data with lowest priority and minimum timestamp and replace it. 3-9 lines use function Get_PRI() to find out the record with lowest priority, and put it into the queue Replace[], 10-16 lines use function Get_T() to find out the record with minimum timestamp from the queue Replace[], and exchange it to the head of the queue, line 17 release the storage space of the first record in queue Replace[].

4 Summary

Cache technology was applied in the food-safety tracing system, which is popular in mobile database system, those "information trees" that were queried frequently should be prefetched and saved to the cache of query terminal. By DP-LRU strategy, which is a replacement strategy designed by using priority and timestamp two attributes, it can weed out those records with lowest priority and minimum timestamp, so that the cache is always effective and have a high access rate.

In short, the cache technology can ensure the cache data in terminal is always useful and have a high access rate, enhance the query efficiency, reduce the pressure of the central server, and significantly improve the operating efficiency and availability of the food-safety tracing system.

References

1. Liu, Y., Cheng, J.: Research on cache management strategy of mobile database technology. Information Technology Institute, Zhe Jiang ShuRen University (2010)
2. Wu, W.: Research and application of cache management in client of mobile database. ChongQing University (2005)

Design and Implementation of Configuration File Automatically Generated

Minggang Wang, Jia Chen, and Yingjie Liao

Transportation Management College, Dalian Maritime University, Dalian, China
wmg267003851@126.com,
chen_jia8008@sina.com, liaoyingjiezhhn@126.com

Abstract. The current system is usually based on three-tier, in order to achieve "high cohesion, low coupling" with modify and expand easily. The ground floor of three-tier is data access layer, in order to achieve low coupling with the upper and convenient access to the database, This paper proposes an implementation mechanism writing the database access information into configuration file, and using a database definition reader to generate the configuration file app.config automatically, while the reader is also implementing the table definition automatically. When the database design changes, or needs to be modified due to require of application, it is very convenient to adjust this require and achieve data access layer and the upper decoupling with this mechanism.

Keywords: configuration file, three-tier architecture, file parsing.

1 Problem Proposed

User configuration file is a collection of environment to load of settings and files when user logs on the computer, or users in the use of software. In the system development process, the use of architecture simplifies the development process, to focus on business rather than technology, architecture can accelerate the development, reduce duplication of development, regular testing, and debate on the technical details, allows output to be expected, behavior control.

Three-tier contains user interface, business logic layer, data access layer, the purpose of different levels is to "high cohesion, low coupling" principle. In order to achieve the independence development of the data access layer, reuse, and decoupling, the data access layer must have a high applicability, it often operates on the database, if the database changes, you need to rewrite the code, this is unreasonable in the real development, therefore, we must process relevant database access information which will change alone, using the configuration file can resolve the issue. In order to facilitate changes to the database access information in the case of unchanged the code, we put some basic information associated with the database access into the configuration file, each time run the system to read the database access information from the configuration file. It is more convenient and flexible when need to change the database access information.

S. Lin and X. Huang (Eds.): CSEE 2011, Part V, CCIS 218, pp. 548–553, 2011.

Configuration file is XML format ,contains the basic information about database tables, in general, the database contains multiple tables, each table contains multiple fields, in the development process, as demand changes, need to constantly adjust the structure of the database. In the system operation and maintenance process, it also needs to adjust the data structure; this will affect the configuration file. But writing configuration file with hands will cost lots of time, make more errors, and disperse the energy of programmers to handle the business logic. Therefore, this paper proposes an automatic generator of configuration file, it can automatically generate the configuration file, implement the automatic generation of table definition and make it more easily to input tables definition into app.config file, so that decouple data access layer and business logic layer.

2 Structural Design of Configuration File

In order to describe the implement and the function of automatically generator of configuration file more clearly, the paper will explain the detail of design and implementation of configuration file first briefly.

3 Design Ideas of Configuration File

Inversion of control (IOC) is an important principle of object-oriented programming to reduce the coupling of computer programs. Inversion of control also have a name called dependency injection (DI).

By IOC model coupling problem can be solved, it moved the coupling out from the code, into a unified XML file. The dependency will be built by a container when needed, in other words, put the interface that is required into the need for its class, this is the source of "dependency injection" claim.

IOC mode, the system can manage the life cycle and dependency of object by IOC container, through the introduction of IOC container which achieved model IOC, making the application configuration and dependency specification separate from the actual application code.

One of the characteristics is through the parts of a text file for configurations interactions between application components, without having to re-edit and compile a specific code.

Using inversion of control method, preparation of the configuration file, can be an effective solution about must modify the code when the database access information modify problem, solve the coupling problem.

4 Design of Configuration File

Configuration file is to facilitate the operation of the database system, The operation of the database is the operation of basic table in substance , so configuration file should contains the messages of basic table, the messages of basic table include: table name(English),field name(Chinese, English),data type(.NET type and DB type),data length, whether primary key. In order to locate each field conveniently, the configuration file plus a display sequence number extra, in addition, separating them with commas, so that the information can be parsed from file accurately.

Based on the above, design solution as follows, each node is some basic information about table:

<add key="Tabled_[TABLENAME]" value="×××" />
TABLENAME: table name
×××:According to the order:

Field English name, field Chinese name,.NET typed type, length, whether primary key, whether foreign key,[;]. By key value, the string TableDef_, read table name ,by';' split field of each table, for information on each field using ',' split, using table-driven method, read the field information, in this way the configuration file to achieve the functions.

5 Configuration File Generator Architecture

With the configuration file design, continue to introduce architecture of configuration file automatic generator. The generator is based on the three-tier, this can make the system more convenient to modify and achieve the purpose of decoupling with actual needs of the system.

6 Three-Tier Architecture

The common sense of the three-tier is to divide the entire business application into: User Interface (UI), Business Logic Layer (BLL), and Data Access Layer (DAL) .The purpose of distinguished levels is "high cohesion, low coupling" thinking.

User Interface: the interface presented to the user, what the user see when using a system.

Business Logic Layer: For specific action, also can be said that the operation to the data layer, business logic processing for data.

Data Access Layer: The transaction done in this layer directly with the database, for the data to add, delete, modify, update, search and so on.

In the software architecture, hierarchical structure is the most common and the most important structure, Microsoft recommends the layered structure which is generally divided into three layers, respectively, from the bottom: Data Access Layer, Business Logic Layer, and User Interface.

7 Structure of the Configuration File Generator Description

In order to describe the system three-tier structure clearly, the class diagram is shown in Fig 1.

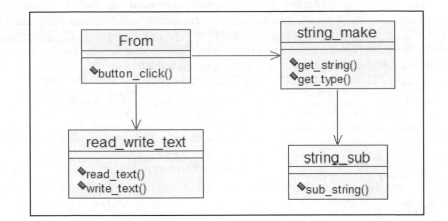

Fig. 1. Class diagram

Form class is the User Interface of three-tier structure, the intuitive system for users, there are small amount of code, mainly about design of display style and event triggers. It doesn't care about business logic and data access processing, thus, achieves separation of the code, which also divide the labor.

Read_write_text class is the Data Access Layer of three-tier structure. The main task is completing the file operations of reading and writing, not involving business logic processing.

String_make class and string_sub class, Business Logic Layer of three-tier structure, is the core of the system implementation. They are in charge of anglicizing and processing of files, and ultimately generating a document to meet the requirements. String_sub class is an encapsulation of common method of the layer, it can reduce repeat code, conveniently to use and modify, while increasing the reuse rate of the code, convenience for the future Software development, reducing development time.

8   Realization of the Function of the Configuration File Generator

Content and functional requirements for system implementation

In short, the db.era file (plain text file) will be parsed to the app.config file as required. db.era file is a report file on the database table generated by Erwin.

It parses the resulting files, and then generates the app.config file to meet the requirements. Each line of the file contains relevant information required to be listed of a table.

Table1 shows what the contents need to be parsed:

Table 1. Table Functional requirements

Db.era	App.config
Table name (English)	TableDef_***
Field name (Chinese, English)	Field name, Field title
Data type	.NET type and DB type
Data length	Data length, As well as a reference data type
If PK	Whether PK
If FK	Is associated with other database tables to display the description text
	Display order number

9 System Implementation

Overall, the implementation of the system is to transfer db.era file format. That is to say, change db.era file into a configuration file that system can be parsed, the configuration file format must be fixed, that is, the above-mentioned configuration file format, so that the system can be successfully resolved, the changes in this file format is actually an analytical processing of a string, so the question focuses on the processing of the string.

There must be some connection between before and after the file changes, A configuration file that corresponds to the db.era file is fixed, therefore, only to find the link between the two documents, then follow this link, certain processing a string, the problem can be solved.

10 Related Applications and Wrapper Class Implementation

The file read-write technology, which achieved the basic read and write capabilities of the file.

String Processing, include the string replacing (Replace Method), matching (StringBuilder method), splitting (Spilt method), intercepting (Substring method) and other methods. Using the above method to parse the file is the most basic technology application of the systems, and also the key to the system.

table-driven method, resolve judgments of NET types and DB types by this method. When need to add the data type without taking into account, you can easily add, very conveniently process.

The wrapper is one of the most characteristics of Object-oriented development thinking, using wrapper idea can reduce the duplication of code, conveniently use and modify, While improve the code reuse rate. It is convenience for the future software development by reducing development time.

11 Conclusion

Configuration file generator decouples the data access layer and business logic layer by shortening the manual time, reducing the error rate of access database. Three-tier framework stresses on the developing task. So that, programmer can focus more on business logic layer; while, when a layer changed, what we only need to do is making a small change to other layers, in other words, Three-tier framework reduces dependence on different layers. But on the other hand, the framework reduces the system performance.

In the software development, the three-tier application is the most common, table-driven method, a variety of string processing method and other methods to read the application document are also very common. File parsing function has applied widely in real system, then how to use the above methods in the system flexibility and reasonability is a issue. Based on the analysis of known files, this paper realizes the function of configuration files automatic gene rationed explains how to process files under the three-tier structure and uses some methods reasonable within the system.

References

[1] http://baike.baidu.com/view/1486379.htm
[2] Duan, S.: Discussion software development on the three-tier, Software Engineering. Tongji University (2010)

Main Factors Influencing College Student Health and Countermeasures Proposal in Network Environment— From Physical Health Education Perspective

Dinghong Mu[1], Wujin Hu[2], and Jinhai Hu[3]

East China University of Technology, Faculty of Physical Education,
330013 Nanchang Jiangxi Province, China
dhmu1970@sina.com

Abstract. This dissertation adopts document-data method, comparative analysis method and Inductive deductive method to analyze main factors influencing college students' physical and mental health from physical health education perspective. It elaborates the significance of physical health education and put up "health first" guideline for promoting health knowledge and cultivate sports skills, creating favorable conditions for physical health education implementation and switching college physical education focus to reform colleges and universities physical education assessment system.

Keywords: college students, health education, factors, sports, strategy.

1 Introduction

College students with long-term overload study and work tend to have central nervous tension, if they do not pay enough attention to psychological adjustment and physical exercise, will result in increased sympathetic activity, endocrine disorders and lead to physical or mental illnesses, which may ultimately reduce learning efficiency and advance caducity. The survey found that the fundamental reason which these students placed less emphasis on health and the whole community lost bearings on youngsters physique level lies in poor health knowledge. Under this circumstance, the Ministry of Education raises the importance of physical health awareness, proposes the "health first" guiding ideology, explores various ways to achieve scientific teaching objectives, increases school sports investment, strengthens the school health education and implements "School Sports Work", "School Health Work" guidance.

2 Health Status of College Students

The 5th National Student Health Survey 2005 showed: 19 ~ 22-year-old, Han nationality, urban male, urban female, rural male, rural female, vital capacity decreased 160 ml, 238 ml, 161 ml, 225 ml respectively, 50-meter race averagely decreased by 0.1 seconds, 0.3 seconds, 0.1 seconds, 0.3 seconds, standing long jump decreased by 3.6 cm, 3.7 cm, 4 cm, 5.2 cm respectively, male chin-up (1 minute sit-

S. Lin and X. Huang (Eds.): CSEE 2011, Part V, CCIS 218, pp. 554–558, 2011.

ups girls) were decreased by 1.5 times, 1.5 times / min, 1.3 times, 2.1 times / min in average, 800 meter race results decreased 10.3 seconds, 12.6 seconds, 9.2 seconds, 9.8 seconds, respectively; overweight and obesity increased 4.61% and 2.63%, which increase 1.2 and 0.4 respectively than in 2000. 82.68% detection rate of poor vision (among which urban was 82.43%, rural 82.95%), which increased by 1.1 % compared to 2000. So we can see even with the rapid development of China's economy, living and medical standards improvement, but many students do not get enough understanding to living quality, their endurance, speed, power and strength further decline, the trend of overweight and obesity detectable rate increase, the high detection rate of poor eyesight and other issues are troubling.

3   Main Factors Influencing College Student Health

Factors of Behavior and Living Style. The so-called behavior and lifestyle factors refer to people's bad behavior and life style which may cause direct or indirect harm to individuals, groups and society's health, and it has potential, cumulative and widespread influence to collectivity. Unhealthy behavior and lifestyle are one of major factors lead to college students health problems such as unhealthy eating lifestyle of smoking, alcohol, overeating, excessive intake of fat, sugar, unhealthy leisure style of unrestrained entertainment, stay up late, lack of sleep, long time watching TV, computer game addiction, unhealthy sport style of lack of exercise or excessive exercise, unhealthy emotional life of contradictory feelings of parents, parents spoil their children and indifference with others, unhealthy psychological activities of self-centered, loneliness, depression, jealousy, selfishness, utilitarianism, materialism, and other unhealthy way to make friends, all of which result in function degradation, low resistance and sub-health generation and spread. Some scholars report that among China's top 10 causes of death diseases, bad behavior and lifestyle factors account for 44.7%.

Environment Factors. Environmental factors refer to outside world of human subject, including natural and social environmental factors, hard factors like material conditions, and soft environment factors like policies, cultural, institutional, legal, ideology and other external conditions. Natural environment is an ecosystem and material basis of human survival. Nowadays, human survival environment has been seriously polluted in rapid modernization development, which will inevitably lead to harm to human health. China has been listed as the world's 13th most water-scarce countries, more than 90% of urban water pollution;4$ skin cancer increase because of Freon destruction to ozone; widespread with toxic heavy metals such as lead, " Technology Food " overflow, pollution, uncontrolled mining and killing of species, all these pollutions together forms chemicals with estrogen features which seriously affects human survival and life quality, in particular cause serious damage to children and young people intellectual development and health.

Social environment includes political, economic, cultural, education and many other factors, which s directly or indirectly affect students' health status. The bidirectional link of health and social development has been proved in many countries and regions. With the development of science and technologies, accelerated pace of social life and employment system reform, people feel pressure from various aspects, in particular, the pressure of complex pressures from professional courses, employment pressures from the contradiction between college enrollment increase and limited employment opportunities, economic pressures from excessive consumption environment, psychological pressure of parents high expectations on children, social responsibility and peer comparisons, These pressures will increase a sense of urgency and anxiety, and if they cannot be resolved appropriately and timely, will lead to serious consequences, but students who just left their homes are hard to resolve psychological anxiety and tension and may cause serious mental illness because they are lack of a more comprehensive guidance. In addition, most college students are the only child in the family, their education is liberal, lack self-discipline and frustration tolerance, low group consciousness, and pay more emphasis on personal development rather than on collaboration, so this kind of psychological state will be hit in their socialization process with the subtle influence of pornography, gambling and other social negative phenomena, which will not only cause students physical, psychological trauma, but also go astray and lead into a life of crime.

Biological Factors. Biological factors are pathogenic microorganisms apart from age, gender and other individual characteristics. Students are living in group and vulnerable to infectious diseases and epidemic. With the abuse of antibiotics and other drugs, part of infectious virus produces a significant resistance to environmental change, some unknown viruses (such as HIV, Ebola, Lassa and Marburg) appear in the tropical rain forest and subtropical grassland regions, a number of viruses have gene mutation (such as the SARS virus), some old diseases resurges (such as cholera, yellow fever, diphtheria and tuberculosis, etc.), which pose a serious threat on human health.

Health Care Factors. Health care refers to a planned and purposive process of health agencies and professionals taking use of health resources and a variety of means to prevent disease, improve health and provide individuals, groups and community service activities in nasopharyngeal carcinoma. Colleges and universities healthcare institutions are not perfect variously, service network incomplete, capital investment insufficient, allocation of health care resources irrational, health care workers not high specialized and many other problems, these factors also have some influence on college students' health.

Individual Health Acknowledge Factor. College students comes in the best physical condition period, they usually have a weak disease acknowledgement, and pay less attention to physical exercise and self-care knowledge accumulation. Students are often lack of self-discipline and unknowingly harm their own bodies. They always consider that no apparent disease is healthy, or even unwilling to see the doctor when they are really sick, which often delaying the best time for treatment.

Countermeasures from Science of Physical Cultural and Sports to Improve College Student Physical Conditions. Many studies confirm that sports have a significant influence on college students' bad behavior intervention, pressures easement, virus resistance enhancement and social negative phenomena erosion reduction. Based on existing research results, the following propose strategies to improve college student health conditions from Science of Physical Cultural and Sports perspective.

Set Correct Guiding Ideology of "health first". "Health First" means that health is the foundation of all educations, sports should be given priority to intellectual, this does not mean that education and learning are not as important as health, but education and learning should be on the basis of health. Establish "health first" guiding principle is to require all schools take student health as start and end-result for education and teaching and take the responsibility of caring student health. Of course, college sports and physical education are duty-bound to take care of student health, and are able to perform their part. In other words, school sports not only teach students scientific exercise methods, but more importantly cultivate student with awareness of physical exercise, habits, and self-training ability to make their own physical exercise schedule based on physical situations, choose training contents and methods, and scientifically arrange exercise amount and level, give right workout evaluation and make necessary medical supervision. Fully understand the guidance ideology background and essence of" health first in school education, take effective steps to strengthen physical education" proposed by the CPC Central Committee and State Council's, actively promote healthy concept of "exercise 1 hour a day, healthy working for 50 years and happy for life", enhance physical and health education curriculum reform, and effectively develop sports and health education function to guide students establishing correct health concepts.

Strengthen Health Knowledge Teaching and Cultivate Sports Skills. Study found that college students' health issue is outstanding, and the fundamental reason is seriously lack of rational cognition on health problems. Therefore, to enhance students health and hygiene education should be a prerequisite for health problem intervention, college students without a knowledge of health and hygiene and their own health status, even if involved in physical exercise, are also blind followers and difficult to have a lasting relatively stable interest, which cannot form into a lifelong habit. Sport skills are foundation to ensure university students with a lasting interest in physical education and health, only emphasizing health and interests cannot form lifelong physical habits without sports skills. Guide students to master certain physical health knowledge, learn 1 or 2 athletic skills, and take use of physical methods are basis to solve college students' health problems.

Create Conditions Conducive to Physical and Health Education. The implementation of Physical Health Education requires competent Physical and Health Education teachers, impeccable equipment and facilities and strong sports culture. Highly qualified faculty is the prerequisite for implementation of physical and health education, teacher's knowledge structure has to switch from "three basic educations" to "healthy education ".Perfect venue, equipment and facilities are the fundamental guarantee of fitness education, increase venue and equipment properly, take reasonable use of existing site and equipments, transform no applicable or idle equipments are all main improvement methods. Cultivate a good Physical health culture by organizing various sports activities, establish health information sites, sports and cultural corridor, poster, radio and other forms of health knowledge can get students' attention to health knowledge and personal health concerns, which may significantly improves health education effect.

Switch College Sports Focus. Colleges and universities must have physical education curriculum at the first and second grade (four semesters with total 144 hours), 18 weeks per semester, one course per week and 2 hours per class. Such curriculum density does not meet students' functional excess recovery principle and sport skills formation memory regular patterns. Therefore, only classroom teaching alone cannot solve problems of athletic skills and health knowledge. The extracurricular sports activities once a day are good for students function level of over-recovery, help students form a memory for sports skills, which enhance students physique and health and master 1 or 2 master athletic skills with multiplier effect. Therefore, the core of school physical education should shift from "physical education" to "extra-curricular physical activities", service to teaching students extracurricular physical exercise.

Assessment System Suitable for Physical Education Objectives. The content and index of physical and health education evaluation assessment have to be formulated by clear education objectives, the ultimate goal is not mainly on physical fitness standards, but also pay more attention to self-care ability, sense of adaptability, sports participation, self training, learning attitude, progress rate as are also in evaluation index, dynamic assessment process should be established for physical evaluation system to truly reflects Physical Health Education goals

References

1. Department of Education: Ministry of Education on the 2005 National Physical Fitness and HealthSurvey results. Education, Sports and Arts (2006)
2. Wangjian, et al.: Health Education, pp. 7–16. Higher Education Press (2006)
3. Juying, D.: Thinking on Health Education of College Students. Wuhan Sports University (11), 114–116 (2005)
4. Ministry of Education: on the issuance of Teaching of Physical Education Curriculum Guidelines, notice, Education, Sports and Arts (2002)
5. Liping, S.: To correct understand the new concept Sports and Health curriculum. Chineseschool sports (5) (2004)

Research on College English Writing on the Macro Discourse Level Based on Web Resources

XiaoGe Jia and JianGuo Tian

Department of Foreign Linguistics and Applied Linguistics,
School of Humanities, Economics and Law, Northwestern Polytechnical University,
Xi'an, Shaanxi, China
lois888777@sina.com, tianjian@nwpu.edu.cn

Abstract. This essay reports part of the results of a questionnaire investigating 74 college students' self-evaluation of their writing behaviors and beliefs on the macro discourse level. Then it moves on to analyze the statistics obtained about students' macro-level writing behaviors and beliefs in terms of making an outline, writing a thesis, providing topic sentences and making conclusions and the purpose for making conclusions. Finally, this essay will present implications on what extra work on college English writing teachers need to do in terms of English writing on the discourse level in order to help college students theoretically and practically master the know-how of English writing.

Keywords: College English writing. Macro discourse level. Thesis. Topic sentence. Conclusion.

1 Introduction

The importance of English writing is self-evident. English wring skill is one of the five skills, namely, listening, speaking, reading, writing and translating required for College students. In the national English proficiency test College English Test Band-4 and Band-6(CET-4, CET-6), the assigned English writing score takes up 15 per cent of the whole test score. What's more, since 1997 it has been provided that if a student's writing score is less than 6, regardless his performance in the other parts, he is definitely to be failed in the exam.

Despite the importance officially attached to English writing, we still do not see an optical picture in students' performance in this aspect. In general, the average writing score for most colleges and universities is around 5, only equal to one third of the total score. Apart from the spelling and grammatical errors, the discourse error is another major factor that contributes to students' poor performance in writing.

This paper intends to first report students' belief on what they do on the discourse level in their writing. Then it will go on analyze the results. On this basis, it will provide findings and implications for teachers teaching English writing. Limitations of this paper are also pointed out and further work is also suggested.

S. Lin and X. Huang (Eds.): CSEE 2011, Part V, CCIS 218, pp. 559–564, 2011.

2 Theoretical Framework

Discourse. It may not be easy for scholars to reach a consensus in defining "discourse". According to Hu Zhuanglin, it seems that American scholars prefer "discourse" to "text", while the European scholars prefer the other way around. In his opinion, the two are the same, referring to both spoken and written passages [1]. This essay uses "discourse" and "text" to refer to written passages.

Macro - level Discourse Analysis. Discourse analysis at this level discusses the qualities of the text as a whole. Neufield holds that a sound essay should have unity, coherence and emphasis in its structure [2]. Ding Wangdao emphasizes unity, coherence and transition in an effective writing [3]. To sum up, we see a good essay at the macro-level should have the following discourse features: for achieving unity, the whole paragraph should concentrate on a single idea which is clearly and precisely stated as a thesis; all the evidence, examples and reasons to develop that idea should be relevant and soundly developed so as to contribute to the completeness of that idea; the conclusion should be short, forceful, substantial, thought-provoking and without new ideas introduced.

3 Methodology

Subjects: The subjects were third-year students (N=74) of German majors with English as their second foreign language drawn from three intact classes. There were 12 male students and 62 female students. Their age ranges from 20 to 24 with an average age of 21.4. Regarding their English proficiency, by the year 2011when the research was conducted, 27 students had not passed CET-4, 38 had passed CET-4 but not CET-6 and 9 had passed both CET-4 and CET-6.

Instrument: The instrument used in this study was a Questionnaire on English Writing Behaviors and Beliefs by which the author aims to investigate some of college students' English writing. The questionnaire includes 13 multiple choices grouped into three groups: English writing on macro discourse level; English writing on micro discourse level; potential reasons for lacking macro/ micro level discourse knowledge. As this essay focuses on the macro-level discourse, it will only report the results for Question 1, 2, 3, 12 and 13 which asked subjects to judge their macro-level English writing behaviors and beliefs. Specifically, these five questions survey in reality how the subjects generally plan for their essay as a whole, including the outline, thesis, topic sentence and conclusion.

4 Results of the Questionnaire and Analysis of the Results

The questionnaires were distributed to the subjects, informing them that the purpose of the questionnaire was to find out some of their English writing behaviors and beliefs and that they were expected to fill out the questionnaire based on the personal situations. They were ensured that they were no right or wrong answers, so all they had to do was to reflect upon their personal writing behaviors concerning the questions on the questionnaire. The subjects turned to be very cooperative and all the 74 questionnaires collected back were valid. Results of the students' response to each question are as follows:

Table 1. Results for Question 1, 2, 3, 12

	A. Never	B. Sometimes	C. Often	D. Always
1. Do you write an outline or at least have one in your mind before you write?	8 (11%)	18 (24%)	35 (47%)	13 (18%)
2. Do you state your thesis explicitly in your introduction paragraph?	2 (3%)	5 (7%)	31 (42%)	36 (36%)
3. Do you give a topic sentence to the paragraph(s) centered on an idea? *[1]	2 (3%)	22 (30%)	37 (49%)	11 (15%)
12. Do you write a conclusion for your essay?*[2]	0 (0%)	3 (4%)	22 (30%)	48 (65%)

Note: *[1] Two subjects for unknown reasons did not make any choice for this question.
*[2] One subject for unknown reasons did not make any choice for this question.

Based on the statistics in the table, we will discuss the following questions:

How do students self-evaluate their performance in their English writing on the macro discourse level? Question 1, 2, 3, and 12 in the questionnaire are designed to stimulate subjects to reflect upon their activities of making a general plan for the whole text, providing an explicit thesis for the whole text in the introduction paragraph, developing a topic sentence for one or several closely related paragraphs and writing a conclusion paragraph for the whole text. These questions are likely to reflect subjects' self-evaluation of their English writing performance on the macro discourse level.

From the above table, we see that 65 per cent of the subjects often or always make an outline for their essay before they write. This demonstrates that these students to some extent have the awareness of planning the overall structure or construction of their essay.

The results also show that 78 per cent subjects state their thesis explicitly in their introduction paragraph. This result does not conform to the discovery of the previous findings. For example, Scollon concluded that Chinese writers rarely had the awareness of stating their point of view directly in a thesis statement [4]. Zhang Zaixin studied that 59 per cent essays of Chinese students did not have a thesis [5].

Regarding the topic sentence, only 48 per cent of the subjects report they often or always give a topic sentence to one or several paragraphs that center on a single idea. It is a common practice for a typical English essay to have a topic sentence for one or several paragraphs that center on a single idea. Brooks compared the topic sentence to "a kind of backbone, a spine" that supported the body of the paragraph and the rest of the paragraph shall be developed around that topic sentence [6]. Zeng Lisha also stated that in the English argumentations and expository essays, up to 60 to 70 per cent of these essays had the paragraph development pattern of "a topic sentence plus the developing materials". Compared the proportion of 60 to 70 per cent, the proportion of 48 per cent indicates that in the aspect of using topic sentence, the subjects in this study is picking up the native English writing habit, but still they have a long way to go and they need even more awareness of and more efforts on this point.

As regards the conclusion, up to 95 students report that they will write a conclusion for an essay. In order to find out subjects' motivation for writing the conclusion, the author designed Question 13. Question 13 and subjects' responses to this question are shown below.

Question 13: Why do I write the conclusion?

A. To sum up the major points in the essay
B. To add some new points
C. To encourage readers to think or act
D. I have no idea why to write the conclusion
E. Other reasons

Table 2. Results for Question 13

	A	B	C	D	E	Total
Frequency of choice	51	1	21	1	0	74
Percentage	70%	1%	28%	1%	0%	100%

Results for Question 13 demonstrate that students write the conclusion for two major reasons, one for summing up the major points in the essay and the other for encouraging readers to think or act. According to Ding Wangdao et al, the end of an essay is important because it is often the part to deeply influence or impress the readers. He mentioned the conclusion of an essay did not need to be a separate paragraph; it can be a single sentence as long as it serves to give readers a sense of completeness [3]. Jordan stated that "drawing a conclusion often involves making a summary of the main points already made. In addition, one's own opinion or viewpoint may be added, if it is appropriate. He observed that sometimes we might make the mistake by adding a conclusion that did not "follow logically from what has been written before" [7]. To sum up, we can see that a conclusion can be long or short, but it is to reiterate the major points elucidated before or the author's opinion logically related to the previous illustrations of viewpoints. Judging from the results for Question 13, up to 98 per cent subjects write a conclusion for summing up the major points in the essay or for encouraging readers to think or act.

5 Findings and Implications

Based on the reported results for the five questions related to subjects' English writing behaviors and beliefs on the macro-discourse level in the questionnaire, we have the following findings:

In this study, statistics show that more than half, or to be exact, 65 per cent of the subjects plan for their essay either by writing down an outline or by weaving one in mind. Such is a good sign showing that these students have the awareness of taking the text as a whole. Undoubtedly, this is a good writing habit on the students' part. The implication for English writing teachers here is that if they will take the trouble to teach students the macro-level discourse knowledge, these students will have better chance of producing high quality essays. In detail, teachers can teach students to comprehensively think about how to put forward their standpoint in a thesis, how to support the thesis with several points summarized in several corresponding topic sentences and how to develop each topic sentence and finally how to conclude the essay with major points emphasized and their own viewpoints proposed clearly.

Statistics also show that 78 per cent subjects reported they often or always stated their thesis explicitly in their introduction paragraph. Different from the previous research findings, the obvious increase awareness of thesis might be due to the fruit of constant in-class emphasis on thesis over recent years, but whether this is the real reason for the increase is open to further and even thorough tests and this will be left to further verifications.

48 per cent of the subjects report they often or always give a topic sentence to one or several paragraphs that center on a single idea. Low as it is, this result is encouraging in indicating growing awareness of the importance of topic sentences. However, also considering the importance of topic sentences in typical English writings, writing teachers still need to continue making efforts to highlight topic sentences in writing lectures by theoretically teaching the knowledge and more importantly practically demonstrate how to write effective and sound topic sentences.

With respect to subjects' behaviors and belief in writing conclusion for their English essay, it is kind of satisfactory and comforting to see 95 per cent of them reported they often or always wrote a conclusion and 98 per cent of them wrote a conclusion in the correct direction, that is, to summarize major points or propose their own opinion based on previous discussions by calling on people to think or act.

However, it must be mentioned here the subjects in this paper is not large enough, which will limit its generalization scale of its findings. For the same reason, some of its findings need further studies to testify.

References

1. Zhuanglin, H.: Discourse Cohesion and Coherence, p. 2. Shanghai Foreign Language Education Press, Beijing (1994)
2. Neufield, R., Baojin, M.: A College English Writing Course. Henan Univertity Press, Henan (1992)
3. Wangdao, D., Bing, W.: A Handbook for English Writing. Foreign Language Teaching and Research Press, Beijing (1994)

4. Scollon, R.: English Legs and One Elbow. Stance and Structure in Chinese English Compositions. In: Paper presented at International Reading Association 2000, Contrastive Discourse in Chinese and English. Foreign Language Teaching and Research Press, Beijing (1991)
5. Zaixin, Z.: Major Problems in English Writing in China. Foreign Language Teaching and Research, 43 (1995)
6. Brooks, C.: Modern Rhetoric, p. 218. Harcourt Brace Jovanovich, Inc., New York (1979)
7. Jordan, R.R.: Academic Writing Course, p. 78. Thomas Nelson and Sons (Hong Kong) Ltd., Hong Kong (1992)

City Bank Employee "Sub-healthy" Reasons of State Association Based on Data Analysis

JianQiang Guo and YingXia Wang

ChangZhou University Jiangsu changzhou China
Jqguo5986@163.com

Abstract. Main commence from reason inquisition analysis become to sub-health, look for it thus of with result that cause of disease vegetable, in order to be placed in sub-healthy bank employee to understand oneself health condition, provide the prevention path of science reasonable for healthy appearance that bank employee improves an oneself.

Keywords: The city, Employee of the bank, Sub-health, Reason.

1 The Preamble

"Sub-health state" means that: although the organism has not have obvious lesion but revealed a dynamic reduce and adapting ability deduce in varying degrees. It is low state of physiological function [1].between health and disease. According to the our earlier research on the bank development and employee health research-- investigation of bank employee sub-health condition in southern city, we draw: bank staff in southern city is" sub-health "high-risk groups, more than half of the bank staff will have some symptoms, such as the waist sour, neck acid aches, shoulder ache, blurred vision, agitating mood and so on. 83.4% of employees are in" sub-health state [2]. We do some research on the related causes of sub-health in such a crowd in order to provide reference for helping them overcome unhealthy habits, lifestyles and improving their health.

2 The Research Objects and Methods

2.1 Research Object

We randomly pick up the staff 588 people (male 340 people, female 248 people) from four commercial bank (bank of China, industrial and commercial bank, agricultural bank of China, China construction bank) and some local bank (such as China merchants bank, city bank, jiangsu bank, etc.) for investigation object in jiangsu southern city (suzhou, wuxi, changzhou, zhenjiang, nantong).We do some investigation, analysis and research. On their work environment, life habits, exercise habits.

S. Lin and X. Huang (Eds.): CSEE 2011, Part V, CCIS 218, pp. 565–569, 2011.

2.2 Research Methods

2.2.1 The Methods of Looking into Materials

Under research need, in Suzhou University Library and Institute of physical education reference room, and Jiangsu industrial College Library and Sports Department reference room for has literature collection, and retrieved work; by network (Internet) and Information Service inspection and gets has related Asia health, and Asia health produced causes, and Asia health and sports activities relationship of file information (as online no is to about leadership borrowing); inspection abroad about Asia health, and Asia health produced causes, and Asia health and sports activities relationship of file information. According to the subject needs to refer to the health and sports, the sports scientific research methods, the physical activity and public health, the social investigation of statistics and projections, the sociological research methods relevant to such works as well as with the study of more than 130 papers.

2.2.2 Survey Method

2.2.2.1 The Questionnaire Method

Respectively, on the Bank of China, industrial and commercial bank, agricultural Bank, construction Bank of China, the four banks and China Merchants Bank, CITIC Bank, Bank staff questionnaire survey in Jiangsu.

2.2.2.2 The Validity and Reliability of the Questionnaire Survey

Before the release of the questionnaire, we test the validity of the questionnaire in the way that the experts agree, after two rounds 'delete, supplement and adjustment, to conform to the requirements and validity inspection. We do the questionnaire reliability tests with the result of investigation by using rectangular relationship reliability test number of Pearson (survey Pearson), Then we calculates the total questionnaire reliability coefficients were R1 = 0.925. It Prove that designed questionnaire has higher reliability.

2.2.2.3 Issuance and Recovery

Combined recycling in person by mail and in person issuing, issued in the form of a questionnaire, and reclaim the questionnaire. Distribution, recycling, are shown in table 1. According to the perspectives of Babi, recovery rate is more than 60% qualified, the survey questionnaire recovery rate exceeds this level, it can completely meet the research needs of this questionnaire.

2.3 Expert Interview

According to the research needs, prepared interview outline, interview the experts concerned during the investigation period, to understand the situation.

2.4 Mathematical Statistics Method

Using SPSS11.5 software on the computer for data statistics and analysis of questionnaires.

2.5 Logical Reasoning Method

To consolidate data collected, using logical reasoning method on analysis of various issues, so as to make relevant recommendations.

3 The Results and Analysis

3.1 Bank Working Environment Survey

According to investigation we can see, bank belongs to the special unit. Staff work environment is relatively special and the living space is relatively narrow. Air pollution, noise pollution, water pollution, light pollution, electromagnetic pollution have many adverse effects on human cardiovascular and nervous system [3]. The room and the office is too narrow and closed, which was settled at artificial environment for a long time constant surroundings. And relative environment and the air circulation are closed. If a person live in this kind of environment for a long time, the body's normal physiological function will be destroyed. And he will lose its specific internal environment stability, form wet wins physique, and produce "sub-health state[4].

3.2 Survey on the Bank Employees' Behaviors, Lifestyles

From the survey on the bank employees' behaviors, lifestyles, we find a quite number of the bank employees have behaviors and lifestyles which are not conducive to health. From chart 3, we can be found that nearly half of the bank employees are often egress social parties. Statistical survey found that nearly half of all bank employees have the habit of smoking, drinking and a minority of people occasionally has the habit of drinking and smoking. We know from the interview that this is needs of the nature of work. All these can be considered the unhealthy lifestyles of bank employees. Bad lifestyles are mainly caused by unhealthy eating habits, stress, smoking, excessive drinking and little sports and other unhealthy lifestyle factors. According to the WHO,as to the human health and longevity, 40 % rely on genetic and objective conditions, including 15 % for genetic, 10 % for social factors, 8 % for medical condition, 7 % for climate conditions, while 60 % depend on ourselves to create a way of life of their own and psychological behaviors [5].

3.3 Survey on Bank Employees' Working Way

More than half of the bank employees have to work overtime, and sometimes stay up late. Because of the particularity of the nature of the work, employees in the bank are required to sit while working. 72.8% bank employees need sitting for close to six hours daily, these can be regarded as not healthy working style. Many generation of professional related disease and chronic has a process, in this process the symptoms tend to be progressive. So prevention is the key .sub-health state was considered a process of generation of professional relevant disease and chronic diseases, so we should had a profound understanding of prevention and deal with the occurrence of sub-health state in advance.

3.4   Survey on Bank Employees' Participation in Sports Exercise

According to investigation, we can see bank employees' participation in sports exercise is inadequate. Regular physical activities can reduce a person's stress reaction and reduce tension, especially appropriate sports activities. We at best consider own actual situation, make physical exercise prescription, follow the exercise principles and laws, insist to take exercise every week not less than three times gradually and persistently, The exercise done every day should not be less than 30min .And aerobic exercise is preferred; it can better enhanced physique, promote the body adjustment, improve qi reconcile widened fat and sugar metabolism, reduce obesity, prevent osteoporosis, enhance immunity [6].

4   Conclusions and Recommendations

4.1   Conclusions

4.1.1. Relatively isolated working environment where the city bank employees worked in, working in the constant surroundings of artificial environment, coupled with the pollution of various environmental decoration materials are the important causes of sub-health.

4.1.2. The city bank employees' bad behaviors, bad living habits make airframe frequently starve, cause the brain anoxia and then cause abnormal endocrine hormone secretion. Nutritional imbalance and junk food, diet etc also creates a lack of a lot of important nutrients, airframes and make obesity increased metabolism disorders, these are among the factors of sub-health [7].

4.1.3. The city bank employees' abnormal work day and accumulating, excessive labor are the main reason for the disorders of human body function. Highly fierce competition in modern society , intricate relationships cause excessive worries, psychological stress and not quiet mind, which not only can cause lack of sleep, but even affect human nerve humoral regulation and endocrine regulation, thus affect the normal physiology function of each system.

4.1.4. The city bank employees often work overtime, inverse sometimes; The human body in the evolutionary process formed the inherent rules of life movement--, clocks. It maintains law of qi operation and metabolism of life movement. If inverse sometimes do, it will destroy the rule and affect the body's normal metabolism.

4.1.5. The city bank employees are lack of exercise; Nowadays, as the urban traffic system are developed, people go out mostly by the car, neglecting the physical exercise. Long-term lack of movement can cause physical deterioration, increased diseases. Life lies in sports, life also lies in sanatorium. Human body has much in common in life movement process, but there are also the individual differences. Therefore, fitness and health should be a strong learning. Everyone in different age stages, his body is in the objective circumstances of dynamic change. If the practice is undeserved, lack of scientific method instruction, it will damage the health of human body [8].

4.2 Recommendation

4.2.1. The city bank employee should pay attention to develop good health habits, improving their working environment hygiene, note ventilated, minimize the contact with all kinds of pollution.

4.2.2. The city bank employee should pay attention to the comprehensive and balanced meal nutrition; In daily life, the daily dietary must ensure that the nutrients supplies which are essential. The nutrition of three meals should be reasonable and we should set up the views of balanced nutrition.

4.2.3. The city bank employees should overcome bad living habits ,such as smoking, drinking, no-limits eating, eating adipose food or overeating, the lack of activity, undesirable sleep, not eating breakfast, etc, which will make the body gradually turned into sub-health state, which eventually led to all sorts of diseases. So we should arrange our work and life reasonably, combine exertion with actively rest, avoid long-term over- fatigue which may damage healthy.

4.2.4. The city bank employee needs to keep a healthy psychological condition and improve psychological quality, which is a powerful weapon against disease. We should establish a correct outlook on life, the values. And we should be indifferent to fame and wealth .As a proverb says :he who is content is always happy. So we should edify sentiment.

4.2.5. The city bank employees need a regular physical exercise, physical exercise should be insist and moderate. The right attitude is a compulsory lesson of the physical exercise.

Acknowledgments. The paper is supported by 2010 liberal arts development fund projects in Changzhou University (No. ZMF100200449).

References

1. Ormel, J., Vonkorll, M.V.: Depressim, anxiety and disalility Ahow synchrony of change. Am J. Pull. Health 86, 385–390 (1996)
2. Guo, J.: Bank development and employee health research-southern city bank employee health survey. Journal of ABC Wuhan training college 4, 46–47 (2007)
3. such as Tianqi Jia. physical therapy and health interventions. Physical education and science 29(3), 51–54 (2008)
4. Yao, Y., Guo, Y.: Sub-healthy reason and prevention. Journal of Anhui Medical College 21(6), 1–2 (2002)
5. Carney, R.M., Freed, L., Sheline, Y.I., et al.: Depression and coronary heart disease. Clin. Cardiology 20, 196–200 (1997)
6. Physical education and science 5, 37–39 (2002)
7. Chen, F., Wang, Z.: Main factors affecting the urban population of sub-health. Journal of preventive medicine in Anhui Province 13(1), 55–56 (2007)
8. Wu, J., Liang, L.: Causes and prevention of sub-health. Journal of Beijing University of physical education 26(2), 206–207 (2003)

Bilingual Teaching Reform and Practice of Engineering Student's "Professional Foreign Language" Based on Multimedia Technology

Zhiqiang Kang[1], Runsheng Wang[2], and Ying Wang[1]

[1] College of Mining Engineering, Hebei United University, HeBei Province Key Laboratory of Mining Development and Safety Technique, Tangshan, 063009 China
[2] Department of Civil Engineering of Tangshan College, Tangshan 063009, China
kzqzsh@163.com, tswangrs@163.com, ying501618@126.com

Abstract. Aiming at the teaching situation of engineering "professional foreign language", I analyze the advantage of the engineering "professional foreign language" combining bilingual teaching mode. What's more, I point out that improving professional foreign language teachers' quality, stimulating study interest, and improving teaching modes and methods are the major approaches of bilingual teaching reform of engineering "professional foreign language" at present, which provides direction for promoting the teaching reform of college engineering "professional foreign language" .

Keywords: Engineering "professional foreign language", bilingual teaching, reform and practice.

1 Introduction

With the rapid development of science and technology today, professional foreign language has become a new field of modern foreign language application and teaching in many countries, so in the field of college teaching, professional foreign language courses also became the compulsory course combined with the professional course which is open for students after the public English learning. However engineering students are the backbone of the technological work in the future, in later learning and work they are not only familiar with the dynamic of domestic and foreign new technology, but also constantly master related new science and technology, and only in this way they can better play the advantage of existing technical knowledge. So opening the professional foreign language course more appear particularly important in engineering professional college students. Bilingual teaching is one of the directions of education reform in colleges and universities, the combination of bilingual teaching and engineering "professional foreign language" teaching can play the positive role of bilingual teaching methods, and also can improve the teaching effect of professional foreign language course. Combining the experiences and lessons engaged in mining engineering foreign language teaching several years, I analyze the teaching situation of engineering professional foreign language and the approach of engineering professional foreign language realizing bilingual teaching reform and practice).

S. Lin and X. Huang (Eds.): CSEE 2011, Part V, CCIS 218, pp. 570–575, 2011.

2 Engineering "Professional Foreign Language" Teaching Status

2.1 Textbooks Normative

With the continuation of engineering professional foreign language curriculum time, teaching materials need experienced a development process that is from scratch, and from freedom selection to normal teaching material.

Initially, professional teachers often freely choose materials, so sources of textbooks are wider range, which are chosen from relevant professional foreign language books and periodicals, or selected from general technology books, newspapers and impurities and so on. But the teaching contents are often too simple, but also can appear sometimes disjointed phenomenon with this professional. With the extension of time and the enhancement of teachers' professional foreign language teaching experience and level, college teachers start to write related professional foreign language teaching material on their own.

On the selection of professional foreign language material, if universities could try their better to have the option of using edition textbooks, this will enable students to systematically understand other country or the professional knowledge by generally accepted in international. But because of the differences between domestic and foreign academic Settings, there are still some difficulties in the selection of original professional English teaching material. Therefore, the specialized subject most college English teaching material selecting is the edition textbook of similar discipline that the author collects and then write by deleting and reorganizing according to the teaching.

2.2 Teacher Resources

At present, engineering "professional foreign language" teaching of most college is undertaken by professional teaching and research office, although professional teachers have deep professional knowledge, English explanation has often the certain difficulty, which affects students' abilities of listening, speaking, writing. There are a few colleges whose professional foreign language teaching is assumed by the foreign language department, these teachers can fluently teach grammar and vocabulary, but they are likely at a loss what to do when meeting the professional, which might make professional foreign language become a language teaching course. I think the current teacher sources of college engineering "professional foreign language" are relatively deficient, and colleges need to introduce young teachers with higher professional knowledge and foreign language level, especially introduce professionals with doctoral degrees, or introduce professionals engaged in relevant technology research in overseas, etc. These personnel do not only have thicker professional knowledge, and have experience of reading foreign scientific literature for many years, and abilities of their listening, speaking, reading and writing in foreign language are higher, which will benefit professional foreign language courses teaching, and easily realize the complement of teaching.

2.3 Teaching Methods

Objectives of setting professional foreign language course is to train their abilities of reading, writing and translating professional materials based on students' previous certain Basic English. But most professional foreign language teaching has stagnated in the traditional teaching method, such as students mainly look textbooks, the teacher explains, analyze sentence features, etc. The effect of this way is not ideal, and teaching content often has the attention to translation of the content, which does not favor the enhancement of professional foreign language ability and the students' study enthusiasm. In the teaching process of mining engineering "professional foreign language", in order to increase the interaction between teachers and students and improve student's enthusiasm, I set aside some time to let the students group discussions in the classroom, then the represents of each group explain the main content of the corresponding paragraphs to everybody, or give a certain time to let the students practice translation using translation forms and so on, as a result I find that the appropriate change of the traditional teaching mode can receive the good result.

3   The Advantage of Engineering "Professional Foreign Language" Combining Bilingual Teaching

Bilingual teaching is one of the development directions of education reform. In 2011, "Several comments about strengthening undergraduate teaching work of higher education institutes and improving the teaching quality" issued by the state point out that we try to make foreign language teaching curriculum courses reach the 5% ~ 10% of bilingual teaching requirements within 3 years, and take bilingual teaching included evaluation index system of common higher undergraduate teaching job level, etc. So far, bilingual teaching of each college has made some achievements, but teaching methods, selection of teaching material and so on still require further exploration, and is still lack of success experience of bilingual teaching.

Bilingual teaching mode was used in engineering "professional foreign language" course, which can play the advantage of both and the role of supplementing each other. Firstly, it reduces the distress of bilingual teaching material selection universities. Professional foreign language courses are open for students combining professional curriculum content after students learning public English for years. For engineering student, professional foreign language study makes students well prepare for future study, consulting foreign materials in work, writing academic papers or going abroad to technical exchanges. Engineering professionals regarding technical has international generality, compared to other subjects, foreign or international general books are more, and it is easy to choose. And if purely for opening bilingual teaching, and no professional direction, its selection difficulty of teaching material is quite large. Secondly, it raises the enthusiasm of student learning "professional foreign language" course. Finally, it improves the ability of professional teachers' bilingual teaching. Bilingual teaching put forward higher request for existing teachers, professional teachers should not only have deep professional theoretical knowledge, but also have the ability of skillfully using foreign languages teaching, asking questions, and solving problems. Although most university professional teachers have master's degree or higher, because of Chinese traditional education mode, especially the engineering university instructors have many experiences of the dumb foreign language learning, so the ability of most teachers' hearing and speaking is bad. Therefore, bilingual teaching of engineering "professional foreign language" is also a process of professional teachers challenging themselves. I have profound experience in this aspect, for example the workload of preparing a bilingual mining engineering "professional foreign language" class is twice as much of preparing for a traditional professional foreign language. In order to better control and vivify classroom atmosphere, students also often collect large and professional relevant foreign sessions and situational essays from Internet or library, etc, in order to enrich students' professional oral English knowledge.

4 Approach to Achieve Bilingual Teaching Reform of "Professional Foreign Language" of Engineering

4.1 To Improve the Quality of Professional Foreign Language Teacher

Professional language teacher should not only have a wealth of professional knowledge, but also a very solid grounding in foreign languages, must be a compound talent in "foreign language + professional". At present, there are not enough professional foreign language teachers who can teach in bilingual language, so schools should strengthen the training for bilingual education teachers to improve the quality of professional foreign language teacher. On the one hand, offer training courses to the existing teacher, such as foreign language speaking training or encourage teachers to study abroad according to the subject's characteristics and so on. On the other hand, introduce more teachers who have doctorate or have the experience of study abroad and have a high level in foreign language to supplement the shortage of professional foreign language teachers.

4.2 Stimulate Students' Interest in Study

Interest plays an important role in learning any course or work. To students, interest is the key to learn any courses, however, sometimes the students' interest in learning requires the guidance of teachers. This phenomenon is more prominent on the study of non-Mandarin language professional courses. Some students of the author once said, "Teacher, to our mining engineering foreign language, you do not need to painstaking prepare bilingual teaching, we junior and senior do not have the pressure of examinations in English, we don't have enthusiasm in learning and listening to professional courses in English. " At present, students are more passive on the process of professional foreign language courses in bilingual education, often don't participate in the teacher's teaching activities by heart. Students are the key point of learning, teachers should play the subjective initiative, fully mobilize students' interest in the implementation of bilingual teaching of professional foreign language courses, such as increase discussion class, moderate difficulty of teaching content, and teaching rhythm shouldn't be too slow or too fast to affect students' enthusiasm.

4.3 Improve Teaching Ways and Means

In the practice of bilingual education for professional foreign language courses, we must improve the existing ways and means of teaching continuously to develop both teachers and students' role to achieve good teaching results. I combined years of foreign language teaching of mining engineering experience, conclude that improve teaching methods and means mainly from the following aspects.

1) Curriculum setting. The teaching time of professional foreign language courses vary by different disciplines, mostly in the third year of undergraduate's first or second semester, extending two to three semesters. In terms of professional foreign language courses, we set this course for engineering in the first semester of third year in our college, 20 hours per semester, a total of 60 hours. However, the first semester of junior year are mostly set basic course, such as mining, student still lack the professional knowledge. The author had to spend a lot of time to explain the professional knowledge in the foreign language class of mining engineering, the corresponding time of the use and the training of English capacity is reduced. Therefore, the setting of professional language curriculum should relate to the professional courses, adjust the setting time according to the professional courses.

2) Teaching methods. In the implementation of bilingual education process, we should try to change the traditional textbook teaching methods, namely, "the original - translation" teaching mode. This mode of teaching is monotonous and boring, is not conducive to the integrated teaching ability of specialized teachers. On the contrary, the use of multimedia in teaching would benefit the implementation of bilingualism in professional foreign language courses. Depending on the difficulty degree of the course, make the foreign language courseware full of information and illustration, this can not only guide the students to active learning, and teachers do not have to spend much time in class to write on the blackboard, it makes the teacher have more time to explain and analyze the content in the Courseware, so that the expertise and foreign language environment make through together. Students listen to the professional knowledge taught by the teacher according to the text and graphics content, and the teaching effectiveness will naturally increase.

3) Use various teaching methods comprehensively. It requires teachers to use various teaching methods comprehensively in the professional Language bilingual education practice, so that the class will be flexible, the subject will be clear. First, stick to the principle of gradual and orderly progress. In bilingual teaching approach, it does not care how much foreign letters and sentences are said in a class. Secondly, the combination of various teaching methods optimizes the teaching mode. Based on modern multimedia information technology design professional language bilingual education mode and take a variety of ways to mobilize the enthusiasm of students, encouraging students to answer questions positively by using the learned professional words, create more opportunities for students to speak foreign language , such as use the form of questions, lectures or discussions and so on.

5   Conclusion

With the rapid development of modern science and technology and international exchange being increasingly frequent today, if engineering colleges want to cultivate professional and technical personnel with high level, extroversion, we must do well teaching work of engineering "professional foreign language". And the bilingual teaching mode is applied to the link of professional foreign language teaching, which can give full play to the advantage of language teaching and professional foreign language teaching, and lay a good foundation for fostering foreign "language + professional" the talents

References

1. HongYan, L., Jing, X.: Petrochemical application 5, 73 (2006)
2. WenFeng, W.: China Science and Technology Information 13, 276 (2008)
3. PengYun, S.: Inner Mongolia financial university journal (comprehensive edition) 4, 60 (2006)
4. QingHua, L., Ming, Y.: Oil education 6, 60 (2004)
5. Fu, S.: Science and Technology Information 16, 349 (2008)
6. FuYu, L., XiangDong, W., Qiang, X.: China electronic education 1, 42 (2006)

Comprehensive to Adjudicate Student's Character Based on Information Analysis

Chunling Sun

School of Information Science and Technology Heilongjiang University
chunling6666@163.com

Abstract. Student's character adjudicating is a typical misty affairs. This text makes use of misty mathematics of comprehensive adjudicate a method, assess the student's grade. Namely according to all the evaluation of that teacher's performance in everyone's noodles to each student makes, carry on comprehensive, then give a personal character level to student. This text leads misty mathematics to enter school production control science and engineering to make, there is good application value.

Keywords: Student's Character, Misty affairs, Educating the evaluation.

1   Introduction

Educating the evaluation is an important realm that educates fulfillment and education research, more and more of the educator, researcher express a tremendous concern and interest to this realm. Educate an evaluation according to the certain purpose and the standard , carry on a description to combine to carry on the activity of value judgment on this foundation towards educating a work and it the status and the results in the relevant factor. Speak from a certain meaning , the course evaluates success or failure that decide course's reform.

It is a more difficult problem to carry on synthesizing to adjudicate to the student's personal character, It is a more typical misty affairs. From the evaluation result ▯ Very good, good, Better, worse, bad, badly, can hardly have a clear boundary badly. How evaluate a student, need to use personal character grade that the method of misty mathematics makes sure a student.

This text be with misty mathematics of comprehensive adjudicate for foundation, synthesize the performance that each teacher is in everyone's noodles to each student adjudicates the student's personal character level the evaluation for doing, give student one is scientific, fair, reasonable of adjudicate a result.

2   Build Up Model

Usually consider a various factor while adjudicating student's personal character, need to make sure index sign. Establish one n index sign, these gathering of index signs are called "adjudicate index sign to gather" record for:

S. Lin and X. Huang (Eds.): CSEE 2011, Part V, CCIS 218, pp. 576–580, 2011.

$U=\{u_1, u_2, \cdots, u_n\}$

Should is divided into some different grades to the evaluation of each index sign, establish m to grow to evaluate grade. Evaluate gathering of grade to be called "the evaluation grade gathers", record for:

$V=\{v1, v2, \cdots, vn\}$

Each adjudicate influence degree of index sign to student personal character is different, for making to adjudicate a result more reasonable, give each the different power that adjudicate index sign respectively according to its influence degree heavy, namely "the power weighs an allotment", record for:

$A= (a1, a2, \cdots, an)$

Among, a_i is u_i to should of power value, and $a_i \geq 0$, $\displaystyle\sum_{i=1}^{n} a_i = 1$. A is U misty son gather.

For each student, should find out them, each adjudicate index sign to gather to mediumly. belong to function in the evaluation, is also want to make sure the student to be each adjudicate index sign to in response to each evaluation grade of belong to a degree. To i index sign to speak, it to should belonging to of each grade degree is a V misty son to gather.

$Ri (ri1, ri2, \cdots, rim)$

Among them, $\displaystyle\sum_{j=1}^{n} r_{ij} = 1$. all adjudicate belonging to of index sign the degree synthesize, then can get the student's evaluation matrix.

$$R = \begin{bmatrix} r_{11} & r_{12} & \cdots\cdots & r_{1m} \\ r_{21} & r_{22} & \cdots\cdots & r_{2m} \\ \multicolumn{4}{c}{\cdots\cdots\cdots\cdots\cdots\cdots} \\ r_{n1} & r_{n2} & \cdots\cdots & r_{nm} \end{bmatrix}$$

In consideration of each power number that adjudicate index sign analysis, it is the misty son of V to gather to then adjudicate B to the student's personal character's synthesizing.

$B = A \Theta R$

According to the algorithm of misty matrix

$$B= (b_1, b_2, \cdots, b_n = a_1, a_2, \cdots, a_n) \Theta \begin{bmatrix} r_{11} & r_{12}\cdots\cdots r_{1m} \\ r_{21} & r_{22}\cdots\cdots r_{2m} \\ \multicolumn{2}{c}{\cdots\cdots\cdots\cdots\cdots\cdots} \\ r_{n1} & r_{n2}\cdots\cdots r_{nm} \end{bmatrix}$$

Among them $b_j = \displaystyle\bigvee_{i=1}^{n} (a_i \wedge r_{ij})$, $j=1, 2, \cdots, m$, The b_j is the student be reviewed for the belonging to of j class a degree, if

$$b\,k = m\,a\,x\,(b\,1,\,b\,2,\,\cdots,\,b\,m)$$

The student's personal character grade then is a k class.

Leading into student's personal concept of character index number is more student's personal character to carry on the precision adjudicates of index sign, for evaluate grade to gather to endow with a value.

Make

$$V1 = (1,2,\ \cdots\cdots,\ m)$$

Call V_1 as to evaluate grade vector, then student's personal character index number

$$a = ARV_1^T$$

What to use is a common matrix multiplication here, the result for gaining at 1 and of m.

It index number is more small, enunciation student personal character level is more high, usually this index sign and student's personal character grade to should of cent value compare for approach.

From above-mentioned analysis, lie in to adjudicating of student personal character key look for to belong to the student of adjudicate matrix R. Usually we make use of all teachers' performance to his each aspects for having something to do with the student the evaluation done to form to adjudicate matrix.

3 An Example

The work carrying on student's personal character's adjudicating generally should include a following step:

(A)Certain the evaluation index sign gather,

U=(Moral qualities, study spirit, study result, research ability, organization discipline, body character, works ability)

(B)Certain the evaluation grade gather

V=(very good, good, better, medium, worse, bad, badly)

V1=(1,2,3,4,5,6,7)

(C) According to school to student's request and student future work need, make sure power between each index signs the number assigns.

A=(0.2,0.15,0.25,0.05,0.1,0.15,0.1)

(D)Please directly teach each teacher of the student and carry on an evaluation to each student and make sure the student's evaluation matrix.

Comprehensive to Adjudicate Student's Character Based on Information Analysis   579

Table 1. 10 teachers are to a student's evaluation form.

	very good	good	better	medium	worse	bad	badly
Moral qualities	1	2	4	2	1	0	0
study spirit	2	1	3	3	0	1	0
study result	0	2	1	4	2	1	0
research ability	0	0	2	3	4	0	1
organization dis-cipline	0	2	2	3	2	1	0
body character	0	3	3	2	1	1	0
works ability	0	0	1	4	4	1	0

Carry on this result to return one processing of turning , get the matrix of adjudicating of student.

$$R = \begin{pmatrix} 0.1 & 0.2 & 0.4 & 0.2 & 0.1 & 0 & 0 \\ 0.2 & 0.1 & 0.3 & 0.3 & 0 & 0.1 & 0 \\ 0 & 0.2 & 0.1 & 0.4 & 0.2 & 0.1 & 0 \\ 0 & 0 & 0.2 & 0.3 & 0.4 & 0 & 0.1 \\ 0 & 0.2 & 0.2 & 0.3 & 0.2 & 0.1 & 0 \\ 0 & 0.3 & 0.3 & 0.2 & 0.1 & 0.1 & 0 \\ 0 & 0 & 0.1 & 0.4 & 0.4 & 0.1 & 0 \end{pmatrix}$$

(E)Compute a student of comprehensive adjudicate B
The student's personal character of comprehensive adjudicate

$B = A \Theta R = (0.15, 0.2, 0.2, 0.25, 0.2, 0.1, 0.05)$

(F) The grade that makes sure the student's personal character according to the B, then take corresponding of the biggest chemical element in the B a time, is the student's personal grade of character level. If when the biggest chemical element in B isn't unique then take the average value that each the biggest chemical element corresponds position, is the student's personal grade of character level.
The biggest chemical element in B is the fourth(0.25) in the originally solid example, past the student's personal character level is "medium ".
(G) Compute student's personal character index number.
In example student's personal character index number is

$\alpha = ArV_1^T = 3.605$

Because the α is smaller than student's personal character "medium " to should of the cent be worth"4", and differ a little bit greatly, explain the student's personal character higher in " medium " .

4 Conclusion

Exploitation misty mathematics that this text puts forward of comprehensive adjudicate principle to carry on a student of personal character adjudicates of method,
strengthened the clarity and public of adjudicating the process, made to adjudicate
result more science, more reasonable. Especially this method student's personal character index number leads to go into and pursues studies schools to carry on three to
living so much, excellent living, judging and deciding of excellent staff graduate with
student of had the initiative allotments to all provide a stronger theory basis. This
method applies scope equal amplitude.

References

1. Yu'an, L., Jianlei, W., Liang, L.: The application of the misty theory in constrcution stage
   quantity control. Journal of Shijiazhuang Institute of Railway AI Technology 4(z1) (2005)
2. Junshan, G., Baiyu., S., et al.: The study of encryption process which is based on chaotic
   theory. Journal Techniques of automation and applications 6(13) (2001)
3. Shunfa, C.: Application of the Fuzzy Comprehensive Evaluation to Materials Selection.
   Machine Design And Research jxsjyyj200201015
4. Matsui, M.: New block encryption algorithm MISTY. In: Biham, E. (ed.) FSE 1997. LNCS,
   vol. 1267, pp. 54–68. Springer, Heidelberg (1997)
5. Nyberg, K., Knudsen, L.R.: Provable Security Against a Differential Attack. Journal of
   Cryptology 8(1), 27–37 (1995)
6. Nyberg, K.: Linear Approximation of Block Ciphers. In: De Santis, A. (ed.) EUROCRYPT
   1994. LNCS, vol. 950, pp. 439–444. Springer, Heidelberg (1995)
7. Matsui, M.: New Structure of Block Ciphers with Provable Security Against Differential
   and Linear Cryptanalysis. In: Gollmann, D. (ed.) FSE 1996. LNCS, vol. 1039, pp. 205–218.
   Springer, Heidelberg (1996)

Research and Practice on Curriculum Construction of the Nonwoven Technology

Wei Zhang and Shouhui Chen

College of Textile, Zhongyuan University of Technology, Zhengzhou,
Henan, 450007, PR China
Henan Key Laboratory of Functional Textiles Material, Zhengzhou,
Henan, 450007, PR China
island0410@gmail.com

Abstract. The curriculum construction of the Nonwoven Technology is based on the training target of the textile engineering talents. The thought and the target of the curriculum construction are set up in order to strength the Connotation Construction, optimize teaching resources and improve teaching quality. The curriculum construction of the Nonwoven Technology includes the building of the teaching staff, the improvement of the teaching methods and the teaching approaches, the innovation and the practice of the practice program and the development of the network-based classroom. Through the curriculum construction of the Nonwoven Technology, the teaching level and the teaching quality could be improved greatly. Besides, the construction of the characteristic specialty of textile engineering will be promoted seriously.

Keywords: Curriculum Construction, Teaching Innovation, Network Based Classroom, Nonwoven Technology.

1 Introduction

The construction of the characteristic specialty of textile engineering would meet the requirement of the training quality and training target for the undergraduate talents. The Nonwoven Technology is one of the platform courses for the textile engineering specialty. The characters of the course show the combination of the theory, the practice and the technology. Besides, the other characteristics of the Nonwoven Technology lie in the theoretical forefront and the discipline-crossing. Therefore the construction target of the Nonwoven Technology was to improve the teaching quality and provide excellent teaching source for the students. The curriculum construction of the Nonwoven Technology has been carried out according to the construction principles of "the recombination of the teaching source, the discipline-crossing comprehensively, the reflection of the modern technology and the tendency of the theoretical forefront". It includes the building of the teaching staff, the improvement of the teaching methods and the teaching approaches, the innovation and the practice of the practice program and the development of the network-based classroom.

S. Lin and X. Huang (Eds.): CSEE 2011, Part V, CCIS 218, pp. 581–584, 2011.

2   The Basic Thought of the Curriculum Construction

The curriculum construction is the combinations of the processes of accumulation, modification, innovation, and improvement. During the curriculum construction, the modern education thought and conception are involved. The modern training methods, means and technology have been introduced into the teaching practice. The training mode of "technology, ability and quality" has been insisted thoroughly. The scheme for the excellent curriculum construction of the Nonwoven Technology is shown is Fig. 1.

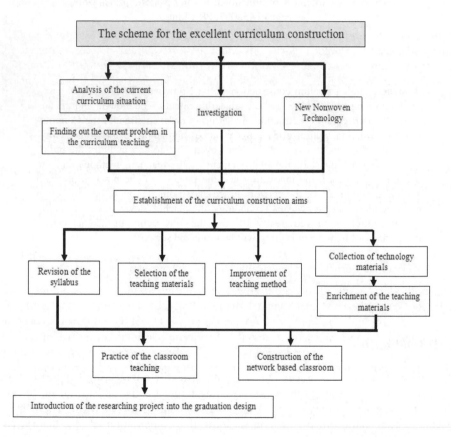

Fig. 1. The scheme for the excellent curriculum construction of the Nonwoven Technology

3   Revision and Perfection of the Syllabus

The syllabus is the core of the classroom teaching. The syllabus has been revised and perfected based on the talent training aims and the curriculum characteristics. Six parts could be found in the new syllabus, shown as in Fig.2.

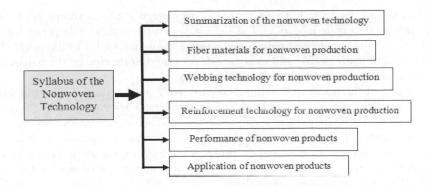

Fig. 2. The revised syllabus of the Nonwoven Technology

4 Teaching Reformation and Practice

In the classroom teaching, for a better understanding of the theory knowledge it is important to guide and to enlighten the students to solve the problem with their own knowledge about the Physics, Mathematics and Eclectics, etc. After the class, the students are asked to search relative literatures on the contents taught and to find what they are interested in. Finally, they could teach themselves and they could learn more actively.

To improve the engineering ability and the practicing ability of the students, the practice teaching has been emphasized. Due to the limitation of the teaching time, two means have been applied. One is the opening of the experimental class, and the other one is encourage students to play a role in the researching project of teachers. Through the practice teaching, the students could have a direct viewing about the nonwoven products. The students could learn the difference of the structure and the performance between the traditional textile products and the nonwoven products.

5 Construction of the Curriculum Learning Website

The curriculum learning website is composed by seven parts: Curriculum introduction, Teachers, Syllabus, Multi-media courseware, Video materials, Teaching resource and Interactive learning. Through the first three parts, the students could learn some information about the curriculum, the main teaching contents and the teaching and researching of the teachers. The multi-media courseware is based on the syllabus totally. The multi-media courseware could be used in classroom teaching and in self-teaching online. The video materials include all kinds of flashes, movies and videos on the equipment, the process and principles. These materials could make the process and the equipment principles much visual, and the professional technology become much easier for understanding. Therefore, the students would have more interest in this curriculum.

The part of teaching resources, including electronical teaching plan, examination database and learning materials, is the important part to encourage the students to learn by themselves. The learning materials recommend the professional books and other information materials, as well as the catalog of the famous enterprises for the production of the nonwoven products and modern equipments all over the world. The students could learn quickly and easily the developing information on the industrials, new products, new equipment and new technology.

The part of the interactive learning could provide an excellent chance and space for the communication of the students and the teachers. They could discuss any subjects about the curriculum online anytime anywhere. The interactive learning part was used as a forum. The students could provide any information, such as the industrial information, the trade information, the professional English, the job information, and the exhibition, etc. The forum would be much popular with the success of the communication between teachers and students.

Besides, the design of the curriculum website shows the comprehension the sharing of all excellent teaching resources. The website was designed as dynamic web pages; therefore, the maintenance and the refresh of the teaching materials become more convenience.

6 Summary

During the curriculum construction, the quick development of the modern textile industrial and the requirement of the applied talents have been taken into consideration. The teaching syllabus has been revised and become more reasonable. The construction of the curriculum learning website inspires the interest of the students in the course of the Nonwoven Technology. Through the construction of the curriculum, the new development of the nonwoven technology has been involved into the theory and classroom teaching by all means, which the students are interested in. Therefore the teaching quality has been improved greatly.

References

1. Chen, X.B.: China Higher Education 7, 23–25 (2007)
2. Guo, J.C.: China Higher Education 2, 17–20 (2007)
3. Zhu, G.Y.: China Higher Medical Education 11, 41–44 (2010)
4. Huang, J.G.: China Higher Education 9, 18–21 (2010)
5. Zhang, H.: China Electric Power Education 3, 6–9 (2010)

Research on Consulting-Type Class with the Aims to Cultivate the Entrepreneur Traits of Students in Schools of Economics and Management Based on Web

Yang Hongtao[1], Liu Dongping[2], and Sun Jingmeng[3]

[1] School of Economics and Management, Harbin Engineering University, China
[2] School of Economics and Management, Harbin Engineering University, China
[3] Physical Education Department, Harbin Engineering University, China
yhttxt@hotmail.com, sallyfeeling@hotmail.com,
sunjingmeng@hrbeu.edu.cn

Abstract. Based on specific analysis of necessity to cultivate current college students' entrepreneur traits, this paper analyzes the feasibility of using consulting-type class to cultivate the entrepreneur traits of students. We aim to proof the effectiveness and innovation significance of using consulting-type class to cultivate students' entrepreneur traits, which greatly mobilizes students' exploring spirit, competition ability, innovation characteristic, scientific quality, social responsibility and other entrepreneur traits' initiative training and effectively achieve three teaching objectives: "cognition, ability, emotion". This paper also shows this class type can be expanded and practiced in other research teaching courses.

Keywords: Consulting-type Class, Students in Schools of Economics and Management, Entrepreneurship Traits, Double-role, Main -body Interaction.

1 Introduction

In china, the employment situation is far more serious than any countries of the world. Owing the world's 9.0% of the natural resources, 9.6% of the capital resources, 1.83% of the technical resources and 1.85% of the international resources, China is expected to create employment opportunities for the world's 26% labor force, which requires that "the graduates are no longer the job seekers, but become the job creators firstly". UNESCO put forward that "the third passport" of education is the entrepreneurship ability, therefore many countries issued a preferential policy to encourage college graduates' self-employed, but this met with bottleneck restriction of the university student's low level entrepreneurship ability. The graduates are lack of entrepreneurship ability, especially the hands-on operation ability, organization ability, management ability, psychological ability and the cooperation spirit; they are also lack of specific market development experience and the relevant knowledge. Therefore, to really make self-employed became the university graduates' effective way of employment, it is imperative for universities to attach great importance to student's

S. Lin and X. Huang (Eds.): CSEE 2011, Part V, CCIS 218, pp. 585–589, 2011.

entrepreneurship spirit and creative ability, which is the cultivation of entrepreneurs' traits: exploring spirit, competitive ability, innovation characteristic, scientific quality and the social responsibility.

1.1 The Feasibility of Using Consulting-Type Class to Cultivate the Entrepreneur Traits of Students

In teaching practice, the cultivation of entrepreneur traits doesn't require to break the current course system to launch specialized entrepreneurship education, it is more important to develop and enhance the entrepreneurship education content with penetrating, combining and strengthening methods in suitable courses (such as marketing). So as front-line teachers, how to train students' entrepreneur traits and improve their innovative ability in specific teaching and form a set of teaching mode which can be in applied and promoted in many courses is the main practice problem. This model need specific implementation carrier, namely the class type. The consulting-type class is just emerged in this environment, the purpose of which is to cultivate students' innovative spirit, practice ability and the lifelong learning ability, and achieve the three teaching objectives – "cognition, ability, emotion", in order to adapt to the requirements of development growing and changing social economy, technology band culture. Therefore, the consulting-type class becomes the main mode of entrepreneurship education course of economy and management.

Consulting-type class type mainly conducts a study from ethics angle such as humanism, constructivism, Curriculum theory, education and psychology. The thinking of consulting-type class is: respecting the students' main position, creating a similar situation and approach as entrepreneurs in the teaching process, making the students explore and research actively, learning to collecting, analyzing and judging from lots of knowledge information, which can enhance students' competition consciousness and exploring spirit, improve the scientific quality and innovative quality, arouse social responsibility, thus to complete the cultivating of entrepreneur traits and improve the entrepreneurship ability.

Judging from the students' cognitive laws, it is a progressive cognitive process from the known to the unknown, from low to high, from the knowledge points to knowledge system. This process should be understood as: a process when students initiatively and selectively work on their learning contents from their own subjective consciousness, based on their existing knowledge and experience to make, and through acquire knowledge and ability through FAQs. And the environment of consulting-type class is very suitable for the need of the cognitive process.

In foreign countries, consulting-type class teaching mode is a highly respected teaching mode of economy and management courses. "Consultation means better control on teaching, which can not only meet the needed of teaching organization flexibility but also improve students' personal satisfaction and ability. Students can put forward some ways of solving the problem, so that the knowledge, skills and experience gained and utilized will benefit the whole participating students."(<Training Strategy and Practice >, Martin Solomon, British). "Consultation made the successful exploration for how to put these points combine: classroom teaching and the extracurricular activities, imparting knowledge and cultivating ability, interest and specialty, teaching and education." (Suhomlinski, The former Soviet Union). "University provides information, but it is imaginative. Classroom centre should lies in students not teachers. Teachers should be guiders, promoters and helpers in class teaching."(A N. Whitehead, British). Consulting-type class just embodies these education spirits.

1.2 The Specific Implementation of Using Consulting-Type Class to Cultivate the Entrepreneur Traits of Students

Consulting-type class teaching method aims to acquire knowledge based on students self-help and communication between teachers and students. In class, students are divided into two or more groups based on practical needs, according to in different doubt on the teaching contents, respectively act as dual leading role of "business consulting experts" and "quasi-entrepreneurs", so the teaching can be conducted between teachers and students, students, students and experts, which is a kind of practical teaching organization class type. In the process, the interaction optimizing relation is embodied, the course form of "reappearance" and "imitation" is changed, the entrepreneur traits training requirements of focusing on innovation and highlighting practice is fully embodied, which is the specific entrepreneurship teaching application class type carrier to cultivate advanced entrepreneur traits.

The implementation of consulting-type class mainly consists of three parts: preparations before class, consulting in class, solutions and teaching reflection, comments and summaries.

1. "Consulting-type class" puts much importance on the students' preparations before class.

After being decorated the curriculum by teachers the students' preview, understand and collecting activities represent, one of the teaching goals is to guide the students generated intense seeking knowledge desire based on the actual perception on specific issue. Teachers consciously offer reference books, teaching materials and other various course resources to the student, this method combines the teaching in class and extracurricular organically, makes the student optimize combination independently and find new information and new knowledge, which can expand the students' learning and life horizons. It emphasizes on students' organic combination, digestion and absorption on knowledge in the learning process, and focuses on the students' cultivation of learning ability, practice ability and innovative ability.

2. "Consulting-type class" can fully mobilize students' learning enthusiasm and initiative, which reflects the dual leading role of "business consulting experts" and "quasi-entrepreneurs".

In class, students are divided into several groups; each group respectively acts as each other's consulting experts and unriddlings for each other. The problems are solved through mutual consultation, if a problem is without complete solutions, closely questions can be asked, the closely questions are more targeted, which require the answerers to give detailed and accurate answers. In this process, teachers should participate in consulting and answering to questions, and make timely guidance, so as to achieve the purpose of organizing teaching.

3. The teaching reflection, comments and summaries of "Consulting-type class" is an important and necessary link.

Teaching reflection before finishing the class aims to collect student's feelings, opinions and learning experiences, which can provide the most direct and valuable reference for the class type further improvement. We fully respect students' feelings, thus laying a solid foundation for so that students in class for application and popularization of each economy and management course, so teaching reflection before finishing the class is very necessary and important.

Through the students' interactive self- consultation, teacher-student interactive consultation, the expert's consultation, internet information consultation, learning team internal consultation, the students' double cognitive roles are reflected: "business consulting experts" and "quasi-entrepreneurs". Especially the "experts" role enormously transfers the students' initiative learning – it is particularly important for the "strong practical application" courses of economy and management. Consulting-type class cultivates students' abilities to collect, analysis and use the information to solve the actual problem, and also cultivates students' language expression, communication skills, comprehensive understanding ability etc. entrepreneur traits, through proposing the problems, analysis, consultation, answering and interactive consultation.

1.3 Main Innovative Points and Training Effectiveness of "Consulting-Type Class"

Judging from the teaching content, Consulting-type Class extracts typical problems before class, is more concentrated generalizations; Judging from the teaching form, it reflects students' leading position in the process teaching fairly clear, students in the process of teaching is a kind of subjective participation and learning; Judging from the role position, students realize the double role in consulting-type class, namely "business consulting experts" and "quasi-entrepreneurs"; Judging from the teaching effect, in consulting-type class , students' active consciousness is strong, they are interested and actively participate in.

1. This is a truly open and practice study. Students oriented, it respects students' main status. Teacher-student interaction, students interaction, teacher's role embodies in the design of class teaching, arrange, guidance, control and summarize. Teaching rows major in students' initiatively seeking, multi-channel consulting and the method to solve problems.

2. Effectively coordinated the relationship between "teacher – directed" with the "student –centered", the method analyzes teaching in the eyes of the characteristics of curriculum and students f active seeking, which has apparent innovation and features, and an obvious practice effect, practical and popularizing value.

3. The strength of consulting-type class is: rich and vivid teaching resources, teaching situations full of consultation and solutions, students' double cognition role can fully mobilize students' learning initiative and enthusiasm, improve students' classroom learning efficiency, improve the teaching quality and teaching efficiency.

Nationally, application of consulting-type class in economy and management teaching in class, we belongs to the first, and respectively successfully completed project approval of "Fifteen Layout" of National Education Science, Heilongjiang province educational reform project in the new century, School important topic in the new century etc. research projects, and wan the first place in "The Third Teachers

Class Type Innovation Class Demonstration of High School in Heilongjiang Province"(Applied course< Marketing>), the first place in excellent lesson plan comparison, the second place in excellent education research. And then we took the second prize of excellent teaching production in Heilongjiang Province in Nov. 2007, which has a great influence in the province. Through reform and practice of this class type, teaching contents are greatly enriched, teaching means are made more perfect, which reflects the strong practicability and operability, has received good teaching effect, and has made a contribution for the promotion of the class type. Meanwhile, the college students' entrepreneurs efficiently training also makes its first appearance, the undergraduates entrepreneurial team accepting of consulting-type training beat the MBA masters and doctors team, who has bagged our college's champion, runners-up and the third place in "May 4th cup" college students business plan competition, and also win the national silver and two bronzes in "The Challenge Cup" national college students business plan competition.

Acknowledgement. Financed by National Social Science Fund (11CSH039);National Natural Science Fund (70972096,70872024); Heilongjiang Province Soft Science Key Project (GB05D101-3); Heilongjiang Province Industry and Informationization committee Soft science Project (GXW20100190); Heilongjiang Province Top Youth Academic Teacher Support Project (1251G016); Heilongjiang Province Higher Education Reform Project; Central University Basic Research Fund (HEUCF100923, 101608).

References

1. Chen, Y.-s.: The Cultivation Orientation of Contemporary Entrepreneurs' Innovative Personality. Modern Enterprise Education (June 2005) (in Chinese)
2. Hu, M.-b., Wang, Z.-x.: Training Mode Study of Efficient Entrepreneurial Type Talents. Journal of Guilin College of Aerospace Technology (January 2005) (in chinese)

The Path to Develop and Utilize University Resources—Evidence from Bengbu University Town

Zhenbo Xu[1] and Rongrong Chen[2]

[1] Bengbu College, lecturer, Bengbu 233000, China
Xuzhenbo74@163.com
[2] Anhui University of Finance & Economics, Bengbu 233000, China
53838847@qq.com

Abstract. In current even the next period, the needs of development and the shortage of funds of higher education in China is still very prominent. In this article, on base of the definition and classification of university resources, and investigation on universities in Bengbu university town, we offered feasibility paths to the relevant departments and universities for reference.

Keywords: University, resources, development, utilization, university town.

Introduction

At present, China's higher education which headed by elite schooling becomes popular. In this process, the needs of development and the shortage of funds of higher education will be very prominent. How to develop and use variety of university resources, improve the efficiency in the use of resources, and make resources optimization disposition, is the focus of educational departments and schools attention, and so is the local government, enterprises and institutions.

"The university resources are the resource elements that maintaining normal operation and maintenance of the continuous development of education undertakings, financial, material in colleges and universities" [1]. Compared with the general social resources, university resources have distinct characteristics of campus. University resources were rooted in the service for teaching and scientific research, development and utilization of resources often want to promote the teaching and research achievements spread. On the other hand, as an important part of social resources, with higher education popularization, university resources should also achieve its own value, and constantly improve exploitation degree, cut the difficult position that running a school, and to promote the good and rapid development in local economy and society.

In recent years, the applied research on university resources has aroused scholars. But overall, always the results are often limited to show the necessity and feasibility of development and utilization in university resources, as for the specific classification of university resources, the actual practice of its development and utilization, there is no involved. Lack of guidance, pertinent and nature of solid exercise, is the biggest problem for colleges and universities.

S. Lin and X. Huang (Eds.): CSEE 2011, Part V, CCIS 218, pp. 590–595, 2011.

1 The Background of Development and Utilization of University Resources

In current even the next period, the needs of development and the shortage of funds of higher education in China is very prominent. Relevant information display, from 1999 to 2006, loans started to the national public, the bank loan of national public universities has reached about 400 billion yuan. Some colleges and universities has carried heavy debt burden, stuck in mud, walked with difficulty. According to Anhui province, "by preliminary statistics which is allowed for the 81 ordinary universities statistics, the colleges and universities total liabilities is 8.35 billion RMB (including bank liabilities 6.398 billion RMB), 24% of the asset-liability ratio by the end of 2006. If base on the year 2006, bank loans by 6% per annum, measuring every provincial public universities reasonable limitation liabilities. A total of 21 universities, 4 junior colleges and 10 high vocational colleges, beyond a reasonable limitation, need to dissolve the debt at least 2.9 billion RMB" [2].

"China's Educational Reform and Development Program" explicitly pointed out, public education funds will still tend to compulsory education. Government funds may not have greatly increased, in this situation, it need multiple sources of funding mechanisms and should "display the superiority in the higher education, use the college technology, intelligences, equipments, facilities and school-run industries etc, carry out foreign service and sales, and increase education funding sources" [3].

On the other hand, from higher education in developed country to see, university resources of society are highly open. For instance, American universities are often called "no fence university". Its library, computer room and so on are basically open to the whole society, many schools even open 24 hours, and provide considerate and convenient service. At the same time, university zone of high-tech companies can make full use of university's information and equipment resources. This not only optimize the allocation of resources, also make the school and social development is an organic whole, the university became a regional economy, social development of intelligence source, radiant source of technology. In turn, these local governments and high-tech companies actively support the development of the school, and guarantee for schools' growth.

In conclusion, develop and use university resources energetically, explore and exploit funds increasing channels actively, China's higher education to become popular, to improve education quality of teaching continuously, to promote the coordinated development of universities and local, is either necessary urgent or feasible.

2 Paths to Develop and Utilize University Resources of Bengbu University Town

The university town, usually refers to "a number of universities as the main body, with the city rely on and supported by sharing resources or function complementary and the road of development, study and research as the main object of emerging community " [4]. In recent years, along with China's higher education rapid expansion, the country has built some university town, or higher education campus (hereinafter collectively referred to as "university town"). Bengbu university town is in eastern outskirts of Bengbu city, Anhui province. Its planning area is 5,800 acres, building area of 1.28 million square meters, has entered into Anhui university of finance and economics, Bengbu medical college, Bengbu college, Anhui electronic information vocational college. Since 2002, Bengbu university town has already begun to take shape, all kinds of school houses, roads, water supply, and other public facilities has invested 610 million RMB. Because of the huge investment, government and universities are facing greater financial pressure.

The following, according to the properties and uses of university resources into different categories, based on the investigation, discuss paths of development and utilization of resources in colleges and universities of Bengbu university town in recent years.

2.1 Natural and Building Resources

Natural resources are referred to the land mountains, lakes, etc owned by the universities; Building resources, include the bridges, channels, squares, spaces, etc.

Bengbu university town is located in eastern outskirts which is on the east side of Longhu lake. In this area, Bengbu college leans against the Lu Mountain in the south, faces the Longzi Lake in the west. Anhui university of finance and economics, Bengbu medical college, and Anhui electronic information vocational college are respectively occupied about 1821, 1300, 849 acres, with a total construction area of 70.1, 33, 21.62 thousand square meters. There are high-rises inside the schools with open squares, well provided teaching facilities and elegant living environment. But the survey found that schools haven't developed and used its natural and building resources very well. Anhui electronic information vocational college, just used its south gate square and space for the cooperation with a driving school. At present it has recruited more students, and better economic benefits.

2.2 School-Run Industry Resources

School-run industry is rely on the college technology and intelligence, established by universities, with scientific and technological achievements transformation, realize the technology innovation as the main characteristics of the economic entity. At present, many universities have such furniture, tools, flowers, horticultural industries resources, such as a science teaching and research base. This achieves the combination of "production, teaching and research", and the important measure of strengthening the quality of education. Furthermore it can turn into economic entity, and bring the real benefit.

Bengbu university town have rich school-run industries resources, including partly realized conversion, create a good economic and social value. For example, Bengbu medical college, played its research and professional advantages, successively established The first and second affiliated hospital. Its popularity and reputation belong to the province-class. Bengbu college also has the metalworking plant, food processing practice institutions in campus. But overall, the survey found that university town haven't exert its technology and intelligence resources advantage very well, didn't have their own school-run industries. In this, the brothers college's successful experience can be learned. Such as Anhui science &technology university actively develop its cultivation, breeding technology park, food processing garden, veterinary hospital, etc. Through the demonstrative leading and technical guidance, the project has many ways for the service of industrialized operation to agriculture, it has won excellent economic and social benefits.

2.3 Operating Resources

University operating resources including campus stadiums, gymnasiums, canteen, water room, bathroom, campus neighboring shops, etc. For sports resources, Bengbu university town have quite sports facilities and field. Such as Anhui university of finance and economics now have 141691 square metres indoor and outdoor sports venues, the per capita indoor sports is 1.46 square meters, and outdoor stadium is 7.25 square meters, also provided with six student health testing rooms, four sets of test instrument. But now these sports facilities are only open to their own teachers and students, as for the neighborhood, such as Huguang district and Longhu Spring, which have many residents, they're actually short of sports resources .The schools can consider to open in moderation, and take an appropriate fee under public service premise to the public. To this, vice minister of education Haoping has emphasized in the meeting of "national school sports venues open to public", "national school sports venues should open first stressed to students, so that the students can benefit from it. It also should actively explore public sports venues for free or preferential open to teenager" [5].

In addition, our universities have such as the canteen, water room, bathroom, campus neighboring shops and other hardware facilities. It is general very well equipped. These resources are profit-making, they can consider to guard the staff and students' life services. At the same time, we can introduce market mechanism appropriately, and make open to the surrounding community.

2.4 Technical Resources

Relying on the powerful research advantage, technical resources is most important part in the university resource. It include obtained patents and the know-how of colleges and universities, etc. Bengbu university town have strong scientific research ability and rich scientific research achievements, they can make full use of the resources according to their own particular situation.

Development and utilization of technical resources actively, which relates to the universities, more closely with local economic and social development. It is gratifying that local government have begun to construct the science park in Bengbu university town. The mayor Xuequn Zhang led Bengbu trade group, and stresses to study the knowledge innovation constructive area in Yangpu district of Shanghai. This area explored university campus, technical park, public community "three zone integration, linkage development, linkage development" mode baked. It's said that Bengbu university science park plans to build in the Bengbu university town, and has completed design of the bidding. The project with a total construction area is about 1.1 million square meters, estimating total investment of about 1.8 billion RMB, two standard workshops which are 53,000 square meters already started to construct [6].

2.5 Cultural Resources

1. Campus media culture resources

Each school in Bengbu university town now has its own web sites, school magazines(physical & electronic)and broadcasting station, most of them are opening and offering to the public, therefore, they reach a very large audience. Every school makes full use of its resource and get economic benefit on condition that without affect the basic functions of the campus media, such as the development of the advertising space in school magazines and school web sites, the sale of the audio advertising time in campus broadcast. A recent survey suggests, "Ancai Youth" of Anhui University of Finance and Economics and "Bengbu college newspaper" regularly reverse advertising space welcome buyer's purchasing.

2. Publishing cultural resources
Many universities have their own publishing cultural resources, like newspaper publishers, magazine publishers and printing factories, some universities even have their own book-publishing houses, electronic audiovisual publishing houses, film and TV studios, etc. "According to a rough statistical analysis, an university with a small and medium-sized publishing house can publish about 150~200 kinds of new books. With the books republished added, the circulation can achieve 400~500 thousand a year. Take into account of those factors, the annual revenue of print and press of a university in medium scale can be up to 14,000,000 RMB [7].

It is not hard to come to the conclusion based on the statistics above that there is a great possibility that universities can put more emphasis on exploring the resource of printing business in order to promote the development of relevant industries. Universities that are qualified in Bengbu University Town, take Anhui University of Finance and Economics as an example, should take certain measures to duplicating, printing, phototypesetting and the publishing of textbooks at the same time as soon as possible.

3. Culture stadiums resources
Culture stadiums are the most overlooked culture resources. Most universities have their own cultural stadiums, such as library, cultural center, science and technology museum, art gallery, museum, movie theater, etc. But they are usually only open for the students of the university and are in idle state during the rest of the time. Meanwhile, the area which the university located in may has its own library, art gallery, movie theater, etc. But they are usually in very high demand due to the short of the available resources.

For that reason, colleges can give full play to their own advantages, meet the societal needs with paid when the culture stadiums resources are in idle state, such as set up reading rooms for external readers and charge per hour or be paid by monthly card and yearly card for the service provided. It is reported that the education park in Chizhou and the library of Chizhou College has been shared with Chizhou Library in our province. As for art gallery, it can undertake large literary performance activities from outside and also can be adaptable for many uses," sports center in University of Edinburgh, for example, is for badminton training from 10 to 12, after 12 it is for children's training with pad and simple protective equipments on the ground; In the afternoon, with the canvas on the wall pulled away, the sports center is unexpectedly used as an indoor rock climbing center [8].

3 Concluding

This article has combed the existing and potential resources of university, it proposed development and utilization of thinking by category, and around some of the universities' thought and actual practice to explore. For other university, its own real resource can be combined with, so as the local economic and social development needs, selectively reference.

In recent years, development and utilization of university town resources in Bengbu have made some actual effect though, but also has the following questions: one is the school itself, not catch university town construction and the development opportunity very well, resource development and utilization is main or simple expansion. The second is different schools, are basically fight alone, not reflect complementary advantages and the coordinated development, existing the integration and sharing of education resources are not up on the agenda; Third is inside the university town, its library, sports hall, movie theaters and other cultural and educational sports facilities using urban didn't coordinate with local public cultural infrastructure; Local government and the universities' relationship is still the traditional closed relationship over the past, conversation, communication, coordination mechanism can not good form. In order to realize the beneficial interaction of talent, funding, community service development ,there are more to be studied.

Throughout the present status of the resources' development and utilization of universities in our country, it is not hard to find that the closed-end form of the long-term running tradition, distinctive campus culture and social psychological estrangement restrict the development, the utilization and the sharing of university resources. We should break the barriers between departments and schools with the principle "use but possess" to promote the open sharing of all kinds of high-quality resources and eventually achieve the ultimate goal which is not only alleviating the financial pressure in universities and improving education quality but also promoting the sound and rapid economic growth in local areas.

References

1. Wang, D.: Modern Commercial 3, 23 (2008)
2. The countermeasure and suggestion of precaution and solving colleges liabilities in our province, http://www.ahpc.gov.cn/info
3. Chen, W.: China Institute for Educational Finance Research 6, 13 (2007)
4. Yang, T.: The Journal of Beijing University of Technology 2, 86 (2003)
5. Xuan, W.: Anhui Daily Version. A2 (September 29, 2010)
6. Hao,Y.: Bengbu Daily Version. A1 (November 15, 2010)
7. Gong, W.: Seek 2, 111 (2003)
8. Wang, Y.: Science Education. 12, 11 (2008)

Research on the Development and Utilization of National Information Resources Based on Marginal Theory and Goal Programming Method—Taking the National Information Resources of Chinese as Example

ZhiTao Du[1], LiHong Liu[2], and GuoQing Huo[2]

[1] Beijing Institute of Science and Technology Information, China
[2] Graduate University of Chinese Academy of Sciences, Beijing, China
du_zhitao@hotmail.com, ddzztt@sina.com

Abstract. National information resources (NIR) as a kind of strategic resources to promote national competitiveness, which is vital to the national economic and social development, possess broad perspectives, foundational and public characteristics. The content system of NIR consists of the layer of information about physical properties, the layer of metadata, the layer of information about national basic data, the layer of classified information and the layer of information for national decisiveness. In order to improve the efficiency and effectiveness for developing and utilizing of NIR, this study discussed the marginal conditions for maximizing value of NIR, depicted the marginal cost curve and marginal benefit curve of NIR, and established investment optimization decision model of NIR based on the goal programming model.

Keywords: National information resources(NIR), Marginal cost, Marginal benefit, Goal programming, Decision model.

0 Introductions

Information resources are a crucial production element of modern society, which plays a more and more important role in the social development. Together with materials and energy resources, the three make the total social resources utilization system. However, due to the complexity of NIR's contents and calculation methods, the content edge system structure as well as the research paradigm of NIR have not reached an agreement yet, which leads to the present extensive-guidance stage of the development and utilization of NIR. We still have a long way to go in the aspect of studying NIR in a more scientific, systematic and quantitative way. Based on this purpose, we study on the limitation of the maximizing value of NIR and the input decisions in this paper in order to support a more scientific and effective NIR planning.

1 The Related Research of NIR and Its Content System

Researchers in and abroad in the NIR field have focused on the following aspects: (1) National Information Policy Aspect. Duffs, Alistair S have studied on the developing

S. Lin and X. Huang (Eds.): CSEE 2011, Part V, CCIS 218, pp. 596–603, 2011.

history and trend of National Information Policy [1]. Henrici, Ingrid [2] Michael Middleton [3], Haines, M [4], Feinberg [5] have studied the information policy of South Africa, Australia, England and "after 911"America respectively. Muir, A and Oppenheim have studied on the national information policy from the copyright, information freedom and data protection aspects [6]. Oppenheim, C has studied the information policies of developed countries from the aspect of electronic government, electronic business, information acquiring, metadata, information freedom, intelligent right, innovation, information education and the legal guarantee aspects [7]. (2) NIR Strategy Aspect. For example, Hart, E T have predicted the changes of American NIR strategy after "911" [8]. (3) NIR Development and Utilization Aspect. For example, Cheryl Marie Cordeiro and Suliman Al-Hawamdeh have studied the IT2000 Scheme of Singapore [9]. (4) Theoretical Model and System Design Aspect. JingChuan Hou has established the structure model for central database and designed its macro conditioning mechanism to network information as well as economy activities [10]. As can be seen from the research above all, the qualitative research to the input-output effectiveness in the NIR construction process is in great need, which makes the maximizing of NIR value hard to achieve.

National Information Resource (NIR) is not all of the information resources of a country, but the strategy information resources, which represents the strength and the level of modernization of a country. NIR has the characteristics of macroscopic, foundation, public, long-term, guidance, decisive etc., which reflects the competitiveness of a country.

NIR is a multi-dimensional concept while its mainframe is built by five layers(Figure 1): (1) The layer of information about physical properties. This layer refers to national information infrastructure. (2) The layer of metadata of NIR. Since metadata could be used to describe NIR's attributes, like elements, scope, quality, source, providing way, and so on, it becomes the integrating tool and connection for the scattered, heterogeneous NIR. (3) The layer of information about national basic data. It's the most fundamental information resources of a nation, which includes data of

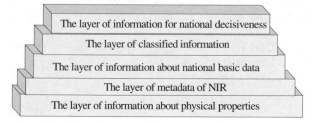

Fig. 1. The Five Layers Model of the Content System of NIR

population, legal person, space & Geographical status, vehicles, buildings, and so on. (4) The layer of classified information. This is the information for all industries, regions and organizations based on the national basic data. (5) The layer of information for national decisiveness. This kind of information is based on the comprehensive induction, deep mining, and systematic integration of each industry, region and organizations' information resources.

2   The Life Cycle of Development and Utilization of NIR Based on Marginal Theory

In order to maximize the value of NIR, NIR must output maximum earnings under the established constraints. To achieve this goal, the necessary and sufficient condition is

NIR's marginal cost equals marginal revenue. Set the total investment cost as C, which promotes the total revenues of NIR, R. There is a functional relation between R and C: C=f (R). Thus the marginal cost MC=$\triangle$C/$\triangle$R=df(R)/dR. If we know C=f (R), then the curves of marginal cost and marginal revenue would be easy to obtain.

The relationship between total investment cost and total revenue of NIR has such characteristics in the nature (Figure 2): when NIR in the initial construction period, due to the large-scale infrastructure construction, the NIR total input costs is greater than the total revenue. Meanwhile, the increasing rate of total investment cost is greater than the increasing rate of total revenue. With large-scale infrastructure investment of NIR gradually completed, the growth rate of NIR's total revenue gradually surpasses the growth rate of total investment. When the infrastructure construction of NIR ends, NIR's total revenue is greater than its total cost, which makes NIR enter the period of benefit. However, in the subsequent NIR utilization process, although information transmission, access, store become more and more easily, the cost to dig out some useful information from the mass of information increases greatly, which gradually reduces the efficiency of NIR when using. Meanwhile, the updating rate of information technology grows faster and faster, which makes the benefit period be in increasingly short duration after infrastructure investment each time.

To compare the relationship between NIR's total revenue and total cost with the relationship between marginal revenue and marginal cost more comprehensively, the intermediate variables Q, which acts on behalf of NIR's integrated output.

Both cost and benefit can be expressed as a function of Q, while the total cost is C(Q) and the total revenue is R(Q). Thus the marginal cost would be: MC(Q) = dC(Q)/dQ while the marginal revenue would be: MR(Q) = dR(Q)/dQ. The life cycle of development and utilization of NIR, and the relations between the total revenue and cost, marginal revenue and marginal cost of each phase of life cycle is shown in Figure 3.

In the term between 0 and Q_2, C(Q)>R(Q), which means NIR is in construction period. Furthermore, this period could be divided into 2 stages: (1) Stage 1: from 0 to

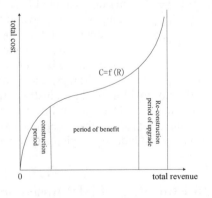

Fig. 2. The relationship between cost and revenue of NIR

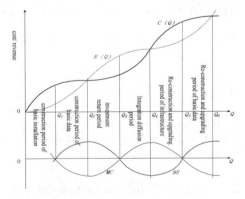

Fig. 3. Lifecycle of Development and Utilization of NIR

Q_1. This stage is the basic installation stage of NIR construction period in which investment to the "hardware" part like the information transmission network is in great need. Thus the growth rate of input greatly outruns that of revenue: MC>MR. This stage is named the construction period of basic installation. (2) Stage 2: from Q_1 to Q_2. This stage puts an emphasis on the "software" part investment like the construction of NIR metadata and national basic database since the large-scale "hardware" construction has been completed gradually. Thus the growth rate of revenue surpasses that of investment: MR>MC. This stage is named "construction period of basic data".

In the term from Q_2 to Q_4, C (Q) <R (Q), which means NIR is in the investment returning period. Furthermore, this period could be divided into two stages: (1) Stage 1: from Q_2 to Q_3. In this stage, the basic installation of NIR has been completed. What's more, R (Q)>C (Q) while MR>MC. The value of NIR has already appeared which makes this stage be named "investment- return period". Maximum total returning has been reached when MC=MR on the point Q_3. It's not difficult to infer that Q_3 is the goal point of maximizing the value of NIR. (2) Stage 2: from Q_3 to Q_4. In this stage, with the deepening development of NIR, the further utilization of NIR becomes more and more difficult and the NIR contents become more obsolete and useless. Thus it's necessary to further strengthen and update the information resources. While total returning of NIR at this stage is still greater than the total input, the NIR growth rate of cost is greater than that of returning, which leads to MC>MR. And this stage is named "Integration Diffusion Period".

In the term from Q_4 to Q_6, C(Q) > R (Q). And NIR is in the reconstruction period, which could be divided into two stages either: (1) Stage 1: from Q_4 to Q_5. In this stage, as information technology advances, some of NIR's infrastructure has lagged behind over time. Thus all hardware resources of NIR must be upgraded or rebuilt, which leads the total cost to surpass the total returning. Also, MC>MR. This stage of NIR shows similar characteristics with the first phase and is named "Re-construction and upgrading period of infrastructure" . (2) Stage 2: from Q_5 to Q_6. Similar to the second stage, this stage is mainly the "soft" resources development of NIR. In this period, MR>MC and this stage is named "Re-construction and upgrading period of basic data".

In reality, the six stages may cross appear, showing the feature of developing when using at the same time. It is important to be clear that Q_3 is the goal point of maximizing the value of NIR and the optimal integrated output of NIR since NIR's marginal returning equals NIR's marginal cost at that point. In order to maximize the value of NIR, we must carry out overall planning, scientific arrangement and optimized allocation to make NIR close to point Q_3.

3 Decision Model for NIR Investment Based on Goal Programming Method

Since integrated output Q could be representative of the various inputs to NIR, the process to find the optimal point Q_3 would be the process to find a variety of building measures under certain established constraints. The main problem of NIR in the current process of development and utilization is uneven development. NIR's systemic and networking characteristics make the only way to maximize value is to achieve a balanced development in all aspects. This kind of balance could be reflected by the equal value of marginal costs of different measures. So to find the best combination of solutions is to find the best combination of measures of marginal cost equalization under a given target of constraints. Based on these analyses, the solutions of maximizing the value of NIR could be got by establishing the following objective programming model.

Set there are n kinds of input measures. Set the cost of i-type measure as $C_i(R_i), i=1,2,\ldots, n$, and n is a continuously differentiable function of the first order. Again set the total budget which can be put into as C. Set the total returning of NIR as R and R^L_i is the returning requirement of i-type measure. Set I^L_i as the capital budget limit of i-type measure.

Thus the multi-objective decision model for maximizing NIR's value is shown below:

$$\min\{P_1 w_1 d_1, P_2 w_2 (d_2^- + d_2), P_3 w_3 (d_3^- + d_4^- + \cdots + d_{n+1}^-), P_4 w_4 (d_{n+2}^- + d_{n+2}^+ + \cdots + d_{2n+1}^- + d_{2n+1}^-), P_5 w_5 (d_{2n+2}^+ + d_{2n+2}^- + \cdots + d_{3n+1}^+ + d_{3n+1}^-)\}$$

s.t
$$R_1 + R_1 + R_2 + \cdots + R_n - d_1^+ + d_1^- = R$$
$$C_1(R_1) + C_2(R_2) + \cdots + C_n(R_n) - d_2^+ + d_2^- = C \qquad (1)$$
$$\left[\frac{dC_i(R_i)}{dR_i} + \cdots + \frac{dC_{i+1}(R_{i+1})}{dR_{i+1}}\right]^2 - d_{i+2}^+ + d_{i+2}^- = \varepsilon \qquad (l = 1,2,\ldots, \text{ n-1})$$
$$R_i - d_{n-1+i}^+ + d_{n+1+i}^- = R_i^L \qquad (l = 1,2,\ldots, \text{ n})$$
$$C_i(R_i) - d_{2n+1+i}^+ + d_{2n+1+i}^- = I_i^L \qquad (l = 1,2,\ldots, \text{ n})$$
$$R_i \geq 0, \qquad\qquad d_k^+, d_k^- \geq 0 \qquad (k = 1,2,\ldots,3n+1)$$

In the above description, d_k^+, d_k^- are Positive and negative deviation variables respectively. P_1, P_2, P_3, P_4, P_5 are the precedence level of each target constraints while w_1, w_2, w_3, w_4, w_5 stand for the weights of designated deviation variables.

The first target constraint formula stands for the total returning requirement of NIR. The second constraint formula is for the limit budget of total fund which can be input. The third constraint formula is for the balance of marginal cost, which means the solution got from this model should satisfy the condition that the marginal cost by each measure should be approximately the same. And ε is the equalization error of marginal cost, which could be designated as any appropriate small number according to the cost magnitude and specific analysis conditions. The fourth constraint formula is for the returning request of each measure. The fifth formula is for the limit of fund which could be input for each measure.

4 Empirical Analysis—Taking Chinese NIR as Example

An objective programming model is established here using the data from "2009 China Information Almanac" [11], "China Statistical Yearbook 2009" [12] and the National Informatization Evaluation Center. Since there is no recognized index system for measuring NIR and the authors' time is limited to collect statistical data from the real economy, the data collected in this paper can only be used as an example of the application of the above model and cannot be indicative of reality.

The main measures to complete the programming target of NIR can be divided into 6 categories: (1) The information infrastructure construction of NIR, including the construction of communication network infrastructure, the construction of public libraries, the construction of network of information and intelligence organizations, the construction of satellite launch and use of project. (2) National basic database construction, including the construction of the natural resources basic database, space & geographic basic database, legal entities' basic database, population as well as vehicles' basic database, etc. (3) Government information resources construction, including the national e-government extranet construction, etc. (4) Macroeconomic and industry information resources construction, including the construction of macroeconomic management information system, the industry information construction of banking supervision, transportation, petroleum & petrochemical, food supply, iron and steel, etc. (5) Information resources construction in areas of people's livelihood, including information construction of minimum living guarantee, culture, national public health, meteorology, earthquakes, environmental protection, etc. (6) National security information resources construction, like construction of military information, golden-shield project, etc. The returning is measured by a set of comprehensive indexes, which get their weighs through the analytical hierarchy process (AHP) separately. The qualitative indexes are got by Delphi Method and then turned into quantitative ones through 7 Likert Scale. As shown in Table 1, all indexes are using percentile scores and standardized.

Table 1. The returning indexes and its measurement of 6 categories of NIR

	Categories	Returning by Categories	Weighs	Before planning		After planning	
				returning	Capital input(100 million yuan)	Returning	Capital input (100 million yuan)
The Total Returning of NIR	①The information infrastructure construction	Coverage and Utilization Level of（R1）	0.1754	70	0.1754	2100	68.5	1661.2
	②National basic database construction	Degree of perfection of the national basic database（R2）	0.1831	68	0.1831	500	71.2	380.4
	③Government information resources construction	Government efficiency（R3）	0.1697	62	0.1697	300	59.8	413.6
	④Macroeconomic and industry information resources construction	NIR's Contribution to GDP （R4）	0.1908	71	0.1908	1500	73.1	1089.4
	⑤Information resources construction in areas of people's livelihood	State of social civilization （R5）	0.0949	88	0.0949	600	83.2	643.1
	⑥National security information resources construction	National Security Index（R6）	0.1861	72	0.1861	1000	70.7	912.3
	Total			70.5		6000	70.2	5100

According to the functional characteristics of marginal returning and marginal cost, Correlation Analysis, Principal component analysis, Factor Analysis, Regression Analysis are applied to deal with these statistical data. Thus the total cost function of the 6 above major initiatives is established as follow:

$$① \quad C_1 = 74(R_1 - 3.45)^3 + 0.62R_1 + 0.75 \quad \text{And} \quad R_1 \geq 3.45 \tag{2}$$

$$② \quad C_2 = 39(R_2 - 6.63)^3 + 0.45R_2 + 0.22 \quad \text{And} \quad R_2 \geq 6.33 \tag{3}$$

③ $C_3 = 15(R_3 - 2.27)^3 + 0.04R_3 + 0.31$ And $R_3 \geq 2.27$ (4)

④ $C_4 = 9(R_4 - 4.57)^3 + 0.52R_4 + 0.09$ And $R_4 \geq 4.57$ (5)

⑤ $C_5 = 11(R_5 - 4.41)^3 + 0.30R_5 + 0.71$ And $R_5 \geq 4.41$ (6)

⑥ $C_6 = 22(R_6 - 7.54)^3 + 0.29R_6 + 0.82$ and $R_6 \geq 7.54$ (7)

In the above formulas, C refers to the input cost of NIR (100 million yuan) while R is the target returning of NIR construction. Now if we want to make the NIR contribution achieve 70.5, at least 600 billion yuan is in need according to the target returning of all measures. If we set the total input budget of NIR construction as 510 billion yuan, then it is necessary to adjust the measures in the context of hard budget constraints.

A decision model is established according to formula (1). The cost constraint of total input, the total target returning limit and the marginal cost equilibrium constraint take the first-level precedence, while the capital input constraint and the target returning limit of respective measure take the second-level precedence. Thus the objective programming model is established as follow:

$\min\{P_1[w_1 d_1^-, w_2(d_2^+ + d_2^-), w_3(d_3^+ + d_4^+ + d_5^+ + d_6^+ + d_7^+)], P_2 w_4(d_8^+ + d_8^- + d_9^+ + d_9^- + d_{10}^+ + d_{10}^- + d_{11}^+ +$
$d_{11}^- + d_{12}^+ + d_{12}^- + d_{13}^+ + d_{13}^- + d_{14}^+ + d_{14}^- + d_{15}^+ + d_{15}^- + d_{16}^+ + d_{16}^- + d_{17}^+ + d_{17}^- + d_{18}^+ + d_{18}^- + d_{19}^+ + d_{19}^-)\}$

s.t

$$R_1 + R_2 + R_3 + R_4 + R_5 + R_6 - d_1^+ + d_1^- = 70.5$$

$74(R_1 - 3.45)^3 + 0.62R_1 + 39(R_2 - 6.63)^3 + 0.45R_2 + 15(R_3 - 2.27)^3 + 0.04R_3$
$+ 9(R_4 - 4.57)^3 + 0.52R_4 + 11(R_5 - 4.41)^3 + 0.30R_5 + 22(R_6 - 7.54)^3 + 0.29R_6 + 2.9$ (8)
$- d_2^+ + d_2^- = 5100$

$$[222(R_1 - 3.45)^2 - 117(R_2 - 6.63)^2 + 0.17]^2 - d_3^+ + d_3^- = \varepsilon$$
$$[117(R_2 - 6.63)^2 - 45(R_3 - 2.27)^2 + 0.41]^2 - d_4^+ + d_4^- = \varepsilon$$
$$[45(R_3 - 2.27)^2 - 27(R_4 - 4.57)^2 - 0.48]^2 - d_5^+ + d_5^- = \varepsilon$$
$$[27(R_4 - 4.57)^2 - 33(R_5 - 4.41)^2 + 0.22]^2 - d_6^+ + d_6^- = \varepsilon$$
$$[33(R_5 - 4.41)^2 - 66(R_6 - 7.54)^2 + 0.01]^2 - d_7^+ + d_7^- - \varepsilon$$
$$R_1/0.1754 - d_8^+ + d_8^- = 70 , \quad R_2/0.1831 - d_9^+ + d_9^- = 68$$
$$R_3/0.1697 - d_{10}^+ + d_{10}^- = 62, \quad R_4/0.1908 - d_{11}^+ + d_{11}^- = 71$$
$$R_5/0.0949 - d_{12}^+ + d_{12}^- = 88, \quad R_6/0.1861 - d_{13}^+ + d_{13}^- = 72$$
$$39(R_2 - 6.63)^3 + 0.45R_2 + 0.22 - d_{15}^+ + d_{15}^- = 500$$
$$15(R_3 - 2.27)^3 + 0.04R_3 + 0.31 - d_{16}^+ + d_{16}^- = 300$$
$$9(R_4 - 4.57)^3 + 0.52R_4 + 0.09 - d_{17}^+ + d_{17}^- = 1500$$
$$11(R_5 - 4.41)^3 + 0.30R_5 + 0.71 - d_{18}^+ + d_{18}^- = 600$$
$$22(R_6 - 7.54)^3 + 0.29R_6 + 0.82 - d_{19}^+ + d_{19}^- = 1000$$
$$R_1 \geq 3.45, \quad R_2 \geq 6.33, \quad R_3 \geq 2.27, \quad R_4 \geq 4.57, \quad R_5 \geq 4.41, \quad R_6 \geq 7.54$$
$$d_k^+ . d_k^- \geq 0 \quad (k = 1,2,...,19)$$

In the above formula, $\varepsilon = 0.0001$. Set w_2=500 while w_3=50 since the input budget belongs to the hard constraint. Set the weight of target returning and other constraint conditions as: w_1=w_4=10. Thus the model's calculation result is: R_1=12.0149; R_2=13.03672; R_3=10.14806; R_4= 13.94748; R_5=7.89568; R_6= 13.15727.

5 Conclusion

Innovation of this paper is not only enriched the content of information resources in theoretical way but also proposed the quantitative, systematic and precision ideas to NIR's decision making process, which provides a new way of thinking to address the extensive, experience of, low efficient in resource allocation problems in the development and utilization of NIR. Of course, this idea is not only for national information resources but can also provide basis for decision making in the information construction of a particular industry or a certain region. All of these will be the direction of future research.

References

1. Duff, A.S.: The Past, Present, and Future of Information Policy. Information, Communication & Society 7(1), 69–87 (2004)
2. Henrici, I.: Approach to the formulation of a National Information Policy for South Africa. South African Journal of Libraries and Information Science 70(1), 30–33 (2004)
3. Middleton, M.: Information Policy and Infrastructure in Australia. Journal of Government Information 24(1), 9–25 (1997)
4. Haines, M.: National Information Policy and National Network Development. Multimedia Information and Technology 26(1), 52–59 (2000)
5. Feinberg, L.E.: Homeland Security: Implications for Information Policy and Practice—First Appraisal. Government Information Quarterly 19(3), 265–288 (2002)
6. Muir, A., Oppenheim, C.: National Information Policy development worldwide IV: Copyright, Freedom of Information and Data Protection. Journal of Information Science 28(6), 467–481 (2002)
7. Oppenheim, C.: Do We Need Fresh Thinking on National Information Policy? Alexandria 14(1), 1–2 (2002)
8. Hart, E.T.: A Look at Changes in Gvernment Information Policies after. IFLA Journal 28(5/6), 273–277 (2002)
9. Cordeiro, C.M., Al-Hawamdeh, S.: National Information Infrastructure and the realization of Singapore IT2000 Initiative. Information Research 6(2), 96 (2001)
10. Hou, J.: Research on Central Information Management and Mechanism for Macroregulating Network Economy. Information Studies:Theory & Application 1 (2005)
11. China Information Yearbook, Beijing China Information Yearbook magazine (2009)
12. China Statistical Yearbook, Beijing China Statistics Press (2009)

Research on the Active Mechanism of the Inter-firm Cooperative Relationship Strength Based on the Game Theory

ZhiTao Du and Hong Fu

Beijing Institute of Science and Technology Information, China
du_zhitao@hotmail.com, ddzztt@sina.com

Abstract. The inter-firm cooperative relations strength (CRS) is an indicator, which measures the extent of cooperation-tightness between firms. Therefore, different CRS results in different business activities. This study, through a simple game model, analyzed the relations between Inter-firm CRS and some other indicators, such as the firm profits, business efficiency, cooperation-contribution, production, product similarity and prices, etc.. The author concluded three regular patterns including the diminishing marginal of cooperation-contribution, cooperation speculation, increasing profits by cooperation. And also proposed the following factors: Firstly, not only the tangible benefits but also the intangible ones after cooperation should be concerned by the firms when they take part in the action of cooperation. Secondly, in order to obtain a more reliable security guarantee, the relatively low efficiency firm should select the tighter cooperation relations. Thirdly, the altruistic behavior during the course of cooperating, which is win-win behavior, should be advocated. It can not only promote the deepening of cooperation relations, but also bring much more benefits to the firm itself. Fourthly, the cooperation should be happened between two firms which have different products. Finally, through cooperation between firms, the cost can be reduced and the capability be enhanced as well, therefore, cooperation is the only way for the development of firms.

Keywords: Firm, Cooperative Relations Strength, Management Behavior, Game Theory.

0 Introductions

As a kind of competitive advantage and unique assets, which could be called relation-assets, of the enterprises, the cooperative-relations have been able to create excess profits for them. The same as other assets of the enterprises, which have to invest higher cost on the relation-assets in advance, and also spend much more time on it as well. The extent of cooperation-tightness between firms is proportional to the costs of the relation-assets. Different CRS results in different decision behaviors. Hence, the enterprises must identify the CRS and make efficient decisions to create maximum relation-profits with minimum relation-costs. Gang Li and ZhiTao Du has established an identified model through the researching of inter-firm CRS [1]. The enterprises can

S. Lin and X. Huang (Eds.): CSEE 2011, Part V, CCIS 218, pp. 604–611, 2011.
© Springer-Verlag Berlin Heidelberg 2011

identify the relations between each other quantitatively based on the model, which provides systematic solutions for the enterprises. This study discussed the impacts on the enterprises' management behaviors brought by different CRS in the light of a simple game model.

1 Definition of Inter-firm CRS

The notion of the strength of relationship tie is derived from sociology. Granovetter, an American scholar, put forward it for the first time in 1973. He defines it as a combination of the amount of time, the emotional intensity, the intimacy (mutual confiding), and the reciprocal service which characterize the tie and holds that the strength of a tie is a kind of tie relationship formed from the communication and contact among individuals and organizations and such relationship may be classified into strong and weak relationships in four aspects, interactive frequency, emotional intensity, intimacy and reciprocal service [2]. Uzzi classifies transaction relationships inside an industrial cluster as arm's length relationship and embedded relationship. He believes arm's length relationship is weak, a business exchange relationship that is non-repeated and pure, with which the exchanging parties lack mutually beneficial cooperation in the long run; and the embedded relationship is strong, with which both parties have high degree of trust and reciprocal expectations and the parties will internalize the external truncation actions [3]. Nooteboom and Gilsing describe the strength of ties with six dimensions, scope, relation-specific investments, duration, frequency of interaction, tie-specific trust and degree of control [4]. Scholars such as Cullen, Johnson, Skano, Sarkar, Echambadi, Cavusgil and Aulakh have opinions similar to Hausman, holding that tie strength consists of mutual trust, reciprocal commitment, and cooperation and communication [5],[6]. This paper argued that inter-firm CRS is an indicator for measuring the extent of inter-firm cooperation-tightness, which forms a continual pedigree from tightest to irrelevance. And the firms will balance between the polar of the pedigree intentionally or otherwise. Then choose an optional CRS with a view to obtain the maximum profits and avoid being held-up by the cooperative relations. The inter-firm CRS is affected both by their decision behavior and the internal and external environment. This study defined the domain of inter-firm CRS as θ and $\theta \in [0, 1]$. If $\theta=0$, it stands for non-cooperation between the firms. If $\theta=1$, it stands for all-round cooperation between firms. If θ is located between 0 and 1, it stands for different extent of cooperation-tightness between firms.

2 The Game Model about CRS Affecting on Management Behavior of Firm

As there are two ways of cooperation, which are longitudinal and latitudinal cooperation between firms, Michael Porter argued that the firm can choose different means of cooperation [7]. This paper just discussed the latter because the former is often stable and easy operation based on the business cooperation in value chain, while the latter is the kind of cooperation based on the level of strategy, so the firms are facing greater risks and difficult to be successful.

2.1 Assumption and the Construction of the Model

The assumption of this paper is that there are two firms (firm i and firm j) with same size in the same market. And both of the two firms would like to cooperate with each other through signing contract. Hence, the firms who participate in cooperation have possibility to negotiate with each other. Product market is Cournot competition. Both sides chose CRS θ at the same time and reach cooperation agreement through contracting at first. Moreover, the two firms invest on the cooperation specifically, such as all kinds of specialization assets of cooperation and monitoring facilities used for supervising both sides during the course of cooperation, based on the CRS θ. Eventually, both sides make the plan of output in the light of the principle of maximum of profit.

q_i and q_j stand for the output of firm i and firm j after cooperation respectively. p_i and p_j stand for product price of the two firms respectively. Furthermore:

$$p_i = a - q_i - \rho q_j \quad p_j = a - q_j - \rho q_i \tag{1}$$

In the equations, $a>0$, ρ stands for the similarity of the product from firm i and firm j, $\rho \in [0, 1]$. If $\rho=0$, it indicates that the product of the two firms is entire irrelevance. If $\rho=1$, it means that the two firms make the same product, which can replace for each other.

After cooperation, the unit cost functions of the two firms are c_i and c_j respectively. Furthermore:

$$c_i = c_i^N - m_i - \theta m_j \tag{2}$$

$$c_j = c_j^N - m_j - \theta m_i \tag{3}$$

In the equations above, c_i^N and c_j^N stand for unit cost of the two firms respectively before cooperation. As unit cost can be shrunk through inter-firm cooperation, m_i and m_j stand for the contribution, made by cooperative relation, on the shrinking of unit cost of the two firms respectively. θm_j stands for the contribution made by the profits of firm i, which brought by cost shrinking through cooperation, on cost shrinking of firm j. And the contribution is the function about CRS and the profit of another cooperative firm.

The profit functions of firm i and firm j satisfy the following equations respectively:

$$\pi_i = (p_i - c_i) q_i \tag{4}$$

$$\pi_j = (p_j - c_j) q_j \tag{5}$$

Given $\dfrac{\partial \pi_i}{\partial q_i} = 0$ and $\dfrac{\partial \pi_j}{\partial q_j} = 0$ will result in the following equations:

$$q_i^* = \frac{a(2-\rho) + \rho c_j - 2c_i}{4-\rho^2} = \frac{a(2-\rho) + \rho(c_j^N - m_j - \theta m_i) - 2(c_i^N - m_i - \theta m_j)}{4-\rho^2} \tag{6}$$

$$q_j^* = \frac{a(2-\rho) + \rho c_i - 2c_j}{4-\rho^2} = \frac{a(2-\rho) + \rho(c_i^N - m_i - \theta m_j) - 2(c_j^N - m_j - \theta m_i)}{4-\rho^2} \tag{7}$$

2.2   CRS and the Profit of Firm

Putting equations (6), (7) into (4), (5) , the consequences are π_i^* and π_j^* , which stand for the optimal expected profits of the two firms respectively. Since both sides, which have the same CRS θ, are the same size and symmetrical, and the impact of cooperation of the two firms are the same. Hence, the following part of the paper will only consider about the situation of firm i.

Solving π_i^* on the first-order partial derivatives of θ as follows:

$$\frac{\partial \pi_i^*}{\partial \theta}=2m_j\frac{a-\rho q_j^*-c_i}{4-\rho^2}=2m_j\frac{p_i-c_i+q_i^*}{4-\rho^2}=\frac{2(c_i^N-m_i-c_i)(a-\rho q_j^*-c_i^N+m_i+\theta m_j)}{(4-\rho^2)\theta} \tag{8}$$

From $\dfrac{\partial \pi_i^*}{\partial \theta} = 2m_j\,\dfrac{p_i - c_i + q_i^*}{4 - \rho^2}$ of the equation (8), we see that when the product price of firm i (p_i) is higher than its unit cost (c_i) of post-cooperation, that's to say that cooperation can bring direct profit for both sides. Then, the tighter of CRS is, the more profit will be brought by cooperation. Meanwhile, even if $p_i-c_i<0$, it will be liable for the firm to participate in cooperation only if $p_i-c_i>-q_i^*$ ($q_i^*>0$). And strengthen cooperative relation will still increase the profit of both sides involved in the cooperation.

Define p_i-c_i as Index of Cooperation Possibility (*ICP*), as shown in figure 1. The higher the *ICP* is, the greater the likelihood of cooperation will be. When $ICP>-q_i^*$, the firms locate in the domain of possibility of cooperation, which indicates that it is possible of cooperation because the potential profit will motivate both sides to participate in co-

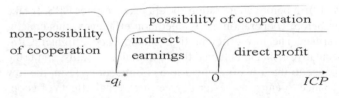

Fig. 1. Index of Cooperation Possibility (ICP)

operation. When *ICP*>0, it means that inter-firm cooperation will bring direct profit for both sides. Furthermore, the larger of investment on cooperative relation is, the more profit brought by cooperation to participated firm will be. When $-q_i^*<ICP<0$, it means that inter-firm cooperation will bring indirect earnings for participated firm, such as the experience and technology of management, but not direct profit. It will still be possible for the firm participating in cooperation. Hence, participated firm will invest on cooperative relation as well. And the more strength the cooperative relation is, the larger earnings for the participated firm will be. When $ICP<-q_i^*$, it stands that both sides locate in the domain of non-possibility of cooperation because there are neither direct profit nor indirect earnings, which motivate both sides to participate in cooperation. It can be concluded as No. 1:

[No. 1] The earnings of inter-firm cooperation is spillover, which indicates that cooperation can bring other income besides profit to participated firm. Although it is not possible for participated firm obtaining direct profit through cooperation, the firm will still likely to choose cooperation with a view to obtain indirect earnings, such as improving management and technology, seizing market etc.. Of course, the risk of loss for the participated firm must be located in an expected domain. Otherwise, the cooperation will be denied by the firm.Conclusion No. 1 may explain why there are many firms, which participate in cooperation actively, though the financial income brought by cooperation isn't so obviously. The reason is that it can bring indirect earnings, such as market sharing, management improving and tacit knowledge etc., for both sides through cooperation.

2.3 CRS and Firm Efficiency

Given $\dfrac{\partial \pi_i^*}{\partial \theta} = 0$ in equation (8), results in the optimal CRS of firm i under the optimal expected profit:

$$\theta^* = \frac{\rho q_j^* - a + c_i^N - m_i}{m_j} = \frac{c_i^N - p_i^* - q_i^* - m_i}{(4 - \rho^2)\theta} \tag{9}$$

Solving θ^* on the first-order partial derivatives of c_i^N as follows:

$$\frac{\partial \theta^*}{\partial c_i^N} = \frac{1}{m_j} > 0 \ \ (c_i^N > 0, \ m_j > 0) \tag{10}$$

From equation (10), we know that the initial cost of firm i before cooperation influences CRS positively. That's to say, the higher the initial cost is, the more strength the cooperative relation will be. It can be concluded as No. 2;

[No. 2] The high cost of firm before cooperation should take a tighter CRS. If take on the initial cost of firm before cooperation as its operation efficiency, this conclusion can be explained further. The low efficient firm should choose tighter CRS, which can reduce the speculative risk and enhance the cooperative benefits, and bring much more reliable insurance to the low efficient firm as a reflection. Then, the low efficient firm will have chance to enjoy a greater degree of external effects of cooperation.As can be seen, cooperation is a "double edged sword". As for the relatively low efficient firm, it can get a greater safety insurance and avoid "opportunism" risks resulted from the other participated firm's speculative behavior, and it can also get a greater risks of being entangled by cooperative relation as well.

2.4 CRS and Cooperative Contribution

Seeking π_i^* on the first-order partial derivatives of m_i and make it to 0:

$$\frac{\partial \pi_i^*}{\partial m_i} = \frac{2(a - \rho q_j^* - c_i^N + m_i + \theta m_j)}{4 - \rho^2} = 0,$$

Solving the equation above, the result is: $m_i^* = -a + \rho q_j^* + c_i^N - \theta m_j$. And then, Solving m_i^* on the first-order partial derivatives of θ, the result is:

$$\frac{\partial m_i^*}{\partial \theta} = -m_j < 0 \ (m_j > 0) \tag{11}$$

As shown in the equation (11), CRS and cooperative relation influence the contribution on shrinking the unit cost of firm negatively. The tighter the CRS is, the smaller the marginal contribution produced by cooperation will be, and vice versa. It can be concluded as No. 3:

[No. 3] Cooperative relation can bring big marginal contribution to participated firms, which are not cooperated closely with each other. As the increasing of the strength of cooperative relation between firms, the marginal contribution on both sides will be reduced. In simple words, if the cooperation of participated firms, which share the same market, has the same size, keep distant relationships, it will produce high benefits to both sides. This article defined this effect as "the law of diminishing marginal contribution of cooperation".

As shown in equation (11) as well, the more contribution on the shrinking of unit cost of other side made by cooperation is, the less the marginal contribution on the own side made by cooperation will be. Therefore, the speculative behavior during cooperation of the participated firms, which have non-complete common interests, can be explained. It can be concluded as No. 4:

[No. 4] As the benefits (especially the tangible gains) produced by cooperation is definite, the participated firm, which will be motivated to be "free rider", would like to take the advantage of other side. This article defined it as "the law of cooperative speculation". Therefore, accomplished restriction mechanism and scientific distribution mechanism must be established by the cooperation community.

2.5 CRS and Output

Put equations (2) and (3) into equation (6), solving q_i^* on the first-order partial derivatives of θ, the result is:

$$\frac{\partial q_i^*}{\partial \theta} = \frac{2m_j - \rho m_i}{4 - \rho^2} \tag{12}$$

As can be seen in the equation (12), if $m_j/m_i > \rho/2$, $\frac{\partial q_i^*}{\partial \theta} > 0$. Define m_j/m_i as QAI

(Quantity Adjust Index), then $\rho/2$ stands for the "adjusting valve" of QAI. Shown as figure 2:When $QAI>\rho/2$, the firm locates in cooperative output-increasing domain, which stands that the tighter the CRS is, the higher the output will be. When $QAI<\rho/2$, the firm locates in cooperative output-reducing domain, which stands that the tighter the CRS is, the lower the output will be. When $QAI=1$, m_i equals m_j, which stands for the equal benefits cooperative output-increasing point. It can be concluded as the following No. 5:

[No. 5] The relation between CRS and output relies on the relation of the contribution, made by cooperation, on shrinking of cost of the other side of the cooperative firm. As for firm I, if $m_j > m_i$, raise CRS will be helpful for the increasing of output of firm i. This article defined it as "the law of cooperative output-increasing". It indicates when cooperation makes much more contribution on shrinking of cost of the other firm, i.e. j, than the own side one, the tighter the CRS is, the higher the output of firm i will be.From No. 5, we can see that the altruistic behavior can promote the cooperation further, and bring much more cooperative earnings for the own side as well.

Moreover, as shown in Figure 3, the point of quantity adjust $\rho/2$ is getting bigger when the product similarity ρ is higher. Shifts up the line of $m_j/m_i=\rho/2$. Cooperative output-increasing domain (domain II) is shrunk, cooperative output-reducing domain (domain I) is broaden. It means that the threshold value of the effect of increasing output by cooperative relation is extended. As ρ stands for the similarity of product between firms, the higher ρ is, it will be more difficult for cooperative relation making positive effect on output increasing.   And vice versa of shifting down the line of $m_j/m_i=\rho/2$. It can be concluded as the following No. 6:

[No. 6] The higher ρ is, it will be more difficult for cooperative relation making positive effect on output increasing. While the lower ρ is, it will be easier for cooperative relation making positive effect on output increasing.Shown in this conclusion of No. 6, ρ plays key roles on the performance of cooperation between firms. When ρ is low, it means that the firms participating in cooperation can be complementary to each other, and will help to improve the cooperative performance.

2.6 CRS and Price

Put equations (2),(3),(6),(7)into equation(1), obtain p_i^* on the first-order partial derivatives of θ:

$$\frac{\partial p_i^*}{\partial \theta} = \frac{(\rho^2 - 2)m_j - \rho m_i}{4 - \rho^2} < 0 \qquad (13)$$

As can be seen from the equation (13), CRS and price are negative correlation, which means the tighter the CRS is, the lower the price of the own side of participated firm will be. Of course, it should be based on the hypothesis of Cournot competition, which excluded the possibility of price fixing. It can be concluded as No. 7:

[No. 7] CRS and price are negative correlation, which means the tighter the CRS is, the lower the price of the own side of participated firm will be.The conclusion of No. 7 proves the effect made by cooperation on the participated firms from the view of price cost. Cooperation can enhance the production efficiency and reduce production costs, allowing participated firms to lower prices.

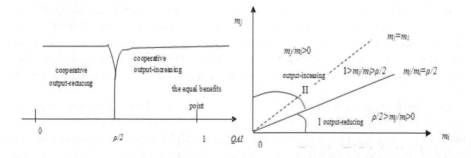

Fig. 2. Quantity Adjust Index (QAI)   **Fig. 3.** The Relationship between ρ and quantity

3 Conclusion

The inter-firm cooperative relations strength (CRS) is an indicator. This study, through a simple game model, analyzed the relations between Inter-firm CRS and some other indicators, such as the firm profits, business efficiency, cooperation-contribution, production, product similarity and prices, etc.. The author proposed three regular patterns including the diminishing marginal of cooperation-contribution, cooperation speculation, increasing profits by cooperation, and drew seven conclusions as well.

References

1. Li, G., Du, Z.: The identification model of the strength of competition-cooperation relationships between enterprises based on AHP and FCE. Journal of Dalian University of Technology(social sciences) 30(2), 22–30 (2009) (in Chinese)
2. Granovetter, M.: The Strength of Weak Ties. American Journal of Sociology 78(6), 1360–1380 (1973)
3. Uzzi, B.: Social structure and competition in interfirm net works: the paradox of embeddedness. Administrative Science Quarterly 42(1), 35–67 (1997)
4. Nooteboom, V.A.G.: Density and Strength of Ties in Innovation Networks: A Competence and Governance View. Ecis (1), 1–44 (2004)
5. Cullen, J.B., Johnson, J.L., Sakano, T.: Success through commitment and trust: The soft side of strategic alliance management. Journal of World Business 35(3), 223–240 (2000)
6. Sarkar, M.B., Echambadi, R., Cavusgil, S.T., Aulakh, P.S.: The influence of complementarity,compatibility,and relationship capital on alliance performance. Journal of the Academy of Marketing Science 29(4), 358–373 (2001)
7. Porter, M.E.: Competitive Advantage. Simon & Schuster Ltd., New York (2004)

Author Index

624   Author Index